Exchange Rate Economics

T0144593

Exchange Rate Economics: Theories and Evidence is the second edition of *Floating Exchange Rates: Theories and Evidence*, and builds on the successful content and structure of the previous edition, but has been comprehensively updated and expanded to include additional literature on the determination of both fixed and floating exchange rates.

Core topics covered include:

- the purchasing power parity hypothesis and the PPP puzzle;
- the monetary and portfolio-balance approaches to exchange rates;
- the new open economy macroeconomics approach to exchange rates; and
- the determination of exchange rates in target zone models and speculative attack models.

Exchange Rate Economics: Theories and Evidence also includes extensive discussion of recent econometric work on exchange rates with a particular focus on equilibrium exchange rates and measuring exchange rate misalignment, as well as discussion on the non-fundamentals-based approaches to exchange rate behaviour, such as the market microstructure approach.

The book will appeal to academics and postgraduate students with an interest in all aspects of international finance and will also be of interest to practitioners concerned with issues relating to equilibrium exchange rates and the forecastability of currencies in terms of macroeconomic fundamentals.

Ronald MacDonald is the Adam Smith Professor of Political Economy, University of Glasgow.

Exchange Rate Economics

Theories and evidence

Ronald MacDonald

 Routledge
Taylor & Francis Group

LONDON AND NEW YORK

First published 2007
by Routledge
2 Park Square, Milton Park, Abingdon, Oxon OX14 4RN

Simultaneously published in the USA and Canada
by Routledge
270 Madison Ave, New York, NY 10016

Routledge is an imprint of the Taylor & Francis Group, an informa business

© 2007 Ronald MacDonald

Typeset in Baskerville by
Newgen Imaging Systems (P) Ltd, Chennai, India

British Library Cataloguing in Publication Data
A catalogue record for this book is available from the British Library

Library of Congress Cataloging in Publication Data
A catalog record for this book has been requested

ISBN13: 978–0–415–14878–8 (hbk)
ISBN13: 978–0–415–12551–2 (pbk)
ISBN13: 978–0–203–38018–5 (ebk)

To Catriona

Contents

Figures

Tables

Preface

This book is the second edition of *Floating Exchange Rates: Theories and Evidence*, first published in 1988. That book was, I believe, the first to present a comprehensive overview of both the theoretical and empirical strands of the exchange rate literature and is still in print today despite much of the material being dated. The changed name for the second edition reflects the changed nature of the subject matter post-1988. Revising a book of this nature is a big undertaking and it certainly would not have been possible were it not for the fact that I was invited to present a course, entitled 'The Economics of Exchange Rates', at the IMF Institute in 1997, and subsequently asked to present revised versions of the course on seven subsequent occasions. This is a five-day course which covers the core material in this book. I am therefore indebted to Mohsin Khan for initially inviting me to present this course and to Andrew Feltenstein for continuing the link since Mohsin's departure from the Institute; without the discipline of preparing this course there is no doubt that this book would never have been completed. I am also grateful to the many IMF staff members and country officials who have indirectly commented on the contents of this book and to the many other participants in central banks, financial institutions and universities who have also commented on the Economics of Exchange Rate course on the many other occasions it has been delivered.

1 Introduction

Some basic concepts and stylised facts and the case for (and against) floating exchange rates

In this book we attempt to produce a coherent overview of the main theoretical and empirical strands in the economics of exchange rate literature and in this chapter we try to set the scene for the rest of the book. Rather than give a blow-by-blow account of succeeding chapters, whose titles listed in the contents page give a firm indication of their contents, we here present some salient issues and a number of important stylised facts which we believe will motivate and set-up the following chapters. In thinking about exchange rate issues, it has become increasingly fashionable in the exchange rate literature to take a microstructural approach to the foreign exchange market (see, for example, Lyons 2001). This approach is very interesting and greatly enhances our understanding of how the main players in the foreign exchange market interact and drive exchange rates, and we consider this approach in some detail in Chapter 14. However, the main theme in this book is that macro-fundamentals are important for explaining exchange rate behaviour and we argue at various points in the book that a macro-fundamental approach can explain the main puzzles in the exchange rate literature.

In the next section we outline some basic definitions of spot and forward exchange rates and we then go on in Sections 1.2 and 1.3 to discuss the main players in the foreign exchange market and the kind of foreign exchange turnover they generate. In Section 1.4 we consider some monetary and balance of payments accounting conditions, under fixed and floating exchange rates, and then go on in Section 1.5 to examine the traditional balance of payments approach to the determination of the exchange rate. In Section 1.6 the covered interest rate parity condition is considered against the backdrop of the Tsiang (1959) analysis of the determination of spot and forward exchange rates, and the related uncovered and closed interest parity conditions are discussed in Section 1.7.

In Section 1.8 we introduce some key stylised facts of the foreign exchange market, namely, the issues of exchange rate volatility – specifically issues of intra- and inter-regime volatility – and the apparent randomness of exchange rate behaviour. These are themes we shall return to on a number of occasions throughout this book and indeed are at the heart of the debate between those economists who favour a macro-fundamentalist approach to exchange rate determination and those who favour a market microstrucure approach.

Although the textbook exposition of, say, the operation of monetary and fiscal policy in an open economy often portrays this in the context of the polar cases of fixed versus floating exchange rates, there are a large range of intermediate regimes between the extremes of fully flexible and rigidly fixed exchange rates and these are considered in Section 1.9, along with some practical issues relating to the measurement of exchange rate regimes.

The advantages and disadvantages of fixed versus flexible exchange rates are considered in Section 1.10, along with some discussion of the empirical evidence on the historical performance of the two kinds of regimes. In Section 1.11 we have a discussion of the determinants of exchange rate regimes while Section 1.12 focusses on currency invoicing practices.

1.1 Exchange rate definitions

There are two types of nominal exchange rates used extensively throughout this book, namely, the spot and forward exchange rate. The bilateral spot exchange rate, S, is the rate at which foreign exchange can be bought and sold for immediate delivery, conventionally 1 or 2 days. The bilateral forward rate, F, is that rate negotiated today (time t) at which foreign exchange can be bought and sold for delivery some time in the future (when a variable appears without a time subscript it is implicitly assumed that it is a period-t variable). The most popularly traded forward contract has a maturity of 90 days and contracts beyond 1 year are relatively scarce. Forward contracts are generally negotiated between an individual – for example, a private customer or commercial organisation – and a bank and the individual has to take delivery of the contract on the specified date. Futures contracts, which are also rates negotiated in the current period for delivery in the future, differ from forward contracts in that they are bought and sold on an organised exchange and the individual holding the contract does not need to take delivery of the underlying asset (it can be bought or sold on the exchange before the delivery date on the exchange). Futures rates are hardly addressed in this book. In general, throughout the book we define nominal exchange rates as home currency price of a unit of foreign exchange. This definition has been chosen since it is the most widely used in the exchange rate literature. It implies that an increase in the exchange rate (a rise in the price of foreign currency) represents a depreciation and a decrease in the exchange rate represents an appreciation. As we shall see, when considering effective exchange rates (both real and nominal), and sometimes for real bilateral rates, the convention is the opposite – a rise in an effective exchange rate represents an appreciation. In general, lower case letters denote the natural logarithm of a variable and so $s = \ln S$ and $f = \ln F$.

These measures of the exchange rate are nominal. A real exchange rate is measured by adjusting the nominal exchange rate by relative prices. For example, the real exchange rate, Q, derived from adjusting the bilateral nominal exchange rate is:

$$Q = \frac{SP^*}{P},$$

or in natural logs:

$$q = s + p^* - p, \tag{1.1}$$

where P denotes the price level in the home country, $*$ denotes a foreign magnitude and lower case letter denote log values.

All of the earlier exchange rate measures are bilateral in nature – the home currency price of one unit of foreign currency (e.g. Japanese yen against US dollars). There are a number of exchange rates which define the home currency against a basket of foreign currencies and these are usually used when trying to obtain an overall measure of a country's external competitiveness, and especially when relating exchange rates to international trade balances. A nominal effective exchange rate (NEER) in essence sums all of a country's bilateral exchange rates using trade weights (NEER $= \sum_{i=1}^{n} \alpha_i S_i$ where α denotes a trade weight, i represents a bilateral paring and, in this context, S is defined as the foreign currency price of a unit of home currency) and these are expressed as an index. With effective exchange rates, the convention is that a rise above 100 represents an exchange rate appreciation, while a fall below 100 represents a depreciation. As in expression (1.1), for the real bilateral exchange rate, a real effective exchange rate (REER) adjusts the NEER by the appropriate composite 'foreign' price level and deflates by the home price level, (REER $= \sum_{i=1}^{n} \alpha_i [(S^i P^j)/P^i]$, where again S is the foreign currency price of a unit of home currency and j represents the home country).[1] A multilateral exchange rate model (MERM), as constructed by the IMF, incorporates trade elasticities, in addition to trade weights, into the calculation of a real effective exchange rate. The idea here is that it is not just the size of trade between two countries that matters, it is also how responsive trade is between two countries with respect to the exchange rate.

1.2   The players in the foreign exchange market

The foreign exchange market differs from some other financial markets in having a role for three types of trade: interbank trade, which accounts for the majority – between 60% and 80% – of foreign exchange trade; trade conducted through brokers (which accounts for between 15% and 35% of trade); and trade undertaken by private customers (e.g. corporate trade), which makes up around 5% of trade in the foreign exchange market. The latter group have to make their transactions through banks since their credit-worthiness cannot be detected by brokers.

The agents within banks who conduct trade are referred to as market makers, so-called because they make a market in one or more currencies by providing bid and ask spreads for the currencies. The market makers can trade for their own account (i.e. go long or short in a currency) or on behalf of a client, a term which encompasses an array of players from central banks, to financial firms and traders involved in international trade. A foreign exchange broker on the other hand does not trade on her own behalf but keeps a book of market makers limit orders

(orders to buy/sell a specified quantity of foreign exchange at a specified price) from which she, in turn, will quote the best bid/ask rates to market makers. The latter are referred to as the broker's 'inside spread'. The broker earns a profit by charging a fee for her service of bringing buyers and sellers together. The foreign exchange market is therefore multiple dealer in nature.

More recently, automated brokerage trading systems have become popular in the foreign exchange market and perhaps the best known is the Reuters 2000–2 automated electronic trading system. This dealing system allows a bank dealer to enter buy and/or sell prices directly into the system thereby avoiding the need for a human, voice based, broker (and it is therefore seen as more cost effective). The D2000-2 records the *touch*, which is the highest bid and lowest ask price. This differs importantly from so-called indicative foreign exchange pages which show the latest update of the bid and ask entered by a single identified bank. The system also shows the quantity that the bank was willing to deal in, which is shown in integers of $1 million. The limit orders are also stored in these systems but are not revealed. A member of the trading system (i.e. another bank) can hit either the bid or ask price via his own computer terminal. The trading system then checks if the deal is prudential to both parties and if it is the deal goes ahead, with the transaction price being posted on the screen. Associated with the price is the change in quantity of the bid (ask) and also in the price offered if the size of the deal exhausts the quantity offered at the previous price. These concepts are discussed in more detail in Chapter 14.

1.3   A snapshot of the global foreign exchange market in 2001

The Bank for International Settlements (BIS) produces a triennial global survey of turnover in the foreign exchange market gathered from data collected by its 48 participating central banks. These surveys have been conducted since 1989 and the latest available at the time of writing was the 2001 survey (see BIS 2001). This showed that average daily turnover in 'traditional' foreign exchange markets – spot transactions, outright forwards and foreign exchange swaps – in 2001 was $1.2 trillion, compared with $1.49 trillion in April 1998, a 19% fall in volume at current exchange rates (a 14% fall at constant exchange rates). The breakdown is shown in Table 1.1, which shows that the biggest hit occurred in terms of spot transactions and foreign exchange swaps, with outright forward contracts increasing slightly.

As the BIS notes, this decline in foreign exchange market turnover does not reflect a change in the pattern of exchange rate volatility (see Table 1.2), but rather the introduction of the euro, the growing share of electronic brokering in the spot interbank market, consolidation in the banking industry and international concentration in the corporate sector (see Galati 2001 for a further discussion).

The share of interbank trading in total turnover in 2001 was 58%, a decline of 5% over the previous survey, a decline attributed to the increased role of electronic brokering, which implied that foreign exchange dealers needed to trade

Table 1.1 Global foreign exchange market turnover[1]

	Daily averages in April (in billions of US dollars)				
	1989	*1992*	*1995*	*1998*	*2001*
Spot transactions	317	394	494	568	387
Outright forwards	27	58	97	128	131
Foreign exchange swaps	190	324	546	734	656
Estimated reporting gaps	56	44	53	60	26
Total 'traditional' turnover	590	820	1190	1490	1200

Source: BIS (2001).

Note
1 Adjusted for local and cross border double-counting.

Table 1.2 Volumes and volatility of foreign exchange turnover[1]

	April 1992		April 1995		April 1998		April 2001	
	Volume	*Volatility*	*Volume*	*Volatility*	*Volume*	*Volatility*	*Volume*	*Volatility*
USD/EUR	192	10.00	254	10.45	290	5.72	354	15.61
USD/JPY	155	8.12	242	17.05	256	11.75	231	10.82
USD/GBP	77	9.66	78	5.65	117	5.31	125	9.08
USD/CHF	49	11.47	61	12.71	79	7.90	57	14.94
EUR/JPY[2]	18	8.73	24	16.76	24	10.99	30	19.97
EUR/GBP[2]	23	5.84	21	8.47	31	6.04	24	8.65
EUR/CHF[2]	13	4.57	18	3.62	18	3.88	12	3.05

Source: BIS (2001).

Notes
1 Volumes in billions of US dollars; volatilities in terms of standard deviations of annualised daily returns computed over calendar months.
2 Prior to 1989, Deutsche mark.

less actively with each other. The share of bank to non-financial customer trading stood at 13% in 2001, a 4% fall from the 1998 figure and the share of activity between banks and non-bank financial customers rose from 20% to 28% in 2001 change and substantially between 1998 and 2001.

The introduction of the euro appears to have reduced turnover because of the elimination of intra-EMS trade: the euro entered on one side of 38% of all foreign exchange transactions, which is higher than the DMs share in 1998, and it is lower than the sum of the euro components in 1998. See Table 1.3 for further details.

The dollar remained the currency with the largest turnover in 2001 (90%), the yen was in third position with a 23% share. The dollar–euro was the most traded currency pair in 2001 (at 30%), followed by dollar–yen (at 20%) and dollar–sterling (at 11%).

Table 1.3 Currency distribution of reported foreign exchange market turnover

Currency	Percentage shares of average daily turnover			
	1989	*1992*	*1995*	*1998*
US dollar	90.0	82.0	83.3	87.3
Euro	—	—	—	—
Deutsche mark	27.0	39.6	36.1	30.1
French franc	2.0	3.8	7.9	30.1
ECU + EMS	4.0	11.8	15.7	17.3
Japanese yen	27.0	23.4	24.1	20.2
Pound sterling	15.0	13.6	9.4	11.0
Swiss franc	10.0	8.4	7.3	7.1
Can dollar	1.0	3.3	3.4	3.6
Aus dollar	2.0	2.5	2.7	3.1
Swedish krone	—	1.3	0.6	0.4
HK dollar	—	1.1	0.9	1.3
Singapore dollar	—	0.3	0.3	1.2
Emerging markets	—	0.5	0.4	3.0
Other	22.0	8.5	7.9	9.3
All currencies	200.0	200.0	200.0	200.0

Source: BIS (2001).

1.4   Some monetary and balance of payments accounting relationships

In this section we consider some monetary and balance of payments relationships and their role in defining fixed and flexible exchange rates. A fixed exchange rate regime may be defined as a commitment by a central bank to defend a particular pegged value of its exchange rate with, in principle, unlimited purchases or sales of foreign exchange. In contrast, in a flexible rate regime the authorities have no such commitment and the exchange rate is free to absorb changes in demand and supply emanating from the balance of payments. The regimes are distinguished, then, in terms of their implications for foreign exchange reserves. This may be demonstrated in the following way. Consider the standard equation for high powered money:

$$M \equiv R + D, \tag{1.2}$$

where M is the stock of high powered, or base, money, R is the foreign-backed component of M, and D is the domestic credit issued by the central bank. On taking first differences of (1.2) we obtain

$$\Delta M = \Delta R + \Delta D \tag{1.3}$$

which on rearranging becomes

$$\Delta R = \Delta M - \Delta D \tag{1.4}$$

where ΔR is the change in the reserves, ΔM is the change in base money and ΔD is the change in the domestic component of the money supply.

Under fixed exchange rates the change in reserves, or the change in the official settlements balance, may alternatively be defined as equal to the sum of the current and capital accounts.

$$\Delta R = CA + CAP \tag{1.5}$$

where

$$CA = NX + i'NFA \tag{1.6}$$

and

$$CAP = SCAP + LCAP \tag{1.7}$$

where CA is the current account, CAP denotes the capital account of the balance of payments, NX is net exports, or the balance of trade, i' is the net foreign interest rate (home minus foreign where the foreign rate is likely some average of foreign interest rates), NFA represents net foreign assets and therefore the term $i'NFA$ represents net interest payments on net foreign assets. As we shall see in succeeding chapters, the interaction between the trade balance and the net foreign asset term plays a crucial role in defining exchange rate dynamics in a number of exchange rate models. $SCAP$ denotes the sum of short-term capital flows (often portrayed as speculative flows and includes items such as short-term Treasury bills and trade credits) and $LCAP$ represents long-term capital flows and has two main categories, namely, portfolio and direct investment. The sum of the current account and the long-term capital account is referred to as the basic balance and was a popular measure of the balance of payments in the 1950s and 1960s because it was thought to reflect the 'fundamental' components of the balance of payments (specifically, it excluded 'speculative' capital flows). It is worth noting at this juncture that both the current and capital accounts of the balance of payments are flow magnitudes.

Under flexible exchange rates, by definition, the authorities do not intervene in the foreign exchange market and thus the change in reserves, ΔR, must equal zero and equation (1.8) must hold:

$$CA = -CAP, \tag{1.8}$$

that is, with a flexible exchange rate the current account surplus equals the deficit on the capital account and the role of the exchange rate in such a regime is to ensure that this condition always holds. Of course, in reality, reserves are likely to be changing since few central banks subscribe to this kind of textbook relationship. Relationship (1.8) clearly has implications for the control of the money supply since from (1.3) we note that if ΔR is zero then there is a one-to-one relationship between domestic credit expansion and the money supply. In other words, with a truly flexible exchange rate it is possible for a country to have an independent monetary policy and this, as we shall see later, is one of the key arguments in favour of flexible exchange rates.

Of course, this also indicates the limits placed on monetary independence with a fixed exchange rate: to the extent that reserves are changing, which is, of course, what adjusts with a fixed exchange rate, there is no longer a unique relationship between domestic credit changes and monetary changes. Indeed, a central proposition of the monetary approach to the balance of payments (see, for example, Frenkel and Johnson 1976) is that a change in the domestic component of the money supply will lead to a broadly offsetting change in reserves, the argument essentially being that from a position of full employment an increase in, say, D results in agents having an excess supply of money which they try to offload by buying goods, services and assets.[2] Since the economy is assumed to be at full employment, this desire may only be fulfilled by purchasing foreign goods and assets. However, as the authorities try to maintain a fixed exchange rate the attempt by domestic residents to purchase foreign goods and assets will result in a loss in reserves which will exactly offset the change in D: this is clearly illustrated by equation (1.4).[3] However, by allowing the exchange rate to float freely the attempt by residents to buy foreign exchange leads to a depreciation of the currency, which means that ΔM and ΔD in equation (1.3) will be equivalent. Thus compared to a regime of fixed exchange rates, flexible exchange rates, by forcing ΔR to be 0, allow a country to pursue an independent monetary policy.[4] We now turn our attention to a discussion of how the exchange rate is determined in the context of a traditional balance of payments perspective.

1.5   A diagrammatic representation of the balance of payments, or flow, model of the determination of the exchange rate

Some of the concepts discussed earlier can be portrayed graphically using the standard flow demand and supply diagram familiar from elementary textbooks. Although familiar, this diagram is useful in motivating some of the more complex models, such as the asset market model and the target zone model, considered elsewhere in the book. The balance of payments approach to the determination of the exchange rate treats the exchange rate as a price, just like any other price, and utilizes the so-called Marshallian scissors of supply and demand in order to analyse its determination. This view is typically known as the balance of payments approach to the determination of the exchange rate because the demand and supply for a currency arise out of the transactions recorded in the balance of payments. Thus a home importer of Japanese colour TVs requires to buy a quantity of Japanese yen in order to make payment to the Japanese exporter and, similarly, a home exporter, by exporting a good, will induce a supply of foreign currency. Equally demand/supply for foreign/home services and assets will result in a corresponding demand/supply for foreign exchange. Concentrating for the moment on the demand/supply for foreign exchange arising from the demand/supply for imports and exports, we

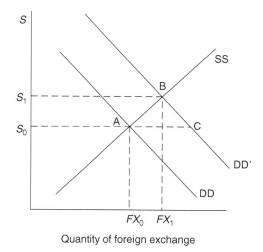

Figure 1.1 The balance of payments model of the determination of the exchange rates.

present in Figure 1.1 a portrait of this determination of the exchange rate, which is set-up with the US as the home country and Japan as the foreign country. Thus underlying DD is the US's demand of imports of goods and services which depends upon the normal factors (on the import demand side consumers' income and tastes, and on the import supply side foreign producers' factor prices). The demand schedule for foreign exchange is downward sloping for the familiar reason that from a position of equilibrium (on the demand curve), an increased quantity of foreign exchange will only be demanded at a lower price. (Note that all of this discussion is from the point of view of the US as the home country.) The exchange rate is determined by the intersection of the demand and supply curves at S_0, with an equilibrium quantity of foreign exchange, FX_0. An increase in the demand for dollars, as a result, say, of a change in tastes or increased income in the US, would shift the demand curve to DD′. At the initial equilibrium at A there would be an excess demand for yen, putting upward pressure on their price, which, in turn, leads to quantity changes until equilibrium is restored at S_1/FX_1. It is worth noting this positive association between income and the exchange rate since, as we shall see in future chapters, it sharply contrasts with the modern asset view of the determination of the exchange rate.

Clearly, in terms of the earlier example, if the exchange rate was not flexible but pegged, as in the Bretton Woods system, the monetary authorities would be forced to intervene in the foreign exchange market to prevent the exchange rate from rising. For example, if in Figure 1.1 we now assume the exchange rate is fixed at S_0, and therefore the central bank has a commitment to buy and sell foreign exchange at this price to defend the currency. With the same change in demand as before, we now have excess demand for foreign exchange at the fixed rate and this has to be satisfied by the US Fed selling foreign exchange at the fixed price. The amount of foreign exchange sales is AB which is equivalent to ΔR in this example. If the change in demand is temporary the central bank may be able to defend the intial pegged rate by simply running down its reserves. However, if the demand change is permanent this could of course result in the central bank loosing all its reserves and having to relinquish the peg. Indeed, in this scenario speculators would in all likelihood try to sell, or short, the domestic currency in a bid to force the Fed's hand (because they anticipate making a capital gain, which may be substantial, by selling an expensive currency and buying it cheap once the devaluation takes place) and their action brings the devaluation forward in time. This kind of behaviour is termed a speculative attack and we consider such attacks, and their timing, in more detail in Chapter 13.

Our discussion of a fixed rate in Figure 1.2 suggests that the exchange rate is rigidly fixed at S_0. However, in reality, and monetary unions aside, there are few historical examples in which exchange rates have been rigidly fixed. For example, in the Classical Gold standard the so-called gold points[5] provided some flexibility and in specific dollar or deutsche mark-based regimes, such as the Bretton Woods and ERM periods, the flexibility has been defined by legislation. This may be illustrated in Figure 1.2 where the bands are represented by $\bar{s}$ (the upper band) and $\underline{s}$ (the lower band) and we superimpose the same demand shock as before. The existence of the flexibility around the central rate clearly restores some independence for monetary policy in the sense that an exchange rate change of AB absorbs much of the demand change, requiring reserve changes of only BC to mop up the remaining excess demand. Of course, if the demand change was permanent the currency may still face the kind of speculative attack referred to in the previous example. However, the existence of some flexibility may play an important role in

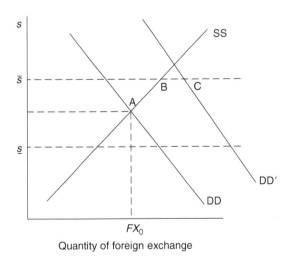

Figure 1.2 Exchange rate bands.

the credibility, and sustainability, of a fixed rate system and this is something that is considered in more detail in Chapter 12.

Another twist to Figure 1.1 relates to the uniqueness of equilibrium. More specifically, as drawn, the supply curve for foreign exchange in Figure 1.1 gives a unique equilibrium. This, however, need not be the case. Thus, if currency supply curves are backward bending, the foreign exchange market may exhibit multiple equilibria.[6] This possibility is shown in Figure 1.3. Points A and C are stable equilibria because the demand curve is downward sloping and the supply curve is upward sloping in the regions of equilibrium. This is not, though, the case at B where a move from this equilibrium would not result in a return to equilibrium but in fact a divergence (to points A or C, in fact). Stability requires that any increase in the exchange rate from equilibrium should produce an excess supply of foreign exchange. This condition is satisfied at both A and C but not B. A sufficient condition for stability is that the so-called Marshall–Lerner condition should hold:

$$\varepsilon_m + \varepsilon_x > 1, \tag{1.9}$$

where ε_m and ε_x refer, respectively, to the domestic elasticity of demand for imports and the foreign elasticity of demand for the country's exports.[7] What this condition states is that an increase in the price of foreign exchange (a depreciation, or devaluation under fixed rates) will result in a reduced home demand for imports and decreased foreign demand for exports which, because of the relatively elastic nature of demand, leads to an increase in total revenues, or, in the present context, an excess supply of foreign exchange which will return the exchange rate to equilibrium: *ceteris paribus* net exports and the current account improves. In most theoretical analyses and, indeed, in many of the models considered in later chapters, a relationship such as (1.9) is assumed to be effective instantaneously following an exchange rate depreciation. But in the real world it is more than

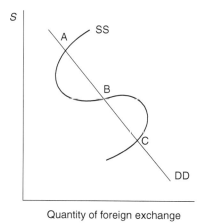

Figure 1.3 Multiple equilibria in the foreign exchange markets.

likely that the relevant elasticities in (1.9) will be highly inelastic (simply because it takes time for existing contracts to be fulfilled and therefore domestic residents cannot instantly buy import-competing goods and foreigners cannot instantly switch towards our cheaper export goods – see, for example, Goldstein and Khan 1985). In the case where the current account worsens in the short term and improves only slowly over time. This pattern of current account behaviour is labelled the J-curve effect.

As we have seen, underlying the demand for foreign currency in Figure 1.1 is the demand and supply of imports and exports of goods and services. But as was noted in the previous chapter, perhaps the most dominant component of day-to-day transactions in foreign exchange markets are (short-term) capital account items. As will be shown in some detail in future chapters, short-term capital movements respond essentially to interest differentials. Thus an increase in the foreign interest rate relative to the domestic rate, *ceteris paribus*, would be expected to lead to a flow of capital to the foreign country, as investors increase their demand for the more profitable foreign interest-bearing assets and decrease their demand for the less profitable home asset(s). In so doing there will clearly be an increased demand for the foreign currency. In terms of Figure 1.1, if the demand and supply schedules underlying the DD and SS curves are the total demand for goods, services and financial assets then the interest differential in favour of the foreign country (Japan in our previous example) would lead to an increased demand for yen represented by the rightward shift in the DD curve to DD′ and a depreciation of the exchange rate from S_0 to S_1. Note therefore that in terms of the balance of payments view of the determination of the exchange rate that an interest differential in favour of the foreign country is associated in the home country with a capital outflow and an exchange rate depreciation. This will be discussed in more detail in later chapters.

1.6   Tsiang's trichotomy of the capital account and covered interest rate parity

Tsiang (1959) proposed analysing the capital account in terms of the behaviour of three different groups of agents: commercial traders, interest arbitrageurs and speculators. Although this approach has not been fashionable for some time, we believe it is, nonetheless, a useful way of integrating the determination of the forward exchange with the determination of the spot exchange rate.[8]

Consider, first, the role of so-called interest arbitrageurs and the concept of interest arbitrage. The object of interest arbitrage is to allocate funds between financial centres in order to realize the highest possible rate of return, subject to the least possible risk. Thus, say, a UK individual had £1000 to invest for 1 year and the current spot exchange rate is £0.60/\$1. She may consider buying a UK treasury bill yielding a 4% rate of interest per annum. Alternatively, the funds could be invested in a similar US treasury bill at a 5% interest rate (the numbers here are taken purely for illustrative purposes). On the face of it, one would expect the investor to put her funds into the US investment since it appears to offer the higher return but is this in fact correct? By investing in the UK the investor would obtain a return after 1 year of £1040 (1000 × 1.04). By selling the £1000 on the spot market would produce $1667 and a return of $1750 after a year (1667 × 1.05). Note that both the sterling return from investing in the UK and the dollar return from investing in the US are certain in the current period (since both interest yields and the current spot exchange rate are known with certainty). However, the sterling return from the dollar investment is not certain since its value depends on the value of the exchange rate in a year's time. If the exchange rate were the same in 1 year's time as today (i.e. 0.6/$1) then the pound return would be £1050 which gives the investor a riskless excess return of £10 – the investor would therefore presumably invest in the US. However, with flexible exchange rates, it is highly unlikely that the same exchange rate which existed at the time the investment was made would also exist at the maturity date. Rather, the exchange rate would in all probability differ. Consider two examples, which are undoubtedly exaggerated but nonetheless make the point. If the exchange rate had depreciated to 0.7 in 1 year the sterling equivalent would be £1225, making the US investment hugely attractive. On the other hand if sterling had appreciated to 0.5 the investor would clearly get less sterling for every dollar invested and the sterling sum would be £875. A risk averse individual (which arbitrageurs are assumed to be) would want to avoid such exchange rate uncertainty and the associated risk, and would at the time of her sale of pounds, simultaneously sell the expected value of the dollar proceeds of her investment (which will be known with certainty today) for sterling. In other words the arbitrageur will buy forward pounds at the current 90-day forward exchange rate and in this way the arbitrageur can avoid foreign exchange risk. This type of foreign exchange transaction is known as covered interest arbitrage.

Clearly, if the spot and forward exchange rates are identical the arbitrageur would, in terms of the earlier example, end up with £1050. But in order to persuade other foreign exchange market participants (and as we shall see later such participants include speculators in this model although in practice they are commercial banks) to buy dollars forward, selling forward pounds, the dollars have to be sold at a discount relative to the spot rate, or conversely looking at it from the buying of pounds, the forward pounds are bought at a premium relative to the pound spot rate. This discount/premium is the 'price' paid to compensate the speculators for the risk involved in holding forward dollars. Thus, in terms of our example, interest arbitrage will be profitable provided that the interest differential in favour of the US is not offset by a discount on the forward dollar. It is usual to refer to the cost of forward cover using the generic label 'forward premium'.

The covered interest arbitrage relationship may be expressed more succinctly in the following way. One unit of the home currency invested in the home country yields $(1 + i)$ or $(1 + i^*)/S$ if invested in the foreign country, and if the latter is converted back to the home currency at the forward rate it will yield $[F(1 + i^*)]/S^{-1}$. In equilibrium, or in an efficient market, these two investment strategies should be equal:

$$\frac{F(1 + i^*)}{S} = (1 + i),$$

or

$$\frac{F}{S} = \frac{(1 + i)}{(1 + i^*)}, \tag{1.10}$$

which is the condition of covered interest parity. Hence if (1.10) holds there will be no incentive for funds to move from the home to the foreign country since the interest differential in favour of the foreign country is offset by the forward premium. Expression (1.10) may be simplified by taking natural logarithms of the terms on the left and right hand sides, that is,

$$i - i^* = f - s, \tag{1.11}$$

and i and i^* are approximately equal to $\ln(1 + i)$ and $\ln(1 + i^*)$, respectively, and $f - s$ is the forward premium. Thus, if $i^* > i$ it is clear from (1.11) that must be less than s; the forward value of the home currency is at a premium and the forward value of the foreign currency is at a discount. It is expected that arbitrage will ensure that equation (1.10/1.11) holds continuously. Thus any slight interest differential in favour of the foreign country will lead to a large quantity of arbitrage funds moving to the foreign country and in doing so will force the forward rate to give a premium on the pound which just offsets the interest differential.

The covered interest parity condition may alternatively be written:

$$CD = i - i^* - f - s = 0, \tag{1.12}$$

where CD is the covered interest differential which indicates that covered arbitrage will only be profitable if the CD is non-zero. In such a case, of course, there would be a riskless profit to be made from covered interest arbitrage.

Consider now the use made by commercial traders of the forward exchange market. In our discussion of the balance of payments model it was implicitly assumed that importers and exporters pay for goods and services immediately. But usually there are lags between the delivery of goods and their actual payment, and under a flexible exchange rate system exporters and importers may wish to guard against the risk of exchange rate changes during this period by hedging in the foreign exchange market. For example, an importer may take delivery today of goods which require payment in 3 months. To avoid the exchange risk inherent in such a transaction, the importer will use the forward exchange market to sell domestic currency for foreign currency in 3 months at a price agreed now. Since the importer holds a foreign currency asset (the foreign currency due in 3 months) and an equal offsetting foreign currency liability, his position is, as in the case of arbitrage, classified as being closed.

In contrast to arbitrageurs and hedgers, speculators deliberately accept a net open position in foreign exchange. Speculation may occur in both the spot and the forward markets, although 'pure' speculation is regarded as being confined to the forward market because little or no funds are required.[9] For the moment we concentrate on pure speculation. If the speculator expects that the future spot rate in 90 days, S^e, will be higher than the current 90-day forward rate she will take a 'long' position (an excess of uncovered foreign exchange claims over liabilities) by purchasing forward foreign exchange. Conversely, if the speculator expects the future spot rate will be less than the current forward rate, she will take a 'short' position (an excess of uncovered foreign exchange liabilities over claims) by selling forward in anticipation of a future spot purchase at a rate lower than the one contracted earlier.

Given these three main types of transactions we can now examine the joint determination of spot and forward exchange rates.

In Figure 1.4 we portray the markets for spot and forward exchange. The DD^c and SS^c schedules denote, respectively, the demand and supply of spot and forward exchange by commercial traders. The schedules reflect the normal commodity demand and supply factors plus, as we have seen, the relationship between interest rates and spot and forward exchange rates. Assuming that speculation is pure, and thus confined to the forward market, there will be some forward rate F at which there will be no speculation, in so far as this rate coincides with the expected future spot rate. If the actual rate is below this rate speculative demand will clearly be a decreasing function of the forward rate. That is, the greater is the extant to which the actual rate falls below the expected future rate the greater will be the demand for the forward foreign currency by speculators. Conversely, if the actual forward rate is above that expected to prevail by speculators their supply will be an increasing function of the current forward rate. The demand/supply of forward pounds by speculators is denoted by the schedule SS^s, which cuts the vertical axis at F. The schedule DD^x is the horizontal summation of speculators' demand and hedgers' demand for forward exchange. By assuming that interest rates are initially equal in the US and UK and that the spot and forward exchange rates coincide at S' and F' we have spot and forward arbitrage schedules denoted by A_s and A_f, respectively, which indicate a perfectly elastic supply of arbitrage funds. Under such conditions the spot and forward markets will be in equilibrium and there will clearly be no interest arbitrage.

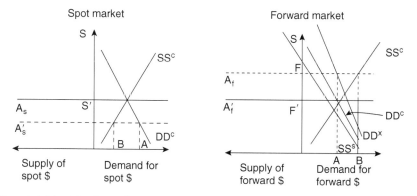

Figure 1.4 The joint determination of the spot and forward exchange rates.

Consider now a fall in the US interest rate relative to that in the UK, which results in interest arbitrageurs selling dollars for pounds spot and, simultaneously, buying forward dollars in return for the proceeds from their investment in pounds. In terms of our diagram this will lead to a downward shift of the A_s schedule to A_s' and an upward shift of A_f to A_f' until the new equilibrium spot and forward rates result in a forward premium which exactly offsets the interest differential. In the new equilibrium, OA of spot currency will be demanded for current account/trade purposes but only OB supplied by commercial transactors, the rest being supplied by the excess supply of dollars resulting from the interest arbitrage. In the forward market the quantity OA will be demanded by speculators and commercial traders and this is clearly less than the quantity OB supplied by hedgers. The difference AB is mopped up by arbitrageurs' forward purchase of dollars. Note that with the perfectly elastic arbitrage schedules utilised in our example, covered arbitrage links the determination of spot and forward exchange rates. This latter view is termed the cambist, or bankers, approach to the determination of the forward exchange rate: in essence, the forward rate is determined, as a residual adjusting to ensure an interest differential is matched by the appropriate forward premium. Indeed, in practice in pricing forward contracts commercial banks simply quote a forward rate on the basis of the known interest differentials and spot exchange rate to ensure that CIP holds. In effect CIP is an identity. An alternative view to the cambist approach is the so-called economists view. In this interpretation the arbitrage schedule is less than perfectly elastic but now the speculators' schedule is perfectly elastic at F in Figure 1.4. In this view the forward and expected spot rates coincide. This view is considered in some detail in Chapter 15. Does the empirical evidence shed any light on these two alternative views of the determination of the forward rate?

There are essentially two ways in which researchers have tested CIP. One relies on simply computing the CD term to determine if it is non-zero, while the other relies on regression analysis using the following type of regression:

$$fp_t = \alpha + \beta(i_t - i_t^*) + \varepsilon_t \tag{1.13}$$

In the context of the latter test (see, *inter alia*, Branson 1969; Marston 1976; Cosandier and Laing 1981; Fratianni and Wakeman 1982) the null hypothesis is $\alpha = 0$ and $\beta = 1$ and, in general, this research may be regarded as unable to reject the null (particularly the key hypothesis that $\beta = 1$). Such regression-based tests seem supportive of CIP. However, it is not clear if equation (1.13) represents a particularly good vehicle for testing CIP since even if $\alpha = 0$ and $\beta = 1$ is supported empirically (and therefore CIP holds on average) the estimated residuals may suggest substantial arbitrage opportunities and therefore CIP may not hold at every point in time. A further problem with this test is that often the different constituent components of CIP – the two interest rates and exchange rates – are not exactly matched in terms of being quoted at the same point in time. More recent tests relying on the CD attempt to address this point.

Frenkel and Levich (1975, 1977) represent one of the first tests of CIP based on calculation of the CD and they demonstrate, using Treasury Bills yields, that there are many non-zero values of the calculated CD for both UK–US and US–Canada combinations, but that 80% of these non-zero observations can be explained by the various transaction costs associated with covered interest arbitrage. Aliber (1973), however, has argued that Tbills are not well suited for the calculation of CIP because they potentially suffer from both sovereign and political risk. Since Euro-denominated bonds do not suffer from such risks they are viewed as a better candidate for the calculation of CIP and when they are used by Frenkel and Levich they report few non-zero values of CD. Taylor (1989) has criticised CIP-based tests which use equation (1.13) or the CD to test CIP because they do not use simultaneous quotes which investors would actually have been working with. When Taylor uses high quality matched data he finds that there are no deviations from CIP. This finding is consistent with the so-called Cambist or Bankers view of covered interest parity which suggests that commercial banks simply price forward rates off the interest differential (given the spot rate). Under this view covered interest rate parity is essentially an identity.

1.7 Open and closed parity conditions

In the earlier analysis, we have argued that it is the uncertainty about the future course of exchange rates that forces arbitrageurs to enter into forward contracts. But if, in contrast, arbitrageurs have complete certainty about the future path of exchange rates, or in the case of uncertainty, arbitrageurs are risk neutral (i.e. they are only concerned with the expected return of their investment and not the risk), what difference would this make to equation (1.11)? Under such circumstances the forward exchange rate in (1.11) may be replaced by the natural logarithm of the expected exchange rate, s_{t+k}^e, and we obtain:

$$i_t - i_t^* = s_{t+k}^e - s_t, \tag{1.14}$$

or in terms of its rational expectations counterpart

$$i_t - i_t^* = E_t s_{t+k} - s_t, \tag{1.14'}$$

where an asterisk denotes a foreign magnitude. That is to say, in the case of certainty and if, for example, $i > i^*$, arbitrageurs will be prepared to move funds from the foreign country to the home country as long as the exchange rate for the domestic currency is not expected to depreciate by as much as, or more than, the interest differential. Equation (1.14) is known as uncovered (or open) interest rate parity (UIP). In a world of certainty the expected change in the exchange rate and the forward premium, or discount, would be identical. In conditions of uncertainty they would differ by an amount equal to the risk premium required to persuade speculators to fulfil forward contracts. It is important to note that although UIP is often portrayed with rational expectations, as in (1.14'), this is an auxiliary assumption.

The empirical evidence on uncovered interest parity is usually indirect in the sense that it involves substituting the forward premium for the interest differential and assuming expectations are rational and therefore $\Delta s_{t+k} = E_t \Delta s_{t+k} + u_{t+k}$. On this basis the following equation can be estimated:

$$\Delta s_{t+k} = \alpha + \beta f p_t + \varepsilon_{t+1}, \tag{1.15}$$

where the null hypothesis is that $\alpha = 0$ and $\beta = 1$. Given, as we have seen, the way commercial banks price forward contracts suggests that CIP is effectively an identity, this may not be a bad way to test UIP, and there is a vast literature on the empirical implementation of equation (1.15) which is considered in Chapter 15. As we shall see there, this literature strongly suggests that UIP does not hold. More direct regression-based tests of (1.14) are based on:

$$\Delta s_{t+k} = \alpha + \beta (i_t - i_t^*) + \varepsilon_{t+1}. \tag{1.16}$$

The early empirical literature which tests 1.16 (see, *inter alia*, Cumby and Obstfeld 1981; Hacche and Townend 1981; Loopesko 1984; Davidson 1985; MacDonald and Torrance 1990) provides clear evidence that the UIP condition is strongly rejected, in the sense that the hypothesis $\alpha = 0$ and $\beta = 1$ is rejected and the error terms are serially correlated in the presence of non-overlapping data (the issue of overlapping data is discussed in Chapter 15). However, it is important to note that tests based on (1.15) and (1.16) rely also on assuming rational expectations and the supposed failure of UIP could in part be due to an expectational issue rather than the failure of the condition per se (this is discussed again in more detail in Chapter 15). More recent tests of UIP have, however, been more supportive of the hypothesis. For example, Chinn and Meridth (2004) find that there is much more support for UIP when 'long horizon' maturity yields of around 10 years are used (traditional tests rely on short-term yields), and Lothian and Wu (2003) find support for UIP between the UK and US when a long time span of data, encompassing two centuries, is used. Lothian and Wu argue that UIP does not perform particularly well for the post-Bretton Woods period because of the exceptional behaviour of the US dollar in the 1980s (i.e. the exceptional appreciation and then subsequent depreciation of the US dollar in that period imparts what amounts to a huge outlier in the data). Chinn (2006) also finds evidence supportive of UIP when he uses survey data expectations to measure the expected change in the exchange rate, rather than impose the rational expectations hypothesis.

Our discussion of UIP leads on to the concept of perfect capital mobility. In the current context, perfect capital mobility is taken to be the joint hypothesis that bonds, identical in all respects apart from their currency denomination, are perfect substitutes and that arbitrage continually ensures the domestic interest equals the foreign rate adjusted for the expected change in the exchange rate (or to put it slightly differently international portfolios adjust instantly). On this basis equation (1.14) may be taken as a representation of perfect capital mobility. Equation (1.12) may not, however, be taken as a measure of perfect capital mobility since, as we have seen, bonds may not be regarded as perfect substitutes if risk is important; that is, there may be a risk premium over and above the expected change in the exchange rate. Other factors, in addition to exchange risk factors, which make bonds imperfect substitutes are: political risk, default risk, differential tax risk and liquidity considerations. Capital may also be imperfectly mobile if portfolios take time to adjust. The definition of perfect capital mobility used here accords with the general usage of the term in the international finance literature (see, *inter alia*, Fleming 1962; Dornbusch 1976; Frenkel and Rodriguez 1982), but contrasts with the definition given by, *inter alia*, Dornbusch and Krugman (1978) and Frankel (1979). The latter take perfect capital mobility simply to mean the instantaneous adjustment of portfolios.[10]

Since we shall be considering in future chapters circumstances where capital is less than perfectly mobile, it will prove useful to define a capital flow function:

$$CAP = \beta[i_t - i_t^* - s_{t+k}^e - s_t], \tag{1.17}$$

where CAP represents a net capital inflow (capital account surplus) and β represents the speed of adjustment in capital markets. Hence if $\beta = \infty$ capital is perfectly mobile, since any change in the uncovered interest differential will lead to a potentially infinite capital movement and clearly (1.14) holds continuously. If, however, β lies between 0 and ∞ capital is less than perfectly mobile and net yield differentials are not continuously arbitraged away. With $\beta = 0$ capital will clearly be completely immobile.

Open or uncovered interest parity relates, as we have seen, to international interest differentials. Closed interest parity, or the Fisher condition, hypothesises that a country's nominal interest rate can be decomposed into a real interest rate plus the expected inflation rate:

$$i_t = r_t^e + \Delta p_{t+k}^e, \tag{1.18}$$

where r_t^e is the *ex ante* real rate of interest, which is often assumed constant, and Δp_{t+k}^e is the expected change in the log price level or the expected inflation rate.

These measures of interest parity are nominal in nature (i.e. nominal interest rates and exchange rates). In Chapter 8 we consider the real interest rate parity condition.

1.8 Some stylised facts about exchange rate behaviour

In this section we consider some stylised facts about exchange rate behaviour. In particular, we consider the time series properties of the first and second moments (mean and variance) of exchange rates and the so-called exchange rate disconnect which relates to both the mean and variance of the exchange rate.

1.8.1   *The level, or first moment, of the exchange rate and the exchange rate disconnect*

It has become something of a stylised fact for financial markets that the uncon-ditional price, or return, distributions of financial assets tend to have fatter tails than the normal distribution. In contrast to the thin-tailed normal distribution, in which the tails decline exponentially, fat-tailed asset market returns decline by a power factor. The so-called fat-tailed result has been confirmed for foreign exchange rates by Westerfield (1977) and Boothe and Glassman (1987) using para-metric methods and Koedijk *et al.* (1990) using semi-parametric methods. De Vries (1994) notes that this fat-tailed phenomenon is more pronounced when exchange rates are managed than in a pure float and he further notes that exchange rate returns of currencies which experience similar monetary policies exhibit no sig-nificant skewness while those with dissimilar polices tend to exhibit skewness (this being most marked in instances where one country is pursuing deflationary policies while its partner is pursuing inflationary monetary policy).[11]

Nominal, and also real, exchange rates, as we shall see in Chapters 3 and 4, are generally regarded as stochastic process containing a unit root; that is, they are $I(1)$ processes. Since the standard range of macroeconomic fundamentals also contain unit roots this has led to most recent empirical analysis of the determinants of the level of nominal exchange rate using non-stationary time series methods, such as cointegration analysis (this is discussed in some detail in Chapter 6).

One of the key themes considered in this book is the so-called exchange rate disconnect of Obstfeld and Rogoff (2000a). This disconnect shows up in two ways. The first is that discussed in the next section and concerns the apparent lack of connection between the volatility of exchange rate fundamentals and the volatility of the underlying macroeconomic fundamentals. The second is in terms of the level of the exchange rate. In particular, since the seminal paper by Meese and Rogoff (1983) it has become something of stylised fact to argue that exchange rate forecasts, based on macroeconomic fundamentals, are unable to outperform a simple random walk. In their survey in the Handbook of International Economics, Frankel and Rose (1995a) argue that 'the Meese and Rogoff analysis of *short hori-zons* [less than 36 months] has never been convincingly overturned or explained. It continues to exert a pessimistic effect on the field of empirical exchange rate modeling in particular and international finance in general' (page 23, emphasis added). Rogoff (1999) has argued something very similar to this.

So it would seem that the level, or mean, of the nominal exchange rate is discon-nected from macroeconomic fundamentals. However, one of the key arguments of this book is our belief that the variability of and the level of the exchange rate is explicable in terms of macro-fundamentals and the disconnect story has been somewhat overplayed.

1.8.2 The volatility, or second moment, of the exchange rate

One of the key features of exchange rates when they are flexible is that they tend to be highly volatile. Such volatility exhibits itself in a number of ways. First, there is the concept of historical or regime volatility (which we discuss in greater detail in the next sub-section). For example, comparing the volatility of exchange rates in the Bretton Woods system to that of the post-Bretton Woods system Hallwood and MacDonald (2000) note that volatility has increased six-fold. At first blush this may not be surprising since the Bretton Woods period was one of fixed but adjustable exchange rates and so one might expect exchange rates to be less volatile than a floating rate regime. However, the original proponents of flexible rate regimes (such as Friedman 1953 and Sohmen 1961) viewed fixed rate regimes as highly unstable regimes prone to speculative attacks and exchange rate realignments, essentially due to the lack of an effective adjustment mechanism, whereas floating rate regimes were thought to be stable regimes since they provided an automatic adjustment mechanism.

Another way in which exchange rates are often described as volatile is with respect to fundamentals within a floating regime – usually referred to as intra-regime volatility and also considered in more detail in the next sub-section. For example, in Table 1.4 we report the coefficients of variation of exchange rates and prices and interest rate differentials. This makes clear that exchange rates are much more volatile than prices, a result which carries over to a whole range of other fundamentals such as money supplies, output levels and current account imbalances (see MacDonald 1988, 1999a). However, notice that Table 1.4 also makes clear that exchange rate volatility is dwarfed by the volatility of interest rates. This suggests, therefore, that exchange rates behave in a manner similar to other asset prices or yields and perhaps the volatility of exchange rates is to be understood by analysing them as asset prices (and, indeed, this is a topic we consider in some detail in Chapters 4–8).

Exchange rates are also regarded as volatile relative to information contained in the expected exchange rate. As we have seen, in the absence of a risk premium the forward exchange rate should be a measure of the expected exchange rate and therefore the forward premium is a measure of the expected change in the exchange

Table 1.4 Coefficients of variation of exchange rates and fundamentals

Country/variable	s	$p - p^*$	$i - i^*$
France	18.16	8.32	199.38
Germany	16.23	2.51	54.52
Japan	14.58	2.79	146.49
Switzerland	16.73	3.78	40.40
UK	22.36	5.17	56.91

Source: MacDonald (1999a).

(a)

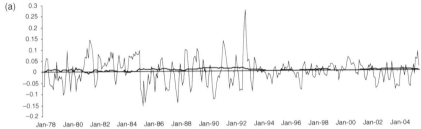

Notes: Heavy line, forward premium; light line, actual change; both series in natural logarithms.

(b)

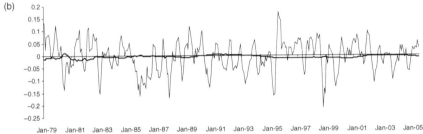

Notes: Heavy line, forward premium; light line, actual change; both series in natural logarithms.

(c)

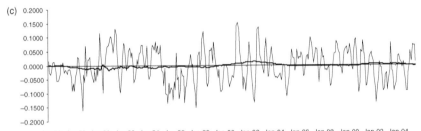

Notes: Heavy line, forward premium; light line, actual change; both series in natural logarithms. After 1998 data refers to
Deutschemark's fixed rate to euro.

Figure 1.5 (a) UK pound sterling per US dollar, actual change and forward premium.
(b) Japanese yen per US dollar, actual change and forward premium. (c) German
Deutschemark per US dollar, actual change and forward premium.

rate. In Figure 1.5a, b and c we plot the exchange rate change against the forward
premium for the bilateral dollar rates of the Japanese yen, German mark and
pound sterling. The figure shows that the forward premium is roughly constant
around zero, while the actual exchange rate change is highly volatile. There are
a number of potential explanations for this result, which is quite general and
applies to numerous exchange rates. One is that there is a lot of news hitting
foreign exchange markets and so the actual exchange rate moves a lot relative to
the expected value set in period t. Such a view is, of course, entirely consistent
with rational information processing. The 'news' approach to exchange rates is

considered in Chapter 15. An alternative, and diametrically opposite view to this is that agents are simply irrational and the excessive volatility of exchange rates relative to the expected exchange rate is a reflection of this. A final interpretation is that there is a time-varying risk premium which moves in an opposite way to the exchange rate change thereby cancelling the effect of the exchange rate volatility when the two are aggregated together in the overall forward premium. The role of the risk premium in the forward premium is also considered in Chapter 15.

The kind of exchange rate volatility that we have been discussing is evident in monthly or even quarterly data. However, when higher frequency data – such as daily or intra-daily data – are considered exchange rates exhibit volatility features which are similar to other asset prices. In particular, one of the key features of financial markets, including the foreign exchange market, is that when high frequency exchange rate data is used to analyse the volatility, or variance, of the exchange rate the price is time-varying and such volatility exhibits clustering or bunching; that is, the phenomenon that large (small) price changes are followed by other large (small) price changes, although of unpredictable sign. The dependency of the second moment of the exchange rate distribution on past values is usually modelled using the autoregressive conditional heteroscedasticity (ARCH) models of Engle (1982) and the generalised autoregressive conditional heteroscedasticty (GARCH) model of Bollerlsev (1986). (See Bollerslev *et al.* 1992 for a literature overview.) For example, using daily data for five bilateral US dollar spot exchange rates Hseih (1988) shows that squared nominal exchange rate returns are highly serially correlated, thereby confirming that conditional volatility is changing over time, and that and ARCH(12) model with linearly declining lag structure captures most of the non-linear stochastic dependence (see also Milhoj 1987; Diebold 1988; Diebold and Nerlove 1989). A number of other papers have gone on to show that GARCH (1,1) models do at least as well as the ARCH class of model in capturing the dependence (see McCurdy and Morgan 1988; Hsieh 1989; Kugler and Lenz 1990). These kinds of results confirm the volatility clustering idea.[12] It is worth noting that the significance of ARCH and GARCH effects for exchange rate returns weakens considerably when the data sampling moves from a daily frequency to a monthly frequency and is usually insignificant at lower frequencies, such as quarterly.

Although the ARCH and GARCH models are able to give a good description of the behaviour of the conditional variance of the exchange rate the estimates referred to earlier do not capture all of the excess kurtosis in the data (see, for example, McCurdy and Morgan 1987; Baillie and Bolerslev 1989; Bollerslev *et al.* 1992). One way of addressing this issue has involved using alternative conditional error distributions, such as the Student-*t* (see, for example, Baillie and Bollerslev 1989) and a normal-Poisson (Hsieh 1989). Lastrapes (1989) and McCurdy and Morgan (1987) suggest that the remaining leptokurtosis is a reflection of outliers associated with policy events and when dummy variables are used to capture such events the leptokurtosis decreases markedly.

Under the maintained assumption of market efficiency, one interpretation of the volatility clustering phenomenon captured in ARCH and GARCH estimates of foreign exchange returns could be that the information reaches the market in clusters or that it takes time for market participants to properly process new information. In Chapter 14, on market microstructure, we consider these interpretations for volatility clustering. We also postpone considering ARCH and GARCH estimates of the foreign exchange risk premium until Chapter 15.

1.8.3 *Intra- and inter-regime volatility*

As we have just seen, one of the key features of a flexible exchange rate regime is the evident volatility of the exchange rate and it is useful to classify such volatility into intra- and inter-regime volatility. Intra-regime volatility refers to the perception, or stylised fact, that in the post-Bretton Woods period nominal exchange rates are more volatile than a standard set of macroeconomic fundamentals (see, for example, Frankel and Meese 1987 and MacDonald 1999). One of the key topics discussed in this book is: can such volatility be explained in terms of traditional macroeconomic fundamentals or is it necessary to move to non-fundamentals, such as noise trading and irrational behaviour or have a paradigm shift away from traditional fundamentals towards the market microstructure interpretation of exchange rate behaviour (see Chapter 14)? Friedman in his classic 1953 essay on floating exchange rates cogently argued that excess volatility should be viewed as a function of instability in the underlying fundamentals:

> instability of exchange rates is a symptom of instability in the underlying economic structure .... a flexible exchange rate need not be an unstable exchange rate. If it is, it is primarily because there is underlying instability in the economic conditions.

Although, as we have said, the issues of excess exchange rate volatility is something of a stylised fact, or widely held belief, in the profession, it is not entirely clear from an empirical perspective that exchange rates are, in fact, excessively volatile relative to macroeconomic fundamentals (and this is something we shall return to in Chapter 7).

One response to the intra-regime volatility argument is to say that if you fix one price, such as the exchange rate, the volatility that was previously observed in it will show up elsewhere in the economic system (say, in terms of increased interest rate volatility). However, the literature on *inter-regime* volatility suggests the opposite, namely, as countries move from fixed exchange rate regimes to flexible exchange rate regimes the volatility of the underlying fundamentals does not change and all that changes is simply the volatility of the (real and nominal) exchange rate (see Mussa 1986; Baxter and Stockman 1989; Flood and Rose 1995, 1999; MacDonald 1999; Arnold, de Vries and MacDonald 2005). For example, Baxter and Stockman (1989) examine the variability of output, trade variables and private and government consumption for both the Bretton Woods and post-Bretton Woods regimes and they concluded that they were 'unable to find evidence that the cyclic behavior of real macroeconomic aggregates depends systematically on the exchange rate regime. The only exception is the well known case of the real exchange rate'. In particular, the real exchange rate is around four times more volatile in a flexible rate regime compared to a fixed rate regime. Flood and Rose (1995, 1999) construct composite measures of macroeconomic fundamentals (relative money supplies and relative outputs) and compare the volatility of this term to the volatility of the exchange rate and are unable to find any discernable difference in the volatility of the fundamentals in the move from fixed to floating, but do find a significant difference in the volatility of the nominal exchange rate in floating rate regimes. We have reproduced the Flood and Rose results here in Figures 1.6 and 1.7. Figure 1.6 is a measure of exchange rate volatility for the bilateral dollar exchange rates of eight currencies over the Bretton Woods and post-Bretton Woods regimes (points to the left of the vertical line superimposed on each figure represent the switch from Bretton Woods – observations to the left – to post-Bretton Woods – points to the right). Figure 1.7 shows the behaviour of a measure of composite fundamentals over the Bretton Woods and post-Bretton Woods periods (the construction of this composite term is discussed in detail in Chapter 6). A visual inspection of Figures 1.6 and 1.7 clearly indicates that in moving from fixed to floating exchange rates the volatility of the fundamentals remains unchanged, while the volatility of the exchange is clearly regime dependent and increases dramatically in the post-Bretton Woods period. A number of researchers (see, for example, Flood and Rose 1995, 1999) have argued that what changes in the move from fixed to floating exchange rates is the structure of the foreign exchange market or the market microstructure and therefore to understand the kind of behaviour portrayed in Figures 1.6 and 1.7 one has to understand the microstructure of foreign exchange markets and this is a topic we consider in Chapter 14. In Chapter 6 we give a macroeconomic interpretation for Figures 1.6 and 1.7.[13]

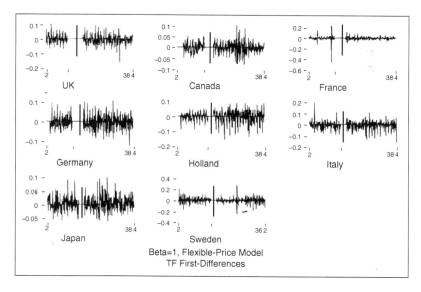

Figure 1.6 Time series of traditional fundamentals, benchmark flexible-price model.

Source: Flood and Rose (1995).

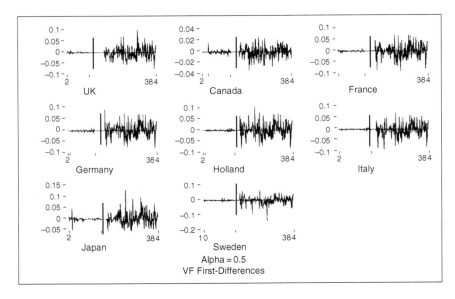

Figure 1.7 Time series of benchmark virtual fundamentals.

Source: Flood and Rose (1995).

1.8.4   *The close correlation between real and nominal exchange rates*

A related point, alluded to in the earlier discussion, concerns the close correlation between real and nominal exchange rates in flexible exchange rate regimes. This is illustrated in Figure 1.8a,b where we plot the real and nominal values of the pound sterling, German mark and Japanese yen. The correlation is clearly extremely close and the actual correlation coefficient is in fact around 0.9 and this result is standard for the real and nominal exchange rates of any industrialised country. Mussa (1986) and others have argued that this close correlation simply reflects the effect of price rigidities on the real exchange rate. For example, if prices are sticky in the short-run and the nominal exchange rate is volatile, due, say, to the classic overshooting story, discussed in Chapter 5, then the real exchange rate will exhibit the same kind of volatility as the nominal exchange rate, which is what we observe in practice. On this view, the feedback runs from the nominal to the real exchange rate. Stockman (1980, 1988) has argued that in a world where prices are flexible and there is preponderance of real shocks, such as technology and preference shocks, the real exchange rate will be volatile and this will impart volatility into the nominal rate. On this view, therefore, feedback runs from the real to the nominal exchange rate. However, one problem with this interpretation is that it seems inconsistent with the stylised fact noted earlier that in moving from

Notes: Heavy line, real exchange rate; light line, actual exchange rate; both series in natural logarithms.

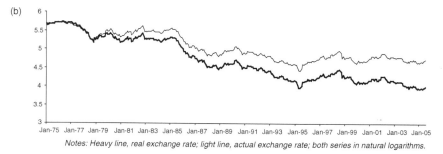

Notes: Heavy line, real exchange rate; light line, actual exchange rate; both series in natural logarithms.

Notes: Heavy line, real exchange rate; light line, actual exchange rate; both series in natural logarithms.
After 1998 data refers to Deutschemark's fixed rate to euro.

Figure 1.8 (a) UK pound sterling per US dollar, nominal and real rates. (b) Japanese yen per US dollar, nominal and real rates. (c) German Deutschemark per US dollar, nominal and real rates.

fixed to flexible exchange rates it is only the volatility of the real exchange rate that changes, the volatility of fundamental shocks does not change. The theoretical underpinnings of the Stockman view are presented in Chapter 4, and empirical evidence on this sticky price versus real shock approach is considered in Chapter 8 and more recent attempts at explaining regime volatility issues are considered again in Chapter 11, after the new open economy model of Obstfeld and Rogoff has been introduced.

1.9 Exchange rate regimes

The standard textbook definition of an exchange rate regime usually makes the stark distinction between fixed and floating, or flexible, exchange rates and on that basis describes a variety of historical exchange rate regimes, namely, the Classical Gold standard, 1870–1914, in which participating countries by fixing their currencies to one ounce of gold fixed their bilateral exchange rates; the inter-war gold exchange (fixed rate) standard; the inter-war floating rate experience; the Bretton Woods fixed, but adjustable, exchange rate regime in which currencies were fixed to the dollar; and the post-Bretton Woods regime in which exchange rates have supposedly been flexible. However, between the textbook cases – what is now referred to as the corner cases – there are various shades of grey and as we shall see the polar case of extreme fixity needs to be more carefully defined.

Nearly all of the empirical studies referred to in this book have used the official or 'standard' classification of an exchange rate regime published by the IMF in its *Annual Report on Exchange Rate Arrangement and Exchange Restrictions*. Until 1997, the IMF asked member states to make a self-declaration of their exchange rate relationship as belonging to four categories, namely, fixed, limited flexibility, managed floating and independently floating.[14] However, as Calvo and Reinhart (2002), Levi-Yeyati and Sturzeneger (2002) and Reinhart and Rogoff (2002) point out, often times when a regime was classified as either independently floating, or a managed float, the reality was rather different in the sense that the country had a *de facto* fixed peg or crawling peg. Furthermore, Reinhart and Rogoff (2002) point out that in the post-World War II period nearly every country has relied at some point in time on either capital controls or dual exchange rates and so the officially reported exchange rate is likely to be 'profoundly misleading'. For example, they report that in 1950, 45% of countries in their sample of 150 countries had dual rates and many more countries had thriving parallel markets. Furthermore, amongst the more important currencies, the UK had multiple exchange rates into the 1970s, Italy in the 1980s and Belgium and Luxembourg until 1990.

Indeed, on using market-determined rates, instead of official rates, Reinhart and Rogoff (2002) find that *de facto* floating was not uncommon during the Bretton Woods period of pegged exchange rates – 45% of countries that were supposedly on pegged regimes were in fact on some form of managed float and they go as far as to suggest that it is difficult to detect any change in exchange rate behaviour between the Bretton Woods and post-Bretton Woods regimes which clearly has important implications for findings of regime volatility discussed earlier and again in Chapters 6 and 11 later.

Since 1997, the IMF has fleshed out the rich variety of intermediate cases between the so-called corner positions of a pure float and a rigidly fixed exchange rate, as exists in a monetary union, and here we follow a similar taxonomy, proposed by Frankel (2003). He distinguishes seven intermediate cases between the two extreme corners of a pure float and participation in a monetary union, each of which can have numerous further variants. In Table 1.5 we present a slightly modified version of Frankel's categorisation.

Table 1.5 Exchange rate regime classifications

Floating corner	Intermediate regimes	Rigidly fixed corner
Pure float	Band	Currency board
Managed or dirty float	Crawling peg	Dollar- and euroisation
	Basket peg	Commodity standard
	Adjustable peg	Monetary union

Source: Frankel (2003).

In the first cell we have the most flexible exchange rate regime and in the bottom right cell we have the least flexible and most rigid regime, in the form of a monetary union. These are the two extreme corner cases. In between there are a range of options distinguished by the degree of flexibility. A managed float can be very close to a pure float if the monetary authorities only intervene occasionally and in small amounts, or it can approximate something closer to an intermediate regime if the authorities intervene on a more or less continuous basis to, say, satisfy an inflation target (such as has been the case in Singapore). Banded regimes are designed to capture the target zone arrangements of Bergsten-Williamson (in which the band is defined around the FEER – see Chapter 9) and Krugman (in which the band is defined around a fixed central parity – see Chapter 12). A crawling peg system is one in which the peg changes usually to accommodate inflation – an indexed crawl – or is a preannouced crawl to maintain competitiveness. A basket peg is where a currency is fixed relative to a basket of its trading partner currencies and an adjustable peg is one in which the currency has a fixed central rate but it can be changed to, say, accommodate disequilibria such as those occurring in the balance of payments (such as occurred in the Bretton Woods system). In the rigidly fixed corner we have the currency board solution which usually involves a country pegging to another currency (the dollar) and allowing the home currency to be transferred into the foreign at the going rate.[15] A commodity standard is where a country fixes its exchange rate rigidly in terms of a commodity such as gold (i.e. the gold standard period) and finally we have the monetary union case which is usually regarded as an irrevocable system of fixed exchange rates, although it may not be in the absence of full political union.

Reinhart and Rogoff (2002) note that the most popular exchange rate regime over recent history has been a pegged rate (33% of observations for the sample 1970–2001) closely followed by a crawling peg, or a variant thereof, which accounts for over 26% of observations. Reinhart and Rogoff (2002) also forcefully argue that it is important to introduce the exchange rate category 'freely falling' which is a floating rate regime in which inflation is over 40% per annum. This type of regime is much more common than the traditional textbook free floating rate regime. This classification makes up 22% and 37% of observations in Africa and Western Hemisphere, respectively, during 1970–2001 and in the 1990s freely falling accounted for 41% of the observations for the transition economies. Hence they argue that given the distortions associated with inflation of 40% and over, any fixed versus flexible rate comparison which does not separate out the freely falling episodes is 'meaningless'.

Using a monthly data set on official and market-determined exchange rates for the period 1946–98, Reinhart and Rogoff (2002) calculate the exchange rate chronologies of 153 countries and using these chronologies and descriptive statistics are able to group episodes into a much finer grid of regimes – 14 in all – than even the recent official IMF classifications and that given in Table 1.5 earlier. As we have noted, this finer classification allows Reinhart and Rogoff (2002) to argue the traditional IMF classification has serious flaws as it has a bias in favour of describing a country's exchange rate regime as a 'peg' when it is not.

1.10 Fixed versus floating exchange rates

In this section we overview the respective cases for flexible and fixed exchange rates and then go on to overview the empirical evidence on the comparative performance of these two regimes. The original, traditional, case for flexible exchange rates was made by Milton Friedman in his classic 1953 essay 'The Case for Flexible Exchange Rates'. We briefly outline here the traditional case for flexible exchange rates, based on Friedman's initial article. First, a flexible exchange rate allows a country to pursue an independent monetary policy, since compared to a fixed rate regime, where monetary policy is constrained to defending the peg, the rate of change of official reserves should, as we saw in Figure 1.5, be zero under a floating rate system. Perhaps the contrast is clearest in the case of a country facing a recession with downwardly rigid prices where a monetary expansion, and the consequent exchange rate depreciation, would produce a boost to aggregate demand (through both the interest rate and the real exchange rate), thereby moving the economy to internal/external balance. In a fixed rate regime the economy has to rely on automatic mechanisms, such as wage and price flexibility, which are likely to be quite slow and long drawn out. Note this argument relies on asymmetric price rigidities – prices are rigid in a downward direction but not up.

The second supposed advantage of a flexible exchange rate is in terms of its insulating properties with respect to real shocks, which show up in the form of trade shocks. For example, a fall in demand in the rest of the world for the home country's exports would automatically be countered by an exchange rate depreciation and a fall in the terms of trade which produced an offsetting stimulus to demand.

A third advantage of a flexible-based regime is that it offers a country stability compared to a fixed rate system such as the Bretton Woods system. This was a key strand in the argument of Friedman in favour of a floating rate system. Because of the lack of an effective adjustment mechanism fixed rate systems were thought to be prone to speculative attacks and periodic crises (speculative attack models are considered in Chapter 13). Indeed, the stabilising nature of expectations under a floating rate system (see Machlup 1972) was seen as a key element in producing a tranquil exchange rate environment.

A fourth advantage of a flexible rate system is that it allows the central bank to maintain two potentially important advantages of an independent central bank, namely, seigniorage and lender-of-last resort. The latter may be important in a banking crises where the ability of the central bank to create unlimited funds may be important in bailing out banks.

A fifth advantage of a floating rate system is in terms of its ability to let the world economy function without recourse to trade barriers and tariffs. The idea being that if the exchange rate is free to equilibrate a country's balance of payments the need for protectionist devices – such as tariffs and quotas – is likely to be limited. A final argument in favour of flexible exchange rates is in terms of the need to hold foreign exchange reserves. In principle, and as we saw in Section 1.4, with a floating exchange rate, the change in official reserves is zero (see Equation 1.8). Since reserves earn a zero, or low, return compared to a longer-term investment there would be some, perhaps small, savings for the national economy (a central bank would still hold reserves in a free float to pay for official commercial transactions).

There is also a long tradition in the economics literature which recognises that macroeconomic performance should be enhanced by having a fixed exchange rate. Perhaps the main traditional advantage of a fixed exchange rate system is to prevent countries pursuing an independent monetary policy, which is seen as imparting an inflationary bias into the economy. If a central bank puts a premium on fighting inflation it may find it advantageous to peg its exchange rate to a hard currency with a strong anti-inflationary reputation (for example, the DM was seen in this light for much of the post-war period) and so 'import' the credibility and low inflation environment. The idea being that in the presence of a credible peg workers and managers will set wages and prices on the basis of an expected low inflation environment in the future (because the currency peg prevents the central bank from expanding the money supply, especially if it is an irrevocable peg), thereby allowing the country to attain a lower inflation rate for any given level of output (Giavazzi and Giovannini 1989; Dornbusch 2001). Edwards and Magendzo (2003) have argued that the harder the peg, the more effective it is in enhancing credibility.

A second advantage of fixed rates is that when exchange rates are flexible they are, as we have noted, highly volatile and such volatility can impart uncertainty into trade and investment decisions, thereby having a negative influence on international trade and investment. Removing this source of uncertainty should therefore encourage international trade and investment. However, an alternative response is to say that trade and investment should be unaffected since agents can hedge the risk in the foreign exchange market. However, forward markets are notoriously incomplete – being non-existent for some developing countries and only existing at very limited maturities for all. Initially, empirical studies failed to reveal a link between exchange rate volatility on trade and investment, but more recent – panel based – estimates do in fact show an important link.

Related to the trade and investment effects of exchange rate volatility is the issue of exchange rate misalignment (see Chapter 9) and its effects on international trade and investment. Misalignment occurs because exchange rates can often spend long periods away from their fundamentals-based equilibrium due to purely speculative influences. For example, the long swings in the dollar in the 1980s – its appreciation down to 1985 and the subsequent depreciation – are generally regarded as being driven by speculative factors. By fixing an exchange rate such misalignments are removed and the deleterious effects on trade and investment are also removed.

A further important advantage of fixed exchange rates is in preventing competitive, or beggar-thy-neighbour, devaluations. Looking back at the inter-war experience of exchange rate flexibility, this was one of the key motivating factors for the architects of the Bretton Woods system who saw a system of fixed exchange rates as a means of obtaining a cooperative solution to the competitive devaluation issue. As Frankel (2003) points out, a recent update of this kind of argument is the currency crises and contagion that occurred in the 1990s where devaluation in one country immediately spread to neighbouring countries because they felt at a competitive disadvantage, but ultimately they did not gain from this.

Aspects of the earlier traditional case for fixed exchange rates have been combined into a prescription that fiscally disciplined emerging markets should fix their currencies to an international money (such as the dollar, euro or yen) and thereby enjoy a rapid accumulation of foreign exchange reserves through export growth, and maintain a high saving ratio which provides certainty to business and profit margins to investors. Such a policy environment will, in turn, lead to a low and stable domestic interest rate which would ensure that the economy maintains the confidence of international investors (see Razin and Rubinstein 2005). However, as Fischer (2001) notes, 'each of the major international capital market-related crises since 1994 – Mexico, in 1994, Thailand, Indonesia and Korea in 1997, Russia and Brazil in 1998, and Argentina and Turkey in 2000 – has in some way involved a fixed or pegged exchange rate regime. At the same time countries that did not have pegged rates – among them South Africa, Israel in 1998, Mexico in 1998, and Turkey in 1998 – avoided crises of the type that afflicted emerging market countries with pegged rates.'

Razin and Rubinstein (2005) argue that a fixed exchange rate regime may be bad for a country if it generates a large increase in the probability of, what they refer to as, a 'sudden stop' crises (i.e. a combination of a financial, or currency, crises and a sharp fall in output) and this dominates the positive effects of a fixed exchange rate on, for example, enhancing trade. Currency and financial crises stemming from fixed exchange rates are considered in some detail in Chapter 13.

Clearly, the practical cost-benefit analysis of an exchange rate regime depends very much on getting the definition of the regime correct. For example, using their reclassification of exchange rate regimes, discussed earlier, Reinhart and Rogoff (2002) show that the performance of a freely floating regime is dramatically different compared to the official IMF classification. For example, the IMF classification, over the period 1970–2001, produces an average annual inflation rate of 174% and an average per capita growth rate of only 0.5% for floating rate regimes, but with the Reinhart and Rogoff (2002) classification free floats deliver average annual inflation of less than 10%, which is the lowest of any exchange rate arrangement, and an average per capita growth rate of 2.3%. Reinhart and Rogoff (2002) argue that this seems to support Friedman's advocacy of the superior properties of floating rate regimes.

Edwards and Yeyati (2003) empirically examine two of the arguments in favour of flexible exchange rates, namely, their role as absorbers of real shocks and the link between this role and the presence of downward rigid prices. Using a *de facto* classification, rather than the IMF *de jure* classification, they find that flexible exchange rate arrangements do help to reduce the impact of terms of trade shocks on GDP growth in both emerging and industrial countries, and found that real output growth is more sensitive to negative than to positive shocks.

There is a large literature which seeks to empirically assess the benefits of, and effects on, macroeconomic performance of different types of exchange rate regimes, particularly fixed versus flexible exchange rate regimes (see, for example, Ghosh *et al.* 1997, 2003; Levy-Yeyati and Sturzeneger 2002). Rogoff *et al.* (2004), using the *de facto* exchange rate classification of Rheinhart and Rogoff, provide a nice overview of the performance of different exchange rate regimes. Their key findings may be summarised as follows. First, mature economies with mature institutional frameworks have the best hope of enjoying the advantages of flexible exchange rates without suffering a loss of credibility. Specifically, their review of the extant studies shows that free floats have registered faster growth combined with relatively low inflation for such countries. This is not so, however, for emerging markets and non-emerging market developing countries, the other country category groups considered by Rogoff *et al.* Since non-emerging market developing countries are not well-integrated into international capital markets, they are probably best able to buy credibility with a fixed exchange rate and, indeed, it would seem that such countries have enjoyed relatively fast growth and low inflation when they have pegged their currencies. However, fixity is not seen as an option for emerging markets and, indeed, the evidence shows that such regimes have had a higher degree of crisis with fixed rate regimes, as noted earlier. This is because emerging markets have strong links with international capital markets, which are similar in nature to mature economies, but this is combined with institutional weaknesses (which shows up in higher inflation, fragile banking systems and debt sustainability) which make their policy makers less than fully credible and so some form of float, such as a crawling peg, is their best option while they learn how to float freely. The analysis of Rogoff *et al.* also shows that macroeconomic performance under all forms of *de facto* regimes was weaker in countries with dual or multiple exchange rates that deviated from official rates, suggesting that important gains may be had from exchange rate unification.

Razin and Rubinstein (2005) argue that in trying to detect the effect of an exchange rate regime on macroeconomic performance, specifically output growth, it is important to include a term which captures the probability of a crisis. They show using a panel data set of 100 low- and middle-income countries that the nature of the exchange rate regime, and also the degree of capital liberalisation, has a negligible effect on a country's economic growth, but that the probability of a crises term has a significantly negative impact on economic growth and that the probability of a crises increases with the switch to a fixed exchange rate.

1.11   The determinants of exchange rate regimes[16]

What are the factors which make a country's policy makers choose a particular exchange rate regime? From a theoretical perspective perhaps the best known guide to this issue is the so-called optimal currency area (OCA) literature. The OCA literature considers the following kind of issue. Consider a country in which there are two regions, A and B, and where the two regions initially have independent monetary policies (i.e. they have independent central banks, interest rates and exchange rates). The countries are considering relinquishing this monetary independence. Should they?

To answer this question, consider the situation where there is a change in demand or supply within the country. If such shocks are asymmetric, that is, they have a differential effect on the two regions, then there may well be an advantage to each of the regions having separate currencies, since, with independent monetary policies, the exchange rate would act as a shock absorber altering the real exchange rate and competitiveness. If, for example, a demand shock entailed a switch in preferences from A goods to B goods, an exchange rate depreciation in favour of A would eventually restore equilibrium by restoring competitiveness. However, if the shock affected the two regions in the same way – the change in preferences, for example, was felt equally across the two regions – there would be no advantage to having separate currencies. Indeed, from our discussions in the previous section there would be a clear advantage to having a single currency. So the issue of joining a monetary union comes down to the question of whether shocks are symmetric or asymmetric. This was the basic insight of Mundell's (1961) seminal paper. If the shocks hitting regions A and B are in fact asymmetric, at least in part, are there any factors which would substitute for the lack of an independent monetary policy if the two regions decided to participate in a monetary union? The OCA literature stresses three key factors.

First, Mundell (1961) argued that in the presence of wage and price stickiness as long as factor mobility, particularly labour mobility, was sufficiently high between the two regions that would assist in restoring equilibrium in the presence of a rigidly fixed exchange rate. In terms of the earlier example, labour and capital would move from region A to region B. If capital and labour are not sufficiently mobile then this would suggest a country should have a flexible exchange rate.

Second, McKinnon (1963) argued that if the two regions have a high degree of openness, in terms of trade as a per cent of GDP, they would not be disadvantaged by having a rigidly fixed exchange rate, especially since they could take advantage of the reduced transaction costs from participating in a monetary union. The nub of the McKinnon argument is that the maintenance of both internal balance (low inflation/high employment) and external balance is much easier to attain with a flexible exchange rate if the economy is relatively closed (i.e. a high proportion of its goods are non-traded), because the necessary resource transfers from the two sectors can occur to maintain internal and external balance. In contrast, if the economy is very open (a small non-traded sector relative to the traded sector) exchange rate flexibility will not be able to maintain equilibrium and the maintenance of internal–external balance (see Chapter 9 for a discussion of this concept) is easier to attain.

Third, Kenen (1963) focused on the degree to which an economy's industrial structure is diversified as the key OCA criterion. For example, if a country, or region, exports a wide variety of goods then in the presence of relative demand shocks and technology shocks, the effect of a shock on output will be less than the effect on individual industries. So a diversified economy will have less need for exchange rate flexibility in order to mitigate against the effects of shocks; conversely, an economy that is little diversified would gain from having a flexible exchange rate.

Taken together these criteria could give conflicting indications of the appropriate exchange rate regime. For example, a country with low labour and capital mobility should have a flexible rate under that criterion, but if it also has a high degree of trade openness it should have a fixed rate regime. Such potential ambiguity of the single criterion approach has been criticised by, for example, Argy and de Grauwe (1990), and although attempts have been made to provide a more general theoretical OCA framework these have not proved to be very satisfactory. Recently, therefore, attention has turned from the single criterion approach to an analysis of the shocks affecting economies or regions, since 'shock absorption' is seen to combine the *net* influence of several of the traditional criteria (Masson and Taylor 1993). There are a number of different aspects to this approach: are shocks symmetric or asymmetric?; are the shocks temporary or permanent?; what are the origins of the shocks – are they real nominal/domestic foreign?

Consider first the evidence on whether shocks are symmetrical or not. The evidence on this issue has focussed on the extent to which business cycles are correlated across regions and countries. A high correlation is taken to be *prima facie* evidence that shocks are symmetrical, whereas a low correlation is thought to be more indicative of asymmetric shocks. A large number of studies have demonstrated that business cycles correlations of European economies in the 1980s became more associated with the German business cycle than the US cycle.

De Grauwe and Vanhaverbeke (1993) are a first cut at regional cycles and they showed that in the 1980s output and employment variability in Europe had been higher at the regional than at the national level (the UK regions were not included in this study). Forni and Reichlin (2001) confirmed this, although they demonstrated that in both the UK and Greece there are strong country-specific cycles. This latter finding was confirmed by Barrios *et al.* (2001) for the UK. They demonstrate that there is only minor cyclical heterogeneity amongst the UK regions, the average correlation coefficient being approximately 0.7. Clark and van Wincoop (2000) confirm that inter-regional business cycle correlation is high – at about 0.7 – for regions within countries, but only in the range of 0.2 to 0.4 for regions at similar levels of economic development across countries.

Usefully, Rose and Engel (2000) present evidence that membership of a monetary union tends to increase the business cycle correlation by about 0.1, and conclude that 'while economically and statistically significant, the size of this effect is small in an absolute sense' (page 19).

In the standard OCA literature, and more specifically the model of Mundell discussed earlier, business cycle relationships are exogenous to monetary policy, in the shape of the monetary union. But in practice it may well be that the OCA criteria are endogenous to the exchange rate regime. Two main linkages are involved in the effect of monetary union on business cycle correlations. One is from the adoption of a common currency to bilateral trade intensity,[17] which then impacts on the business cycle correlation[18] through a variety of mechanisms, discussed later.[19] The second source of endogeneity relates to nominal shocks and, in particular, the role of the exchange rate as a source of extraneous shocks rather than a shock absorber.

Frankel and Rose (1998) examined the interrelationship between two optimum currency area criteria: the amount of bilateral trade integration and business cycle correlation. They find a strong positive association between country pair-wise correlation of economic activity and trade intensity.[20] However, there is another dimension to this argument that relates to sectoral specialisation: if sector specific demand and supply shocks are an important component of macroeconomic fluctuations (business cycles) then regions with similar sectoral structures will have relatively symmetric business cycles (Kenen 1963; Barrios *et al.* 2001). However, models of international trade and specialisation would predict reduced trade costs resulting from monetary integration will lead to an increase in sectoral level specialisation due to comparative advantage or agglomeration type arguments. Indeed, Krugman (1993) predicted that agglomeration would be an implication of monetary integration in Europe, with the consequent clustering of industries producing greater asymmetry of macro shocks.[21] In this view of the world monetary integration would undermine its own desirability. However, Ricci (1999) presents a new economic geography model in which the opposite effect occurs: monetary integration leads to a geographical dispersion of sectors and a more symmetric relationship between inter-regional macro shocks.[22] Devereux *et al.* (2001) showed, using a disaggregate sectoral data base, that relative specialism patterns in the UK had remained very stable over the period 1985–91. Similarly, Barrios *et al.* (2001) used GDP correlations and two indices of sectoral dissimilarity (one is an index for all sectors, while the other is an index for manufacturing industries on their own) and they showed that the UK regions had stable and remarkably similar indices with respect to the rest of the UK (Scotland had one of the lowest) over the period 1966–97.

In terms of the second source of endogeneity – nominal shocks – both Buiter (2000) and Layard *et al.* (2000) have argued that due to high international capital market integration exchange rates tend to be a source of shocks rather than acting as a shocks absorber (see also Artis and Ehrmann 2000). Regions should therefore pool their monetary policy in instances where they have high capital mobility. Under this view OCAs become endogenous because the pooling of monetary sovereignty removes one of the main causes of asymmetric macro shocks.

A second issue relating to shocks relates to whether they are permanent or transitory or not. Temporary or transitory shocks could, in principle, be cushioned by financing, whereas permanent shocks would require adjustment. A large number of papers have used the structural vector autoregression methods of Blanchard and Quah (1989) to assess this issue for groups of ERM countries. For example, using this methodology Cohen and Wyplosz (1989) show that symmetric shocks to France and Germany are permanent.

A large number of studies have attempted to empirically test the determinants of exchange rate regimes using the traditional OCA criteria, discussed earlier, and also other macroeconomic fundamentals such as monetary, foreign price shocks and a country's inflationary potential (see, *inter alia*, Heller 1978; Melvin 1985; Cuddington and Otoo 1990; Frieden *et al.* 2001). Most of such studies use a *de jure* exchange rate classification and Rogoff *et al.* (2004) survey this extensive literature and report that the results do not appear to be robust with respect to country coverage, sample period and regime classification: 'For example, openness – the most frequently analysed variable – is found to be significantly associated with floating rate regimes by three studies, significantly associated with fixed rate regimes by three studies and not significantly associated with any particular regime by another five studies.' The only terms which did produce a consistent relationship with the exchange rate regime were economy size and inflation.

1.12 Currency invoicing patterns and vehicle currency issues

As we shall see on a number of occasions in this book, particularly in our discussion of PPP and the effects of monetary and fiscal policy in an open economy context, an important issue in the economics of exchange rates is the currency used by exporters to invoice their products. In this regard, there are essentially three choices: the exporter can invoice in her own currency – referred to as producer's currency pricing or PCP – in the currency of the importer – labelled local currency pricing, LCP – or in a third currency, which is termed vehicle currency pricing, VCP. In an early contribution, Swoboda (1968, 1969) argued that transaction costs would be an important determinant of whether a currency would be used as an international medium of exchange – low transaction costs, signifying a high degree of liquidity would make a currency more likely to be used as a vehicle currency (see Rey 2001 for a recent theoretical exposition of this view). McKinnon (1979) focussed on industry characteristics as being an important determinant of a vehicle currency: goods that are homogeneous and traded in specialised markets are likely to be invoiced in a single low transaction cost currency. Krugman (1980) argued that intertia was an important determinant of a vehicle currency. That is, once a dominant currency has become established as a key vehicle currency in a specific market a firm in that market will have no incentive to use an alternative currency as it would incur higher transaction costs. More recent work has focussed on macroeconomic variability as the key determinant of a vehicle currency and some of this work is considered in chapter 11 (see, for example, Giovannini 1988; Devereux *et al.* 2001; Bacchetta and van Wincoop 2002; Goldberg and Tille 2005).

Goldberg and Tille (2005) exploit data on invoice currency use in exports and imports for 24 countries to show that the US dollar is the currency of choice for most transactions involving the US. They also find that the dollar is extensively used as a vehicle currency involving transactions of goods that do not directly involve the US but that are traded on organised exchanges or that are referenced priced international trade flows. They argue that industry herding and hysteresis appear to be the dominant characteristics for industries which have highly substitutive goods; variances and covariances amongst macroeconomic fundamentals are less important for invoicing patterns in such industries. However, Goldberg and Tille (2005) also demonstrate that business cycle volatility is important in the invoicing of diversified products.

2 Purchasing power parity and the PPP puzzle[1]

In this chapter and the next we consider the proposition of purchasing power parity (PPP). This concept has been widely used to measure the equilibrium values of currencies and is often the one an economist will first turn to when asked if a currency is over- or undervalued or not. PPP is also a relationship which underpins other exchange rate models, such as the monetary model considered in Chapters 4–6. In his comprehensive 1982 survey of the PPP literature, Jacob Frenkel referred to the 'collapse' of the PPP hypothesis. It is therefore perhaps surprising that since Frenkel's survey there has been a huge resurgence of interest in the PPP hypothesis. Much of this interest has arisen because of the development of new econometric methods, such as cointegration and non-stationary panel methods, and the application of these methods to testing PPP. The recent PPP literature has produced the so-called PPP puzzle (Rogoff 1996), which concerns the reconciliation of the high short-term volatility of the real exchange rate with the slow mean reversion speed of the real exchange rate. As we shall see in succeeding chapters, the volatility of the real exchange rate can be explained by, *inter alia*, speculative bubbles, portfolio effects and liquidity effects. The PPP puzzle arises because if it is indeed, say, liquidity effects which drive real exchange rate volatility then the mean reversion speed of the real exchange rate would be expected to be relatively rapid (standard macro-theory suggests that in the presence of sticky prices, the real effects of liquidity shocks on real magnitudes should be dissipated after around 2 years), but in practice mean reversion speeds are painfully slow.[2]

In this chapter we start by outlining the PPP hypothesis and then go on to survey the extant empirical evidence on PPP. In terms of the latter, we consider first what we refer to as 'the early evidence', that is, empirical estimates conducted in the 1960s through to the 1980s, and then go on to consider more recent empirical tests which rely largely on unit root and cointegration testing. In the next chapter, we focus on the rich variety of explanations offered in the literature to explain the PPP puzzle, and particularly the slow mean reversion speed. These explanations range from the pricing to market behaviour of multinational firms, the role of 'real' variables, such as productivity differentials and expenditure effects, and frictions due to transaction costs.

A useful starting point for our discussion of PPP is Figure 1.1 which portrays real and nominal exchange rates for the recent floating period. As we noted in

Chapter 1, the striking feature of this figure is the very close correlation between real and nominal exchange rates (the correlation coefficient is in excess of 0.9 and this is a common finding, regardless of the currency studied). As we shall see, this close correlation immediately calls into question the existence of purchasing power parity on a continuous, period-by-period basis. However, Figure 1.1 does not necessarily rule out the existence of PPP as a longer run concept and that is one of the key aspects of the PPP literature that we try to assess in this chapter and the next.

The outline of the remainder of this chapter is as follows. In the next section we consider the PPP concept in more detail, and discuss some important reasons why it may not be expected to hold in both the short and longer term. Section 2.2 contains an overview of the early empirical literature on PPP, while Section 2.3 contains a review of more recent tests of PPP, which rely on panel unit root and panel cointegration testing methods. Section 2.4 contains a discussion of the power of unit root tests and how issues of power have been addressed in the PPP literature.

2.1   Purchasing power parity: traditional PPP versus efficient markets PPP and the PPP puzzle

2.1.1   Absolute and relative PPP

The starting point of the traditional PPP hypothesis is the so-called law of one price (LOOP). Consider a two-country world in which the home and foreign country each produce a homogeneous traded good. Absent any impediments to international trade, such as transportation costs and tariffs, the LOOP says that the homogeneous good should sell for the same price in the home and foreign country, when converted at the market exchange rate:

$$P_t^i = S_t P_t^{i*}, \tag{2.1}$$

where P^i denotes the price of the homogeneous good i, S is the nominal exchange rate (home currency price of one unit of foreign currency) and, as before, an asterisk denotes a foreign magnitude. The mechanism that forces the LOOP condition is arbitrage. Thus, if the domestic price level is greater than the quotient of the foreign price level and the exchange rate it would be profitable to ship the good from the foreign to the home country. The continuation of this process would ensure that the LOOP was eventually restored (i.e. prices would fall in the home country and rise in the foreign country).

If it is further assumed that there are n goods produced in each country and each of these goods has as its counterpart a homogeneous equivalent in the foreign country, then by summing across the n goods a measure of the overall price level in each country may be obtained as:

$$P_t = \sum_{i=1}^{n} \alpha^i P_t^i, \tag{2.2}$$

and

$$P_t^* = \sum_{i=1}^{n} \alpha^i P_t^{i*}, \tag{2.2'}$$

where α denotes the weight used to aggregate the individual prices, $\sum_{i=1}^{n} \alpha_i = 1$ and it is assumed the weights are identical across countries. Using these price levels we may derive the condition of absolute PPP as:

$$S_t = \frac{P_t}{P_t^*}. \tag{2.3}$$

Absolute PPP (APPP) says that a country's nominal exchange rate is determined as the ratio of the overall price levels in the home and foreign country. So a country with a relatively high price level will have a depreciated exchange rate relative to its trading partners. As in the simple LOOP condition in (2.1), arbitrage is the mechanism which ensures APPP holds and therefore APPP is usually thought of as a long-run relationship (i.e. after the arbitrage process has been completed). We will say more about the time dimension of PPP later, when we discuss the time series properties of real exchange rates. Equation (2.3) may alternatively be expressed in logs as:

$$s_t = p_t - p_t^*, \tag{2.3'}$$

where lower case letters denote a natural log transformation has been used.

An alternative way of thinking about the proposition of absolute PPP is in terms of the definition of the real exchange rate, Q, introduced in Chapter 1:

$$Q_t = \frac{S_t P_t^*}{P_t} = 1. \tag{2.4}$$

So if APPP holds the real exchange rate should equal unity. Alternatively, the log of the real exchange rate should equal zero:

$$q_t = s_t - p_t + p_t^* = 0. \tag{2.4'}$$

Referring back to Figure 1.1, we see now why the close correlation between real and nominal exchange rates represents a violation of PPP. Clearly, if PPP holds for a currency, the log of the real exchange rate would not vary – it would be independent of the nominal exchange rate. But it is not and this is true for any real and nominal exchange rate comparison.

The restrictiveness of absolute PPP is immediately apparent from the earlier discussion. First, it presupposes that goods are identical across countries (i.e. good i produced in the home country is a perfect substitute for good i produced in the foreign country). It is not hard to imagine many (indeed most) instances where this is not the case. For example, a washing machine produced in the home country is unlikely to be identical to a washing machine produced in a foreign country, even if it is produced by the same (multinational) company. We shall discuss the issue of imperfectly substitutable goods in more detail later. A second key assumption necessary to derive (2.3) is that the weights – the α's – used to construct the price levels are the same across countries. This may not be too unreasonable for countries at a similar level of development (i.e. the kind of basket of goods consumed in, say, France and Italy is probably similar, although by no means identical). However, it is clearly unreasonable for countries at different levels of development and, furthermore, the weights used are likely to evolve over time. A third issue relating to the construction of (2.3) is the absence of transaction costs for those involved in arbitraging goods across countries. It is relatively easy to modify PPP to allow for constant transportation costs or other (constant) impediments to trade, by introducing a factor π into the earlier expressions. For example:

$$s_t = \pi + p_t - p_t^*, \tag{2.5}$$

where π represents the cost of shipping the good(s) into the home country.[3] Assuming such costs are symmetrical between the home and foreign country facilitates defining a neutral band for the log of the real exchange rate. Within this neutral band non-zero values of the real exchange rate – that is, deviations from PPP – would be permissible as in:

$$-\pi \leq q_t \leq \pi. \tag{2.6}$$

The neutral band concept is illustrated in Figure 2.1 where the existence of transportation costs means that points such as A and B would not be profitable to arbitrage away, while points such as C and D would be. As we shall see later, the

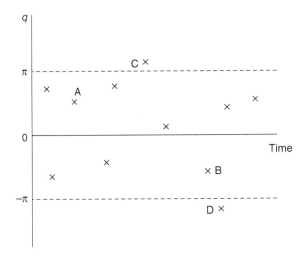

Figure 2.1 PPP and the neutral band.

existence of transaction costs can have more complex, non-linear, implications for the PPP hypothesis and the behaviour of the real exchange rate.

An alternative version of PPP, referred to as relative PPP, is obtained by expressing the variables in (2.5) in terms of changes:

$$\Delta s_t = \Delta p_t - \Delta p_t^*, \tag{2.7}$$

where a Δ denotes a first difference operator. Relative PPP indicates that countries with relatively high inflation will experience a depreciating currency. Compared to absolute PPP this variant of PPP is relatively uncontroversial.

A final issue relating to the construction of absolute PPP concerns the assumption earlier that all goods entering the overall price levels are traded. Few aggregate price measures include only traded goods and that is especially true of the price measures many researchers have used to test PPP (which indeed are in index form rather than levels – we shall return to this point later). The issue of whether a price measure that includes non-traded goods is suited to a test of PPP has long been debated in the international finance literature.[4] Frenkel (1976) has a nice discussion of this issue, and the following few paragraphs draw on his contribution. For example, a number of the original proponents of APP advocated the use of only traded goods prices in the computation of PPP (e.g. Pigou 1920; Angell 1922; Viner 1937) while another group advocated using a price measure that covers a broad range of commodities, including non-traded goods (see, for example, Hawtrey 1919; Cassel 1928). Frenkel notes that those who advocate a PPP computation based only on traded goods prices emphasize the role of commodity arbitrage, while an asset approach to the determination of exchange rates underpins the view of those who propose a broader price measure (the asset approach is discussed in Chapters 4–7) – an x per cent rise in the supply of money should lead to an equiproportionate rise in all prices in an economy, both traded and non-traded (this view is considered in some detail in Chapter 4). For example, Samuelson (1964) underscores the view that the equilibrium exchange rate is determined by a spatial arbitrage process from which non-traded goods are excluded:

> Patently, I cannot import cheap Italian haircuts nor can Niagara-Falls honeymoons be exported.

On the other hand, the asset view of PPP takes it as given that arbitrage forces the LOOP and argues that if the PPP hypothesis only applies to traded goods then:

> The purchasing power parity doctrine presents but little interest . . . (it) simply states that prices in terms of any given currency of the same commodity must be the same everywhere . . . . Whereas its essence is the statement that exchange rates are the index of monetary conditions in the countries concerned.
>
> (Bresciani-Turrono 1934)

The extreme asset view of PPP advocates the separation of exchange rate determination from traded prices and recommends a focus on non-traded prices:

> Strictly interpreted then, prices of non-internationally traded commodities only should be included in the indices in which purchasing power pars are based.
>
> (Graham 1930)

An even more extreme version of this idea advocates the use of wage rate parity, the wage being the price of the least traded commodity (Rueff 1926; Cassel 1930).

We now present a definition of what we, and others, refer to as 'traditional' PPP. It is fair to say that few proponents of PPP would be wedded to such a strict definition of PPP as given in expressions (2.3) or (2.4). Rather, proponents of PPP such as Gustav Cassel, who is generally regarded as the proponent of the version of PPP discussed here, would argue that absolute PPP is a level to which an exchange rate gravitates, but it can be away from this level for some time, due to factors such as foreign exchange market intervention or non-zero interest differentials (see Officer 1976, for example, for an extended discussion of this issue). One way of capturing this idea is to say that instead of the log of the real exchange rate being equal to zero, as in (2.4′), it should be mean-reverting:

$$q_t = \rho q_{t-1} + \beta + \varepsilon_t, \quad 0 < \rho < 1, \tag{2.8}$$

where ρ is the parameter of mean reversion, ε_t is a random error term and β is a constant. If we write the log of the equilibrium exchange rate as $\bar{q}$ and if we define this as the unconditional expectation of the process in (2.8) then (assuming $\rho < 1$):

$$\bar{q} = \frac{\beta}{1 - \rho}.$$

Long-run PPP is violated if $|\rho| = 1$ and if ρ and/or β are not time-invariant constants (our discussion here follows Abuaf and Jorion 1990). If long-run PPP holds, short-run PPP is violated whenever $q_t \neq \bar{q}$ and, as we have said, factors which would prevent a continuous equality between short- and long-run PPP would be non-zero interest differentials and foreign exchange market intervention.[5] Traditional PPP focuses on the existence of long-run PPP and, more specifically, how long it takes for a currency to settle at its long-run PPP value. In other words: how fast is mean reversion in expression (2.8)? To answer this question it is useful to introduce the concept of a half-life; that is, how long does it take for half of a shock to PPP to be extinguished? If a and b denote the initial and final deviations from equilibrium, respectively, the number of intervals from a to b will be given as $(\ln b - \ln a) / \ln \rho$ and therefore the formula for a half-life is given as:

$$hl = \frac{\ln(0.5)}{\ln(\hat{\rho})}. \tag{2.9}$$

In the traditional form of PPP money neutrality probably suggests hl should be around 1 year, and this would imply a value for ρ of 0.5, with annual data.

However, and as we shall see in more detail later, estimated half-lives are much higher than 1 year. For example, for the post-Bretton Woods period when currencies are examined on an individual basis, ρ turns out to be statistically indistinguishable from unity. However, when data from prior to the post-Bretton Woods regime, or when panel data are used for the post-Bretton Woods, there is clear evidence of statistically significant mean reversion and the half-life falls within the range of 3 to 5 years (see MacDonald 1995a; Rogoff 1996). Rogoff (1996) has labelled such mean reversion speeds, combined with the large volatility of real exchange rates as the PPP puzzle:

> How can one reconcile the enormous short-term volatility of real exchange rates with the extremely slow rate at which shocks appear to damp out? Most explanations of short-term exchange rate volatility point to financial factors such as changes in portfolio preferences, short-term asset price bubbles and monetary shocks. Such shocks can have substantial effects on the real economy in the presence of sticky nominal prices. Consensus estimates for the rate at which PPP deviations damp, however, suggest a half-life of three to five years, seemingly far too long to be explained by nominal rigidities. It is not difficult to rationalize slow adjustment of real shocks if real shocks – shocks to tastes and technology – are predominant. But existing models based on real shocks cannot account for short-terms exchange-rate volatility.
>
> (Rogoff 1996: 647–8)

As we shall see, one useful way of trying to understand and explain the PPP puzzle is to decompose the overall (CPI-based) real exchange rate into two relative price components, an internal and external component. To do this, we introduce non-traded prices into our previous set-up in the following way. Assume that the overall price level, p, is made up of a price level for traded goods, which, in turn, is the sum of the n traded goods produced in the home and foreign country, and the price level for non-traded goods, which is the sum of the m non-traded goods produced:

$$p_t = \beta_t p_t^T + (1 - \beta_t) p_t^{NT}, \quad 0 < \beta < 1, \tag{2.10}$$

$$p_t^* = \beta_t p_t^{T^*} + (1 - \beta_t) p_t^{NT^*}, \quad 0 < \beta < 1, \tag{2.10'}$$

where p_t^T denotes the price of traded goods, p_t^{NT} denotes the price of non-traded goods, the βs denote the share of traded goods in the economy and lower case letters again indicate that a log transformation has been utilised. The existence of non-traded goods can impart an important bias into the determination of the equilibrium exchange rate. This may be seen in the following way. Consider again the definition of the real exchange rate, defined with respect to overall prices, given previously:

$$q_t \equiv s_t - p_t + p_t^*, \tag{2.11}$$

and define a similar relationship for the price of traded goods as:

$$q_t^T \equiv s_t - p_t^T + p_t^{T*}.$$ (2.11′)

By substituting (2.10), (2.10′) and (2.11′) into (2.11) we can obtain:

$$q_t = q_t^T + (\beta_t - 1)[(p_t^{NT} - p_t^T) - (p_t^{NT*} - p_t^{T*})]$$ (2.12)

or

$$q_t = q_t^T + q_t^{NT,T}$$

where $q_t^{NT,T} = (\beta_t - 1)[(p_t^{NT} - p_t^T) - (p_t^{NT*} - p_t^{T*})]$, the relative price of non-traded to traded goods in the home country relative to the foreign country is usually referred to as the relative internal price ratio.

From the perspective of trying to unravel the sources of deviations from PPP, expression (2.12) is quite neat because it indicates that there are two potential sources of systematic movements in real exchange rates (which is another way of thinking about deviations from PPP): one is through movements in the relative price of traded goods, captured in q^T, and the other is movements in the internal price ratio, $q^{NT,T}$. In a world where all macroeconomic shocks are nominal, the existence of non-traded goods would have no impact on the real exchange rate since all prices, both traded and non-traded, would move in proportion to, say, a monetary disturbance. However, in a world where there are both real and nominal disturbances, real shocks can lead to movements in $q^{NT,T}$ which are independent of q^T, thereby producing a violation of PPP. In this regard, perhaps the best known real shock is a total factor productivity shock which occurs in the traded sector and gets transmitted into p^{NT} and, ultimately, the CPI-based real exchange rate. This is the so-called Balassa–Samuelson hypothesis, which we discuss in the next chapter. We shall return to expression (2.12) when we discuss the recent empirical literature on PPP.

As Rogoff (1996) notes, and as we will demonstrate further later, the q^T term is highly volatile and its variance innovation dominates the variance innovation of $q^{NT,T}$. Since $q^{NT,T}$ is usually taken to be driven by 'real shocks', such as taste and technology shocks, which are likely to be highly persistent, the variance behaviour of $q^{NT,T}$ makes it difficult to explain the behaviour of q in terms of $q^{NT,T}$. In sticky-price models such as those considered in Chapter 5, the volatility of the nominal exchange rate gets transferred on a one-to-one basis into the volatility of q^T. But how do we explain then the persistence of q^T? Much of the current chapter is devoted to an explanation of that question.

2.1.2 *Efficient markets PPP*

Although traditional PPP predicts that real exchange rates should be strongly mean-reverting, an alternative version of PPP suggests that mean reversion should be zero and the real exchange rate should follow a random walk process. This version, which has been popular in the finance literature (see, for example, Roll 1979), is labelled here as efficient markets PPP (EMPPP). In contrast to traditional PPP, this approach relies on arbitrage on the capital account, rather than arbitrage on the trade account. Capital market arbitrage is captured by the assumption of perfect capital mobility, as expressed in the uncovered interest rate parity (UIP) condition:

$$E_t(\Delta s_{t+k}) = (i_t - i_t^*). \tag{2.13}$$

Using the relative Fisher condition (i.e. subtracting equation (1.18) from its foreign counterpart) to decompose the nominal interest rates into real and expected terms inflation terms – $i_t - i_t^* = (E_t r_{t,t+k} - E_t r_{t,t+k}^*) + (E_t \Delta p_{t+k} - E_t \Delta p_{t+k}^*)$ – and substituting out for the nominal interest differential in (2.13) we get:

$$(s_t - p_t + p_t^*) = -(E_t r_{t,t+k} - E_t r_{t,t+k}^*) + (E_t s_{t+k} - E_t p_{t+k} + E_t p_{t+k}^*), \tag{2.14}$$

or

$$q_t = -(E_t r_{t,t+k} - E_t r_{t,t+k}^*) + E_t q_{t+k}. \tag{2.14'}$$

This expression states that the real exchange rate is determined as the negative of the expected real interest rate differential and the real rate expected in period $t + k$, where the latter rate is usually interpreted as the equilibrium rate, $\bar{q}_t$. By rearranging expression (2.14′) we may obtain:

$$E_t \Delta q_{t+k} = (E_t r_{t,t+k} - E_t r_{t,t+k}^*). \tag{2.15}$$

Assuming that expectations in expression (2.15) are formed rationally implies:

$$E_t \Delta x_{t+k} = \Delta x_{t+k} + \varphi_{t+k}.$$

By further assuming that relative expected interest rates are equalised up to a constant it follows that the evolution of the real exchange rate can be described by a simple random walk process with drift:

$$q_t = q_{t-1} + \alpha + \varphi_{t+k}, \tag{2.16}$$

where α is the drift term. Superficially, expression (2.16) is similar to what we have referred to earlier as traditional PPP. However, the important difference is that under the EMPP view of real exchange rates there is no mean reversion: a shock to the real exchange rate is permanent. Clearly, such a view is not very appealing since it has unattractive implications for the current account of the balance of payments, but it is useful for motivating some of the time series results considered later.

2.2   The early empirical evidence on PPP and the LOOP

In this section we consider what we refer to as the early empirical evidence on PPP and the LOOP. By this we mean empirical work implemented using traditional econometric methods (i.e. tests conducted prior to the development of cointegration and unit root testing methods) in the 1970s and early 1980s for the post-Bretton Woods and inter-war experiences with floating exchange rates. One of the first tests of the LOOP was conducted by Isard (1977) who compared disaggregate prices across countries. In particular, he tested the LOOP using export transaction prices for 2 to 5 digit STIC categories between the US and Germany and export unit values in 7 digit A and B groupings between the US and Canada, Germany and Japan. On the basis of a regression analysis, Isard demonstrated that large and persistent deviations of the LOOP occured for all of these price comparisons. Isard also demonstrated that a positive correlation existed between contemporaneous dollar exchange rates and relative dollar prices. A similar study to Isard's, although at a more disaggregate level, was conducted by Kravis and Lipsey (1978) and they also fail to find any evidence supportive of the LOOP. Giovannini (1988) compares Japanese and US export prices for disaggregated traded goods, and also for manufactured goods which are close to being commodities, and again confirms Isard's result: there are large and persistent deviations from the LOOP and these are strongly correlated with the nominal exchange rate.

Early tests of absolute and relative PPP focus on the following two expressions:

$$s_t = \beta + \alpha_0 p_t + \alpha_1 p_t^* + \varphi_t, \tag{2.17}$$

$$\Delta s_t = \beta + \alpha_0 \Delta p_t + \alpha_1 \Delta p_t^* + \varphi_t. \tag{2.18}$$

Frenkel (1980, 1981) presents estimates of equations (2.17) and (2.18) for the inter-war experience with floating exchange rate for the dollar–pound, franc–dollar and franc–pound exchange rates, using both CPI and WPI price measures, over the period February 1921–May 1925. Results supportive of both hypothesis are reported in the sense that estimated coefficients are statistically different from zero and numerically and statistically close to their prior values. For example, a representative result for the franc–dollar exchange rate from Frenkel (1981) is:

$$s_t = \underset{(0.16)}{1.183} + \underset{(0.11)}{1.091}(p_t - p_t^*), \quad \text{SER} = 0.054, \quad \text{DW} = 1.70 \tag{2.19}$$

(2.19) where standard errors are in brackets and wholesale price indices have been used.[6] This result makes clear the fact that the coefficient on the relative price term is insignificantly different from unity. However, Frenkel's (1981) estimates of (2.17) and (2.18), for a variety of currencies for the recent floating period, produce unsatisfactory estimates in the sense that coefficient estimates are often far from their prior values (although see discussion later). For example, consider the estimate from Frenkel (1981) for the dollar–franc rate over the period June 1973–July 1979:

$$s_t = \underset{(0.027)}{1.521} + \underset{(0.37)}{0.184}(p_t - p_t^*), \quad \text{SER} = 0.029, \text{DW} = 2.30. \tag{2.20}$$

This kind of result led Frenkel (1981) to refer to 'the collapse of purchasing power parities during the 1970s'. Krugman (1978) also presents estimates of (2.17) and (2.18) for both the inter-war and recent floating periods and his results are unfavourable to PPP in both periods. He concludes, 'There is some evidence then that there is more to exchange rates than PPP. This evidence is that the deviations from PPP are large, fairly persistent and seen to be larger in countries with unstable monetary policy.'

However, two early studies estimated (2.17) and (2.18) using panel methods, that is, pooled time series – cross-section estimators, and report results which are favourable to PPP even for the 1970s period. Panel estimates of PPP rely on the following framework:

$$s_{it} = \alpha_i + \beta'(p_{it} - p_{it}^*) + \left\{ \sum_i \gamma_i D_i \right\} + \left\{ \sum_t \delta_t D_t \right\} + u_{it}, \tag{2.21}$$

where the i subscript indicates that the data has a cross-sectional dimension (running from 1 to N), D_i and D_t denote, respectively, country-specific and time-specific fixed effect dummy variables (although not noted here it is straightforward to incorporate random effects into (2.21)). In a standard panel setting a number of modelling strategies are available for the disturbance term, ranging from a purely random term to autoregressive processes (with either common autoregressive terms across individual panel members or different autoregressive terms across members), or it may be spatially correlated, or some combination of these assumptions may be used.

One clear advantage to using panel methods to estimate PPP has been noted by Frankel and Rose (1995). Their argument is as follows. Since PPP is unlikely to hold continuously, deviations from PPP – that is, the error term in equation (2.17) – will be correlated with relative prices, that is, Cov $(\phi, p - p^*) \neq 0$. If this covariance is non-zero it will introduce a standard errors-in-variable bias producing biased and inconsistent estimates of the αs. However, this bias will vanish in circumstances where u becomes sufficiently small relative to the total variation in the data (see also Davutyan and Pippenger 1985). In the context of a PPP study, Frankel and Rose (1995) demonstrate that for panel data sets defined for the recent floating period the cross-sectional variability dominates the time series variability. Therefore Cov $(\phi, p - p^*)$ is likely to go to zero in a panel framework.

The earliest application of panel methods to testing PPP was that of Hakkio (1986), who used a monthly data set for the period March 1973–April 1982 to estimate equation (2.16) for the UK pound, French franc, Canadian dollar and Japanese yen (all against the US dollar). A systems estimator was used which incorporated the correlation of the error term across countries and Hakkio found that the coefficients on relative prices (i.e. α_0 and α_1) to be equal and opposite and insignificantly different from unity.

MacDonald (1988b) also used panel methods to estimate (2.17) and (2.18). The key point in this paper was the recognition that since PPP was a long-run phenomenon the most appropriate way to estimate it was by using low frequency data, such as annual data. Such data was argued to be preferred to monthly or quarterly data because it had a higher signal-to-noise ratio. Of course the problem with using annual data to estimate PPP relationships for the recent float is the relatively small number of annual observations available. MacDonald therefore proposed using a panel estimator to increase the number of observations. In particular, he used a time wise autoregressive/cross-sectionally heteroscedastic estimator and found that for a panel of five countries over the period 1973–85 the coefficients in both (2.17) and (2.18) were insignificantly different from unity, in absolute terms. To our knowledge MacDonald (1988b) was the first to test PPP in a panel context using annual data. As we shall see later, nearly all of the recent panel estimates of PPP rely on annual data.

2.3   The recent empirical evidence on PPP and the LOOP

Recent tests of PPP have focussed on using cointegration methods to test the relationship between the nominal exchange rate and relative price relationship, and unit root methods have been used to determine if real exchange rates are mean-reverting processes and, in particular, estimate half-life adjustment speeds. Before considering these type of tests we look at the sources of volatility in real exchange rates in terms of the two key components q^T and $q^{NT,T}$.

2.3.1   *Real exchange rate volatility and systematic movements of the real exchange rate: q^T versus $q^{NT,T}$*

As noted in Section 2.2, the early tests of the LOOP showed that there are significant violations of the hypothesis. More recent tests of the LOOP have followed on from the work of Engel (1993) who calculated the relative importance of the two components in (2.12) by comparing the conditional variances of relative prices within countries – $V(p_i - p_j)$ – and across countries – $V(p_i - s - p_i^*)$. Four dissaggregated indices of the CPI are used, namely, energy, food, services and shelter. These indices are chosen to capture different degrees of tradability, with food taken to be the traded good and the remaining components the non-traded elements. The data are collected for the G7, over the period April 1973–September 1990 and comparisons are made between the G6 and the US. The startling result to emerge from Engel's work is that out of a potential 2400 variance comparisons, 2250 have the variance of the relative price within the country smaller than the variance across countries for the same type of good; that is, $V(p_i - p_j) < V(p_i - s - p_i^*)$. This would seem to indicate that it is violations in the LOOP that are responsible for the major part of the volatility of CPI-based real exchange rates.

Rogers and Jenkins (1995) push Engel's original analysis further by considering finer disaggregations of the prices entering the CPIs of 11 OECD countries (in contrast to Engel their price series are mutually exclusive and collectively combine to give the total CPI), for the sample period 1973:4 to 1991:12. They also use cointegration methods to assess the relative importance of the two terms in (2.12). In particular, if sticky prices explain the time series behaviour of CPI-based real exchange rates, then q_t and q_t^T should be cointegrated, since the second component on the RHS of (2.12) should be stationary. However, if the Balassa–Samuelson model is correct, q_t and the relative price of traded to non-traded prices should be cointegrated and q_t^T should be stationary. They demonstrate, first, that, on average, 81% of the variance of the real CPI exchange rate is explained by changes in the relative price of traded goods, rather than the relative price of non-traded goods. This confirms Engel's (1993) results. Second, using food prices as the most tradable price they find little evidence of stationarity of q_t^T, which would seem to be evidence against the Balassa–Samuelson hypothesis. Further, although there are a small number of instances where q_t and q_t^T are cointegrated, they do not regard this as sufficiently convincing to support the Balassa–Samuelson proposition.

As Rogers and Jenkins recognise, however, the food index used as their measure of traded goods prices is not composed entirely of tradable items (this criticism also applies to Engel's work since the traded components of the CPI will contain, possibly substantial, non-traded elements) and this may introduce a bias into the calculations. To tackle this issue they also analyse a highly disaggregate data set of relative prices for defined the US–Canada. They find that although some relative prices are stationary (8 out of 54) the majority (46) appear non-stationary. Interestingly, the real rates that are non-stationary relate to highly non-tradable items like haircuts and highly tradable items such as frozen vegetables. Rogers and Jenkins conclude by arguing that although a small proportion of real exchange rate variability is explicable in terms of a Balassa–Samuelson effect, the overwhelming majority comes from price stickiness and hysteretic effects.

Engel (1999) provides an update of his original study. Here, in addition to using OECD disaggregate price indices for the G6 currencies against the USD for the period January 1962–December 1995, Engel also uses output prices from the OECD and personal consumption deflators from national income accounts to construct the q_t^T and $q_t^{NT,T}$ terms. Instead of calculating variance ratios, as in the original study, Engel calculates Mean Square Error statistics for k differences up to a horizon of $k = 406$. The key finding in the paper is that over 95% of US dollar bilateral real exchange rates are explained by the q_t^T component of the real exchange rate.

Froot *et al.* (1995) show that the kind of deviations from the LOOP, reported by Engel and others, is not a recent – post-Bretton Woods – phenomenon. In particular, they use transaction prices on eight commodities sourced in England and Holland and the pound–shilling exchange rate, spanning the late thirteenth century up to the twentieth century, to test the LOOP. Strikingly, they find that 'the magnitude and persistence of deviations from the law of one price are not dramatically different today than they were during the middle ages.' They also find some (limited) evidence in favour of the Balassa–Samuelson proposition.

The price-based tests reported in this section supports the view that it is the q^T component of the real exchange rate that is responsible for the majority of the variability and systematic movement in the overall CPI-based real exchange rate. However, this evidence does not, of course, mean that the Balassa–Samuelson effect is unimportant. In the next chapter we consider a number of papers which seek to test the Balassa–Samuelson hypothesis directly.

2.3.2   *Cointegration-based tests*

Cointegration-based tests of PPP has concentrated on the application of cointegration methods to an equation such as (2.17). In contrast to the earlier tests, discussed in Section 2.3, cointegration-based tests focus on the properties of the residual term in (2.17). In particular, if s_t, p_t and p_t^* are integrated of order one – I(1) – then so-called weak-form PPP (MacDonald 1993) exists if the residual term from an estimated version of (2.17) is found to be stationary, or I(0). Strong-form PPP exists if, in addition to weak-form holding, homogeneity is also satisfied; that is, $\alpha_0 = 1$ and $\alpha_1 = -1$. If the estimated coefficients are equal and opposite then this implies relative prices affect the exchange rate in a symmetrical fashion; that is, $\alpha_0 = -\alpha_1$. The distinction between weak- and strong-form PPP is important because the existence of transportation costs and different price weights across countries means that 'there are no hypothesis regarding the specific values of α_0 and α_1 except that they are positive and negative' (Patel 1990). We now illustrate the effects that differing price indices and transportation costs can have on (2.17) using two simple examples from Patel (1990).

To illustrate the effects of transportation costs on regression-based tests of PPP, we assume that the price series in (2.17) are defined for tradeable goods only (the discussion goes through, with suitable modification, for more general price series) and transportation costs are defined by the parameter φ for the home country and φ^* for the foreign country (where both φ and φ^* are assumed greater than unity). Consider the following 'exchange rates', s_t^1 and s_t^2:

$$s_t^1 = p_t - \varphi^* p_t^*, \tag{2.22}$$

$$s_t^2 = \varphi p_t - p_t^*. \tag{2.23}$$

Now if the actual exchange rate s_t is less than s_t^1 there will be a profitable arbitrage opportunity from importing foreign goods into the home country, while if s_t is greater than s_t^2 profitable arbitrage would exist in terms of exporting goods from the home country to the foreign country. If in long-run equilibrium s_t approximates to the arithmetic mean of s_t^1 and s_t^2, equations (2.22) and (2.23) imply:

$$s_t = ((\varphi + 1)/2)p_t - ((\varphi^* + 1)/2)p_t^*. \tag{2.24}$$

In terms of the earlier discussion, this means that relative measured prices need not have an equiproportionate effect on the exchange rate and this will be compounded if transaction and trade restrictions are important – in terms of regression equation (2.17) α_0 and α_1 need not equal plus and minus unity, respectively.

A further explanation for why α_0 and α_1 need not equal unity, in absolute terms, relates to the construction of the price series (see Patel 1990). Assume a representative agent, i, for whom PPP prevails. Therefore:

$$s_t = \zeta p_t^i - \zeta^* p_t^{*i}, \tag{2.25}$$

where p_t^i and p_t^{*i} are the 'true' prices facing the representative agent in the home and foreign country and, by definition, $\zeta = \zeta^* = 1$. In terms of measured price indices, p_t and p_t^*, the weights used to construct them will differ from country to country:

$$p_t = \sum_{j=1}^{N} \omega_{jt} p_{jt}, \tag{2.26}$$

$$p_t^* = \sum_{j=1}^{N} \omega_{jt}^* p_{jt}^*, \tag{2.27}$$

where ω_j denotes the weight given to commodity j in the construction of the price index and this will differ from country to country; that is, $\omega_j \neq \omega_j^*$ (the potential time-variation of ω implies that the α terms are also potentially time-varying). Hence if the weights are not equal across countries, the only inference that may be tested on the α's in (2.17) is that they are positive (because the weights are, by definition, positive).

The basic message from cointegration-based tests of (2.17) is that the estimator used matters. For example, the application of the two-step Engle–Granger method, in which symmetry is generally imposed, produces little or no evidence of cointegration – see, for example, Baillie and Selover (1987), Enders (1988), Mark (1990) and Patel (1990) for evidence of a variety of bilateral currencies from the recent floating period. MacDonald (1995a) applies this test to a consistent data base for nine bilateral US dollar exchange rates for the recent floating experience and for illustrative purposes his results are presented in Table 2.1. This table contains a set of point estimates of the coefficients in (2.17), along with augmented Dickey–Fuller statistics. The sample period used to construct these numbers runs from March 1973 to December 1992 and both wholesale and consumer prices (WPI and CPI) are used as the price measures.

Using the WPI as the price measure we note that all of the α_0 and α_1 coefficients are correctly signed (positive and negative, respectively) while with the CPI, 7 of the 9 currencies produce correctly signed values of these coefficients and this seems to suggest that the WPI measure is the more appropriate. However, it is clear that most of the estimated coefficients are far from their hypothesised values of $+1$ and -1 (although as we have seen this is not particularly damaging to the PPP hypothesis in the presence of transaction costs). Of more concern, however, is the fact that none

Table 2.1 Engle–Granger two-step cointegration tests

	CPI			WPI		
	α_0	α_1	ADF	α_0	α_1	ADF
Canada	−0.00001	0.223	−2.400	0.783	−0.672	2.100
France	3.157	−3.662	−2.260	1.709	−1.192	−2.350
Germany	5.552	−3.266	−1.620	3.144	−2.250	−1.420
Italy	1.916	−2.892	−2.050	0.668	−0.365	−1.470
Japan	1.088	−1.390	−2.670	2.161	−1.621	−2.920
Netherlands	1.681	−1.275	−2.150	2.111	−1.593	−1.310
Sweden	−0.318	0.921	−1.950	0.929	−0.809	−1.180
Switzerland	0.382	−0.758	−2.360	2.254	−1.355	−1.650
United Kingdom	0.614	−0.579	−2.350	0.517	−0.478	−2.060

Notes

The countries in the first column denote the home currency component of the nominal exchange rate used in the Engle–Granger two-step regression (in all cases the foreign currency is the US dollar). The entries in the columns labelled α_0 and α_1 denote estimated coefficients and ADF denotes the augmented Dickey–Fuller statistic calculated from the residuals of the cointegration regression. The critical value for the latter is −2.98. The labels CPI and WPI indicate the use of a consumer or wholesale price measure in the cointegrating regression.

of the estimated augmented Dickey–Fuller statistics are significant at the 5% level (indeed, none are significant at even the 10% level). Taylor and McMahon (1988) use the Engle–Granger two-step test to evaluate the PPP hypothesis for inter-war exchange rates; however, see Ahking (1990) for a critique of this work.

However, as is now well known the two-step method of Engle and Granger suffers from a number of deficiencies, such as having poor small sample properties and, in the presence of endogeneity and serial correlation, the asymptotic distribution of the estimates will depend on nuisance parameters (see, for example, Banerjee *et al.* 1986). Since Johansen's (1988, 1995) full information maximum likelihood method produces asymptotically optimal estimates (because it has a parametric correction for serial correlation and endogeneity) a number of researchers have applied this method to testing the PPP hypothesis. Thus, Cheung and Lai (1993), Kugler and Lenz (1993), MacDonald (1993, 1995a) and MacDonald and Marsh (1994a) all report strong evidence of cointegration, and therefore support for weak-form PPP, but little evidence in favour of strong-form PPP when US dollar bilateral exchange rates are used, since homogeneity restrictions are usually strongly rejected. MacDonald (1993, 1995a) reports more evidence in favour of strong-form PPP when DM-based bilaterals are used.

For illustrative purposes, we present Table 2.2 which contains a representative set of Johansen-based PPP results from MacDonald (1995a) (these estimates are constructed using the same data sets underlying the numbers in Table 2.1 for the Engle–Granger tests, discussed earlier).

Table 2.2 should be read in the following way. The numbers in the column labelled 'Trace' are estimates of Johansen's Trace test for the hypothesis that there are at most r distinct cointegrating vectors. The estimates of the normalised cointegrating vectors are contained in the two columns under α_0 and α_1, the entries

Table 2.2 Multivariate cointegration tests of PPP

	Trace			α_0	α_1	γ	LR3	LR4
Canada								
CPI	5.43	13.65	35.54*	−10.88	−0.12	−0.02	11.9*	12.2*
WPI	2.53	9.76	39.72*	−1.12	0.01	−0.01	15.0*	25.0*
France								
CPI	4.04	15.02	35.45*	−2.95	0.03	−0.07	0.1	0.3
WPI	...	...	...	...	...	...	—	—
Germany								
CPI	0.04	6.59	19.62	−0.37	0.01	−0.02	—	—
WPI	0.00	9.26	24.16	−84.6	0.46	−0.00	—	—
Italy								
CPI	6.17	14.91	35.79*	−5.8	0.09	−0.01	10.6	11.1*
WPI	0.82	6.25	25.06	7.11	−0.10	−0.01	—	—
Japan								
CPI	4.64	18.29	45.98*	−22.9	0.11	0.01	0.02	6.18
WPI	1.71	12.18	31.87*	−2.42	1.78	−0.04	4.28*	15.29*
Netherlands								
CPI	4.21	17.15	36.92*	6.60	−0.00	−0.01	0.01	5.51
WPI	1.13	11.49	36.30*	20.46	−0.10	−0.01	9.09*	15.97*
Sweden								
CPI	0.07	17.53	23.37	2.84	−0.04	0.07	—	—
WPI	2.34	12.52	26.52	8.49	−0.13	−0.01	—	—
Switzerland								
CPI	0.16	7.60	27.03	2.28	−0.00	−0.05	6.23*	11.27*
WPI	0.92	11.38	41.43*	4.38	0.00	−0.01	9.67*	19.41*
United Kingdom								
CPI	10.08	24.05	43.79*	−0.59	0.01	−0.06	0.34	6.96*
WPI	3.35	16.28	40.91*	0.27	0.01	−0.03	0.01	3.17

Source: MacDonald (1995a).

in the γ column are the estimated adjustment coefficients from the exchange rate equation and the entries in the LR3 and LR4 columns are likelihood ratio tests statistics for testing, respectively, proportionality and symmetry. An asterisk indicates that a statistic is significant at the 5% significance level. On the basis of the Trace test there is evidence of one significant cointegrating vector for each country, apart from Sweden and Germany. We note further that although many of the estimated coefficients are correctly signed, many coefficient values are far from their numerical values of unity in absolute terms. It is not surprising, therefore, that the proportionality and symmetry restrictions are convincingly rejected for most currency price combinations. Therefore, the evidence in Table 2.2 provides support for weak-form PPP, but not strong-form PPP.

One interesting feature of the results reported in Table 2.2 is the speed with which the exchange rate adjusts to its equilibrium value. With two exceptions, all of the estimated γs are negative (and only one of the positive values is statistically significant). The average of the adjustment speeds across currencies (for those currencies that produce a negative adjustment speed) is approximately -0.02, which indicates that, on average, 2% of a deviation from the error correction mechanism (ECM) is corrected within 1 month. On the basis of this number, the half-life of a deviation from the ECM is 36 months (i.e. $(1 - 0.02)^{36}$). Compared with some of the other adjustment speeds discussed in this chapter this represents a relatively rapid adjustment back to equilibrium. However, it is important to note that adjustment here does not represent an adjustment to strict PPP (i.e. where proportionality holds), but rather to a mongrelised version of PPP in which the coefficients on relative prices are not at their hypothesised values.

MacDonald and Moore (1996) use the methods of Phillips-Hansen (1990) and Hansen (1992) as an alternative (to Johansen) way of addressing issues of simultaneity and temporal dependence in the residual of (2.17). They also report strong evidence of weak-form PPP for US dollar bilaterals, while strong-form PPP holds for most DM-based bilaterals.

The superior performance of PPP when DM-based exchange rates are used is a recurring theme in the empirical literature and was first noted by Frenkel (1981) in the context of the traditional regression-based tests of PPP, discussed earlier. The effect may be attributed to a number of factors. First, the existence of the ERM has attenuated the volatility of DM bilaterals relative to US dollar bilaterals, thereby producing a higher signal-to-noise ratio. Second, the geographical proximity of European countries facilitates greater goods arbitrage and therefore makes it more likely that PPP will occur. Third, the openness of European countries, in terms of their trade making up a greater proportion of their collective national output than in the US, means that the arbitrage process is more likely to occur, thereby forcing the LOOP.

Pedroni (1997) has proposed panel cointegration methods as an alternative to panel unit root tests. The construction of such a test is complicated because regressors are not normally required to be exogenous, and hence off-diagonal terms are introduced into the residual asymptotic covariance matrix. Although these drop out of the asymptotic distributions in the single equation case, they are unlikely to do so in the context of a non-stationary panel because of idiosyncratic effects across individual members of the panel. A second difficulty is that generated residuals will depend on the distributional properties of the estimated coefficients and this is likely to be severe in the panel context because of the averaging that takes place. Pedroni (1997) proposes statistics which allow for heterogeneous fixed effects, deterministic trends, and both common and idiosyncratic disturbances to the underlying variables (and these, in turn, can have very general forms of temporal dependence). Applying his methods to a panel of nominal exchange rates and relative prices for the recent float, he finds evidence supportive of weak-form PPP. Pedroni (2001) confirms this panel evidence in favour of weak-form PPP using group mean panel estimators.

The evidence in this section may be summarised as suggesting that on both a single currency basis and on the basis of panel tests, for the recent floating experience, weak-form PPP holds for dollar bilateral pairings and strong-form PPP holds for many DM-based bilaterals. Although a finding in favour of weak-form

PPP would now seem to be widely accepted in the literature, it is important to note that the implied mean reversion from the studies discussed in this section is often painfully slow.

2.3.3 Unit root based tests of PPP

Most other recent tests of the PPP proposition have involved an examination of the time series properties of the real exchange rate. In order to test if the autoregressive parameter in an estimated version of equation (2.10) is significantly different from unity, a number of researchers (see, *inter alia*, Roll 1979; Darby 1980; MacDonald 1985; Enders 1988; Mark 1990) have used an augmented Dickey–Fuller (ADF) statistic, or a variant of this test, to test the unit root hypothesis for the recent floating period. A version of an ADF statistic for the real exchange rate is given as:

$$\Delta q_t = \gamma_0 + \gamma_1 t + \gamma_2 q_{t-1} + \sum_{j=1}^{n-1} \beta_j \Delta q_{t-j} + v_t,$$

where n is the lag length from a levels autoregression of the real exchange rate. As is standard in this kind of test, evidence of significant mean reversion is captured by a significantly negative value of γ_2. However, in practice the estimated value of γ_2 is insignificantly different from zero implying that the autoregressive coefficient in (2.8) is statistically indistinguishable from unity. This, therefore, has been taken by some (see Darby 1980, for example) as evidence in favour of the EMPPP discussed in Section 2.1. However, as Campbell and Perron (1991), and others, have noted univariate unit root tests have relatively low power to reject the null when it is in fact false, especially when the autoregressive component in (2.8) is close to unity.

Alternative tests for a unit root have therefore been adopted in a bid to overturn this result. The variance ratio test, popularised by Cochrane (1988), is potentially a more powerful way of assessing the unit root characteristics of the data, since it captures the long autocorrelations which are unlikely to be captured in standard ADF tests, and which will be important for producing mean reversion. Under the null hypothesis that the real exchange rate follows a random walk, the variance of the kth difference should equal k times the first difference. That is,

$$\text{Var}(q_t - q_{t-k}) = k\text{Var}(q_t - q_{t-1}).$$

On rearranging this expression we have:

$$V_k = (1/k) \cdot [(\text{Var}(q_t - q_{t-k})) \cdot (\text{Var}(q_t - q_{t-1}))^{-1}] = 1, \tag{2.28}$$

where V_k denotes the variance ratio, based on lag k. So a finding that an estimated value of V_k equals unity would imply that the real exchange rate follows a random walk. However, if V_k turns out to be less than unity this would imply that the real exchange rate was stationary and mean reverting. The intuition for this is straightforward – if the underlying process driving the real exchange rate is mean-reverting the variance of the series would decrease as k becomes larger. Alternatively, if V_k turns out to be greater than one the real exchange rate would exhibit 'super-persistence'.

Huizinga (1987) calculates the variance ratio test for 10 (industrial) currencies and 120 months of adjustment, and finds that the average V_k implies a permanent real exchange rate component of around 60%, with the remaining 40% being transitory; however, on the basis of standard errors, constructed using the $T^{1/2}$ formula, none of the estimated variance ratios are significantly below one.

Glen (1992) and MacDonald (1995a) demonstrate that on using Lo and MacKinlay (1988) standard errors, which are robust to serially correlated and heterogeneous errors, significant rejections of a unitary variance ratio may be obtained, but that the extent of any mean reversion is still painfully slow. For example, on the basis of WPI constructed real exchange rates, MacDonald finds that the Swiss franc, pound sterling and Japanese yen all have variance ratios which are approximately 0.5 after 12 years (and these values are significantly less than unity). So on a single currency basis for the recent float the evidence from mean reversion in real exchange rates suggests that adjustment to PPP is painfully slow.

2.4   Econometric and statistical issues in unit root based tests and in calculating the half-life

2.4.1   The power of unit root tests and the span of the data

One natural way of increasing the power of unit root tests is to increase the span of the data. Intuitively, what this does is to give the real exchange rate more time to return to its mean value, thereby giving it greater opportunity to reject the null of non-stationarity. In increasing the span, it is insufficient, as Shiller and Perron (1985) have indicated, to merely increase the observational frequency, from, say, quarterly to monthly data for a particular sample period. Rather, what is important for power purposes is to increase the span of the data using long runs of low frequency, or annual, data. For example, moving from, say, approximately 30 years of annual data for the post-Bretton Woods period to 30 years of monthly data for the same period is unlikely to increase the lower frequency information necessary to overturn the null of no cointegration or the null of a unit root.

For example, assume the estimated value of ρ is 0.85, and its estimated asymptotic standard error is $[(1 - \rho^2)/X]^{1/2}$, where X equals the total number of observations. With 30 years of annual data the standard error would be approximately 0.1, with an implied t-ratio which is insufficient to reject the null of a unit root (i.e. the t-ratio for the hypothesis $\rho = 1$ is 1.5). However, with 100 annual observations the standard error falls to 0.05, implying a t-ratio for the hypothesis $\rho = 1$ of 6.8. Defining $X = N \cdot T$, where T denotes the time series dimension and N denotes the number of cross-sectional units, then this example makes clear that expanding the span in a time series dimension increases the likelihood of rejecting the null of a unit root. The span may also be increased by holding T constant and increasing N. We now consider each of these alternatives.

2.4.1.1 Increasing NT by increasing T: long time span studies

A number of researchers (see, for example, Frankel 1986, 1988; Edison 1987; Abuaf and Jorion 1990; Grilli and Kaminsky 1991; Lothian and Taylor 1995) have implemented a real exchange rate unit root test using approximately 100 years of annual data. In contrast to comparable tests for the recent floating period, these tests report evidence of significant mean reversion, with the average half-life across these studies being around 4 years. Diebold *et al.* (1991) also use long time spans of annual data, ranging from 74 to 123 years, to analyse the real exchange rates of six countries. In contrast to other long time span studies, the authors use long memory models to capture fractional integration processes. They find considerable evidence that PPP holds as a long-run concept and report a typical half-life of 3 years.

As an alternative to examining the time series properties of real exchange rates, some long-run studies have examined the nominal exchange rate/relative price relationship and find that homogeneity restrictions hold, although the implied half-life is longer than that recovered from real exchange rate autoregressions. For example, Edison (1987) uses annual data on the UK pound–US dollar exchange rate over the period 1890–1978 and reports the following error correction model:

$$\Delta s_t = \underset{(0.08)}{0.135} + \underset{(0.17)}{0.756}[\Delta(p - p^*)_t] - \underset{(0.04)}{0.086}(s - p - p^*)_{t-1}. \qquad (2.29)$$

where standard errors are in parenthesis. The coefficient on the change in relative prices is insignificantly different from unity and the coefficient on the error correction term indicates that approximately 9% of the PPP gap is closed each year, implying a half-life of 7 years.

Although studies which extend the span by increasing T are obviously interesting, they are not without their own specific problems since the basket used to construct the price indices is likely to be very different at the beginning and end of the sample period. This may be viewed as the temporal analogue to the spatial problem that arises in comparing price indices at a particular point in time and makes the interpretation of the results difficult. Also, such studies suffer from spanning both fixed and flexible rate regimes with the inclusion of data from the former regime making mean reversion more likely. Additionally, Froot and Rogoff (1995) raise the problem of 'survivorship', or sample selection, bias in these studies. Such bias arises because the countries for which very long spans of data are available are countries which have been wealthy for relatively long periods of time and are more likely to produce evidence in favour of PPP because their relative price of non-traded goods have not changed that much. Countries which only comparatively recently became wealthy (such as Japan) or countries which were once wealthy but are no longer (such as Argentina) have not featured in the studies mentioned earlier. However, such countries are more likely to produce a violation of PPP over long time spans because their relative price of non-traded goods have changed dramatically (Froot and Rogoff (1995) have presented some empirical evidence to suggest that there is some support for this hypothesis). For these reasons attention has turned from expanding T, the time series dimension, to extending N, the cross-sectional dimension.

2.4.1.2   *Increasing* NT *by increasing* N: *panel studies*

In contrast to the early empirical literature, the more recent panel exchange rate literature has involved testing for the stationarity of the residual series in (2.21) or reparameterising the equation into an expression for the real exchange rate and testing the panel unit root properties of real exchange rates. The first paper to test mean reversion of the real exchange rate in a panel setting was Abuaf and Jorion (1990). In particular, using a ZSURE estimator they implement a Dickey–Fuller style test for 10 US dollar-based real exchange rates for the period 1973–87, and they are only able to reject the null hypothesis of a unit root using a 10% significance level. More recent tests of the panel unit properties of real exchange rates have been conducted using the test(s) proposed by Levin and Lin (1992, 1994), who demonstrated that there are 'dramatic improvements in statistical power' from implementing a unit root test in a panel context, rather than performing separate tests on the individual series. The panel equivalent of the univariate ADF is:

$$\Delta q_{it} = \gamma_i + \delta_i q_{i,t-1} + \sum_{j=1}^{l-1} \beta_{ij} \Delta q_{i,t-j} + v_{it}, \tag{2.30}$$

where, as before, i denotes the cross-sectional dimension.

The Levin and Lin approach involves testing the null hypothesis that each individual series is I(1) against the alternative that all of the series as a panel are stationary. Their approach allows for a range of individual-specific effects and also for cross-sectional dependence by the subtraction of cross-sectional time dummies. Frankel and Rose (1995), MacDonald (1995b), Oh (1995), Wu (1995) and Wei and Parsley (1995) have all implemented variants of the Levin and Lin panel unit root test on 'overall' price measures (such as WPI and CPI) and find evidence of mean reversion which is very similar to that reported in long time spans of annual data, namely, half-lives of 4 years. Another feature of these studies, which is quite similar to the long time span studies, is the finding of price homogeneity when PPP is tested in a panel context using nominal exchange rates and relative prices. Oh (1996) and Wei and Parsley (1995) have examined the unit root properties of panel data for the Summers-Heston data set and tradable sectors, respectively, and report similar results to those based on aggregate data.

Bayoumi and MacDonald (1998) examine the panel unit root properties of inter- and intra-national exchange rates. The former are defined for a panel of CPI and WPI based real exchange rates for 20 countries, over the period 1973–93, while the intra-national data sets are constructed from Canadian regional and

US federal data for the same period and the same number of real rates. The argument in the paper is that, if indeed, the predominant source of international real exchange rate movements is monetary, observed mean reversion should be more rapid in international data than in intra-national data because monetary shocks are transitory relative to real shocks. This is, in fact, borne out by the panel data sets: for the international data set there is clear evidence of stationarity on the basis of the Levin and Lin test, while for the intra-national panel sets real rates are non-stationary and only very slowly mean-reverting.

Goldberg and Verboven (2005) use the Levin and Lin panel unit root test to examine what they refer to as the absolute and relative forms of the LOOP.[7] Their data set comprises the prices of 150 car vehicle makes in five separate European markets over the period 1970–2000. They demonstrate that there are substantial deviations from the absolute version of the LOOP, which they explain within the framework of a structural product differentiation model, and report half-lives of approximately 8.3 years. For the relative version of the LOOP they find much less evidence of deviations and much faster half-lives, of between 1.3 and 1.6 years. Clearly, the latter are much faster speeds than those found using aggregate price data.

One problem with the Levin and Lin test is that it constrains the δ parameter to be equal across cross-sectional units (although the dynamics are not constrained to be equal across the units). Im *et al.* (1995) propose two statistics which do not suffer from this constraint, namely, the standardised *t*-bar and *LR*-bar statistics. The standardised *t*-bar statistic involves calculation of:

$$\Lambda_{\bar{t}} = \frac{\sqrt{N(T)}[\bar{t}_T - E(t_T)]}{\sqrt{\text{Var}(t_T)}}, \tag{2.31}$$

where $\bar{t}_T$ denotes the average of the *t*-ratios on δ from individual (i.e. country-by-country) ADF tests, and $E(t_T)$ and $\text{Var}(t_T)$ are the asymptotic values of the mean and variance, respectively, as tabulated by Im *et al.* (1995). The standardised *LR*-bar statistic is based on the average of the log-likelihood ratio statistics for testing the null of a unit root in the individual ADF tests and has the form:

$$\Lambda_{\bar{LR}} = \frac{\sqrt{N(T)}[\bar{LR}_T - E(LR_T)]}{\sqrt{\text{Var}(LR_T)}}, \tag{2.32}$$

where $E(LR_T)$ and $\text{Var}(LR_T)$ are the asymptotic values of the mean and variance, respectively, again tabulated by Im *et al.* (1995). On the basis of stochastic simulations, Im *et al.* demonstrate that these statistics have substantially more power than the standard ADF test and the Levin and Lin panel test.

Coakley and Fuertes (1997) implement (2.31) and (2.32) on a panel data set comprising 10 countries for the post-Bretton Woods period, and are able to 'comfortably reject the unit root null', thereby providing further evidence of the power of the panel.

Liu and Maddalla (1996) and Papell (1997) both highlight the importance of residual correlation in panel unit root tests, a feature absent from the first set of critical values tabulated by Levin and Lin (1992) (used by Frankel and Rose 1995; Oh 1995; Wu 1995) although not in the Levin and Lin (1994) paper (used by MacDonald 1995). Papell (1997) finds that for a number of different panels the null of a unit root cannot be rejected when monthly data are used, although it can be using quarterly data. O'Connell (1998b) also takes the Levin and Lin test to task by noting that the power of the test relies on each new bilateral relationship added to the panel generating new information. Although each relationship added may indeed contain some new information it is unlikely that this will be one-to-one given that the currencies are bilateral rates, often defined with respect to the US dollar, and therefore will contain a common element. Correcting for this common cross-correlation using a GLS estimator (although assuming that the errors are iid over time), O'Connell (1998b) finds that the significant evidence of mean reversion reported in earlier studies disappears.

The observation, referred to in Section 2.2, that PPP works better for DM-based bilaterals than US dollar bilaterals is confirmed in a panel context by Jorion and Sweeney (1996) and Papell (1997), who both report strong rejections of the unit root null (CPI) based real exchange rates when the DM is used as the numeraire currency. This result is confirmed by Wei and Parsley (1995) and Canzoneri *et al.* (1996) using tradable prices. Papell and Theodoridis (1997) attempt to discriminate amongst the potential reasons for the better performance of DM rates by taking the candidates referred to earlier – measures of volatility, openness and distance. Using a panel data base constructed for 21 industrialised countries, over the period 1973–96, they find that it is both volatility and distance which are the significant determinants of this result; openness to trade proves to be insignificant. Lothian (1997) has given another reason why US dollar bilaterals are likely to work less well in a panel context and that is because they are dominated by the dramatic appreciation and depreciation of the dollar in the 1980s (therefore the informational content of adding in extra currencies is less for a dollar-based system than a mark-based system).[8] Papell and Theodoris have confirmed this result and, in particular, show that the evidence in favour of PPP for the dollar strengthens the more post-1985 data is included in the sample.

In a bid to gain further insight into the robustness of the panel unit root findings discussed earlier, Engle *et al.* (1998) analyse a panel data base constructed from prices in 8 cities, located in 4 countries and in 2 continents. They use this panel data set to address some of the perceived deficiencies in other panel tests. For example, their panel estimator allows for heteroscedastic and contemporaneously correlated disturbances, differing adjustment speeds of real rates and the model structure used means that their results are not dependent on which currency is picked as the base currency (which, as we have seen, is an issue in some tests). In implementing this general panel structure, they are unable to reject the null of a unit root for the period September 1978–September 1994. However, and as they recognise, it is unclear if their failure to reject the null is due to the fact that their panel is much smaller than that used in other studies and also is defined for prices in cities, rather than country wide price measures which are used in most other studies (also, they do not allow the disturbance terms to have different serial correlation properties, which, as we have seen, may be important).

In the context of panel PPP tests, Taylor and Sarno (1998) argue that the kind of panel unit root tests discussed earlier may be biased in favour of rejection of the null hypothesis of a unit root if as few as one series in the panel are stationary. Their work is based on Monte Carlo simulations. As an alternative to the Levin and Lin and Im *et al.* tests discussed earlier, Taylor and Sarno propose using the FIML methods of Johansen to test the number of unit roots in a panel of real exchange rates. There are at least two difficulties with the approach proposed by Taylor and Sarno. First, there is the practical difficulty that the VAR-based method of Johansen can only be applied to panels with a relatively small cross-sectional dimension, certainly much smaller than the panels discussed earlier. More damaging, however, is that they have an unconstrained constant term in their VECM specification which means they implicitly allow for linear trends under the null. Of course, such a null cannot provide a test of PPP since the existence of a time trend means that what is really under test is PPP modified to include a Balassa–Samuelson effect.

2.4.2   Half-lives and size biases

Engel (2000a) has argued that the unit root tests used to extract half-lives are likely to have serious size biases and are therefore unreliable. His argument is based on the work of Cochrane (1991) and Bough (1992) that there is always a non-stationary representation for a time series which is arbitrarily close to any stationary representation and this can introduce a size bias into the kind of extended span tests discussed earlier. The argument runs as follows. As before, decompose the real exchange rate into traded and non-traded components as:

$$q_t = x_t + y_t, \quad \text{where,} \ x_t = q_t^T \ \text{and} \ y_t = q_t^{NT}. \tag{2.33}$$

The relative price of traded goods is assumed to be a stationary random variable, but permanent shocks to productivity could introduce a non-stationary component into the relative price of non-traded goods. The stochastic processes for x and y are therefore assumed to be given by:

$$y_{t+1} = y_t + w_{t+1}, \tag{2.34}$$

and

$$x_{t+1} = \phi x_t + m_{t+1}, \tag{2.35}$$

where w and m are mean zero, iid, serially uncorrelated but contemporaneously correlated random variables (with variances σ_w^2 and σ_m^2). These assumptions imply a univariate ARMA representation for Δq_t as:

$$\Delta q_{t+1} = \phi \Delta q_t + \xi_{t+1} + \mu \xi_t, \tag{2.36}$$

where

$$\mu = -\left[1 + (1 + \phi^2)S^2 + (1 + \phi)SR - 0.5\sqrt{(1 - \phi^2)}S^4 + 4(1 - \phi)S^2 \right.$$
$$\left. + 4(1 - \phi^2)(1 - \phi)S^3R\right]/\left[1 + \phi S^2 + (1 + \phi)RS\right],$$

and where S is the variance ratio, σ_w^2/σ_m^2, and R is the correlation between m and w, that is, $\sigma_{mw}^2/\sigma_w^2\sigma_m^2$. This expression implies that as S goes to 0 (i.e. when the unit root component gets very small) μ goes to minus 1 and therefore the importance of the moving average component increases. In practice this means that when constructing a standard ADF test a large number of lags would have to be included to control for the MA effect. However, tabulated critical values (such as those of Dickey and Fuller 1979) are calibrated for low-order autoregressive processes and so the size of the ADF test will not be correct (similar biases can be shown to occur for Phillips–Perron type tests). Using a Monte Carlo exercise Engel shows that with 100 years of annual data and a y – that is, non-traded – component of 42%, the true size of the ADF test is 0.90 rather than the 5% that is commonly used. Therefore the probability of rejecting a unit root is 90% when a 5% critical value is used.

2.4.3 Imprecision of half-lives

Cheung and Lai (2000) have focussed on the imprecision of half-life estimates. Using an impulse response analysis they demonstrate, for the CPI-based real exchange rates of France, Germany, Italy and the UK vis-a-vis US, that half-life estimates have a high degree of imprecision because the estimated confidence intervals are very wide (e.g. for the franc–USD the value of hl is 3.86 with 95% confidence intervals which span values of 1.58 to 8.52). Cheung and Lai also show that convergence to PPP is non-monotonic (a hump-shaped response with initial amplification) and this is responsible for substantially prolonging the adjustment process. They argue that such non-monoticity is not consistent with the price adjustment in a standard Dornbusch overshooting model (Engel argues that the size bias will equally apply in panel data sets).[9]

2.4.4 Product aggregation bias

A number of papers have sought to determine if the slow mean reversion of CPI-based real exchange rates reflects an aggregation bias, by studying the actual prices of individual products across countries. For example, Cumby (1996) examines the price of hamburgers across countries, Ghosh and Wolf (1994, 2001) and Knetter (1997) the price of magazines and Crucini et al. (1998) the prices of a broad group of consumer goods. These studies find substantial evidence that the LOOP does not hold at a point in time, although Cumby (1996) and Ghosh and Wolf (1994) do find some evidence of significant mean reversion for hamburgers and magazines. Haskel and Wolf (2001) examine the relative prices of 100 identical goods sold in 25 countries by IKEA. They report significant common currency price divergences across countries for a given product and across products for a given country pair and they interpret this as reflecting pricing to market. Haskel and Wolf also report evidence of significant mean reversion for deviations from the LOOP, although such mean reversion is relatively slow (they obtain a mean reversion coefficient of 0.89).

Imbs *et al.* (2002) argue that differentiated goods prices mean-revert at different rates and aggregating across goods will introduce a positive bias into aggregate half-lives. This may be seen by assuming the relative price of individual traded goods, i, follows an AR1 process:

$$q_{it}^T = \rho_i q_{t-1}^T + \beta_i + \varepsilon_{it}, \tag{2.37}$$

where ε_{it} is $\sim$ iid, $E(\varepsilon_{it}) = 0$ and $E(\varepsilon_{it}^2) = \sigma_i^2$ and the slope coefficients vary across sectors according to:

$$\rho_i = \rho + \eta_i, \tag{2.38}$$

where η_i is the sectoral specific component and has mean zero and a finite variance. Ims *et al.* assume that each sector receives equal weight in the aggregate price index in all countries and that the relative price term, $q_t^{NT,T}$, is zero. This kind of set up can be used to address two related questions: what happens when the autoregressive parameter is constrained to be equal in a panel context and what happens when relative sectoral prices are aggregated into the real exchange rate? In terms of the former question, consider the following panel equation where a common slope is imposed for all sectors:

$$q_{it} = \rho q_{it-1} + \beta_i + v_{it}, \tag{2.39}$$

and $v_{it} = \varepsilon_{it} + \eta_i q_{it-1}$ which indicates that error term includes lagged relative prices and will, as a result, be correlated with the regressor (instrumental variables will not be able to address this issue because any useful instruments must be correlated with q_{it-1} and therefore also with the error term). Imbs *et al.* demonstrate that the bias of the pooled estimator can be expressed as:

$$\hat{\rho} - \rho = \frac{E\left(\eta_i/(1 - \rho_i^2)\right)}{E\left(1/(1 - \rho_i^2)\right)} \tag{2.40}$$

where $\hat{\rho}$ denotes the probability limit of the fixed-effects estimator of ρ. This bias will be zero in the absence of heterogeneity and unambiguously positive when $0 < \hat{\rho}_i < 1$. They also demonstrate that the magnitude of the bias is increasing with the degree of sectoral heterogeneity. Estimates of half-lives generated from the kind of panel studies referred to earlier will overstate the half-life of the real exchange rate and this will be especially so if mean reversion speeds are highly heterogeneous across goods.

Imbs *et al.* also demonstrate that this kind of bias holds for estimates based on the aggregate real exchange rate. On the assumption that each sector receives equal weight in aggregate price index for all countries, the aggregate real exchange rate is then given by:

$$q_t = \frac{1}{N} \sum_{i=1}^{N} q_{i,t}. \tag{2.41}$$

In this context the error term from estimating the standard AR1 process, $q_t = \rho q_{t-1} + \beta + \varepsilon_t$, is given by:

$$\varepsilon_t = \bar{\varepsilon}_{it} + \frac{1}{N} \sum_{i=1}^{N} \eta_i q_{it-1}^T, \tag{2.42}$$

where $\bar{\varepsilon}_{it} \equiv 1/N \sum_{i=1}^{N} \varepsilon_{it}$. Since the error term contains the lagged dependent variable, through unaccounted heterogeneity, the error term will again be correlated with the regressor producing inconsistent estimates of the AR1 coefficient and of the half-life.

Using CPI-based real exchange rates and the sectoral disaggregate components of these prices collected from Eurostat, over a sample period 1975–96, Imbs *et al.* estimate half-lives for the CPI-based real exchange rates of around 4 years, which is in the usual range, and half-lives for the diaggregate data of between 4 months and 2 years. They also demonstrate that the degree of heterogeneity is much more marked for the relative price of traded goods than the relative price of non-traded to traded goods and, indeed, homogeneity restrictions on the persistence properties of real exchange rates cannot be rejected. They also demonstrate that the apparent dominant role of traded goods at long horizons can be traced back to the same aggregation bias that solves the PPP puzzle.

However, Chen and Engel (2005), using new empirical evidence and theoretical reasoning, argue that 'aggregation bias does not explain the PPP puzzle'. They demonstrate using a simulation analysis that if q_t^T is constrained to be nonexplosive $-1 \le \hat{\rho}_i$ – then the size of the aggregation bias is much smaller than Imbs *et al.* claim. Furthermore, in the presence of measurement error in q_t^T, which is additive, and not very persistent, they show that this can make relative prices appear less persistent than they actually are. Using the same data set as Imbs *et al.*, but with corrections for data entry errors, Chen and Engel show that half-life estimates are in fact in line with Rogoff's consensus estimates. Additionally, using two different bias correction methods they find that the half-life deviations from PPP for this data set turn out to be even higher than Rogoff's consensus estimates.

2.4.5   Time aggregation bias

Taylor (2000) argues that the use of low frequency data, such as the annual data used in nearly all of the panel data sets referred to earlier, does not, by definition, permit the identification of high frequency adjustment. The kind of time aggregation Taylor refers to is time averaging, rather than observational aggregation (i.e. having a daily price process which is only observed on a weekly basis), which is well known from Working (1960) can introduce severe biases into statistical tests. Taylor demonstrates how such time averaging imparts an important bias into half-life estimates of the real exchange rate. In particular, Taylor demonstrates, both theoretically and via a simulation exercise, that when the degree of temporal aggregation is greater than the half-life this bias is likely to be very great.

2.4.6 Using Big Mac data to avoid product and time aggregation biases

In order to study the dynamic behaviour of the real exchange rate in a setting that is free of the time aggregation bias issue raised by Taylor (2001), the product aggregation bias of Imbs *et al.* (2002), and also to reassess Engel proposition that deviations from the LOOP are the key explanation for systematic real exchange rate movements, Parsely and Wei (2003) use the Economists's data set on the price of a Big Mac in a number of capital cities. In particular, Parsely and Wei match Big Mac prices with the prices of the underlying ingredients of a Big Mac across countries, which then allows them to decompose Big Mac real exchange rates into tradable, q^T, and non-tradable, q^{NT}, components.

Parsely and Wei (2003) demonstrate that adjustment speeds for real exchange rate calculated using the tradable components of the Big Mac are much lower than that for non-tradables (average half-lives of 1.4 years and 3.4 years, respectively) and the half-life of Big Mac deviations is 1.8 years which is, as we have seen, much smaller than the kind of half-lives reported in the literature using CPI-based real exchange rates. In terms of Engel's explanation for real exchange rate behaviour – that it is the relative price of traded goods, rather than the relative price of non-traded to traded goods which dominates – they show that his finding does not hold in general and that factors such as reduced exchange rate volatility, lower transport cost, higher tariffs and exchange rate pegs generally weaken this explanation.

Concluding comments

In this chapter we have overviewed the PPP hypothesis, introduced the PPP puzzle and reviewed the relevant empirical evidence. We have shown that, especially for the post-Bretton Woods experience, PPP is not a very useful construct from the perspective of explaining medium to long-run exchange rate behaviour and that even expanding the span of the data, either cross-sectionally or using long time series spans of data, does not resolve the PPP puzzle. In the next chapter we look at what we refer to as economic explanations of the puzzle.

3 The economics of the PPP puzzle

In this chapter we consider some economic explanations for the PPP puzzle, introduced in the previous chapter. As we shall see, these explanations may be categorised in terms of the real exchange rate decomposition introduced in Chapter 2, as equation (2.12), and repeated here:

$$q_t = q_t^T + q_t^{NT,T}.$$

The first explanation we consider focuses on q_t^T and concerns the importance of transaction costs in driving a wedge between the home price of good i and its foreign price equivalent. As we saw in Chapter 2 the existence of such costs can create a neutral band within which it is not profitable to exploit deviations from the LOOP. Here the main focus is on the role of transaction costs in creating a non-linear adjustment process for the real exchange rate and the role this, in turn, can have in explaining the PPP puzzle. Section 3.2 contains a discussion of the well-known Balassa–Samuelson hypothesis and its explanation for systematic movements in real exchange rates. As we shall see, this explanation focuses on systematic movements on the relative internal price ratio, $q_t^{NT,T}$, as the key determinant of systematic movements in real exchange rates. Finally, in Section 3.3, we consider a number of explanations related to the role of market structure in explaining the PPP puzzle. These explanations again focus on the term q_t^T. The first of these is the issue of pricing to market and the associated concept of pass-through. Pricing to market is considered from both a theoretical and empirical perspective. A second aspect of market structure we consider is the role a country's distribution sector (i.e the wholesale and retail trade) can play in explaining systematic movements of the real exchange rate. That the distribution sector is an important aspect of market structure in most countries is evidenced by the fact that it accounts for approximately 20% of value added and employment of developed countries and often accounts for a much larger proportion of the final price of goods (as much as 40% in many countries – see MacDonald and Ricci 2001).

3.1   Transaction costs, the neutral band and non non-Linear mean reversion

A number of researchers (see, *inter alia*, Heckscher 1916, Dumas 1992 and Sercu, Uppal and Van Hulle 1995) have argued that the existence of transaction costs, due largely to the costs of transportation, are a key explanation for the relatively slow adjustment speeds evident in PPP calculations and, in particular, as an explanation for the failure of the law of one price to hold. For example, and as we noted in Chapter 2, in the presence of transaction costs, the price of good i in location j, p_j^i may not be equalised with its price in location k, p_k^i. If there are transportation costs, k, π^i, the relative price could fluctuate in a range:

$$-\pi_i \leq \frac{p_j^i}{p_k^i} \leq \pi_i. \tag{3.1}$$

Further, if the transportation costs depend positively on distance, the range of variation in the relative price will also depend on that distance. In this section we explore the effects of transactions costs in two ways: first, by examining how important transportation costs are relative to other factors and, particularly, nominal exchange rate volatility; second, we examine the implications of transaction costs for non-linear exchange rate behaviour.

3.1.1   Transactions costs versus nominal exchange rate volatility

Wei and Parsley's (1995) is an attempt to decompose the sources of the real exchange rate exchange rate volatility, noted in the previous section, into that relating to transportation costs, and other related impediments to trade, and a single macroeconomic factor, namely nominal exchange rate volatility. More specifically, Wei and Parsley focus on the first difference of the real exchange rate:

$$q_{ij,k,t} = \ln\left[\frac{P_{i,t}}{P_{j,t}S_{ij,t}}\right] - \ln\left[\frac{P_{i,t-1}}{P_{i,t-1}/P_{j,t-1}S_{ij,t-1}}\right], \tag{3.2}$$

where ij denotes the country pairing and k denotes the sector. They use annual data, 1973–86, covering 14 countries and 12 tradable sectors (chosen on the basis of an export-to-production ratio greater than 10). They define the standard deviation of $q_{ij,k,t}$ as $V_{ij,k}$ and use as explanatory variables for transaction costs the distance between trading centres, a dummy for a common border (which should reduce variability, to the extent that it reduces transaction costs), a dummy if two countries are separated by sea (which should increase variability because it increases transactions costs), dummies to represent free trade areas (EEC and EFTA), which should be significantly negative, a language dummy to represent cultural differences (i.e. a common language should directly facilitate transactions). Finally VS, exchange rate volatility, is included to represent a sticky price or macro effect. A representative result from Wei and Parsley is:

$$V_{ij} = \underset{(0.002)}{0.0064} \, \text{LogDistance} - \underset{(0.005)}{0.0058} \, \text{Border} + \underset{(0.005)}{0.0260} \text{Sea}$$

$$+ \underset{(0.0668)}{0.2315} \, VS - \underset{(0.0068)}{0.0048} \text{EEC} + \underset{(0.0069)}{0.0361} \text{EFTA} + \underset{(0.0035)}{0.021} \text{Lang.} \qquad (3.3)$$

This reveals that the distance between the major cities in the sample is statistically significant and, in particular, indicates that a 1% increase in distance is associated with a rise in the variability of price differences of approximately 0.01. The Border variable is wrongly signed, although insignificant, while the Sea variable is correctly signed and significant. Nominal exchange rate volatility, VS, has a significantly positive effect and, in terms of absolute magnitude, has the biggest impact. Having controlled for transport and exchange rate volatility, free trade areas do not seem to significantly reduce deviations from PPP relative to other OECD countries, since the EEC and EFTA dummies are both insignificant. The Lang dummy which takes on a value of 1 if two countries share common language (i.e. UK and US, Belgium and France) is positive, which is the wrong sign, although insignificant. So the upshot of the work of Wei and Parsley is that transportation costs and exchange rate volatility are the key explanations for PPP deviations, although clearly exchange rate volatility is the dominant determinant.

Engel and Rogers (1996) seek further clarification of the transportation cost issue by using consumer price data, disaggregated into 14 categories of goods, for 9 Canadian cities and 14 cities in the United States. The basic hypothesis they test is that the price of similar goods between cities should be positively related to the distance between those cities if transportation costs are important. On holding distance constant, volatility should be higher between two cities separated by a national border (because of the influence of exchange rate volatility). For each good i there are 228 city pairs and for each city pair they construct standard deviations as their measure of volatility. Cross border pairs do exhibit much higher volatility than within country pairings (although the volatility of US pairings is generally higher than that for Canadian pairings). Their regressions seek to explain the relative price volatility using the following type of equation:

$$V\left(\frac{p_j^i}{p_k^j}\right) = \beta_1^i r_{j,k} + \beta_2^i B_{j,k} + \sum_{m=1}^{n} \gamma_m^i D_m + u_{j,k}, \qquad (3.4)$$

where $r_{j,k}$ is the log of the distance between locations, $B_{j,k}$ is a dummy to represent the border between Canada and the US the D_m represent city dummies. The estimated values of β_1 and β_2 are expected to be positive. Using both single equation methods, for each of the 14 categories of price, and also panel methods, Engel and Rogers find strong evidence that both distance and the border terms are highly significant explanatory variables for real exchange rate volatility and each has the correct sign. It turns out that the border term is the relatively more important in that to generate as much volatility by distance as generated by the border term, the cities would have to be 75,000 miles apart. Engel and Rogers work therefore confirms the findings of Wei and Parsley that a national border (which in this context is a proxy for the nominal exchange rate), rather than distance, is the key determinant of real exchange rate volatility.

3.1.2   *Transactions costs and non-linear adjustment*

Transportation costs have been used in another way to rationalise deviations from PPP. In particular, Dumas (1992) has demonstrated that for markets which are spatially separated, and feature proportional transactions costs, deviations from PPP should follow a non-linear mean-reverting process, with the speed of mean reversion depending on the magnitude of the deviation from PPP. The upshot of this is that within the transaction band, as defined in (3.1), say, deviations are long-lived and take a considerable time to mean revert: the real exchange rate is observationally equivalent to a random walk. However, large deviations – those that occur outside the band – will be rapidly extinguished and for them the observed mean reversion should be very rapid. The existence of other factors, such as the uncertainty of the permanence of the shock and the so-called sunk costs of the activity of arbitrage may widen the bands over and above that associated with simple trade restrictions (see, for example, Dixit 1989 and Krugman 1989). Essentially the kind of non-linear estimators that researchers have applied to exchange rate data may be thought of as separating observations which represent large deviations from PPP from smaller observations and estimating separately the extent of mean reversion for the two classes of observation.

Obstfeld and Taylor's (1997) attempt to capture the kind of non-linear behaviour imparted by transaction costs involves using the so-called Band Threshold Autoregressive (B-TAR) model. If we reparametrise the standard AR1 model, $q_t = \beta q_{t-1} + \varepsilon_t$ as:

$$\Delta q_t = \lambda q_{t-1} + \varepsilon_t, \tag{3.5}$$

where the series is now assumed to be demeaned (and also detrended in the work of Obstfeld and Taylor, because the do not explicitly model the long-run systematic trend in real exchange rates) and $\lambda = (\beta - 1)$. Then the B-TAR is:

$$\Delta q_t - \begin{cases} \lambda^{\text{out}}(q_{t-1} - \pi) + \varepsilon_t^{\text{out}} & \text{if } q_{t-1} > \pi; \\ \lambda^{\text{in}} q_{t-1} + \varepsilon_t^{\text{in}} & \text{if } \pi \geq q_{t-1} \geq \pi; \\ \lambda^{\text{out}}(q_{t-1} + \pi) + \varepsilon_t^{\text{out}} & \text{if } -\pi > q_{t-1}; \end{cases} \tag{3.6}$$

where $\varepsilon_t^{\text{out}}$ is $\mathcal{N}(0, \sigma_t^{\text{out}})^2$, $\varepsilon_t^{\text{in}}$ is $\mathcal{N}(0, \sigma_t^{\text{out}})^2$, $\lambda^{\text{in}} = 0$ and λ^{out} is the convergence speed outside the transaction points. So with a B-TAR, the equilibrium value for a real exchange rate can be anywhere in the band $[-\pi, +\pi]$ and does not necessarily need to revert to zero (the real rate is demeaned). The methods of Tsay (1989) are used to identify the best-fit TAR model and, in particular, one which properly partitions the data into observations inside and outside the thresholds. This involves a grid search on π to maximise the log likelihood ratio, LLR $= 2(L_a - L_n)$, where L is the likelihood, the subscript n denotes the null model and a is the alternative TAR model. This is computationally simple, since for a given value of π, TAR estimation in this context amounts to an OLS estimation on partitioned samples – sets of observations with q_{t-1} wholly inside or wholly outside the thresholds.

Using the data set of Engel and Rogers (1996), discussed above, Obstfeld and Taylor find that for inter-country CPI-Based real exchange rates, the adjustment speed is between 20 and 40 months, when a simple AR1 model is used, but only 12 months for the TAR model. When dissagregate price series are used to test the law of one price the B-TAR model produces evidence of mean reversion which is well below 12 months, and indeed as low as 2 months in some cases. Obstfeld and Taylor also show that measures of economic distance – distance itself, exchange rate volatility and trade restrictions – are all positively related to the threshold value and these variables also have a consistent inverse relationship with convergence speed.

Michael *et al.* (1997) apply the exponentially autoregressive (EAR) model of Haggan and Ozaki (1981) (see also Granger and Teravirta (1993)) to a monthly inter-war data base and a data base consisting of two centuries of annual real exchange rate data. For each of the exchange rates considered, they are able to reject linearity in favour of an EAR process. An interesting further feature of the work of Michael *et al.* is that the estimated EAR parameters are consistent with Dumas's hypothesis; in particular, real exchange rates behave like random walks for small deviations from PPP, but are strongly mean-reverting for large (positive or negative) deviations.

In contrast to both Obstfeld and Taylor and Michael *et al.* O'Connell (1998a) tests a TAR model for the post Bretton Woods period and finds that there is no difference between large and small deviations from PPP – both are equally persistent. The difference between O'Connell's result and those reported above may relate to the fact that he does not use a search algorithm to locate the thresholds (they are simply imposed) or to the fact that he uses aggregate price data (although this was also used in the above studies). In a bid to determine if these points are indeed responsible for the O'Connell's finding, O'Connell and Wei (1997) use a B-TAR model and disaggregate US price data set to test the law of one price. As in Obstfeld and Taylor, they confirm the finding that large deviations from the law of one price are band reverting whilst small deviations are not.

Bec *et al.* (2006) argue that the definition of the transaction bands is problematic in many B-TAR studies since the real exchange rate is itself non-stationary. They show how to set up a B-TAR model for the real exchange rate using a real interest differential (a stationary process) to define the bands. The approach is implemented for the CPI-based real exchange rates of six industrialized countries against the US dollar for the post-Bretton Woods period. Clear non-linear relationships are reported for all the currencies and the maximum half-life is 13 months (the shortest being 3 months). Taylor *et al.* (2001) apply the smooth transition autoregressive (SETAR) model to four bilateral real exchange rates for the recent floating period and show that for large deviation from PPP mean reversion is relatively rapid (i.e under 1 year for a shock of 40% to the real exchange rate).

Using a Monte Carlo analysis, El Gamal and Ryu (2006) demonstrate that the use of non-linear models to solve the PPP puzzle is unnecessary because in actuality the linear AR model captures most of the features of more sophisticated parametric and non-parametric models. They find that shocks to real exchange rates decline exponentially fast under all models thus supporting the long-run PPP hypothesis and suggesting there is no PPP puzzle.

The work overviewed in this section indicates that transaction costs are a significant determinant of real exchange rate volatility, although nominal exchange rate volatility dominates. Of more significance, however, is the import of transportation costs for the mean-reverting behaviour of real exchange rates. To the extent that such costs are responsible for introducing non-linearities into exchange rate data it would seem that this can explain the relatively slow mean reversion of the real exchange rate that we noted in the previous chapter. However, as we have seen other (linear) explanations can explain the slow mean reversion of real exchange rates, and this is discussed further in Chapter 8, and so we sound a cautionary note about non-linear estimators since they are something of a black box. Furthermore, these kind of models are based on the premise that the LOOP should hold once the non-linearities implied by the existence of transactions costs are allowed for. However, as we have argued, the stylised facts suggest that the kinds of goods entering international trade are imperfect substitutes and not perfect substitutes as suggested in the LOOP. Additionally, the LOOP relies crucially on the activity of arbitrage. But who carries out such arbitrage? Clearly, although individuals can take advantage of price differences when they travel internationally, this will only have a very limited, if any, effect on the equalisation of goods prices across countries. Wholesalers seem a more natural unit to take advantage of price differences across countries. However, this is only likely to be feasible for goods which are regarded as generic (cereals, for example, and perhaps also certain electronic components may be regarded in this way), but for the vast majority of goods there will likely be institutional or legal constraints which limit the ability of even wholesalers to engage in the goods arbitrage process. The absence of an effective arbitrage process in modern international trade makes it difficult to interpret non-linear results which rely on such a process.

3.2   Productivity differences and the relative price of non-traded to traded goods

3.2.1   The Balassa–Samuelson hypothesis

The previous section suggests that although real exchange rates have been mean-reverting for the recent floating period, they have been highly persistent. How, though, may this persistence be explained? As we noted earlier, in terms of our decomposition of the CPI, such persistence may either be explained by systematic movements of the external relative price, q^T, or the internal price ratio, $q^{NT,T}$.

Perhaps the best known explanation of the latter is the so-called Balassa–Samuelson (BS) productivity hypothesis, which we now outline. The BS effect is usually derived from a two sector – traded and non-traded – small open economy model. Capital is assumed to be perfectly mobile between the two sectors and across countries. Labour is also assumed to be mobile across the two sectors, but crucially it is not mobile internationally. The law of one price is assumed to hold for the prices of traded goods and nominal wages are determined in the tradable sector.[1]

More specifically, it is assumed that capital and labour are fully employed:

$$L^{NT} + L^T = L, \tag{3.7}$$

$$K^{NT} + K^T = K, \tag{3.8}$$

where K and L denote, respectively, the total capital stock and labour supply and, as before, the T and NT superscripts denote traded and non-traded sectors, respectively. Capital and labour are combined to produce output using a constant returns to scale Cobb-Douglas production technology:

$$y^T = H(K^T)^{(1-\lambda)}(L^T)^{\lambda} \equiv HL^T f(k^T), \tag{3.9}$$

$$y^{NT} = N(K^{NT})^{(1-\delta)}(L^{NT})^{\delta} \equiv NL^{NT} f(k^{NT}), \tag{3.10}$$

where H and N denote total factor productivity in the traded and non-traded sectors and $k^T \equiv K^T/L^T$ and $k^{NT} \equiv K^{NT}/L^{NT}$. Both capital and labour receive their respective marginal products which, in turn, equal the interest rate and wage, respectively. For a small open economy, the world interest rate is given at i, and the marginal product of capital in each sector is given as:

$$i = H(1 - \lambda)(k^T)^{-\lambda}, \tag{3.11}$$

and

$$i = q^{NT,T} N(1 - \delta)(k^{NT})^{-\delta}, \tag{3.12}$$

where, as before, $q^{NT,T}$ is the relative price of non-tradables. The capital-labour ratio in tradables (k^T) is given by (3.11). With two factors of production the factor price frontier can be solved by the maximisation of profit – $(F(K, L) - WL - rk)$ – which generates factor-demand functions in each sector. The assumption of a linearly homogeneous production technology allows us to write the wage as:

$$W = H\left[f(k^T) - f'(k^T)k^T\right] = H\lambda(k^T)^{\lambda-1}. \tag{3.13}$$

Solving for k^T from (3.11) and substituting this into (3.13) yields the wage equation as:

$$W = H\lambda(i/H(1 - \lambda))^{(\lambda-1)/-\lambda}, \tag{3.14}$$

which indicates that for this small open economy the wage is determined entirely by factor productivity in tradables. Our final relationship, which ties down the internal price ratio/productivity relationship may be derived in the following way. Solving the capital-labour ratio in non-tradables from (3.12) gives:

$$k^{NT} = (i/[q^{NT,T} N(1-\delta)])^{1/-\delta}. \tag{3.15}$$

Perfect competition in the non-tradable sector requires that the following condition holds:

$$q^{NT,T} Nf(k^{NT}) = ik^{NT} + W. \tag{3.16}$$

For a given interest rate it follows from (3.10), (3.14) and (3.15) that the relative price of non-tradables is:

$$\hat{q}^{\overline{NT},T} = \delta \hat{w} - \hat{v} = \frac{\delta}{\lambda} \hat{\eta} - \hat{v}, \tag{3.17}$$

where we have expressed the variables in log changes, with lower case letters denoting log values (i.e. $\eta = \log H$ and $v = \log N$), and a circumflex denoting a change. The basic message from this equation is that deviations from PPP – movements in the internal price ratio – are driven by productivity differences between the traded and non-traded sectors. To quote Balassa (1964):

> The greater are productivity differentials in the production of tradable goods between countries, the larger will be differences in wages and in the prices of services and correspondingly the greater will be the gap between purchasing power parity and the equilibrium exchange rate.

The intuition for this result may be explained in the following way. Productivity developments tend to be concentrated in the tradable sector but a shock to total factor productivity in this sector cannot affect the price of the traded good, by assumption (the LOOP rules out any changes in the relative price of traded goods). Therefore to ensure the real wage continually equals the marginal product of labour in the traded sector, the wage in the traded sector rises and this pulls up the economy wide wage in proportion (i.e. wages in the traded and non-traded sectors are equalised). The rise in the wage in the non-traded sector raises the price of non-traded goods, the relative price of traded to non-traded goods and hence the CPI-based real exchange. Rogoff (1992) and Obstfeld and Rogoff (1996) modified the original Balassa–Samuelson story to be consistent with forward-looking, optimising agents and their modification is considered in Chapter 10.

3.2.2 *Testing for the Balassa–Samuelson effect*

Tests of the BS hypothesis have proceeded in one of two ways. The first set of tests are indirect and rely on testing which of the two relative price effects embedded in expression (2.12) dominates the behaviour of the overall real exchange rate: is it movements in the relative price of traded goods (i.e. violations of the LOOP) or the relative price of traded to non-traded goods? These tests were discussed in the last chapter and, broadly speaking, are not supportive of the BS proposition since they indicate that it is movements in the relative price of traded goods which, in large measure, explain the time series behaviour of real exchange rates. However, these indirect tests do not preclude a significant direct relationship between productivity and exchange rate movements. The second set of tests rely on building measures of productivity in the traded and non-traded sectors and regressing the CPI-based real exchange rate and/or the internal price ratio onto these productivity measures.

3.2.3   Testing the Balassa–Samuelson proposition directly using measures of productivity

In this section we consider some direct tests of the Balassa–Samuelson proposition. Hsieh (1982), Marston (1990) and DeGregorio and Wolf (1994) examine the relationship between the CPI-based real exchange rate and productivity in growth terms. Results favourable to the Balassa–Samuelson hypothesis are reported, in the sense that the coefficients on productivity in the two sectors are statistically significant and correctly signed.[2] As Chinn and Johnston (1999) point out, however, the use of growth rates in these papers allows for permanent shocks to the relationship in levels, which is perhaps undesirable. Canzoneri *et al.* (1999) use panel cointegration methods to test the relationship between the relative price of non-traded to traded goods and relative productivity in the traded to non-traded sectors, where productivity is measured using labour productivity differentials. Canzoneri *et al.* report results supportive of the Balassa–Samuelson proposition, in the sense that the relative price of non-traded to traded goods is cointegrated with productivity differentials.

Ito *et al.* (1997) report a statistically significant relationship between the real exchange rate change and the change in per capita GDP, their proxy for the Balassa–Samuelson effect, for a group of Asian currencies. However, they do not find an association between the per capita differential and the relative price of non-traded to traded goods. As they recognise, one explanation for this latter result could be that per capita GDP is not a good proxy for productivity differences. Chinn and Johnston (1999) use OECD sectoral total factor productivity to analyse the relationship between CPI-based real exchange rates and the relative price of traded to non-traded goods and productivity differences. They report significant cointegrating relationships, suggesting long-run relationships and point estimates, which are supportive of the Balassa–Samuelson proposition.[3]

MacDonald and Ricci (2001) also use the OECD sectoral data base to build productivity measures which are then used in panel regressions of the CPI-based real exchange rate. They find that when the difference between productivity in the traded and non-traded sector is entered as a differential it is correctly signed, strongly significant and has a plausible magnitude (in particular, they find a point estimate on relative productivity of around 0.8, which is consistent with its interpretation as the share of expenditure on non-traded goods). However, MacDonald and Ricci demonstrate that the Balassa–Samuelson prediction that the coefficients on productivity in the traded and non-traded sectors are equal and opposite is strongly rejected. Furthermore, when the wage is entered into the panel regressions the coefficient on productivity on the traded sector becomes significantly negative. If the Balassa–Samuelson hypothesis is correct the introduction of the wage, which is the conduit through which productivity in the traded sector influences the CPI-based real exchange rate, should render the coefficient on tradable productivity to be zero. MacDonald and Ricci interpret this effect as indicating that the LOOP does not hold. This point is discussed in more detail in Sections 3.4 and 3.5. One other interesting aspect of MacDonald and Ricci's work is that by conditioning the real exchange rate on productivity differentials, and other 'real' determinants of the real exchange rate, nearly all of the PPP puzzle may be explained.

3.2.4 The demand side and the internal price ratio

The Balassa–Samuelson model discussed earlier, and our discussion so far, has suggested that the key influence on the internal price ratio, and the CPI-based real exchange rate, comes from the supply side, in the form of productivity differentials. Demand side influences can, however, have a similar effect on the internal price ratio. Why might demand side influences impinge on the internal price ratio? One way such an effect can arise is if preferences are non-homothetic across traded and non-traded goods: with positive income growth this would lead, ceteris paribus, to a rise in the relative price of non-traded to traded goods and an appreciation of the CPI-based real exchange rate. Alternatively, in the context of the Balassa–Samuelson model presented above, if capital and labour are mobile across sectors in the long-run, but not in the short run, then demand side factors can have a short run impact on the real exchange rate.

3.3 Market structure and the real exchange rate

Dornbusch (1987) and Krugman (1987) were the first to argue that market structure may be important in explaining deviations from PPP. The market structure story is an attempt to explain systematic movements in the real exchange rate in terms of the relative price of traded goods, q_t^T. In this section we consider two aspects of the market structure story. Perhaps the best known is pricing to market and we consider some of the theoretical and empirical evidence on that hypothesis in the next two subsections. We then consider some recent work which looks at the role of a country's distribution sector – its wholesale and retail sectors – in explaining the PPP puzzle.

3.3.1 Pricing to market and pass-through

Why should the price of a good produced in a foreign country, but sold in the domestic country not reflect the full change in any exchange rate change? That is to say, what explains price stabilisation in the local currency (or relatedly the degree of pass-through)? A number of hypotheses have been given in the literature to explain this phenomenon. Among them are imperfect competition, costs of adjustment in supply, menu costs, concern for market share and the role of particular currencies in the international financial system. In terms of the latter, if the price which is used to invoice an export is the home currency then exchange rate fluctuations will not affect the home currency price and there will be zero pass-through from the exchange rate to domestic prices. Since so many traded goods are invoiced in terms of US dollars, perhaps the US is the best example of a country where LCP is likely to be effective. However, for countries whose currencies are not widely used for invoicing purposes, pricing to market (PTM) (a term introduced by Krugman (1987)) the existence of differentiated products and imperfectly competitive firms, who price discriminate across export markets, can also generate a stabilisation of local currency prices and zero pass through. For example, such firms may alter the mark-up of price over marginal cost as the exchange rate changes in order to protect their market share in a particular location. However, it is worth noting that the alternative paradigm of a perfectly competitive firm structure can also generate this result. For example, say there is an appreciation of a country's currency and this appreciation is correlated with a rise in world demand, which pulls up marginal costs. In this case pass through would also be less than complete (i.e. the tendency for the local currency price to fall as the exchange rate appreciated would be offset by the rising marginal cost).

3.3.2   *Pricing to market: theory*

The concept of PTM can be illustrated using the following simple partial equilibrium model of exporter behaviour taken from Knetter (1989). An exporting firm is assumed to sell to N foreign destinations and demand in each destination is assumed to have the same general form:

$$x_{it} = f_i(s_{it}p_{it})v_{it}, \quad i = 1,\ldots,N \ t = 1,\ldots,T, \tag{3.18}$$

where x_{it} is the quantity demanded by destination market i in period t, p_{it} is the price in terms of the exporters currency, s is the exchange rate (foreign, or destination currency, per unit of exporters currency) and v is a random (demand) shift variable. The exporter's costs are assumed to be given by:

$$C_t = C\left(\sum x_{it}\right)\delta_t, \tag{3.19}$$

where C_t measures costs in home currency units, the summation runs over all i destination markets and δ_t is a random variable that may shift the cost function – due perhaps to a change in input prices. The period-t profit of the exporter is:

$$\Pi_t = \sum p_{it}x_{it} - C\left(\sum x_{it}\right)\delta_t. \tag{3.20}$$

By substituting the demand functions into the profit function and maximising this with respect to the price charged in each market gives the following set of first-order conditions:

$$p_{it} = c_t \left(\frac{\varepsilon_{it}}{\varepsilon_{it} - 1} \right) \quad i = 1, \ldots, N \ \ t = 1, \ldots, T \tag{3.21}$$

where c_t denotes the marginal cost of production in period t $(= C'\delta)$ and ε_{it} is the elasticity of demand with respect to local currency price in destination market i. The system of equations in (3.21) captures the basic result of price discrimination: the price in the exporter's currency is a mark-up over marginal cost, where the mark-up is determined by the elasticity of demand in the various destination markets.

On the basis of (3.21) if the exporter faces a constant elasticity of demand schedule then the price charged over marginal cost will be a constant mark-up and in this case there will be complete pass-through; that is, the price in terms of the exporters currency will stay unchanged as the exchange rate depreciates and so the price in terms of the destination market will fully reflect the exchange rate change. However, in this example although marginal cost is common across destinations, it may nonetheless vary over time and the mark-up can therefore vary across destinations. For a monopolist who discriminates across export markets, demand schedules that are less convex (i.e. more elastic) than a constant-elasticity schedule will produce a stabilisation of local currency price and therefore pricing to market: as the exchange rate depreciates the mark-up will fall. However, if the monopolist's demand schedule is more convex (inelastic) than a constant-elasticity schedule will produce the opposite effect – mark-ups increase as the buyer's currency depreciates.

The specific form of PTM in which sellers reduce the mark-up to buyers whose currencies have depreciated, thereby stabilising the price, is known as local currency price stability (LCPS).

Equation (3.21) could also be used to represent export behaviour in a perfectly competitive environment. In this case the demand elasticities are infinite and independent of destination and the firm chooses the level of output at which marginal cost is equated to world price.

In the model considered above, the price of the good is invoiced in the exporters own currency. What are the implications when the exporter invoices the price in the importers currency? One implication is that if the firm is risk averse it will try to offload at least some of the risk of currency movements by hedging in the forward market. Feenstra and Kendall (1997) proposed a variant of the model considered above to capture the different invoicing possibilities and also the cost of hedging. In this model the exporter sets price (in the importers currency) in period $t - 1$ for period t but the period-t exchange rate is unknown, making the currency revenue from trade uncertain. The uncertainty, though, can be offset by selling the importers currency on the forward market. More specifically, when invoicing in the importer's currency, the exporter maximises the expected utility of profits in its own currency as:

$$\text{Max } E_{t-1}\{U[(s_t p_t - c_t^*)x(p_t, v_t, \mathcal{Z}_t) + y_t(f_{t-1}^t - s_t)]\}, \tag{3.22}$$

where U is the firms utility function, p_t is the price in the importing country set in period $t-1$ for t, c^* cost of production (average and marginal) in the exporters currency, x is the demand function for imports where v (a scaler) is the price of import-competing goods[4] and $\mathcal{Z}$ is consumer expenditure. The last term in (3.22) represents the cost of forward cover where y is the amount of the importers currency sold on the forward market. The nominal exchange rate, s, defined in units of the exporter's currency, is assumed to be the only stochastic term entering (3.22). The first-order condition from this maximising problem is:

$$p_t\left(1 - \frac{1}{\eta_t}\right) = \left(\frac{E_{t-1}c_t^*}{t - \upsilon f_t}\right), \tag{3.23}$$

where the price elasticity of demand, $\eta, \equiv -\delta \ln(E_{t-1}x_t)/\delta \ln p_t$. In this expression the exporter's marginal costs, $E_{t-1}c_t^*$, are converted to the importing country's currency using the forward exchange rate and so the forward rate, along with the elasticity of demand, is now a determinant of the optimal price. This is an illustration of the separation theorem of Ethier (1973) that the variance of the spot rate does not affect the optimal price. Feenstra and Kendal (1997) demonstrate that the comparable first order condition for a firm which invoices in its own (i.e the exporters) currency is:

$$p_t^*\left(1 - \frac{1}{\eta_t^*}\right) = \left(E_{t-1}c_t^*\right), \tag{3.24}$$

where p_t^* is the price in the exporters currency, $\eta_t^* \equiv -\delta \ln[E_{t-1}x(p_t^* z_t - \upsilon f_t, q_t, z_t)]/\delta$ where the forward rate enters the elasticity formula and, again, as in the case of invoicing in the importing country's currency, the variance of the exchange rate does not affect the optimal price chosen by the exporting firm.

3.3.3   *Pricing to market: some empirical evidence*

Mann (1986) analysed a data set consisting of the movement of four-digit industry US import prices relative to a trade weighted average of foreign production costs and found that profit margins are adjusted to mitigate the impact of exchange rate changes on dollar prices of US imports. Interestingly, she found that US exporters did not adjust mark-ups in response to exchange rate changes. The latter finding was confirmed by Knetter (1989).

Knetter (1989) presents an empirical framework which is capable of distinguishing between three alternative hypotheses: the fully competitive integrated market model and two non-competitive alternatives. These hypotheses may be motivated using the following panel regression equation:

$$\ln p_{it} = \theta_t + \lambda_t + \beta_i \ln s_{it} + u_{it}, \tag{3.25}$$

where θ_t is a time effect, λ_t is a country effect and u_{it} is a regression disturbance. If the null hypothesis is a single competitive world market for exports then the null requires price equal to marginal cost and export prices will be equalised across destinations. Hence in the context of (3.25), the time effects will measure the common price that obtains in each period and there would be no residual variation in the data which could be correlated with country effects or exchange rates so the fixed effects and β_i coefficient should be zero.

An alternative null hypothesis to perfect competition would be the imperfect competition structure and price discrimination referred to above. In the case of a constant elasticity of demand with respect to the local currency price in destination markets, the price charged over marginal cost is, as we have seen, a fixed mark-up over marginal cost in each destination market, although this could vary over time. In this case the country, or fixed, effects in (3.25) will capture the fact that mark-ups can vary across destinations, the time effects should measure the marginal cost movements exactly and the β_i coefficient should be zero. Under either of these hypotheses, shocks to either cost or demand will leave the conclusion that export prices are independent of the exchange rate unchanged. This is because under the null the only affect on price is via a change in marginal cost and since marginal cost is common across destinations it cannot have an idiosynchratic effect on price.

A finding of a significantly non-zero β_i coefficient in (3.25) would be inconsistent with either the full perfect competition model and a constant elasticity of demand in the imperfect competition/price discrimination hypothesis. As the partial equilibrium model underpinning (3.21) shows, if demand elasticities change with changes in the local currency price then export prices will depend on exchange rates. As we have seen, the idea is that pricing to market is dependent on the convexity of the demand curve facing the firm and the general rule is as follows: (from Knetter (1989)) if demand, as perceived by the firm, becomes more (less) elastic as local currency prices rise, then the optimal mark-up charged by the exporter will fall (rise) as the buyer's currency depreciates and this is true irrespective of the market structure assumed. Of course this interpretation assumes that the exchange rate only affects the mark-up by affecting the local currency price. Outside the null, there may be a non-zero covariance between the exchange rate and the disturbance term if, for example, cost shocks are correlated with the exchange rate. Kendall argues that the inclusion of time dummies will mop up this effect, especially if there is some heterogeneity in the convexity of the demand curve across countries. However, exchange rates could be correlated with the disturbance if there are macroeconomic variables which systematically influence elasticities. In support of this, Knetter cites Meese and Rogoff (1983) to argue exchange rates are unrelated to macroeconomic fundamentals, although as we shall see in Chapter 6 this conclusion is contentious.

The data set considered by Knetter consists of quarterly data for six US export products and ten German export products, the sample period running from 1978:1 to 1986:1 for US exports and 1977:1 to 1985:4 for German exports. Sixteen separate industry models are estimated. For the US data set, Knetter finds that the country effects are statistically significant in nearly all instances. The regressions which have the nominal exchange rate as a regressor indicate that 21 export markets violate the invariance of export prices to exchange rates implied by the constant-elasticity model. Another puzzling aspect of the results is that the coefficient on the exchange rate is more often positive than negative. This indicates that if there is an exchange rate depreciation in the foreign country the US exporters actually adjust dollar prices to further increase the price. As we have noted, this is optimising behaviour only if exporters perceive demand schedules to be more convex than a constant elasticity of demand schedule (i.e. inelastic).

With the German data base, Knetter finds that in over half of the equations the coefficient on the exchange rate term is significant (irrespective of the definition) and, in contrast to the US data, negative coefficients occur about three times more frequently than positive coefficients. One particularly interesting finding is the fact that that the coefficient on the exchange rate is consistently negative across export categories when the US is the destination market. How may the different results between German Exporters to the US and US exporters to Germany and other countries be explained? One explanation may lie in the size of the US market. The US is obviously a large market and German exporters may be more concerned with market share in the US than US exporters, especially since export markets are small relative to the US market. Another explanation for this kind of pattern is that although markets in the US are imperfectly competitive, the number of competing firms in the US is much larger than in other markets so the price stabilisation may be an indication of the near competitive nature of the US market. Another explanation for these results may be found in invoicing patterns – normally exporters invoice in their own currency but to the US may invoice in dollars and if invoice prices are fixed in the short run then local currency prices are also fixed.

In a further paper, Knetter (1993) uses data on annual value and quantity of exports for a number of seven-digit industries in the US, UK, Japan and Germany. The sample period is 1973–87 for US and Japanese exports, 1974–87 for most UK exports and 1975–87 for German exports. The equation estimated is similar to (3.25), only now the price series and exchange rate enter as first differences:

$$\Delta p_{it} = \theta_t + \beta_i \Delta s_{it} + u_{it}, \tag{3.26}$$

where, as before, $i = 1, \ldots N$ and $t = 1, \ldots, T$ index the destination of exports and time, respectively, and where p is the log of export price. The error term is assumed to be *iid* with zero mean and constant variance. As in Knetter (1989), θ_t is a time effect designed to capture the variation of marginal costs over time. A zero value of β implies that the mark-up to a particular destination is not responsive to fluctuations in the value of the exporters currency against the buyer's – changes in currency values are fully passed through, in this case to the buyer. Negative values of β imply that mark-up adjustment is associated with LCPS, while positive values of β correspond to the case in where destination-specific changes in mark-ups amplify the effect of destination-specific exchange rate changes on the price in units of the buyer's currency. The economic interpretation of β depends, of course, on the assumptions made about the underlying market structure.

The percentage of point estimates that imply LCPS are as follows: Germany 89%, Japan 79%, the UK 67% and the US 45%. One of the papers most striking results is that, in contrast to Knetter (1989), there is very little evidence that the destination market is important in determining the extent of LCPS. In particular, there is little evidence to suggest that foreign exporters treat the US differently to any other market. This suggests that the large swings observed in the dollar are not responsible for the existence of PTM. Also, and in contrast to other research in this area, there is little evidence of differences in behaviour within common industries. However, there is clear evidence of different behaviour across US and UK industries and Knetter argues that future research should look at industry characteristics rather than, for example, focusing on trying to understand exchange rate behaviour using atheoretical methods, such as the permanent and transitory decompositions of exchange rates considered in Chapter 8.

Giovannini (1988) presents evidence that the relative export price (the export price, in foreign currency relative to the domestic price) of a narrow sectoral set of Japanese manufacturers prices – things like ball bearings, nuts and bolts – fluctuate widely over the period 1973–83 (+/ − 20%), and on many occasions these appear to be systematically related to the exchange rate (the yen-dollar rate). These kind of movements are suggestive of some form of price discrimination. The novelty of Giovannini's work is that it provides a neat way of unravelling whether these effects arise from *ex ante* discrimination or they could not have been predicted and are simply the outcome of exchange rate surprises. In the first stage of his analysis, Giovannini uses a set of forecasting equations to determine if deviations from the LOOP (i.e. the relative export price scaled by the nominal exchange rate) are predictable. These equations involve projecting the deviation from the LOOP onto information publicly available in period t. The regressions clearly demonstrate that there is predictablity in these deviations and this implies that firms either discriminate *ex ante* or prices are preset for more than 1 month in advance, or both. In a second stage these two effects are unravelled by estimating relative price equations which incorporate price staggering. The results show that, even allowing for price staggering, there is clear evidence that firms engage in *ex ante* price discrimination.

Ghosh and Wolf (2001) have criticised the standard pass through equation noted above. In particular, they argue that in the context of equations such as (3.25) and (3.26) that it is difficult to distinguish between pricing to market and menu cost pricing. For example, with menu costs the expectation is that there would be a long sequence of non-zero pass-through followed by a single price change with complete pass-through of the cumulative change in the exchange rate since the last price change. If menu costs differ across products and price changes are staggered then a regression of aggregate price on the exchange rate will, since it averages the two sets of observations across many products, likely yield a non-unitary and non-zero estimate of price pass-through, which is similar to pricing to market. The two alternative explanations for a lack of complete pass have very different implications for PPP. The LOOP remains valid, in the long term, with menu costs, while deviations from the LOOP are permanent in most models of strategic pricing.

In order to address the relative importance of menu costs and pricing to market in explaining imperfect pass-through, Ghosh and Wolf (2001) examine the properties of the prices of the Economist and Business Week using a panel of 11 countries for the period January 1973 to December 1995 (the *Economist*) and January 1980 to December 1995 (for *Business Week*). Their analysis of this data set reveals the following. First, they find a small pass through from contemporaneous exchange rates to prices (3% and 11% for the *Economist* and *Business Week*, respectively). Second, they find a much larger pass through of cumulative exchange rate changes since the last price adjustment to the current price change. Third, the pass through elasticity increases sharply if the sample is restricted to those months in which prices are changed, although the elasticity is well below unity. The conclusions Gosh and Wolf draw from this evidence is that menu costs play an important role in addition to strategic pricing decisions.

Goldberg and Knetter (1997) provide a useful survey of the degree of exchange rate pass-through and note a consensus estimate of the pass-through from the exchange rate to import prices for the US of 60%, although lower-long run estimates for the US are suggested in Campa and Goldberg (2002) (approximately 30% pass-through for the US). Campa and Goldberg (2002) report pass-through percentages of 40% and 80%, respectively, for Germany and Japan.[5]

Feenstra and Kendall (1997) use quarterly data over the period 1974:1 1994:4 to test equations (3.23) and (3.24) for the bilateral (home currency to) US dollar exchange rates of Canada, Germany, Japan and UK. In order to operationalise these expressions, they take a log-linear specification of the two demand functions (defined in exporters and importers currency) and by aggregating them and exploiting the covered interest parity condition they obtain:

$$\ln s_t = \beta_0 + (\ln c_t^* - \ln l_t) - \beta_1 [\lambda(\ln P_t - \ln l_t) + (1 - \lambda)$$
$$\times (\ln P_t^* - \ln c_t^*)] + (i_t - i_t^*) + \beta_3 u_t \qquad (3.27)$$

where the exchange rate is the foreign currency price of the dollar (the dollar being the home currency c^* denotes marginal and average costs in the foreign currency (measured using the foreign currency WPI) l is the price of import-competing goods (taken as the US WPI), P and P^* denote the import and export price indices, respectively and the term in square brackets has the interpretation of an average traded price, the interest differential is the 90-day interest differential and the β's are reduced form parameters.

The Johansen multivariate cointegration method is used to test for evidence of long-run relationships amongst the variables entering (3.27) and evidence of three significant cointegrating vectors is found in each case (although in some cases this finding is ambiguous). For each country, the first vector is normalised on the exchange rate and the coefficients on the relative WPI term (which is essentially the PPP term in this relationship) are all statistically significant and close to their hypothesised values of +/−1 for the UK, Canada and Japan but far away for Germany (in the majority of cases the coefficients are also insignificantly different from unity). The coefficient on the average traded price turns out to be highly significant in each case (since this can be of either sign and still be consistent with pricing to market not regarded as an issue). The interest differential is correctly signed in each case, but usually only weakly significant. To interpret the remaining vectors, Feenstra and Kendall (1997) sum the first and second vector to produce a relationship without the interest differential (again normalised on the exchange rate) and by summing all three vectors they produce a third relationship which is absent both the interest differential and the average traded goods price.

To gain further insight into the cointegrating relationships Feenstra and Kendall calculate the standard deviations of the residuals from each of these vectors. The standard deviation of the first two vectors is always much smaller than the third and a comparison of the residuals from the first and second suggest that it is the PTM term which is producing the reduced standard deviation. In particular, they show the PTM term explains about one-sixth of the deviations from PPP for Canada, and more than one-third for Japan and the UK. The exception is Germany where the inclusion of the interest differential is crucial in reducing the residual standard deviation. Feenstra and Kendall further demonstrate that their results are not sensitive to the choice of the aggregation parameter used to construct the PTM term.

Cheung, Chinn and Fujii (1999) seek to explore the consequences of market structure for the *persistence* of deviations from PPP. They capture persistence using the mean reversion coefficient for industry i of country j as:

$$\text{MRC}_i^j = 1 + \delta.$$

This is then regressed onto two measures of market structure and a number of macroeconomic variables. The first measure of market structure is the price cost margin (PCM) which approximates profits of an industry and is intended to give a measure of how competitive an industry is:

$$\text{PCM}_{i,t}^j = \frac{V_{i,t}^j - M_{i,t}^j - W_{i,t}^j}{V_{i,t}^j} \tag{3.28}$$

where V is the value of total prod, M is cost of materials and W is the wage. The second measure is the intra-industry trade index (IIT) defined as:

$$\text{ITT}_{i,t}^j \equiv 1 - \frac{|\text{EX}_{i,t}^j - \text{IM}_{i,t}^j|}{(\text{EX}_{i,t}^j + \text{IM}_{i,t}^j)} \tag{3.29}$$

where EX and IM represent sectoral exports and imports. A large value of ITT represents a high level of market power due to product differentiation.

Using sectoral real exchange rate data (for 9 manufacturing sectors) from 15 OECD countries over the period 1970–93, Cheung *et al.* show that both market structure effects are significantly positively related to the mean reversion speed and robust to different specifications; the macro variables are, however, not robust to different specifications. They also show that industries with high PCMs have slowest mean reversion.

3.4   Market structure and the role of the distribution sector

As noted in the introduction, the distribution sector plays an important role in industrial countries where it often reaches 20% of industrial activity both in terms of value added and of employment and might therefore account for a large component of prices. For example, using US input–output data, Burstein *et al.* (2000) show that consumption goods in the US contain distribution services accounting for about 47% of the final price in the agricultural sector and 42% in manufacturing. Dornbusch (1989) mentions the importance of the distribution sector in influencing the RER via 'the service content of the consumer prices of goods'. Recent studies of the Balassa–Samuelson effect, which use sectoral data to derive measures of relative productivity of tradables and non-tradables, include the distribution sector in the non-tradable sector (see the discussion above). Both Devereux (1999) and Burstein *et al.* (2000) explicitly discuss the role of the distribution sector in explaining the RER, but still treat the sector as a non-tradable (in both papers it is assumed to influence the domestic consumption price of tradables, after international price equalization). Obstfeld and Rogoff (2000) briefly mention, but do not pursue, the role of the distribution sector as an alternative explanation for the relatively slow mean reversion in RERs. Engel (1999) has suggested the distribution sector as one explanation for the variability of the relative price of non-traded goods in explaining US CPI-based RER movements.

MacDonald and Ricci (2001, 2005) empirically examine the role of the distribution sector on the real exchange rate and, in particular, whether productivity in the distribution sector influences the real exchange rate through the tradable or non-tradable channels. In order to motivate their empirical tests MacDonald and Ricci introduce the distribution sector into a variant of the Balassa–Samuelson model considered in Section 3.2.1 and we briefly overview their model here. The model assumes constant returns to labor in all primary activities, that is production of intermediate inputs (I), of distribution services (D), of non-tradables goods (N) and of the aggregation services (A) necessary to manufacture tradables from intermediate inputs.[6,7] The technology for secondary activities are Cobb-Douglas: in goods I, D and A, for the production of tradables (T); and in goods T and D in order to make tradables available to consumers (TC). The model is then completed by assuming different technologies in the primary activities across countries, identical Cobb-Douglas preferences in tradables and non-tradables across countries, wage equalisation within countries, international price equalisation for tradables, and non-tradability of intermediate inputs. In formulas, for country i ($i = 1, 2$):

$$Y_{ki} = \frac{L_{ki}}{\beta_{ki}}, \quad k = I, D, N, A \tag{3.30}$$

$$Y_{Ti} = \frac{Y_{Ii}^{\gamma\eta}\, Y_{Di}^{1-\gamma}\, Y_{Ai}^{\gamma(1-\eta)}}{(\gamma\eta)^{\gamma\eta}\,(1-\gamma)^{1-\gamma}\,(\gamma(1-\eta))^{\gamma(1-\eta)}}, \tag{3.31}$$

$$Y_{TCi} = \frac{Y_{Ti}^{1-\phi} \, Y_{Di}^{\phi}}{\phi^{\phi} \, (1-\phi)^{1-\phi}}, \tag{3.32}$$

$$U_i = \frac{y_{Ni}^{\alpha} \, y_{TCi}^{1-\alpha}}{\alpha^{\alpha} \, (1-\alpha)^{1-\alpha}}, \tag{3.33}$$

where L_{ki} and β_{ki} represent, respectively, employment and unit labour input requirement prevailing in sector k and country i (for $k = I, D, N, A$), and Y_{ki} is the output in sector k of country i (for $k = I, D, N, A, T, TC$); U_i and y_{ki} stand for, respectively, the utility of one individual of country i and her/his demand for good k (for $k = N$, TC).

In equilibrium, given firms and consumer maximisation problems and goods market clearing, the following equations for the price of the various goods and services of the two countries must hold:

$$p_{ki} = \beta_{ki} w_i, \quad k = I, D, N, A, \tag{3.34}$$

$$p_{Ti} = p_{Ii}^{\gamma\eta} \, p_{Di}^{1-\gamma} \, p_{Ai}^{\gamma(1-\eta)} = w_i \, \beta_{Ii}^{\gamma\eta} \, \beta_{Di}^{1-\gamma} \, \beta_{Ai}^{\gamma(1-\eta)}$$

$$\equiv w_i \, \beta_{Ti}^{\gamma} \, \beta_{Di}^{1-\gamma}, \tag{3.35}$$

$$p_{TCi} = p_{Ti}^{1-\phi} \, p_{Di}^{\phi}, \tag{3.36}$$

$$p_{T1} = e \, p_{T2}, \tag{3.37}$$

$$p_i = p_{Ni}^{\alpha} \, p_{TCi}^{1-\alpha}, \tag{3.38}$$

$$\text{RER} \equiv \frac{p_1}{e \, p_2} = \frac{p_{N1}^{\alpha} \, p_{TC1}^{1-\alpha}}{e \, p_{N2}^{\alpha} \, p_{TC2}^{1-\alpha}}, \tag{3.39}$$

where w_i is the wage prevailing in country i, $\beta_{Ti} \equiv \beta_{Ii}^{\eta} \, \beta_{Ai}^{1-\eta}$ is the average productivity of the two stages of production of tradable goods in country i, and e is the nominal exchange rate (units of currency 1 for one unit of currency 2).

Price equalization of tradable goods determines relative wages and provides the familiar relation for the RER, which is now augmented for the distribution sector:

$$\frac{w_1}{e \, w_2} = \left(\frac{\beta_{T2}}{\beta_{T1}}\right)^{\gamma} \left(\frac{\beta_{D2}}{\beta_{D1}}\right)^{1-\gamma}, \tag{3.40}$$

$$\text{RER} = \left(\frac{w_1}{e w_2}\right)^{\alpha+(1-\alpha)\phi} \left(\frac{\beta_{N1}}{\beta_{N2}}\right)^{\alpha} \left(\frac{\beta_{D1}}{\beta_{D2}}\right)^{(1-\alpha)\phi}$$

$$= \left(\frac{\beta_{T2}}{\beta_{T1}}\right)^{\alpha\gamma+(1-\alpha)\phi\gamma} \left(\frac{\beta_{N2}}{\beta_{N1}}\right)^{-\alpha} \left(\frac{\beta_{D2}}{\beta_{D1}}\right)^{(1-\gamma)\alpha-(1-\alpha)\phi\gamma}$$

Hence, the RER of country 1 versus 2 will appreciate with the relative productivity of tradables (β_{T2}/β_{T1}) and will depreciate with the relative productivity of non-tradables (β_{N2}/β_{N1}). It will also appreciate with the relative productivity of the distribution sector (β_{D2}/β_{D1}), if this sector plays a bigger role in delivering goods in the tradable industry rather than to consumers. This is because the productivity of the distribution sector has two effects: on the one hand, it tends to lower the price of tradables (by lowering the cost of distributing intermediate inputs), thus raising the relative wage and appreciating the RER (similar to the effect of the productivity of tradables); on the other hand, it lowers the consumer price of tradables, depreciating the RER (similar to the effect of the productivity of non-tradables).[8,9]

The data set used by MacDonald and Ricci consists of a panel of 10 OECD for the period 1970–91 (annual data). The dependent variable in their study is the logarithm of the CPI-based real exchange rate and the explanatory variables are the relative productivity in tradables and non-tradables, relative productivity in the distribution sector, the wage (see Section 3.2.3 for a discussion of the role of the wage in a Balassa–Samuelson framework) and two macroeconomic control variables, net foreign assets and the real interest differential. A typical result, estimated using panel DOLS, from MacDonald and Ricci is:

$$q_t = \underset{(3.97)}{-0.003 nfa_t} + \underset{(2.74)}{0.007(r_t - r_t^*)} - \underset{(2.78)}{0.253 \text{prod}_t^T} - \underset{(6.08)}{0.306 \text{prod}_t^{NT}}$$
$$+ \underset{(4.47)}{0.230 \text{prod}_t^D} + \underset{(16.45)}{0.580 w_t^T} \tag{3.41}$$

where variable names have their usual interpretation, prod is productivity (in traded, T, non-traded, NT, and distribution, D) and w^T is the wage in the traded sector. Productivity in the distribution sector has a significantly positive impact on the real exchange rate and this is independent of the influence of the regular Balassa–Samuleson productivity effects from the traded and non-traded sectors. The positive influence on the real exchange rate suggests that productivity in the distribution sector influences the real exchange rate in a manner akin to productivity in the traded sector, rather than as a non-traded effect. Note, that as discussed in Section 3.2.3, the coefficient on productivity in the traded sector is negative, instead of positive as predicted under the standard Balassa–Samuelson framework. MacDonald and Ricci interpret this as *prima facie* evidence of a violation of the LOOP and argue that the Balassa–Samuelson model is not well suited to understanding how productivity differences impact on the real exchange rate.

3.5   Productivity redux and the imperfect substitutability of internationally traded goods

As we have seen in previous sections the empirical evidence suggest that the assumption that goods entering international trade are perfect substitutes, which as we have seen is at the heart of the Balassa–Samuelson proposition, is untenable. A number of recent papers have therefore attempted to revisit the effects of productivity differences on the exchange rate in the absence of homogeneous traded goods (see, for example, MacDonald and Ricci 2003 and Benigno and Thoenissen 2003). Here we illustrate this approach using the model and empirical evidence of MacDonald and Ricci (2003). In sum, this model features differing productivity levels across countries and sectors (as in a standard Balassa–Samuelson approach), imperfect substitutability of internationally traded goods, different levels of product market competition – or of economies of scale – in different countries (which are two key ingredients of the several trade theory models, particularly since Helpman and Krugman 1985 and Krugman 1990), and home bias in demand.[10,11]

The model encompasses two countries (1 and 2), each with a tradable (T) and a non-tradable sector (N). Each of these sectors is composed of many varieties which enters the utility function in a Dixit–Stiglitz (1977) form. Each variety is produced by a different firm under increasing returns to scale with a fixed cost and a constant marginal cost, both in terms of labor. Trade is assumed to be free. Labour mobility within countries ensures domestic wage equalisation across sectors. International labour immobility prevents agglomeration effects.[12] Preferences are similar across countries: Cobb-Douglas in tradables and non-tradables, CES between domestic and foreign tradables and CES of the Dixit–Stiglitz type among varieties of each sector.

A representative individual of country k ($k = 1, 2$) is assumed to maximise the following preferences:

$$
U_k = \left\{ \delta \left[\sum_{i=1}^{n_{Tk}} \left(c_{Tki}^k \right)^{\theta_{Tk}} \right]^{\theta/\theta_{Tk}} + (1 - \delta) \left[\sum_{j=1}^{n_{Tk'}} \left(c_{Tk'j}^k \right)^{\theta_{Tk'}} \right]^{\theta/\theta_{Tk'}} \right\}^{(1-\gamma/\theta)}
$$

$$
\times \left[\sum_{h=1}^{n_{Nk}} \left(c_{Nkh}^k \right)^{\theta_{Nk}} \right]^{\gamma/\theta_{Nk}} .
\tag{3.42}
$$

Subject to:

$$
\sum_{i=1}^{n_{Tk}} p_{Tki}^k c_{Tki}^k + \sum_{j=1}^{n_{Tk'j}} p_{Tk'j}^k c_{Tk'j}^k + \sum_{h=1}^{n_{Nk}} p_{Nkh}^k c_{Nkh}^k = w_k L_k,
$$

where $\{c_{Tki}^k, c_{Tk'j}^k, c_{Nkh}^k\}$ are, respectively, the consumption from the part of the representative consumer of country k of the $\{i\text{th}, j\text{th}, h\text{th}\}$ variety of the $\{$tradables produced in country k, tradables produced abroad – that is in country k' – and non-tradables produced in country $k\}$. Similarly $\{p_{Tki}^k, p_{Tk'j}^k, p_{Nkh}^k\}$ are the prices in location k of the varieties as respectively listed above. Prices of foreign varieties in the domestic market will equal foreign prices multiplied by the nominal exchange rate, e.[13] The labour supply and the wage rate of location k are denoted by L_k and w_k, respectively.

MacDonald and Ricci assume that relative weights of domestic and foreign tradables are assumed to be such that, *ceteris paribus* (i.e. if prices were identical), expenditure on domestic goods would be at least as large as expenditure on foreign goods ($0 < 1 - \delta \leqslant \delta < 1$). This introduces an expenditure bias on domestic tradables to the extent that $\delta > 1 - \delta$.[14] Crucially, the parameters $\theta_{T1}, \theta_{T2}, \theta_{N1}, \theta_{N2}$ allow for the elasticity of substitution of demand to differ across sectors and countries.

The Consumers' maximisation problem implies that consumers will spend a share γ and $1 - \gamma$ of their income on non-tradable and tradable goods, respectively. Within tradable goods, the relative expenditure between domestic and foreign tradables will depend on the relative (domestic versus foreign) prices as well as on the expenditure bias towards domestic goods. Within each of the three sub-utility consumption baskets (domestic tradables, foreign tradables and non-tradables), expenditure will be allocated equally among varieties, as the latter are all symmetric. Formally, the optimal expenditure functions of the representative consumer of country k on the typical varieties of domestic tradables (c_{Tk}^k), foreign tradables $(c_{Tk'}^k)$ and domestic non-tradables (c_{Nk}^k) are given by:

$$c_{Tk}^k = (1/n_{Tk}) \left[(n_{Tk})^{[\theta/(\theta-1)][(\theta_{Tk}-1)/\theta_{Tk}]} \left(p_{Tk}^k \right)^{1/(\theta-1)} (\delta)^{1/(1-\theta)} \right]$$

$$\bigg/ \left[(n_{Tk})^{[\theta/(\theta-1)][(\theta_{Tk}-1)/\theta_{Tk}]} \left(p_{Tk}^k \right)^{\theta/(\theta-1)} (\delta)^{1/(1-\theta)} \right.$$

$$\left. + (n_{Tk'})^{[\theta/(\theta-1)][(\theta_{Tk'}-1)/\theta_{Tk'}]} \left(p_{Tk'}^k \right)^{\theta/(\theta-1)} (1 - \delta)^{1/(1-\theta)} \right] (1 - \gamma) E_k,$$

$$(3.43)$$

$$c_{Tk'}^k = (1/n_{Tk'}) \left[(n_{Tk'})^{[\theta/(\theta-1)][(\theta_{Tk'}-1)/\theta_{Tk'}]} \left(p_{Tk'}^k \right)^{1/(\theta-1)} (1 - \delta)^{1/(1-\theta)} \right]$$

$$\bigg/ \left[(n_{Tk})^{[\theta/(\theta-1)][(\theta_{Tk}-1)/\theta_{Tk}]} \left(p_{Tk}^k \right)^{\theta/(\theta-1)} (\delta)^{1/(1-\theta)} \right.$$

$$\left. + (n_{Tk'})^{[\theta/(\theta-1)][(\theta_{Tk'}-1)/\theta_{Tk'}]} \left(p_{Tk'}^k \right)^{\theta/(\theta-1)} (1 - \delta)^{1/(1-\theta)} \right] (1 - \gamma) E_k,$$

$$(3.44)$$

$$c_{Nk}^k = \frac{1}{n_{Nk} p_{Nk}^k} \gamma E_k. \qquad (3.45)$$

The firm's maximisation problem, which is taken from a Dixit–Stiglitz formulation, produces the following first-order condition:

$$p_{sk}^k = \frac{w_k}{\pi_{sk} \theta_{sk}}, \qquad (3.46)$$

where π_{sk} represent the marginal productivity of labour in the respective sector of each country, w is the wage and as is usual in the Dixit–Stiglitz framework, θ_{sk} (a parameter of the utility function) equals the inverse of the optimal mark-up, and this is refered to as a measure of product market competition in the respective sector.[15]

The various equilibrium conditions facilitates derivation of the following expression for the real exchange rate:[16]

$$q = \left(\frac{(n_{N1})^{(\theta_{N1}-1)/\theta_{N1}}}{(n_{N2})^{(\theta_{N2}-1)/\theta_{N2}}} \frac{w}{\theta_N \pi_N} \right)^\gamma$$

$$\times \left(\frac{N_{T1} (w/\theta_T \pi_T)^{\theta/(\theta-1)} (v)^{1/(1-\theta)} + N_{T2}}{N_{T1} (w/\theta_T \pi_T)^{\theta/(\theta-1)} + N_{T2} (v)^{1/(1-\theta)}} \right)^{(1-\gamma)(\theta-1)/\theta} . \quad (3.47)$$

Which shows in the absence of an expenditure bias (i.e. if $v = 1$), the real exchange rate would depend only on the relative price of non-tradables. By differentiation, and after some manipulation the following reduced from equation for the exchange rate can be derived:

$$\hat{q} = \phi_{\pi T} \hat{\pi}_T + \phi_{\pi N} \hat{\pi}_N + \phi_{\theta T} \hat{\theta}_T + \phi_{\theta N} \hat{\theta}_N \quad (3.48)$$

where, recalling the definition of v,

$$\phi_{\pi T} = \frac{\gamma \left[(\delta/(1-\delta))^{1/(1-\theta)} ((1+\theta)/(1-\theta)) - 1 \right] + 1 - (\delta/(1-\delta))^{1/(1-\theta)}}{\left[(\delta/1-\delta)^{1/(1-\theta)} ((1+\theta)/(1-\theta)) + 1 \right]},$$

$$\phi_{\pi N} = -\gamma, \quad \phi_{\theta T} = (1-y_T)\phi_{\pi T}, \quad \phi_{\theta N} = -\gamma(1-y_N).$$

Equation (3.48) provides several implications for the behaviour of the real exchange rate.

First, the impact on the real exchange rate of the relative productivity in tradables is smaller than that of the relative productivity in non-tradables (i.e. $\phi_{\pi T} < \gamma$). This as we have seen differs from the usual Balassa–Samuelson theoretical result. In fact, the imperfect substitutability of tradables implies that the productivity of tradables also has a direct negative impact on the prices of tradables in addition to the indirect positive impact – via wages – on the price of non-tradables. To the extent there is an expenditure bias towards domestic tradables, the direct negative impact would produce a depreciation of the real exchange rate (as domestic prices fall more than foreign ones). Such an effect would go against the usual positive impact on the real exchange rate of the indirect effect (via the wage) of the productivity of tradables.

The second implication of this model is that the overall impact of the productivity of tradables on q is positive, unless the share of expenditure on non-tradables is very small; that is $\phi_{\pi T} > 0$, only if γ is not too small. If the share of expenditure on non-tradables were to be too small, the direct negative impact of productivity of tradables on the real exchange rate can be larger than the indirect positive impact via wages. As discussed below, MacDonald and Ricci find empirically that $\phi_{\pi T} > 0$.

Third, the impact of relative product market competition in the tradable (non-tradable) sector on the real exchange rate is similar to the impact of relative productivity in the tradable (non-tradable) sector, if the price effect of changes in the number of varieties of tradables (non-tradables) captured by y_T (y_N) is neglected. The intuition for this is that absent the price effect product market competition affects prices – and hence the real exchange rate – in a similar way to productivity (incorporating the price effect would generate the opposite effect on the exchange rate.

MacDonald and Ricci (2003) test equation (3.48) using the same data set as discussed in the last section, along with a new variable *comp*, relative product market competition, which is the inverse of the mark-up and equals the equilibrium ratio of variable employment to total employment (this term is also directly related to the elasticity of substitution and inversely related to the equilibrium economies of scale).

Summarising their complete set of results, MacDonald and Ricci conclude the following. First, the coefficient of the relative productivity of tradables is significantly lower than the coefficient of the relative productivity of non-tradables, in absolute terms, as predicted by the model. Second, the coefficient of the relative productivity of tradables changes sign if the wage is introduced into the estimation. These two results are consistent with the hypothesis of imperfect substitutability of tradables, coupled with an expenditure bias towards domestically produced tradables. An increase in productivity in tradables has two effects: first, a direct negative impact on the price of tradables, and therefore pressure towards a depreciation of the real exchange rate. Second, the lower price induces a larger demand and hence a higher wage (the standard Balassa–Samuelson effect), which instead tends to appreciate the real exchange rate via an increase in the price of non-tradables. The first effect ensures that the direct impact of the productivity of tradables on the real exchange rate – that is net of the wage channel – is negative.

Third, MacDonald and Ricci (2003) find that the coefficient of productivity on non-tradables drops when the wage enters the regression. This result is likely to be due to the impossibility of deriving perfect measure of tradables and non-tradables: some components of non-tradables index (such as the utilities) might be used as intermediate inputs and therefore be indirectly traded. Productivity in these components would thus behave as productivity of tradables and would slightly offset other components. Fourth, a measure of product market competition in the tradable sector is significant and positive and this suggests that an increase in product market competition of tradables acts exactly like an increase in productivity, which is consistent with the model if the effect of the change in the number of varieties is neglected (i.e. if we believe that the CPI-based real exchange rate cannot capture the effect of the change in the number of varieties on the true price index – the price of one unit of marginal utility). Fifth, the coefficient of product market competition in the tradable sector remains significant and positive, although it drops in size, when the wage is introduced.[17] MacDonald and Ricci argue that this result cannot be explained in terms of their model and requires further investigation of the mechanism through which product market competition affects the real exchange rate, as it suggests that the product market competition in tradables does not have the same transmission mechanism as the productivity of tradables.

Concluding comments

In this chapter we have presented a number of economic explanations for the PPP puzzle. We have argued that in trying to understand the puzzle non-linear models, although interesting in themselves, cannot realistically explain persistent deviations from PPP, since such models are reliant on the goods entering international trade being perfectly substitutable and agents having no impediments to goods arbitrage. We would argue that the alternative explanations considered in this chapter, namely market structure and the 'real determinants' of real exchange rates, in the form here of productivity differences, offer a more realistic explanation for the PPP puzzle. We have also discussed models which relax the assumption that goods are perfectly substitutable internationally. In succeeding chapters, the role of additional real determinants of the real exchange rates, such as net foreign assets and terms of trade effects, are considered in some detail.

4 The flexible price monetary approach to the exchange rate

In this and the next two chapters we turn to a fundamentals-based approach to modelling the nominal exchange rate which has become something of a workhorse in the exchange rate literature, namely, the monetary approach to the exchange rate. As we shall see, this approach builds on the PPP construct considered in the last chapter and that is especially true of the flexible price variant of the monetary model considered in this chapter, where PPP is assumed to hold continuously. The sticky-price variants of the monetary model, considered in the next chapter, assume that PPP is violated in the short-run, although it is assumed to hold in the long-run.

The variants of the monetary model discussed in this chapter and the next yield important insights into the issue of exchange rate volatility, particularly the issue of excess exchange rate volatility first introduced in Chapter 1. Although the various guises of the monetary approach considered – most notably the flex-price and sticky-price approaches – rely on PPP, their motivation is quite different since they view the exchange rate as the relative price of two monies (i.e. assets), rather than as the relative price of commodities. Interpreting the exchange rate as an asset price yields important insights into why floating exchange rates are more volatile than underlying economic fundamentals. This may be illustrated by referring back to Table 1.4 of Chapter 1, where the coefficients of variation of three series are presented for a number of representative countries.

From Table 1.4 we note that exchange rates are between 2 and 8 eight times more volatile than relative prices. This kind of result is often cited to make the point that exchange rates are much more volatile than economic fundamentals, and, of course, the finding is entirely consistent with what we said in the last chapter (this kind of result would also occur if we took other standard fundamentals such as money supplies and current accounts). However, the key thing to note from Table 1.4 is that interest differentials are much more volatile than exchange rates. Indeed, the excess volatility of interest rates with respect to exchange rates is similar in magnitude to the excess volatility of exchange rates with respect to prices, the range for the former being between 2 and 10. So Table 1.4 makes the point that in trying to understand the behaviour of exchange rates it is more appropriate to take an asset price perspective, rather than a commodity price perspective.

The insight that exchange rates should be thought of as asset prices is a fundamental contribution of the asset approach to the exchange rate (see MacDonald 1988). Within the asset approach there are two competing classes of models: the monetary approach and the portfolio-balance approach. In the former class of models non-money assets – namely bonds – are assumed to be perfect substitutes, while in the latter they are assumed imperfectly substitutable. As noted earlier, the focus in this chapter is on monetary models; aspects of the portfolio-balance model are discussed in Chapters 7 and 15. One key contribution of the asset approach is that exchange rates are inherently forward looking – today's price is inextricably linked to the price in the next period, and so on. This forward-looking aspect of exchange rates is brought out in our theoretical discussions of the models.

The outline of this chapter is as follows. In the next section we consider what we refer to as the *ad hoc* flex-price monetary approach (FLMA), which explains excessive exchange rate volatility in terms of a magnified response of the current exchange rate to expected future excess money supplies. The approach is referred to as *ad hoc* because it is derived on the basis of money market equilibrium conditions rather than the optimising behaviour of agents. We also consider the implications of rational speculative bubbles for exchange rate volatility using the FLMA. In Section 4.3 we consider the Lucas–Stockman variant of the flexible price monetary model. This version has at its core the optimising behaviour of agents and offers another explanation for exchange rate volatility which is consistent with rational behaviour.

4.1   The flex-price monetary approach

A popular variant of the monetary approach is the, so-called, flex-price monetary approach (FLMA). This model is usually presented as a two-country, two money, two bonds and a single homogenous traded good (alternatively, absolute PPP holds continuously for identical baskets of goods). Crucially, bonds are assumed to be perfect substitutes, and so uncovered interest rate parity holds continuously:

$$E_t(\Delta s_{t+k}) = (i_t - i_t^*). \tag{4.1}$$

The perfect substituability of home and foreign bonds means they may be lumped together into a composite bond term and the wealth constraint effectively features three assets, namely, domestic money, foreign money and the composite bond. Since the bond market may be thought of as a residual,[1] attention then focuses on money market equilibrium conditions. Money demand relationships are given by standard Cagan-style log-linear relationships of the following form:

$$m_t^D - p_t = \beta_0 y_t - \beta_1 i_t, \quad \beta_0, \beta_1 > 0, \tag{4.2}$$

$$m_t^{D*} - p_t^* = \beta_0 y_t^* - \beta_1 i_t^*, \tag{4.2'}$$

where, for simplicity, the income elasticity, β_0, and the interest semi-elasticity, β_1, are assumed equal across countries. If it is additionally assumed that money market equilibrium holds continuously in each country:

$$m_t^d = m_t^s = m_t,$$

$$m_t^{*,d} = m_t^{*,s} = m_t^*,$$

then using these conditions in (4.2), and rearranging for relative prices, we obtain:

$$p_t - p_t^* = m_t - m_t^* - \beta_0(y_t - y_t^*) + \beta_1(i_t - i_t^*). \tag{4.3}$$

On further assuming that PPP (or the LOOP) holds for the relative prices (see Chapter 2) we obtain a base-line monetary equation as:

$$s_t = m_t - m_t^* - \beta_0(y_t - y_t^*) + \beta_1(i_t - i_t^*). \tag{4.4}$$

In words, the nominal exchange rate is driven by the relative excess supply of money. Holding money demand variables constant, an increase in the domestic money supply relative to its foreign counterpart produces an equiproportionate depreciation of the currency. Changes in output levels or interest rates have their effect on the exchange rate indirectly through their effect on the demand for money. So, for example, an increase in domestic income relative to foreign income, *ceteris paribus*, produces a currency appreciation, while an increase in the domestic interest rate relative to the foreign rate generates a depreciation. Although some proponents of the flex-price monetary model view equation (4.4) as holding continuously it seems more appropriate to think of it as a long-run equilibrium relationship, where the nominal interest rates, via the Fisher condition, capture expected inflation.

4.1.1   *The forward-looking monetary relationship and the magnification effect*

One of the useful features of the monetary model is that it includes forward-looking expectations and this introduces the possibility of excessive exchange rate movements relative to fundamentals. This may be seen more clearly in the following way. By noting from (4.1) that the expected change in the exchange rate is equal to the interest differential in (4.4), we may rewrite (4.4) as:

$$s_t = m_t - m_t^* - \beta_0(y_t - y_t^*) + \beta_1 E_t(s_{t+1} - s_t), \tag{4.5}$$

which, in turn, may be rearranged for the current exchange rate as:

$$s_t = z_t + \theta E_t(s_{t+1}), \tag{4.5'}$$

where:

$$z_t = (1 + \beta)^{-1}[m_t - m_t^* - \beta_0(y_t - y_t^*)],$$

and

$$\theta = \beta_1(1 + \beta_1)^{-1}.$$

With rational expectations the expected exchange rate in period $t + 1$ may be obtained by leading (4.5′) one period and taking conditional expectations:

$$E_t s_t = E_t z_{t+1} + \theta E_t s_{t+2}.$$

By recursively substituting out the expected exchange rate for all future periods the forward extension of the monetary model may be obtained as:

$$s_t = \sum_{i=0}^{\infty} \theta^i E_t[z_{t+i}], \qquad (4.6)$$

where the transversality or terminal condition $- \lim_{i \to \infty} \theta^i E_t s_{t+i+1} = 0 -$ is assumed to hold. A key implication of (4.6) is that changes in current fundamentals can have a more than proportionate, or magnified, effect on s to the extent they influence the future profile of expectations. This may be seen more clearly by posing the following example: what does a current change in the money supply signal to agents? To answer this question we assume the time series properties of the composite fundamental term to have an AR1 representation:

$$z_t = \phi z_{t-1} + u_t \quad |\phi| < 1.$$

Using this expression in (4.6) a closed form solution for the exchange rate may be derived as:

$$s_t = (1 - \phi\theta)^{-1} z_t, \qquad (4.7)$$

and since the term $(1 - \phi\theta)^{-1}$ is greater than unity a current change in m will have a magnified effect on s_t. So in answer to the earlier question, a current change in the money supply, by signalling to agents through (4.7) further changes in the future, produces a more than proportionate movement in the current exchange rate relative to current fundamentals.

On the basis of this, one potential explanation for the apparent excess volatility of the exchange rate with respect to current fundamentals is that such a comparison misses the dramatic effect that expectations can have on exchange rate volatility. In discussing exchange rate volatility it is useful to introduce the so-called variance inequality of variance bounds relationship, popular from the stock market literature. If we denote the solution (4.6) as market fundamentals or 'no-bubbles' and label it $\hat{s}_t$, where:

$$\hat{s}_t = \sum_{i=0}^{\infty} \theta^i E_t[z_{t+i}]. \qquad (4.6')$$

Expression (4.6') may be rewritten as:

$$\hat{s}_t = E_t s_t^*, \qquad (4.6'')$$

where s_t^* has the interpretation of the perfect foresight exchange rate (the rate that would prevail if there is no uncertainty):

$$s_t^* = \sum_{i=0}^{\infty} \theta^i z_{t+i}.$$

With rational expectations it follows that:

$$s_t^* = \hat{s}_t + u_t, \qquad (4.8)$$

or

$$s_t^* = s_t + u_t, \qquad (4.8')$$

where u_t is a purely random forecast error. Taking the variance of the left and right hand sides of (4.8') we obtain:

$$\text{Var}(s_t^*) = \text{Var}(s_t) + \text{Var}(u_t).$$

Since the error term is a purely random term it must follow that $\text{Cov}(\hat{s}_t, u_t) = 0$ and therefore:

$$\text{Var}(s_t^*) \geq \text{Var}(s_t). \qquad (4.9)$$

If the magnification story is correct then the variance of the perfect foresight exchange rate should be at least as large as the variance of the actual exchange rate. In Chapter 6 we consider ways of testing this proposition empirically.

4.2   Rational speculative bubbles

Another explanation for exchange rate volatility can be derived from the forward monetary model by relaxing the terminal condition assumption. In particular, if $\lim_{i \to \infty} \theta^i E_t s_{t+i+1} = 0$, does not hold, then there are potentially multiple solutions to (4.5') each one of which may be written in the form:

$$s_t = \hat{s}_t + b_t. \qquad (4.10)$$

For (4.10) to be a rational bubble, and therefore a solution to (4.5') it must evolve in the following way:

$$b_t = \theta E_t b_{t+1}. \qquad (4.11)$$

This is regarded as a rational bubble because it provides a solution to the model which is equivalent to (4.5'). The existence of an explosive bubble violates the transversality condition which may be seen by substituting (4.11) into the limit condition for the final period expected exchange rate condition:

$$\theta^{t+k} E \hat{s}_{t+k} = \theta^{t+k} E_t s_{t+k} + \theta^{t+k} E_t b_{t+k} = b_t.$$

The bubble term will eventually dominate the exchange rate process and push it away from the fundamental path. The implications of a rational speculative bubble for excess volatility of the exchange rates can be demonstrated by constructing a 'variance inequality' which is comparable to (4.9). In the presence of speculative bubble we know from (4.10) that $\hat{s}_t = s_t - b_t$ and so we have to replace (4.8) with:

$$s_t^* = s_t - b_t + u_t. \tag{4.12}$$

Since, *a priori*, a correlation between b_t and s_t cannot be ruled out, the variance decomposition now has the following form:

$$\text{Var}(s_t^*) = \text{Var}(s_t) + \text{Var}(b_t) + \text{Var}(u_t) - 2\text{Cov}(s_t, b_t), \tag{4.13}$$

which indicates that in presence of speculative bubbles, exchange rates may be excessively volatile relative to fundamentals-based values. In other words, if a researcher were to test the inequality (4.9) and find it were reversed, then such violation would represent *prima facie* evidence of a speculative bubble.

A further implication of a speculative bubble, from the perspective of testing the FLMA, is that it will impart an explosive element into the right hand side of (4.5). For example, if all of the variables entering (4.5) are integrated of order 1, $I(1)$, the FLMA with the transversality condition imposed implies that s should form a cointegrating set with the RHS variables. That is:

$$z_t = s_t - m_t + m_t^* + \beta_0(y_t - y_t^*) \sim I(0). \tag{4.14}$$

If, however, z_t turns out to be $I(1)$ the interpretation is that transversality condition is violated and this is *prima facie* evidence of a speculative bubble. Issues relating to the empirical testing of (4.13) and (4.14) are considered again in more detail in Chapter 6.

4.3　The Lucas monetary model

Although the flex-price monetary model considered earlier has become something of a workhorse in international finance, particularly for analysing exchange rate issues, it is nonetheless *ad hoc* since it is derived using Cagan-style money market relationships which do not arise from the optimising behaviour of individuals. However, both Stockman (1980) and Lucas (1982) have demonstrated how a version of the flexible price monetary equation may be derived from a model with fully optimising agents. In the context of this model, Stockman (1980) has emphasised how, in contrast to the sticky-price model, real exchange rate changes are driven by real shocks rather than the interaction of exchange rate overshooting and sticky prices. We now consider this variant of the flex-price model.

The Lucas model is essentially a barter economy model into which money is introduced through a cash-in-advance constraint. We therefore first consider the barter version of the model before going on to consider the introduction of a cash-in-advance constraint into the model. The barter economy aspects are considered in Section 4.3.1 and money is introduced into this barter set-up in Section 4.3.1.1.

4.3.1   The Lucas barter economy

The model comprises two countries, each country producing a single good and where the representative agent in each country has an intertemporal utility function given by:

$$U = E_t \left(\sum_{t=0}^{\infty} \beta^t U(C_t, C_t^*) \right), \quad 0 < \beta < 1, \tag{4.15}$$

where C_t represents consumption in the home country of the home good and C_t^* is home consumption of the foreign good, β is the subjective discount rate and the usual assumptions are assumed to hold for $U(.)$.[2] The foreign representative agent is assumed to have the same kind of utility function.[3] Firms produce the two homogeneous (non-storable) goods – y and y^* – using no capital or labour inputs and therefore the goods are pure endowment goods. Production evolves over time according to a first order autoregressive processes, which is known to agents:

$$y_t = \delta y_{t-1}, \tag{4.16}$$

and

$$y_t^* = \delta^* y_{t-1}^*, \tag{4.17}$$

where δ and δ^*, in turn, evolve according to a stochastic process known to agents. All of the output produced in each country is paid out to individuals in the form of dividends and it is assumed that the home good, y, is the numeraire good and q_t is the real exchange rate defined as the price of y^* in terms of y (P^*/P). The value of domestic wealth that the domestic agent has at the start of period t is:

$$W_t = \omega_{y_{t-1}}(y_t + e_t) + \omega_{y_{t-1}^*}(q_t y_t^* + e_t^*), \tag{4.18}$$

where $\omega_{y_t} + \omega_{y_t^*}$ are the shares of home and foreign firms held by domestic residents, e is the ex-dividend market value of the firm and so the terms in brackets are the with dividend value of the home and foreign firms. In period t, the agent is then assumed to allocate wealth towards new consumption and share prices as:

$$W_t = e_t \omega_{y_t} + e_t^* \omega_{y_t^*} + C_t + q_t C_t^*. \tag{4.19}$$

The consolidated budget constraint may be obtained by equating (4.18) with (4.19):

$$c_{y_t} + q_t c_{y_t^*} + e_t \omega_{y_t} + e_t^* \omega_{y_t^*} = \omega_{y_{t-1}}(y_t + e_t) + \omega_{y_{t-1}^*}(q_t y_t^* + e_t^*). \tag{4.20}$$

Maximising equation (4.15) subject to the consolidated budget constraint for the home country yields a standard consumption Euler equation of the form:

$$q_t = \frac{u_{c_t}^*}{u_{c_t}}. \tag{4.21}$$

Equation (4.21) relates the relative price of the two goods to their marginal rate of substitution (where u_{c_t} is the marginal utility of consumption of the y good and $u_{c_t}^*$ is the corresponding marginal utility of y^* consumption).[4] A standard implication of this kind of first order condition is that if the agent is behaving optimally then a reallocation of x units C for C^* should not result in any change to total utility. Similar first order conditions (not reported here) also hold for domestic holdings of home and foreign equity, and a similar set of first-order conditions are assumed to hold for the foreign country as well.

Following Mark (2001) the use of an explicit form of the utility function makes the result in (4.21) more concrete. In particular, if the period utility function is assumed to be of the constant relative risk aversion (CRRA) form:

$$u(C, C^*) = \frac{X_t^{1-\gamma}}{1 - \gamma}, \tag{4.22}$$

where X is a Cobb–Douglas index of the two goods ($X_t = C_t^\theta C_t^{*1-\theta}$) equation (4.22) can be rewritten as

$$q_t = \frac{1-\theta}{\theta} \frac{y_t^{\theta-1}}{(y_t^*)^{-\theta}} \tag{4.23}$$

and by dividing the numerator and denominator by $(\theta - 1)$ we get

$$q_t = \frac{1-\theta}{\theta} \frac{y_t}{y_t^*}, \tag{4.23'}$$

which indicates that in the barter economy the real exchange rate is determined by relative output levels.

4.3.1.1   *Introduction of a cash-in-advance constraint into the barter model*

Money can be introduced into this model by assuming a so-called cash-in-advance constraint; that is, agents are required to use money for the purchase of goods (an alternative way to get money into this class of model is through the utility function and this kind of model is considered in some detail in Chapters 10 and 11). In the Lucas (1982) model the cash-in-advance constraint means that consumers have to set aside money in period t to satisfy all of their purchases in $t+1$. This is rationalised by thinking of the representative agent as a household with two individuals, one specialising in production and the other in consumption. In period t the producer sells her output and in period $t+1$ the consumer spends the proceeds of that output. At the end of $t+1$ the household's producer and consumer only get together again after markets have closed.

Specifically, assume that the total outstanding stock of the home and foreign money are M_t and M_t^* (these are assumed to evolve according to a first-order AR process, known to agents), P_t is the home price of y and P_t^* is the foreign price of y^*. The current values of y, y^*, M and M^* are known in advance so domestic (and foreign) residents know in advance how much home and foreign money is needed to finance current consumption plans. The cash-in-advance constraints for the home agent have the following form:

$$m_{1t-1} \geq P_t C_t, \tag{4.24}$$

and

$$m_{1t-1}^* \geq P_t^* C_t, \tag{4.24'}$$

where m_1 and m_1^* denote, respectively, the domestic agent's holdings of home and foreign money. These constraints imply that agents have to set aside at least as much money as they plan to spend on purchases of goods. However, given that there is no uncertainty about how much money will be required to finance period-t purchases, these constraints will be binding (i.e. agents don't hold excess money balances) in the presence of a positive nominal interest rate. The binding cash-in-advance constraints are:

$$m_{1t} = P_t C_t \tag{4.25}$$

and

$$m_{1t}^* = P_t^* C_t. \tag{4.25'}$$

By adding the two monies into the respective consolidated budget constraint, the Euler equation in the presence of a cash-in-advance constraint can be demonstrated to be:

$$\frac{S_t P_t^*}{P_t} = \frac{u_{c_t}^*}{u_{c_t}}. \tag{4.26}$$

This expression is not our desired result since it does not feature money. To introduce money into (4.26) we note that the adding-up constraints for the two monies are:

$$M = m_1 + m_2, \tag{4.27}$$

$$M^* = m_1^* + m_2^*, \tag{4.27'}$$

where m_2 and m_2^* are, respectively, the foreign country holdings of domestic and foreign money. These adding-up constraints, combined with the binding cash-in-advance constraints, imply a unitary velocity of money in each country:

$$M_t = P_t y_t \tag{4.28}$$

and

$$M_t^* = P_t^* y_t^* \tag{4.28'}$$

using (4.28) in (4.26) we obtain:

$$\frac{S_t M_t^*}{M_t} \frac{y_t}{y_t^*} = \frac{u_{c_t}^*}{u_{c_t}}, \tag{4.29}$$

and on rearranging this equation we may get an expression for the nominal exchange rate as:

$$S_t = \frac{u_{c_t}^*}{u_{c_t}} \frac{M_t}{M_t^*} \frac{y_t^*}{y_t}. \tag{4.30}$$

As in the flex-price monetary model, we see that the nominal exchange rate is here determined by relative money supplies and output, but in contrast to the FLMA, the exchange rate now depends on marginal utilities (preferences) and does not explicitly depend on future expectations (although they could be brought in). As Stockman (1980) notes, the fact that the exchange rate depends here on marginal utilities can have an important bearing on understanding exchange rate behaviour, particularly the behaviour of the real exchange rate. To illustrate this, we consider an example from Stockman (1980).

In Figure 4.1 we have an initial equilibrium at point A. Some exogenous shock then occurs which alters the home and foreign endowments to y_2 and y_2^*, respectively. Given nominal money supplies, the new price levels will be determined by M/y_2 and M^*/y_2^*, respectively. Suppose at the *old* nominal exchange rate this results in a relative price P_2/SP_2^* given by *ll* in Figure 4.1. Clearly, the highest indifference curve that can be reached at B is **U**. If the exchange rate stayed unchanged the representative agent would attempt to move along *ll* to a preferred position by buying less of the home good and more of the foreign good. This process will result in the representative agent in the home country increasing their demand for foreign exchange and those in the foreign country decreasing their demand for foreign exchange. This process will result in a change in export prices and the nominal exchange rate until the real

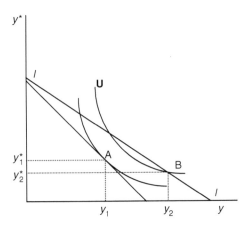

Figure 4.1 An endowment change in the monetary model.

exchange rate changes to ensure point **B** is a tangency point with **U**. These changes can be made more concrete by considering a worked example from Stockman (1980).

Suppose the utility function of the representative agent is $U = 5(c + c^*) - (c^2 + c^{*2}) + 5cc^*$ and the initial allocation of production is $y = 2$ and $y^* = 3$. Production then changes to $y = 3$ and $y^* = 2$. In the initial equilibrium the relative price of the two goods would be 16/9. Since the nominal exchange rate in this set-up is determined by the simple quantity theory equations (4.28) and (4.28′) the nominal exchange rate equation is:

$$s = \frac{M}{M^*} \frac{3}{2} \frac{9}{16} \propto \frac{27}{32}.$$

With the money supplies constant the production change produces an exchange rate change which is proportional to 2/3 times 16/9, or 32/27, and the new relative price of the home good in terms of the foreign good is 9/16. So the home money price of the home good falls by about one-half, the foreign price of the foreign good increases by about one-third, and the nominal exchange rate depreciates by around two-thirds: as noted earlier each of these three variables moves to provide the new equilibrium.

Some further implications follow on from the earlier example. First, the lower is the marginal rate of substitution between home and foreign goods, the larger will be the depreciation of the nominal exchange rate. If, as is often assumed in this class of model, the marginal rate of substitution is greater in the long run than in the short run, the exchange rate will depreciate more in the short run than in the long run. As in the Dornbusch model, the short-run exchange rate overshoots its long-run equilibrium value. In contrast to the Dornbusch model, however, the overshooting in this model is an equilibrium phenomenon.

As we saw in Chapter 2, real exchange rates are highly persistent. Stockman has argued that this is *prima facie* evidence in favour of his view that it is real shocks which drive real exchange rates, rather than liquidity shocks interacting with sticky prices. This is because nominal shocks should only have a short-lived effect on the real exchange rate (i.e. we note in Chapter 2 that a half-life for the real exchange rate of around 1 year is consistent with a traditional interpretation of PPP) while in actuality real exchange rates display considerable persistence (a half-life which is typically between 3 and 5 years).

A second implication of this model is that government intervention in the foreign exchange market cannot affect the real exchange rate. The reason for this is that in the earlier example the change in the nominal exchange rate did not cause the real exchange rate, it was merely one of the ways in which the real exchange rate change occurred. Of course, this impotence of foreign exchange intervention relies on the absence of uncertainty in this model. Recognising that agents are uncertain about whether an exchange rate change is associated with a real or nominal disturbance, could allow a foreign exchange intervention to have a real effect.

5 The sticky-price monetary model

In this chapter we consider a number of sticky-price variants of the monetary model. Our discussion starts, in Section 5.1, with the classic Mundell–Fleming model in which prices are rigidly fixed and therefore this model may be viewed as the polar opposite to the flex-price monetary model. In Section 5.2 we go on to discuss the Dornbusch (1976) extension of the Mundell–Fleming model, which we label the sticky-price monetary approach (SPMA). This latter model offers an explanation for excess exchange rate volatility in terms of the assymetrical adjustment of goods and asset markets. In Section 5.3 we consider a stochastic version of the Mundell–Fleming–Dornbusch model. Much as in the previous chapter, the variants of the monetary model mentioned here are all *ad hoc*, relying primarily on money market equilibrium conditions rather than on the optimising behaviour of agents. In Section 5.4 we therefore consider the sticky-price analogue to the Lucas model introduced in the previous chapter.

5.1 The Mundell–Fleming model

In this section we examine a model which has had a fundamental influence on international monetary economics, particularly the branch dealing with floating exchange rates: namely, the Mundell–Fleming (MF) model (the original references to this model are: Fleming (1962); Mundell (1963, 1968); Sohmen (1967); more recent references are: MacDonald (1988); Obstfeld and Rogoff (1996); Mark (2000)). The basic focal point of the MF model is a small open economy with unemployed resources, a perfectly elastic aggregate supply curve, static exchange rate expectations and perfect capital mobility. Given such assumptions it can be demonstrated that with flexible exchange rates monetary policy is extremely powerful in altering real output but fiscal policy is completely impotent. The inefficacy of fiscal policy under floating exchange rates has been one of the most enduring results in international economics, although it is of course crucially contingent on the underlying assumptions of the basic model.

Indeed, the base-line MF has come in for some considerable criticism because it is relatively *ad hoc* and, for example, it is essentially static in nature, both in terms of its failure to model expectations and also because dynamic interactions stemming from current account imbalances are not addressed. Despite this, the model is still often used, especially as a first cut at addressing macroeconomic issues in an open economy (see, for example, Krugman 2001). For this reason we give an overview of the basic model in this chapter. We then go on to address some of the deficiencies of the model by considering variants due to Dornbusch (1976) and Obstfeld (1985). Although such variants address some of the more glaring omissions of the MF model they nonetheless are still regarded as *ad hoc* variants because they do not have any micro foundations.

The MF model is a model of a small open economy facing a given world interest rate and a perfectly elastic supply of imports at a given price in terms of foreign currency. More specifically, in the MF model there are assumed to be four assets: a domestic and a foreign bond, each having an identical maturity, and a domestic and a foreign money. As in the FLMA of the previous chapter, the bonds are assumed to be perfect substitutes while the money in the home and foreign countries are assumed to be non-substitutable and thus only held in the country of issue (models in which domestic and foreign residents are allowed to hold both currencies are termed currency substitution models – such models are discussed in Chapter 7). Expectations are assumed to be static (i.e. the expected change in the exchange rate is equal to zero) and arbitrage is assumed to ensure that bond yields are continually equalised. These assumptions imply that the domestic rate of interest must continually equal the foreign rate:

$$i = i^*,\tag{5.1}$$

which is a representation of perfect capital mobility in the MF model.

The money market equilibrium, or LM curve, for the domestic economy is given by:

$$m - p = m^D - p = \beta_0 y - \beta_1 i, \quad \beta_0, \beta_1 > 0,\tag{5.2}$$

where variable names and symbols have the same interpretation as in the previous chapter.

Underlying the condition for goods market equilibrium in the standard MF model are the assumptions of unemployed resources, constant returns to scale and fixed money wages, resulting in a typically Keynesian 'deep depression' aggregate supply schedule (i.e. perfectly elastic).

Equilibrium in the goods market is given by the following IS curve:

$$y = d = g + \gamma_1(s - p) + \gamma_2 y - \gamma_3 i, \quad \gamma_1 > 0, 0 < \gamma_2 < 1, \gamma_3 > 0,\tag{5.3}$$

where output is demand determined, g is government spending, $s \quad p$ is a competitiveness term and influences aggregate demand through its effect on net exports, y_t captures the effect of income on consumption spending and i_t influences demand through its effect on investment spending and consumption. The (simplified) balance of payments equilibrium condition in the MF model is given by:

$$b = \vartheta_0(s - p) + \vartheta_1 y + \vartheta_2 y^* + \vartheta_3 i + n, \quad \vartheta_0, \vartheta_2 > 0, \vartheta_1 < 0, \vartheta_3 \to \infty.\tag{5.4}$$

In this simplified balance of payments condition net interest rate payments on net foreign assets are ignored, and the first three terms represent the effects of the real exchange rate and home and foreign income, respectively, on the trade balance. The second last term represents the effect of the domestic interest rate on capital flows and, in particular, shows that capital is here assumed to be perfectly mobile. The last term, n, is an exogenous shift factor. The small country assumption, along with the assumption that expectations are static, implies that only the domestic rate of interest enters this relationship.

By substituting (5.1) in (5.2) and (5.3), totally differentiating the result and rearranging we can obtain the following two-equation system which can be used to compute the system's comparative statics:

$$dy = \frac{1}{1 - \gamma_2} dg + \frac{\gamma_1}{1 - \gamma_2} ds - \frac{\gamma_3}{1 - \gamma_2} di^*, \tag{5.5}$$

$$dm = \frac{\beta_0}{1 - \gamma_2} dg + \frac{\beta_0 \gamma_1}{1 - \gamma_2} ds - \left[\beta_1 + \frac{\beta_0 \gamma_3}{1 - \gamma_2} \right] di^*, \tag{5.6}$$

where we have used the assumption that prices are constant to set $dp = 0$.

The workings of the MF model, and particularly the comparative statics, can be illustrated graphically in the following way. In part A of Figure 5.1 the schedule XX represents the locus of points of exchange rates and income levels along which

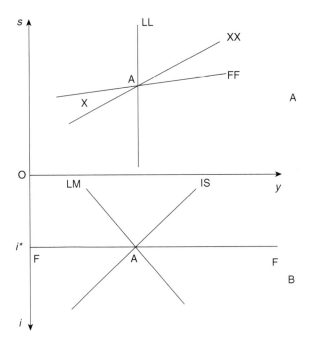

Figure 5.1 The Mundell–Fleming model.

there is equilibrium in the goods market. It has an upward slope because a higher level of output will, with a marginal propensity to spend of less than unity, lead to an excess supply of goods which necessitates an exchange rate depreciation (a rise in s) to maintain goods market equilibrium (the rising exchange rate improves the trade balance – assuming that the Marshall–Lerner condition holds – diverting demand towards domestic goods). The LL schedule represents the locus of s and y consistent with money market equilibrium: for a given rate of interest, equation (5.1), there will be only one income level at which the money market clears (bearing in mind that the price level is constant).

In Figure 5.1 B the curve IS represents the locus of interest rates and income along which there is equilibrium in the goods market. The curve LM is the locus of i and y consistent with equilibrium in the money market. The slopes of the IS and LM schedules in $i - y$ space should be obvious to those familiar with the basic IS–LM analysis.

The FF schedule represents combinations of s and y consistent with equilibrium in the balance of payments. In quadrant B, the perfectly elastic external balance schedule reflects the assumption of perfect capital mobility. Thus the balance of payments can only be in equilibrium when the domestic interest rate, i, equals the foreign interest rate, i^*; if for some reason i was above i^* the net capital inflow would be potentially infinite and swamp the current account (trade balance). The FF schedule in s/y space is upward sloping since an increase in income, by causing the current balance to deteriorate, requires an increase in s (depreciation), to maintain equilibrium in the balance of payments. The FF curve in s/y space is drawn for the initial rate of flow of capital imports.

That the XX schedule is drawn steeper than the FF schedule reflects the assumed stability of the system. Thus if FF were drawn steeper than XX and the economy was at a disequilibrium point such as X, movements in s and y would push the system away from the equilibrium, A. Initially, equilibrium pertains at point A. We shall now consider two types of shock: an increase in the money supply and an expansionary fiscal policy.

5.1.1 A monetary expansion in the MF model

An expansionary monetary policy, conducted by an open market purchase of bonds by the central bank, shifts the money market equilibrium schedule in Figure 5.2 from LM to LM′. At the initial levels of income and interest rate the expansionary monetary policy must imply an excess of domestic liquidity. With the domestic interest rate effectively fixed at the world level (equation (5.1)) and prices assumed constant the only way money market equilibrium can be restored is via an increase in income, from y_1 to y_2. The latter will occur because the expansionary monetary policy leads to an *incipient* decline in the domestic interest rate which, in turn, leads to a capital outflow and exchange rate depreciation. The rising price of foreign exchange will, via the Marshall–Lerner condition, result in an improved trade balance and have an expansionary effect on income as demand is switched from foreign goods to home goods: income will continue rising, and IS will shift

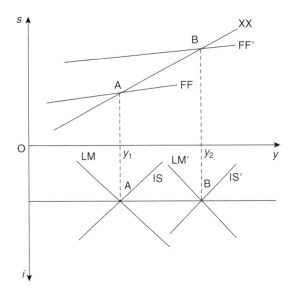

Figure 5.2 Monetary expansion in the MF model.

rightwards, until money market equilibrium has been restored at point B. Since the marginal propensity to spend in our variant of the model is less than unity, the current account must be in surplus at B and the capital account in deficit; the capital account deficit implies that FF shifts upwards to FF′. The effects of monetary policy on income and the exchange rate may be affirmed by deriving the following money multipliers from the system (5.5) and (5.6): $dy/dm = 1/\beta_0 > 0$ and $ds/dm = [(1 - \gamma_2)/\beta_0\gamma_1] > 0$.

With fixed exchange rates the conclusion that monetary policy has powerful effect on income is reversed. Thus the monetary expansion of LM to LM′ results in an incipient fall in the interest rate and a capital outflow, which does not in this case have any beneficial effect on income since the exchange rate implies that the authorities must be loosing reserves. As they intervene to support the currency the money supply will fall (assuming no sterilisation) and the LM schedule will shift back to intersect IS at A, since only at the initial equilibrium will there be no incipient change in the interest rate. The income multiplier in this case is therefore $dy/dm = 0$.

5.1.2   *Expansionary fiscal policy in the MF model*

Consider now an increase in government spending, financed purely by issuing bonds. This shifts the XX and IS curves to XX′ and IS′, respectively, in Figure 5.3 A and 5.3 B. With a fixed exchange rate an increase in government spending which shifted IS to IS′ would be effective in raising income. For example, an increase

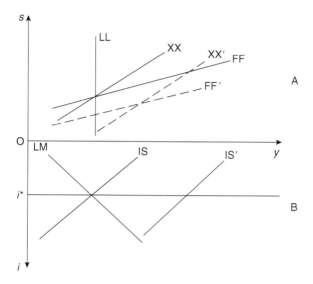

Figure 5.3 Fiscal policy and the MF model.

in g by raising income would increase the demand for money and the rate of interest. The latter would attract a potentially infinite inflow of capital, shifting LM rightwards and increasing income by the full multiplier. Since the interest rate is jammed at the world level, and the exchange rate is fixed, we have an expansion of income analogous to the expansionary effects of fiscal policy in the classic textbook liquidity trap case. However, with floating exchange rates the increased rate of interest leads to an exchange rate appreciation which worsens the trade balance by crowding out exports and sucking in imports, pushing the IS′ curve back to IS. In the top quadrant the FF curve shifts to FF′ with no change in output.[1] An alternative way to see this result is to consider the effect of the fiscal shock on the velocity of money. Since fiscal policy cannot alter the domestic interest rate, it cannot alter the velocity of circulation $(y - m)$ and hence there is only one level of output (the initial level) which can be supported by the given money supply.

The effects of a change in government spending on income and the exchange rate, with a flexible exchange rate and perfect capital mobility, are given by the following multipliers: $dy/dg = 0$ and $ds/dg = 1/\gamma_1$. With fixed exchange rates, the corresponding multipliers are $dy/dg = [1/(1 - \gamma_2)] > 0$ and $dm/dg = [\beta_0/(1 - \gamma_2)] > 0$.

5.1.3 The insulation properties in the MF model

In this section we consider how well both fixed and flexible exchange rates insulate a country against foreign interest rate and income shocks.

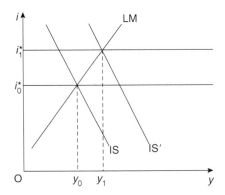

Figure 5.4 The insulation properties of the MF model with respect to a foreign interest
rate shock.

An increase in the foreign rate of interest is illustrated in Figure 5.4, with the
foreign interest rate rising from i_0^* to i_1^*. (The higher foreign interest rate results in
agents reallocating their portfolios and switching from domestic to foreign bonds,
pulling up the domestic interest rate until it equals the foreign rate (equation (5.1).)
The arbitrage process will also result in an exchange rate depreciation. Both the
higher interest rate and the depreciated exchange rate will have offsetting effects
on income, with the higher price for foreign currency boosting income through the
trade account and the higher interest rate curtailing the income expansion. Which
effect dominates? In the ensuing equilibrium, with a given money supply, the higher
interest rate implies excess money balances which can only by absorbed by a rise
in income – the IS schedule moves to IS′ in Figure 5.4 and income expands from
y_0 to y_1. The multiplier derived from (5.5) and (5.6) is: $dy/di^* = [\beta_1/\beta_0] > 0$. Thus
a flexible exchange rate with perfect capital mobility does not insulate the small
country from a foreign interest rate shock. Under fixed rates a rise in i^* also leads to
a capital outflow, a fall in the money supply and an equal rise in i which induces a
fall in the level of income. In this case the multiplier is $dy/di^* = -(\gamma_3/(1-\gamma_2)) < 0$.

The insulation properties of a floating exchange can also be considered with
respect to an exogenous change in the demand for the home country's exports.
Say, for example, that there is a world recession and a fall in the demand for home
country exports, represented by a fall of n in equation (5.4). The export fall will
induce an exchange rate depreciation which, in turn, results in a fall in imports
and a rise in the exchange rate related component of exports. With perfect capital
mobility the interest rate remains at i_0^* and for a given stock of money so too must
the level of income: the exchange rate moves to stabilise income in the case of an
export shock (under fixed exchange rates the export shock is transmitted to the
domestic economy).

So a flexible exchange rate in the context of the simple MF model only insu-
lates the home economy from a shock to net exports. The high degree of capital

mobility ensures that the effects of a foreign interest rate shock are transmitted to the domestic economy.

5.1.4 Imperfect capital mobility and the MF model

With perfect capital mobility and flexible exchange rates the MF model suggests that monetary policy is extremely powerful and fiscal policy is completely impotent. If, however, capital is less than perfectly mobile (i.e. $C_i < \infty$) it can be demonstrated that both monetary *and* fiscal policy are efficacious with floating exchange rates (although the former policy will now be less effective). Thus the policy multipliers dy/dg and dy/dm are both positive. The effect of less-than-perfect capital mobility on our MF diagrams is to render the slope of the FF curve less than perfectly elastic, since a small rise in the domestic interest rate no longer leads to a massive capital inflow, swamping the trade balance: the trade account is no longer a mere appendage to the balance of payments, as it is when capital is perfectly mobile. In Figures 5.5 and 5.6 FF is the locus of i and y consistent with equilibrium in the balance of payments and its slope can be understood by considering points A and B in Figure 5.5 and an initially fixed exchange rate. At point B, income is relatively high and thus the trade balance deficit will be greater than at point A; to keep the overall balance of payments in equilibrium we require a relatively large capital account surplus at B and thus a relatively higher interest rate. FF has been drawn with a flatter slope than the LM schedule implying that, even with imperfect capital mobility, capital flows are more elastic than money demand to the rate of interest (i.e. $\vartheta_3 > \beta_1$). Points above the FF schedule represent points of balance of payments surplus with fixed exchange rates and an appreciated exchange rate with floating rates. Points below the FF schedule represent balance of payments deficit with fixed exchange rates and a depreciated exchange rate with floating exchange rates. In Figures 5.5 and 5.6 we consider the two policy shocks discussed earlier for the perfect capital mobility case, namely, an increase in the money supply and a fiscal expansion.

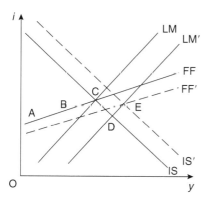

Figure 5.5 Monetary expansion and imperfect capital mobility.

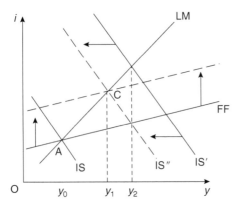

Figure 5.6 Fiscal expansion and imperfect capital mobility.

From an initial equilibrium at C in Figure 5.5, monetary expansion shifts the LM curve rightwards. A new equilibrium could be thought of at D where both the domestic goods and money markets are in equilibrium. However, D is, for a given exchange rate, not consistent with balance of payments equilibrium since it implies a balance of payments deficit. Hence the exchange rate must depreciate, which will push the IS curve rightwards, but with less than perfectly mobile capital this will also push the FF schedule downwards (i.e. the trade balance improves). A new long-run equilibrium is given at E where income is higher, the interest rate is lower, and the trade balance has improved. The position of the final equilibrium will clearly depend upon the relative elasticities of the schedules.

A fiscal expansion from an equilibrium of A in Figure 5.6 leads, as in the perfect capital mobility case, to a rightward shift in the IS schedule. At the intersection of the IS' and LM curves at B we have a tendency for the exchange rate to appreciate. The latter, via its effect on the trade balance, shifts the FF schedule upwards and the IS schedule back from IS' to, say, IS''. Point C is suggestive of the system's final equilibrium, with an expansionary fiscal policy having generated higher income, an appreciation of the exchange rate, and a current account deficit which is offset by the effect of a higher interest rate on the net capital inflow. As in the perfect capital mobility case, some of the extra government spending is crowded out by a fall in private expenditure – the move from y_2 to y_1 – but that crowding out is *not* complete. Clearly then, the effectiveness of monetary and fiscal policy with flexible exchange rates depends crucially on the mobility of capital. This is an issue to which we return in Chapter 7.[2]

5.2 The sticky-price variant of monetary approach

Although the basic MF model is still often used to make policy prescriptions about the operation of monetary and fiscal policy in an open economy (see, for example,

Krugman 2003) it has a number of well known deficiencies, amongst these are the complete rigidity of prices and the lack of any dynamic adjustment to the 'long-run'. Dornbusch (1976) proposed a variant of the MF model in which the kind of outcomes discussed in the previous section occur in the short-run while in the long-run the exchange rate solution is given by the FLMA, in which prices are continuously flexible. Dornbusch's model is labelled the sticky-price monetary approach (SPMA). As we have said, in the long-run equilibrium is defined as in the FLMA, but in the short-run commodity prices are assumed to be sticky and take time to adjust to their equilibrium values. In contrast, asset prices – bond prices and the exchange rate – are continuously flexible and this asymmetry between goods and asset price adjustment produces the celebrated overshooting result. This may be formalised in the following way.

We follow Dornbusch (1976) in assuming the domestic country is small and so takes the foreign price level and interest rate as given. The perfect foresight version of uncovered interest parity (i.e. where the expected exchange rate change is equal to the actual exchange rate change) is assumed to hold continuously:

$$\dot{s}_t = (i_t - i_t^*), \tag{5.7}$$

where an overdot indicates a continuous time change, ds/dt. Equation (5.7) is one of the key dynamic adjustment equations of the model. The domestic money market equilibrium condition is as defined in the MF, and is repeated here as:

$$m_t - p_t = \beta_0 y_t - \beta_1 i_t. \tag{5.8}$$

In long-run equilibrium prices are perfectly flexible and are determined by the long run money market equilibrium condition:

$$m_t - \bar{p}_t = \beta_0 y_t - \beta_1 i_t, \tag{5.9}$$

where an overbar denotes a long-run magnitude. PPP is assumed to hold in the long-run (i.e. after price adjustment is complete):

$$\bar{s}_t = \bar{p}_t - \bar{p}_t^*. \tag{5.10}$$

By subtracting (5.9) from (5.8) we may express the deviation of the current price from its long-run level as:

$$p_t - \bar{p}_t = \beta_1 (i_t - i_t^*). \tag{5.11}$$

On using (5.7), expression (5.11) may alternatively be expressed as:

$$\dot{s}_t = \beta_1^{-1} (p_t - \bar{p}_t), \tag{5.12}$$

which is the first dynamic equation of the model. Prices are assumed to adjust to long-run PPP in terms of a standard Phillips excess demand relationship:

$$\dot{p}_{t+1} = \pi (d_t - y_t), \quad \pi > 0, \tag{5.13}$$

where d_t denotes the log of aggregate demand and π is the speed of adjustment parameter. Aggregate demand, in turn, is assumed to be given by equation (5.3) rewritten here as:

$$d_t = \gamma_0 + \gamma_1 (s_t - p_t) + \gamma_2 y_t - \gamma_3 i_t, \quad \gamma_0, \gamma_1, \gamma_3 > 0 \text{ and } 0 < \gamma_2 < 1, \tag{5.14}$$

where g has been replaced by γ_0 which represents an exogenous shock. By substituting (5.14) into (5.13) we obtain:

$$\dot{p}_{t+1} = \pi(d_t - y_t) = \pi[\gamma_0 + \gamma_1(s_t - p_t) + (\gamma_2 - 1)y_t - \gamma_3 i_t]. \tag{5.15}$$

In long-run equilibrium this may alternatively be expressed as:

$$\pi[\gamma_0 + \gamma_1(\bar{s}_t - \bar{p}_t) + (\gamma_2 - 1)y_t - \gamma_3 i_t] = 0. \tag{5.16}$$

On subtracting (5.16) from (5.15) a price adjustment equation, in terms of deviations from long-run equilibrium, may be obtained as:

$$\dot{p}_t = \pi\gamma_1(s_t - \bar{s}_t) - \pi(\gamma_1 + \gamma_3/\beta_1)(p_t - \bar{p}_t). \tag{5.17}$$

This is the second dynamic equation of the SPMA system. Expressing equations (5.12) and (5.17) in matrix form we have:

$$\begin{bmatrix} \dot{s}_t \\ \dot{p}_t \end{bmatrix} = \begin{bmatrix} 0 & 1/\beta_1 \\ \pi\gamma_1 & -\pi(\gamma_1 + \gamma_3/\beta_1) \end{bmatrix} \begin{bmatrix} s_t - \bar{s}_t \\ p_t - \bar{p}_t \end{bmatrix}. \tag{5.18}$$

The necessary and sufficient condition for (5.18) to have a unique solution is for the coefficient matrix to have a negative determinant, which indeed it does:

$$-\pi\gamma_1/\beta_1.$$

In Figure 5.7 the $\dot{p}$ and $\dot{s}$ schedules represent, respectively, equations (5.12) and (5.17). The arrows of motion allow us to infer the saddle path, the models stable solution, as the schedule SP. Given rational expectations the economy will always be located at a point on the saddlepath. More formally, the saddle path is derived as the solution to the earlier system:

$$\lambda^2 + \pi(\gamma_1 + \gamma_3/\beta_1)\lambda - \pi\gamma_1/\beta_1$$

which has the following two solutions:

$$\lambda_1, \lambda_2 = 0.5\left\{-\pi(\gamma_1 + \gamma_3/\beta_1) \pm \sqrt{[\pi^2(\gamma_1 + \gamma_3/\beta_1)^2 - 4(\pi\gamma_1/\beta_1)]}\right\}.$$

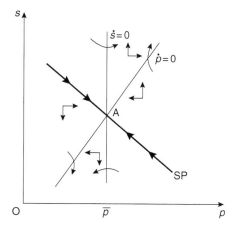

Figure 5.7 The phase diagram representation of the SPMA model.

Thus the two eigenvalues have opposite signs. The unique saddle-point path in Figure 5.7 is given by the negative root, λ_1, say, in (5.18). The equation of motion for s must then satisfy:

$$\dot{s}_t = \lambda_1 (s_t - \bar{s}_t). \tag{5.19}$$

Substituting (5.19) into (5.12) gives:

$$s_t = \bar{s}_t + (\beta_1 \lambda_1)^{-1} (p_t - \bar{p}_t), \tag{5.20}$$

which is the equation describing the saddle path.

Assume that the initial equilibrium in Figure 5.8, at A, is disturbed by a decrease in the money supply. With sticky commodity prices, asset 'prices' or yields – the exchange rate and the interest rate – move, or jump, to clear the asset markets. In terms of Figure 5.8, this involves the saddle path moving to SP_2 and the exchange rate moving from s_1 to s_2. The gap s_2–s_3 is the extent of exchange rate overshooting. Referring to equation (5.15) we know that at B, aggregate demand will have decreased, both because of the effect of the exchange rate appreciation on competitiveness, and also because the interest rate will have risen. As the economy moves from the sticky-price period to one in which prices are flexible, this will result in falling prices, a declining interest rate which, in turn, will depreciate the currency. Eventually, the system converges to the new equilibrium at point C. It is possible to demonstrate that the parameter from a regressive expectations equation for the exchange rate is consistent with the assumption of perfect foresight used in the model (see, for example, Dornbusch 1976). For example, a standard regressive expectations equation is:

$$\dot{s}_t^e = \varphi(\bar{s}_t - s_t), \quad 0 < \varphi < 1. \tag{5.21}$$

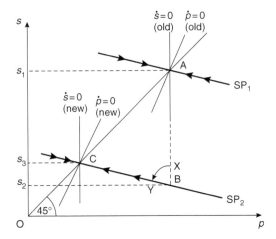

Figure 5.8 Unanticipated and anticipated decreases in the money supply.

With perfect foresight, $\dot{s}_t^e = \dot{s}_t$ and therefore it is clear from (5.19) that for there to be no expectational errors φ must equal $-\lambda_1$. Given the formula for λ_1 we see that with perfect foresight, the parameter φ depends on all the models structural parameters. Indeed, with equation (5.21) defining the dynamic evolution of the exchange rate, it is possible to demonstrate that the extent of exchange rate overshooting is governed by the following equation:

$$ds/dm = 1 + 1/\beta_1\varphi.$$

This equation demonstrates that a change in the money supply will produce a more than proportionate change in the exchange rate and that this overshooting will be determined by β_1 and φ. In particular, the smaller are β_1 and φ, the greater is the extent of any exchange rate overshooting. Thus, for a given fall in the interest rate (required to clear the money market), the current exchange rate has to move by more (relative to its long-run equilibrium) the smaller is the interest rate semi-elasticity of demand for money and the smaller is the regressive expectations parameter. We therefore have a further potential explanation for intra-regime volatility: in this model a current change in the money supply has a more than proportional effect on the exchange rate because of the interaction between liquidity impulses and sticky prices. A researcher observing the change in the exchange rate and the change in money will observe that $\Delta s_t > \Delta m_t$ and this is entirely consistent with rational forward-looking expectations.

5.2.1 *Anticipated monetary policy changes and the sticky-price model*

So far the changes in the money supply we have considered have all been completely unanticipated by market participants. But often governments make announcements about their money supply intentions in order to affect agents' expectations. For example, this was one of the main objectives of the monetary targeting regimes of central banks such as the Bundesbank and Bank of England in the 1980s: conditional on the credibility of the policy, the announcement of a future monetary contradiction could, it was argued, modify wage bargainers' price expectations, making a disinflation policy less painful. In practice, such targeting was, of course, concerned with reducing monetary *growth* rates (as have been the monetary targets adopted by other central banks). Although we shall discuss the effect of an anticipated reduction in monetary growth in a version of the SPMA in Section 5.2.3, it will, nonetheless, be useful to analyse the effect of an anticipated once-for-all decrease in the money supply at this stage.

Consider, again, the version of the SPMA model as portrayed by Figure 5.8 with steady-state equilibrium initially at A. The monetary authorities then announce in period t_0 that they will reduce the money supply in period t_1. What effect does this have if the new steady-state equilibrium is at C? Agents in period t_0, although governed by the initial steady-state equilibrium, will, nevertheless, be expecting an exchange rate appreciation. Thus when the money supply announcement is made the exchange rate jumps and appreciates to a point such as X (notice that the $\dot{s} = 0$ schedule only moves when the money supply is actually decreased). The exchange rate must appreciate immediately after the monetary announcement, otherwise there will be potentially large capital gains to be made. Point X is chosen so that s and p follow their dynamic trajectories and will be on SP$_2$ when the actual money supply decrease takes place. Thus from X the initial exchange rate appreciation will, through equation (5.14), lead to a reduction in aggregate demand and a falling price level. The latter effect will increase real money balances, and reduce the rate of interest which, for UIP, requires an expected appreciation of the currency. Hence between t_0 and t_1 the economy moves from X to Y in terms of Figure 5.8, and is then on the new stable saddle path when the change in the money supply is actually implemented. The economy thereafter moves along the saddle path SP$_2$ as in the case of the unanticipated policy.

An anticipated monetary shock therefore has important implications in terms of this simple model. Hence even before a reduction in the money supply takes place, aggregate demand falls short of its full employment level, resulting in an economic contraction and presumably unemployment. (For a further discussion of anticipated monetary policy in small rational expectations models see Blanchard, 1981, 1984, for the closed economy; Gray and Turnovsky 1979; Wilson 1979, Blanchard and Dornbusch 1984, for the open economy.)

5.2.2   *A resource discovery and the SPMA model*

In this section we utilise the SPMA model to analyse the effects of a resource discovery on a small open economy. For example, this analysis was originally designed to be suggestive of the effects of an oil discovery for countries such as the UK and Norway and the discovery of natural gas in the Netherlands – the so-called Dutch disease – but is equally applicable to similar discoveries in other countries. In a standard neoclassical model the discovery of oil would present no special macroeconomic problems since wage and price flexibility ensures that an oil discovery only leads to a change in relative prices: domestic output does not deviate from its steady-state natural rate (see, for example, Minford 1977). But in the Keynesian tradition of short-run price stickiness there may be important short-run consequences of an oil discovery and the SPMA model should be useful in illustrating this. The SPMA model has been utilised for this purpose by, *inter alia*, Buiter and Miller (1981a), Eastwood and Venables (1982), Buiter and Purvis (1983) and Sheffrin and Russell (1984). In analysing the effect of a resource discovery in the SPMA model we follow Sheffrin and Russell (1984) and modify the model in the following way.

In particular, we rewrite our money demand and aggregate demand schedules, respectively, as:

$$m = \alpha_0 p + (1 - \alpha_0)s + \alpha_1 y - \alpha_2 i + \alpha_3 \hat{x}; \quad 0 < \alpha_0 < 1, \alpha_3 > 0 \tag{5.22}$$

and

$$d = \beta_1 (s - p) + \alpha_4 x \quad \alpha_4 < 0 \tag{5.23}$$

where the deflator for real money balances is now a weighted average of the price of domestic output, p, and the price of imports, given by s. The terms x and $\hat{x}$ are oil-related: the former represents the permanent income stream from oil and the latter current income from oil. Notice that, for simplicity, in deriving (5.23) we have set γ_0, γ_2 and γ_3 equal to zero. The model's steady-state solution may be derived by setting $\dot{p}$ and $\dot{s}$ equal to zero in (5.7) and (5.13) and solving (5.22) and (5.23) simultaneously with d and y equated and i set equal to i^*:

$$p = \frac{(1 - \alpha_0)}{\beta_1} (\alpha_4 x - y) + \alpha_2 i^* - \alpha_1 y - \alpha_3 \hat{x} + m, \tag{5.24}$$

$$s = \frac{-\alpha_0}{\beta_1} (\alpha_4 x - y) + \alpha_2 i^* - \alpha_1 y - \alpha_3 \hat{x} + m. \tag{5.25}$$

Consider now the phrase diagram representation of this version of the SPMA model for *no* initial oil wealth. The model's dynamics are again portrayed by two equations: a $\dot{p}$ and $\dot{s}$ equation. Thus on substituting (5.7) in (5.22) and (5.23) in (5.13) we obtain:

$$\dot{s} = \frac{1}{\alpha_2} [\alpha_0 p + (1 - \alpha_0)s + \alpha_1 y - m] - i^*, \tag{5.26}$$

$$\dot{p} = \pi[\beta_1(s - p) - y]. \tag{5.27}$$

The phase diagram representation of these two equations is given in Figure 5.9. From (5.27) it is clear that the locus of s and p satisfying $\dot{p} = 0$ will be a positively

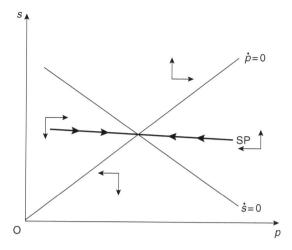

Figure 5.9 The dynamic behaviour of the exchange rate and price level, when the exchange rate is a deflator of real money balances.

sloped 45° line: for the goods market equilibrium an increase in the exchange rate requires an equal increase in p to maintain competitiveness constant and ensure no excess demand. The locus of s and p satisfying $\dot{s}=0$ in (5.26) will clearly be negative. Thus on setting $\dot{s}=0$ in (5.26) and, on rearranging, we obtain:

$$p = \frac{1}{\alpha_0}[m - (1-\alpha_0)s - \alpha_1 y + \alpha_2 i^*], \qquad (5.28)$$

which clearly shows the negative relationship between p and s when $\dot{s}=0$. The economic intuition behind this is that from a position where the domestic interest rate equals the foreign rate, and therefore $\dot{s}=0$, an increase in the price level requires a reduction in s to maintain real balances, and therefore i, constant. The horizontal arrows point towards the $\dot{p}=0$ schedule for the reasons given earlier, and the vertical arrows point away from the $\dot{s}=0$ schedule because, from a point on the $\dot{s}=0$ schedule, a rise in s means that real money balances have fallen, the domestic interest rate is above the foreign rate and the exchange rate must be expected to depreciate (below the $\dot{s}=0$ locus the domestic interest rate is below the foreign rate and the exchange rate is expected to appreciate). Consider now the effects on the phase diagram in Figure 5.9 of an oil discovery.

In terms of this version of the SPMA model one can distinguish the adjustments from the old to new equilibrium depending on whether the impact of oil is stronger in the goods market or in the money market, as portrayed in Figure 5.10. On the discovery of oil the exchange rate jumps from A on to the new saddle-point path at B and continues to appreciate towards the new equilibrium at C. Thus with a strong wealth effect in the aggregate demand function the relative price of domestic

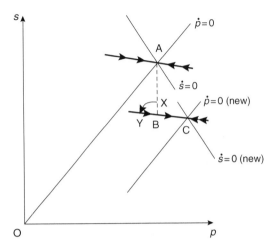

Figure 5.10 Goods market wealth effect dominates money market wealth effect.

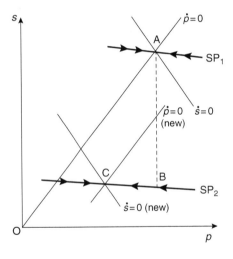

Figure 5.11 Money market wealth effect dominates goods market wealth effect.

output must rise, which with sticky prices in the short term can only be achieved by a (sharp) exchange rate appreciation. The latter, since it is part of the deflator of nominal money balances, increases real money balances, lowers the domestic interest rate requiring, via (5.26), a continuing exchange rate appreciation as we move out of the short-run period. Outwith the short-run period the effect on demand of the increased oil wealth results in a steadily rising price level to the new equilibrium at C. Figure 5.11 illustrates the situation where the oil discovery dominates the demand for money. The exchange rate again appreciates from

A to B. But because the wealth effect on the demand for money is so strong, the domestic interest rate has to rise to equilibrate the money market and this necessitates, via (5.7), a depreciating exchange rate as illustrated in the move from B to C. Thus regardless of whether the oil effect dominates the demand for money and demand for domestic output, the exchange rate sharply appreciates in the impact period. The two scenarios may, however, be distinguished by the response of the domestic interest rate, which rises when the money market effect is strong and falls when the goods market effect dominates.

To summarise: in the new equilibrium following an oil discovery the real exchange rate will have appreciated. Clearly, if we had a more disaggregated goods sector, in terms of traded and non-traded goods, the traded goods sector would suffer unemployed resources as a consequence of this real appreciation (assuming factor prices do not continually clear factor markets).[3] Such unemployment will be exacerbated if there is a lag between the resource discovery and the spending of the oil revenue.

Following on from our discussion in the previous section, what happens if asset market participants know about the oil discovery and correctly anticipate the future spending effect? The 'oil anticipation effect' is illustrated using Figure 5.10 (i.e. we assume that in the new steady state, the goods market effect dominates the money market effect). For simplicity, it is assumed that from time t_0 (the time of the oil discovery) to T (the time when the oil revenue effects aggregate demand) there is zero effect of the oil on aggregate demand. Thus from t_0 to T the system is governed by the initial steady state at A, while from time T on the system is governed by the new steady state, C. At the time of the discovery asset market participants expect the exchange rate to appreciate in the future and therefore the actual rate will appreciate and aggregate demand and the price level will fall as represented by the path XY: the economy suffers from a period of deflation as a consequence of the oil discovery.

5.2.3 *Money growth, inflation and the SPMA model*

Although the perfect capital mobility version of the SPMA model gives some important insights into exchange rate behaviour, it is nevertheless somewhat unrealistic in that in the short-run, sticky-price, period, inflation is assumed to be zero. Although inflation rates in most OECD countries are currently at historically low levels, they are nonetheless non-zero. We now consider a version of the sticky-price model which allows for non-zero expected inflation. It also has the further advantage that it incorporates changes in the growth of the money supply; the variant of the sticky-price model considered hitherto only features in one-shot changes in the *level* of the money supply. However, in the real world monetary changes are often means by which Western governments have attempted to control inflation. What effect then does the incorporation of an inflation term and a money growth term into the SPMA model have on its conclusions? Some answers to this question are provided by Buiter and Miller (1981a) and we present here a simplified version of their model, which we christen SPMA II; henceforth we

label the sticky-price monetary model without money growth/inflation effects as
SPMA I.

The SPMA II model shares equation (5.8) – the money market equilibrium –
and the perfect foresight version of UIP as given by equation (5.7) with the SPMA I
model. The aggregate demand and inflation equations, however, differ slightly to
equations (5.13) and (5.14) and are reported here as equations (5.29) and (5.30):

$$d = \gamma_1 (s - p) - \gamma_3 (i - \dot{p}), \tag{5.29}$$

$$\dot{p} = \pi (d - y) + \mu, \tag{5.30}$$

$$\mu = \dot{m}, \tag{5.31}$$

where the aggregate demand function now explicitly recognises the effect of the
real interest rate – the inflation-adjusted nominal interest rate, $i - \dot{p}$ – on aggregate demand (for simplicity, we ignore here the effects of income and oil wealth
on demand). Thus an increase in the real interest rate is hypothesised to have a
depressing effect on aggregate demand. Inflation is equal, as before, to an excess
demand component plus core, or trend, inflation, μ. The latter variable is, in turn,
equal to the rate of monetary growth, $\dot{m}$, as in (5.31). Therefore (5.30) postulates
that if aggregate demand is greater than capacity output, inflation will increase
by more than the rate of growth of the money supply. This expression may be
interpreted as an expectations-augmented Phillips curve, where μ is the expected
inflation term. In order to analyse the model's short-run dynamics it will prove
useful to define real money balances, $m - p$, as l and the real exchange rate, $s - p$,
as q. Real liquidity, l, is a predetermined, or in Buiter and Miller's terminology, a
backward looking variable: it only jumps in the short-run in response to discontin-
uous changes in m. The real exchange rate, q, is in contrast to l, a forward looking
variable and jumps whenever the nominal exchange rate, s, jumps in response
to new information. As in the SPMA I model, prices are assumed sticky in the
short-run and neither the price level nor the rate of change of prices is assumed to
change in response to a change in the level of the money supply.

Consider, first, the model's long-run steady-state properties. In the SPMA I
model the expected (and actual) change in the exchange rate equalled zero in
steady state. In the SPMA II model, however, the presence of core inflation implies
a non-zero exchange rate change in the steady state. This follows because in the
steady state the nominal interest rate will, via the familiar Fisher relationship, equal
the real interest rate plus the core inflation rate in order to induce agents to hold
the domestic non-money asset, that is:

$$i = r + \mu. \tag{5.32}$$

Since UIP is a property of the SPMA II model, μ will also equal $\dot{s}$ in the steady
state. Setting $\dot{p}$ equal to zero and equating d and y and on using (5.32) and (5.8) in

(5.29) we obtain the steady-state exchange rate as:

$$\bar{s} = m + \left(\frac{1}{\gamma_1} - \alpha_1\right)y + \left(\alpha_2 + \frac{\gamma_3}{\gamma_1}\right)i^* + \alpha_1\mu, \tag{5.33}$$

and on using (5.32) in (5.8) we obtain the steady-state price level as:

$$\bar{p} = m - \alpha_1 y + \alpha_2 i^* + \alpha_2\mu. \tag{5.34}$$

Using expressions (5.33) and (5.34) we may define the long-run levels of competitiveness and real balances as:

$$\bar{q} = \bar{s} - \bar{p} = \frac{1}{\gamma_1}y + \frac{\gamma_3}{\gamma_1}i^* \tag{5.35}$$

and

$$\bar{l} = \bar{m} - \bar{p} = \alpha_1 y - \alpha_2(i^* + \mu). \tag{5.36}$$

Equation (5.35) shows that the long-run level of competitiveness is constant and makes clear why if there is any long-run core inflation the exchange rate must change to offset it. The SPMA II model's dynamics, and, in particular, its adjustment to the steady-state conditions, may be captured by two key equations. On setting y equal to unity and using (5.31) in (5.30) we get

$$\dot{l} + \pi d = 0, \tag{5.37}$$

and by substituting (5.7) in (5.30) we obtain:

$$\dot{q} + \pi d - i = \mu - i^*, \tag{5.38}$$

and on using equations (5.8) and (5.29) to eliminate d and i and after some manipulation the following expression can be obtained:

$$\begin{bmatrix} \dot{i} \\ \dot{q} \end{bmatrix} = \frac{1}{\Lambda}\begin{bmatrix} \pi\gamma_3 & \pi\alpha_2\gamma_1 \\ 1 & \gamma_1(\pi\alpha_2 - \alpha_1) \end{bmatrix}\begin{bmatrix} 1 \\ q \end{bmatrix} + \frac{1}{\Lambda}\begin{bmatrix} \pi\alpha_2\gamma_3 & 0 \\ \alpha_2 & -\Lambda \end{bmatrix}\begin{bmatrix} \mu \\ i^* \end{bmatrix}, \tag{5.39}$$

where $\Lambda = \beta_0(\pi\alpha_2 - \alpha_1) - \alpha_2 < 0$. The dynamic equations in (5.39) are illustrated in Figure 5.12.

The locus $\dot{l} = 0$ represents combinations of l and q that satisfy a stationary level of real money balances and we see from (5.39) that it has a negative slope.[4] The schedule $\dot{q} = 0$ is the locus of l and q which gives a stationary level of competitiveness and its slope can be seen to depend upon the aggregate demand adjustment coefficient, π.[5] For low values of π, $\dot{q} = 0$ has a positive slope and for high values (corresponding to rapid goods market adjustment) $\dot{q} = 0$ will be negatively sloped. We assume here that $\dot{q} = 0$ has a positive slope. The horizontal arrows indicate that from a position of equilibrium on the $\dot{l} = 0$ schedule a point to the right (left), implies higher (lower) real money balances, a lower (higher) nominal interest rate

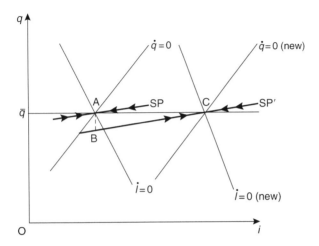

Figure 5.12 Unanticipated reduction in the rate of monetary growth in the Buiter–Miller model.

and therefore excess demand (excess supply) which reduces (increases) real money and pushes the system back to the schedule. The vertical arrows point away from the $\dot{l}=0$ schedule because a point directly to the right (left) indicates high liquidity, low (high) interest rates and appreciating (depreciating) exchange rate which worsens (improves) competitiveness. The stable saddle-point path is given by SP.[6]

Consider, first, an unanticipated reduction in the rate of monetary growth which is announced and implemented simultaneously. Such a shock may be regarded as the kind of policy adopted by many Western governments in the late 1970s and 1980s (the UK being a particular case in point)[7] and is illustrated in Figure 5.12. From equation (5.39) we know that a monetary contraction shifts the $\dot{l}=0$ and $\dot{q}=0$ schedules rightwards. From equation (5.35) we note that the steady-state value of competitiveness is unchanged by a change in μ and therefore the new equilibrium will be along the horizontal line through $\bar{q}$. From equation (5.31) we also note that because real money balances depend negatively on the core rate, in the long run the demand for real money balances must have increased. The new steady-state equilibrium is represented therefore at point C and the corresponding stable saddle path as SP′. However, the assumption of differential speeds of adjustment in goods and asset markets ensures that this equilibrium cannot be achieved instantly. In the short-run period prices are sticky and at the time of the monetary announcement (i.e. at the original steady state A) the stock of real money balances will be unchanged. But because μ must enter (5.8) through l, the demand for real money balances has increased and the lower interest rate must be offset by the expectation of an exchange rate appreciation. Thus the exchange rate, and hence competitiveness, both jump on to the new saddle path at B – as in the simple SPMA model the exchange rate has overshot its equilibrium value. The money market is cleared at B by a fall in output which, in turn, is induced by the real exchange rate appreciation and an increase in the real interest rate (i falls by less than p). Once we move from the short-run period into one in which prices are free to move, prices will be falling (due to the effect on aggregate demand of the decline in competitiveness and the increase in the real interest rate), the nominal interest rate will also be falling and the exchange rate depreciating as we move to the new equilibrium. The increased demand for real money balances is satisfied in the new equilibrium because the inflation-adjusted interest rate has fallen, making interest-bearing assets less attractive. In fact, real money balances in the new equilibrium will have increased by the interest semi-elasticity of the demand for money times the monetary contraction (i.e. $\alpha_2 \mu$), whilst all real variables stay unchanged; in the long-run the model therefore exhibits standard neoclassical properties.[8]

Consider, finally, an unanticipated increase in the *level* of the money supply, the announcement and implementation of which are simultaneous. Since the price level and the exchange rate in this model are homogeneous of degree 1 in the money supply, the new steady-state equilibrium must be one in which q and l are unchanged. Thus in terms of Figure 5.13 the original and 'new' long-run equilibria are at a point such as A, and the saddle path SP_1 is relevant for both before and after the change in the money supply. Hence starting from l_1 the increase in the money supply increases liquidity to l_2 (i.e. $l_1 = m_1 - p_1$, $l_2 = m_2 - p_1$ where $m_2 > m_1$). The real exchange rate must therefore jump to q_2 and, since the exchange rate will be expected to appreciate to equilibrium, the nominal interest rate will fall on impact and output will expand. Over time this increases the price level, reduces real money balances, raises the interest rate and appreciates the exchange rate: eventually the system returns to A. The story is similar to that portrayed earlier for the simple SPMA model. The earlier shock does, however, allow us to tell a rather interesting story (due to Buiter and Miller 1981b).

We have seen that a reduction of the monetary growth rate results in a painful adjustment of output to the new steady state. The basic reason for this is that the

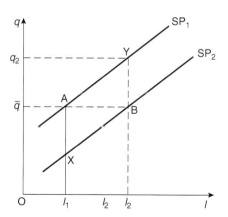

Figure 5.13 Level and growth changes in the money supply.

reduced monetary growth rate increases, as we have seen, agents' demand for real money balances, but with the level of the money supply given the only way the real money supply can increase is via a fall in p. The latter, due to the specification of the price adjustment equation, cannot happen instantly: p falls because $d < y$. Clearly, one way to circumvent this would be to increase the level of the money supply in tandem with the decrease in the growth of the money supply. This is illustrated in Figure 5.13 where $\bar{q}$ is the level of competitiveness consistent with equilibrium before and after the change in the money supply and SP_2 is the stable path associated with the new equilibrium at B. As we have seen, a reduction in m moves the system from A to X in the short-run period, the economy gradually adjusting to B over time. If, however, the authorities simultaneously increase the level of the money supply by the correct amount (i.e. to l_2) the system would move immediately to B (i.e. a level only increase puts the system to Y). Buiter and Miller (1981b) argue that the UK authorities' decision not to claw back the sterling M3 overshoot in the second half of 1980 amounted to the type of joint policy illustrated in Figure 5.13 and this prevented the economy from suffering further deflation.

5.3 A stochastic version of the Mundell–Fleming–Dornbusch model

In this section we present a stochastic version of the Mundell–Fleming–Dornbusch model. This model is based on Obstfeld (1985) and Clarida and Gali (1994) and since most of the relationships are familiar from previous chapters, our discussion here will be relatively brief. The open economy IS equation in the model is given by:

$$y_t^{d'} = d_t' + \eta(s_t - p_t') - \sigma(i_t' - E_t(p_{t+1}' - p_t')), \tag{5.40}$$

where a prime denotes a relative (home minus foreign) magnitude. The expression indicates that the demand for output is increasing in the real exchange rate and a demand shock (which captures, say, fiscal shocks) and decreasing in the real interest rate. The LM equation is familiar from our previous discussions

$$m_t^{s'} - p_t' = y_t' - \lambda i_t', \tag{5.41}$$

where the income elasticity has been set equal to one. The price-setting equation is taken from Flood (1981) and Mussa (1982) and is given as:

$$p_t' = (1 - \theta)E_{t-1}p_t^{e'} + \theta p_t^{e'}. \tag{5.42}$$

Expression (5.42) states that the price level in period t is an average of the market-clearing price expected in $t - 1$ to prevail in t, and the price that would actually clear the output market in period t. With $\theta = 1$ prices are fully flexible and output is supply-determined while with $\theta = 0$, prices are fixed and predetermined one period in advance. The final equation in this model is the standard UIP condition:

$$i_t' = E_t(s_{t+1} - s_t). \tag{5.43}$$

The stochastic properties of the relative supply of output, $y_t^{s'}$, d_t' and m_t', are assumed to be given by:

$$y_t^{s'} = y_{t-1}^{s'} + z_t, \tag{5.44}$$

$$d_t' = d_{t-1}' + \delta_t - \gamma \delta_{t-1}, \tag{5.45}$$

$$m_t' = m_{t-1}' + v_t, \tag{5.46}$$

where z_t, δ_t and v_t are random errors. Therefore on this basis both relative money and output supply are random walks and the relative demand term contains a mix of permanent and transitory components (i.e. a fraction, γ, of any shock is expected to be offset in the next period).

By substituting (5.44) and (5.45) into (5.40) a flexible price rational expectations equilibrium, in which output is supply-determined, for the expected real exchange rate ($q = s - p$) is given by:

$$q_t^e = (y_t^s - d_t)/\eta + (\eta(\eta + \sigma))^{-1}\sigma\gamma\delta_t \tag{5.47}$$

which indicates that the flex-price real exchange rate depreciates with respect to a supply disturbance and appreciates in response to a demand disturbance. With $\gamma > 0$, the expectation that the demand disturbance will be partially offset in the future produces the expectation of real depreciation which, in turn, dampens the magnitude of the appreciation in the present.

From the definition of the real exchange rate and (5.41) the equilibrium price that would prevail in the flexible price rational expectations equilibrium, $p^{e'}$, must satisfy:

$$(1 + \lambda)p_t^{e'} = m_t' - y_t^{s'} + \lambda(E_t q_{t+1}^e - q_t^e) + \lambda E_t p_{t+1}^{e'} \tag{5.48}$$

On using (5.44) to (5.46) and (5.47) in (5.48) we can obtain:

$$p_t^{e'} = m_t' - y_t^{s'} + \lambda(1 + \lambda)^{-1}(\eta + \sigma)^{-1}\lambda\delta_t. \tag{5.49}$$

From (5.49) we see that the flexible price relative price level rises in proportion to the monetary shock, declines in proportion to the supply shock and rises in response to the temporary component in the demand shock. In contrast, a permanent demand shock will have no effect on $p_t^{e'}$. This follows because by driving up the common level of both real and nominal interest rates, it must drive up home and foreign prices in proportion. The flexible price solution to the model may therefore be characterised by (5.47), (5.49) and:

$$y_t^{e'} = y_t^{s'}. \tag{5.50}$$

This characterisation makes clear that in the flexible price equilibrium the levels of relative output, the real exchange rate and relative national price levels are driven by three shocks: a supply shock, z, a demand shock, δ, and a monetary shock, v.

A comparable sticky-price equilibrium may be derived in the following way. By Substituting (5.49) into (5.40) the following expression for the evolution of the price level may be derived:

$$p'_t = p_t^{e'} - (1 - \theta)(v_t - z_t + \alpha\gamma\delta_t), \tag{5.51}$$

where $\alpha \equiv \lambda(1 + \lambda)^{-1}(\eta + \sigma)^{-1}$. A positive money or demand shock produces a rise in the relative price level which is less that the flexible price case, $p^{e'}$. With a positive supply shock the price level falls but by less than the flexible price case. An expression for the real exchange rate may be derived by substituting (5.40) and (5.43) into (5.41) and using (5.49):

$$q_t = q_t^e + v(1 - \theta)(v_t - z_t + \alpha\gamma\delta_t), \tag{5.52}$$

where $v \equiv (1 + \lambda)(\lambda + \sigma + \eta)^{-1}$. We note that as in the non-stochastic version of the MFD model the existence of sticky price adjustment means that the real exchange rate is influenced by monetary shocks. The short-run level of demand determined output can be generated by substituting (5.52) into (5.40) to get:

$$y'_t = y_t^{s'} + (\eta + \sigma)v(1 - \theta)(v_t - z_t + \alpha\gamma\delta_t). \tag{5.53}$$

As expected, with sluggish price adjustment demand and monetary shocks, in addition to supply shocks, influence y_t in the short-run. Although all three shocks influence all three variables in the short-run, the long-run response of y, q and p to the shock is triangular. That is, only the supply shock influences the long-run level of relative output; supply and demand shocks influence the long-run level of the real exchange rate; and all three shocks influence the long-run level of prices at home and abroad. We return to this stochastic version of the MFD model in Chapter 8 where we consider empirical work which seeks to decompose real exchange rate variability into supply, demand and monetary shocks.

5.4   The Lucas monetary model with sticky prices

The final version of the sticky-price model we consider in this chapter is a variant of the Lucas model, due to Grilli and Roubini (1992), in which there are liquidity effects. As we shall see, such effects can produce exchange rate overshooting as in the Dornbusch model. In contrast to that model, however, this overshooting arises in a general equilibrium model with optimising agents. Our discussion here follows the model presented in Grilli and Roubini (1992) in which liquidity effects in asset markets are modelled by introducing a cash-in-advance constraint into asset markets, in addition to the cash-in-advance constraint existing in goods markets. The two cash-in-advance constraints are motivated by assuming that the representative household has three members. The first member takes the period-t endowment and sells it to other households and makes this available to the other two individuals in the household to spend in the next period. The second individual takes a proportion, ρ, of the household's initial money holdings (both home and foreign) and uses this to buy domestic and foreign goods from other households. The third member of the household takes the remaining proportion, $1 - \rho$, of the initial money holdings and uses them to transact in asset markets. The asset markets in this variant of the Lucas model comprise home and foreign money and home and foreign government securities, labelled B_t and B_t^* respectively, where the securities are assumed to be one-period pure discount bonds.

The representative agents in the home and foreign country are assumed to have the same intertemporal utility function, and associated properties, as given in equation (4.19) of the previous chapter, repeated here:

$$U = E_t \left(\sum_{t=0}^{\infty} \beta^t U(C_t, C_t^*) \right), \quad 0 < \beta < 1. \tag{5.54}$$

The agent (number 2) who transacts in asset markets faces the same cash-in-advance constraints used in the flex-price version of the model, discussed in the previous chapter (see 4.24):

$$m_{1t-1} \geq P_t C_t. \tag{5.55}$$

The agent who transacts in the asset market faces the following cash-in-advance constraint:

$$\mathcal{Z}_t + s_t \mathcal{Z}_t^* \geq \kappa_t B_t + s \kappa_t^* B_t^*, \tag{5.56}$$

where κ and κ^* denote, respectively, the domestic and foreign currency prices of the domestic and foreign discount bond, $\mathcal{Z} = M_1 - m_1$ and $\mathcal{Z}^* = M_1^* - m_1^*$ and $M_1(M_1^*)$ denotes the total amount of money of the home (foreign) country held by the home resident and given the cash-in-advance constraint (5.55), $\mathcal{Z}$ ($\mathcal{Z}^*$) is the amount of money held by the home agent for transactions in the home (foreign) asset market (similar relationships are assumed to hold in the foreign country).

Maximising the utility function subject to the consolidated budget constraint from this model produces an exchange rate equation of the form:

$$S_t = \frac{P_t}{P_t^*} \frac{u_{c_t}^*}{u_{c_t}} \frac{M_t}{M_t^*} \frac{\kappa_t}{\kappa_t^*}. \tag{5.57}$$

This expression clearly closely parallels equation (4.30) in that the nominal exchange rate is driven by relative prices and relative marginal utility. Additionally, however, this variant of the Lucas model has a direct role for relative money and the relative price of bonds in the equilibrium exchange rate equation. The final exchange rate equation may be derived from (5.57) by substituting out for relative commodity prices. Equilibrium prices in this model are determined by a monetary relationship of the form:

$$P = (1 - z) \cdot (y)^{-1}, \tag{5.58}$$

where z is ratio of money held by the representative agent for asset market purposes, as proportion of total money held (i.e. $z = \mathcal{Z}/M$). This expression indicates that the equilibrium price depends on the money supply, income, as in a standard quantity theory relationship, but also the share of money used for asset purposes (this comes from the second cash in advance constraint for assets). Using this measure of the equilibrium price in (5.57) produces the following measure of the equilibrium exchange rate:

$$s = \frac{1 - z}{1 - z^*} \frac{y_t^*}{y_t} \frac{u_{c_t}^*}{u_{c_t}} \frac{M}{M^*} \frac{\kappa}{\kappa^*}. \tag{5.59}$$

Grilli and Roubini (1992) decompose (5.59) into two components. The first is labelled the 'fundamental' Fisherian component:

$$\frac{1 - z}{1 - z^*} \frac{y_t^*}{y_t} \frac{u_{c_t}^*}{u_{c_t}}, \tag{5.60}$$

and is the component which prevails absent any liquidity effects. It is referred to as Fisherian because it consists of expected inflation and the ratio of time preferences. The second component is the ratio of bond prices and this is referred to as the 'non-fundamental' equilibrium component. The latter is the liquidity effect and is driven by government operations in the bond markets. In particular, the only role for government in this model is to engage in open market operations with government bonds. More specifically, the government in the home (foreign) country issues bonds equal to a proportion, x_t, of the period-t money supply: that is, $B_t = x_t M_t$. It is assumed that the proportion x is a serially uncorrelated random variable and is the only source of uncertainty in the model. Bond prices, in turn, are determined by the equilibrium conditions for security markets, that is:

$$z_t = x_t \kappa_t, \tag{5.61}$$

and

$$z_t^* = x_t^* \kappa_t^*, \tag{5.61'}$$

which, in turn, implies that the ratio of securities prices is given by:

$$\frac{\kappa}{\kappa^*} = \frac{z}{x} \frac{x^*}{z^*}. \tag{5.62}$$

The stochastic nature of x makes the relative bond prices stochastic as well.

The 'liquidity' model has the following implications, additional to those discussed earlier for equation (5.59). First, the equilibrium exchange rate (and prices) depend upon the share of money used in asset transactions, z. Since the price of goods is driven by the amount of money available for goods transactions, a decrease in this quantity through an open market operation will reduce the equilibirum price in home country and appreciate the exchange rate currency.

Second, stochastic open market operations which lead to an increase in the supply of bonds in the home country (i.e. an increase in x) will produce an appreciation of the exchange rate through a familiar route: bond prices fall as a result, the home interest rate rises and the currency appreciates. However, in contrast to the standard liquidity effect in the MFD model, the liquidity effect here is 'pure' in the sense the rate of growth of money is held constant (by assumption, using a tax) which means that in (5.59) the expected inflation rate is constant, as is the rate of time preference.

Third, the model has implications for the excess volatility of nominal exchange rates. This can be demonstrated in the following way. Write the equilibrium exchange rate in (5.54) in logs as:

$$\ln s = k + \ln(x^*) - \ln(x), \tag{5.63}$$

where the constant term, k, includes all non-stochastic components of the exchange rate (i.e. relative money supplies, relative prices, the rate of time preference and relative output levels). The constancy of the Fisherian fundamentals would, on their own, imply a constant value of the exchange rate. However, with stochastic interest rate shocks, due to stochastic Open Market Operations, the exchange rate becomes excessively volatile relative to the non-stochastic fundamentals:

$$\text{Var}(\ln s) = \text{Var}[\ln(x^*)] + \text{Var}[\ln(x)]. \tag{5.64}$$

Of course this result presupposes the two shocks are uncorrelated. In the presence of a non-zero correlation, expression (5.64) has to be modified to:

$$\text{Var}(\ln s) = \text{Var}[\ln(x)] + \text{Var}[\ln(x^*)] - 2\text{Cov}(\ln(x), \ln(x^*)), \tag{5.65}$$

It is worth noting that this relationship implies that in the presence of unexpected liquidity shocks, the variance of the exchange rate could be reduced to zero if the monetary policies of the two countries are perfectly correlated such that (x) and (x^*) are perfectly correlated. In the presence of such liquidity shocks the model therefore predicts that exchange rate stability can only be achieved if monetary policies are tightly coordinated across countries.

6 The monetary approach to the exchange rate

An empirical perspective

In this chapter we consider the empirical evidence on variants of the monetary model, considered in previous chapters, and specifically, evidence on the floating exchange rate variant of the monetary model. Other evidence on the monetary model, in terms of its role in explaining, for example, speculative attacks against currencies and the behaviour of exchange rates in target zones are considered in other chapters. Although the bulk of the empirical evidence considered in this chapter relates to the recent (i.e. post-Bretton Woods) regime, evidence for the inter-war experience with floating rates shall also be discussed. The outline of the remainder of the chapter is as follows. In the next section we sketch the basic reduced forms that have become workhorses for estimating the monetary model and the so-called early estimates of the model (these relate to the period immediately after the inception of the post-Bretton Woods regime, especially the 1970s and early 1980s) and then go on in Section 6.2 to consider the so-called early estimates of the model; we include in these early estimates the seminal Meese and Rogoff (1983) out-of-sample forecasting paper. More recent work on out-of-sample forecasting and empirical estimates of the monetary model which rely on cointegration-based methods are considered in Section 6.3. Estimates of the forward-looking monetary model are presented in Section 6.4. Empirical evidence on issues of intra and inter-regime volatility are considered in Section 6.5.

6.1 Some monetary approach reduced forms and the early post-Bretton Woods evidence

6.1.1 The flex-price monetary reduced form

Although, as we shall see, the monetary model has been estimated structurally, by far the most popular way of estimating variants of the model is as a reduced form. The most widely exploited reduced form is that derived from the flex price monetary approach (FLMA), considered in Chapter 4, and repeated here:

$$s_t = \beta_0(m_t - m_t^*) + \beta_1(y_t - y_t^*) + \beta_2(i_t - i_t^*) + \varphi_t, \tag{6.1}$$

where φ_t is a random disturbance term and, following on from our discussion in Chapter 4, it is expected that $\beta_0 = 1$, $\beta_1 < 0$ and $\beta_2 > 0$. A variant of this reduced form, which is more in line with the optimising models of the previous chapter, and the forward-looking model of Chapter 4, would exclude the interest differential:

$$s_t = \beta_0(m_t - m_t^*) + \beta_1(y_t - y_t^*) + \varphi_t, \tag{6.1'}$$

where the interpretation of the β_0 and β_1 parameters would be as in the FLMA. Most researchers (although many do not explicitly say so) expect coefficients on income and the rate of interest to have values close to those found in estimates of closed economy money demand equations. Thus, for example, Bilson (1978b) posits that β_1 is expected to lie in the range between 0.5 and 1.5 and β_2 is expected to lie between 0 and 3.

6.1.2 The sticky-price reduced form

An alternative two-country monetary approach reduced form may be derived utilising the structural equations from the perfect capital mobility version of the sticky-price monetary approach (SPMA). In particular, consider the key equations from the sticky-price model:

$$m_t' - p_t' = \beta_0 y_t' - \beta_1 i_t', \tag{6.2}$$

$$d = \gamma_0 + \gamma_1(s - p') + \gamma_2 y' + \gamma_3 i', \quad \gamma_0, \gamma_1, \gamma_2, \gamma_3 > 0, \tag{6.3}$$

$$p_{t+1}' - p_t' = \pi(d_t - y_t'), \quad \pi > 0, \tag{6.4}$$

where a prime denotes a relative (home to foreign) magnitude and where the interpretation of these relationships is the same as that discussed in the previous chapter. We follow Driskell (1981) and assume that money market equilibrium obtains each period and that the relative money supply term follows a random walk:

$$m_t' = m_{t-1}' + \varepsilon_t,$$

which means that the best prediction of next period's money supply is the current period's money supply. Combining equations (6.2), (6.3) and (6.4), the following reduced-form price equation can be obtained:

$$p_t' = b_1 y_{t-1}' + b_2 p_{t-1}' + b_3 m_{t-1}' + b_4 s_{t-1} \tag{6.5}$$

where $b_1 = \pi(1 - \gamma_2) + \beta_0 \gamma_3/\beta_1$, $b_2 = 1 - \pi \gamma_3/\beta_1 - \pi \gamma_1$, $b_3 = \pi \gamma_3/\beta_1$ and $b_4 = \pi \gamma_1$. By assuming that the equilibrium exchange rate, $\bar{s}$, is determined by equilibrium relative excess money supplies, m', and given the random walk assumption for the money supply, the standard regressive expectations equation $\Delta s_t^e = \theta(\bar{s}_t - s_t)$ may be rewritten as:

$$\Delta s_t^e = \theta(m_t - s_t) \tag{6.6}$$

and on combining (6.2) with (6.5) and (6.6) with the standard UIP condition ($\Delta s_t^e = i_t'$) the following reduced form may be derived:

$$
\begin{aligned}
s_t = \pi_0 + \pi_1 s_{t-1} + \pi_2 m_t' + \pi_3 m_{t-1}' + \pi_4 p_{t-1}' + \pi_5 y_t' \\
+ \pi_6 y_{t-1}' + \pi_7 \varepsilon_t' - \pi_8 \varepsilon_{t-1}',
\end{aligned}
\tag{6.7}
$$

where the following constraints can be shown to hold on the coefficients: $\Sigma_{i=1}^4 \pi_i = 1, \pi_1 < 0, \pi_2 > 1, \pi_3 < 0, \pi_4 < 0, \pi_5 < 0$ and $\pi_6 < 0$. The first constraint says that PPP must hold in the long-run. Note, particularly, the sign on π_2 which suggests that an increase in the money supply leads to a more than proportionate rise in the exchange rate, which is a key prediction of the sticky price monetary model (i.e. that there is exchange rate overshooting). Also note that the error term in the final reduced form is predicted to follow a first-order moving average (MA1) process, rather than the random error assumed in equation (6.1). An interesting feature of the earlier derivation is that by substituting for i' we end up with a reduced-form exchange rate equation purged of the effects of a relative interest rate term on the exchange rate. Driskell demonstrates that if capital is less than perfectly mobile an equivalent reduced form to (6.7) may be derived, where the prediction is that the coefficient on m only needs to be positive (i.e. there does not need to be overshooting in the less-than-perfect capital mobility version of the sticky-price model).

6.1.3   The hybrid monetary model, or RID

The hybrid, or real interest differential (RID), model was first popularised by Frankel (1979), and essentially attempts to combine elements of the sticky-price model with the flex-price approach in a manner which is amenable to econometric testing. In particular, and following Frankel (1979), we modify the regressive expectations formulation to have the following representation:

$$
\Delta s_{t+1}^e = \varphi(\bar{s}_t - s_t) + \Delta p_{t+1}',
\tag{6.8}
$$

which simply says that in long-run equilibrium, when the actual exchange rate is at its equilibrium level, $\bar{s}_t = s_t$, the exchange rate is expected to change by an amount equal to the long-run inflation differential. The equilibrium short-run exchange rate may be obtained by substituting (6.8) into the UIP condition ($\Delta s_t^e = i_t'$), and rearranging to get:

$$
s_t = \bar{s}_t - \varphi^{-1}(i_t' - E_t \Delta p_{t+1}').
\tag{6.9}
$$

Equation (6.9) indicates that the current exchange rate, s_t, may be above or below $\bar{s}_t$ depending on the real interest differential. Hence if the domestic real interest rate is above the foreign real interest rate the currency will appreciate relative to its equilibrium value; this captures the spirit of overshooting in the sticky-price model. It is usual to assume that $\bar{s}_t$ in equation (6.9) is determined by the FLMA. Combining these two elements, and assuming that equilibrium values are determined by current actual values, allows the following expression to be derived:

$$s_t = m_t - m_t^* - \beta_0(y_t - y_t^*) + \beta_1(\Delta p_t^e - \Delta p_t^{e*})$$
$$+ \varphi^{-1}[(i_t - \Delta p_{t+1}^e) - (i_t^* - \Delta p_{t+1}^{e*})]. \tag{6.10}$$

On assuming that short interest rates capture real interest rates (i.e. the liquidity impulses of monetary policy) and long bond yields capture expected inflation we may rewrite this reduced form as:

$$s_t = \alpha_0(m_t - m_t^*) + \alpha_1(y_t - y_t^*) + \alpha_2(i_t^s - i_t^{s*}) + \alpha_3(i_t^l - i_t^{l*}) + u_t. \tag{6.11}$$

Equation (6.11) represents a useful way of distinguishing amongst the different categories of monetary models, and this is summarised in Table 6.1.

In particular, the fact that all three models are in the monetary tradition is reflected in the unitary coefficient on the relative money supply term, and the negative coefficient on the income elasticity. The key difference between the models occurs with respect to the two interest rate semi-elasticities. In the FLMA there is a one-to-one relationship between inflation and interest rates and so there is no real interest rate effect; that is, $i_t = E_t \Delta p_{t+k}$. In contrast, in the sticky-price monetary model interest rates purely reflect liquidity effects and so there is no role for expected inflation differentials as given by long bond yields. Finally, the Frankel RID nests both approaches within it and facilitates a role for both short and long interest rates. As we shall see, equation (6.11) has been estimated for a number of different currencies and time periods.

In estimating the reduced forms (6.1), (6.7) and (6.11) there are, of course, a number of important econometric issues that arise. The first batch of estimates of these equations, discussed in the next section, generally treated them as static relationships and estimated them using OLS, or OLS with an autocorrelation correction. In some instances researchers used instrumental variables to address potential simultaneous equation biases stemming from the money supply and interest rates. More recent studies of the monetary class of models have shown the advantages of using dynamic modelling methods and, in particular, recognised the potentially non-stationary nature of the variables. We shall consider these kind of econometric issues in more detail as we consider the different results.

Table 6.1 Summary of different monetary models

	α_0	α_1	α_2	α_3
FLMA	1	−	0	+
SPMA	1	−	−	0
RID	1	−	−	+

6.2 Early empirical evidence on the monetary model

In this section we review the empirical evidence on the monetary model from the first two decades of the post-Bretton Woods period, that is, using data from the 1970s and early 1980s.

6.2.1 The 1970s in-sample empirical evidence

The reduced forms (6.1), (6.7) and (6.11) were extensively researched in the 1970s and 1980s using data from the 1970s and early 1980s (see MacDonald 1988). It was standard in this early literature to analyse the equations in a traditional static framework although some limited dynamics in the form of a one-period partial adjustment mechanism were sometimes employed. In terms of their in-sample performance – judged by their 'goodness-of-fit' and coefficients being correctly signed – these equations seemed to work pretty well for the 1970s. Two representative examples are reported here for, respectively, the FLMA and RID, as equations (6.12) and (6.13):

$$s_t = \underset{(0.51)}{1.52}\, m_t - \underset{(0.56)}{1.39}\, m_t^* - \underset{(0.45)}{2.23}\, y_t + \underset{(0.38)}{0.073}\, y_t^* + \underset{(1.17)}{2.53}\, i_t$$

$$+ \underset{(0.67)}{1.93}\, i_t^* \quad [\text{Hodrick (1978)}] \tag{6.12}$$

$$R^2 = 0.66; \text{DW} = 1.61; \text{SER} = 0.37;$$

estimator: OLS; currency: DM–USD, July 1972–June 1975

$$s_t = \underset{(0.21)}{0.97}\,(m_t - m_t^*) - \underset{(0.22)}{0.52}\,(y_t - y_t^*) - \underset{(2.04)}{5.40}\,(i_t^s - i_t^{s*}) + \underset{(3.33)}{29.40}\,(i_t^l - i_t^{l*}),$$

$$\tag{6.13}$$

$$R^2 = 0.91; \rho = 0.46; \text{estimator: instrumental variables} \quad [\text{Frankel 1979}]$$

where numbers in brackets are standard errors, R^2 denotes the coefficient of determination, DW is the Durbin Watson statistic, SER the standard error of the regression and ρ is the first-order autoregressive coefficient.

In equation (6.12) all of the coefficients enter unconstrained and all, with the exception of that on the foreign interest rate, are correctly signed. Furthermore, most have values which are close to the hypothesised priors and all but one are statistically different from zero. For example, the coefficients on the domestic and foreign money supplies are numerically close to $+1$ and -1 and, indeed, a formal t-test indicates that they are insignificantly different from plus and minus one. The R^2 is deemed sufficiently high to indicate that the equation has good in-sample explanatory power, although the DW statistic indicates there may be some residual autocorrelation. A similar story pertains to the estimate of the RID reported as equation (6.13). In this equation all of the coefficients are again correctly signed and statistically significant and, most notably, both interest rate effects are statistically significant implying that both the flex-price (expected inflation) and sticky-price (liquidity effect) interest rate effects are in the data for this sample period. In estimating the reduced form, Frankel used a first-order Cochrane type correction to correct for serial correlation, and this was indicative of some form (perhaps dynamic) of misspecification. Other tests supportive of the monetary model for this early period are Dornbusch (1979) and Putnam and Woodbury (1980).

The SPMA reduced form (6.11) has also been tested by a number of researchers for the early post-Bretton Woods period. Driskell (1981), for example, presents an estimate of equation (6.11) for the Swiss franc–US dollar for the period 1973–7 (quarterly data) which is reported here:

$$s_t = \underset{(2.82)}{2.22} + \underset{(3.65)}{0.43}\, s_{t-1} + \underset{(5.73)}{2.37}\, m_t' - \underset{(5.60)}{2.45}\, m_{t-1}' + \underset{(2.23)}{0.93}\, p_{t-1}' + \underset{(1.37)}{0.35}\, u_{t-1}'$$

$$R^2 = 0.99; \quad \text{Durbin's } h = 0.21,$$

(6.14)

where, due to the unavailability of a quarterly income series, the y terms were dropped in the estimated version of (6.11) and the presence of first-order auto-correlation necessitated estimation using the Cochrane–Orchutt procedure. Note that $\Sigma \pi_i$ equals 1.28 (see discussion surrounding equation (6.11)) which is insignificantly different from unity at the 5% level and thus PPP holds as a long-run phenomenon. Interestingly, although the coefficient on m_t' is greater than unity, which is clearly supportive of the perfect capital mobility version of the SPMA model, the coefficients on s_{t-1} and p_{t-1}' are both positive, which turns out to be supportive of the imperfect capital mobility version of the SPMA model.[1]

Other tests of the SPMA reduced form have been conducted by Wallace (1979), Hacche and Townend (1981) and Backus (1984). Wallace estimates, using OLS, an unconstrained version of equation (6.11) for the Canadian dollar–US dollar over the period 1951 Q2 to 1961 Q1. Results supportive of the SPMA are presented, in the sense that the coefficients are statistically significant and, interestingly, it is shown that the coefficient on the domestic money supply is significantly less than unity which is supportive of the imperfect capital mobility version of the model. Backus (1984) tests equation (6.11) for the same exchange rate as Wallace for the recent Canadian floating experience (1971 Q1 to 1980 Q4, quarterly data), and in support of the earlier results finds no evidence of overshooting. However, Backus's OLS results differ from those of Wallace in that he finds few statistically significant coefficients.

Estimates of a dynamic error correction version of equation (6.11) by Hacche and Townend (1981) for the UK pound effective exchange rate, May 1972 to February 1980, are suggestive of exchange rate overshooting, but in other respects the estimated equation is unsatisfactory: many coefficients are insignificant and wrongly signed and the equation does not exhibit sensible long-run properties. The version of the SPMA model due to Buiter and Miller (1981a), which we discussed in Chapter 5, has been empirically implemented by Barr (1984) and Smith and Wickens (1990). In Barr (1984) the Buiter–Miller model is reduced to a two-equation system in competitiveness and liquidity, and the model is tested on UK data for the recent floating period (1973 Q1 to 1982 Q1); results supportive of the Buiter–Miller model are reported. Further favourable empirical estimates of the Buiter–Miller model are presented in Smith and Wickens (1990) who estimate the model structurally for sterling's effective exchange rate (period 1973–91). In simulating the model, Smith and Wickens find that the exchange rate overshoots by 21% in response to a 5% change in the level of the money supply.[2]

In sum, the different variants of the monetary model seem to work reasonably well for the early part of the recent floating period, at least on the basis of the criteria adopted by researchers at the time (namely, the satisfaction of coefficient restrictions and in-sample fit). However, even such apparently successful early results for the monetary model were probably fragile, in the sense that although the coefficients were correctly signed and the R^2 statistics reasonably high, the estimates still suffered from serial correlation which was indicative of some form of misspecification.

6.2.2 *The second-period tests of the monetary reduced forms*

As data for the 1980s became available researchers showed that the monetary class of model failed in terms of their in-sample fit and coefficients being wrongly signed. For example, estimates of the RID model by Dornbush (1980), Haynes and Stone (1981), Frankel (1983) and Backus (1984) cast serious doubt on its ability to track the exchange rate in-sample: few coefficients are correctly signed, the equations have poor explanatory power in terms of the coefficient of determination, and autocorrelation is an endemic problem. One particularly disturbing feature of their estimated equations is that the sign on the relative money supply term is negative, suggesting that a money supply leads to an exchange rate *appreciation*! This latter phenomenon, of the price of the mark rising as its supply is increased, has been labelled by Frankel (1982c) as the 'mystery of the multiplying marks' (we shall return to this phenomenon later).

How do we explain the earlier poor performance of the monetary approach equations as we move into the 1980s? Haynes and Stone (1981) have suggested that the root of the problem may be traced to restricting the coefficient on home and foreign monies, incomes and interest rates to have equal and opposite signs, restrictions often imposed by researchers. The imposition of such constraints may be justified on the grounds that if multicollinearity is present, constraining the variables will increase the efficiency of the coefficient estimates. However, Haynes and Stone (1981) show that the subtractive constraints used in monetary approach equations are particularly dangerous because they may lead to biased estimates and also (in contrast to additive constraints) to sign reversals: that is, this could explain the 'perverse' negative sign on the relative money supply. Indeed, when Haynes and Stone estimate an unconstrained version of the RID model they find that coefficient values are broadly supportive of the RID model and, in particular, the sign on the relative money term is as predicted by the theory. However, Haynes and Stone's estimated equation produces a textbook example of multicollinearity: high R^2 combined with few statistically significant variables.

A second explanation for the poor performance of the monetary model has been given by Frankel (1982c): he attempts to explain the mystery of the multiplying marks by introducing wealth into the money demand equations. The justification for this inclusion is that Germany was running a current account surplus in the late 1970s and this was redistributing wealth from US residents to German residents thus increasing the demand for marks, and reducing the demand for dollars, independently of the other arguments in the money demand functions. By including home and foreign wealth (defined as the sum of government debt and cumulated current account surpluses) in equation (6.11), and by not constraining the income, wealth and inflation terms to have equal and opposite signs, Frankel (1982c) reports a monetary approach equation in which all variables, apart from the income terms, are correctly signed and most are statistically significant; the explanatory power of the equation is also good.

A further explanation for the failure of the monetary approach equations may be traced to the relative instability of the money demand functions underlying reduced forms such as (6.1). Thus a number of single-country money demand studies strongly indicate that there have been shifts in velocity for the measures of money utilised by the researchers mentioned earlier (see Artis and Lewis 1981 for a discussion). In Frankel (1984), shifts in money demand functions are incorporated into equation (6.11) by introducing a relative velocity shift term $v - v^*$, which is modelled by a distributed lag of $(p + y - m) - (p^* + y^* - m^*)$. The inclusion of the $v - v^*$ term in equation (6.11) (along with a term capturing the real exchange rate – the inclusion of such a term in an asset reduced form will be considered in the next chapter) for five currencies leads to most of the monetary variables becoming statistically significant and of the correct sign. However, significant first-order serial correlation is a problem in all of the reported equations.

Driskell and Sheffrin (1981) argue that the poor performance of the monetary model can be traced to a failure to account for the simultaneous bias introduced by having the expected change in the exchange rate (implicitly through the relative interest rate term) on the right hand side of monetary equations. However, taking account of this in a rational expectations framework Driskell and Sheffrin (1981) find no support for the RID monetary model and suggest that the reason for its failure may lie in an assumption underlying all the monetary models: namely, that assets are perfect substitutes. The latter suggestion implies that an additional variable, such as a risk premium, may need to be included into a monetary model. This line of argument supports our earlier contention that the persistent autocorrelation reported in monetary models is suggestive of model misspecification.

6.2.3   *Out-of-sample evidence: the Meese and Rogoff critique*

As we have seen, once observations from the 1980s are included into estimated reduced-form monetary exchange rate models, the in-sample performance of the models break down. Perhaps the most devastating indictment against the monetary model to come from the early empirical evidence was that of Meese and Rogoff (1983), who examined the out-of-sample forecasting performance of the model.

Ever since the publication of the Meese and Rogoff paper the ability of an exchange rate model to beat a random walk has become something of an acid test, indeed, *the* acid test of how successful an exchange rate model is. It has become the equivalent of the *R* squared metric by which an exchange rate model is judged.

In sum, Meese and Rogoff (1983) take the FLMA and RID model, and variants of these models (the Hooper–Morton variant of the monetary model which is discussed in Chapter 7), and estimate these models for the dollar–mark, dollar–pound, dollar–yen and the trade weighted dollar. The sample period studied was March 1973 to November 1980, with the out-of-sample forecasts conducted over the sub-period December 1976 to November 1980. In particular, the models were estimated from March 1973 to November 1976 and 1- to 12-step ahead forecasts were conducted. The observation for December 1976 was then added in and the process repeated up to November 1980. Rather than forecast all of the right-hand-side variables from a particular exchange rate relationship simultaneously with the exchange rate, to produce real time forecasts (i.e. forecasts which could potentially have been used at the time), Meese and Rogoff gave the monetary class of models an unfair advantage by including actual data outcomes of the right-hand-side variables. Data on the latter variables were available to them due to the historical nature of their study, but of course they would not have been available at the time of forecasting to a forecaster producing 'real time' forecasts. To produce the latter all of the right-hand-side variables would have had to be forecast simultaneously with the exchange rate. Out-of-sample forecasting accuracy was determined using the mean bias, mean absolute bias and the root mean square error criteria. The benchmark comparison is, as we have noted, a simple random walk with drift:

$$s_t = s_{t-1} + \kappa + \varepsilon_t, \tag{6.15}$$

where κ is a constant (drift) term and ε_t is a random disturbance. Since the RMSE criterion has become the measure that most subsequent researchers have focussed on we note it here as:

$$\text{RMSE} = \sqrt{\frac{\sum (F_t - A_t)^2}{n}},$$

where F is the forecast and A is an actual outcome. By taking the ratio of the RMSE obtained from the model under scrutiny, to the RMSE of the random walk process, a summary measure of the forecasting performance can be obtained as:

$$\text{RMSE}^r = \frac{\text{RMSE}^m}{\text{RMSE}^{rw}}, \tag{6.16}$$

where RMSE^r is the root mean square error ratio (this is equivalent to the Theil statistic).

In sum, Meese and Rogoff were unable to outperform a random walk at horizons of between 1 and 12 months ahead, although in 4 instances (out of a possible 224) the VAR model produced a ranking which was above the random walk at longer horizons (1 outperformance at 6 months and 3 outperformances at 12 months), although this is still a number which is less than that expected by chance. The reason why the Meese and Rogoff finding has been interpreted as a particularly telling indictment against fundamentals-based models is because they deliberately gave their models an unfair advantage by using actual data outcomes of the fundamentals, rather than forecasting them simultaneously with the exchange rate. The Meese and Rogoff result has been confirmed more recently by Mark (1995) and Chinn and Meese (1995), although these researchers do find that predictability kicks in at 'longer horizons', that is, horizons of 36 months and above. We return to the forecast performance of the monetary model in the next section.

6.3   Recent empirical evidence on the monetary model

6.3.1   Cointegration-based studies

As in the PPP literature considered in Chapter 2, more recent work on the monetary model has involved the use of cointegration methods to test its long-run properties. One reason for the popularity of cointegration methods in testing the monetary model is that they address the issue of the potential non-stationarity of the data. This would seem to be especially important in the context of this model since, as we have seen, many of the earlier studies featured estimates which had a high $\bar{R}^2$ combined with a low Durbin Watson (DW) statistic, or some evidence of serial correlation. The combination of a high $\bar{R}^2$ and low DW is often taken as a classic symptom of a spurious regression equation. The application of cointegration techniques seems especially relevant for the standard FLMA and its forward-looking variant, since price flexibility is usually thought of as a long-run phenomenon. Indeed, in the sticky price variant of the monetary model equation (6.1) provides the long-run exchange rate. However, a number of researchers have also advocated testing the RID using cointegration methods, although this seems less clear-cut given that the derivation of this relationship exploits a *short-run* adjustment mechanism. Consider again equation (6.1), repeated here:

$$s_t = \beta_0(m_t - m_t^*) + \beta_1(y_t - y_t^*) + \beta_2(i_t - i_t^*) + \varphi_t.$$

The essential idea underlying cointegration-based studies is to estimate this relationship and check the order of integration of the error term, φ. The null hypothesis of no cointegration is that the error term is $I(1)$ (integrated of order 1), $H_0 : \varphi \sim I(1)$. The second area of interest in a cointegration-based study is whether the estimated cointegrating vector, that is, the estimated coefficients, conforms to the monetary model. The use of cointegration methods has a further advantage in the context of the monetary model. As we have noted, one potential problem with the early estimates of the monetary model is that they are likely to suffer from simultaneous equation bias due to the likely two-way relationship between exchange rates and money and interest rates. This follows on because of the super consistency result for cointegrated processes: instead of converging at the rate $T^{1/2}$, in the case of stationary processes, least squares estimates of non-stationary but cointegrated processes converge at a rate T. This means that, asymptotically, endogeneity will have a negligible effect on the coefficient estimates (in finite samples, however, endogeneity biases can still be significant – see Banerjee *et al.* 1986).

Again, paralleling the cointegration-based studies of PPP discussed in Chapter 2, the first set of cointegration studies of the monetary model relied on the Engle–Granger two-step method, while later studies used fully modified estimators such as the Johansen (1995) full information maximum likelihood method. A summary of a selection of the studies which have used these methods is contained in Table 6.2. There are a couple of key results generated by this table. First, when the Engle–Granger two-step method is used, the null of no cointegration is usually not rejected. However, when the Johansen estimator or other estimators which include a correction for endogeneity and/or serial correlation of the error term are used the null of no cointegration is rejected. Indeed, notice that when the Johansen method is used there is clear evidence of multiple cointegrating vectors.

To illustrate the results obtained for the monetary model using cointegration methods we take as an example MacDonald and Taylor (1991), who used the cointegration methods of Johansen (1995) to test model for the German mark–US dollar exchange rate. In particular, define the monetary vector:

$$x_t' = [s_t, m_t, m_t^*, y_t, y_t^*, i_t, i_t^*], \tag{6.17}$$

and assume it has a VAR representation of the form:

$$x_t = \eta + \sum_{i=1}^{p} \Pi x_t + \varepsilon_t, \tag{6.18}$$

where η is a $(n \times 1)$ vector of deterministic variables, and ε is a $(n \times 1)$ vector of white noise disturbances, with mean zero and covariance matrix Ξ. Expression (6.18) may be reparameterised into the vector error correction mechanism (VECM) as:

$$\Delta x_t = \eta + \sum_{i=1}^{p-1} \Phi_i \Delta x_{t-i} + \Pi x_{t-1} + \varepsilon_t, \tag{6.19}$$

where Δ denotes the first difference operator, Φ_i is a $(n \times n)$ coefficient matrix (equal to $-\sum_{j=i+1}^{p} \Pi_j$), Π is a $(n \times n)$ matrix (equal to $\sum_{i=1}^{p} \Pi_i - I$) whose rank determines the number of cointegrating vectors. If Π is of either full rank, n, or zero rank, $\Pi = 0$, there will be no cointegration amongst the elements in the long-run relationship (in these instances it will be appropriate to estimate the model in, respectively, levels or first differences).

If, however, Π is of reduced rank, r (where $r < n$), then there will exist $(n \times r)$ matrices α and β such that $\Pi = \alpha\beta'$ where β is the matrix whose columns are

Table 6.2 Cointegration results for the monetary model

Source, currencies, period	m	m*	y	y*	i^s	i^{s*}	i^l	i^{l*}	Cointegrated? Method?
Baillie–Selover (1987); Y–$ 1973:3–1983:12	0.065	—	0.458	—	0.005	—	0.035	—	No Engle–Granger
Baillie–Selover (1987) C$–$, 1973:3–1983:12	−0.466	—	−0.047	—	0.010	—	−0.003	—	No Engle–Granger
Kearney–MacDonald (1990) A$–$ 1984:1–1988:12	0.186	—	0.946	—	0.022	—	−0.012	—	Yes Engle–Granger
MacDonald–Taylor (1993) DM–$, 1976:1–1990:12	1	—	−1	—	0.049	−0.050	—	—	Yes Johansen
MacDonald–Taylor (1994) £–$, 1976:1–1990:12	−0.471	1.06	−0.733	−0.284	—	—	−0.052	0.004	No Engle–Granger
MacDonald–Taylor (1993) £–$, 1976:1–1990:12	0.209	−0.49	−0.098	0.646	—	—	0.035	0.086	Yes Johansen
Cushman et al. 1997 Turkish lira–$ 1981Q3–1992Q4	0.21	—	−1.13	—	1.14	—	—	—	Yes Johansen
Kouretas (1997) C$–$ 1970:6–1994:5	−0.12	−0.79	−0.32	0.32	0.08	−0.02	—	—	Yes Dynamic OLS

Source: MacDonald and Swagel (2000).

Note
When a single coefficient is reported in two adjacent columns, this indicates that the coefficient has been constrained to be equal and opposite across the two variables.

the linearly independent cointegrating vectors and the α matrix is interpreted as the adjustment matrix, indicating the speed with which the system responds to last period's deviation from the equilibrium level of the exchange rate. Hence the existence of the VECM model, relative to say a VAR in first differences, depends upon the existence of cointegration.

The existence of cointegration amongst the variables contained in x is determined by two tests proposed by Johansen. The likelihood ratio, or Trace, test statistic for the hypothesis that there are at most r distinct cointegrating vectors is

$$TR = T \sum_{i=r+1}^{N} \ln(1 - \hat{\lambda}_i), \tag{6.20}$$

where $\hat{\lambda}_{r+1}, \ldots, \hat{\lambda}_N$ are the $N - r$ smallest squared canonical correlations between x_{t-k} and Δx_t series (where all of the variables entering x_t are assumed $I(1)$), corrected for the effect of the lagged differences of the x_t process (for details of how to extract the λs see Johansen 1988, and Johansen and Juselius 1990).

In Table 6.3 we report the estimated Trace statistics from MacDonald and Taylor (1991), along with the corresponding 5% critical values, and these indicate that there are up to three significant cointegrating vectors for the mark.[3]

The finding of multiple cointegrating vectors when the methods of Johansen are applied is a common one in the exchange rate literature, and is something we discuss later. MacDonald and Taylor focus on the first cointegrating vector and test hypotheses of the form:

$$\text{Hypothesis}: \ \beta = \{H_1 \phi_1\}.$$

In particular, they test if the coefficients on the home and foreign money supplies are equal to plus and minus unity and if the income elasticity of money demand is equal to minus one. These restrictions in fact go through for the mark–dollar rate, since the appropriate likelihood ratio test statistic is 18.77 with a p-value of 0.72

Table 6.3 Cointegration results for the mark–dollar exchange rate

Null hypothesis	Trace	5% critical
System consists of: $[s, m, m^*, y, y^*, i, i^*]$		
$r \leq 6$	1.43	0.09
$r \leq 5$	6.33	19.96
$r \leq 4$	18.17	34.91
$r \leq 3$	39.19	53.12
$r \leq 2$	77.10	76.07
$r \leq 1$	115.8	102.1
$r \leq 0$	159.8	131.7

Source: MacDonald and Taylor (1993).

(the statistic has an approximate χ^2 distribution with 12 degrees of freedom). The normalised vector with the constraints imposed is:

$$s_t = (m_t - m_t^*) - (y_t - y_t^*) + 0.049i_t - 0.050i_t^*. \tag{6.21}$$

This relationship clearly closely conforms to the flex-price monetary model and perhaps the success in getting such a tightly defined relationship for the mark reflects, at least in part, the relative success of the Bundesbank in controlling the German money supply during the sample period (1976–90). However, as is made clear in Table 6.2, for other countries where there is evidence of cointegration the estimated coefficients are often far from their expected values and cannot be restricted in the way they are in (6.21) (see, for example, MacDonald and Taylor 1991 and 1994; Sarantis 1994; Kouretas 1997). Cushman *et al.* (1997) have argued that the critical values used by MacDonald and Taylor to determine the number of significant cointegrating vectors are only valid for much larger samples than those available to MacDonald and Taylor. When Cushman *et al.* use a small sample correction the existence of cointegration disappears. However, given that cointegration tests, such as the Johansen maximum likelihood method, have relatively low power to reject the null of no cointegration, it may be preferable to use a lower significance level than the standard 95% level. Indeed, Juselius (1995) has argued that this is especially relevant if the researcher can interpret the cointegration vector (*s*) in an economically meaningful way (see also La Cour and MacDonald 2000).

Using cointegration-based methods, Chrystal and MacDonald (1996) compare the properties of divisia money (DIM) to simple sum money (SSM) in the context of a monetary reduced form (for STG–USD). They find that the DIM outperforms SSM in the sense of producing sensible long- and short-run relationship.

La Cour and MacDonald (2000) attempt to address the issue of multiple cointegrating vectors in the monetary model using a 'specific-to-general' approach which also allows for deviations of the nominal exchange rate from PPP. Consider first the following nine-dimensional vector:

$$x_t^{g'} = [s_t, p_t, p_t^*, m_t, m_t^*, i_t^l, i_t^{l*}, \Delta p_t, \Delta p_t^*], \tag{6.22}$$

which contains a menu of variables consistent with the monetary approach, broadly defined (it may also, of course, be consistent with other exchange rate models).[4] The vector is labelled a 'gross' vector since from it a number of sub-systems, discussed later, may be constructed

Rather than starting with a reduced form based on (6.22), La Cour and MacDonald advocate a 'specific-to-general' approach. The latter involves starting with the equilibrium relationships underlying the monetary model conditions and trying to interpret these in an economic and statistical sense before estimating the final relationship. A natural starting point in the monetary model is the money market equilibrium condition. Using a data set for the ECU against the US dollar, and a sample period of January 1982–December 1994, La Cour and MacDonald (2000) use the econometric methods of Johansen (1995) to determine the number of significant cointegrating vectors and also to place interpretable restrictions on the data. The money market relationship for the EU and US areas is analysed using the following vector, which represents a subset of the gross vector (6.22):

$$x_t^{m'} = [(m_t - p_t), y_t, i_t, \Delta p_t]',$$

(6.23)

where variables have the same interpretation as before.[5] Using the trace test of Johansen there was evidence of two significant cointegrating vectors for the EU and US systems and La Cour and MacDonald then implement joint hypothesis tests of the following form on the full cointegrating space (see Johansen and Juselius 1992):

Hypothesis : $\beta = \{H_1\phi_1, H_2\phi_2\}$,

this can be seen as the joint selection of two stationary relationships which are fully specified and identified. The results from this testing strategy produces a simple money market equation for the EU of the form

$$m_t - p_t = -10.55^* i_t.$$

(6.24)

Equation (6.24) indicates that real money balances are negatively related to the opportunity cost variable, as standard monetary theory would predict. The fact that income is insignificant in this money demand relation was unexpected, and probably reflected the small variation in this variable for the relatively short time span of the sample period. For the second vector, a stationary relationship between inflation and the interest rate, as suggested by the Fisher relationship, was shown to hold[6] and the test of the joint hypothesis that these two vectors define the cointegration space has a test statistic of 0.93, with a *p*-value of 0.63. A similar relationship is shown to hold for the US. Following this specific-to-general approach, La Cour and MacDonald are able to identify the five significant cointegrating vectors in the gross system (6.22):

$$m_t - p_t = -\underset{(0.66)}{3.50} i_t,$$

(6.25)

$$m_t^* - p_t^* = -\underset{(1.15)}{15.78} i_t^*,$$

(6.25′)

$$\Delta p_t = i_t,$$

(6.26)

$$\Delta p_t^* = i_t^*,$$

(6.26′)

$$s_t - p_t + p_t^* = -\underset{(1.63)}{19.51} i_t + \underset{(2.77)}{46.58} i_t^*,$$

(6.27)

where standard errors are in brackets. Equations (6.25) and (6.25′) represent EU and US money demand relationships, respectively, and they have the same specification as that recovered from the partial system discussed earlier.

Equations (6.26) and (6.26′) are Fisher conditions for the EU and US, respectively, where the coefficients on interest rates could be restricted to unity. The final relationship in this system is an exchange rate equation which explains deviations from PPP in terms of relative interest rates, where the coefficients on the interest rates indicate a traditional capital flow interpretation: a rise in the domestic interest rate appreciates the real exchange rate (this is the so-called UIP–PPP relationship discussed later in this chapter and again in Chapter 9). On the basis of the reported standard errors, all of the coefficients are statistically different from zero and, furthermore, it proved possible to impose the same structure on the gross system as existed in the sub-systems (the test statistic that the five vectors define the cointegration space has a value of 5.75, with a p-value of 0.22). The earlier discussion has illustrated how multiple cointegration vectors from an exchange rate model can be interpreted. We shall see in the next section that this model also has desirable out-of-sample forecasting properties.

Finally, in this section we consider some of the studies which use panel cointegration methods to test the monetary model. A panel formulation of the flex-price monetary equation is:

$$s_{it} = \alpha_i + \theta_t + \beta_1(m_{it} - m_{it}^*) + \beta_2(y_{it} - y_{it}^*) + \beta_3(i_{it} - i_{it}^*) + u_{it}, \tag{6.28}$$

where now a cross-sectional dimension has been added $-i = 1, \ldots, N -$ in addition to the time dimension $-t = 1, \ldots, T -$ and where α_i is a fixed effect, θ_t a common time effect and u_{it} is an idiosyncratic error. Husted and MacDonald (1998) were the first to estimate the monetary equation in a panel setting and they did so for four groups of countries: a panel of 21 OECD countries relative to the US and Japan, and a panel of 17 European countries relative to the US and Germany. The sample period is 1973, quarter 1 to 1994, quarter 4. A variety of two-step estimators and error correction forms were used to estimate the model and for all the panels clear evidence of cointegration was reported. However, in terms of the magnitudes and signs of the coefficients, the panels defined relative to Germany performed best and this result therefore parallels the numeraire issue discussed in our chapter on PPP (Chapter 2).

Using a two-step estimator, Groen (2000) estimates (6.28) (without the interest rate differential) for a number of panels against the US dollar and German mark, over the period 1973, quarter 1 to 1994, quarter 4. For the DM-based panels clear evidence of cointegration is found using a 5% significance level, although the evidence of cointegration is more fragile for US based panels (cointegration is found at the 10% level). In both panels the point estimates for β_1 and β_2 are close to their prior values and this is particularly so for the DM-based panels (e.g. the estimates of β_1 in these panels are very close to plus one).

Mark and Sul (2001) use the panel DOLS methodology to estimate the monetary model for a panel of 18 countries (against three countries, the US, Japan and Switzerland) over the sample 1973:1 to 1997:4. They also assume that the interest differential in (6.28) is zero and impose β_1 and β_2 to be plus and minus unity, respectively. For all three panels the null hypothesis of no cointegration between the exchange rate and monetary fundamentals is rejected at the 5% level. Mark and Sul then go on to use these panels to construct out-of-sample forecasts and this part of their exercise is discussed in more detail in the next section.

6.3.2   *Out-of-sample forecasting revisited*

The Meese and Rogoff (1983) finding has had an enduring impression on the economics profession. For example, surveying the post-Meese and Rogoff literature Frankel and Rose (1995a) argue (emphasis added): 'the Meese and Rogoff analysis of *short horizons* [less than 36 months] has never been convincingly overturned or explained. It continues to exert a pessimistic effect on the field of empirical exchange rate modeling in particular and international finance in general.'

One potential reason why Meese and Rogoff may have been unable to beat a random walk is because all but one of their empirical relationships were either static or had very limited dynamics. However, we know from our discussions of the PPP proposition, which as we have seen underpins the monetary model, that exchange rate dynamics tend to be quite complex and adjustment to PPP takes a considerable number of periods. A similar story is true for the money market relationships which are so central to the monetary model – all of the available evidence from money demand studies indicates that adjustment to equilibrium is often quite complex. Clearly, for an empirical exchange rate model to be successful it should incorporate these kind of dynamics. As we shall now demonstrate, when these dynamics are accounted for in the estimation process the random walk model is convincingly beaten.

One potential reason for the dynamics in the relationships underpinning the monetary model is structural instability. One way of allowing for such instability would be to let the coefficients in the reduced-form equation evolve over time and this has been done in a number of studies, such as Wolff (1987) and Schinasi and Swamy (1987). These studies report a consistent outperformance of the random walk model at horizons as short as 1 or 2 months.

Another way of addressing the dynamic adjustments underlying (6.1), (6.7) and (6.11) is to use a modelling method such as the so-called general-to-specific dynamic modelling approach proposed by Hendry and Mizon (1993) and others. Although in one of their estimated models, Meese and Rogoff did allow for rich dynamic interactions using a VAR, it is likely that such a system is over-parameterised in terms of its use of information and such systems generally do not forecast well. Interestingly, Meese and Rogoff in a footnote cite this as a potential reason for the poor performance of the VAR-based implementation of the model. The general-to-specific approach can be used to produce parsimonious VARs or parsimonious VECM models.

The general-to-specific approach to exchange rate modelling, and its implications for exchange rate forecastability, can be illustrated using the approach of MacDonald and Taylor (1991). In particular, they take the significant cointegrating vector discussed earlier as equation (6.21) and produce a dynamic error correction equation of the following form:

$$\Delta s_t = \underset{(0.073)}{0.244} \, \Delta s_{t-2} - \underset{(0.235)}{0.417} \, \Delta_2 \Delta m_t - \underset{(0.343)}{0.796} \, \Delta y_t$$

$$- \underset{(0.003)}{0.008} \, \Delta^2 i_t^* - \underset{(0.013)}{0.025} \, z_{t-1} + \underset{(0.003)}{0.005} \, . \tag{6.29}$$

This equation was shown to pass a standard set of in-sample diagnostic tests (not reported here). Of perhaps more significance, however, is the ability of this model to outperform a random walk in an out-of-sample forecasting exercise. In order to produce truly dynamic out-of-sample forecasts, MacDonald and Taylor implemented a dynamic forecasting exercise over the last 24 observations using the procedure of Meese and Rogoff (1983); that is, they sequentially re-estimated the model for every data point from 1989:1 onwards, computing dynamic forecasts for a number of forecast horizons. The root mean square error (RMSE) statistics for these horizons, along with comparable RMSEs from a random walk model, are reported in Table 6.4.

The results are in marked contrast to those of Meese and Rogoff, in the sense that the random walk model is beaten at all of the estimated horizons, even at 1 month ahead (remember the consensus view according Frankel and Rose is that the benchmark random walk model cannot be beaten at horizons of less than 36 months). However, despite the apparent success in beating a random walk, MacDonald and Taylor continue to use the actual right-hand-side variables in their forecasting exercise and therefore although this is consistent with the original Meese and Rogoff article, these forecasts could not have been used by practitioners to make 'real time' exchange rate forecasts. Furthermore, although the RMSE ratios are less than unity, it is not clear that they are significantly less than one. In order to address these kind of issues MacDonald and Marsh (1997) propose a modelling technique which produces fully simultaneous forecasts of all of the model variables and they also provide significance levels for the RMSE ratios. MacDonald and Marsh take the so-called UIP–PPP approach, which involves combining relative interest rates with the nominal exchange rate and relative prices to produce a

Table 6.4 Dynamic forecast statistics

Horizon (months)	RMSE from dynamic ECM	RMSE from random walk	RMSE ratio
12	0.131	0.148	0.88
9	0.103	0.112	0.91
6	0.081	0.088	0.92
3	0.043	0.053	0.81
2	0.032	0.040	0.80
1	0.028	0.030	0.93

Source: MacDonald and Taylor (1993).

stationary (cointegrating) relationship and is discussed in some detail in Chapter 9 (this approach is also referred to as Casselian PPP since in his writings the leading proponent of PPP, Gustav Cassel, recognised that exchange rates could be away from their PPP determined values because of interest differentials). That is, they focus on the following vector:

$$x' = [s, p, p^*, i^l, i^{l*}].$$

The modelling approach involves the structural econometric modelling of Hendry and Mizon (1993) and Johansen and Juselius (1994). Essentially, this involves moving from the kind of VECM representation, described in (6.19), to a con-strained VAR (CVAR), a parsimonious VAR (PVAR) and finally to a simultaneous equation model (SEM). The CVAR arises because the imposition of restrictions on the cointegrating vector or adjustment matrix will change the estimated short-run dynamics of equation (6.19) and the coefficients of the deterministic variables. These new coefficients are denoted by a tilde, and the constrained CVAR can be written as:

$$\Delta x_t = \tilde{\eta} + \sum_{i=1}^{p-1} \tilde{\Phi}_i \Delta x_{t-i} + \tilde{\Pi} x_{t-1} + v_t. \tag{6.30}$$

The CVAR is an intermediate stage in the modelling of the system. The next step is to make the system more parsimonious by exclusion restrictions on Φ_i. After the imposition of all such unrejected restrictions the PVAR can be written as:

$$\Delta x_t = \hat{\eta} + \sum_{i=1}^{p-1} \breve{\Phi}_i \Delta x_{t-i} + \tilde{\alpha} \beta' x_{t-1} + u_t, \tag{6.31}$$

where a breve denotes a new matrix of coefficients following these restrictions. The final stage in the procedure is to move from this reduced-form PVAR to simultaneous econometric models (SEMs) of the individual equations in the system.

$$A_0 \Delta x_t = \hat{\eta} + \sum_{i=1}^{p-1} A_i \Delta x_{t-i} + \alpha \hat{\beta} x_{t-1} + \mu_t. \tag{6.32}$$

In the final SEM, each equation is fully specified in that it may have contemporane-ous as well as lagged dynamic terms, and may contain long-run equilibria ($\beta' x_{t-1}$) where the speed of adjustment is given by the coefficients in α. A key advantage of this SEM modelling strategy is that it results in a full system of equations, rather than a single reduced form, and can therefore be used to provide forecasts for all of the variables in the model. The essential point made by MacDonald and Marsh is that an exchange rate model which incorporates a sensible long-run equilibrium and dynamic properties, which are rich enough to capture the underlying data generating process, should do better than a static model or one with very simple dynamics (which is essentially the kind of model used by other researchers).

MacDonald and Marsh focus on the yen, mark and pound against the US dollar, over the period January 1974–December 1992, with the last 24 observations held back for forecasting purposes. The forecasts constructed are fully simultaneous and dynamic and could therefore have been used by a potential forecaster. The success of the forecasts is gauged in three ways. First, using the $RMSE^r$ criterion, discussed earlier. Second, in terms of the directional ability calculated as:

$$D = \frac{(1 \text{ if forecast direction} = \text{actual, else } 0)}{n}. \tag{6.33}$$

On the basis of chance D is expected to be 0.5, and therefore any number above 0.5 means that the model does better in terms of its predictive ability than simply tossing a coin. Finally, RMSE ratios were constructed for the model projections relative to a panel of 150 professional forecasts, located in the G7 financial centres, and as collected by Consensus Economics of London (gauged using the $RMSE^r$ criterion).

In Table 6.5 we present a representative SEM model for the UK–USD. This table should be read in the following way. The dependent variable for each equation is noted in the first column (so, for example, the first equation is for the change in the exchange rate). The cells in the columns under A_0 contain contemporaneous (i.e. period t) interactions amongst the variables, while the cells in the A_i block contain the coefficients on the lagged variables. Finally, the coefficients on the ECM terms (i.e. the α coefficients) are contained in the final two columns. The estimated system reported in Table 6.5 reveals that there are a number of significant simultaneous interactions, complex dynamic relationships that drive the dependent variables and also the importance of the error correction terms which are numerous and also highly significant in all cases. The forecasting results are summarised in Table 6.6. We note that for the pound sterling the model beats the random walk at 2 months ahead, while for the yen and mark forecastability kicks in at 3 and 4 months ahead, respectively. Note that many of the RMSE ratios are significantly less than unity and this is especially so for the pound sterling. All of the models seem to have very good directional forecasting powers and across the three currencies and forecast horizons, our models outperform the professional forecasters. It is also worth noting that the RMSE ratio of our SEM model relative to a VAR in first differences is always less than unity. This would seem to underscore the point that such models are likely to underperform, both because they are over-parameterised and also because of their failure to incorporate the 'long-run' information contained in the cointegrating vector.

In a follow-up paper, MacDonald and Marsh (1999) extend their earlier analysis by using a tripolar model of the yen, dollar and German mark (the long-run relationships for this model are discussed in Chapter 9). An example of one of the

Table 6.5 SEM equations: United Kingdom

	A_0					A_i								A	
	ΔS_t	Δp_t	Δp_t^*	Δi_t	Δi_t^*	Δp_{t-1}	Δp_{t-3}	Δp_{t-1}^*	Δi_{t-1}	Δi_{t-1}^*	Δi_{t-2}^*	Δi_{t-3}^*	Δi_{t-4}^*	$ECM1_{t-1}$	$ECM2_{t-1}$
Δs_t	-1	—	-5.541 (3.826)	2.959 (3.354)	—	—	—	—	—	—	—	—	—	—	-0.076 (4.410)
Δp_t	-0.119 (3.014)	-1	—	0.433 (2.508)	-0.551 (2.304)	0.266 (4.734)	0.157 (3.006)	—	—	—	—	—	—	-0.006 (6.104)	—
Δp_t^*	0.053 (2.930)	0.097 (2.193)	-1	—	—	—	—	0.646 (9.426)	—	—	—	0.125 (2.928)	—	—	—
Δi_t	—	—	—	-1	0.441 (2.684)	0.122 (2.254)	—	—	0.362 (6.036)	—	—	—	—	0.007 (5.744)	—
Δi_t^*	—	—	0.476 (4.047)	—	-1	—	—	—	—	0.195 (2.929)	-0.297 (4.324)	—	-0.124 (1.949)	-0.010 (4.178)	—

Source: MacDonald and Marsh (1997).

Table 6.6 Dynamic forecasting performance

Horizon (months)	German mark		Pound sterling		Japanese yen	
	R.W. (1)	Direct. (5)	R.W. (1)	Direct. (5)	R.W. (1)	Direct. (5)
1	1.081	0.500	1.007	0.553	1.059	0.500
2	1.059	0.541	0.990	0.649	1.034	0.541
3	1.003	0.583	0.929	0.694	0.974	0.528
4	0.929	0.657	0.871	0.829	0.952	0.514
5	0.894	0.735	0.854	0.882	0.957	0.618
6	0.877	0.818	0.854	0.788	0.949	0.656
7	0.879	0.781	0.853	0.750	0.912	0.750
8	0.881	0.710	0.837	0.774	0.843	0.742
9	0.901	0.700	0.812	0.767	0.818	0.833
10	0.914	0.655	0.806	0.793	0.771	0.897
11	0.903	0.571	0.802	0.786	0.682	0.929
12	0.889	0.556	0.805	0.741	0.618	0.963

Source: MacDonald and Marsh (1997).

Notes
The numbers in the column labelled R.W. are the ratio of the RMSE from the model to that of a random walk and the numbers in the column labelled Direct. are an indication of directional forecasting ability (see text).

dynamic equations from this model (for the DM–USD) is reported here:

$$\Delta s_t^{\text{ger}} = \gamma_0 + \sum_{i=1}^{i=l} \gamma_{1i} \Delta s_{t-i}^{\text{ger}} + \sum_{i=1}^{i=l} \gamma_{2i} \Delta s_{t-i}^{\text{jap}} + \sum_{i=1}^{i=l} \gamma_{3i} \Delta p_{t-i}^{\text{ger}}$$

$$+ \sum_{i=1}^{i=l} \gamma_{4i} \Delta p_{t-i}^{\text{jap}} + \sum_{i=1}^{i=l} \gamma_{5i} \Delta p_{t-i}^{\text{us}} + \sum_{i=1}^{i=l} \gamma_{6i} \Delta i_{t-i}^{\text{ger}} + \sum_{i=1}^{i=l} \gamma_{7i} \Delta i_{t-i}^{\text{jap}}$$

$$+ \sum_{i=1}^{i=l} \gamma_{8i} \Delta i_{t-i}^{\text{us}} + \alpha_1 \beta^{\text{ger}} x_{t-1} + \alpha_2 \beta^{\text{jap}} x_{t-1},$$

which reveals rich dynamic interaction spilling over from Germany, Japan and the US and the existence of two error correction terms (represented by the x_{t-1} terms). The out-of-sample forecasting results from this exercise are reported in Table 6.7 and demonstrate once again the ease with which the random walk model can be beaten in an out of sample forecasting context once appropriate dynamics and long-run relationships have been incorporated into an exchange rate model.

La Cour and MacDonald (2000) show that the random walk model can be beaten in a dynamic error correction model in which the long-run cointegrating relationships are fully specified (as discussed in the previous section). They construct their out-of-sample forecasts using the 24 data points saved from the complete data set, namely, for the period December 1992–December 1994. The criteria used to gauge the relative performance of the model with that of a random walk is the

Table 6.7 Forecasting performance from a tripolar model

Horizon (months)	German mark		Japanese yen	
	RMSE ratio	Direction	RMSE ratio	Direction
1	0.969	56	1.120	52.0
2	0.952	76	1.072	68.0
3	0.973	60	0.912	80.0
4	0.928	64	0.811	80.0
5	0.891	62.5	0.759	83.3
6	0.885	69.6	0.721	78.3
7	0.876	63.6	0.624	90.9
8	0.908	57.1	0.540	95.2
9	0.917	65	0.545	100
10	0.901	73.7	0.529	94.7
11	0.902	77.8	0.465	100
12	0.906	88.2	0.440	100

Source: MacDonald and Marsh (2004).

Table 6.8 Root mean square error ratios for the monetary model of La Cour and MacDonald

Horizon (months)	1	4	6	8	12
Ratio	1.77	1.05	0.78	0.58	0.51

industry standard, namely, the root mean squared error criterion. As we note from Table 6.8, the RMSE is above 1 for 1 and 4 months ahead but falls below unity at horizons beyond 4 months.[7]

Mark and Sul (2001) use their panel estimates of the monetary model, discussed in the previous section, to construct 1 and 16 quarter ahead out-of-sample forecasts and compare these to forecasts produced using a random walk model, in terms of the $RMSE^r$. Using the US dollar as the numeraire, the root mean squared error ratio has a model value of unity at the one quarter horizon. However, at 16 quarters the monetary model dominates a random walk for 17 out of the 18 exchange rates and this difference is statistically significant. For the other two numeraire currencies (the yen and Swiss franc) the monetary model also significantly outperforms a random walk for the vast majority of countries. In contrast to the US results, however, the majority of RMSE ratios for the one quarter forecasts, using the Swiss franc as numeriare, are significantly below unity, while the number of ratios below unity for the yen is slightly below half of the total number of countries. Mark and Sul conclude by noting: 'There is a preponderance of statistically superior predictive performance by the monetary model exchange rate regression.'

Cheung *et al.* (2005) estimate a monetary approach reduced forms and variants, which incorporate 'real' factors such as a Balassa–Samuelson effect. Their sample period is 1973, quarter 2 to 2000, quarter 4 and they consider five currencies against the US dollar and Japanese yen. They report that 'no model consistently outperforms a random walk, by a mean squared error criterion; however, along a direction-of change dimension, certain structural models do outperform a random walk with statistical significance.' In the light of our discussion earlier this result seems surprising especially since Cheung *et al.* use an error correction specification, in addition to a first difference specification. However, crucially, the error correction models estimated are not rendered parsimonious by the deletion of insignificant dynamics and MacDonald and Marsh have shown this aspect of exchange rate modelling is extremely important in the process of obtaining accurate exchange rate forecasts.

We believe that the research presented in this section demonstrates clearly that the random walk paradigm no longer rules the roost in terms of exchange rate forecasting. There is now a sufficient body of evidence to suggest that the random walk can be beaten in a large variety of samples and for a number of different currencies. This of course is not to say that the random walk model can always be beaten, but it does, at least, indicate that the pessimism that many have levelled against fundamentals-based exchange rate models is unwarranted.

6.4   Does the forward-looking monetary model explain exchange rate volatility?

As we saw in Chapter 4, the forward-looking monetary model offers a potentially attractive way of explaining exchange rate volatility. In this section we consider some of the empirical evidence which seeks to test the forward-looking variant of the monetary model.

The earliest test of the forward-looking monetary model was conducted by Huang (1981) who implemented so-called variance inequality tests of the form:

$$\Delta s_t \leq \Delta x_t,$$

that is, the volatility of the monetary fundamentals, as captured by the variance, should be at least as great as the volatility of the exchange rate. Using monthly data for the period March 1973–March 1979, Huang for three bilateral exchange rates (US dollar–DM, US dollar–pound sterling and pound–DM) demonstrated that the inequality was in fact reversed: exchange rates are much more volatile than fundamentals.

Arnold *et al.* (2005) examine the issue of intra-regime volatility for the post-Bretton Woods regime. Specifically, they construct standard deviations of Δs and Δf, where f is a composite measure of fundamentals, such as $[(m - m^*) - (y - y^*)]$, using both the US and Germany as alternate numeraires, for the post-Bretton Woods period. The striking result from this study is that the order of magnitude for the volatility in the total fundamentals is not very different to exchange rate volatility.

Other tests of the forward-looking model rely on imposing restrictions on vector autoregressive models. Such tests may be distinguished with respect to whether they include cointegration restrictions in their tests or not. Tests which do not impose cointegrating restrictions are: Hoffman and Schlagenhauf (1983) and Kearney and MacDonald (1987). We illustrate these tests by using the approach of Hoffman and Schlagenhauf (1983). Consider the forward-looking monetary equation from the previous chapter, repeated here as:

$$s_t = (1 + \beta_1)^{-1} \sum_{i=0}^{\infty} [\beta_1/(1+\beta_1)]^i E_t[x_{t+i}]. \tag{6.34}$$

In order for this equation to have a closed-form solution some assumption has to be made about the time series properties of the fundamental variables. Hoffman and Schlagenhauf, for example, assume the following first-order (vector) autoregressive process for the evolution of the fundamentals term:

$$\Delta x_t = \rho \Delta x_{t-1} + \mu_t. \tag{6.35}$$

Given an estimate of (6.35) a conditional forecast for any future j-period can be obtained as:

$$E_t x_{t+j} = x_t + \sum_{i=1}^{j} \rho_m^i \Delta x_t \tag{6.36}$$

and by substituting this into equation (6.34) a closed-form solution of the following form may be derived as:

$$s_t = x_t + \frac{\beta_1 \rho}{1 + \beta_1 - \rho\beta_1} \Delta x_t, \tag{6.37}$$

which, since all of the variables are observable can be estimated. By considering an unconstrained version of (6.37) a set of cross-equation restrictions, often regarded as the hallmark of rational expectations models, may be imposed on (6.36). The unconstrained version of (6.37) is:

$$s_t = x_t + \Theta \Delta x_t. \tag{6.38}$$

Hoffman and Schlagenhauf (1983) estimate this for the period June 1974 through to December 1979 (which corresponds to what we have referred to as the 'early' floating rate period) for the Deutschemark, French franc and pound sterling, all against the US dollar. They find that 'the restrictions implied by the rational expectations hypothesis and those typically associated with the monetarist approach are consistent with the data.'

One important problem with the implementation of the forward-looking restrictions in the earlier noted tests of the model is that they use a VAR-based approach in which variables enter as first differences and this will be misspecified if cointegration exists between the exchange rate and the fundamentals. This is because in the presence of cointegration a VAR in differences will exclude information contained in the levels of the variables (see, for example, Engle and Granger 1987).

Since, as we have seen, there is considerable evidence to support cointegration in the context of the monetary model, MacDonald and Taylor (1993) propose using a vector error correction methodology, first proposed in the context of a present value stock pricing formula by Campbell and Shiller (1987), to test the forward-looking model in the presence of cointegration. We now present a description of the methods of MacDonald and Taylor and this first involves some manipulation of the basic relationships. Consider again the basic equation of the monetary model:

$$s_t = x_t + \beta_1 E_t(\Delta s_{t+1}). \tag{6.39}$$

On subtracting x_t from both sides of this expression we may obtain

$$s_t - x_t = \beta_1 E_t(\Delta s_{t+1}). \tag{6.40}$$

Since s_t is an $I(1)$ process, Δs_t must be stationary and, if the monetary model is valid, it must follow that the left hand side of (6.40) is also stationary; that is, s and x are cointegrated, $CI(1, 1)$. Using the forward-looking monetary equation with the transversality condition imposed, we may write the expected change in the exchange rate as:

$$\beta_1 E_t(\Delta s_{t+1}) = \beta_1 \left[(1 - \theta) \sum_{j=0}^{\infty} \theta^j E_t x_{t+1+j} - (1 - \theta) \sum_{j=0}^{\infty} \theta^j E_t x_{t+j} \right],$$

$$= \sum_{j=1}^{\infty} \theta^j E_t \Delta x_{t+j}, \tag{6.41}$$

(where note that $\theta = \beta_1(1 - \theta)$). Following Campbell and Shiller (1987), MacDonald and Taylor label $s - x$ as the spread, ζ_t, and therefore (6.40) and (6.41) imply:

$$\zeta_t = s_t - x_t = \sum_{j=1}^{\infty} \theta^j E_t \Delta x_{t+j}. \tag{6.42}$$

That is to say if the model fundamentals are $I(1)$ processes (they need to be differenced to achieve stationarity) the model implies that the spot exchange rate should be cointegrated with the fundamentals. This could be regarded as a first test of the present value model – if these variables are not cointegrated then it suggests that there is an additional explosive term on the right hand side of (6.39) due, say, to a speculative bubble. Expression (6.42) may be rewritten as:

$$\zeta_t = E_t \hat{\zeta}_t, \tag{6.43}$$

where:

$$\hat{\zeta}_t = \sum_{j=1}^{\infty} \theta^j \Delta x_{t+j},$$

which is the so-called prefect foresight spread, and parallels the perfect foresight exchange rate discussed in the previous chapter. In words, equation (6.42) implies that the spread is the present discounted value of the expected change in future fundamentals and is the optimal predictor of the expected future change in fundamentals – in an empirical sense, ζ_t should Granger cause the change in fundamentals. The Granger causality of ζ_t with respect to Δx_t may be regarded as a second test of the present value model. A more formal test of the model may be conducted in the following way.

If both Δx_t and ζ_t are stationary then they must have a Wold representation which may be approximated using a VAR with lag length, q.[8] In companion form the VAR is:

$$
\begin{bmatrix} \Delta x_t \\ \Delta x_{t-1} \\ \vdots \\ \Delta x_{t-p+1} \\ \zeta_t \\ \zeta_{t-1} \\ \vdots \\ \zeta_{t-p+1} \end{bmatrix} = \begin{bmatrix} \rho_1 \rho_2 \cdots \rho_p & \vdots & \lambda_1 \lambda_2 \cdots \lambda_p \\ & \vdots & \\ I_{p-1} & \vdots & 0 \\ & \vdots & \\ \delta_1 \delta_2 \cdots \delta_p & \vdots & \omega_1 \omega_2 \cdots \omega_p \\ & \vdots & \\ 0 & \vdots & I_{p-1} \\ & \vdots & \end{bmatrix} \begin{bmatrix} \Delta x_{t-1} \\ \Delta x_{t-2} \\ \vdots \\ \Delta x_{t-p} \\ \zeta_{t-1} \\ \zeta_{t-2} \\ \vdots \\ \zeta_{t-p} \end{bmatrix} + \begin{bmatrix} \eta_t \\ \vdots \\ 0 \\ \vdots \\ \varepsilon_t \\ \vdots \\ 0 \end{bmatrix},
$$

(6.44)

or:

$$ z_t = A z_{t-1} + v_t. \tag{6.45} $$

We now define two selection vectors:

$$ \Delta x_t = h' z_t, $$

where h' is a $(1 \times 2p)$ row vector with a 1 in the first element and zeros elsewhere and

$$ \zeta_t = g' z_t, $$

where g' is a $(1 \times 2p)$ row vector with a 1 in row $p \times 1$ element. The standard multi-period forecasting formula can be used to forecast z in any future period, as:

$$ E[z_{t+k}/H_t] = A^k z_t, \tag{6.46} $$

where H_t is the so-called econometrician's information set, consisting of only lagged values of ζ_t and Δx_t. By projecting both sides of (6.45) onto H_t and applying the law of iterated mathematical projections, and using the past three equations, we can obtain:

$$g'z_t = \sum_{i=1}^{\infty} \left(\frac{\beta_1}{1 + \beta_1} \right)^i h' A^i z_t,$$

$$= h'\phi A(I - \phi A)^{-1} z_t, \tag{6.47}$$

where $\phi = (\beta_1/1 + \beta_1)$. If equation (6.47) is to hold non-trivially, the following $2p$ parameter restrictions can be imposed on the VAR:

$$g' - h'\phi A(I - \phi A)^{-1} = 0, \tag{6.48}$$

and post-multiplying (6.48) by $(I - \phi A)$ we can get a set of non-linear restrictions on the VAR for $(\zeta_t, \Delta x_t)'$:

$$H_0 : g'(I - \phi A) - h'\phi A = 0. \tag{6.49}$$

The non-linear restrictions test is the third formal first test of the forward-looking monetary model. Fourth, a variance bounds test, popularised by Shiller (1980) in the context of the stock market literature, may be calculated using this framework. For example, if expectations are rational then it must follow that:

$$\hat{\zeta}_t = \zeta_t + u_t, \tag{6.50}$$

where u_t is a random error and with rational expectations must be uncorrelated with ζ_t. Given that variances cannot be negative, it must further follow that:

$$\mathrm{Var}(\zeta_t) \leq \mathrm{Var}(\hat{\zeta}_t). \tag{6.51}$$

Such a test is seen as an improvement over the basic variance bounds tests used by, for example, Huang (1981) as it addresses the issue of non-stationarity in the presence of cointegration. A final test of the model can be obtained by noting that the perfect foresight spread, $\hat{\zeta}_t$, may be calculated as:

$$\hat{\zeta}_t = h'\phi A(I - \phi A)^{-1} z_t.$$

Campbell and Shiller argue that a simple graphical comparison of the calculated perfect foresight spread with the actual spread will give a qualitative measure of how well the model fits

In terms of the first test of the model, we saw in the previous section that a number of studies support cointegration of the exchange rate with monetary fundamentals particularly when the methods of Johansen or panel methods are used. Consider again the results of MacDonald and Taylor (1993), who use a data period spanning January 1976–December 1990 for the DM–USD. As we noted in Section 6.3.1, clear evidence of cointegration was found for the general system which included relative interest rates. The evidence of cointegration also existed for the base-line forward-looking model in which interest rates are excluded from the cointegrating set and a very tightly defined relationship of the following form could be recovered:

$$s_t = m_t - m_t^* - (y_t - y_t^*),$$

where the restriction that the coefficients on the relative money supply and income terms were unity could not be rejected. The monetary model therefore passes the first of the present value tests. However, the remaining set of tests are not so favourably deposed to the model.

The forward-looking restrictions were implemented for a range of four different values for the semi-interest elasticity of the demand for money and in each case the restrictions were rejected with a p-value of 0.00. Furthermore, the variance inequality (6.51) was actually reversed in each case – that is, empirically it turns out that $\text{Var}(\zeta_t) \geq \text{Var}(\hat{\zeta}_t)$. Finally, in Figure 6.1 we plot the actual spread alongside its theoretical counterpart and it is clear that both $\hat{\zeta}_t$ and ζ_t are very different, and therefore the model would also seem to fail this qualitative test.

Engel and West (2003) also exploit a Campbell–Shiller type present value model to demonstrate that under certain assumption one implication of this model is that the exchange rate should Granger cause fundamentals. Using quarterly data for the G7 over the period 1974:1–2001:3 they demonstrate quite a bit of evidence of Granger causality running from the US dollar bilateral exchange rates and fundamentals extracted from a standard monetary model (i.e. relative money supplies

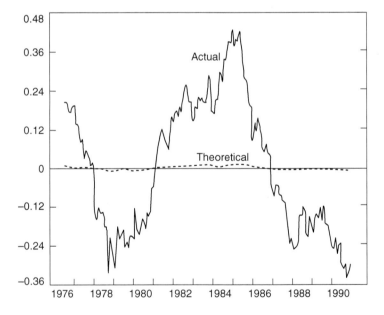

Figure 6.1 Actual and theoretical spread.

Source: MacDonald and Taylor (1993).

and relative income levels) and a monetary model extend to include a Taylor rule (which introduces relative interest rates as an extra fundamental). However, they find little evidence of causality running in the opposite direction, from fundamentals to exchange rates, which seems to confirm the exchange rate disconnect. The Granger causality results are shown to be robust with respect to both bivariate and multivariate pairings. Engel and West, however, recognise that since the present value model is a reduced-form relationship the Granger causality between exchange rates and fundamentals could be reflective of other factors (i.e. it could be that exchange rates Granger cause money supplies because central banks react to the exchange rate in setting monetary policy). Engel and West also demonstrate analytically that in the context of a rational expectations present value model that the exchange rate can exhibit near random walk behaviour if fundamentals are $I(1)$ and the discounting factor, from the present value relationship, is close to unity.

In sum, the forward-looking monetary model does not seem to offer the means of explaining the phenomenon of intra-regime volatility. The forward-looking model is considered again in Chapter 11, after we have introduced the New Open Economy Macroeconomic models, and as we shall see there, variants of the model to appear to offer an interesting explanation for intra-regime exchange rate volatility in terms of uncertainty. We close this Chapter by asking the question: can the monetary model be used to explain the issue of inter-regime volatility first introduced in Chapter 1?

6.5   Inter-regime volatility

Baxter and Stockman (1989) were the first to examine the variability of output, trade variables and private and government consumption across the Bretton Woods and post-Bretton Woods experience and they were:

> unable to find evidence that the cyclic behavior of real macroeconomic aggregates depends systematically on the exchange rate regime. The only exception is the well known case of the real exchange rate.

That is to say as countries move from fixed to flexible exchange rates the volatility of macroeconomic fundamentals does not change but the volatility of the real (and nominal) exchange rate does change. Flood and Rose (1995) re-examine the issue of inter-regime volatility using the monetary model. Specifically, Flood and Rose (1995) construct what they refer to as Virtual Fundamentals (*VF*) and Total Fundamentals (*TF*). Consider again the base-line monetary equation:

$$s_t = m_t - m_t^* - \beta_0(y_t - y_t^*) + \beta_1(i_t - i_t^*),$$

which can be rearranged as:

$$s_t - \beta_1(i_t - i_t^*) = m_t - m_t^* - \beta_0(y_t - y_t^*),$$

where the left hand side is the 'Virtual Fundamental', $VF_t = [s_t - \beta_1(i_t - i_t^*)]$, and the right hand side becomes the 'Traditional Fundamental', $TF_t = [m_t - m_t^* - \beta_0(y_t - y_t^*)]$. Flood and Rose also consider adding a disturbance term to the money market equilibrium conditions to obtain an augmented traditional fundamental, $ATF_t = [m_t - m_t^* - \beta_0(y_t - y_t^*) + (\varepsilon_t - \varepsilon_t^*)]$. The virtual and total fundamentals are calculated for estimated values of the βs and the results are shown to be robust to different values of these coefficients.

Flood and Rose calculate the conditional volatility of the VF and TF and ATF terms for the Bretton Woods and post-Bretton Woods periods. The countries studied are: UK, Canada, France, Germany, Holland, Italy, Japan, Sweden. The results (reported as Figures 1.6 and 1.7) show that the volatility of VF increases dramatically as countries move from fixed to floating, but the volatility of the TF and ATF terms does not. These results are confirmed formally using variance ratio statistics. So on their view standard monetary fundamentals cannot explain the volatility of exchange rates in the move from fixed to floating exchange rates and attention has to be focussed on what does change in the fixed to floating move, namely, the market microstructure of the foreign exchange market (this view is considered in some detail in Chapter 14).[9]

Inter-regime issues have recently been revisited by Arnold, de Vries and MacDonald (2005) (AVM). In trying to understand inter-regime volatility issues, AVM argue that it is important to introduce distortions, which are likely to be prevalent in fixed rate regimes, such as Bretton Woods, into monetary exchange rate equations. Their variant of the monetary equation is given as:

$$s = E[m_j - m_j^*] - E[x_j - x_j^*] + \ln\frac{R}{I} - \ln\tau\frac{\tau^*\omega^*}{\omega}$$
$$+ E[\ln\tau_j + \ln\omega_j^* - \ln\omega_j] + \Omega,$$

where of terms which do not have an obvious interpretation, τ is a capital control distortion, ω is a trade distortion and Ω is the risk premium comprising the sum of variances and covariances of the individual variables.

Arnold, de Vries and MacDonald (2005) tackle the inter-regime volatility issue by focussing on two key distortions, namely, IMF support and capital controls. In a fixed rate regime, and from a monetary perspective, the key volatility term should be volatility in reserves and AVM show, using a specific case study for the UK, that IMF credit facilities are quantitatively important enough to include in an analysis of the volatility trade-off and when it is included fundamental volatility increases in fixed rate regimes.

AVM also use the offshore–onshore interest rate differential as a measure of capital controls and show for the UK during the Bretton Woods striking how marked the volatility of the onshore–offshore differential is and indeed it is almost the reverse of the stylised exchange rate volatility – that is, highly volatile in Bretton Woods and hardly any volatility in the floating rate period. AVM also demonstrate that capital controls, in the form of the onshore–offshore differential, are an important source of volatility for France and Italy during the period when capital controls were in force in the ERM (i.e. 1979–83).

AVM also demonstrate, using data from the ERM period, that the magnitude of exchange rate volatility is clearly dependent on whether exchange rate realignments are excluded or not. With realignments included, exchange rate volatility is much greater compared to the non-realignment position. Flood and Rose (1995, 1999), and others, do not include exchange rate realignments in their work.

Concluding comments

In this chapter we have presented an overview of the empirical evidence relating to the monetary model. We summarise this evidence in the following way. First, the early tests of the model (i.e. tests which rely on traditional econometric methods) are not supportive of the model in either an in-sample or out-of-sample context. In terms of the former tests coefficients are often wrongly signed, have values which are far from their priors and have low explanatory power. Following Meese and Rogoff (1983) the out-of-sample properties of these models are no better than a random walk, even when actual data outcomes of the right-hand-side variables are used. However, more recent tests of the monetary model are more favourably disposed. For example, using cointegration methods there is ample evidence to suggest that monetary model provides a well-defined long-run relationship. Furthermore, using these long-run relationships, and an econometric modelling strategy which explicitly recognises the complex short- to medium-run dynamics that exist in foreign exchange markets, the random walk paradigm can be beaten at horizons as short as 2 months ahead and the models can also be shown to have good directional ability. Recent econometric modelling methods, however, do not reveal the forward-looking version of the model in a particularly good light. Nonetheless, recent empirical works suggest that both the intra- and inter-regime volatility issues may be understood using monetary fundamentals.

7 Currency substitution models and the portfolio balance approach to the exchange rate

7.1 Introduction

In this chapter we move away from the monetary class of model, where non-money assets such as bonds are perfect substitutes, to the portfolio balance class of model in which non-money assets are imperfectly substitutable. Before considering this class of model, however, we first of all consider some currency substitution (CS) models. Although such models have much in common with the monetary class of models considered in the last three chapters, they also provide a nice link with the portfolio balance models because they emphasise the importance of risk and diversification, introduce a role for wealth effects into an exchange rate relationship and also highlight the key interaction between current account adjustment, the evolution of net foreign assets and wealth effects. As we shall see, such interactions are also at the heart of some of the models of real exchange rate determination, considered in Chapter 7 and the new open economy macroeconomic models of Chapters 9 and 10.

7.2 Currency substitution models

The monetary models considered in the last three chapters constrained home and foreign residents to hold only their own monetary stock – there was no allowance for the phenomenon of CS,[1] in which residents are allowed to hold money issued in both the home and foreign country (or 'monies' in a multi-country setting).[2] However, in a regime of floating exchange rates, multinational corporations, involved in international trade and investment, and speculators (such as commercial banks) have an incentive to hold a *basket* of currencies in order to minimise the risk of revaluation effects of potential exchange rate changes on their wealth[3] (i.e. economic agents will, *ceteris paribus*, shift their currency balances away from dollars if they expect the dollar to depreciate). Thus, much as in traditional portfolio balance theory, considered below, foreign exchange market participants have an incentive to hold a basket of currencies, the proportions of the various currencies in the portfolio varying with the risk and expected rates of return of the specific currencies. The ability of foreign exchange market participants to substitute between different currencies has been made possible due to the lifting of exchange controls in the post-Bretton Woods period by most of the participating members of the generalized float.

The kind of currency substitution referred to above, where agents hold a basket of home and foreign currencies and switch between these currencies in response to expected currency movements, is usually referred to as direct currency substitution. In practice it is likely that only a small proportion of a country's non-interest-bearing money stock would be held by non-nationals.[4] Before considering models which seek to model this kind of direct CS, it is worth noting that an indirect form of CS, which is closely related to the more familiar concept of capital mobility, may quantitatively be more important than direct capital mobility. Thus, expectations of an exchange rate change will induce substitution between non-money assets, such as bonds, and this will result in a form of currency substitution. This indirect form of CS may be illustrated with the following example from McKinnon (1982). For example, assume that the world consists of two countries, home and foreign, and uncovered interest parity is maintained between their non-money assets.

$$i - i^* = \dot{s}^e, \tag{7.1}$$

The two countries are assumed to have issued bonds, V, and the interest rates in each country are determined as:

$$i = i^w + (1 - a)\dot{s}^e, \tag{7.2}$$

$$i^* = i^w - a\dot{s}^e, \tag{7.3}$$

where i^w is the nominal world yield on bonds and is given by:

$$i^w = ai + (1 - a)i^*,$$

where a is the financial weight of the home country (in this case the US) in the world financial markets as measured by the ratio of dollar to total bonds outstanding – $a = V/V^*$. If a is assumed to be, say, 0.5 and s is the home currency price of foreign currency then an expected depreciation of the home currency of 10% will result in an increase in the home rate relative to the world rate of 5% and a reduction in the foreign rate of 5%. If expectations are commonly held, significant capital flows need not take place since the rates will adjust immediately to eliminate arbitrage incentives. However, the higher (lower) interest rate in the home (foreign) country results in agents holding less home currency and more foreign currency. To put this differently, the capital outflow from the home to foreign country is an exact reflection of the reduced demand for the cash of the home country and the increased demand for the cash of the foreign country. McKinnon (1982) argues that quantitatively this indirect form of currency substitution may be more important than the direct form of currency substitution: 'Massive capital flows can easily be induced even when the interest differential remains "correctly" aligned to reflect accurately the change in expected exchange depreciation.'[5] Although *indirect* CS may be the more important form of CS, it would clearly be impossible to distinguish it from ordinary capital mobility.

We now examine the implications of CS for the determination of the exchange rate in a monetary approach framework. The models we consider share the common feature that domestic residents can hold their wealth, W, in a portfolio of either domestic money, M, or foreign money, M^*:

$$W = M + M^*. \tag{7.4}$$

The proportions of the two currencies held depends on the expected change in the exchange rate, and changes in the expected rate lead to attempts by portfolio holders to substitute between currencies. The variant of the flex-price monetary model considered in Section 7.2.1 highlights the importance of risk/returns factors (and their determinants) as a basis for agents' decisions to substitute between currencies. In Section 7.2.2 two currency substitution models are discussed which tackle a deficiency that has characterised the exchange rate models considered hitherto, namely their lack of stock–flow interactions. A general equilibrium CS model is sketched in 7.2.3.

7.2.1   Currency substitution (CS) and the flex-price monetary approach

In the monetary models of the exchange rate considered so far, monetary services are only provided by the domestic currency. However, and as we have argued, this is probably an unrealistic assumption; various international companies have an incentive to hold a variety of currencies and therefore monetary services may be provided by other currencies. This may be illustrated by rewriting the kind of money demand function used in other chapters as:

$$M^D/P = \Omega(Y, i), \tag{7.5}$$

where Ω is the proportion of monetary services provided by domestic money. Clearly if $\Omega = 0$ we are in the sticky/flex price monetary approach world. In a world of CS Ω is assumed to lie between zero and unity, and hence $1 - \Omega$ gives the proportion of monetary services provided by foreign money.

Following King *et al.* (1977), the share of foreign currency, for a given institutional structure, depends upon exchange rate expectations and the uncertainty, Γ, with which these expectations are held:

$$\Omega = f(\dot{s}^e, \Gamma), \quad f_1 < 0, f_2 < 0, \tag{7.6}$$

where f_1 and f_2 are partial derivatives ($f_1 = \delta\Omega/\delta\dot{s}^e$). Thus expectations of an exchange rate depreciation tend to decrease holdings of domestic money as does increased uncertainty. Exchange rate expectations are argued to depend on the expected future monetary growth for a given structure of foreign monetary policy $\dot{s}^e = \dot{m}^e$ and uncertainty is assumed to be a function of the variability, or variance, of domestic money supply: increased variance raises the level of exchange rate uncertainty associated with portfolio holdings of domestic currency. Thus we may rewrite (7.6) as:

$$\Omega = g[\dot{m}^e, \; var \; \dot{m}^e], \quad g_1 < 0, \; g_2 < 0, \tag{7.7}$$

where $\dot{m}^e$ is the expected monetary expansion, and thus an expected increase in the domestic money supply will cause investors to want to hold more foreign money.[6] A similar argument applies to an increase in the variance of $\dot{m}^e$.

For simplicity, it is assumed that the conditions underlying the simple flex-price monetary model considered in Chapter 4 hold here, namely PPP and UIP, and additionally, the home country is assumed to be small. Using a log-linear version of (7.5) it is straightforward to obtain (where we have normalised P^* to unity and i^* to zero):

$$s = m - \Omega - \alpha_1 y + \alpha_2 \dot{s}^e. \tag{7.8}$$

Equation (7.8) is a monetary currency substitution reduced form. Notice that the inclusion of Ω implies that changes in currency preferences will have an independent, and direct, effect on the exchange rate. Given the above assumptions about $\dot{s}^e$ and Ω (equation (7.7)), equation (7.8) may be pushed further. Thus, by assuming equation (7.7) has the form:

$$\Omega = \beta_0 \dot{m}^e + \beta_1 \; var \; \dot{m}; \quad \beta_0 < 0, \; \alpha_1 < 0, \tag{7.9}$$

and on substituting for Ω in (7.8), and using the fact that $\dot{s}^e = \dot{m}^e$, we obtain

$$s = m - \alpha_1 y + (\alpha_2 - \beta_1) \; var \; \dot{m}^e \tag{7.10}$$

where, since $\beta_0 < 0$, $\alpha_s - \beta_2 > 0$. Thus, in addition to the traditional monetary effects of m and y on the exchange rate equation (7.10) also demonstrates the effect of CS. The coefficient of $\dot{m}^e$ is larger than it would be in the absence of CS (i.e. $\alpha_2 - \beta_0 > \alpha_2$) because of the ability of agents to substitute between domestic and foreign money, exacerbating pressure for a currency depreciation or appreciation. This effect will be reinforced if the expected variability of monetary policy, var $\dot{m}^e$, changes in tandem with the expected change in $\dot{m}$.

7.2.2 *Wealth effects and two CS models*

One of the criticisms of the MF model and its extensions, noted in Chapter 4, is that positions of equilibrium are consistent with non-zero current account positions and continual flows across foreign exchange markets. For example, following a monetary expansion in the flexible exchange rate version of the MF model, the small open economy runs a balance of payments surplus. This surplus must, over time, be changing the country's stock of assets: under a flexible exchange rate domestic residents will be accumulating foreign assets (i.e. a capital account deficit will be the counterpart of a current account surplus) and financial wealth must be changing. Such wealth effects would be expected to have implications for spending, if wealth enters the consumption function, and also equilibrium in asset markets, if money demand is a function of wealth. Such wealth effects will also ensure that the so-called equilibrium in the MF model can only be temporary: the wealth-induced spending and asset demand effects will push the economy to a *new stock* equilibrium where flows are equal to zero. But in neither the MF nor the sticky price monetary model does wealth enter the money demand equations or the expenditure functions, and thus the loop from the real sector to the asset sector and back again to the real sector is ignored.

The above discussion also has relevance for the FLMA model where the role of the current account in affecting asset equilibrium is ignored. Although there is nothing inconsistent with a country running a current account surplus or deficit in the FLMA model, such imbalances are not allowed to affect money demand since wealth does not enter as a scale variable. We now consider the incorporation of such wealth effects into a CS model and in Section 7.3 we consider the role that wealth plays in the context of the portfolio balance approach. Two CS models are used to discuss wealth effects and stock–flow interactions. A common feature of both models is that agents can only accumulate or decumulate foreign currency by the home country using a current account surplus or deficit.

In the first model, due to Kouri (1976), wealth is included as a scale variable into the money demand equation and an explicit role is given to the current account. Current account surpluses or deficits, by changing wealth, result in changes in the demand for the home and foreign currency and, as a corollary, changes in the exchange rate. Model 1 is useful in that it illustrates the dynamics of the exchange rate in an asset model once allowance has been made for the current account. However, as we shall see, it is somewhat limited because trade flows respond passively to conditions of stock equilibrium. In model 2, due to Calvo and Rodriguez (1977), model 1 is pushed further by allowing the current account to depend upon the real exchange rate. Both models assume that asset markets adjust instantaneously following a shock.

In the model of Kouri (1976) it is assumed that the home country is small and produces a single traded good, which is a perfect substitute for the foreign traded good. The foreign price is assumed constant and equal to unity so that the exchange rate and the domestic price level are equivalent,

$$S = P^T, \tag{7.11}$$

where P^T is the price of the traded good and it is further assumed that the economy is fully employed and thus domestic output, Y^T, is constant. Domestic residents can hold their real wealth, w, in either non-interest-bearing foreign real money balances M^* (with $P^{T*} = 1$) but foreign residents cannot hold domestic money balances, that is,

$$w = M' + M^*, \tag{7.12}$$

where $M' = M/S$. The home demand for the domestic and foreign moneys is assumed to depend upon the expected change in the exchange rate (for simplicity we ignore the risk term, Γ, discussed in the previous section). On equating the asset demands with their supplies we obtain:

$$M^{D'} = L'(\dot{s}^e) = M',$$
(7.13)

$$M^{D*} = L^*(\dot{s}^e) = M^*.$$
(7.13')

By substituting the definition of wealth into (7.13) a condition for asset market equilibrium may be obtained as:[7]

$$L'(\dot{s}^e) = M'.$$
(7.14)

For given values of $\dot{s}^e$, M and M^* condition (7.14) gives the market clearing value for the exchange rate, S (noting $M' = M/S$). Since foreigners cannot hold domestic currency the only way that domestic residents can accumulate foreign assets is by running a current account surplus and the latter is equal to the excess of output over consumption:

$$\dot{M}^* = CA = Y^T - C^T(w), \quad c_w > 0$$
(7.15)

where $\dot{M}^*$ is the accumulation of foreign money (or the absolute value of the capital account), CA is the current account, C^T represents domestic consumption, or absorption, of the traded good (assumed to be a positive function of real wealth), and $Y^T - C^T$ is savings.

The long-run equilibrium, or steady-state conditions, for the model are as follows. First, the stock of real wealth and its components are unchanging, which necessitates that the current account be equal to zero. Second, the stock of wealth is held in desired proportions. Third, the expected change in the exchange rate equals the growth in the money stock. Using Figure 7.1, the model's short-run equilibrium and movement to the steady state is illustrated. The model is based on the crucial dichotomy, used in Chapter 5, of instantaneous adjustment of asset markets and relatively slow goods market adjustment (although prices are continuously flexible in this model). The inelastic schedule $Y^T Y^T$ represents the exogenously given full employment level of output (i.e. $Y^T Y^T$ is basically a 'classical' aggregate supply curve). The MM schedule, given by equation (7.14) (holding M and $\dot{s}^e$ constant), represents asset market equilibrium. Thus from a position of equilibrium on the MM schedule an increase in the supply of foreign money, M^*, necessitates an exchange rate appreciation (fall in S) to maintain wealth constant (see equation (7.12)). The $C^T C^T$ schedule gives domestic absorption as a function of the exchange rate and is negatively sloped since an exchange rate depreciation decreases wealth (equation (7.12)) and this in turn will reduce consumption (see equation (7.15)). Steady-state equilibrium is given at a point such as A where the current account is balanced, the stock of wealth is constant, and domestic residents hold M_0^* of foreign money at an exchange rate S_0.

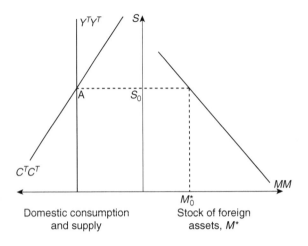

Figure 7.1 Equilibrium in dynamic currency substitution model 1.

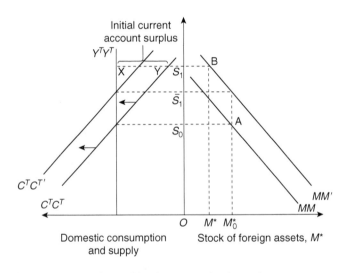

Figure 7.2 Open market purchase of foreign money for domestic money.

Assuming that exchange rate expectations are static, and therefore $\dot{s}^e = 0$, an unanticipated purchase of $M^*M_0^*$ of foreign money from domestic residents, with domestic money, by the central bank (i.e. central bank intervention in the foreign exchange market) would shift the MM curve to MM′ in Figure 7.2. Since the supply of foreign assets to domestic residents has been cut by $M^*M_0^*$, the only attainable point of MM′ is B: the exchange rate depreciates from S_0 to S_1. The exchange rate depreciation, in turn, reduces the value of real financial wealth and thus absorption, so that via (7.15) the current account moves into surplus by the amount XY. Point B is, however, only one of short-run equilibrium. The current account surplus will be changing wealth and this will shift the $C^T C^T$ curve leftwards; the exchange rate will be appreciating, which in turn will further increase absorption. The new equilibrium is reached at $\bar{S}_1$ where the current account and portfolio are balanced and real wealth is constant: the final equilibrium differs from the initial equilibrium by a higher value for S (in proportion to the money supply change). Other magnitudes, including foreign assets, are identical to the initial equilibrium.

Notice that this model gives another example of exchange rate overshooting: to maintain asset market equilibrium the exchange rate overshoots its final equilibrium. This follows because of the assumed nature of expectations. Thus with static expectations the exchange rate has to depreciate more than proportionately to the money supply increase for the following reason. A proportionate increase in S would restore money balances to the original level, but with a lower stock of foreign assets (due to the foreign exchange intervention) the exchange rate has to depreciate more than proportionately to the increase in the money supply. This overshooting crucially depends on the static nature of expectations. If expectations were rational, no exchange rate overshooting would occur, since immediately after the unanticipated foreign exchange intervention, agents would revise their expectations about the future exchange rate to be consistent with the new equilibrium.[8]

The above model is useful in so far as it allows a role for the current account within the framework of the asset approach. The model is, however, rather limited in that trade flows are a mere appendage to the stock adjustment process; that is, trade flows adjust passively to the stock equilibrium conditions. But what happens if a fairly standard trade equation is introduced into the model and PPP does not hold in the short-run so that changes in the nominal exchange rate are real changes resulting, if the Marshall–Lerner elasticities condition holds, in trade flows? We now consider a version of the monetary CS model which incorporates a current account equation and has trade flows responding to the real exchange rate. The model, which we christen model 2, is due to Calvo and Rodriguez (1977) and the exposition in Frenkel and Rodriguez (1982). An interesting feature of this CS model is that exchange rate overshooting occurs even when agents are endowed with perfect foresight.

The definition of wealth and the money demand equations used in model 2 are identical to those of model 1 (equations (7.12) and (7.13)). Since it is assumed that agents have perfect foresight in model 2 the expected change in the exchange rate is equal to the actual change in the exchange rate. The asset equilibrium condition is rewritten in the form

$$M'/M^* = L(\dot{s}); \quad L_{\dot{s}} < 0 \tag{7.16}$$

and thus the desired ratio of home to foreign money declines when the domestic currency is expected to depreciate. As in model 1, the home currency is assumed to be non-traded, and although foreign money is traded, it can only be accumulated over time by the home country running a trade surplus.

In common with model 1, the country is assumed to produce a traded good, is small in relation to world trade, and equation (7.11) holds. In contrast to model 1, however, the domestic economy produces, in addition to the traded good, a non-traded good. The relative price of traded to non-traded goods, P^T/P^N, governs production decisions and since (7.11) holds this may be written as $q = S/P^N$, where q is the real exchange rate. Thus we have:

$$Y^T = Y^T(q), \quad Y_q^T > 0, \tag{7.17}$$

$$Y^N = Y^N(q), \quad Y_q^N < 0, \tag{7.18}$$

where Y^N denotes the demand for non-traded goods and the partial derivatives denote the effect of an increase in the real exchange rate on production. Thus an increase in the real exchange rate leads to an increased in production of the traded good and decreased production of the non-traded good. The demand for each good, denoted as C^T and C^N, depends upon q and real wealth:

$$C^T = C^T(q, w), \quad C_q^T < 0, \; C_w^T > 0, \tag{7.19}$$

$$C^N = C^N(q, w), \quad C_q^N > 0, \; C_w^N > 0, \tag{7.20}$$

where the partial derivatives indicate that an increase in the real exchange rate results in reduced consumption of the traded good and increased consumption of the non-traded good, and an increase in real wealth results in an increase in the demand for both goods. The accumulation of foreign money, in turn, is given by the difference between the consumption and production of traded goods:

$$\dot{M}^* = CA = Y^T(q) - C^T(q, w) \tag{7.21}$$

Since prices are assumed to by fully flexible in model 2, equilibrium in the market for non-traded goods will hold continuously and is given by:

$$Y^N(q) = C^N(q, w). \tag{7.22}$$

The assumed values of the partials for Y^N and C^N implies a specific relationship between w and q. In particular, a rise in real wealth must be accompanied by a fall in the real exchange rate:

$$q = q(w), \quad q_w < 0 \tag{7.23}$$

On substitution of (7.23) into (7.21) we can obtain a further expression for the accumulation of foreign money in terms of the value of assets:

$$\dot{M}^* = f(w) \tag{7.24}$$

The change in real wealth is given by

$$\dot{w} = \dot{M} + \dot{M}^*, \tag{7.25}$$

where the $\dot{M}^*$ term is given by (7.24). The $\dot{M}'$ term may be expressed in the following way. Denote the percentage change in the nominal money supply, $\dot{M}/M$, by ϕ and, since $M' = M/S$, we have

$$\dot{M} = M'(\phi - \dot{s}). \tag{7.26}$$

Expression (7.26) may be pushed further in the following way. First substitute for M' from (7.12) (i.e. $M' = w - M^*$) to get

$$\dot{M}' = w - M^*(\phi - \dot{s}). \tag{7.26'}$$

Second, we use the inverse of (7.16) for $\dot{s}$ (i.e. $\dot{s} = l(M'/M^*) < 0$), and since $M' = w - M^*$ we can obtain the following expression from (7.25)

$$\dot{w} = (w - M^*)\left[\phi - 1\left(\frac{w - M^*}{M^*}\right)\right] + f(w) \tag{7.27}$$

Equations (7.24) and (7.27) characterise the dynamics of model 2 and are represented graphically in Figure 7.3. The schedule $q(w)$ in the left hand side of Figure 7.3 represents combinations of w and q consistent with equilibrium in the non-traded goods market and therefore satisfies equation (7.23) (a rise in w must be associated with a fall in q). In the right hand side of Figure 7.3 the schedules $\dot{w} = 0$ and $\dot{M}^* = 0$ represent the loci of w and M^* which satisfies equations (7.24) and (7.27), respectively. The initial steady state which is characterised by $M^* = \dot{w} = 0$, $(f(w) = 0$, equation (7.24); and $\phi = \dot{s}$, equation (7.27)), is represented in Figure 7.3 by w_0. M_0^* and via equation (7.23), q_0. The trajectory SP is the perfect foresight saddle path which satisfies the laws of motion and the initial conditions. Consider now an increase in the rate of monetary expansion (i.e. from ϕ_0 to ϕ_1, where $\phi_1 > \phi_0$), which from (7.27), shifts the $\dot{w} = 0$ schedule rightwards,

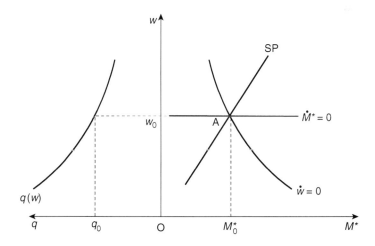

Figure 7.3 Currency substitution with perfect foresight and non-traded good.

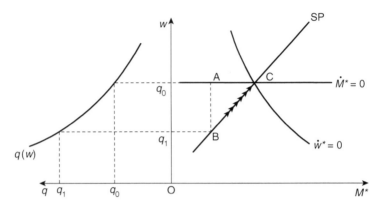

Figure 7.4 Increased monetary expansion in currency substitution model 2.

with the new steady state at point C.[9] This is illustrated in Figure 7.4 (where A corresponds to the equilibrium in Figure 7.3).

The increase rate of monetary growth leads to an instantaneous expectation of an exchange rate depreciation and a desire on the part of asset holders to substitute foreign currency for domestic currency. Point C, however, cannot be reached instantly, since we have assumed that M^* can only be accumulated by running a current account surplus; B is the only point of short-run equilibrium consistent with the stable path to the new steady state at C. At point B real wealth has fallen since the only way asset holders' desire to hold a greater proportion of M^* in their portfolios can be satisfied is, for given initial values of M^* and M', for S to rise, as in model 1, resulting in a reduction in M'. For equilibrium in the non-traded goods market to be maintained this fall in wealth must be offset by a rise in the real exchange rate to q_1 (i.e. $S > P^N$). As Calvo and Rodriguez (1977) point out, if the overall price level is a weighted average of S and P^N the exchange depreciates by more (i.e. 'overshoots') than the price level. The initial depreciation of the real exchange rate results in an incentive for domestic producers to produce traded rather than non-traded goods, and a switch in consumption by consumers from traded to non-traded: the short-run reduction of wealth reduces the consumption of both traded and non-traded goods (see equations (7.19) and (7.20)). The resulting current account surplus moves the economy from the short-run equilibrium at B to the new steady state C with the economy accumulating M^* and the real exchange rate appreciating.

Since the accumulation of foreign currency in model 2 is equivalent to claims on the stock to traded goods, asset holders after the monetary expansion are effectively using traded goods as an inflation hedge. As Frenkel and Rodriguez (1982) demonstrate, in the context of the above model, if the non-traded good is the inflation hedge, the exchange rate will *undershoot* the average price level as the price of non-traded goods rises.

7.2.3   A general equilibrium model of CS

Much as in our discussion in the previous two chapters the above models have been criticised as ad hoc. Here we briefly consider a general equilibrium CS model due to Canzoneri and Diba (1993). Their model consists of a world in which there are two currencies and utility depends upon consumption of a single perishable good and an index of effective real balances:

$$U = E_t \sum_{\tau=t}^{\infty} \beta^{\tau-t} u(c_\tau, x_\tau), \quad 0 < \beta < 1, \tag{7.28}$$

where terms have their usual interpretation and x_τ is an index of effective real money balances, determined by a constant elasticity of substitution transaction technology:

$$x_t = [0.5(M_\tau/p_\tau)^{(1-1/\sigma)} + 0.5(M_\tau^*/p_\tau^*)^{(1-1/\sigma)}]^{(1-1/\sigma)^{-1}}, \tag{7.29}$$

where, of terms not already defined, σ is the elasticity of substitution. The household is assumed to have stochastic endowment, y_τ of the consumption good and can hold both currencies and nominal bonds (B) denominated in the two currencies and the household budget constraint is:

$$c_\tau + M_\tau/p_\tau + M_\tau^*/p_\tau^* + B_\tau/p_\tau + B_\tau^*/p_\tau^*$$
$$\leqslant y_\tau - T_\tau + M_{\tau-1}/p_\tau + M_{\tau-1}^*/p_\tau^* + (1 + i_{\tau-1})B_{\tau-1}/p_\tau$$
$$+ (1 + i_{\tau-1}^*)B_{\tau-1}^*/p_\tau^* \tag{7.30}$$

where i denotes the net nominal interest rate on the bonds, issued in period $\tau - 1$ and maturing in τ and T is tax, or subsidy, by the household's government. The first order conditions for an interior solution to the household's utility maximisation imply:

$$0.5u_x(c_t, x_t)[x_t p_t/M_t]^{1/\sigma} = u_c(c_t, x_t)i_t/(1 + i_t) \tag{7.31}$$

$$0.5u_x(c_t, x_t)[x_t p_t^*/M_t^*]^{1/\sigma} = u_c(c_t, x_t)i_t^*/(1 + i_t^*) \tag{7.32}$$

where $u_c(c_t, x_t)$ and $u_x(c_t, x_t)$ are the partial derivatives of $u(c_t, x_t)$ and assuming these partials exist in equilibrium (7.31) and (7.32) imply:

$$M_t^* S_t = M_t[i_t/(1 + i_t)]^\sigma [i_t^*/(1 + i_t^*)]^{-\sigma}, \tag{7.33}$$

where $S_t - p_t/p_t^*$ is the exchange rate between the two currencies. As long as households of all countries share the same transaction technology and the same interest rates and exchange rate it is possible to aggregate (7.33) across households and interpret the monies appearing in (7.33) as aggregate stocks of the two currencies. By taking the natural logarithms of both sides of (7.33) and linearising the term involving the interest rates around the same steady state value $\bar{i}$ we obtain:

$$m_t^* - m_t + s_t = \alpha(i_t - i_t^*), \tag{7.34}$$

where $\alpha = \sigma/\bar{i}(1 + \bar{i})$. Equation (7.34) indicates that relative currency demands depend upon interest rates rate differentials and the responsiveness of relative demands to interest differentials increases with the degree of CS, if an increase in σ leads to an increase in $\alpha = \sigma/\bar{i}(1 + \bar{i})$. Exploiting the UIP condition, may be rewritten as:

$$s_t = m_t - m_t^* + \alpha(i_t - i_t^*), \tag{7.35}$$

which is a similar, two country, variant of (7.10), although here derived in a general equilibrium setting. On the basis of (7.35), Canzoneri and Diba (1993) stress that any conclusion about the relationship between currency substitution and α depends upon an assumption about monetary policy. For example, an increase in σ could conceivably induce new monetary policies that raise $\bar{i}$ enough to lower α.

In this section we have introduced the concept of CS. Although the CS concept is clearly an appealing one,[10] it would probably be more realistic to allow agents to hold a portfolio of money *and* non-money assets. This is the topic to which we now turn.

7.3   The portfolio balance approach to the exchange rate

In the previous section some stock-flow interactions were considered in the context of two CS models. Although, as was demonstrated, such models offer some interesting exchange rate dynamics, they nevertheless concentrate on a narrow range of assets, in particular, home and foreign money supplies. In this section we expand the range of assets available to portfolio holders to include domestic and foreign bonds and use the stock-flow framework to analyse the effects of various asset market changes. The model outlined in this chapter may therefore be viewed as an extension of the Mundell–Fleming–Dornbusch model, which properly incorporates stock-flow interactions and also allows for the imperfect substitutability of assets. The portfolio balance model has its origins and development in research conducted by McKinnon and Oates (1966), Branson (1968, 1975) and McKinnon (1969). The portfolio model has been applied to the determination of the exchange rate by, *inter alia*, Branson (1977), Allen and Kenen (1978), Genberg and Kierzkowski (1979), Isard (1980) and Dornbusch and Fischer (1980). The portfolio model presented here is a synthesis of the models contained in these papers.

In contrast to the variants of the monetary model considered in previous chapters, the domestic and foreign bonds in the portfolio balance approach are *not* assumed to be perfect substitutes. There are in fact a number of factors (such as differential tax risk, liquidity considerations, political risk, default risk and exchange risk) which suggest that non-money assets issued in different countries are unlikely to be viewed as perfect substitutions by investors. Thus, just as international transactors are likely to hold a portfolio of currencies to minimise exchange risk (i.e. currency substitution), risk-averse international investors will wish to hold a portfolio of non-money assets, the proportions of particular assets held depending on risk/return factors. This implies that uncovered interest parity will not hold and should instead be replaced with a risk-adjusted version, such as:

$$i_t - i_t^* - \Delta s_{t+k}^e = \lambda_t \tag{7.36}$$

where λ_t is a risk premium. In this context if international investors decide that a currency has become riskier, they are likely to reallocate their bond portfolios in favour of less risky assets.

7.3.1 The portfolio balance model

The asset sector of our small country portfolio balance model is outlined as equations (7.37) to (7.40):

$$W = M + B + SF, \tag{7.37}$$

where M denotes domestic money, B, domestic bonds, and, F, and foreign bonds. Since the bonds are assumed to be very short term assets, rather than Consols, we do not need to consider capital gains or losses induced by interest rate changes.

Demand for the three assets depends upon the domestic and foreign rate of interest, which are assumed to be exogenously given, and are homogenous of degree 1 in normal wealth:[11]

$$M = m(i, i^* + \Delta s^e)W, \quad m_i < 0, m_{i^* + \Delta s^e} < 0, \tag{7.38}$$

$$B = b(i, i^* + \Delta s^e)W, \quad b_i > 0, b_{i^* + \Delta s^e} < 0, \tag{7.39}$$

$$SF = f(i, i^* + \Delta s^e)W, \quad f_i < 0, f_{i^* + \Delta s^e} > 0. \tag{7.40}$$

The partial derivatives in (7.38) to (7.40) indicate that for any asset an increase in the own rate leads to an increase in demand and an increase in a cross rate leads to a decrease in demand. It is also assumed that the bonds are gross substitutes (i.e. $b_i > f_i$ and $f_{i^* + \Delta s}^e > b_{i^* + \Delta s}^e$) and a greater proportion of any increase in domestic wealth is held in domestic bonds rather than foreign bonds. To simplify the analysis, the asset demand equations are not dependent upon income. As Allen and Kenen (1980) point out, this introduces an important asymmetry into a portfolio balance model, namely that while conditions in goods markets do not have a direct effect on asset markets, asset market conditions directly affect goods markets since the exchange rate, S, features in both sectors. Although domestic residents can hold all three assets, foreign residents can only hold foreign bonds (and presumably also foreign money which is non-traded). As in our CS models the only way residents of the small country can accumulate F is by running a current account surplus (which as we shall see below, equals positive savings). The supplies of both M and B are exogenously given by the authorities.

The real sector of the model is described by equations (7.41) and (7.44) and is identical in specification to the real sector of the CS, model 2, in the previous section. Prices are assumed to be continuously flexible and the economy operates at full employment. Equation (7.45) represents domestic residents' disposable income which is assumed equal to income derived from traded and non-traded goods plus interest earnings on foreign bonds.[12] Equation (7.47) describes the small country's price level which is given by a simple Cobb–Douglas formulation.[13]

$$Y^T = Y^T(q), \quad Y^T_q > 0 \tag{7.41}$$

$$Y^N = Y^N(q), \quad Y^N_q < 0, \tag{7.42}$$

$$C^T = C^T(q, w), \quad C^T_q < 0, \ C^T_w > 0, \tag{7.43}$$

$$C^N = C^N(q, w), \quad C^N_q > 0, \ C^N_w > 0, \tag{7.44}$$

$$Y^D = Y^T + Y^N + (i^* + \Delta s^e)(SF), \tag{7.45}$$

$$C = C^T + C^N, \tag{7.46}$$

$$P = P^\alpha_N S^{1-\alpha} \tag{7.47}$$

where $q = S/P^N$, $S = P^T$ and $w = W/P = M/P + B/P + SF/P$.

The current account of the balance of payments is given as the difference between the consumption and production of traded goods (the trade balance) plus the interest earnings from the holdings of the foreign asset. The capital account of the balance of payments is simply the accumulation over the relevant period of the foreign asset:

$$\Delta F = CA = Y^T(q) - C^T(q, w) + (i^* + \Delta s^e)SF. \tag{7.48}$$

Therefore the foreign asset can only be accumulated by the country running a current account surplus. Equation (7.48) differs from equation (7.15) by the addition of the interest earnings term and the fact that the capital account is now equal to the accumulation of the foreign bond, not the foreign money. The equilibrium condition for the non-traded good is given as

$$Y^N(q) = C^N(q, w). \tag{7.49}$$

Since, by definition, the non-traded good can only be consumed at home, relative price movements will ensure that (7.49) holds continuously.

The current account surplus, or deficit, can be shown to be linked to the economy's savings or dissavings in the following way. If agents are assumed to have a *constant* desired target level of real wealth, $\bar{w}$, then savings, a, may be represented as the excess of desired over actual real wealth, that is,

$$a = \beta(\bar{w} - w), \quad \beta > 0. \tag{7.50}$$

Hence if actual wealth is below desired wealth agents will be saving, and conversely if w is greater than $\bar{w}$ agents will be dissaving. Since a is simply the difference between disposable income and consumption (i.e. $Y^D - C$) we have:

$$a = (Y^T - C^T) + (i^* + \Delta s^e)SF, \tag{7.51}$$

where we have used condition (7.49) to justify the exclusion of $(Y^N = C^N)$. Equation (7.51) is simply an alternative representation of equation (7.48): the current account surplus/deficit is equal to savings/dissavings.

Before considering the workings of the model we must say a little about expectations. At all points of time, asset prices – the domestic interest rate, the exchange rate and the expected change in the exchange rate (noting the foreign interest rate is assumed to be exogenous) – are determined by the outstanding asset shocks. But the asset system (7.37)–(7.40) will, on its own, be indeterminate, since we have three equations, only two of which are independent, and three unknowns. Thus we need to introduce a further relationship to capture expectations. Two assumptions are common in this vintage of model: either static expectations where $\Delta s^e = 0$, or rational expectations where we require the further equation

$$\Delta s^e_{t+1} = \Delta s_{t+1} + \varepsilon_{t+1} \tag{7.52}$$

which says that the expected change in the exchange rate equals the actual change plus a white-noise error. Given some expectational assumption, the asset sector determines the spot exchange rate, S, and the domestic interest rate, i. In this chapter we shall assume that expectations are static.[14]

To illustrate the effects of various shocks in our asset market model, it will prove useful, for pedagogic purposes, to think of the model in terms of three separate periods: an impact period, a short-run adjustment period and long-run equilibrium. The impact period is concerned with the instantaneous adjustment of the asset markets following a shock. The short-run period is one in which the prices determined in the impact period have 'real' effects and result in changes in flows over time. In particular, the asset prices determined in the impact period will have implications for the overall price level and this will result in a discrepancy between actual and desired wealth, which, in turn, has consequences for savings and the current account. Such flow magnitudes will eventually force the economy to a new long-run steady-state equilibrium with zero savings and a zero current balance.

The workings of the model can be illustrated diagrammatically in the following way. Consider, first, the asset sector. Figure 7.5 shows combinations of i and S which hold the demand for money equal to its supply (equation (7.38)) (MM), the demand and supply of domestic bonds in equality (equation (7.39)) (BB) and the demand and supply of foreign assets in equality (equation (7.40)) (FF). An intuitive explanation of the relative slopes of the schedules in Figure 7.5 is as follows. Taking money M and bonds B first, from a position of portfolio equilibrium an increase in the price of foreign currency will increase wealth by revaluing the foreign asset (i.e. making it larger in home currency terms) in equation (7.37) and thus will create an increased demand for both M and B to restore portfolio equilibrium.

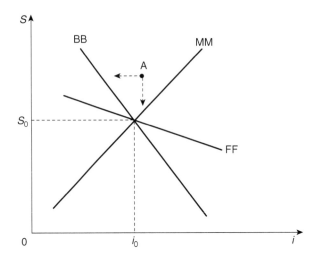

Figure 7.5 Asset market equilibrium.

As the demand for money rises, for a given supply, i (the opportunity cost of holding money) must rise to maintain money market equilibrium – hence the positive MM curve in S–i space. The BB curve has a negative slope since the increased demand for bonds, for a given supply, raises their price and results in a lower rate of interest. The negative slope of the FF schedule may be explained by a fall in i which increases the attractiveness of foreign assets leading to a rise in S. Then BB is steeper than FF because domestic demand for domestic bonds is more responsive than domestic demand for foreign assets to changes in the domestic rate of interest (this follows from the assumed gross substitutability of assets).

The three schedules in Figure 7.5 will shift in response to various asset disturbances. For example, an increase in the money supply will shift the MM schedule to the left since, for a given value of S, the interest rate must fall to restore portfolio balance. An increase in the supply of bonds shifts the BB schedule to the right since, for a given value of S, the interest rate on bonds must rise (price must fall) for the supply to be willingly held. An increase in the foreign asset F will result in the downward movement of FF since, for a given value of i, the maintenance of portfolio balance requires an exchange rate appreciation.

Because of the wealth constraint (7.37), we know that only two of the three asset equations are independent. Thus, if a given change restores equilibrium in two markets, the third market must also be in equilibrium. In order to analyse various shocks it is therefore legitimate to concentrate on only two schedules. In what follows we concentrate either on the combination of BB and MM or on BB and FF. Using the combination BB and FF we may illustrate that the portfolio system is globally stable. Consider point A in Figure 7.5, a point which is above the BB–FF intersection. For a given value of S the interest rate is too high for bond market equilibrium. This will generate an excess demand for such bonds, a rise in their price and a fall in their yield, namely i. Similarly, for a given i the exchange rate at A is too high for foreign asset market equilibrium: agents will attempt to sell foreign assets and convert the proceeds into domestic currency. This process will cause the exchange rate to appreciate (S falls). Hence at A the arrows of motion point towards the BB and FF schedules. Using similar reasoning, we may infer the arrows of motion for the other sectors in the diagram. So starting from a point such as A, the system may be expected to follow the path indicated by the broken line.

In Figure 7.5 we have examined the short-run determination of the domestic interest rate and exchange rate from the point of view of asset market equilibrium. To illustrate goods market equilibrium, we introduce Figure 7.6 which shows the domestic production and consumption of traded goods ($Y_T Y_T$ and $C_T C_T$) as, respectively, positive and negative functions of the exchange rate. Thus, for a given price of non-traded goods, an increase in the price of traded goods leads to a reduction in consumption as consumers switch from traded to non-traded goods (see equations (7.43) and (7.44)) and an increased relative production of traded goods (see equations (7.41) and (7.42)). An increase (decrease) in wealth shifts the $C_T C_T$ schedule to the right (left) and leaves $Y_T Y_T$ unaffected. An increase (decrease) in the price of non-traded goods shifts the $C_T C_T$ schedule to the right and the $Y_T Y_T$ schedule to the left. These latter shifts occur because, while we have S on the vertical axis in Figure 7.6, a change in P^N for given S will also impact the real exchange rate as $q = S/P^N$. This, in turn, will affect the allocation of consumption and production between traded and non-traded goods. As we shall see later, P^N will vary under pressure from excess demand for non-traded goods.

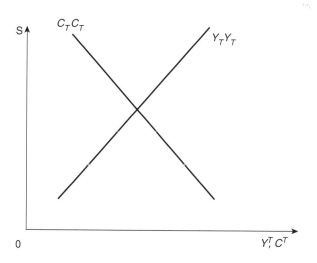

Figure 7.6 Goods market equilibrium.

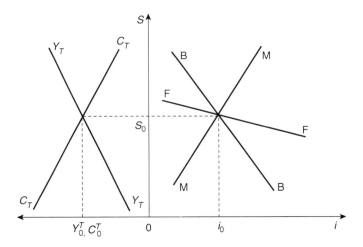

Figure 7.7 Asset and goods market equilibrium in the portfolio balance model.

In Figure 7.7 we combine Figures 7.5 and 7.6 to give a representation of joint asset and goods market equilibrium as i_0, S_0, Y_0^T, C_0^T. Consider now a number of shocks which upset the system's initial equilibrium. In particular, we consider an open market swap of money for bonds, an increase in the supply of bonds and an asset preference shift between home and foreign bonds.

7.4   Open market purchase of bonds: monetary policy

7.4.1   *Impact period*

We first consider the impact effect on asset markets of an open market purchase of bonds for money. An open market purchase of bonds for money by the central bank, in the impact period, will shift the BB and MM curves leftwards to BB′, MM′ in Figure 7.8. At the initial equilibrium, X, the open market purchase of bonds leaves asset holders with an excess supply of money and excess demand for bonds. In their attempts to buy bonds, investors will push the domestic interest rate down and this, in turn, will lead to an increased demand for foreign bonds which will push the exchange rate upwards until the excess demand for foreign bonds is eliminated. If it is assumed that the domestic interest elasticity of demand for money is less than the domestic interest elasticity of the demand for foreign bonds, then the percentage change in the demand for foreign bonds will be greater than the percentage increase in the money stock. Given that there is a one-to-one relationship between S and F, this implies that the exchange rate change will be larger than the money supply change: the exchange rate overshoots. The impact period equilibrium is given at point Y.

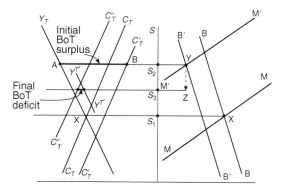

Figure 7.8 An open market purchase of bonds for money.

Note
BoT: balance of trade.

7.4.2 The short-run adjustment period and the move to the new long-run equilibrium

Although the valuation effect of the exchange rate on the foreign asset will on impact result in a rise in nominal wealth, once we move to the short-run period this will be offset by the effect the exchange rate overshoot has on the price index and thus real wealth: actual real wealth in the short-run period will fall short of desired real wealth. This mismatch of desired and actual real wealth implies, via equation (7.50), that agents must be saving and thus running a current account surplus (see equation (7.48)) during the adjustment period. Thus the desire to restore the initial value of desired wealth can only be realized by the country running a current account surplus and accumulating the foreign asset. This is possible since in the impact period relative prices have moved in favour of the traded goods sector, inducing a switch in production from non-traded goods. The current account surplus over time forces the price of foreign currency downwards (i.e. F is rising and so S must be falling), leading to a diminution of the savings rate until equilibrium is restored.

The shifts in the $C_T C_T$ and $Y_T Y_T$ functions are shown in Figure 7.8:

1 $C_T C_T$ initially shifts to the right to $C'_T C'_T$ (meaning less consumption of T goods) as residents increase their saving rate to restore their real wealth.
2 As real wealth increases back to its initial level, and the desire to save declines, $C_T C_T$ gradually regains its initial position. However,
3 $C_T C_T$ will shift further left beyond its initial position because the price of non-traded goods (P^N) has increased under the pressure of excess demand for non-traded goods (caused by the depreciation of S). Finally,
4 the increased P^N also causes the $Y_T Y_T$ function to shift to the right – meaning lower production of T goods.

Notice that at the new equilibrium the country is running a trade balance deficit. This may be explained in the following way. If, in the initial equilibrium, the price of traded goods equalled the price of non-traded goods, in the new equilibrium the relative price of traded goods will have fallen: the increase in the money supply has not led to a proportionate increase in the price level. This follows because in the adjustment period the home country has been accumulating foreign assets and in the new equilibrium interest receipts on the foreign assets must be greater than the initial equilibrium. Since the current account is the sum of the trade balance plus interest earnings and since a zero current balance is a condition of steady-state equilibrium, the positive interest earnings must be offset by a trade balance deficit. The latter is induced by a fall in the real exchange rate (i.e. P^N rises relative to P^T).[15] Isard (1977) has described this effect as the 'knock-out punch' to PPP!

The adjustment of the asset equilibrium schedules in Figure 7.8 from the impact equilibrium to the new long-run equilibrium is indicated by the arrow from Y to Z. Thus the accumulation of the foreign asset during the adjustment period will require an exchange rate appreciation for the maintenance of foreign asset equilibrium: the FF schedule shifts downwards. The accumulation of F over time also increases the size of the portfolio and thus the demand for bonds and money will rise. The increase in the demand for the former will lead to a leftward shift of the BB' curve (i.e. for a given exchange rate, the increased demand for bonds will force the price up and the interest rate down) and the increased demand for money will push MM' to the right over time.

In summary, the open market purchases set off portfolio and asset price adjustments. On *impact*, i falls and S depreciates, overshooting in fact, as the excess of money causes substitution into both domestic and foreign bonds. In the *short run*, as wealth on balance has fallen, residents increase their rate of saving via a current account surplus. As actual wealth now increases towards the desired level, the rate of saving falls and with it the size of the current account surplus – causing S to appreciate. In the *long-run* asset markets adjust, with the accumulation of foreign bonds setting off a desire to hold more money and domestic bonds.

In Figure 7.9 the profiles of the exchange rate, the trade balance and the capital account of the balance of payments are illustrated for the monetary shock. The monetary expansion takes place in period t_0 and the system has returned to long-run equilibrium in period t_n. In Figure 7.9(c) the initial sharp depreciation of the exchange rate is denoted as the move from S_0 to S_1. As we have seen, the exchange rate appreciates during the adjustment period and because of the non-homogeneity of the system does not return to its initial equilibrium by t_n. The trade account initially moves into surplus at t_0, but over time the effect of the appreciating exchange rate means that the country will be running a trade account deficit. In the new long-run equilibrium t_n, the country runs a trade deficit which is 'financed' by the interest earnings from the foreign asset. Since the condition of long-run equilibrium is that the current account equals zero, the capital account must also be balanced at t_n. Notice therefore that in contrast to the Mundell–Fleming model the expansionary monetary policy only has a transitory effect on the capital account: the stock–flow nature of the model ensures that this must be so.

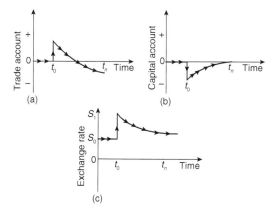

Figure 7.9 The adjustment profiles of (a) the trade account, (b) the capital account and (c) the exchange rate.

7.4.3 An increase in the supply of domestic bonds: fiscal policy

Consider now a once-and-for-all increase in the supply of bonds. (Although we have not explicitly modelled the public sector, this could follow from a bond-financed increase in government expenditure.) An increase in the supply of bonds increases wealth and, for a given domestic interest rate i, requires an increase in the exchange rate S to maintain the foreign exchange market in equilibrium; thus, the FF schedule in Figures 7.10 and 7.11 shifts rightwards to FF'. For a given value of the exchange rate the increased supply of domestic bonds will require an increase in the domestic interest rate to maintain bond market equilibrium: the BB schedule shifts rightwards and the new equilibrium is at Y. The increased bond supply exceeds any wealth-induced increase in bond demand and the domestic interest rate is unambiguously raised.

The effect on the exchange rate of an increase in the stock of domestic bonds is in fact ambiguous. This is because the rise in the domestic interest rate will induce a reduced demand for foreign assets and this will tend to offset the increased demand for foreign fixed price bonds due to the wealth effect. The ultimate effect depends on whether F and B or B and M are the closer substitutes.

7.4.3.1 New bond issue and currency depreciation

Assuming that B and M are better substitutes than F and B, the issue of B causes currency depreciation at Y in Figure 7.10, despite higher i attracting some capital inflow. This comes about because residents are, by assumption, not strongly attempting to swap foreign bonds, F, for B to obtain the higher rate of interest. The adjustment from Y to the new long-run equilibrium at, say, Z will be the same as for the open market operation – lower wealth reducing the demand for B and F.

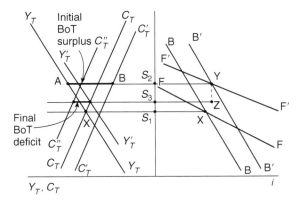

Figure 7.10 An increase in the supply of bonds and currency depreciation.

Note
BoT: balance of trade.

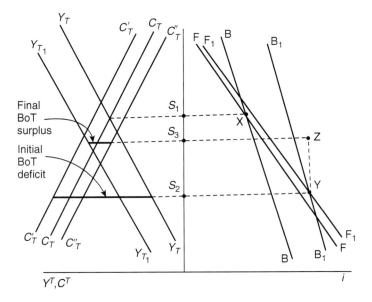

Figure 7.11 An increase in the supply of bonds which causes currency appreciation.

Note
BoT: balance of trade.

On the production and consumption side too, the outcome is the same as with the open market operation. Thus, at Y real wealth will have fallen, agents will be saving and real wealth will be reaccumulated over time, pushing $C_T C_T$ first to the right and then back to the left as the level of actual wealth recovers. Moreover, as the price of non-traded goods will have risen owing to excess demand for them at the depreciated exchange rate S_2, the substitution effect out of non-traded into traded goods will have the economy ending up with $C_T''C_T''$. On the production side, the rise in P^N works against traded goods production and Y_TY_T shifts to $Y_T'Y_T'$. Thus, the initial balance of trade surplus at S_2 turns into an ultimate trade deficit at S_3, which is financed by interest income on the foreign bonds accumulated through the earlier trade surplus.

7.4.3.2 *New bond issue and currency appreciation*

If F and B are regarded as better substitutes for each other then the exchange rate will be appreciated (lower) at Y in Figure 7.11 because the shift in demand from F to B as a result of the rise in i will be greater the closer are F and B regarded as substitutes (relative to B and M). This coupling of appreciation and bond financing actually occurred in the US during the period 1981–5.

With the issue of new bonds raising wealth, FF and BB shift so that S appreciates to S_2, the price level falls, and actual wealth increases relative to desired wealth. These events set off the following adjustments:

1   C_TC_T shifts left to $C_T'C_T'$ owing to the wish to reduce actual real wealth to the desired level – which is achieved through a trade and current account deficit and capital inflow at S_2.
2   As actual real wealth gradually falls back to its desired level, $C_T'C_T'$ steadily shifts back to C_TC_T.
3   However, the consumption of traded goods will fall even more than this to $C_T''C_T''$ because the relative price of non-traded goods has fallen.
4   Finally, Y_TY_T shifts left to $Y_T'Y_T'$ due to the lower price of non-traded goods which encourages greater traded goods production.

Thus, the initial position at S_1 is one of trade balance (assuming no accumulation of foreign assets). Following the issue of bonds the currency appreciates to S_2 when there is a payments deficit financed by capital inflow. This is a version of the famous 'twin deficits'. But S_2 cannot be sustained as interest payments must be made on the accumulated foreign debt. The exchange rate depreciates from its overshot position at S_2 to S_3 so creating a balance of trade surplus exactly equal to the interest payments. At which point the current account is balanced so that actual wealth remains at its desired level.

In the long-run, a higher exchange rate than S_2 is needed due to the increase in wealth raising the demand for F and B so BB and FF again shift to pass through Z.

7.4.4 *Asset preference shift*

If, due to a perceived increased riskiness, domestic bonds become more attractive than foreign bonds, what effect will this have in the impact period and in the short-run adjustment to a new equilibrium? Such a shock is illustrated in Figure 7.12.

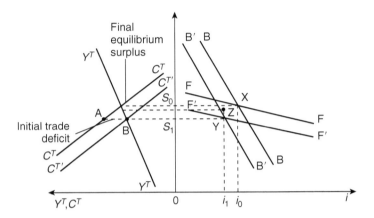

Figure 7.12 A shift in asset preferences.

At the initial equilibrium, the increased demand for domestic bonds can only be satisfied by a reduction in the rate of interest, giving the leftward shift from BB to BB′. Equally the attempt to move out of foreign bonds can, in the impact period, only be satisfied by a leftward shift of the FF schedule. Thus the impact effect of a change in asset preferences from foreign to domestic bonds results in a reduction in the interest rate and the exchange rate: from i_0 to i_1 and from S_0 to S_1.

Moving from the impact period to the short-run adjustment period, we find that private sector wealth has increased due to the fall in the price of the traded good and thus w must be greater than $\bar{w}$ and agents dissaving. This is illustrated in the left hand side of Figure 7.12 where the initial current account deficit is equal to AB. Over time this deficit will result in a loss of the foreign asset and a reduction in wealth which pushes $C_T C_T$ to the right and the exchange rate upwards. If the domestic economy lost foreign assets during the adjustment period it would end up with a final equilibrium at a point such as Z.

7.5   Empirical evidence on currency substitution

As was demonstrated earlier in this chapter, the concept of CS has an important bearing on the insulation properties of a floating exchange rate system. Thus it seems worthwhile to ascertain if the hypothesis is empirically verifiable. Before considering the empirical studies which attempt to directly test for CS it is worth noting that Bilson (1979a) has interpreted the coefficient on the relative interest rate term in monetary approach equations as a measure of the substitutability of currencies. But as Bilson recognizes, it is impossible to discern whether this reflects substitution between currencies, between the home currency and bonds, or between the home currency and goods. As we shall see, this problem plagues nearly all the empirical studies of CS.

One of the first empirical studies of CS was conducted by Miles (1978). Out of a total portfolio of assets (money and non-money) the private sector decides to hold M_0 cash balances. Since the CS literature predicts that both domestic and foreign money provide money services, the problem is to decide the proportion of M_0 to be held in M and M^*. The choice between domestic and foreign money is captured by Miles (1978) in the following way. Following the functional form used by Chetty (1969) in his study of the nearness of near-moneys, Miles assumes that domestic and foreign real money balances are inputs into a constant elasticity of substitution (CES) production function for money services. This production function is then maximised subject to an 'asset constraint' of the form

$$\frac{M_0}{P} = \frac{M}{P}(1+i) + \frac{M^*}{P^*}(1+i^*), \tag{7.53}$$

which reflects the assumption that there is an opportunity cost to holding real balances, i, and that this opportunity cost may differ between two types of balances, i^*. By maximising the money services production function subject to the asset constraint and assuming that PPP holds, Miles obtains:

$$\log(M/M^*S) = a + \sigma \ln(1 + i^*/1 + i), \tag{7.54}$$

where σ is a measure of the elasticity of substitution between the home and foreign money balances. Equation (7.54) has been estimated by Miles (1978) for the Canadian dollar–US dollar, and in Miles (1981) for US dollar and German mark holdings relative to foreign currency holdings (the interest rates being treasury bill rates). The results are reported in Table 7.1 for the fixed and floating period.

Notice that for the three countries considered, the elasticity of substitution term is large and statistically significant (marginally so for Canada–US) in the floating period, but relatively small and insignificant in the fixed rate period. Miles concludes from this that in periods of fixed exchange rates central banks make currencies perfect substitutes on the supply side, and thus agents do not need to substitute on the demand side, but that in periods of floating exchange rates and little or no government intervention agents have to undertake the substitution mechanism themselves.

But Miles has been taken to task over his implementation of the CS model by a number of researchers. For example, Bordo and Choudri (1982) argue that the same problem with interpreting the coefficient in monetary approach equations as an elasticity of substitution applies to equation (7.54). Thus, for example, if the foreign rate of interest rises we would expect domestic residents to substitute away from both domestic and foreign currency towards foreign bonds. The significant positive coefficient in the estimated version of equation (7.54) may simply reflect a greater elasticity in the demand for foreign currency with respect to foreign interest rates. By respecifying equation (7.54), in an attempt to capture the separate effects of currency substitution and currency bond substitution, Bordo and Choudri (1982) show that σ becomes insignificant and wrongly signed for the Canadian dollar–US dollar. Laney *et al.* (1984) criticise Mile's results from a slightly different perspective.

Table 7.1 Some currency substitution evidence

	c	σ	R^2	DW	ϱ
Canada–US					
1962 $Q3 - 1970$	2.31	2.66	0.78	1.41	0.9
Q2	(12.7)	(0.79)			
1970 $Q3 - 1975$	2.79	5.78	0.79	1.27	0.8
Q4	(16.1)	(1.83)			
US–Foreign currency					
1967 $Q1 - 1971$	5.89	0.14	0.44	1.97	0.65
Q2	(59.10)	(0.04)			
1971 $Q3 - 1978$	5.61	5.08	0.72	1.96	0.81
Q3	(39.34)	(3.38)			
Germany–Foreign currency					
1965 $Q1 - 1967$	4.48	1.51	0.69	2.0	0.81
Q2	(26.71)	(0.51)			
1971 $Q3 - 1978$	3.71	2.78	0.89	2.28	0.97
Q3	(5.71)	(2.23)			

Source: Miles (1978, 1981).

Note
t ratios in parentheses.

They argue that actual foreign currency holdings are extremely small relative to domestic money holdings. For example, in 1981 US foreign currency holdings amounted to $3 billion whereas total narrowly defined money amounted to over $400 billion. Additionally, well over a half of the US foreign currency holdings are designed as short-term investments rather than deposits and thus they may be more reflective of international capital mobility rather than CS (although see McKinnon's (1982) argument discussed in Section 7.2). Thus the effect of CS on the domestic money supply is likely to be trivially small. Indeed when Laney *et al.* use Miles's elasticity of substitution estimate in a standard demand for money function, they show that the elasticity of domestic interest rates is only affected by an amount equal to −0.003 due to currency substitution, which is much less than typical estimates of domestic interest rate elasticity (namely, −0.100).

A number of other studies attempt to determine the effects of CS on the demand for a currency using either single-equation money demand functions (see Hamburger 1977: Hamburger and Wood 1978; Broughton 1979; Alexander 1980; Vaubel 1980; Brittain 1981; Bordo and Choudri 1982; Howard and Johnson 1982; Johnson 1982); or portfolio models (see Chrystal 1977 and Brillembourg and Schadler 1979). This evidence has been usefully summarized by Spinelli (1983) in the following way:

1   The CS is never found to be close to infinite, or just high, not even for two highly integrated economies, such as the United States and Canada (Alexander 1980; Bordo and Choudri 1982) or of countries with no contraint

at all on capital movements, such as Switzerland (Vaubel 1980; Howard and Johnson 1982).

2   Statistically significant cross elasticities are not at all easy to detect. To quote from Brillembourg and Schadler (1979, p. 527), 'Of the off-diagonal terms of the matrix [of elasticities], only about one-fifth are significantly different from zero at the 95% confidence level …'

3   Generally speaking (Chrystal 1977 gives a few exceptions), the estimated values for the cross elasticities are so low that they tend to fall between 1/4 and 1/10 of those for the own elasticities.

4   It is not quite clear what the pattern of CS is. However, if the most weight is attached to the results by Brillembourg and Schadler (1979), one could infer that the demand for US dollars and Japanese yen is relatively unaffected by changes in the rates of return on foreign currencies, while there appears to be some degree of complementarity between the US dollar and the Deutsche mark. Hence, the case for a monetary union between the US, Japan, and the Federal Republic of Germany is far from obvious.

It would seem difficult to conclude, from the evidence presented above, that the CS hypothesis is particularly well supported by the data. It may be argued that this is because of the difficulty a researcher faces in actually discriminating between CS and traditional capital mobility. Cuddington (1983) attempts to isolate the two effects by specifying and estimating a general portfolio balance model where domestic residents demand for foreign money is distinguished from their demands for foreign non-monetary assets. Cuddington's empirical results 'bring into question the empirical as well as theoretical relevance of currency substitution' (see also Cuddington 1982). In sum, the empirical literature seems to indicate that the concept of CS offers does not offer any insights that cannot be gained from taking a conventional capital mobility perspective.

More recent work on CS has focussed on the concept of dollarisation (see Carlos and Vegh 1992 and Guidotti and Rodriguez 1992), the process of substituting a foreign currency for a domestic currency in order to satisfy the medium of exchange function of money (dollarisation can also fulfil the store of value function of money). Dollarisation can be either *de jure*, where a country officially adopts the currency of a foreign nation to wholly replace its currency (see Feige 2003) or *de facto* where economic agents voluntarily choose to substitute a foreign currency for the domestic currency as a means of payment or as a store of value. The latter may arise because of a loss of confidence in the domestic currency or to the growth of underground or unrecorded economic activity. Advocates of dollarisation argue that the adoption of a strong foreign currency provides inflation disciplining, and thereby prevents currency and balance of payments crises emerging which, in turn, affects the level and volatility of interest rates and stimulates economic growth (Feige and Dean 2002). Critics of dollarisation point to the loss of seigniorage and a loss of an independent monetary policy.

Fiege (2003) evaluates the available evidence on the total amount of US dollars held abroad and concludes that roughly 50% of US currency was held abroad at the end of 2001, 29% of which was held in transition, or central European, countries. Feige also shows that such transition countries also hold considerable amounts European legacy countries currencies and eleven transition countries have more than 50% of their total currency supply in the form of foreign currency. Fiege (2003) argues that the traditional IMF dollarisation index understates the magnitude of dollarisation because it relies exclusively on foreign currency deposits and does not take account of foreign currency in circulation (for measures of dollarisation and euroisation for transition countries see Feige and Dean (2002)). There is evidence that once dollarisation exists within a country it can become persistent and indeed irreversible (see Guidotti and Rodriguez 1992 and Oomes 2001).

7.6   Econometric evidence on the portfolio balance approach

In testing the portfolio balance approach Branson *et al.* (1977) and Branson and Haltunen (1979) propose using variants of the following reduced form, which is derived from the asset sector of a two-country variant of the model considered in Section 7.4:

$$S_t = f(M_t, M_t^*, B_t, B_t^*, F_t, F_t^*) \qquad (7.55)$$

In a two-country setting asset accumulation emanating from the current account will have the same effect on the exchange rate as in the small country case as long as domestic residents' preference for the domestic bond is greater than their preference for the foreign bond.

Branson *et al.* (1977), arbitrarily drop the B and B^* terms from equation (11.19), and econometrically estimate the following equation for the deutschmark–US dollar exchange rate, over the period August 1971 to December 1976 (the sign of the effects of asset changes on the exchange rate are represented by a plus or minus sign above the assets and are interpretable in terms of our discussion in the theoretical section):

$$s_t = \alpha_0 + \alpha_1 m_t - \alpha_2 m_t^* - \alpha_3 f_t + \alpha_4 f_t^*, \qquad (7.56)$$

where the money supply terms are defined as M_1 and the foreign asset terms are proxied by cumulated current account balances. Although all of the estimated coefficients had the hypothesised signs, after correction for autocorrelation only one coefficient was statistically significant. To allow for any potential simultaneity bias induced by foreign exchange market intervention by the German authorities (i.e. $M_t = F_t + D_t$ and thus, if F_t is changed to modify S_t, M_t will be correlated with the error term, introducing simultaneous equation bias), Branson *et al.* (1977) estimated equation (11.20) using two stage least squares, but this did not lead to a substantial improvement of the results.

In Branson and Haltunen (1979), equation (7.56) is estimated for the mark–dollar rate for the larger sample period from August 1971 to December 1978, but the results are very similar to those in the earlier paper. In a further paper, Branson and Haltunen (1979) estimate equation (7.56) for the Japanese yen, French franc, Italian lira, Swiss franc and the pound sterling (all relative to the US dollar) for the period from July 1971 to June 1976. Their ordinary least squares results show most equations with statistically significant coefficients and signs which are consistent with the priors noted in equation (7.56). However, little reliance can be placed on their results since they suffer from acute autocorrelation. The latter could reflect a dynamic misspecification of the model or the exclusion of variables relevant to the portfolio approach. Indeed, Bisignano and Hoover (1983), in their study of the Canadian dollar, include domestic non-monetary asset stocks and report moderately successful econometric results. A further problem with the Branson *et al.* implementation of the portfolio model is that the use of bilateral exchange rates and cumulated current accounts implies that third country assets and liabilities are perfect substitutes. Bisignano and Hoover (1983) use strictly bilateral asset stocks in their study and this could be a further reason for their successful results (the use of cumulated current accounts by researchers is usually out of necessity and not choice: few countries publish the details of the ownership of assets).

Alternative tests of the portfolio balance approach have exploited the insight of Dooley and Isard (1982) that the portfolio model can be solved for a risk premium. It is argued that the risk premium term λ_t is a function of the factors that determine the supply of outside assets, that is government bonds. Thus, λ_t may be written as a function of the relative supplies of bonds:

$$\lambda_t = \frac{1}{\beta} \frac{B_t}{F_t S_t}. \tag{7.57}$$

The idea being that an increase in the relative supply of domestic bonds requires an increased risk premium for these assets to be willingly held in international portfolios. On substituting (7.57) into equation (7.36) the following equation is obtained:

$$\frac{B_t}{F_t S_t} = \beta(i_t - i_t^* - \Delta s_{t+k}^e), \tag{7.58}$$

or, re-expressing the left-hand side in logs,

$$b_t - s_t - f_t = \beta(i_t - i_t^* - \Delta s_{t \mid k}^e). \tag{7.59}$$

Thus, in order to diversify the resultant risk of exchange rate variability, investors balance their portfolios between domestic and foreign bonds in proportions that depend on the expected relative rate of return (or risk premium). Following Frankel (1983), equation (7.59) can be used to derive a generalised asset market representation of the exchange rate which is econometrically testable.

By rearranging equation (6.8) as

$$\varphi(s_t - \bar{s}_t) = \Delta p_{t+1} - \Delta p_{t+1}^* - \Delta s_{t+1}^e, \tag{7.60}$$

and by simultaneously adding the interest differential to $-\Delta s^e_{t+k}$, subtracting $(\Delta p^e_{t+k} - \Delta p^{e*}_{t+k})$ from the differential and solving for s_t the following equation is obtained:

$$s_t = \bar{s}_t - \frac{1}{\phi}[(i_t - \Delta p^e_{t+k}) - (i^*_t - \Delta p^{e*}_{t+k})] + \frac{1}{\phi}(i_t - i^*_t - \Delta s^{e*}_{t+k}) \tag{7.61}$$

which states that the exchange rate deviates from its long-run value by an amount proportional to the real interest differential and the risk premium. Furtheremore, substituting the standard monetary equation, rewritten here

$$\bar{s}_t = \beta_0(m_t - m^*_t) - \beta_1(y_t - y^*_t) + \beta_2(\Delta p^e_{t+k} - \Delta p^{e*}_{t+k}),$$

for the long-run equilibrium exchange rate (and again assuming that long-run values are given by their current actual values), the following equation can be derived:

$$s_t = \beta_0(m_t - m^*_t) - \beta_1(y_t - y^*_t) + \beta_2(\Delta p^e_{t+k} - \Delta p^{e*}_{t+k})$$
$$- \frac{1}{\phi}[(i_t - \Delta p^e_{t+k}) - (i^*_t - \Delta p^{e*}_{t+k})] + \frac{1}{\phi}(i_t - i^*_t - \Delta s^{e*}_{t+k}) \tag{7.62}$$

Relative bond supplies enter equation (7.62) via the last term. Thus, by substituting (7.59) into the last term in (7.62) and solving for s_t the following reduced-form relationship may be obtained:

$$s_t = \omega_0(m_t - m^*_t) + \omega_1(y_t - y^*_t) + \omega_2(\Delta p^e_{t+k} - \Delta p^{e*}_{t+k})$$
$$+ \omega_3(i_t - i^*_t) + \omega_4(b_t - f_t) \tag{7.63}$$

where the ω's are the reduced-form parameters, which are related in an obvious way to the underlying structural parameters. Note that this relationship is simply a version of the real interest differential model, discussed in the previous chapter, extended to include the relative bond supply term. Therefore the signs of ω_0 to ω_3 have the same interpretation as in the last chapter and the positive sign on ω_4 implies that an increase in the supply of domestic bonds relative to foreign bonds should result in an exchange rate depreciation because domestic bonds have become relatively risky.

Frankel (1983) tests equation (7.63) for the dollar–mark exchange rate in the period from January 1974 to October 1978 and a representative equation is reported here:

$$s_t = \underset{(0.31)}{0.50}(m_t - m^*_t) - \underset{(0.21)}{0.056}(y_t - y^*_t) - \underset{(0.47)}{0.36}(i_t - i^*_t)$$
$$+ \underset{(0.69)}{1.85}(\Delta p^e_{t+k} - \Delta p^{e*}_{t+k}) + \underset{(0.05)}{0.31}(b^*_t - f_t),$$

where standard errors are in parentheses. In this equation it is assumed that the US is the home country and Germany is the foreign country; however, b^*_t and f_t are, respectively, German holdings of the domestic (i.e. German) and home

(US) bond (this is why the labelling is perhaps a little confusing) and therefore the coefficient on $(b^* - f)_t$ should have a negative sign if the above modelling strategy is appropriate. The signs on money, income, interest rates and the inflation rate are all correct, although only the last-mentioned term is statistically significant. The risk premium term, $(b^* - f)_t$, although statistically significant is wrongly signed: an increase in the foreign asset relative to the home bond leads to an exchange rate depreciation, in contrast to the prior expectation. Thus, Frankel's estimates, at best, give somewhat mixed support to the portfolio balance approach.

A version of equation (7.63) has also been estimated by Hooper and Morton (1983) for the dollar effective exchange rate over the period 1973.II–1978.IV and they found that the risk premium term, assumed a function of the cumulated current account surplus (net of the cumulation of foreign exchange intervention) was neither significant nor correctly signed. However, both Blundell-Wignall and Browne (1991) and Cushman *et al.* (1997) find statistically significant exchange rate influences from cumulated current account balances.

The above-noted tests of the portfolio model all use 'in-sample' criteria to assess the model's performance. In addition to testing the out-of-sample performance of the monetary models considered in Chapter 9, Meese and Rogoff (1983) also assessed the out-of-sample forecasting performance of the portfolio model represented by equation (7.63) (see Chapter 6 for details of the Meese and Rogoff methodology). In common with their findings for the simple monetary models, Meese and Rogoff demonstrated that the portfolio balance variant of the equation was unable to beat the simple random walk. However, it is important to re-emphasise the point made in Chapter 6 that this could simply reflect the failure to take account of the underlying data dynamics.[16]

Cushman (2006) tests the portfolio balance model for the Canadian–US exchange rate using better asset data than in most of the earlier studies, discussed above, and he also addresses non-stationarity issues, using the methods of Johansen (1995) (none of the studies discussed above address issues arising from the non-stationarity of the data). The empirical implementation of the model produces two statistically significant cointegrating vectors, which are shown to be close approximations for the home and foreign asset demand functions of the theoretical model. The cointegrating relationships are then used to build a parsimonious error correction model which is shown to outperform a random walk in an out of sample forecasting exercise.

A somewhat different approach to assessing the validity of the portfolio model than using in-sample or out-of-sample criteria, is that proposed by Obstfeld (1982). He proposes estimating a four equation structural version of the portfolio model for the deutschmark–US dollar exchange rate over the period 1975–81 (the four equations are for money demand, money supply and home and foreign bond market equilibrium). The idea is to simulate the model over the sample period, under conditions of perfect foresight, and assess whether sterilized intervention (which amounts to a swap of domestic bonds for foreign bonds, with no implication for the money supplies in the home or foreign countries) would have been successful. If the portfolio balance model is appropriate such intervention should be effective in changing the exchange rate since bonds are assumed to be imperfect substitutes. In fact Obstfeld finds that sterilized intervention only has a miniscule effect on the exchange rate compared with non-sterilized intervention, which has a big effect. However, Kearney and MacDonald (1986) implement a similar methodology for the sterling–dollar exchange rate over the period 1973–83 and find that sterilized intervention does seem to have a relatively big effect on the exchange rate. The effectiveness of sterilized intervention in the UK relative to Germany is attributed by Kearney and MacDonald to the UK's investment currency scheme whereby foreign exchange reserves were rationed throughout the period up to 1979.

In sum, the above selection of empirical studies on the portfolio balance approach are not particularly supportive of the model. But perhaps this should not be surprising: the paucity of good data on non-monetary aggregates (in particular their distribution between different countries), and, as noted above, the relatively primitive specifications of the reduced forms tested, perhaps do not give the portfolio balance approach a fair 'crack of the whip'. We return to some empirical evidence on the validity of the portfolio balance model in Chapter 15 where we examine the literature which seeks to model the risk premium.

The evidence presented in this chapter offers rather mixed support for the portfolio balance model, although the recent work of Cushman (2006) suggests that when an estimation method which recognises the non-stationarity of the data is used, along with good quality data on asset stocks, results supportive of the portfolio model can be recovered.

8 Real exchange rate determination

Theory and evidence

In this chapter we move away from the long-run exchange rate framework provided by PPP and the monetary model to a more eclectic exchange rate model, which combines both real and nominal factors. In particular, we have seen from our discussion of the recent literature on PPP that it takes about 8 years for a deviation from PPP to be extinguished. As we noted in Chapter 3, part of the explanation for this slow mean reversion might lie in the existence of transportation costs which introduce non-linear thresholds. An alternative explanation is that there may be 'real' factors (one of these being the Balassa–Samuelson effect, considered in Chapter 2) which introduce systematic variability into the behaviour of real and nominal exchange rates and in this chapter we examine some recent work which seeks to model this systematic variability. Also considered in this chapter are a number of other issues relating to real exchange rates such as real exchange rate volatility and real interest rate parity.

This chapter has four main sections. In Section 8.1 we present a model, due to Mussa (1984) and Frenkel and Mussa (1986), which neatly introduces some of the key determinants of exchange rates when PPP does not hold continuously. We refer to this model as an eclectic exchange rate model (EERM) because it combines elements of the asset market approach considered in Chapters 4–7, along with traditional balance of payments characteristics and forward-looking expectations. In Section 8.2 we present some empirical estimates of exchange rate models, starting with the real interest parity condition and then moving on to some direct estimates of the EERM model and variants of this model. Finally, in Section 8.3 we present an overview of the literature that seeks to decompose real exchange rates into permanent and transitory components and, relatedly, real and nominal sources. The main objective of this literature is to assess if the source of real exchange rate volatility lies in the assymetrical adjustment between goods and asset markets (asset markets adjust instantly while goods markets adjust slowly), as suggested by Dornbusch (1976) and others, or if it is real shocks which drive the real exchange rate, along the lines suggested by Stockman (1988).

8.1 An eclectic real exchange rate model

In this section we discuss a model of the exchange rate which combines asset market attributes with traditional balance of payments characteristics. The model may be viewed as a general equilibrium model of the exchange rate and we label it the eclectic exchange rate model (EERM). It has a number of attractions. First, since it incorporates aspects of the asset market approach, like the monetary models discussed in the last chapter, it captures key features of exchange rate behaviour, such as the current spot price being closely tied to the expected price. Second, by incorporating concepts from the balance of payments equilibrium condition, flow elements, such as those suggested in the portfolio balance approach to the exchange rate, are introduced into the process of exchange rate determination. In particular, the model recognises that changes in net foreign asset holdings and real shocks generate changes in the balance of payments that may require real exchange rate adjustment, even in equilibrium. This seems a particularly attractive feature of the model since, as we noted in Chapter 2, PPP on its own does not seem sufficient to explain the equilibrium behaviour of exchange rates. A further advantage of the explicit modelling of a balance of payments sector, in combination with a monetary sector, is that it introduces issues of sustainability in a natural way (a characteristic emphasised in the fundamental equilibrium exchange rate (FEER) approach to exchange rate modelling discussed in the next chapter).

A useful starting point for our discussion here is the definition of the real exchange rate introduced previously as:

$$q = p - (s + p^*), \tag{8.1}$$

where p denotes the logarithm of the domestic price of domestic goods, p^* denotes the logarithm of the foreign price of foreign goods and s the logarithm of the domestic price of one unit of foreign exchange. When a variable is not explicitly dated in this section it is assumed to be contemporaneous, that is, period t. The logarithm of the general price level, P, in the home country is assumed to be a weighted average of p and $s + p^*$:

$$P = \sigma p + (1 - \sigma) \cdot (s + p^*) = s + p^* + \sigma q, \tag{8.2}$$

where σ denotes the weight of domestic goods in the domestic price index. Expression (8.2) may be used to define the expected nominal exchange rate in period n, as:

$$E_t s_n = E_t P_n - E_t p_n^* - \sigma E_t q_n. \tag{8.3}$$

This decomposition of the expected nominal exchange rate illustrates three key channels of exchange rate determination in this model; two of these, P and p, are consistent with the exchange rate continually tracking PPP, whilst the third is clearly not. We now consider each of these channels in a little more detail.

8.1.1   The general price level channel and the demand and supply for money

As in standard monetary models of the balance of payments and exchange rate, we assume that the general price level is determined by the interaction of the demand and supply of money. In contrast to the standard money demand function that was used in Chapter 4, we follow Mussa (1984) in our use of a richer specification for this function. In particular, this specification includes, in addition to conventional domestic variables, currency substitution and portfolio balance (i.e. open economy) effects, as suggested by our discussions in Chapter 7. In particular, the logarithm of the home demand for money is assumed to be given by:

$$m^D = K + \alpha_1 P + \alpha_2 A + \alpha_3 s + \alpha_4 q - \alpha_5 i - \alpha_6 E_t \Delta s,$$
$$\alpha_1, \alpha_2, \alpha_3, \alpha_5, \alpha_6 > 0 \quad \text{and} \quad \alpha_4 <> 0, \tag{8.4}$$

where K captures all of the exogenous influences on the demand for money, such as real income effects, and A denotes the stock of net foreign assets (defined in terms of foreign currency – the foreign good) which is assumed to have a positive effect on the demand for money because it represents a wealth effect. The nominal exchange rate has a positive effect on the demand for money because a currency depreciation, by revaluing net foreign assets in domestic currency terms, increases domestic wealth. The relative price of domestic goods in terms of imported goods can affect the demand for money through a variety of channels (one being because of the effect on the value of domestic product). Both the domestic interest rate and the expected exchange rate change are negatively associated with the demand for money through the standard opportunity cost channel; in the case of $E_t \Delta s$, an expected depreciation of the domestic currency will, through a currency substitution argument, result in a switch out of domestic assets into foreign assets.

It is further assumed that the domestic interest rate is given by the familiar risk-adjusted uncovered interest rate parity condition:

$$i = i^* + E_t \Delta s + \lambda, \tag{8.5}$$

where λ denotes an exogenous risk premium. On using equations (8.1) through (8.5) we may express the condition of money market equilibrium, in which the demand for money is equal to the supply, as:

$$m = l + \gamma s + \phi E_t \Delta s, \tag{8.6}$$

where m denotes the supply of money, $\gamma = \alpha_1 + \alpha_3 > 0$, $\phi = \alpha_5 + \alpha_6 > 0$ and

$$l = K - \alpha_3 p^* - \alpha_5(i^* + \lambda) + (\alpha_4 - \sigma\alpha_3)q + \phi E_t \Delta p^* + \phi\sigma E_t \Delta q + \alpha_2 A. \tag{8.7}$$

If it is assumed that p^*, i^*, q and A are determined independently of the money supply we may obtain the following expression for the expected price level in period n.

$$E_t P_n = (1/(\gamma + \eta)) \cdot \sum_{j=0}^{\infty} \eta/(\gamma + \eta)^j \cdot E_t[m_{n+j} - l_{n+j}]. \tag{8.8}$$

In words (8.8) simply says that the expected price level in any period is the present discounted value of the present and expected stream of the excess demand for money. Changes in either the expected or unexpected component of this general price level will result in exchange rate changes which are consistent with PPP. Equation (8.8) also illustrates under what circumstances the nominal exchange rate may be more volatile than current fundamentals. Thus, if a current change in fundamentals signals to agents a revision in expected future fundamentals, this may generate excess volatility in the nominal exchange rate – the so-called magnification effect discussed in Chapter 4. Such effects are a key feature of asset market prices. As expression (8.3) makes clear, however, there is likely to be more to exchange rates than PPP in this model. The issue of how real factors affect the nominal exchange rate, independently of their effects through the demand for money, may be introduced by discussing the evolution of A and q.

8.1.2   The balance of payments and the real exchange rate

In this section we discuss how the term $\sigma E_t q_n$ may impinge on the nominal exchange rate using a balance of payments model of the determination of the exchange rate. The current account surplus of the balance of payments, ca, is defined as:

$$ca = \beta(z - q) + r^* A, \quad \beta > 0, \tag{8.9}$$

where, of variables not previously defined, z summarises the exogenous real factors that affect domestic excess demand and foreign excess demands for domestic goods and β is a reduced form parameter containing the relevant relative price elasticities.[1] Because the foreign country (or the rest of the world) is assumed to willingly absorb changes in assets in exchange for foreign goods, at the fixed foreign real interest rate r^*, the capital account deficit, cap, denotes the desired rate of accumulation of net foreign assets by domestic residents. The capital account deficit is assumed to be a function of the discrepancy between private agents' target level of net foreign assets, $\hat{A}$, and their current actual level, A, and the expected change in the real exchange rate:

$$cap = \mu(\hat{A} - A) - \alpha E_t \Delta q, \quad \mu, \alpha > 0. \tag{8.10}$$

There are two ways of interpreting the $E_t \Delta q$ term in (8.10). The first is to say it captures the influence of expected changes in the value of foreign goods, measured in terms of the domestic good, on the desired accumulation of foreign assets, or simply the influence of domestic real interest rates on desired savings (i.e. there is a condition of real interest parity between $E_t \Delta q$ and relative real interest rates).[2] The condition of balance of payments equilibrium requires that the current account surplus be matched by the capital account deficit:

$$\beta(z - q) + r^* A = \mu(\hat{A} - A) - \alpha E_t \Delta q. \tag{8.11}$$

Since the capital account position is driven by the desired accumulation of net foreign assets, we may interpret any current account imbalance given by (8.11) as sustainable. The issue of sustainability is a central feature of the internal–external balance view of the determination of the exchange rate considered in the next chapter. If we additionally assume that the evolution of net private holdings of foreign assets is determined by the current account surplus (in the absence of official holdings of foreign assets):

$$\Delta A = \beta(z - q) + r^* A, \tag{8.12}$$

then the two forward-looking difference equations (8.11) and (8.12) provide a solution for the two endogenous variables, A and q. The solution for the current (equilibrium) real exchange rate is given by:

$$q_t = \bar{q}_t + \tau(A_t - \bar{A}_t), \tag{8.13}$$

where a bar denotes an equilibrium, or desired, value. More specifically, we have:

$$\bar{q}_t = \bar{z}_t + (r^*/\beta)\bar{A}_t, \tag{8.14}$$

$$\bar{z}_t = (1 - \phi) \cdot \sum_{j=0}^{\infty} \phi^j \cdot E_t \bar{z}_{t+j},$$

$$\bar{A}_t = (1 - \phi) \cdot \sum_{j=0}^{\infty} \phi^j E_t \hat{A}_{t+j},$$

$$\phi = (1/(1 + \eta)) \text{ and } \tau = (\eta/\beta) - (1/\alpha) > 0,$$

and where η has the interpretation of a 'discount rate'. In the current context this may be shown to reflect the sensitivity of the current account surplus to the level of q and the sensitivity of the capital account deficit both to the expected change of q and to the divergence of net foreign assets from their target level.[3]

This framework usefully illustrates the dependence of the current value of the real exchange rate on two key factors. First, the current estimate of the long-run equilibrium real exchange rate, $\bar{q}_t$. This is the rate expected to be consistent with current account balance, on average (in present and future periods) and is driven by forward looking weighted averages of present and expected NFA and the exogenous real factors. As we saw in Chapter 7 the interaction between net foreign assets and the real exchange rate is a key factor in the portfolio balance class of models. This first factor emphasises the key aspect of an asset pricing relationship – changes in the expected stream affect the current price.

The second factor is the divergence between the current value of net foreign asset holdings and investors' current estimate of the long-run desired level of these holdings, $\bar{A}_t$. This may be thought of as a type of error correction of mechanism – the greater is A the lower the price which agents hold the stock, so the higher is q (i.e. the relative price of domestic to foreign goods). Given exogenous factors, the higher is q lower is trade balance surplus and the slower is the accumulation of foreign assets. So discrepancies between A and $\bar{A}_t$ introduce important dynamic interactions into the model.

As Mussa (1984) has emphasised, it is important to note that this model goes far beyond the traditional flow balance of payments view of the determination of the exchange rate outlined in Chapter 1. This is because $\bar{q}_t$ depends on the discounted sum of present and expected future z's, where it is assumed that such expectations are consistent with the economic forces that will actually determine the future real exchange rate, and also $\bar{A}_t$.

Net foreign assets are a crucial term in the EERM model. Masson, Kremers and Horne (1993) present a succinct summary of the long-run determinants of a country's net foreign asset position. In particular, they cite demographic factors, which reflect the age-structure of the population and have a bearing on cross-country variations in savings rates and hence net foreign asset positions. Second, in a world in which Ricardian equivalence is broken, a higher level of government debt, *ceteris paribus*, is associated with a lower net foreign asset position.

We therefore have two channels through which real factors can affect the nominal exchange rate, defined by (8.3). If the real factors have their affect solely through the demand for money, l, they will induce movements in the nominal exchange rate consistent with PPP. If, however, the real changes have their influence through q this will necessitate a change in the exchange rate and relative price configuration that implies a deviation from PPP. Nominal exchange rate movements associated with expected or unexpected changes in the discounted present value contained in P will be those consistent with PPP.

8.1.3   *The foreign price level*

The third, and final, determinant of $E_t s_n$ is $E_t p_n^*$, and movements in the latter variable will also generate expected nominal exchange rate movements which are consistent with PPP.

The above model is, we believe, an extremely useful conceptual framework for thinking about the determination of a country's exchange rate. It captures the effect of current and expected relative excess demand for money on the exchange rate in the way suggested by the asset approach to the exchange rate. Additionally, it allows for real exchange rate changes and, in particular, captures issues concerning the sustainability of current account imbalances and their implications for real and nominal exchange rates. In the next section we overview research which uses the kind of variables highlighted by the model presented in this section to model long- and short-run real and nominal exchange rates.

8.2 Empirical tests of real exchange rate models

8.2.1 Real interest rate parity

In order to examine the systematic components of real exchange rates, a number of researchers have focused on just one of the relationships of the model presented in the last section, namely the uncovered interest parity condition (8.5), expressed here in real terms, by subtracting the expected inflation differential from both the expected change in the exchange rate and the interest differential and setting the risk premium to zero:

$$E_t(q_{t+k} - q_t) = (_k r_t - _k r_t^*). \tag{8.15}$$

In expressing (8.15) in a form suitable for econometric testing most researchers follow Meese and Rogoff (1984) and assume the following adjustment equation for the real exchange rate:

$$E_t(q_{t+k} - \bar{q}_{t+k}) = \theta^k(q_t - \bar{q}_t), \quad 0 < \theta < 1, \tag{8.16}$$

where $\bar{q}_t$ is interpreted as the long-run or systematic (permanent) component of the real exchange rate. By assuming $\bar{q}_t$ follows a random walk:

$$E_t \bar{q}_{t+k} = \bar{q}_t \tag{8.17}$$

and on substituting (8.16) in (8.15), the following expression may be obtained:

$$q_t = \alpha_k(E_t q_{t+k} - q_t) + \bar{q}_t \tag{8.18}$$

where $\alpha_k \equiv 1/(\theta^k - 1)$. Noting that α_k goes to -1 as k tends to infinity, we get:

$$\bar{q}_t = q_t + \lim_{k \to \infty}(E_t q_{t+k} - q_t), \tag{8.19}$$

or, equivalently:

$$\bar{q}_t = \lim_{k \to \infty} E_t q_{t+k}.$$

On combining (8.15) with (8.19) the following expression may be obtained:

$$q_t = \alpha_k(_k r_t - _k r_t^*) + \bar{q}_t. \tag{8.20}$$

One strand of the literature based on (8.20) assumes it is the sticky price representation of the monetary model. If one is prepared to make the further assumption that *ex ante* PPP holds then $\bar{q}_t$ may be interpreted as the flexible price real exchange rate (which, as was implied by our earlier discussion, must simply equal a constant, or zero in the absence of transaction/transportation costs) and so (8.20) defines the deviation of the exchange rate from its long-run equilibrium in terms of a real interest differential. Papers that follow this interpretation are Baxter (1994) and Clarida and Galli (1994).

Regression-based estimates of the relationship between the real exchange rate and the real interest differential may conveniently be split into two sets: those which assume the equilibrium real rate is equal to a constant, and therefore do not explicitly model the underlying determinants of $\bar{q}_t$, and a group of papers which explicitly focus on trying to model such determinants.

Papers which assume the equilibrium real rate is constant focus on the following regression equation:

$$q_t = \beta_0 + \beta_1 r_t + \beta_2 r_t^* + \varphi_t, \qquad (8.21)$$

which may be derived from (8.20) by assuming $\bar{q}_t = \beta_0$. In an estimated version of (8.21) it is expected that $\beta_1 < 0$ and $\beta_2 > 0$. Some researchers put some structure on these coefficients. For example, when (8.21) is derived as a representation of the sticky price monetary model (see Edison and Melick 1995), the assumption of regressive exchange rate expectations implies that the coefficients β_0 and β_1 should be above plus 1 and minus 1, and inversely related to the underlying maturity. However, the reduced form relationship in 8.21 between real exchange rates and real interest rates can be derived without imposing regressive expectations and given possibly substantial measurement error, the only requirement on the estimated coefficients from (8.21) is that they be negative and positive, respectively.

Estimates which allow for a time varying equilibrium exchange rate assume that the latter is a function of variables like net foreign assets and productivity and include these variables into a regression equation like (8.21), in addition to the real interest rate terms.

8.2.2   Cointegration-based estimates of the RERI

By far the most popular method used to estimate (8.21), and its variants, involves using cointegration methods. For example, a variety of researchers have used Engle–Granger cointegration methods (see, *inter alia*, Meese and Rogoff 1988; Coughlin and Koedijk 1990; Edison and Pauls 1993; Throop 1994),[4] and have failed to uncover a statistically significant link between real exchange rates and real interest differentials[5] However, paralleling the work with PPP and unit root testing in real exchange rates, these results seem to be estimation-specific. When the Johansen method is used to tie down the real exchange rate–real interest rate relationship, clear evidence of cointegration is found.

For example, Edison and Melick (1995), MacDonald (1997) and MacDonald and Swagel (2000) used Johansen multivariate cointegration methods and found evidence of a unique cointegrating vector between a variety of real exchange rates and real interest rates; Edison and Melick find that this result only holds with long rates, while MacDonald and Swagel find it holds for both short and long rates.

Relatedly, Johansen and Juselius (1990) and MacDonald and Marsh (1997) find that when PPP is tested jointly with UIP, again using Johansen methods, strong evidence of cointegration is found (up to two significant vectors) which is evidence supportive of a relationship between real exchange rates and real interest rates.

MacDonald and Nagayasu (2000) use the panel cointegration methods of Pedroni to test the constant real equilibrium exchange rate variant of real interest rate parity. A panel of 14 industrialised countries relative to the US is used for the period 1976–97. Clear evidence in favour of the constant equilibrium variant of the RERI model is reported, in the sense of the existence of a cointegrating relationship and estimated slope coefficients which are in conformity with the model (are inversely related to maturity yield of the underlying bonds). Using a different panel approach Chortareas and Driver (2001), however, find no evidence of a long-run relationship in the context of a panel data set.

A number of researchers allow $\bar{q}_t$ to systematically change over time in response to, *inter alia*, productivity effects, fiscal imbalances, net foreign asset accumulation and terms of trade effects. The theoretical justification for the inclusion of these kinds of variables is taken from the kind of model discussed in Section 8.1. As in the estimates of the constant equilibrium variant of the model, the estimator used is important in determining the RERI link. Using the Engle–Granger two-step estimator, Meese and Rogoff (1988), Edison and Pauls (1993) and Coughlin and Koedjik (1990) fail to find any evidence of cointegration. For example, Coughlin and Koedjik (1990) sequentially regress the real exchange rate on the various candidates noted above and find no evidence of a cointegrating relationship for six bilateral real exchange rates. In contrast, using multivariate cointegration methods, Meese and Rogoff (1988) also find no evidence of cointegration and, additionally, confirm that their celebrated dictum that nominal exchange rate models cannot outperform a random walk, also holds for real rates.

In contrast to the above, Throop (1992), Edison and Melick (1995), MacDonald (1997) and Clark and MacDonald (1998) find clear evidence of cointegration in RERI relationships which allow $\bar{q}_t$ to systematically vary over time. For example, Throop (1992) uses both a two-step estimator and a dynamic error correction model, over the period 1982 quarter 1 to 1990 quarter 3, to reveal significant evidence of cointegration in systems containing the effective US dollar, and the US bilaterals of the yen, the mark and the pound sterling. Interestingly, the US effective is shown to dominate a random walk, in an out-of-sample forecasting contest, at horizons of one to eight quarters; however, the evidence for bilaterals is more mixed – in one-half of the horizons it is able to beat a random walk. Using the multivariate cointegration methods of Johansen (1995), Edison and Melick (1995) find some evidence of cointegration between real interest rates and bilateral real exchange rates, although they demonstrate that the cointegration result arises from the stationarity of the real interest differential. MacDonald (1997) also uses the Johansen cointegration estimation method and produces clear evidence of a significant cointegrating relationship for the effective rates of the mark, yen and dollar. Furthermore, these are shown to produce dynamic real exchange rate models capable of outperforming a random walk at horizons as short as 2 quarters.

In their systems, Clark and MacDonald (1998) report evidence of two significant cointegrating vectors, for the effective systems of the US dollar, the German mark and the Japanese yen. An example, for the effective US dollar over the period 1960 to 1996, here indicates the kind of relationships that may be recovered from this kind of system.

$$q_t = \underset{(0.04)}{0.084} \, l\text{tot} + \underset{(0.33)}{2.701} \, bs + \underset{(0.10)}{1.237} \, \text{nfa} - \underset{(0.01)}{0.004} \, \lambda + \underset{(0.014)}{4.595} \tag{8.22a}$$

$$r_t - r_t^* = \underset{(0.003)}{-0.014} \tag{8.22b}$$

where $l$tot is the log of the terms of trade, bs is a Balassa–Samuelson effect (measured as the ratio of CPI to WPI in the home country relative to the foreign country), nfa is net foreign assets, λ is a risk premium and standard errors are in parenthesis. All of the coefficients are correctly signed and all, apart from that on the relative debt term (the proxy for the risk premium), are statistically significant. The $\chi(4)$ test of whether the chosen restricted vectors span the cointegrating space has an estimated value of 5.49 and a marginal significance level of 0.24; the restrictions are easily satisfied at standard levels of significance.

The cointegration-based empirical evidence on the RERI relationship may be summarised as offering rather mixed support for the hypothesis, especially when it is not augmented with additional variables. However, Baxter (1994) was the first to note that there is in fact an inconsistency in estimating the RERI using cointegration-based methods and that this inconsistency may explain the failure of some researchers to find empirical support for the approach. Hoffman and MacDonald (2005) have elaborated this point and we follow their discussion here. Consider again equation (8.15) with rational expectations imposed

$$(q_{t+1} - q_t) = (r_t - r_t^*) + u_{t+1}, \tag{8.23}$$

where a one-period maturity is assumed and u_{t+1} is a random error term combining errors in forecasting inflation and the exchange rate. Since the disturbance term in (8.23) is stationary, it must follow that the left and right hand sides of the equation are integrated of the same order. Since, as we have seen, real exchange rates on a univariate basis are $I(1)$ processes, or close to $I(1)$ processes, $q_{t+1} - q_t$ must be $I(0)$ and therefore so too must $r_t - r_t^*$. However, with $r_t - r_t^*$ stationary it follows that the real exchange rate and the real interest differential cannot be cointegrated, unless in a 'trivial' sense where in an unconstrained regression of q_t, r_t and r_t^* the real interest rates cointegrate to become a stationary differential.

8.2.3   *Other tests of the RERI relationship*

Baxter (1994) forcefully argues that the failure of many empirical studies of the real interest rate/real exchange rate relationship to capture a significant relationship has to do with the use of a first difference operator to induce stationarity in the vector of variables. As we noted earlier, although the use of the difference operator ensures that $I(1)$ variables are transformed into stationary counterparts, it also removes all of the low frequency information from the data, some of which may be useful for tying down a desirable relationship. Moreover, from a theoretical perspective transforming the data using a first difference operator presupposes that the effect of real interest rates on the real exchange rate is permanent; however, to the extent that (8.21) represents a reduced form representation of the sticky price monetary model the relationship between the two variables would only be expected to be transitory.

In order to better understand the RERI model Baxter (1994) proposes an alternative specification to (8.21), namely one which relates the transitory component of the real exchange rate to the real interest differential (she assumes real interest rates are stationary). In regression equation form this is given as:

$$q_t^T = \alpha + \beta_k(_kr - {_kr_t^*}) + u_{kt}. \tag{8.24}$$

Such a relationship can be derived by assuming the real rate comprises permanent (q_t^P) and transitory (q_t^T) components and that the permanent component follows a random process. Using, alternatively, univariate and multivariate Beveridge–Nelson decompositions to derive q_t^T, and *ex post* and *ex ante* measures of the real interest differential, Baxter estimates (8.24) for a number of bilateral country pairings. The majority of her estimates of β turn out to be significantly negative, the only exception being those for the UK. Further, the majority of point estimates reported by Baxter are above unity, which (her version of) the model predicts, and it is noteworthy that this is the only paper on the RERI which establishes this result. MacDonald and Swagel (1998) use band pass filters to extract the business cycle component from both real exchange rates and real interest rates for bilateral and real effective exchange rates. They find very strong evidence of the real interest rate/real exchange rate relationship in the sense that coefficients are correctly signed and statistically significant.

Hoffman and MacDonald (2005) propose a correlation-based approach to estimating the RERI. This may be illustrated in the following way. Rewrite equation (8.15) as:

$$\lim_{k \to \infty} E(q_{t+k} - q_t) = -\alpha_k(_kr_t - {_kr_t^*}). \tag{8.25}$$

This equation indicates that the current real interest differential contains sufficient information for forecasting the expected long-run change in the real exchange rate. Hence although an econometrician may not have access to all of the information used by economic agents in their forecasting process, equation (8.25) indicates that current real interest rates should embody all of that information. Hoffman and MacDonald therefore extract two measures of the expected change in the real exchange rate from a VAR system comprising the real interest differential and the real exchange rate. For a selection of six currencies over the period 1978 quarter 1, to 1997 quarter 4, they report clear evidence that the real interest differential is closely correlated with the real interest differential.

8.2.4   Tests of the EERM

Based on the EERM model of Mussa (1984), discussed earlier, Faruqee (1995) uses the cointegration methods of Johansen to estimate equilibrium real exchange rate equations for the US and Japan. The real exchange rate used is the CPI-based real effective exchange rate and the conditioning variables are net foreign assets as a proportion of GNP, an index of the terms of trade. Two measures of productivity were additionally used as conditioning variables. They are the relative price of traded to non-traded goods, TNT, and comparative measure of labour productivity, PROD. Clear evidence of at least on cointegration is reported for both the US and Japanese systems. Focusing on the first significant vector the following result is obtained for the US:

$$\text{REER}_t = 1.47\text{nfa}_t + 0.91\text{tnt}_t - 0.30, \tag{8.26}$$

and, similarly, for Japan

$$\text{REER}_t = 0.66\text{PROD}_t, \tag{8.27}$$

these results were obtained by implementing exclusion restrictions on the full set of variables, indicated above.

MacDonald (1999b) tests the EERM using the methods of Johansen. In particular, expression (8.3) is rearranged into one which is analytically equivalent, namely:

$$s_t = (1/(\gamma + \eta)) \cdot \sum_{j=0}^{\infty} (\eta/(\gamma + \eta))^j \cdot E_t[m_{t+j} - k_{t+j}], \tag{8.28}$$

where we have set $t = n$ and

$$k = K + \alpha_1 p^* - \alpha_5(i^* + \lambda) + (\alpha_4 + \sigma\alpha_1)q + \alpha_2 A.$$

Expression (8.28) is useful from an estimation perspective for two key reasons. First, in the context of a present value model such as (8.28) if the dependent variable and the right hand side variables are integrated of order 1, $I(1)$, then it follows (see, for example, Campbell and Shiller (1987) and MacDonald and Taylor (1993)) that for the model to be valid s must be cointegrated with the right hand side variables. Second, the existence of cointegration facilitates the construction of a dynamic error correction model of the short-run exchange rate and its dynamic adjustment to the long-run equilibrium.

The long-run equilibrium relationship, or cointegrating vector, implied by (8.28) is given as:

$$\bar{s} = \beta_0 \bar{m} + \beta_1 \bar{y} + \beta_2 \bar{p}^* + \beta_3(\bar{i}^* + \bar{\lambda}) + \beta_4 \overline{\text{tnt}} + \beta_5 \overline{\text{tot}} + \beta_6 \bar{A}, \tag{8.29}$$

where

$$\beta_0, \beta_3 > 0, \quad \beta_1, \beta_2, \beta_4, \beta_5, \beta_6 < 0$$

and, for expository purposes, we have used a bar to denote a long-run equilibrium value, y, real income, has been substituted for K, tnt, the relative price of non-traded goods, and tot, the terms of trade, have been substituted for the real exchange rate and the β's are reduced form coefficients. In testing relationship (8.29) MacDonald used the multivariate cointegration methods of Johansen (1995) and finds clear evidence of cointegration in systems for the effective exchange rates of the US dollar, German mark and Japanese yen, over the period 1973 to 1993. In particular, the US dollar exhibited one cointegrating vector, the German mark two cointegrating vectors and the Japanese yen four cointegrating vectors. MacDonald attempted to interpret these vectors using the approach of Johansen and Juselius (1992). In particular, for a system with four cointegrating relationships this identification procedure amounts to the joint selection of four stationary relationships of the form:

$$\beta = \{H_1\phi_1, H_2\phi_2, H_3\phi_3, H_4\phi_4\}, \tag{8.30}$$

where H_1 to H_2 represent the specific hypothesis implemented on each of the cointegrating vectors and this can be interpreted as the joint selection of four stationary relationships which are fully specified and identified (in terms of the Johansen (1995) rank condition). The restricted vectors for Japan are reported in Table 8.1.

The idea underlying the identification in Table 8.1 is that the first vector is interpreted as an exchange rate relationship, the second as a money market system, the third as an expression for net foreign assets and the final vector represents the interaction between the terms of trade and the relative price of non-traded to traded prices. Imposing this structure across the four vectors produced a Wald statistic of 17.46 and a p-value of 0.06.

Table 8.1 Restricted cointegrating vectors for the Japanese yen effective exchange rate

S	y	P^*	i^*	tnt	tot	nfa	M
-1	0	-1.47	0.06	-1.08	0	0	0
		(0.08)	(0.004)	(0.16)			
0	2.13	0.11	0	0	0	0	-1
	(0.03)	(0.02)					
0	0	0	0	0	5.26	-1	0
					(0.29)		
0	0	0	0	-1	0.34	0	0
					(0.02)		

Source: MacDonald (1999b). Check coefficient on p in second coin vector of EERM.

Note
Standard errors in parenthesis.

Gagnon (1996) uses the panel equivalent to the single equation Phillips–Loretan estimator to estimate equilibrium exchange rate relationships. In particular, using an annual data set for 20 bilateral DM rates, over the period 1960 to 1995, he examines the effect of Balassa–Samuelson, NFA, and share of government consumption in total output. Two alternative measures of a Balassa–Samuelson effect are used – real per capita income and the ratio of CPI to WPI in the home relative to the foreign country – and only the relative price measure proves to be statistically significant. The government consumption ratio also does not exhibit any explanatory power. The only variable found to have a robust and significant relationship with the exchange rate, in both the short- and long-run, is the NFA term; an increase in NFA produces a real exchange rate appreciation of 24% in the short run and an approximate 10% appreciation in the long-run. Adjustment speeds in his different specifications range from -0.23 to -0.5, with the average being -0.4.

Kawai and Ohare (1998) examine monthly bilateral real exchange rates (defined using both CPI and WPI measures) for the G7 countries 1973–96. They also use the Johansen cointgeration method to demonstrate considerable evidence of cointegration amongst real exchange rates and the kinds of explanatory variables discussed above. For example, relative labour productivity is statistically significant and correctly signed in over one-half of the country pairs for which they define cointegration (productivity measure as industrial productivity per labour employed in the industrialised or manufacturing sector).

8.3 Decomposing real exchange rates into permanent and transitory components

In this section we present an overview of papers which seek to decompose real exchange rates into permanent and transitory components. A number of researchers have used the univariate and multivariate Beveridge–Nelson (BN) decompositions to decompose real exchange rates into permanent and temporary components. For example, Huizinga (1987) uses univariate BN decompositions to extract the permanent components of his chosen currencies. On average, he finds that around 90% of real exchange rate movements are permanent. As we shall see in Chapter 9, Huizinga proposed interpreting the permanent component of the real exchange rate as a measure of equilibrium and deviations from this permanent value as a measure of exchange rate misalignment.

Cumby and Huizinga (1990) use a multivariate BN decomposition (MBN) based on a bivariate VAR of the real exchange rate and the inflation differential and present a set of plots of the permanent component of the real exchange rate against the actual real rate for the $–DM, $–Yen, $–Sterling and $–C$. In general, the permanent components of these real rates are shown to exhibit substantial time-variability, but to be more stable than the actual real exchange rate. Their key message is that there are often large and sustained deviations of real exchange rates from their permanent values and such deviations are interpreted as being driven by the business cycle component.

Clarida and Gali (1994) present both univariate and multivariate (the latter are generated from a trivariate VAR consisting of the change in the real exchange rate, the change in output and the inflation rate) BN decompositions of the real exchange rates of Germany, Japan, Britain and Canada. On the basis of the average univariate results, it would seem that around 0.8% of the variance of the real exchange rate is permanent and only 0.2% is transitory. Interpreting the latter as the business-cycle-related component implies that only a very small percentage of individual country real exchange rate movements are business cycle driven. However, for Germany and Japan the picture changes quite dramatically when the multivariate decompositions are used: now for Germany and Japan 0.7% and 0.6%, respectively, of the variance of the real exchange rate change is due to transitory, or business cycle, components. Clarida and Gali attribute this difference to the fact that in the $–DM and $–Yen systems, inflation has significant explanatory power, in a Granger causality sense, over and above past values of lagged real exchange rate changes and lagged output changes.

Baxter (1994) also reports univariate and multivariate BN decompositions for a number of currencies, and on the basis of the univariate tests she finds that the permanent component of the real exchange rate always exceeds the transitory component and it is greatest in the case of the pound–dollar (this is consistent with the Clarida and Gali analysis which also finds the pound sterling has the largest permanent component). However, her multivariate decompositions – consisting of the real exchange rate and inflation differential – reveal that the transitory component dominates in three of the currency pairings. The finding that the transitory component is much greater in the multivariate decompositions is in accord with Clarida and Gali. Baxter (1994) also presents correlations of the permanent and transitory components across countries. For the univariate models all of the permanent components are strongly correlated across countries (having correlation coefficients in excess of 0.5), but the transitory components show no such clear-cut pattern; some are positively correlated (German mark–Swiss franc and French franc–Swiss franc), but most are zero or negative. The multivariate correlations, however, reveal much stronger evidence of positive correlations across countries; interestingly, the only currency pairings to produce negative correlations are those involving sterling. So on the basis of the multivariate results there is much more evidence of an international business cycle.

Campbell and Clarida (1987) apply an unobserved components model to the real exchange rate–real interest rate model (8.20) and extract the permanent and transitory components. They demonstrate that the majority of movements in the real exchange rate (at least 79%) are driven by movements in the permanent component of the real rate and the remainder due to the transitory element.

In sum, univariate decompositions of real exchange rates into permanent and transitory components indicate the dominance of permanent elements, although multivariate representations give a far more even split between the two components. Since the univariate results exclude information which may be an important determinant of real exchange rates, we believe that the multivariate results give a more accurate picture of the importance of the business cycle in driving real exchange rate movements. Another way of interpreting the multivariate decompositions is to say that they illustrate the importance for fundamentals to explain the real exchange rate and this finding would seem to contrast with the pessimism in some quarters regarding the importance of fundamentals in explaining exchange rate behaviour.

8.4   Structured VARS: demand, supply and monetary shocks

As we noted in the introductory chapter, one of the key issues in the economics of real exchange rates is the extent to which movements in real rates are driven by underlying real factors, such as preferences and technology, or nominal factors such as asset market disturbances. Most of the evidence that is cited in support of one camp or the other on this issue relates to the relative importance of permanent and transitory components of real exchange rates. For example, Stockman (1988) appeals to some of the univariate evidence on real exchange rates to support his contention that it is real factors which drive real rates, whereas Mussa (1988) cites the kind of evidence discussed in Chapter 1. However, this kind of evidence is, at best, merely suggestive of the relative importance of real and nominal shocks in driving real exchange rates. Starting with Lastrapes (1992), a number of researchers have sought to explicitly model the relative importance of real and nominal shocks using a 'structural VAR' approach; that is, a VAR with the kind of long-run identification restrictions of Blanchard and Quah (1989) imposed. The most influential paper in this genre is that of Clarida and Gali (1994) and we spend some time on their methods in Section 8.4.2. Before detailing the literature started by Clarida and Gali we briefly outline the mechanics of the SVAR approach.

8.4.1   The SVAR approach

The SVAR approach may be illustrated in the following way. Assume the vector x_t has a VAR representation of the following form:

$$B(L)x_t = \varepsilon_t, \tag{8.31}$$

where ε_t is an $n \times 1$ vector of reduced form disturbances, with $\mathrm{Var}(\varepsilon_t) = \Sigma, B(L)$ is a matrix polynomial in the lag operator L, for simplicity deterministic elements are ignored and the variables entering the x_t vector are assumed to be stationary. If $B(L)$ is invertible it will have a moving average representation of the following form:

$$x_t = F(L)\varepsilon_t, \tag{8.32}$$

where $F(L) = B(L)^{-1}$. Assuming (8.31) is estimated appropriately, the residuals will be serially uncorrelated. If e_t is defined as an $n \times 1$ vector of *structural* disturbances, which are also generated from an invertible autoregressive representation, and C_0 is an $n \times n$ matrix which describes the contemporaneous correlations among the disturbances:

$$x_t = C_0 e_t + C_1 e_{t-1} + C_2 e_{t-2} + \cdots \tag{8.33}$$

Identifying an estimated reduced form VAR system, such as (8.31), becomes a matter of choosing a unique value for C_0. Since C_0 contains $n \times n$ elements, identification requires imposing n^2 restrictions. The structural disturbances and the reduced form residuals are related as $e_t = C_0^{-1} \varepsilon_t$, and so the choice of C_0 also implies the choice of the covariance matrix:

$$\Lambda = C_0^{-1} \Sigma C_0^{-1'},$$

where Λ is the variance covariance matrix of structural disturbances. Maximum likelihood estimates of Λ and C_0 can be obtained through sample estimates of Σ. As we have said, identification requires choosing n^2 elements of C_0. Almost all approaches to identifying VAR models start with restricting the $n(n+1)/2$ parameters of the covariance matrix Σ. The first n of these usually come from normalising the n diagonal elements to be unity, while the remaining $n(n-1)/2$ restrictions come from assuming that the structural shocks are mutually uncorrelated or orthogonal. Taken together, these restrictions on C_0 imply:

$$C_0^{-1} \Sigma C_0^{-1'} = I,$$

where I is the identity matrix. This leaves a further $n(n-1)/2$ restrictions on C_0 to fully identify the model. The approach adopted in all of the papers in the SVAR literature is to assume that C_0 is equal to $C(1)$, the long-run coefficient matrix on the structural shocks, and to impose the remaining restrictions by assuming that this is lower triangular. This means that the long-run coefficient matrix has a Wold representation and the particular ordering of variables is achieved by appealing to economic theory.

Latrapes (1992) was the first to apply an SVAR decomposition to real exchange rate behaviour. In particular, he estimated bivariate VAR models consisting of real and nominal exchange for five US dollar bilateral rates over the period March 1973–December 1989. Using the identification methods described earlier, he extracted two shocks – a real and nominal – and he restricted the nominal shock to have a zero long-run impact on the level of the real exchange rate. A set of variance decompositions showed that real shocks were the predominant source of both real and nominal exchange rate behaviour for the sample, and he interprets this as evidence favouring the Stockman–Lucas view of exchange rate determination (see Chapter 4). However, as Lastrapes recognises, his results may be a reflection of the two dimensional nature of his system: with multiple real and nominal shocks the results could turn out to be different. Clarida and Gali (1994) use the SVAR approach to decompose real exchange rate behaviour into three shocks and since there work has become something of a benchmark in this literature, we consider it in some detail here.

8.4.2 The Clarida–Gali SVAR approach

In order to understand the structural restrictions used by Clarida and Gali (1994) we first present a stochastic version of the Mundell–Fleming–Dornbusch model. This model is based on Obsfeld (1985) and Clarida and Gali (1994) and since most of the relationships are familiar from previous chapters, our discussion here will be relatively brief. The open economy IS equation in the model is given by:

$$y_t^{d'} = d_t' + \eta(s_t - p_t') - \sigma(i_t' - E_t(p_{t+1}' - p_t')), \tag{8.34}$$

where a prime denotes a relative (home minus foreign) magnitude. The expression indicates that the demand for output is increasing in the real exchange rate and a demand shock (which captures, say, fiscal shocks) and decreasing in the real interest rate. The LM equation is familiar from our previous discussions

$$m_t^{s'} - p_t' = y_t' - \lambda i_t', \tag{8.35}$$

where the income elasticity has been set equal to one. The price setting equation is taken from Flood (1981) and Mussa (1982) and is given as:

$$p_t' = (1 - \theta)E_{t-1}p_t^{e'} + \theta p_t^{e'}. \tag{8.36}$$

Expression (8.36) states that the price level in period t is an average of the market-clearing price expected in $t - 1$ to prevail in t, and the price that would actually clear the output market in period t. With $\theta = 1$ prices are fully flexible and output is supply determined while with $\theta = 0$, prices are fixed and predetermined one period in advance. The final equation in this model is the standard UIP condition:

$$i_t' = E_t(s_{t+1} - s_t). \tag{8.37}$$

The stochastic properties of the relative supply of output, $y_t^{s'}$, d_t' and m_t' are assumed to be:

$$y_t^{s'} = y_{t-1}^{s'} + z_t, \tag{8.38}$$

$$d_t' = d_{t-1}' + \delta_t - \gamma\delta_{t-1}, \tag{8.39}$$

$$m_t' = m_{t-1}' + v_t, \tag{8.40}$$

where z_t, δ_t and v_t are random errors. Therefore both relative money and output supply are random walks and the relative demand term contains a mix of permanent and transitory components (i.e. a fraction γ of any shock is expected to be of offset in the next period).

By substituting (8.38) and (8.39) into (8.34) a flexible price rational expectations equilibrium, in which output is supply determined, for the expected real exchange rate ($q = s - p$) is given by:

$$q_t^e = (y_t^s - d_t)/\eta + (\eta(\eta + \sigma))^{-1}\sigma\gamma\delta_t, \tag{8.41}$$

which indicates that the flex-price real exchange rate depreciates with respect to a supply disturbance and appreciates in response to a demand disturbance. With $\gamma > 0$, the expectation that the demand disturbance will be partially offset in the future produces the expectation of real depreciation which in turn dampens the magnitude of the appreciation in the present.

From the definition of the real exchange rate and (8.35) the equilibrium price that would prevail in the flexible price rational expectation equilibrium, $p^{e'}$ must satisfy:

$$(1 + \lambda)p_t^{e'} = m_t' - y_t^{s'} + \lambda(E_t q_{t+1}^e - q_t^e) + \lambda E_t p_{t+1}^{e'}. \tag{8.42}$$

On using (8.38) to (8.40) and (8.41) in (8.42) we can obtain:

$$p_t^{e'} = m_t' - y_t^{s'} + \lambda(1 + \lambda)^{-1}(\eta + \sigma)^{-1}\lambda\delta_t. \tag{8.43}$$

From (8.43) we see that the flexible price relative price level rises in proportion to the monetary shocks, declines in proportion to the supply shock and rises in response to the temporary component in the demand shock. In contrast a permanent demand shock will have no effect on $p_t^{e'}$. This follows because by driving up the common level of both real and nominal interest rates, it must drive up home and foreign prices in proportion. The flexible price solution to the model may therefore be characterised by (8.41), (8.43) and:

$$y_t^{e'} = y_t^{s'}. \tag{8.44}$$

This characterisation makes clear that in the flexible price equilibrium the levels of relative output, the real exchange rate and relative national price levels are driven by three shocks: a supply shock, z, a demand shock, δ and a monetary shock, v.

A comparable sticky price equilibrium may be derived in the following way. By substituting (8.43) into (8.36) the following expression for the evolution of the price level may be derived:

$$p_t' = p_t^{e'} - (1 - \theta)(v_t - z_t + \alpha\gamma\delta_t), \tag{8.45}$$

where $\alpha \equiv \lambda(1 + \lambda)^{-1}(\eta + \sigma)^{-1}$. A positive money or demand shock produces a rise in the relative price level which is less than the flexible price case, $p^{e'}$. With a positive supply shock the price level falls but by less than the flexible price case. An expression for the real exchange rate may be derived by substituting (8.34) and (8.37) into (8.35) and using (8.43), the following expression may be obtained:

$$q_t = q_t^e + v(1 - \theta)(v_t - z_t + \alpha\gamma\delta_t), \tag{8.46}$$

where $v \equiv (1 + \lambda)(\lambda + \sigma + \eta)^{-1}$. We note that as in the non-stochastic version of the MFD model the existence of sticky price adjustment means that the real exchange rate is influenced by monetary shocks. The short run level of demand determined output can be generated by substituting (8.46) into (8.34) to get:

$$y_t' = y_t^{s'} + (\eta + \sigma)v(1 - \theta)(v_t - z_t + \alpha\gamma\delta_t). \tag{8.47}$$

As expected, with sluggish price adjustment demand and monetary shocks, in addition to supply shocks, influence y_t in the short run. Although all three shocks influence all three variables in the short run, the long-run response of the y, q and p is triangular. That is, only the supply shock influence the long-run level of relative output; supply and demand shocks influence the long-run level of the real exchange rate; and all three shocks influence the long-run level of prices at home and abroad.

Clarida and Gali (1994) use an SVAR approach to estimate the stochastic version of the open economy MFD model discussed above. As in that model, the three key variables modelled are the change in relative output levels, the change in the real exchange rate and a relative inflation rate (changes are used to address the non-stationarity of the level of output, the real exchange rate and the price level) and more specifically, let

$$x_t \equiv [\Delta y_t, \Delta q_t, \pi_t]', \tag{8.48}$$

where the estimated covariance matrix, Σ, will have dimensions 3×3. Assuming the shocks are mutually orthogonal and normalising the n diagonal elements to be unity, the remaining $3(= n(n-1)/2)$ restrictions on C_0 may be obtained by assuming it is lower triangular:

$$C_0 = \begin{bmatrix} c_{11} & 0 & 0 \\ c_{21} & c_{22} & 0 \\ c_{31} & c_{32} & c_{33} \end{bmatrix}.$$

Bearing in mind the ordering of the variables in (8.48), this amounts to only the first shock, which is labelled a supply shock, having a long-run effect on all three variable, the second shock, labelled the demand shock, having a long-run effect on both the real exchange rate and relative inflation and the third shock, the nominal or monetary shock, only having and effect on the relative inflation term. This lower triangular representation of course follows from the stochastic version of the MFD model considered above. The 3×1 vector of structural shocks is:

$$e_t \equiv [z_t, \delta_t, v_t]', \tag{8.49}$$

where z_t represents the supply shock, δ_t is the demand shock and v_t is the nominal shock.

The expected sign patterns of the real shock on output, the real exchange rate and the price level generated by the MFD model are as follows. A permanent demand shock should permanently appreciate the currency, increase the price level and output in the short run. A supply shock should produce a depreciation of the currency, a fall in prices and a rise in output. Finally, a nominal shock should also produce a nominal depreciation of the currency which, with sticky prices, will also generate a real depreciation; however, in contrast to the supply side shock this will not be permanent. The nominal shock also produces a rise in the price level and a, perhaps, transitory effect on output.

Given this kind of framework, Clarida and Gali seek to answer two questions: what have been the sources of real exchange rate fluctuations since the inception of floating exchange rates and how important are nominal shocks relative to real shocks? To answer these questions they use their estimated structural VAR models to estimate variance decompositions of the real exchange rate, impulse response functions of the set of VAR variables, to the underlying shocks and compute 'real time' historical decompositions of the real exchange rate. Clarida and Gali estimate this model for the dollar bilaterals of the German mark, Japanese yen, UK pound and Canadian dollar, over the period 1974q1 to 1992q1.

The impulse response analysis of CG indicates that the responses of relative output, relative inflation and the real exchange rate to the underlying structural model are, in general, consistent with the underlying theoretical structure of the MFD model. For example, US–German impulse response indicates that in response to a one-standard deviation nominal shock, the real exchange rate initially depreciates by 3.8% (the nominal overshoots by 4%), US output rises relative to German output by 0.5% and US inflation rises relative to German inflation by 0.3% rise. The output and real exchange rate effects of a nominal shock take between 16 and 20 quarters to die out. In response to a one-standard deviation relative demand shock, the dollar initially appreciates in real terms by 4%, relative output rises by 0.36% and there is a 0.44% rise in US inflation relative to foreign inflation. The effect on the exchange rate is permanent and after 20 quarters the real rate appreciates by 6%. A one-standard deviation relative supply shock produces a (wrongly signed) 1% dollar appreciation in quarter 2 and this quickly goes to zero (after 20 quarters the appreciation is only 0.2%). Other currency pairings produce similar results and, in particular, the perverse supply side effect appears for the other currencies as well which would seem to indicate an unsatisfactory aspect of their modelling.

Following MacDonald and Swagel (2000), if we interpret the business cycle related component as the sum of the demand and money shock then CG's variance decompositions demonstrate that for all four real exchange rates the business cycle component constitutes approximately 90% of the variance of the exchange rates at quarter 40. Of this total, almost all is attributable to demand shocks in the case of the UK and Canada, while for Japan the split is 60% demand and 30% monetary with the split being approximately equal for the German mark. The proportion of the forecast error variance due to the supply shock is statistically insignificant at all forecast horizons. The very small supply side specific component reported by CG has become something of stylised fact in the literature on the economics of real exchange rates.

Chadha and Prasad (1997) apply the Clarida–Gali approach to the Japanese yen–US dollar exchange rate over the period 1975 quarter 1 to 1996 quarter 1.

Their impulse response analysis indicates a permanent real exchange rate depreciation in response to a supply shock (of around 8%), while a demand shock produces a permanent appreciation (of around 8%). The nominal shock produces an initial real depreciation which is eventually offset with the real rate settling down to zero by quarter 8. The fact that all shocks have a correctly signed effect on the Japanese yen exchange rate contrasts with the findings of CG and may be a reflection of the longer sample period used by Chadha and Prasad. Their variance decomposition analysis reveals a somewhat different split between the different shocks at quarter 40. In particular, the business cycle shocks total 78% (compared to 90% in CG), with the supply-side shock accounting for the remainder. Interestingly, supply and demand shocks each contribute about one-fourth of the forecast error variance after quarter 8, with nominal rates explaining the remainder. In contrast to CG, Chadha and Prasad find that the proportion of the forecast error variance due to the supply shock is statistically significant at all forecast horizons. Chadha and Prasad interpret their findings as suggesting that monetary and fiscal policy can have a substantial effect on the real exchange rate at business cycle frequencies, whereas the role of technology and productivity shocks is relatively small.

Ghosh (1991) also uses a Blanchard–Quah decomposition to identify a simple VAR model for Dollar–Yen and Dollar–mark for the period 1972–87. He considers five shocks: home and foreign supply; home and foreign money and a relative demand shock (these are essentially the same shocks as in CG, although they constrain the first two to enter in relative terms). In contrast to CG, Ghosh allows all of these shocks to affect the real exchange rate in the long-run (the restrictions appear in the other equations: only supply-side shocks can affect output, although both supply and monetary shocks are allowed to affect inflation). The variance decompositions from his estimated VARs indicate that Keynesian factors predominate in the short-run, but supply side factors dominate the long-run behaviour. For example, at a four quarter horizon, 25% of the yen real rate is accounted for by monetary changes, and 57% by aggregate demand shocks, with the remainder being split between supply-side shocks (8%) and exogenous oil shocks (5%). In contrast, at the 10-year horizon Japanese supply-side shocks account for 83% of the variance, combined monetary shocks the remaining 7% and relative demand 7%. So although monetary shocks are allowed to affect the long-run value of the yen they only have a very small effect. Ghosh's results for the DM are similar to the yen results.

Clarida and Gali's results for the real US bilateral rates of the German mark, Japanese yen and UK pound are confirmed by MacDonald and Swagel (1998) for a longer sample period (1973–97); the sum of demand and nominal shocks – the business cycle related components – dominate, as in CG, explaining approximately 90% of the variance of the mark and yen exchange rates after 40 quarters, with demand shocks being by far the most important component, especially for the UK. For the German mark, however, the business cycle component explains 70% of the forecast error variance with the supply side shock explaining the remaining 30%. Interestingly, all of the forecast error variances are statistically significant at all forecast horizons and this is also the case for horizons of quarter 12 and above for the yen (all of the supply shock forecast error variances for UK pound are insignificant). Furthermore, MacDonald and Swagel also confirm the perverse sign of a supply-side shock on the real exchange rate and the statistically insignificant forecast error variances due to the supply-side shock. Interestingly, however, when considering real effective exchange rates (of the US dollar, UK pound and Japanese yen) the supply-side shocks become correctly signed with respect to the exchange rate and, although the aggregate effect of the business cycle component is similar to the bilaterals at quarter 40 (explaining 85% of the variance, rather than 90%), the composition of the business cycle component is different. For example, for the UK bilateral 73% of the residual variance is due to the demand shock, 14% to the nominal, while for the effectives the relative proportions are 59% and 25%. For the Japanese yen the difference is more marked, since the demand component moves from a 47% share in the bilateral to 25% in the effective, with the nominal share moving from 40% to 59%. The use of effective rates would therefore seem to be important in measuring the relative importance of demand shocks, but not supply shocks which have a very similar influence to their role in the bilateral case.

Two further studies seek to address the issue of the relative dominance of demand shocks by specifying a richer menu of shocks, particularly on the supply side. For example, Rogers (1999) expands the *x*vector in (8.48) to include the change in the ratio of government spending to output, and replaces inflation as the nominal variable with base money and the base money multiplier. The particular identification restrictions imposed allow him to construct fiscal and productivity shocks (both of which should produce a long-run appreciation on the real exchange rate), a demand shock (a long-run depreciation, due to having a model in which traded/non-traded distinction is made) and a monetary shock (no long-run effect). This particular specification is implemented on an annual data set for the UK pound–US dollar exchange rate over the period 1859–1992. The impulse response analysis reveals that 50% of the variance of the real exchange rate is due to monetary shocks (with a roughly equal split between money multiplier shocks and the monetary base shock), productivity (supply) shocks account for approximately 35% with the remainder coming from the demand side. So supply shocks put in a more respectable performance in this paper. In a bid to discern if this is dependent on the sample period or the richer shock specification, Rogers implements his VAR specification for the same data sample as that used in CG, and the CG specification for his longer sample. In terms of the latter exercise, he finds that the longer sample docs not increase the role of the supply side shock, although it does increase the role of the monetary shock at the expense of the demand shock (interestingly, this is similar to the extended sample findings of MacDonald and Swagel). Implementing his model structure on the CG data set produces a similar result: the business cycle shocks dominate the total but the composition changes from the demand shocks being the dominant shocks to the nominal shocks contributing about one-half the total for all of the currencies considered by CG.

Weber (1998) also extends the CG model by specifying a richer menu of shocks. In particular, he splits supply shocks into labour supply and productivity components and segments monetary shocks into both money demand and money supply; additionally, he also includes a relative aggregate demand shock. His vector becomes:

$$\Delta x_t \equiv [\Delta l_t, \Delta y_t, \Delta q_t, (\Delta m_t - \Delta p_t), \pi_t]'. \tag{8.50}$$

In terms of the real exchange rate, the long-run restrictions are that the real exchange rate depreciates in response to both a relative productivity and relative labour supply shocks and the real exchange rate appreciates in response to a relative demand disturbance. The long-run restrictions are imposed using the Blanchard–Quah decomposition. The data set consists of the three real bilaterals: US dollar–German mark, US dollar–Japanese yen and German mark–Japanese yen and the period spanned is 1971 month VIII to 1994 month XII. Weber's results essentially confirm the findings of CG – demand shocks are the dominant force driving real exchange rates, although for the two cross rates involving the Japanese yen supply side shocks (in the form of labour market shocks) do contribute a much larger fraction of the forecast error variance (around one-third) compared to the original CG study; and this result confirms the findings of Chadha and Prasad (1997). However, Weber notes that the demand shocks are highly correlated with the real exchange rate and, indeed, for the US dollar–German mark this is on a one-to-one basis; most intriguingly he demonstrates that the relative demand shock does not have a significant impact on output, which presumably it should have if it is to serve any purpose in representing a demand shock. Weber concludes by arguing that the AD shock is simply a 'catch-all' term which reflects what is left of real exchange rate movements that cannot be forecast from the other variables in the system. It is therefore questionable to interpret such shocks as AD shocks when they contain such a large share of the residual variance.

The basic CG model suffers from other deficiencies in addition to those noted by Weber.[6] First, the basic identification procedure used forces all of the temporary shocks to have a monetary origin. Of course in practice, or in the data, this is unlikely to be the case. This means that a whole range of temporary supply shocks – oil price shocks, changes in fiscal policy – are subsumed as a monetary shock. The same kind of argument could be made for temporary demand shocks. Second, in setting up the identifying assumptions, it is assumed that the innovations to demand and supply are uncorrelated, which, for a variety of reasons, seems implausible (i.e. an increase in AD raises I, which raises the future capital stock and supply, as well as demand). Third, in the original CG study nominal shocks only have a miniscule effect on relative output and this raises the question of whether it is the way nominal shocks are specified, rather than the absence of important nominal effects that is to blame. Sarte (1994) has demonstrated that identification in structural VARs can be very sensitive to identifying restrictions particularly when residual series are used as instruments for the variables for which they are intended as instruments.[7]

The empirical work on structural VAR relationships may be summarised in the following way. The basic message from the original paper by Clarida and Gali is that supply-side shocks explain a miniscule and insignificant proportion of the variance of key real exchange rates. Extending the sample from that in CG seems to have the effect of increasing the importance of nominal shocks at the expense of demand shocks, while leaving the role of supply-side shocks unchanged, although supply-side shock do seem to be important for the Japanese yen. The measurement of shocks also seems to be important, especially on the demand side: defining the monetary variable to be monetary rather than price has an important bearing on the relative split between demand and nominal. The use of effective rates rather than bilateral measures seems to make a difference, particularly with respect to achieving correctly signed impulse response functions.

8.4.3   *Other VAR-based studies of real exchange rate behaviour*

In the presence of sticky prices, both the MFD model and optimising models, such as those considered in Chapter 5, predict a liquidity effect: that is, a contractionary monetary policy increases the nominal and real interest rates and the nominal and real exchange rate appreciates as a consequence. However, empirical evidence from closed economy VAR models (see, for example, Christiano and Eichenbaum 1992) suggests that interest rates seem to fall in response to a liquidity contraction. This has been labelled 'the liquidity puzzle'. Open economy variants of these VAR models have created two related puzzles which we group under the same label, namely the exchange rate puzzle: *on impact* a decrease in liquidity depreciates non-US-dollar currencies (although the sign is correct for the US dollar); after the impact period currencies persistently appreciate in contrast to what would be expected under UIP. In this section we consider this literature.

Eichenbaum and Evans (1995) use an unrestricted VAR approach to examine the effects of three different measures of monetary policy on the nominal and real US bilateral exchange rates (defined as the dollar price of one unit of the other currency) of the Japanese yen, German mark, Italian lira, French franc and UK pound for the period January 1974 to May 1990. The vector is

$$x' = [y^{us}, p^{us}, m^{us}, i - i^{us}, q], \tag{8.51}$$

where variables have an obvious interpretation and note the only variable to appear in differential form, apart from the real exchange rate, is the interest differential. Three measures of the US money supply are used and entered (sequentially) into the VAR system: the ratio of the log of non-borrowed reserves to total reserves (nbrx), the Federal Funds rate and the Romer and Romer index of monetary policy. The variables enter the VAR in levels (i.e. they are not first differenced) and no cointegrating restrictions are tested or imposed. The VARS are left unrestricted and the only identifying restriction used is the Choleski decomposition in which the ordering is as in equation (8.51). This ordering corresponds to the assumption that the US monetary authority looks at the contemporaneous values of p and y when setting the monetary variable, but not the interest rate term or the real exchange rate.

Using *nbrx* as the measure of monetary policy, Eichenbaum and Evans find the following. First, a one-standard-deviation contractionary shock to US monetary policy produces, on average across the 5 currencies, a 36 basis-point decline in the interest differential and that this effect is persistent. The shock also produces a persistent appreciation of the nominal and real US dollar exchange rates and the two series are very closely correlated with each other. In contrast to the Dornbusch overshooting story, the maximal impact of the monetary shock occurs, on average, 35 months after the initial impulse. This kind of pattern is, of course, inconsistent with UIP, but nevertheless consistent with the so-called forward premium puzzle (see Chapter 15); that is, the time-t expected one-period return from holding the foreign rather than the US asset is lower both because the interest differential is lower and also because the dollar is expected to appreciate rather than depreciate between t and $t+1$ (they show that these excess returns are persistent and are consistent with the fact that future changes in the exchange rate tend to be negatively related to the forward premium).

Eichenbaum and Evans also demonstrate that monetary shocks significantly explain between 18% (the UK) and 43% (Yen) of the variability of the nominal exchange rate and argue, that in conjunction with their other findings, this highlights important shortcomings of monetised international real businness cycle models. The results using the other measures of monetary policy are qualitatively very similar to those obtained using nbrx.

Grilli and Roubini (1992) analyse the following vector using VAR methods:

$$x' = [y, \Delta p, y^{\text{us}}, \Delta p^{\text{us}}, i, i^{\text{us}}, s], \tag{8.52}$$

where the variables again have an obvious interpretation. The data sample is monthly, 1974–91 and the Currencies considered are US dollar bilaterals (home currency–dollar) of the German mark, French franc, Italian lira, UK pound, Japanese yen and Canadian Dollar. The VAR is identified using a Choleski decomposition and the ordering given in (8.52). Their results show clear evidence of an exchange rate puzzle. That is, following a monetary contraction (defined as an increase in the short-term interest rate) the French franc, German mark and Italian lira all depreciate on impact and this is significant in the cases of the latter two currencies but not for the French franc. Although the remaining currencies appreciate on impact none of these appreciations are statistically significant. However, in contrast the US dollar always appreciates significantly on impact following a monetary tightening. The impulse response analysis of Grilli and Roubini also shows a persistent appreciation of the currencies rather than the depreciation that would be implied from the UIP condition.

Grilli and Roubini (1996) offer two explanations for the exchange rate puzzle. One is the idea that the US is the 'leader' country in the setting of monetary policy for the G7, while the other countries act as followers. The other explanation is that interest rate innovations in the non-US countries occur as an endogenous policy reaction to inflationary shocks that, in turn, cause an exchange rate depreciation. In particular, having current and past inflation rates in the VAR may not be sufficient to capture expected inflation. Therefore having a better proxy for inflationary expectations – explicitly testing for exogeneity, is therefore one way of trying to solve this puzzle. Grilli and Roubini (1996) pursue this interpretation by including long rates in addition to short rates in the vector analysed and the monetary variable now becomes the spread between the short- and long-term interest rates. This addition seems to do the trick – for FF, DM, JY, CD and UK pound the puzzle is now solved in the sense that the currencies now appreciate on impact. However, Grilli and Roubini (1996) still recognise that there are a number of shortcomings of this approach. First, the recursive ordering in such systems seems unrealistic from a real world policy-making perspective. For example, to get an impact effect of the interest rate on the exchange rate the latter variable has to be put after the interest rate in the ordering and this of course implies that monetary policy cannot react contemporaneously to the exchange rate. This seems unappealing since the monetary authority of a small open economy is likely to react quite quickly to the effects of an exchange rate depreciation on its inflation rate (indeed, even a large open economy, such as the euro zone, may react quickly). Second, the so-called price puzzle was not fully explained in Grilli and Roubini. Third, the identification used in Eichenbaum and Evans and Grilli and Roubini still produces a 'delayed overshooting' or forward discount bias puzzle – the currency continues to appreciate for some time after the initial monetary contraction.

Kim and Roubini (2000) attempt to addresss these remaining puzzles in the context of a structured VAR model. In particular, they consider a data vector which is similar to those in the earlier-noted papers, apart from the inclusion of the price of oil and the foreign interest rate:

$$x' = [i^s, m, p, y, oilp, i^{\text{us},s}, s]. \tag{8.53}$$

These variables are included in order to try to identify exogeneous monetary policy changes; that is, they are designed to remove monetary reactions to supply-side shocks or to US monetary impulses. Structural Bernanke–Sims identification restrictions are used. For all six currencies studied they find a statistically significant appreciation of the exchange rate in response to a monetary contraction. Furthermore, in almost all cases the initial appreciation is followed quite quickly by a depreciation after 2 months and the confidence invervals are such that there is no indication of significant appreciation during this period. In sum, the shape of the subsequent exchange rate profile is much more in accord with the standard UIP condition than the other studies referred to above. This is confirmed by the fact that they find little evidence of significant persistent deviations from UIP for their sample period. The key to understanding why this result differs from previous papers is is that their identification scheme of Kim and Roubini is able to distinguish the components of interest rate shocks due to Fisherian effects from those due to 'true' monetary tightening – it is only the latter effect that leads to the expected impact appreciation of the nominal exchange rate suggested by liquidity models (and this is robust to the choice of different monetary aggregates).

MacDonald (1999b) uses the empirical estimates of the EERM model, discussed earlier, to unravel the sources of real and monetary shocks for the effective exchange rates of the US dollar, Japanese yen and German mark. Variance decompositions (and impulse response functions) are constructed subject to the cointegration constraint (Blanchard–Quah style restrictions, as in CG are not imposed). For the US dollar, the largest proportion of the quarter 1 error variance, somewhat surprisingly, is explained by the foreign price term. In terms of magnitude, this is closely followed by the terms of trade and relative productivity, other variables having a small effect in the initial quarter. In sum, what are referred to as real variables explain slightly less of the first quarter error variance than the nominal variables (19.9% against 23%). Moving through the quarters the relative importance of the variables is little changed apart from net foreign assets and the Balassa–Samuleson effect (as represented by tnt). By quarter 20 (the final quarter) the proportion of the exchange rate error variance explained by the real factors dominates (being 30.50 against 22.46 for the nominal).

The variance decompositions for the Japanese yen perhaps not surprisingly show relative productivity as the dominant component in quarter 1, although by quarter 20 the net foreign asset term explains an almost equivalent proportion of the error variance. Perhaps, not surprisingly, real factors are the key determinants of the quarter one variance (41.6% against 12.68% nominal) and also the quarter 20 outcomes (49.97% real against 16.57% nominal). The productivity and terms of trade effects turn out to be the dominant explanatory variables in explaining the German mark decomposition throughout, although foreign magnitudes and net foreign assets are also relatively important. In quarter 1 real factors explain 48.47 (against a nominal total of 15.3), and by quarter 20 real factors explain 47.5 (against 18.5 nominal).

Concluding comments

In this chapter we have focused on models which take an explicitly real approach to exchange rate determination. We first outlined an EERM, which combines elements of a traditional balance of payments flow approach with the forward-looking nature of the asset market approach considered in Chapters 4 and 5. We noted that this EERM model is supported by the extant empirical evidence. Empirical evidence on the real interest rate parity condition was also considered in this chapter and we argued that when an appropriate estimation strategy is used evidence in favour of this key parity condition is reported. Another theme explored in this chapter is the decomposition of real exchange rates using structural VARs. The empirical evidence from this literature indicates that when simple three variable VARs are used, supply-side shocks explain only a small proportion of the variance of real exchange rates; the main source of real exchange rate variability is demand and nominal components. However, when SVAR models are used which have a richer specification for the supply side, the split between the three categories of shocks is more evenly balanced. The final theme discussed in this chapter was the VAR based literature which seeks to unravel liquidity effects on real and nominal exchange rates.

9 Equilibrium exchange rates
Measurement and misalignment

9.1 Introduction

In this chapter we return to the issue of equilibrium exchange rates. The chapter is intended to have two main themes. First, we noted in Chapters 2 and 3 that PPP does not seem to provide a good measure of a country's equilibrium exchange rate. Are there any alternative measures that can be used for this purpose? As we saw in Chapter 3, one explanation for the poor performance of PPP is that there are real factors driving real exchange rates and once the real rate is conditioned on these factors many of the puzzles associated with PPP disappear. In this chapter we provide an overview of different alternative approaches to measuring equilibrium exchange rates that rely on such real factors. The second theme we address here is how to use an equilibrium exchange rate to assess if a currency is overvalued or not.

Calculating equilibrium exchange rates and assessment issues have become especially topical of late for a variety of reasons. First, a number of countries – such as the current group of accession countries, and the UK and Sweden – have an interest in knowing the appropriate exchange rate for entry into the euro area (either in terms of the rate at which to participate in an ERM II arrangement or the appropriate rate at which to lock a currency permanently to the euro). Second, the behaviour of certain currencies, such as the initial sharp and sustained fall in the external value of the euro immediately after its inception in 1999, the sustained appreciated value of sterling in the late 1990s and the post 2005 behaviour of the Chinese renminbi against the US dollar, has generated a debate about the sources of exchange rate movements. Does such behaviour represent movements in the underlying equilibria, and therefore the currencies are correctly priced, or do they represent misalignments? Clearly, to answer these kinds of questions requires some measure of the equilibrium exchange rate. Knowledge of equilibrium exchange rates is also desirable in the wider context of reform of the international monetary system (IMS). For example, proposals for introducing a greater degree of fixity into the IMS (such as those of Williamson 1988 and McKinnon 1988) – between the yen, dollar and euro – requires knowledge of the appropriate rate at which to lock currencies or the appropriate central rate of a target zone/crawling peg arrangement.

Purchasing power parity (PPP) is often the measure economists first turn to when asked to think about the issue of equilibrium exchange rates and exchange rate misalignment. But as we saw in Chapters 2 and 3, PPP on its own is not a particularly good measure of an equilibrium exchange rate and in this chapter we consider a number of alternative measures of equilibrium which are suitable for assessment purposes. Since the construction of an equilibrium exchange rate often relies on using recently developed econometric methods we present a brief overview of such methods where appropriate.

The outline of the remainder of this chapter is as follows. In the next section we introduce a simple balance of payments model of the exchange rate and also address the issue of exchange rate misalignment. In Section 9.3 measures of equilibrium which rely on combining PPP with uncovered interest parity are discussed. Section 9.4 contains a discussion of so-called behavioural equilibrium exchange rates. Section 9.5 overviews measures of equilibrium which rely on a permanent and transitory decompositions of the real exchange rate. The internal–external balance approach to measuring equilibrium exchange rates is discussed in Section 9.6; in particular, we discuss here the fundamental equilibrium exchange rate model, the IMF real exchange rate model and the natural real exchange rate model. In Section 9.7 we consider how the new open macroeconomic model of Obstfeld and Rogoff (1995) may be used for assessment purposes. A concluding section summarises the advantages and disadvantages of the different approaches.

9.2   Measuring exchange rate misalignment

In order to illustrate the concept of exchange rate misalignment, we formalise the balance of payments exchange rate relationship introduced in Chapter 1:[1]

$$s_t - p_t + p_t^* = (\alpha_2/\alpha_1)y_t - (\alpha_3/\alpha_1)y_t^* - \alpha_1^{-1}(i_t' \text{nfa}_t)$$
$$- \mu/\alpha_1(i_t - i_t^* - E_t\Delta s_{t+k}), \tag{9.1}$$

where variable definitions are as before and we have redefined the dependent variable as the real exchange rate. Equation (9.1) does not represent a 'true' steady state equilibrium, because it is not stock-flow consistent (although as we shall see later variants of the internal–external balance approach essentially use (9.1) to identify a medium-run equilibrium) but it is useful for illustrating some of the concepts considered in succeeding sections. Following Clark and MacDonald (1998), we define Z_{1t} as a set of fundamentals which are expected to have persistent effects on the long-run real exchange rate and Z_{2t} as a set of fundamentals which have persistent effects in the medium-run, that is over the business cycle. In terms of (9.1) Z_{1t} would contain the relative output terms and net foreign assets, while Z_{2t} would contain interest rate yields. Given this, the actual real exchange rate may be thought of as being determined in the following way:

$$q_t = \beta_1' Z_{1t} + \beta_2' Z_{2t} + \tau' T_t + \varepsilon_t, \tag{9.2}$$

where T is a set of transitory, or short-run, variables and ε_t is a random error. Following Clark and MacDonald (1998), it is useful to distinguish between the actual value of the real exchange rate and the current equilibrium exchange rate, q_t'. The latter value is defined for a position where the transitory and random terms are zero:

$$q_t' = \beta_1' \mathcal{Z}_{1t} + \beta_2' \mathcal{Z}_{2t}. \tag{9.3}$$

The related current misalignment, *cm*, is then given as:

$$cm \equiv q_t - q_t' = q_t - \beta_1' \mathcal{Z}_{1t} - \beta_2' \mathcal{Z}_{2t} = \tau' T_t + \varepsilon_t, \tag{9.4}$$

and so *cm* is simply the sum of the transitory and random errors. As the current values of the economic fundamentals can deviate from the sustainable, or desirable, levels, Clark and MacDonald (1998) also define the total misalignment, *tm*, as the difference between the actual and real rate given by the sustainable or long-run values of the economic fundamentals, denoted as:

$$tm_t = q_t - \beta_t' \bar{\mathcal{Z}}_{1t} - \beta_2' \bar{\mathcal{Z}}_{2t}. \tag{9.5}$$

The calibration of the fundamentals at their desired levels may either be achieved by the user placing some judgement on what values the actual variables should have been during the sample period or, perhaps, using some sort of statistical filter, such as the Hodrick-Prescott filter. By adding and subtracting q_t' from the right hand side of (9.5) the total misalignment can be decomposed into two components:

$$tm_t = (q_t - q_t') + [\beta_1'(\mathcal{Z}_{1t} - \bar{\mathcal{Z}}_{1t}) + \beta_2'(\mathcal{Z}_{2t} - \bar{\mathcal{Z}}_{2t})], \tag{9.6}$$

and since $q_t - q_t' = \tau' T_t + \varepsilon_t$, the total misalignment in equation (9.6) can be rewritten as:

$$tm_t = \tau' T_t + \varepsilon_t + [\beta_1'(\mathcal{Z}_{1t} - \bar{\mathcal{Z}}_{1t}) + \beta_2'(\mathcal{Z}_{2t} - \bar{\mathcal{Z}}_{2t})]. \tag{9.7}$$

Expression (9.7) indicates that the total misalignment at any point in time can be decomposed into the effect of the transitory factors, the random disturbances, and the extent to which the economic fundamentals are away from their sustainable values. In the BEER approach considered in Section 9.4, the distinction between these two measures of equilibrium is made explicit. As we shall see, other approaches to the equilibrium real exchange rate do not make the distinction explicit – the FEER and PEER approaches focus on measures of total misalignment, while the CHEERS approach focuses on current misalignment.

9.3   UIP and PPP: capital enhanced measures of the equilibrium exchange rate – CHEERS

If we assume that $\mu \to \infty$ in (9.1), and capital is therefore perfectly mobile, we may recover the uncovered interest parity (UIP) condition as:

$$E_t(\Delta s_{t+k}) = (i_t - i_t^*). \tag{9.8}$$

A number of researchers (see, for example, Brigden *et al.* 1997) have used this expression to calculate a measure of the (short- to medium-run) equilibrium exchange rate. For example, absent a risk premium, if the interest rate in the home country is x% above that in its trading partner its currency will be expected to depreciate by x% over the maturity of the bonds used to define i and i^*. On the basis of this relationship it should therefore be possible to say where an exchange rate will be in period k (the maturity period). However, as we noted in Chapter 1 (and as is discussed again in Chapter 15) there is little empirical support for this relationship on its own and therefore drawing inferences purely on the basis of (9.8) is hazardous.

A related approach to explaining the persistence in real exchange rates, and also in obtaining well-defined measures of the equilibrium exchange rate, involves combining an interest differential with PPP. This approach has been popularised by Johansen and Juselius (1990), Juselius (1995), MacDonald and Marsh (1997, 1999) and Juselius and MacDonald (2004, 2007). We refer to this approach as a capital enhanced equilibrium exchange rate, or CHEER. The approach captures the basic Casselian view of PPP, discussed in Chapter 6, that an exchange rate may be away from its PPP determined rate because of non-zero interest differentials. In terms of expression (9.1), therefore, the approach focuses on the interaction between the real exchange rate and the capital account items; it ignores the relative output terms and net foreign assets (and indeed any other 'real' determinants). Unlike the pure form of Casselian PPP, in which non-zero interest differentials only have a transitory impact on the real exchange rate, here the interest rates can have a medium-run, or business cycle, effect. The essential proposition of this approach is that the long-term persistence in the real exchange rate is mirrored in the interest differential. We consider the CHEERs approach first from a statistical perspective and then from an economic perspective.

Since interest differentials are usually empirically found to be $I(1)$ processes (see, for example, Juselius and MacDonald 2004, 2007) some combination of an appropriate interest differential and the real exchange rate may cointegrate down to a stationary process. More specifically, if the expected exchange rate in (9.8) is used to determine the relative prices, as in an absolute PPP condition, we may use (9.8) to derive the following relationship:

$$(i_t - i_t^*) = \omega_2(p_t - p_t^*) - s_t, \tag{9.9}$$

or, less restrictively, as:

$$[\omega_1(i_t - i_t^*) - \omega_2(p_t - p_t^*) + s_t] \sim I(0). \tag{9.10}$$

The reason why an appropriate interest differential and real exchange rate may cointegrate is as follows. For a period such as the recent float we know that there have been large current account imbalances (this is especially clear when the US dollar is the bilateral numeraire) and these have been driven in large measure by national savings imbalances, such as fiscal imbalances. The fact that real exchange rates have been so persistent, and therefore any adjustment of the current account to relative prices is painfully slow (see Juselius and MacDonald 2004, 2007), means that the current account imbalances have to be financed through the capital account of the balance of payments. This, in turn, means that the persistence observed in real exchange rates should get transferred through into persistence in a nominal interest differential (in particular, an interest differential with a similar maturity to the evident persistence in real exchange rates). The CHEERs approach, therefore, involves exploiting the following vector:

$$x'_t = [s_t, p_t, p^*_t, i_t, i^*_t].$$ (9.11)

In MacDonald and Marsh (1999) equation (9.11) is estimated using the methods of Johansen for the US dollar bilateral rates of the DM, pound sterling and Japanese yen over the period January 1974 through to December 1992. For each country evidence of two significant cointegrating vectors is found and in each case the first vector can be identified to have a similar form to that of the German mark–US dollar exchange rate:

$$s_t = p_t - p^*_t - 7.33(i_t - i^*_t),$$ (9.12)

which indicates that the coefficient on relative prices can be constrained to have a coefficient of plus and minus unity and the coefficient on the interest differential has a traditional capital flow interpretation. Potentially then this relationship could be used as a measure of the equilibrium exchange rate. However, one problem with this initial approach is that the second significant cointegrating vector could not be identified. This issue was solved in MacDonald and Marsh (2004) where it was argued that to be able to identify both vectors in a system like (9.11) the close linkages in currency markets should be recognised in any econometric exercise by modelling currencies and their determinants jointly. Taking the tripolar relationship between Germany, the US and Japan as an example, this means modelling the following vector:

$$x'_t = \left[s^{ger}_t, s^{jap}_t, p^{ger}_t, p^{jap}_t, p^{us}_t, i^{ger}_t, i^{jap}_t, i^{us}_t \right].$$ (9.13)

MacDonald and Marsh (2004) demonstrate that two significant cointegrating vectors exist amongst the variables in (9.11) and by testing hypotheses on this vector they demonstrate how it may be partitioned into two stationary relationships for Germany and Japan of the form:

$$\beta^{ger} x = [\omega_1(i^{ger} - i^{us}) - \omega_2(p^{ger} - p^{us}) + s^{ger}],$$
$$\beta^{jap} x = [\omega_3(i^{jap} - i^{us}) - \omega_4(p^{jap} - p^{us}) + s^{jap}],$$ (9.14)

where ω_2 and ω_4 could be restricted to unity in both equations and ω_1 and ω_3 were estimated significantly positive (i.e. significantly negative in equation form). These relationships indicate that although no *direct* spillovers appear in the long-run relationships, the wider conditioning information set proved important in recovering sensible point estimates – *indirect* spillovers are important in the long-run (direct spillovers appear in the dynamic equations derived from (9.2) and this was mentioned in Chapter 5).

In Juselius and MacDonald (2007) the vector in (9.11) is extended to include both short- and long-term interest rates and the system is analysed for the German mark–US dollar system. Sensible and stable equilibrium relationships are shown to exist for this country pairing, although the nature of the equilibrium is slightly different to that reported in MacDonald and Marsh. In particular, the relationship between exchange rates and interest rates is between the real exchange rate and real interest differential (rather than the nominal differential, as in MacDonald and Marsh). In Juselius and MacDonald (2004) a similar analysis is conducted for the Japanese yen–US dollar pairing.

In summary, the advantages of the CHEERs modelling approach are, at least, two-fold. First, well-founded measures of equilibrium may be recovered from either (9.11) or (9.13), in the sense that the composite term is stationary and degree one homogeneity restrictions can often be imposed on the relative price terms and the coefficients on the interest differential are consistent with a capital account inter-pretation. Thus the estimated CHEER gives a different measure of equilibrium to that which would be obtained by simply using the UIP condition (a positive relationship would be expected in the latter approach). Furthermore, the speed of mean reversion of the adjustment term is often much faster than the univariate PPP-based adjustment referred to earlier and the out-of-sample exchange rate forecasts can be constructed which dominate a random walk at horizons as short as 2 months ahead (this is considered in Chapter 5). As a measure of the equilibrium exchange rate it is clearly a 'medium-run' concept in the sense that it does not impose stock-flow consistency. This may be seen as a disadvantage of the approach for assessment purposes. However, it may, nevertheless, provide a useful measure of equilibrium in circumstances where data on net foreign asset positions and other fundamentals are not available (see, for example, the application in MacDonald 1997 to the exchange rates of formerly centrally planned countries).

9.4   Behavioural equilibrium exchange rates – BEERs

The BEER approach of Clark and MacDonald (1998) is not based on any specific exchange rate model and in that sense may be regarded as a very general approach to modelling equilibrium exchange rates. However, it takes as its starting point, though the proposition that real factors are a key explanation for the slow mean reversion to PPP observed in the data. In contrast to some of the FEER-based approaches, discussed later, its specific modus operandi is to produce measures of exchange rate misalignment which are free of any normative elements and one in which the exchange rate relationship is subject to rigorous statistical testing. To illustrate their approach, Clark and MacDonald (1998) take the risk adjusted real interest parity relationship, which has been used by a number of researchers to model equilibrium exchange rates (see, for example, Faruqee 1995 and MacDonald 1997), and which was also discussed in the context of the efficient markets version of PPP in Chapter 2:

$$\Delta q_{t+k}^e = -(r_{t,t+k}^e - r_{t,t+k}^{*e}) + \lambda_t, \tag{9.15}$$

since the BEER approach is normally applied to real effective exchange rates, the real exchange rate is now expressed as the foreign currency price of a unit of home currency. Expression (9.15) may be rearranged as an expression for the real exchange rate as:

$$q_t = q_{t+k}^e + (r_{t,t+k}^e - r_{t,t+k}^{*,e}) - \lambda_t, \tag{9.16}$$

and if q_{t+k}^e is interpreted as the 'long-run' or systematic component of the real exchange rate, $\bar{q}_t$ and rearranging (9.16), with rational expectations imposed, we get:

$$q_t = \bar{q}_t - (r_t - r_t^*). \tag{9.17}$$

By assuming that $\bar{q}_t$ is, in turn, a function of net foreign assets, nfa, the relative price of traded to non-traded goods, tnt, and the terms of trade, tot, an expression for the real exchange rate may be written as:

$$q_t = f[r_t - r_t^*, \text{nfa}_t, \text{tot}_t, \text{dtnt}_t]. \tag{9.18}$$

Using the multivariate cointegration methods of Johansen (1995), Clark and MacDonald estimate (9.18) for the real effective exchange rates of US dollar, Japanese yen and German mark, over the period 1960–96 (annual data). For each of the currencies they find evidence of two cointegrating vectors and attempt to interpret one of the vectors as an exchange rate relationship and the other as a stationary relationship for the interest differential. For illustrative purposes we focus on the results for the US dollar:

$$q_t = \underset{(0.04)}{0.084}\, l\text{tot} + \underset{(0.33)}{2.701}\, l\text{tnt} + \underset{(0.10)}{1.237}\, \text{nfa} - \underset{(0.01)}{0.004}\, \lambda + \underset{(0.014)}{4.595}$$

$$r_t - r_t^* = \underset{(0.003)}{-0.014}. \tag{9.19}$$

All of coefficients in equation (9.19) are correctly signed and all, apart from that on the relative debt term (our proxy for the risk premium), are statistically significant. The χ (9.1) test that the chosen restricted vectors span the cointegrating space has an estimated value of 5.49 and a marginal significance level of 0.24; the restrictions are easily satisfied at standard levels of significance. Using the associated alpha adjustment matrix the US dollar real exchange adjusts significantly to both disequilibrium errors (with an alpha coefficient of -0.374 on the first error correction term and -0.434 on the second).

In Figure 9.1 we report the BEER calculated from (9.19). In terms of our discussion in Section 9.2, Figure 9.1 shows the current equilibrium rate, that is q_t'.

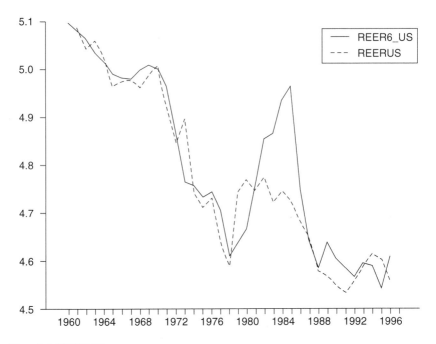

Figure 9.1 US BEER.

Perhaps the most striking feature of the figure is the extent to which the dollar was overvalued in the period 1980–6. It is worth noting that this finding is common to other BEER estimates (see, for example, Faruqee 1995; MacDonald 1997 and Stein 1999). As discussed earlier, the US BEER plotted in Figure 9.1 reflects a behavioural equilibrium. However, since it is possible for the fundamentals to be away from their equilibrium values it is also possible to calibrate the BEER with some normative structure placed on the fundamentals. For example, in Figure 9.2 a BEER calculation in the spirit of the FEER approach is performed. In particular, the NFA position of the US is set at a 'sustainable level' (equal to its 1980 level) and the total misalignment calculated. This shows that the sharp depreciation of the dollar over the post-1980 period was an equilibrating response to the deterioration in the net foreign asset position of the US. Alberola *et al.* (1999) and Clark and MacDonald (1998) have advocated the Granger and Gonzalo decomposition as an alternative way of calibrating the total misalignment.

Papers which have used the BEER approach to modelling the equilibrium exchange rates of mature economies are: Clostermann and Friedmann (1998) who estimate a BEER relationship for the German mark real effective exchange rate (1975 first quarter – 1996 fourth quarter); Wadhwani (1999) for the equilibrium UK pound–German mark exchange rate using a variant of the BEER; Clostermann and Schnatz (2000) who construct a real synthetic euro for the period 1975–98; MacDonald (2002) constructs a BEER for the real effective exchange rate of New Zealand.

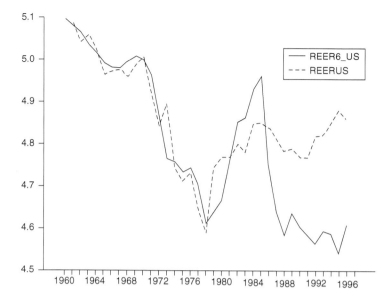

Figure 9.2 US BEER, Counterfactual L, NFA at 1980 values (post-1980).

The BEER approach has also been widely used for developing countries and emerging markets. In such studies the conditioning variables are often slightly different to those used in the studies developed earlier. One of the pioneering studies for developing countries was that of Edwards (1989) who used data from 12 developing countries over the period 1962–84 to estimate the following specification.

$$q_{it} = f(\Delta\%\text{TFPROD}, \text{TOT}, \text{GC/GDP}, \text{OPEN}, \text{CAPCON}, s, q_{it-1}),$$

where $\Delta\%\text{TFPROD}$ is the rate of growth of total factor productivity, TOT is the terms of trade, GC is government consumption, OPEN is a proxy for a trade regime, CAPCON is the severity of capital controls.

Edwards approach has been updated, using the kind of cointegration methods discussed earlier, by Elbadawi (1994), for seven Latin American Countries, Montiel (1999), for five Southeast Asian countries, Husted and MacDonald (1998) and Chinn (1998), for East Asian countries (see the collection of papers in Hinkle and Montiel 1999), MacDonald and Ricci (2004) for the South African effective rate.

A large number of BEER studies have been conducted for the Central European countries (see Egert *et al.* (2005) for a survey). Applications of the BEER approach to these countries is highly topical given some are already members of the EU, and are in the transition process to full membership of the euro area. All of these countries started the transition process with relatively large undervaluations, in terms of PPP, and most have undergone dramatic appreciations in the post-1990 period, with some of this reaction being a reaction to the initial undervaluation.

A group of early studies argued that such trend appreciation was driven largely by a Balassa-Samuelson effect. But recent evidence indicates that the LOOP does not hold for these countries and this is reflected in the fact that the PPI-based real exchange rate has appreciated at the same rate as the CPI rate and in any case the non-traded sector is relatively small in these countries (of the order of 20–30%). Egert *et al.* (2005), for example, report that only around 2% of these countries, appreciations can be explained in this way. One explanation for the dramatic PPI appreciation for these countries is that it may simply reflect a 'catching up' phenomenon, in terms of a quality adjustment bias and a demand shift to domestic produced tradables.

MacDonald and Wojcik (2004) argue that regulated price increases, particularly in the non-traded sector, seem to be an important component in explaining the appreciation important and indeed this effect is shown to dominate the productivity effect.

9.5   Permanent and transitory decompositions of real exchange rates – PEERS permanent and transitory components of real exchange rates

A somewhat different way of measuring equilibrium exchange rates is to use a time series estimator to decompose a real exchange rate into its permanent and transitory components:

$$q_t = q_t^P + q_t^T,$$

where q_t^P is the permanent component and q_t^T is the transitory component of the real exchange rate. The permanent component is then taken to be the measure of equilibrium – the permanent equilibrium exchange rate, or PEER. As we saw in the previous chapter there are a number of alternative ways of extracting the permanent component from an economic series, one of the most widely used being the Beveridge-Nelson decomposition.

9.5.1   Beveridge-Nelson decompositions

Huizinga (1987) was the first to plot the permanent component derived from a univariate BN decomposition against the actual real rate and then make inferences about the extent of over or undervaluation of particular currencies. His analysis shows the dollar to have been overvalued for the 2-year period 1976–8, undervalued for the 4-year period from late 1978 to late 1982 and overvalued for the 3-year period from early 1983 to early 1986. He estimates the post-1985 depreciation of the dollar to have been just right in terms of returning it to its current long-run value against the pound.

As we saw in Chapter 8, Cumby and Huizinga (1990) apply multivariate BN decomposition (MBN) to the real exchange rates of the $–DM, $–Yen, $–Sterling and $–C$. The permanent components generally vary considerably over time but are somewhat more stable than the actual exchange rate, often leaving large and sustained deviations of these real rates from the predicted 'equilibrium' values.

However, Clarida and Gali (1994) sound a cautionary note about using BN type decompositions to generate measures of exchange rate misalignment. In particular, they present both univariate and multivariate BN decompositions of the real exchange rates of Germany, Japan, Britain and Canada. As we saw in Chapter 8, on the basis of the average univariate BN results, around 0.8% of the variance of the real exchange rate is permanent and only 0.2% is transitory. For Japan and Germany, however, the picture is quite different when multivariate BN decompositions are used. In this case 0.6 (for Japan) and 0.7 (for Germany) of the variance of the real exchange rate is attributable to transitory factors (Baxter 1994 confirms this finding). Clarida and Gali show that this can make a big difference to the measure of misalignment in the sense that the two measures can give conflicting signals. We believe that this finding emphasises the importance of fundamentals in explaining exchange rate behaviour and the importance of conditioning on an appropriate set of fundamentals in any exercise where exchange rate assessment issues arise.

9.5.2   *Structured vector autoregressions*

As we noted in Chapter 8, Clarida and Gali (1994) propose an SVAR approach to extracting demand and supply shocks (taken to be the permanent components of the real exchange rate) and nominal shocks (taken to be the transitory components of real exchange rates). They then construct figures to show the importance of the three shocks on the real exchange rates of the US dollar bilateral rates of the Canadian dollar, German mark, Japanese yen and UK pound. This is illustrated in Figure 9.3, reproduced from Clarida and Gali (1994), for the DM. In this figure newsslogq represents the actual real exchange rate with the cumulative effect of the three shocks netted out and it is plotted against the evolution of the real exchange rate if only one shock had prevailed (monetary shocks in the first segment, demand shocks in the second and supply shocks in the third). So the top panel in the figure compares the actual path of the dollar–DM real exchange rate with the path that would have existed if only nominal shocks had hit the system. The figure indicates, for example, that nearly all of the real depreciation of the dollar against the DM in the late 1970s was attributable to demand shocks, while the real appreciation in the first half of the 1980s was attributable to demand shocks.

MacDonald and Swagel (2000) apply the Clarida–Gali method to the real effective exchange rates of the German mark, Japanese yen, UK pound and US dollar (and also the bilateral US dollar exchange rates of the German mark, pound sterling and Japanese yen). They interpret the cyclical, or business cycle, component as the sum of the demand and nominal shocks and netting this out from the

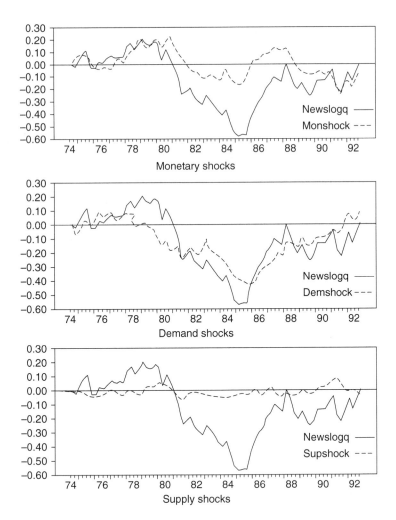

Figure 9.3 Sources of $/DM real exchange rate fluctuations.

Source: Clarida and Gali (1994).

actual real exchange rate, produces an alternative measure of the permanent (i.e. supply side) component of the real exchange rate. These permanent components are plotted against the actual effective rates in Figure 9.4. For the DM, for example, supply side movements explain the movement in the effective rate up to 1984 and then cyclical factors account for the subsequent weakness and then appreciation and depreciation through 1989. Supply side factors explain the appreciation of the mark from 1991 to 1994 while the appreciation from 1994 to 1995 is explained by a relatively strong cyclical position.

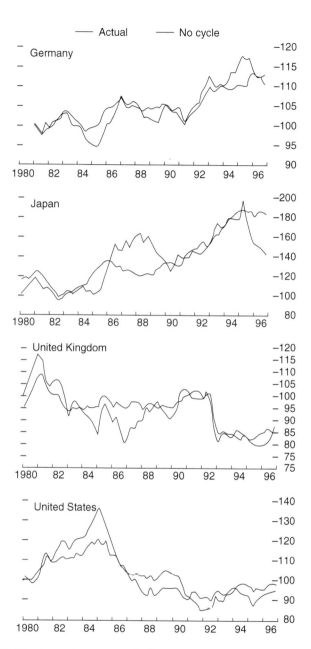

Figure 9.4 Effective exchange rate misalignments.

Source: MacDonald and Swagel (2000).

Detken *et al.* (2000) augment the basic Clarida–Gali model to include a relative employment term, the difference in the ratio of government consumption over GDP and the long-term interest differential. They apply this model to the real effective exchange rate of a synthetic euro for the period 1973–98. They find that the various shocks have a correctly signed effect on the exchange rate and around one-half of the contemporaneous forecast errors in the real exchange rate are accounted for by nominal shocks, although in the long-run, despite having a relatively rich supply side, real demand shocks dominate the evolution of the real exchange rate.

9.5.3   *Cointegration-based PEER estimates*

Clark and MacDonald (2000) also propose using the permanent component calculated from a VAR system and interpret this as measure of equilibrium, which is referred to as the permanent equilibrium exchange rate (or PEER). In contrast to the studies that use SVARS the PEER does not rely on Blanchard–Quah style restrictions, but it does require the existence of cointegration amongst the variables entering the VAR. Clark and MacDonald (2000) interpret the PEER as one way of calibrating a BEER and for reasons that shall become clear, they interpret the misalignment calculated from the PEER as a total misalignment. The approach may be illustrated in the following way. Johansen (1995) has demonstrated that a vector error correction model, such as that used by most of the researchers who have estimated a BEER, has a vector moving average representation of the following form:

$$x_t = C \sum_{i=1}^{t} \varepsilon_i + C\mu t + C^*(L)(\varepsilon_t + \mu), \tag{9.20}$$

where

$$C = \beta_\perp \left(\alpha'_\perp \left(I - \sum_{1}^{k-1} \Gamma_i \right) \beta_\perp \right)^{-1} \alpha'_\perp,$$

and where $\alpha_\perp$ determines the vectors defining the space of the common stochastic trends and therefore should be informative about the key 'driving' variable(s). The $\beta_\perp$ vector gives the loadings associated with $\alpha_\perp$ (i.e. the series which are driven by the common trends).

If the vector X is of reduced rank, r (i.e. if there exists cointegration) then Granger and Gonzalo (1995) have demonstrated that the elements of X can also be explained in terms of a smaller number of $(n - r)$ of $I(1)$ variables called common factors, f_t, plus some $I(0)$ components, the transitory elements:

$$X_t = A_1 f_t + \tilde{X}_t. \tag{9.21}$$

The identification of the common factors may be achieved in the following way. If it is assumed that the common factors, f_t, are linear combinations of the variables X_t:

$$f_t = B_1 X_t, \tag{9.22}$$

and if $A_1 f_t$ and $\tilde{X}_t$ form a permanent–transitory decomposition of X_t then from the VECM representation the only linear combination of X_t such that $\tilde{X}_t$ has no long-run impact on X_t are:

$$f_t = \alpha'_\perp X_t, \tag{9.23}$$

where $\alpha'_\perp \alpha = 0$. As Granger and Gonzalo point out, these are the linear combinations of ΔX_t which have the 'common feature' of not containing the levels of the error correction term z_{t-1} in them. This identification of the common factors enables Granger and Gonzalo to obtain the following permanent–transitory decomposition of X_t:

$$X_t = A_1 \alpha'_\perp X_t + A_2 \beta' X_t, \tag{9.24}$$

where, of terms not previously defined, $A_1 = \beta_\perp (\alpha'_\perp \beta_\perp)^{-1}$ and $A_2 = \alpha(\beta'\alpha)^{-1}$. It is straightforward to demonstrate that the common factor, f_t, corresponds to the common trend in the analysis of Stock and Watson (1988). This has the advantage that it is easier to estimate and also hypotheses on the common trends can be tested.

Clark and MacDonald (2000) estimate BEERs and PEERs for the real effective exchange rates of the US dollar, the Canadian dollar and UK pound, for the period 1960–97. The model is simpler than that used in Clark and MacDonald (1998) since both the terms of trade and the risk premium are dropped from the analysis. The relevant vector analysed therefore becomes:

$$x'_t = [q_t, (r_t - r_t^*), \text{nfa}_t].$$

For all three currencies studied there is evidence of one statistically significant cointegration vector and this is therefore consistent with three common trends. For both the US and Canadian dollars a close association is found between the BEER and the PEER. For these currencies therefore the value added in using the PEER approach lies in its ability to detect the source of the common trends, and the orthogonal decomposition of alpha and beta suggested that they are driven predominantly by the net foreign asset and Balassa–Samuelson terms. For the UK pound, however, the implied time path of the BEER and PEER turn out to be very different and the UK BEER is much more volatile than the actual real exchange rate, particularly in the first half of the sample period, whereas the PEER is smoother than the BEER. An analysis of the permanent and transitory components of the other variables reveals that the source of the difference is that the actual real interest differential contains a substantial transitory element in the case of the UK (the correlation between the actual and transitory real interest rates for the UK is 0.8, while for the

US it is only 0.06) and the PEER measure, by definition, filters this out of the data leaving only the permanent component. Clark and MacDonald (2000) therefore argue that supplementing the BEER approach with a PEER decomposition may be useful for assessment purposes, especially if the driving fundamentals contain important transitory elements.

Alberola *et al.* (1999) estimate BEER type relationships (the cointegrating vector comprises the real exchange rate, net foreign assets and a Balassa–Samuelson term) for a variety of industrial country real effective exchange rates, using the Engle–Granger two-step method. PEERs are then constructed to gauge the extent of currency misalignments. For example, at the end of 1998 they estimated that the euro was undervalued by 4.5%, the dollar overvalued by 7.5% and the pound sterling is overvalued by 15.7%. Bilateral estimates of equilibrium were then constructed and these show that the euro was undervalued against the dollar at the end of 1998 by 7.5%, and this had widened to an undervaluation of around 20% by the end of 1999. Similarly, the dollar proved to be strongly overvalued against the yen, by 13.64% and to a lesser extent against the Canadian dollar by 4.63%.

Makrydakis *et al.* (2000) use the methods of Johansen to estimate BEER relationships for a synthetic times series of the euro, over the period 1980Q1–99Q2. The conditioning variables are a relative productivity term (the ratio of GDP to total employment), net foreign assets and a real interest differential. All of the coefficients on these variables enter with the correct sign and their magnitude is similar to those obtained for the original EMU currencies, such as the German mark, although the net foreign asset term is statistically insignificant. The implied PEER is then calculated using the methods of Granger and Gonzalo (1995) and this is interpreted as the equilibrium exchange rate. They show that the euro was 1.5% above its equilibrium at the end of the first quarter in 1999, although this had declined to a misalignment of only 0.34% by the second quarter of 1999. Makrydakis *et al.* also use their estimated PEER to describe the historical evolution of the real synthetic euro.

Hoffman and MacDonald (2000) present PEER estimates which are subject to both a cointegration constraint and to the additional constraints implied by a structural VAR. In particular, they consider a vector comprising a real income differential, the real effective exchange rate and the real interest differential (this choice being motivated by an extended Mundell–Fleming–Dornbusch model). Six country systems are considered (the US, Japan, Germany, France, Italy, the UK and Canada) and the estimation period is 1978, quarter 2 to 1997 quarter 4. In contrast to the studies considered in the previous sub-section, permanent and transitory components are identified solely from the cointegration information in the data. Real and nominal shocks are then disentangled using the identification methods of Blanchard and Quah. In sum, Hoffman and MacDonald find that the majority of real exchange rate variation is explained by real shocks, although nominal shocks have an important role to play as well.

Using the Granger–Gonzalo decomposition, Hoffman and MacDonald generate permanent and transitory decompositions and they find that the bulk of exchange rate movements are permanent. For the US effective rate, practically all of the appreciation of the US dollar in the 1980s would seem to be permanent, and this contrasts with the findings of Clark and MacDonald (2000). Japan has the largest misalignment of the countries studied (being around 10% of the permanent component) and all misalignments tend to be very persistent, with autocorrelations ranging between 0.6 (for Canada) and 0.96 (for Italy). Hoffman and MacDonald also explore the sources of the shocks and find that, on average, between one-quarter and one-third of the misalignment forecast error variance is due to nominal permanent shocks. The role of real shocks, however, tends to be more varied across countries. For example, in the cases of the US and France it accounts for almost two-thirds of misalignment variance, but plays little role for Germany and Canada.

9.6   The internal–external balance (IEB) approach

The internal–external balance (IEB) approach has perhaps been the most popular way of estimating an equilibrium exchange rate in which deviations from PPP are explicitly recognised. In that sense it has some similarities to the BEER approach. However, the key difference with the BEER approach is that the IEB usually places more structure, in a normative sense, on the determination of the exchange rate. In particular, and in general terms, the equilibrium real exchange rate is defined as that rate which satisfies both internal and external balance. Internal balance is usually taken to be a level of output consistent with full employment and low inflation – say, the NAIRU – and the net savings generated at this output level have to be equal to the current balance, which need not necessarily equal zero in this approach. The general flavour of the IEB approach may be captured by the following equation:

$$S(W) - I(X) = CA(\hat{q}, Y) = -\text{CPA}(Z), \tag{9.25}$$

where S denotes national savings, I denotes investment spending and W, X, Y and Z are vectors of variables, to be discussed later, and $\hat{q}$ is the real exchange rate consistent with internal balance and the value chosen for CAP (the external balance objective). All of the approaches discussed in this section use a variant of this relationship.

9.6.1   *Fundamental equilibrium exchange rates – FEERS*

In the internal–external balance approach of Williamson (1983a) the equilibrium exchange rate is labelled a fundamental equilibrium exchange rate (FEER). This is an explicitly medium-run concept, in the sense that the FEER does not need to be consistent with stock-flow equilibrium (the medium-run is usually taken to be a period of earlier 5 years in the future), and in that sense is in the spirit of the balance of payments model presented in Chapter 1 and restated earlier as equation (9.1). The FEER approach has been refined and developed by Wren-Lewis (1992).

The definition of internal balance used in this approach is as given earlier – high employment and low inflation. External balance is characterised as the sustainable desired net flow of resources between countries when they are in internal balance. This is usually arrived at judgementally, essentially by taking a position on the net savings term in (9.25) which, in turn, will be determined by factors such as consumption smoothing and demographic changes. The use of the latter assumption, especially, has meant that the FEER is often interpreted as a normative approach and the calculated FEER is likely to be sensitive to the choice of the sustainable capital account. It also means that the misalignment implied by the FEER is a total misalignment.

There are essentially two approaches to estimating a FEER. The first involves taking an estimated macroeconometric model, imposing internal and external balance, and solving for the real exchange rate which is then classified as the FEER. However, by far the most popular method of generating a FEER involves focussing on a current account equation and setting it equal to a sustainable capital account (see Wren-Lewis 1992). For example, consider again the current account relationship underpinning equation (9.1) and set this equal to a sustainable capital account term:

$$\alpha_1(s_t + p_t^* - p_t) - \alpha_2 \bar{y}_t + \alpha \bar{y}_t^* + i' \bar{\text{nfa}}_t = \bar{\text{cap}}_t^{st} \tag{9.26}$$

where symbols have their usual interpretation (i' is the net interest payments on net foreign assets, nfa) an overbar denotes that a variable has been calibrated at a desired, or sustainable, level and cap is the measure of the capital account. It is important to note that Williamson's definition of the latter excludes speculative capital flows and focuses on structural capital flows, hence the superscript st on cap. Given that variables are set at desired values in (9.26), and assuming estimates of the α terms are available, the equation may be solved for the real exchange rate, which is the FEER. The other popular, although less tractable, way of estimating a FEER is to impose internal and external balance on a full blown macroeconometric model and solve for the real exchange rate.

Barrell and Wren-Lewis (1989) demonstrate that in calculating the FEER it is very important to allow for revaluation effects through the net foreign asset term, especially if the Marshall–Lerner condition just holds. As Wren-Lewis (1992) emphasises, this implies that the real interest rate has settled at its long-run equilibrium value in the medium-run. Clearly, this is a strong assumption, since it places a constraint on monetary policy in the medium-run. Furthermore, Wren-Lewis (1992) notes that the FEER is a 'method of calculation of a real exchange rate which is consistent with medium term macroeconomic equilibrium'. That is to say, the FEER approach does not embody a theory of exchange rate determination. Nonetheless, there is the implicit assumption that the actual real effective exchange rate will converge over time to the FEER. Hence embedded in this approach is a medium-run current account theory of exchange rate determination. That is, it is assumed that a divergence of the actual real rate from the FEER will set in motion forces that will eventually eliminate this divergence, but as the approach characterises only the equilibrium position, the nature of the adjustment forces is left unspecified.

In addition to the difficulty in measuring a sustainable capital account, the calculation of trade elasticities has often meant that an extra layer of judgement has to be imposed before the FEER can be calculated. This is because the estimated trade elasticity (or elasticities) (the α_1 in (9.26)) often turn out to be effectively zero (see Goldstein and Khan 1985). Furthermore, what has been described by Driver (2000) as the 'Achilles heel' of the FEER approach is the hysteresis introduced into the FEER due to interest payments on the net foreign asset term. Bayoumi *et al.* (1994) consider this effect in some detail. To illustrate, assume that in the initial period the current exchange rate is at the FEER level and internal and external balance obtains. The actual real exchange rate then depreciates in the next period, thereby improving the current balance and improving the country's net foreign asset position. The latter, in turn, implies that in future periods the real exchange rate, consistent with medium-run capital accumulation, will no longer be the FEER; in particular, the FEER needs to appreciate to squeeze out the effects of the net asset accumulation. This hysteresis effect is a necessary consequence of viewing the exchange rate as a medium-run concept. Taking a stock measure of equilibrium would of course rule out this kind of effect.

Driver and Wren-Lewis (1999) assess the sensitivity of FEER calculations of the US dollar, Japanese yen and German mark to different formulations and assumptions. They find that two key factors impart a considerable amount of uncertainty into FEER type calculations. For example, changes in the assumed value of the sustainable capital account (as a proportion of GDP) of 1% can produce changes in the value of the FEER of around 5%. Since such changes in the capital account could easily be due to measurement error, this suggests caution in interpreting point estimates of the FEER. For example, in using a FEER to define the equilibrium rate with which to lock two currencies together, some sort of confidence interval should be applied to the point estimate (this uncertainty is one of the reasons why Williamson argues that crawling peg arrangements should feature wide exchange rate bands). Driver and Wren-Lewis also show that it is often difficult to produce well-defined estimates of the trade equations, and therefore the underlying trade elasticities, which are so central to the FEER. Inevitably, this means that the FEER estimate will be sensitive to the chosen elasticity.

Barrell *et al.* (1991) estimated a FEER for the UK pound and demonstrated that the central parity rate at which the UK entered the ERM was overvalued. This finding contrasted sharply to an estimate based on PPP that showed the pound correctly valued on entry. Driver and Wren-Lewis (1998) present estimates of the FEER for the G7 in the year 2000. They find, *inter alia*, that the FEER estimates for 2000 differ in important respects from the rates prevailing in early 1998 (at the time the study was written). In particular, they find that the US dollar was substantially overvalued, the yen grossly undervalued, while the pounds value was about correct against the dollar, although overvalued against European currencies.

9.6.2   The IMF variant of the internal–external balance approach

One of the key objectives of the recent IMF implementation of the IEB approach (see, for example, Isard and Faruqee 1998 and Faruqee *et al.* 1999) is to produce a more satisfactory measure of the desired capital account term. One important element in this approach is the recognition that the equilibrium current account can be viewed as the difference between desired saving and investment, $\bar{S} - \bar{I}$, which, in turn, is equal to the sustainable capital account in (9.25). The equilibrium real exchange rate is then calculated as the real effective exchange rate that will generate a current account equal to $\bar{S} - \bar{I}$. More specifically, the IMF works with the following variant of (9.25):

$$S(\text{def}, \text{gap}, \text{dep}, (y - y^*)) - I(\text{gap}, \text{dep}, (y - y^*)) = CA(q, \text{gap}, \text{gapf}) \tag{9.27}$$

where, of variables not previously defined, def is the government deficit, gap is the difference between actual and potential output and gapf is the difference between foreign and actual and potential output and dep is the dependency ratio. The IMF's IEB approach defines two measures of equilibrium. A medium-run current account equilibrium (a flow equilibrium rather than a stock equilibrium) is defined as a position where domestic and foreign output gaps are eliminated and the current exchange rate is expected to remain into the indefinite future. A longer-run equilibrium is one in which the underlying current account position is compared with a stable ratio of NFA to GDP, where the latter is designed to measure stock equilibrium.

The mechanics of calculating the medium-run equilibrium exchange rate are as follows. First, dynamic savings and investment equations are estimated, along with a dynamic current account equation. These equations are then solved for the long-run equilibrium and output gaps are set equal to zero and the fiscal deficit is cyclically adjusted. The resulting savings–investment gap is then compared with the estimated current account position and if there is a discrepancy the exchange rate is assumed to move to equilibrate the two relationships. The latter exchange rate is interpreted as the medium-run equilibrium. For example, if the savings–investment relationship produces a surplus of 1% of GDP, while the current account relationship suggests a deficit of -1% of GDP, the exchange rate would have to depreciate in order to bring about an improvement of the current account of 2% of GDP. One of the appealing components of this approach is that the required exchange rate changes required across countries are ensured to be internally consistent on a multilateral basis by an appropriate normalisation.

9.6.3   The natural real exchange rate – the NATREX

In the NATREX approach of Stein (1994, 1999), Stein and Allen (1995) and Stein and Sauernheimer (1997) the starting point is again equation (9.25). As in the FEER approach, Stein excludes speculative capital flows from his measure of the capital account, and the sustainable capital account term is assumed equal to social saving less planned investment. The key determinant of social savings is the rate of time preference, tp, while the key determinant of investment is Tobin's 'q'. The latter in turn is determined by productivity, ω, and the real exchange rate:

$$S(tp, \text{nfa}) - I(\omega, q, k) = CA(q, k, \text{nfa}). \tag{9.28}$$

Aditionally, savings are assumed to be a function of net foreign assets and invest-ment a function of the capital stock, k. The inclusion of stocks in the flow relationships enables an equilibrium to be derived that is stock-flow consistent. Stein (1999) proposes two forms of NATREX equilibrium. In 'long-run' equilib-rium the following criteria have to be satisfied. First, net foreign assets are constant and, in a non-growing economy, the current account is equal to zero. Second, the capital stock is constant and the rate of capacity utilisation is at its stationary mean. Real interest rate parity prevails, in the sense that real interest rates are equalised (since the real exchange rate is also in equilibrium, the expected change in the real exchange rate is zero). Finally, there are no changes in reserves or speculative capital movements. The difference between the medium- and long-run NATREX relates to the evolution of net foreign assets and the capital stock. For example, in the medium-run the current account can be non-zero to the extent that *ex ante* savings minus *ex ante* investment is non-zero. Such imbalances get integrated into the stocks and these ultimately drive the system to a long-run equilibrium where intertemporal budget constraints are satisfied. In both the long- and medium-run equilibria, internal balance is assumed to hold.

Using a VECM model, Stein (1999) empirically implements the NATREX in a single equation context for the real US dollar effective exchange rate against the G7 for the post-Bretton Woods period. Time preference is measured as the ratio of social (sum of public and private) consumption to GDP and the productivity of capital is measured as a four-quarter moving average of the growth of real GDP. These are the two key explanatory variables that Stein uses to model the long-run real exchange rate. The long-run estimates (using the Johansen method) are:

$$q_t = \underset{(88.93)}{-404.97}\, tp_t + \underset{(202.87)}{1207.98}\, tp_t^* + \underset{(1.06)}{2.044}\, pr_t - \underset{(0.50)}{2.211}\, pr_t^*. \tag{9.29}$$

All of the variables are seen to be correctly signed in terms of the NATREX – an increase in US (G7) time preference depreciates (appreciates) the US dollar, while an increase in US (G7) productivity appreciates (depreciates) the US dol-lar. The implied equilibrium here is clearly a current equilibrium since none of the fundamentals are calibrated at desired levels. Furthermore, none of the stock levels, which are so crucial in defining the longer-run NATREX, appear in (9.29). Stein also presents estimates of a medium-run equilibrium exchange rate in which an interest differential and the deviation of capacity utilisation from its mean are included in addition to the variables mentioned earlier.

9.6.4   *The new open economy macroeconomics approach to equilibrium exchange rates*

As we shall see in the next chapter, the basic idea in the new open economy (NOEM) class of model is that the optimising behaviour of consumers has implications for the current account which, in turn, has implications for exchange rates. Obstfeld and Rogoff (2001) have shown how this approach may be used to assess whether currencies are overvalued or not and we follow their example here. The approach has more in common with the FEER-based approach than the other approaches considered in this chapter since it does not produce a *measure* of the equilibrium exchange rate. Rather, it asks the question: how much would the exchange rate have to move to reduce a current account imbalance to zero?

The first assumption in the NOEM is that the authorities have an internal balance objective, as in the internal–external balance approach, in which they seek to reduce the current account deficit to zero. Consumers are assumed to have a CES utility function of the form:

$$\left[\gamma C_T^{(\theta-1)/\theta} + (1-\gamma)C_N^{(\theta-1)/\theta} \right]^{\theta/(\theta-1)}, \tag{9.30}$$

where θ is the price elasticity, C_T is the consumption of traded goods and C_N is the consumption of non-traded goods. When $\theta = 1$, (9.30) simplifies to the simple log form:

$$\gamma \log C_T + (1-\gamma) \log C_N. \tag{9.31}$$

The domestic production of both tradables and non-tradables is assumed exogenous at Y_T and Y_N, respectively, and so the consumption of non-traded goods must match the production of non-traded goods, that is $C_N = Y_N$. However, the existence of international trade means that the consumer's consumption of the traded good is not tied to production – $C_T \neq Y_T$.

If prices are assumed fully flexible then it follows that the relative price of non-traded to traded goods – $p = P_{NT}/P_T$ – is determined in the following way.

$$p = \left(\frac{1-\gamma}{\gamma} \right)^{1/\theta} \left(\frac{C_T}{Y_N} \right)^{1/\theta} \tag{9.32}$$

and it follows that the exact CPI, in terms of the traded good, is:

$$P = \left[\gamma + (1-\gamma)p^{(1-\theta)} \right]^{1/(1-\theta)} \tag{9.33}$$

Given the earlier set-up, calculation of the required exchange rate change – real and nominal – to remove a current account imbalance hinges on having numerical values for θ and C_T/Y_N. For the parameter θ, Ostry and Reinhart (1991) have reported point estimates of around one for short- to medium-run horizons, although the figure is likely to be higher in the long-run. An estimate of C_T/Y_N may be obtained from the current account ratio:

$$\frac{CA}{Y} = \frac{Y_T - C_T - iD}{Y},\qquad(9.34)$$

where Y (GDP) and D (net external debt) are expressed in terms of traded goods. Taking the situation of the US in 2001, where a current account deficit as a proportion of GDP of 4.4% existed, Obstfeld and Rogoff assume Y_T/Y is 25% and iD/Y is 1.2% (which implies an interest rate of 6% and a GDP to net debt ratio of 20%). If for external balance, the ratio of the current account to income, CA/Y, falls to zero the drop in net imports of tradables would need to be 16% (i.e. 4.4 / 28.2). With prices fully flexible and θ equal to unity, the relative price of non-traded to traded goods, p, has to fall by 16%, otherwise there would be an excess supply of non-traded goods which would conflict with the internal balance assumption.

The impact of the rise in the relative price of traded goods (p falls) on the CPI depends on the Fed's price stabilisation policy. If the Fed tries to stabilise the CPI then with $Y_{NT} = 75\%$ and $Y_T = 25\%$ a 12% rise in traded prices would be required and a 4% fall in non-traded prices. Since P_T is set in world markets this implies a 12% depreciation of the exchange rate.

The effects of current account changes depend crucially on the underlying assumptions. For example, if the parameter θ equalled 0.5, instead of 1, this would imply a nominal exchange rate depreciation of 24%. Alternatively, a value of Y_T/Y of 15% would imply a 20% exchange rate depreciation. If the assumption of price flexibility is swapped for one of some price stickiness this will alter the current account implications for the exchange rate further. For example, if exporters only pass-through one-half of any exchange rate change to importers, the Fed would have to let the dollar depreciate by 24% to stabilise the CPI and the level of employment in the non-traded sector. With price stickiness of traded and non-traded goods, and if imports account for about half of all traded goods consumed, then a US dollar depreciation of between 40% and 50% would be required.

The upshot of the Obstfeld and Rogoff analysis is that there is an important short–long distinction in the effects of the current account on the exchange rate. In the long run with price flexibility and a higher value of θ, the required exchange rate change would be much smaller than the short-run where the combination of price stickiness and a relatively small value of θ would produce a large exchange rate change. Since their approach requires little in the way of data, the NOEM approach would seem to offer a tractable way of calculating how much required exchange rate adjustment is necessary to achieve current account objectives. It therefore may be an appealing method of calculating equilibrium exchange rates for developing countries or transition economies where data constraints may make it difficult to implement some of the other approaches outlined in this chapter.

Conclusions

In this chapter we have overviewed different ways of constructing an equilibrium real exchange rate. These approaches all take as their starting point the view that, for the reasons given in Chapter 2, PPP on its own is not sufficient for calculating an equilibrium exchange rate. We argued that purchasing power parity and atheoretical constructs are unlikely to be well-suited for this purpose. However, we have also argued that there are a variety of approaches which do provide well-defined measures of equilibrium. A strictly medium-run measure of the equilibrium exchange rate is provided by the capital enhanced extension of PPP. This approach has been demonstrated to produce mean reversion speeds that are much faster than that produced by PPP on its own. The approach may also be extended in a straightforward fashion to incorporate other financial effects such as the yield gap and, say, stock market revaluations. More structured approaches to defining the medium-run equilibrium exchange rate are provided by the different variants of the internal–external balance approach. In this approach the key characteristic of the medium-run is that any current account imbalance must be sustainable. The internal–external balance approach also provides a measure of the long-run exchange rate which is usually defined as a position where net foreign assets are constant. One key feature of the internal–external balance approach is that it usually contains a substantial normative element, in terms of what is meant by sustainability and internal balance. The behavioural equilibrium approach seeks to provide a measure of the equilibrium exchange rate which is stock-flow consistent and which is independent of assumptions about sustainability. However, the approach can be used to provide a measure of equilibrium in which fundamentals are calibrate at sustainable levels, although this is quite a separate exercise. We have also argued that further insight into the nature of a behavioural equilibrium exchange rate may be gauged from a decomposition of the real exchange rate into its permanent and transitory components.

10 The new open economy macroeconomics and exchange rate behaviour

In this chapter, and the next, we consider exchange rate models based on the so-called new open economy macroeconomics (NOEM) of Obstfeld and Rogoff. In this chapter we consider two base-line models: the two-country and small-country variants of the NOEM. As in the variants of the Lucas monetary model considered in Chapter 3, the NOEM class of models have at their heart the optimising behaviour of agents, although in the NOEM this is combined with monopolistic producers who set prices one period in advance in their own currency (i.e. there is producer pricing and complete pass-through). The monopolistic element of these models means price exceeds marginal cost and, even with short-run price stickiness, the monopolist is prepared to supply more output in response to increases in demand. Output is therefore demand determined in this class of model. One of the major advantages of this approach is that it readily facilitates the analysis of the welfare effects of macroeconomic policy. The approach stemmed from Svensson and van Wijnbergen (1989) and was further developed and fleshed out by Obsfeld and Rogoff (1995, 1996, 2000a,c). A more tractable variant of the model is presented in Corsetti and Pensetti (2001) and Lane (2001) provides a useful survey of this literature.

The outline of our discussion of the NOEM is as follows. In the next section we analyse the two-country redux exchange rate model of Obstfeld and Rogoff (1995). This is essentially a variant of the Mundell–Fleming–Dornbusch model, with optimising individuals and prices preset in an imperfectly competitive market. Our discussion of the model is as complete as we think it necessary to impart the basic tenor of the key results. However, since we have not adopted the NOEM as the main framework in our book some short cuts have been taken and if the reader finds some elements rather opaque they are directed to the original source material (particularly Obstfeld and Rogoff 1995, 1996). In Section 10.2 roles for both productivity and government spending are introduced. In Section 10.3 the small-country variant of the NOEM is presented. Here we revisit the issue of exchange rate overshooting and the effects of monetary policy on the current account and the real exchange rate. Throughout the book we have used upper case letter to denote the level of a variable and lower case letters the log level. The rule does not apply in this chapter where we need lower and upper case letters to signify individual and composite terms, respectively. In the next chapter we consider some extensions to the NOEM which have an important bearing on the issue of exchange rate volatility.

10.1   The two-country redux model

10.1.1   *The base-line two-country model*

The redux model is a two-country model and in each country there is a continuum of consumer–producers (sometimes referred to as yeoman farmers) that produce differentiated goods $(0, n)$ in the home country and $(n,1)$ in the foreign country (the discussion here follows Obstfeld and Rogoff 1995, 1996 and Lane 2001). Agents have perfect foresight and have monopoly power and, crucially, charge a price above marginal cost. This is an important assumption in this model because it means that output is at less than the socially optimum level and therefore expansionary monetary policy, say, can have a permanent effect on output. In our presentation of the model we will generally focus on the home relationships and only introduce foreign relationships where it is helpful for the discussion. However, it is important to bear in mind that paralleling each of the home country relationships is usually an equivalent foreign country relationship. The preferences of the representative home agent, j, are assumed to be given by the following function:

$$U_t^j = \sum_{s=t}^{\infty} \beta^{s-t} \left(\log C_s^j + \eta \left(\frac{M_s}{P_s} \right)^{1-\varepsilon} - \frac{\kappa}{2} y_s(j)^2 \right), \tag{10.1}$$

where β is the subjective rate of time preference $(0 < \beta < 1)$, C is a constant elasticity of substitution (CES) consumption index of the following form:

$$C = \left[\int_0^1 c^j(z)^{(\theta-1)/\theta} dz \right]^{\theta/(\theta-1)}, \qquad \theta > 1, \tag{10.2}$$

where $c^j(z)$ is the consumption of good z by individual j, θ is the consumption (intra-temporal) elasticity of substitution, M denotes money balances, P is the consumption-based price index (defined below), ε is the consumption elasticity of money demand $(\varepsilon > 0)$ and it is (implicitly) assumed that the inter-temporal elasticity of substitution is equal to unity (we return to this point in the final section). As we shall see later, θ is also the price elasticity of demand facing the monopolist producer and the reason this is assumed to be greater than unity is to be consistent with the assumption of monopolistic competition.[1]

From equation (10.1) we see that agents derive positive utility from consumption and real money balances, M/P (because the latter reduce transactions costs), and disutility from work, which is assumed positively related to output. More specifically, suppose the disutility from work, l, is given by $-\phi l$ and the production function is $y = Al^{\alpha}$ or, alternatively, in inverted form $l = (y/A)^{1/\alpha}$. Then if $\alpha = 1/2$ and $\kappa = 2\phi/A^{1/\alpha}$ we obtain the output term in equation (10.1).

The home price index associated with the consumption index is the price index which measures the minimum value of expenditure which buys one unit of the consumption index. Formally, minimising the expenditure function, or nominal budget constraint $\mathcal{Z}$:

$$\min_{c(z)} \mathcal{Z} = \int_0^1 p(z)c(z)dz,$$

(where $p(z)$ is the home currency price of good z) subject to:

$$\left[\int_0^1 c(z)^{\theta/(\theta-1)}dz \right]^{\theta/(1-\theta)} = 1,$$

yields the home money price level:

$$P = \left[\int_0^1 p(z)^{1-\theta}dz \right]^{1/(1-\theta)}. \tag{10.3}$$

If the law of one price is assumed to hold for individual commodities, expression (10.3) may be rewritten as:

$$P = \left[\int_0^1 p(z)^{1-\theta}dz \right]^{1/(1-\theta)}$$

$$= \left[\int_0^n p(z)^{1-\theta}dz + \int_n^1 [Sp^*(z)]^{1-\theta}dz \right]^{1/(1-\theta)}, \tag{10.3a}$$

and the equivalent expression in the foreign country is:

$$P^* = \left[\int_0^1 p^*(z)^{1-\theta}dz \right]^{1/(1-\theta)}$$

$$= \left[\int_0^n [p(z)/S]^{1-\theta}dz + \int_n^1 [p^*(z)^{1-\theta}dz \right]^{1/(1-\theta)}, \tag{10.3b}$$

where 0 to n goods are made in the home country and the rest produced abroad. It is worth noting that if we compare equation (10.3a) and (10.3b) domestic prices are related to foreign prices by absolute PPP – $P = SP^*$. This follows in this model because preferences are identical across countries and because the LOOP is assumed to hold initially. However, and as we shall see, terms of trade changes are important in this model and so changes in the relative prices of individual goods can take place. The period-by-period nominal budget constraint for the representative individual is written in nominal terms as:

$$P_t F_{t+1}^j + M_t^j = P_t(1+r_t)F_t^j + M_{t-1}^j + p_t(j)y_t(j) - P_t C_t^j - P_t \tau_t, \tag{10.4}$$

where r denotes the real interest rate on bonds between $t-1$ and t, $y_t(j)$ is output of good j for which agent j is the sole producer and $p(j)$ is its domestic currency price.

The variable F is a riskless real bond denominated in the consumption commodity good (this is assumed to be the only traded asset in the model and therefore equals C) and τ denotes lump sum taxes. The government is assumed to balance its budget:

$$\tau_t + \frac{M_t - M_{t-1}}{P_t} = 0, \tag{10.5}$$

and in the absence of government spending this means that all seignorage revenues are returned to the public in the form of transfers. By maximising (10.2) subject to the nominal budget constraint the following expression may be obtained

$$\int_0^1 p(z)c(z)dz = \mathcal{Z}, \tag{10.6}$$

where $\mathcal{Z}$ is any fixed total nominal expenditure on goods. It can be demonstrated that for any two goods z and z':

$$c(z') = c(z)\left[\frac{p(z)}{p(z')}\right]^\theta, \tag{10.7}$$

which indicates that relative consumption depends only on relative prices, which is intuitive enough given that preferences are assumed to have a CES form. By substituting (10.7) into (10.6) and using (10.3) the representative agents' demand for good z is given by:

$$c^j(z) = \left[\frac{p(z)}{P}\right]^{-\theta}\frac{\mathcal{Z}^j}{P} = \left[\frac{p(z)}{P}\right]^{-\theta}C^j. \tag{10.8}$$

By integrating demand for good z across all agents (taking a population weighted average of home and foreign demands) and making use of the LOOP for individual prices and absolute PPP (which combined mean that for any good $z, p(z)/P = p^*(z)/P^*$) a constant-elasticity demand curve for the output of the (monopolistic) consumer–producer may be obtained as:

$$y(z) = \left[\frac{p(z)}{P}\right]^{-\theta}C^w, \tag{10.9}$$

where $C^w(= nC + (1-n)C^*)$ is aggregate global consumption.[2] This relationship implies that output is demand determined in this model and, as we shall see in more detail later, with price stickiness and marginal cost given, an exchange rate depreciation increases marginal revenue and results in an expansion of output.

As is standard in this kind of model, the representative agent must decide on her optimal choice of consumption, money holdings, labour supply and optimal price.

The model may be solved by using the demand curve (10.9) to substitute for $p_t(j)$ in the budget constraint (10.4) then using the resulting expression to substitute for C_t^j in (10.1). This gives the unconstrained maximisation problem (the individual takes C^w as given):

$$\max_{y(j), M^j, B^j} U_t^j = \sum_{s=t}^{\infty} \beta^{s-t} \left\{ \log \left[(1+r_s)F_s^j + \frac{M_{s-1}^j}{P_s} + y_s(j)^{(\theta-1)/\theta}(C_s^w)^{1/\theta} \right. \right.$$

$$\left. \left. - \tau_s - F_{s+1}^j - \frac{M_s^j}{P_s} \right] + \eta \log \left(\frac{M_s^j}{P_s} \right) - \frac{\kappa}{2} y_s(j)^2 \right\}. \qquad (10.10)$$

The first-order conditions derived from this maximising problem are:

$$C_{t+1} = \beta(1+r_{t+1})C_t, \qquad (10.11)$$

$$\frac{M_t}{P_t} = \eta C_t \left(\frac{1+i_{t+1}}{i_{t+1}} \right)^{1/\epsilon}, \qquad (10.12)$$

$$y_t^{(\theta+1)/\theta} = \frac{\theta-1}{\theta\kappa}(C_t^w)^{1/\theta} \frac{1}{C_t}, \qquad (10.13)$$

where the j index has been suppressed and i_{t+1} is the nominal interest rate for home country loans between t and $t+1$.[3] Equation (10.11) is the familiar first-order consumption Euler equation for the composite consumption index (note the inter-temporal elasticity of substitution is assumed to be unity). The first-order condition for real money balances simply indicates that in equilibrium agents should be indifferent between consuming a unit of consumption in period t or using the same funds to raise cash balances, enjoying the derived transactions utility in period t and converting this into consumption in period $t+1$. The first-order condition for the labour–leisure trade-off in equation (10.13) ensures that the marginal utility cost of producing an extra unit of output (in terms of the foregone leisure) equals the marginal utility from consuming the added revenue that an extra unit of output brings.[4]

The technique adopted by Obstfeld and Rogoff (1995, 1996) to solve the model involves solving for the steady state and then examining the dynamic effects of a monetary shock by taking a log-linear approximation around this steady state. Before proceeding, it is worth noting that in the steady state, where consumption and output are constant, the Euler equation (10.11) ties down the real interest rate as:[5]

$$\bar{r} = \delta \equiv \frac{1-\beta}{\beta},$$

where the overbar indicates a steady-state value.

If it is assumed that all producers in a country are symmetric, that is, they set the same price and output in equilibrium, then (10.3a) and (10.3b) may be simplified to:

$$P = \left[np_t(h)^{1-\theta} + (1-n)[S_t p_t^*(f)]^{1-\theta} \right]^{1/(1-\theta)}, \tag{10.3a'}$$

$$P^* = \left[n[p_t(h)/S_t]^{1-\theta} + (1-n)p_t^*(f)]^{1-\theta} \right]^{1/(1-\theta)}. \tag{10.3b'}$$

10.1.2 Log-linearising around the steady state

In solving the model we follow Obstfeld and Rogoff and log-linearise the earlier equations around the steady state. The log-linear approximations of (10.3a') and (10.3b') around the initial steady state are:

$$\hat{P}_t = n\hat{p}_t(h) + (1-n)[\hat{S}_t + \hat{p}_t^*(f)], \tag{10.3a''}$$

and

$$\hat{P}_t^* = n[\hat{p}_t(h) - \hat{S}_t] + (1-n)[\hat{p}_t^*(f)], \tag{10.3b''}$$

where the hats denote a percentage change around the steady-state equilibrium: that is, $\hat{X}_t = dX_t/\bar{X}_0$, where $\bar{X}_0$ is the initial steady-state value.

The log-linear first-order conditions for consumption (from equation (10.11)) in the home and foreign country are:

$$\hat{C}_{t+1} = \hat{C}_t + (1-\beta)\hat{r}_t, \tag{10.14}$$

$$\hat{C}_{t+1}^* = \hat{C}_t^* + (1-\beta)\hat{r}_t, \tag{10.15}$$

and the corresponding log-linear money demand equations are:

$$\hat{M}_t - \hat{P}_t = \frac{1}{\epsilon}\hat{C}_t - \beta\left(\hat{r}_t + \frac{\hat{P}_{t+1} - \hat{P}_t}{1-\beta}\right), \tag{10.16}$$

$$\hat{M}_t^* - \hat{P}_t^* = \frac{1}{\epsilon}\hat{C}_t^* - \beta\left(\hat{r}_t + \frac{\hat{P}_{t+1}^* - \hat{P}_t^*}{1-\beta}\right). \tag{10.17}$$

Comparing these equations to money market relationships used in other chapters, we note that a key feature of these equations is that the scale variable is consumption rather than income. Log-linear versions of equation (10.9) and its foreign counterpart are:

$$\hat{y}_t = \theta[\hat{P}_t - \hat{p}_t(h)] + C_t^w, \tag{10.18}$$

$$\hat{y}_t^* = \theta[\hat{P}_t^* - \hat{p}_t^*(f)] + C_t^w. \tag{10.19}$$

By subtracting (10.19) from (10.18) and making use of the PPP relationship for the overall price series the following relative output relationship may be derived:

$$\hat{y}_t - \hat{y}_t^* = \theta[\hat{S}_t + \hat{p}_t^*(f) - \hat{p}_t(h)]. \tag{10.20}$$

The log-linear versions of the home and foreign counterpart to (10.13) are:

$$(\theta + 1)\hat{y}_t = -\theta\hat{C}_t + \hat{C}_t^w, \tag{10.21}$$

$$(\theta + 1)\hat{y}_t^* = -\theta\hat{C}_t^* + \hat{C}_t^w, \tag{10.22}$$

and on subtracting (10.22) from (10.21) we obtain an alternative measure of relative income, which we use later:

$$\hat{y}_t - \hat{y}_t^* = -\frac{\theta}{1 + \theta}(\hat{c}_t - \hat{c}_t^*), \tag{10.23}$$

In sum equations (10.3a″), (10.3b″), (10.14), (10.15), (10.16), (10.17), (10.18), (10.19), (10.21) and (10.22) define the model. Before presenting a solution of the model we must first discuss the wealth interactions and the current account.

10.1.3 Wealth transfers and the current account

A crucial aspect of the model, as we shall see in more detail later, is the effect that wealth transfers, through the current account, can have on the steady state. Because of this, the model contains important similarities with the portfolio-balance and currency substitution models discussed in Chapter 7 and the eclectic exchange rate model in Chapter 8. In both countries steady-state consumption must equal steady-state real income:

$$\bar{C} = \delta\bar{F} + \frac{\bar{p}(h)\bar{y}}{\bar{P}}, \tag{10.24}$$

$$\bar{C}^* = -\left(\frac{n}{1 - n}\right)\delta\bar{F} + \frac{\bar{p}^* - (f)\bar{y}^*}{\bar{P}^*}, \tag{10.25}$$

where the log-linearised counterparts of (10.24) and (10.25) are:

$$\acute{c} = \delta\acute{F} + \acute{p}(h) + \acute{y} - \acute{P}, \tag{10.26}$$

$$\acute{c}^* = -\left(\frac{n}{1 - n}\right)\delta\acute{F} + \acute{p}^*(f) + \acute{y}^* - \acute{P}^*, \tag{10.27}$$

where the over prime denotes the percentage change in the steady-state values; that is, $\acute{X} = d\bar{X}/\bar{X}_0$. On subtracting (10.27) from (10.26) we obtain:

$$\acute{C} - \acute{C}^* = \left(\frac{1}{1 - n}\right)\delta\acute{F} + \acute{y} - \acute{y}^* - [\acute{S} + \acute{p}^*(f) - \acute{p}(h)]. \tag{10.28}$$

The effects of wealth transfers may now be seen by using the steady change equivalents of (10.20) and (10.23) (i.e. rewriting these with over primes above each of the variables) into (10.28) to obtain:

$$\acute{C} - \acute{C}^* = \left(\frac{1}{1-n}\right)\left(\frac{1+\theta}{2\theta}\right)\delta\acute{F}. \tag{10.29}$$

Expression (10.29) indicates that steady-state domestic consumption can be greater than foreign consumption by an amount determined as the product of the two bracketed terms times $\delta\acute{F}$. If output was exogenous in the model the effect on consumption would simply be determined by the first term in brackets $(1-n)^{-1}$. However, with endogenous income this effect is attenuated by the second term in brackets (remember $\theta > 1$). The intuition for this latter result is simply that a positive wealth transfer to the domestic economy means that domestic agents consume more leisure while in the foreign country agents consume less leisure and work harder. By substituting (10.23) into (10.20), rearranging for relative consumption and using (10.29) to substitute for relative consumption, the following steady-state terms of trade relationship may be obtained:

$$\acute{p}(h) - \acute{S} - \acute{p}^*(f) = \left(\frac{1}{1-n}\right)\left(\frac{1}{2\theta}\right)\delta\acute{F}. \tag{10.30}$$

Equation (10.30) shows that the home country's terms of trade will improve as a result of a positive transfer and this improvement is again driven by the labour–leisure decision. We are now in a position to look more closely at the exchange rate relationship implied by the model and the effects of monetary policy.

10.1.4   *The exchange rate and unanticipated monetary shocks*

Subtracting equation (10.15) from (10.14) gives:

$$\hat{C} - \hat{C}^* = \acute{C} - \acute{C}^*. \tag{10.31}$$

Equation (10.31) indicates that shocks to relative per capita consumption have a permanent effect and this is nothing other than open economy analogue of the random walk model of consumption (see Hall 1978). The $t+1$ time subscripts have been dropped here since we follow Obstfeld and Rogoff in assuming that the economy gets back to steady state after a disturbance in one period. Hence all $t+1$ subscripted variables can be replaced with percentage changes in steady state. With this assumption, hatted variables can be interpreted as short-run values, while over prime variables are long-run. Similarly, assuming PPP – $\hat{S}_t = \hat{P}_t - \hat{P}_t^*$ – holds continuously (i.e. in the short- and long-run) the money demand equations (10.16) and (10.17) can be manipulated to get:

$$\hat{S} = \hat{M} - \hat{M}^* - \frac{1}{\epsilon}\left(\hat{C} - \hat{C}^*\right) + \frac{\beta}{(1-\beta)\epsilon}\left(\acute{S} - \hat{S}\right).^{[6]} \tag{10.32}$$

Note the similarity between equation (10.32) and the flex-price monetary equation of Chapter 4, despite the fact that the current model uses a sticky price assumption. Consumption enters this equation rather than income because in the present model the opportunity cost of money is determined by the marginal utility of consumption. As Obstfeld and Rogoff note, this has potentially important empirical implications: in this class of model the attempts by agents to smooth consumption leads to borrowing and lending through the capital account of the balance of payments and this, in turn, means transitory shocks which induce permanent consumption movements will have permanent exchange rate effects (because they have permanent current account effects). By leading (10.32) one period we obtain the long-run, or steady-state, exchange rate relationship:

$$\hat{S} = \hat{M} - \hat{M}^* - \frac{1}{\epsilon}\left(\hat{C} - \hat{C}^*\right). \tag{10.33}$$

We now reconsider the classic Dornbusch exercise, discussed in Chapter 5, of an unanticipated permanent rise in the relative home money supply. Before examining this shock in detail, a couple of preliminaries. First, in the short-run the home currency price of home goods and the foreign currency price of foreign goods are fixed (they are preset one period in advance) and home output becomes demand determined through (10.9). Since a monopolist always prices above marginal cost it will be profitable for him to meet unexpected demand at the preset price. It is important to note, though, that although prices are preset in terms of the producer's own currency, the foreign currency price of a producer's output must change if the exchange rate changes. This can be seen from (10.3a″) and (10.3b″), which imply:

$$\hat{P} = (1 - n)\hat{S},$$

and

$$\hat{P}^* = -n\hat{S}.$$

In the parlance of the pricing to market literature discussed in Chapters 3 and 4, there is complete pass-through of an exchange rate change to domestic prices (note from (10.18) and (10.19) that this will feed through into the home (and foreign) short-run demand functions).

A second difference between the short- and long-run (steady state) is that in the latter period the current account has to balance but in the short-run income need not equal expenditure and the current account need not equal zero. The short-run current account surplus is given by:

$$F_{t+1} - F_t = r_t F_t + \frac{p_t(h)y_t}{P_t} - C_t. \tag{10.34}$$

The linearised current account equations for the home and foreign country are:

$$\acute{F} = \hat{y} - \hat{C} - (1 - n)\hat{S}, \tag{10.35}$$

and

$$\left(\frac{-n}{1-n}\right)\acute{F} = \acute{F}^* = \hat{y}^* - \hat{C}^* + n\hat{S}, \tag{10.36}$$

where we have used (10.3a″) and (10.3b″) and the fact that $p(h)$ and $p^*(f)$ are preset. It is worth noting that steady-state values of F appear in (10.35) and (10.36). This is because with one-period price setting, whatever net foreign asset stocks arise at the end of the first period become the new steady-state values from period 2 onwards.

The implications of an unanticipated monetary shock may be seen by substituting (10.33) into (10.32), using (10.31) and noting that $\acute{M} - \acute{M}^* = \hat{M} - \hat{M}^*$ (because the money supply shock is permanent):

$$\hat{S} = \hat{M} - \hat{M}^* - \frac{1}{\epsilon}\left(\hat{C} - \hat{C}^*\right). \tag{10.37}$$

Comparing (10.37) with (10.33) it must follow that the exchange rate moves immediately to its new long-run value – there is no exchange rate overshooting. The intuition for this is quite simple – if agents expect that the consumption differential is constant (as in (10.31)) and that the money differential is also constant then a constant exchange rate must also be expected.

10.1.5   A graphical portrayal of the NOEM model

A graphical portrayal of the effect of an unanticipated increase in the money supply is presented in Figure 10.1. The MM schedule represents equation (10.37) and captures the equilibrium relationship between home–foreign consumption and

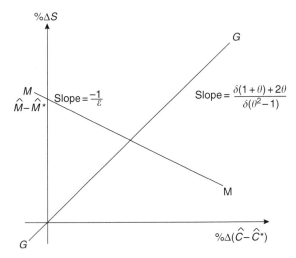

Figure 10.1 Short-run equilibrium in NOEM.

the exchange rate that arises from the money market equilibrium conditions. It is downward sloping because an increase in the home country's relative consumption raises the demand for money in that country which, in turn, must lead to a fall in its relative price level and a currency appreciation. The schedule intersects the vertical axis at $m - m^*$, which is the equilibrium exchange rate response if prices are fully flexible.

The schedule GG captures the effect of the home–foreign consumption differential on the exchange rate stemming from the current account relationship and provides an important link between the short-run equilibrium (where the current account is not required to be in equilibrium) and the long-run (where the current account must be in balance). The GG schedule is positively sloped because home consumption can rise relative to foreign consumption if the exchange rate depreciates in the short-run, permitting home output to rise above foreign output (see equations (10.20) and (10.23)). More precisely this may be seen in the following way. Subtract (10.36) from (10.35) we obtain:

$$\acute{F} = (1 - n)\left[(\hat{y} - \hat{y}^*) - (\hat{C} - \hat{C}^*) - \hat{S}\right].$$

(10.38)

Using (10.20) to eliminate the output differential in (10.38), which with short-run price stickiness simply equals:

$$\hat{y}_t - \hat{y}_t^* = \theta\hat{S}_t,$$

(10.39)

and using (10.29) to substitute out for f', and noting (10.31) we obtain:

$$\hat{S} = \frac{\delta(1 + \theta) + 2\theta}{\delta(\theta^2 - 1)}(\hat{C} - \hat{C}^*).$$

(10.40)

This relationship indicates that the GG schedule is upward sloping because home consumption can rise relative to foreign consumption only if the exchange rate depreciates in the short-run which permits home output to rise relative to foreign output. The short- and long-run equilibrium exchange rate and consumption differential lie at the intersection of the MM and GG schedules. The formal solution for this intersection is:

$$\hat{S} = \frac{\epsilon[\delta(1 + \theta) + 2\theta]}{\delta(\theta^2 - 1) + \epsilon[\delta(1 + \theta) + 2\theta]}(\hat{M} - \hat{M}^*) < (\hat{M} - \hat{M}^*),$$

(10.41)

where the inequality holds because $\theta > 1$. Note that since the prices of domestic goods are preset, this expression also represents the terms of trade. In Figure 10.2, point A represents the initial equilibrium and B the equilibrium after a monetary expansion with the M'M' schedule representing the post-shock monetary expansion. Note that the exchange rate effects of a monetary impulse are smaller, the larger is the price elasticity of aggregate demand. As θ approaches infinity the GG schedule becomes horizontal (i.e. as home and foreign goods become very close substitutes, small exchange rate changes lead to very large shifts in demand with preset prices).

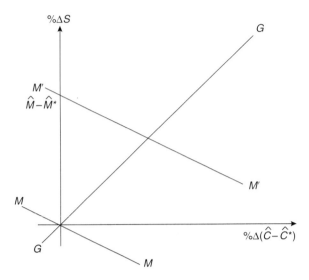

Figure 10.2 Unexpected relative rise in home money in NOEM.

The effects of the monetary shock are as follows. In the short-run, with preset prices, the home country terms of trade worsens and the world real interest rate falls. Both of these effects stimulate consumption in the foreign country. In the home country output and consumption rise, but the latter does not rise by the same amount as the increase in income, due to consumption smoothing, and therefore the domestic current account moves into surplus. Much as in the portfolio balance model of Chapter 7, the latter effect implies a permanent improvement in net foreign assets and in the new steady state this allows the trade account to be in deficit: the positive net investment flow allows domestic consumption to be permanently above domestic income. The wealth effect of the net foreign asset position is such as to reduce domestic labour supply and output and this produces a permanent improvement in the terms of trade. The latter may be seen formally in the following way. By combining (10.37) and (10.41) we get:

$$\hat{C} - \hat{C}^* = \left(\frac{\epsilon \delta (\theta^2 - 1)}{\delta (\theta^2 - 1) + \epsilon [(1 + \theta) + 2\theta]} \right) (\hat{M} - \hat{M}^*). \tag{10.42}$$

The short-run current account (which by assumption also equals the long-run change in net foreign assets) may be obtained by substituting the short-run output gap relationship $\hat{y} - \hat{y}^* = \theta \hat{S}$ along with (10.37), (10.41) and (10.42) into (10.38) to get:

$$\hat{F} = \left(\frac{2\theta \epsilon (1 - n)(\theta - 1)}{\delta (\theta^2 - 1) + \epsilon [\delta (1 + \theta) + 2\theta]} \right) (\hat{M} - \hat{M}^*). \tag{10.43}$$

By combining equation (10.30) with (10.43) one may obtain the steady-state terms of trade as:

$$\hat{p}(h) - \hat{S} - \hat{p}^*(f) = \left(\frac{\epsilon \delta (\theta - 1)}{\delta (\theta^2 - 1) + \epsilon [\delta (1 + \theta) + 2\theta]} \right) (\hat{M} - \hat{M}^*). \quad (10.44)$$

There are two aspects of (10.44) worth noting. First, comparing (10.41), which with sticky prices gives the short-run fall in the terms of trade, with (10.44), which gives the long-run improvement, we see that in absolute terms the short-run effect dominates the long-run effect. Second, the impact of a monetary shock on the long-run terms of trade is of an order of magnitude given by the real interest rate ($=\delta$). Note from (10.29) that the exchange rate depreciates less than proportionately to the money supply change, even in the long-run (remember $\hat{S} = \bar{S}$ for a permanent money supply shock). The intuition for this is simple – since the home country's real income and consumption rise in the long-run, the nominal exchange rate does not need to depreciate as much as it would under fully flexible prices. Obstfeld and Rogoff (1996) are careful not to overstate this long-run non-neutrality result. In particular, they argue that in an overlapping generation's version of the model the real effects of the monetary shock would eventually die out, although over a relatively much longer time span than the price frictions.

10.2 Government spending and productivity effects

In this section we introduce a role for government spending into the base-line NOEM. Although the introduction of government spending affects most of the equations introduced in the previous section, we focus only on a few of the key relationships here (in general the introduction of government spending affects the equations additively). Following Obstfeld and Rogoff (1995) we assume that the government's consumption index takes the same basic form as the private sectors:

$$G = \left[\int_0^1 g^j(z)^{(\theta - 1)/\theta} dz \right]^{\theta/(\theta - 1)}, \quad \theta > 1, \quad (10.45)$$

where the government's elasticity of substitution is assumed to be the same as the private sectors. Both the government budget constraint and current account relationship also have to be modified. The former is:

$$\tau_t + \frac{M_t - M_{t-1}}{P_t} = G_t, \quad (10.46)$$

and the short-run current account relationship is:

$$F_{t+1} - F_t = r_t F_t + \frac{p_t(h) y_t}{P_t} - C_t - G_t. \quad (10.47)$$

The steady-state expression for the effects of a permanent (tax-financed) government spending shocks on relative consumption is (this parallels the derivation of

(10.29), only now world government spending is added to (10.18), (10.19), (10.21) and (10.22)):

$$\acute{C} - \acute{C}^* = \left(\frac{1}{1-n}\right)\left(\frac{1+\theta}{2\theta}\right)\delta\acute{F} - \left(\frac{1+\theta}{2\theta}\right)(\acute{G} - \acute{G}^*). \tag{10.48}$$

Equation (10.48) indicates that relative home consumption falls by less than the rise in relative government spending because agents respond to the rise by substituting out of leisure and into work. Similarly, the steady-state terms of trade equation (10.30) is modified in the presence of government spending to:

$$\acute{p}(h) - \acute{S} - \acute{p}^*(f) = \left(\frac{1}{1-n}\right)\left(\frac{1}{2\theta}\right)\delta\acute{F} - \left(\frac{1}{2\theta}\right)(\acute{G} - \acute{G}^*). \tag{10.49}$$

This expression indicates that a rise in relative government spending deteriorates the home country's steady-state terms of trade (because it induces a rise in relative home output).

To analyse the short-run effects of government spending we return to Figure 10.1. Since government spending does not affect the money demand or private sector consumption Euler equations, it does not affect the MM schedule. However, since it does affect the current account it will affect the GG schedule, which becomes:[7]

$$\hat{S} = \frac{\delta(1+\theta) + 2\theta}{\delta(\theta^2 - 1)}(\hat{C} - \hat{C}^*) + \frac{1}{\theta - 1}\left[\hat{G} - \hat{G}^* + \frac{1}{\delta}(\acute{G} - \acute{G}^*)\right], \tag{10.50}$$

where the first component in square brackets represents the temporary component of government spending and the second term represents the permanent component. With a purely temporary rise in home government spending (financed by an increase in taxes) the GG schedule in Figure 10.3 shifts to G′G′ while MM remains unchanged. The currency depreciates as a result of this shock. This is because home consumption falls, which implies lower money demand and this, in turn, raises the price and depreciates the currency. Because the increase in government spending and tax is temporary, consumption falls by less than the increase in G and the home country runs a current account deficit. There is in fact a partially offsetting effect on the current account here because the exchange rate depreciation produces a rise in home relative to foreign output (although home output rises, the leisure–labour trade-off does not change by enough to offset the rise in taxes) country.

A permanent increase in home government spending (i.e. a shock to $\acute{G}$) will cause a similar chain of events, although the effect on the exchange rate is larger in this case: that is, the intercept on the basic figure now changes. In contrast to the effects of a temporary shock to government spending, the current account moves into surplus here because home income in the short-run rises by more than its long-run counterpart and so domestic residents adjust current consumption down by more than the change in government spending. A final point to note here is

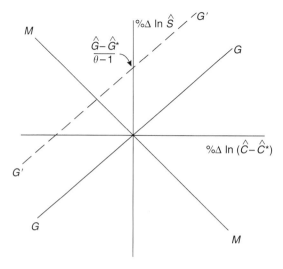

Figure 10.3 An unexpected temporary increase in home G.

the magnitude of the exchange rate change with respect to changes in government spending when prices are sticky. Since the equation for MM holds under both sticky and flexible prices, the exchange rate change *impact* of a government spending increase is proportional to the consumption differential, irrespective of whether prices are sticky or not. But both temporary and permanent fiscal shocks have smaller absolute effects on relative consumption with sticky prices and they must have smaller absolute exchange rate effects as well.

10.3 Productivity shocks revisited

In Chapter 3 we considered the effects of differential productivity growth on exchange rates using the Balassa–Samuelson framework. Here we revisit the effects of productivity growth on the exchange rate using the NOEM (we revert to the variant of the model in Section 10.1; that is, prior to the introduction of government expenditure). Productivity shocks are captured in this framework by the κ parameter in the utility function, which we repeat here:

$$ U_t^j = \sum_{s=t}^{\infty} \beta^{s-t} \left(\log C_s^j + \eta \left(\frac{M_s}{P_s} \right)^{1-\epsilon} - \frac{\kappa}{2} y_s(j)^2 \right). \tag{10.1}$$

Higher productivity is represented by a fall in κ – less labour is required to produce a given quantity of output. All of the linearised equations of the model stay the same except for the labour–leisure trade-off equations, represented by (10.21) and (10.22), which now become:

$$(\theta + 1)\hat{y}_t = -\theta\hat{C}_t + \hat{C}_t^w + \theta\hat{a}_t, \tag{10.51}$$

$$(\theta + 1)\hat{y}_t^* = -\theta\hat{C}_t^* + \hat{C}_t^w + \theta\hat{a}_t^*, \tag{10.52}$$

where $a_t \equiv -(\kappa_t - \bar{\kappa}_0) \cdot \bar{\kappa}_0^{-1}$ and the relative income equation (10.23) now becomes:

$$\hat{y}_t - \hat{y}_t^* = -\frac{\theta}{1+\theta}(\hat{C}_t - \hat{C}_t^*) + \frac{\theta}{1+\theta}(\hat{a}_t - \hat{a}_t^*), \tag{10.53}$$

and the relative steady-state consumption difference equation (10.29) is now modified to:

$$\hat{C} - \hat{C}^* = \left(\frac{1}{1-n}\right)\left(\frac{1+\theta}{2\theta}\right)\delta\acute{F} + \left(\frac{\theta-1}{2\theta}\right)(\acute{a} - \acute{a}^*). \tag{10.54}$$

This expression indicates that, on holding net foreign assets constant, a rise in the steady-state value of home productivity relative to foreign productivity increases relative home consumption, but proportionately less than the rise in home productivity. The reason for this is partly because home residents respond by consuming more leisure and partly because the relative price of home output falls. That the relative home price falls can be seen from the modified terms of trade equation:

$$\acute{p}(h) - \acute{S} - \acute{p}^*(f) = \left(\frac{1}{1-n}\right)\left(\frac{1}{2\theta}\right)\delta\acute{F} - \left(\frac{1}{2\theta}\right)(\acute{a} - \acute{a}^*). \tag{10.55}$$

To analyse the effect of a permanent increase in relative productivity on the exchange rate, we return to a modified version of Figure 10.1. As in the case of a government spending shock, the MM schedule remains unchanged. Using (10.31) and (10.39) we obtain a new GG schedule as:

$$\hat{S} = \left(\frac{\delta(1+\theta)+2\theta}{\delta(\theta^2-1)}\right)(\hat{C} - \hat{C})^* - \left(\frac{1}{\delta(1+\theta)}\right)(\acute{a} - \acute{a}^*). \tag{10.56}$$

As is clear from Figure 10.3, holding money constant, the effect of an improvement in productivity is to appreciate the exchange rate. The intuition for this is as follows. In the short-run output is demand determined and so the productivity shock is absorbed by a rise in home leisure, but in the long-run a permanent shock increases output (but less than proportionately since there is some increase in the consumption of leisure). The anticipated long-run rise in output means agents attempt to smooth consumption by dissaving. The latter raises current consumption, increases money demand and appreciates the exchange rate. The latter generates a current account deficit, decreases net foreign assets and reduces

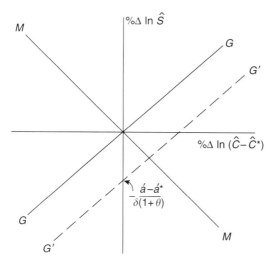

Figure 10.4 Unexpected relative rise in domestic productivity.
Source: Obstfeld and Rogoff (1995).

home relative to foreign consumption through (10.54), but not by enough to reverse the initial increase. The intersection of MM and GG is now given by:

$$\hat{S} = \left(\frac{\delta(1+\theta) + 2\theta}{\theta\delta(1+\theta) + 2\theta} \right)(\hat{m} - \hat{m})^* - \left(\frac{\theta - 1}{\theta\delta(1+\theta) + 2\theta} \right)(\acute{a} - \acute{a}^*). \quad (10.57)$$

An unanticipated temporary rise in relative home productivity would have no effect in this model because the whole of the productivity increase is absorbed by an increase in leisure. This is because in the short-run, with prices preset, output is entirely driven by demand, so agents keep supply constant in the presence of a rise in productivity and consume more leisure.

10.4   The small-country variant – exchange rate overshooting revisited and the relationship between the inter- and intra-temporal elasticity of substitution

In the variant of the NOEM model considered so far, the inter-temporal elasticity of substitution was assumed to be equal to the intra-temporal elasticity of substitution, and all goods are assumed to be traded. In this section we present a variant of the model in which allowance is made for non-traded goods. What difference do these two modifications to the model make to the operation of monetary and fiscal policy? The model is based on the appendix to Obstfeld and Rogoff (1995), Obstfeld and Rogoff (1996) and especially Lane (2000).[8] The model is one of a small open economy with a traded and non-traded sector. The former sector is assumed perfectly competitive (and there is complete price flexibility), its output is given as an endowment, $Y_T,$[9] and this is a perfect substitute for the traded good produced in the rest of the world. The non-traded goods sector is monopolistically competitive, with preset nominal prices. The objective function (10.1) is modified to:

$$U_t^j = \sum_{s=t}^{\infty} \beta^{s-t} \left(\frac{\sigma}{\sigma - 1} C_s^{(\sigma-1)/\sigma} + \frac{\eta}{1 - \varepsilon} \left(\frac{M_s}{P_s} \right)^{1-\varepsilon} - \frac{\kappa}{2} y_s(j)^2 \right), \qquad (10.58)$$

where $\beta \in (0, 1)$, aggregate consumption is assumed to have a CRRA form, σ represents the elasticity of inter-temporal substitution (assumed positive), real money balances now enter the utility function with a general isoelastic function and ε (assumed positive) is interpreted as the reciprocal of the consumption elasticity of money demand and, as before, $\kappa > 0$. Aggregate consumption is taken to be a CES index across traded and non-traded goods:

$$C_t = \left[\gamma^{1/\theta} C_{Tt}^{(\theta-1)/\theta} + (1 - \gamma)^{1/\theta} C_{Nt}^{(\theta-1)/\theta} \right]^{\theta/(\theta-1)}, \qquad \theta > 0, \qquad (10.59)$$

θ is the (intra-temporal) elasticity of substitution between traded and non-traded goods. As we shall see later, the relationship between σ and θ has an important bearing on the effects of monetary shocks on the current account. The index function of non-traded goods has the now familiar CES form and is given as:

$$C_N = \left[\int_0^1 c_N(z)^{(\mu-1)/\mu} dz \right]^{\mu/(\mu-1)}, \qquad \mu > 1, \qquad (10.60)$$

where μ is the elasticity of substitution between non-traded goods. The consumption price index is given by:

$$P_t = \left[\gamma P_{Tt}^{1-\theta} + (1 - \gamma) P_{Nt}^{1-\theta} \right]^{1/(1-\theta)}, \qquad (10.61)$$

and the index for non-traded prices is:

$$P_N = \left[\int_0^1 p_N(z)^{(1-\mu)} dz \right]^{1/(1-\mu)}. \qquad (10.62)$$

Bonds are denominated in terms of the traded good and the budget constraint for agent j, modified to reflect the traded–non-traded split, is:

$$P_{Tt} F_{t+1} + M_t = P_{Tt}(1 + r_t) F_t + M_{t-1} + p_{Nt}(j) y_{Nt}(j)$$
$$+ P_{Tt} \bar{y}_T - P_{Nt} C_{Nt} - P_{Tt} C_{Tt} - P_t \tau_t. \qquad (10.63)$$

The government budget constraint is again given by (10.5) and the demand curve for non-traded goods is:

$$y_N^d(j) = \left[\frac{p_N(j)}{P_N}\right]^{-\mu} C_N^A, \quad \mu > 1, \tag{10.64}$$

where C_{Nt}^A is aggregate home consumption of non-traded goods which producers take as given. Maximising (10.58) subject to (10.63) and (10.64) and assuming the absence of speculative bubbles we obtain the following first-order conditions, where, as before, it is assumed that $(1 + r)\beta = 1$:

$$\frac{C_{Tt+1}}{C_{Tt}} = \left[\frac{(P_t/P_{Tt})}{(P_{t+1}/P_{Tt+1})}\right]^{\sigma-\theta}, \tag{10.65}$$

$$\frac{C_{Nt}}{C_{Tt}} = \frac{1-\gamma}{\gamma}\left(\frac{P_{Nt}}{P_{Tt}}\right)^{-\theta}, \tag{10.66}$$

$$\left(\frac{M_t}{P_T}\right) = \left[\frac{\chi\, C_t^{1/\sigma}}{1 - (\beta P_{Tt}/P_{Tt+1})}\right]^{1/\varepsilon}, \tag{10.67}$$

and

$$y_{Nt}^{(\mu+1)/\mu} = \left[\frac{(\mu-1)}{\mu\kappa}\right] C_t^{-(1/\sigma)} (C_{Nt}^A)^{1/\mu}\left(\frac{P_{Nt}}{P_t}\right). \tag{10.68}$$

In the consumption Euler condition, (10.65), consumption between the current and next period depends upon the price of the aggregate price index to the price of traded goods in period t relative to $t + 1$. This relative price has been labelled the 'consumption based real interest rate' by Dornbusch (1983). If this relative price is low in period t relative to $t + 1$, consumption will be encouraged in the current period. However, such a relative price configuration will also encourage consumption from traded to non-traded goods, and the former effect dominates the latter if the inter-temporal elasticity of substitution is greater than the intra-temporal elasticity of substitution ($\sigma > \theta$). Equation (10.66) indicates that with a relative price of non-traded to traded goods of unity, the relative consumption of non-traded goods is larger the smaller is the parameter γ. The demand for real money balances in equation (10.67) is increasing in the level of consumption and declining in the nominal interest rate. The Euler condition for the equilibrium supply of non-traded goods (10.68), indicates that the higher the consumption index, C, the lower is the level of production because agents increase leisure in line with the consumption of other goods.

In the symmetric steady-state equilibrium we follow Lane (2001) in assuming the relative price of non-traded to traded goods is unity ($P_N/P_T = 1$) which, in turn, implies that $y_T = \gamma/(1 - \gamma)$ and $C^A_{Nt} = y_{Nt} = (1 - \gamma)C_t$. The steady-state production and consumption of non-traded goods is given by:

$$y_N = C_N = \left[\frac{\mu - 1}{\mu\kappa}\right]^{\sigma/(\sigma+1)} (1 - \gamma)^{1/(1+\sigma)}, \tag{10.69}$$

which indicates that the production of non-traded goods will be greater the larger is μ, the competitiveness of the non-traded sector, the smaller is κ, the less taxing is work effort, and the larger is the weight placed on consumption of non-traded goods in the utility function (given by $1 - \gamma$).

Consider again an unanticipated permanent expansion of the money stock: $\hat{M} = M' > 0$. The stickiness of prices in this variant of the NOEM relates to prices of non-traded goods, which are again set one period in advance; that is, $\hat{P}_N = 0$. Using a log-linear version of expression (10.64), we see that C'_T and $\hat{C}_T$ are linked by:

$$C'_T - \hat{C}_T = (\sigma - \theta)(\hat{p} - \hat{p}_T) - (\sigma - \theta)(P' - P'_T), \tag{10.70}$$

and the relationship between C'_N and $\hat{C}_T$ is governed by:

$$C'_T = -r\hat{C}_T, \tag{10.71}$$

which indicates that the price of increasing the consumption of tradables in the short-run by 1% is $-r$%. Expression (10.71) follows from the fact that the steady-state consumption of traded goods (given the constant endowment assumption) can only be increased by the income earned from the accumulation of foreign assets, which is:

$$C'_T = r\frac{dF}{C_0},$$

where as before the zero subscript indicates an initial value and the accumulation of foreign assets is, in turn, governed by:

$$\frac{dF}{C_0} = \hat{y}_T - \hat{C}_T = -\hat{C}_T.$$

The linearised version of (10.66) is:

$$C'_N - C'_T = \theta(P'_N - P'_T). \tag{10.72}$$

In steady state the change in non-traded consumption is simply equal to the steady-state change in non-traded production. From the Euler condition for supply and the optimised relationship between C_N and C we may obtain:

$$C'_N = y'_N = \frac{(\sigma - \theta)\gamma}{1 + \sigma}(P'_N - P'_T). \tag{10.73}$$

By combining (10.72) and (10.73) the steady-state change in tradables consumption as a function of the steady-state change in the relative price of non-traded goods in terms of traded goods is:

$$C'_T = \left[\theta + \frac{(\sigma - \theta)\gamma}{1 + \sigma}\right](P'_N - P'_T). \tag{10.74}$$

In the short-run with sticky prices non-traded production is driven purely by the level of demand as given by (10.66):

$$\hat{y}_N = \hat{C}_N = \theta\hat{P}_T + \hat{C}_T. \tag{10.75}$$

The short-run and steady-state monetary equilibrium conditions may be derived from a log-linearised variant of (10.67):

$$\varepsilon(M' - \hat{p}) = \frac{\theta}{\sigma}\left[\hat{P}_T - \hat{P}\right] + \frac{1}{\sigma}\hat{C}_T - \frac{1}{r}(P'_T - \hat{P}_T), \tag{10.76}$$

$$\varepsilon(M' - P') = \frac{\theta}{\sigma}\left[P'_T - P'\right] + \frac{1}{\sigma}C'_T. \tag{10.77}$$

Equations (10.70) to (10.77) can be used to solve both the short-run and steady-state effects of an unanticipated monetary surprise, which are:

$$\hat{p}_T = \beta_1 M' \tag{10.78}$$

$$P'_T = \beta_2 M', \tag{10.79}$$

$$\hat{y}_N = \hat{C}_N = \beta_3 M', \tag{10.80}$$

$$y'_N = C'_N = -\beta_4(\sigma - \theta)^2 M', \tag{10.81}$$

$$\hat{C}_T = \beta_5(\sigma - \theta)M', \tag{10.82}$$

$$C'_T = -\frac{\beta_6(\sigma - \theta)}{r}M', \tag{10.83}$$

$$P'_N - P'_T = -\beta_7(\sigma - \theta)M', \tag{10.84}$$

where the reduced form parameters, $\beta_1, \beta_2, \beta_3, \beta_4, \beta_5, \beta_6, \beta_7 > 0$, are a function of the underlying structural parameters. We are now ready to analyse the effect of divergences in the inter- and intra-elasticities of substitution on the current account. In the 'base-line' case where $\sigma = \theta$, a positive monetary shock results in an expansion in the nontraded sector (equation (10.80)) and the price of traded goods rises in both the short- and long-run (equations (10.78) and (10.79)). With the two elasticities cancelling out by assumption, there can be no spillover to consumption in the traded sector (from (10.82) and (10.83)) and so the current account must stay in balance. As in the base-line case, when $\sigma > \theta$ the monetary stimulus will raise short-run production of the non-traded good and produce a rise in the price of the traded good (which by assumption represents a nominal depreciation).

Since the elasticity of substitution between tradables and non-tradables is relatively low, the increased consumption of non-tradables stimulates consumption of tradables (10.81) and the current account goes into deficit. In the new long-run steady state the current account must be balanced and so the long-run consumption of tradables needs to fall (equation (10.82)) in order to generate the trade surplus required to finance negative net foreign assets resulting from the monetary shock, and these negative net foreign assets, in turn, require a long-run depreciation of the real exchange rate – the relative price of non-tradables in terms of tradables must fall (equation (10.84)).

With $\sigma < \theta$, the initial exchange rate depreciation (real and nominal), and fall in the consumption of traded goods, produces a current account surplus. The latter, in turn, facilitates an increased consumption of the traded good in the long-run, from (10.71), and a rise in the relative price of non-tradables (the real exchange rate rises). Note that in this example, as in the case where $\sigma > \theta$, production and consumption of the traded good falls in the new steady state. As in the portfolio balance model of Chapter 7, this is due to the accumulation/decumulation of net foreign assets which has a wealth effect on the desired level of consumption of the non-traded good and the optimal supply of labour in the non-traded sector. In particular, the former effect is inversely related to θ, the intra-temporal elasticity of substitution, while the strength of the latter depends inversely on σ, the inter-temporal elasticity of substitution. The former effect dominates when $\sigma > \theta$. More specifically, when $\sigma > \theta$ net foreign assets, as we have seen, become negative and the implied wealth effect on the consumption of non-tradables (their desired level falls) is greater than its effect on labour supply (the desired level rises). When $\sigma < \theta$ the reverse happens: the increased net foreign asset position increases the desired consumption of non-traded goods, but this is offset by the desired contraction of labour supply.

Following Obstfeld and Rogoff (1995) the small open economy model can be used to revisit the exchange rate overshooting result of Dornbusch. Remember that in the Dornbusch model money is neutral in the long-run. To achieve that result in the small-country model, as we have seen, the elasticity of inter-temporal substitution has to equal the intra-temporal elasticity of substitution, $\sigma = \theta$. Making this assumption, equation (10.76) simplifies to:

$$\varepsilon(\hat{M} - \hat{P}) = \left[\hat{P}_T - \hat{P}\right] + \frac{1}{r}(\hat{P}_T - P_T'), \qquad (10.85)$$

where with money neutral the change in consumption will be zero (the level is constant). Long-run money neutrality also implies:

$$P_T' = M' = \hat{M}, \qquad (10.86)$$

and log differentiating equation (10.61) with the price of the non-traded good, assumed constant, we obtain:

$$\hat{P} = \gamma \hat{P}_T. \qquad (10.87)$$

Using (10.87) and (10.86) in (10.85), rearranging the resulting expression and noting the law of one price holds continuously, we obtain:

$$\hat{P}_T = \hat{S} = \frac{r\varepsilon + 1}{(1 - \gamma + \varepsilon\gamma)r + 1}\hat{M}, \tag{10.88}$$

which shows that with $\varepsilon > 1$ the nominal exchange rate overshoots its long-run level – that is, $\hat{S} > \hat{M} = M'$. The intuition for this result is as follows. A 1% rise in P_T will raise C_N proportionately and this, in turn, will raise real consumption by $1 - \gamma$ (since P_N is fixed). With $\varepsilon > 1$, the consumption elasticity of demand $(1/\varepsilon)$ dictates that the demand for real balances will rise less than proportionately than the supply if $\hat{P}_T = \hat{M}$. Hence P_T and the exchange rate must move more than proportionately with respect to the change in the money supply.

In this chapter we have overviewed the so-called two-country redux model of Obstfeld and Rogoff and its small-country variant and emphasised the implied exchange rate behaviour stemming from these models. In the next chapter we consider a number of extensions to these base-line new open economy macroeconomic models.

11 The new open economy macroeconomic model

Pricing to market and exchange rate volatility redux

The NOEM model considered in the previous chapter has had an important and significant impact on open economy macroeconomics in general, and the economics of exchange rates, in particular. A number of researchers have taken variants of the basic two-country and small-country models considered in the last chapter and used them to revisit a number of the issues considered previously in this book, such as pricing to market and intra-regime volatility. In this chapter we consider some of these extensions to the basic NOEM model.

In the next section we consider variants of the base-line NOEM model in which exporter's invoice in the currency of the importer's currency, in the form of local currency pricing, rather than invoicing their product in their own currency, as in the base-line model. The fixed versus floating exchange rate issue is revisited in Section 11.2 and in Section 11.3 we consider extensions to the NOEM which examines the optimal currency invoicing strategy of a company engaged in international trade and the issue of endogenous exchange rate pass-through. In Section 11.4 we consider models which embed the NOEM in a stochastic environment and, specifically, focus on the issue of exchange rate volatility. In the final section we overview papers which attempt to empirically test the NOEM.

11.1 Pricing to market and the NOEM

In the variant of the NOEM set-up in the last chapter, prices are set in the exporter's currency and therefore there is an automatic 100% pass-through of an exchange rate change to the local price level in both the short- and long-run. A number of papers have adopted the NOEM framework but have made the opposite assumption with respect to pricing policy: in particular, prices are set in the importing, or buyer's, currency. This is referred to as local currency pricing (LCP) and with sticky prices in the short-run, means that the pass-through in response to an exchange rate change is zero (see Chapter 3 for a further discussion of pricing to market).

Betts and Devereux (1996) analyse the implications of PTM for real exchange rate variability using a variant of the NOEM model considered in the previous chapter. The key differences that the assumption of PTM makes to that model relate to the price functions and we focus on these here. In the PTM variant of the NOEM each of the n goods in the model are assumed to be sold exclusively by price-setting firms and a fraction, v, of firms in each country can price-discriminate across countries – referred to as PTM goods. The remaining $1 - v$ goods can be freely traded across countries so firms must set a unified price for these goods and the LOOP holds. A critical assumption, considered again later, is that consumers are assumed to be unable to trade PTM goods across countries and therefore cannot restore LOOP relationships. This assumption results in the home (and correspondingly the foreign) country CPIs (equation 10.3) now being modified to:

$$P = \left[\int_0^n p(z)^{1-\theta} dz + \int_n^{n+(1-n)s} p^*(z)^{1-\theta} dz + \int_{n+(1-n)s}^n sf^*(z)^{1-\theta} dz \right]^{1/(1-\theta)},$$

$$(11.1)$$

where p represents home prices and f represents foreign currency prices. Here $p(z)$ is the home currency price of the home produced good, $p^*(z)$ is the home currency price of a foreign PTM good, z, and $f^*(z)$ is the foreign currency price of a foreign non-PTM good.

As in the model of the previous chapter, firms operate a simple linear production technology:

$$y(z) = Ah(z), \tag{11.2}$$

where $y(z)$ is the total output of the firm, $h(z)$ is employment and A is a constant. For PTM firms, total output is divided between output sold domestically – $x(z)$ – and output sold abroad – $n(z)$. The firm hires labour domestically and the PTM firm chooses $p(z)$ and $f(z)$ separately to maximise the following profit function:

$$\pi(z) = p(z)x(z) + sf(z)n(z) - (W/A)(x(z) + n(z)), \tag{11.3}$$

where the firm faces a similar demand schedule to that given in equation (10.8):

$$c(z) = \left[\frac{v(z)}{P} \right]^{-\theta} C, \tag{11.4}$$

where $v(z)$ is equal to either $p(z)$, $p^*(z)$ or $sf^*(z)$. Given this the firm then sets prices in the two markets as a mark-up over MC such that:

$$p(z) = sf(z) = \frac{\theta}{\theta - 1} \frac{W}{A}, \tag{11.5}$$

where $\theta/1 - \theta$ represents the mark-up. Since the elasticities of demand are same in each market, the LOOP and PPP must hold even for PTM goods if prices are continuously flexible. Indeed, in the flex-price world PTM has no implications for any variable irrespective of the source of the shock. However, PTM does have an effect when prices are set one period in advance as in the basic NOEM model.

With sticky prices it is straightforward to show that home and foreign price indices, log linearised around the initial steady state, are:

$$\hat{P} = (1 - n)(1 - v)\hat{s}, \tag{11.6}$$

$$\hat{P}^* = -n(1 - v)\hat{s}. \tag{11.7}$$

These relationships indicate that with sticky prices the response of aggregate price indices to an exchange rate depreciation is lower the greater the share of goods subject to PTM, and as $v \to 1$, P and P^* are entirely unaffected by an exchange rate depreciation. Using these pricing relationships, and assuming real money balances enter the utility function with an isoelastic form as in (10.58), the following variant of (10.33) may be obtained:

$$\hat{S}(1 - v) = \hat{M} - \hat{M}^* - \frac{1}{\varepsilon}\left(\hat{C} - \hat{C}^*\right), \tag{11.8}$$

where, in contrast to (10.33) the size of v determines the magnitude of the deviations from PPP. Using the remaining equations of the sticky-price solution of the model (i.e. the demand and current account equations) the following relationship may be derived:

$$\hat{s} = \frac{\hat{C} - \hat{C}^*}{(1 - v)(\theta - 1) + v}. \tag{11.9}$$

The intuition for this relationship may be seen by assuming complete PTM (i.e. $v = 1$). In this instance, a positive depreciation of the exchange rate allows domestic consumption to be above foreign consumption because the depreciation, although having no effect on relative prices, increases the home currency earnings of home firms and reduces the foreign currency earnings of foreign firms. This income redistribution allows the home country to consume more relative to its trading partner. Combining the last two equations yields the following exchange rate relationship:

$$\hat{s} = \frac{(\hat{M} - \hat{M}^*)}{(1 - v)(\varepsilon + \theta - 1) + v}. \tag{11.10}$$

In this relationship a rise in v will increase the response of the exchange rate so long as $\varepsilon > 2 - \theta$. Since $\theta > 1$ this condition implies that the existence of PTM will increase the volatility of the exchange rate so long as the consumption elasticity of money demand, ε, is 'not too high'. Furthermore, if in addition the consumption elasticity of demand is below unity the presence of PTM not only increases exchange rate volatility, it also generates exchange rate overshooting.

Bergin and Feenstra (2000) also study pricing to market in the context of a NOEM model, but in contrast to Betts and Devereux they model demand using translog preferences, rather than the standard constant elasticity of demand schedules. The main difference this makes is to generate variable mark-ups over marginal cost, rather than a constant mark-up. Additionally, they introduce intermediate goods into the production process and allow firms to set prices in a staggered fashion, rather than the standard one-period-in-advance assumption of the Redux model. In this kind of set-up Bergin and Feenstra demonstrate that monetary shocks can have persistent effects on real exchange rates even after firms have had the opportunity to change the price of the good. There are two reasons for this: firms are reluctant to change price if other firms keep their prices fixed, both because they will loose market share and their total marginal cost does not change quickly (with the price of intermediate goods fixed). The variable mark-up over marginal cost in this model means that deviations from the LOOP are also persistent, in contrast to the Betts and Devereux model in which the LOOP is re-established once firms are free to adjust prices, and this produces a larger accumulation of net foreign assets during the adjustment period and, consequently, there is a bigger long-run impact on the real exchange rate. Bergin and Feenstra also demonstrate that the persistence of the real exchange rate can raise the volatility of the exchange rate by increasing exchange rate overshooting.

In the two-country Redux model considered in the previous chapter, financial markets were incomplete in the sense that agents can only trade in a riskless real bond and therefore risk-sharing is incomplete. Lane (2001) notes that with complete financial markets and the LOOP, full risk-sharing means that there are no shifts in wealth arising from monetary shocks. Hence the crucial result of the Redux model that current account/wealth changes can have a permanent effect on relative prices and the real exchange rate will be ruled out.

In the context of a pricing to market model variant of the Redux model, Chari *et al.* (1998) compare the effects of monetary shocks with complete financial markets versus incomplete financial markets where only a noncontingent domestic currency nominal bond is traded. Interestingly, they demonstrate that in this variant incompleteness of financial markets makes little difference to the persistence effects of monetary policy, essentially because equilibrium current account movements are small. Betts and Devereux (2000) produce a similar result, while Tille (2001) shows that the financial structure does generally qualitatively alter the current account response to a monetary shock under pricing to market.

11.2 Exchange rate regime issues

Devereux and Engel (1998) extend the stochastic version of the NOEM model set out in Obstfeld and Rogoff (2000c) and, in particular, investigate the welfare properties of fixed versus floating with respect to foreign monetary shocks. It turns out that the optimal exchange rate regime depends crucially on the pricing policy of exporters. With LCP the variance of home consumption is not affected by foreign monetary shocks under floating exchange rates and a float is shown to always dominate a fixed rate regime. However, under producer currency pricing, shocks get transmitted to consumption under both fixed and flexible exchange rates and the latter regime may or may not dominate. For example, since the price paid by home residents for goods changes as the exchange rate changes, foreign monetary shocks can affect domestic consumption. In this case the variance of consumption is still lower with flexible exchange rates compared to fixed rates (as in the original Friedmanite case for flexible exchange rates), but exchange rate volatility reduces the average level of consumption because firms set higher mark-ups (to offset the raised expected marginal cost). Indeed, when risk aversion is very high, exchange rate variability is so costly in welfare terms that fixed rates tend to dominate. An important feature of the model of Devereux and Engel is that the exchange rate regime affects not just the variance of consumption and output, but also their average levels. Other recent papers which explore LCP and exchange rate regime issues are Bergin (2000) and Bergin and Feenstra (2000).

Obstfeld and Rogoff (2000b) criticise pricing to market in its LCP form as 'highly implausible because the assumptions and predictions appear grossly inconsistent with many other facts'. For example, they argue that non-traded items such as rents, distribution and advertising, which appear in consumer price indexes of tradable goods, give deviations from the LOOP and it is therefore not necessary to have the extreme assumption of PTM–LCP. Furthermore, price stickiness induced by currency invoicing (which has a maximum lag of 90 days) is not enough on its own to explain persistent macro fluctuations – wage stickiness is also required. Finally, Obstfeld and Rogoff note that the national (i.e. exporter's) currency is still the principal currency for invoice denomination, although that trend is changing: for Japan the figure is 17%, for UK 43% and for Italy 34% (the US is an exception, with 80% of imports invoiced in USD).

11.3   The optimal invoicing currency

In Chapter 1 we noted that there are a number of potential determinants of the optimal currency used by an exporting firm when invoicing. A recent strand in the optimal invoicing literature model has involved using the NOEM to determine the optimal currency invoicing strategy. In order to illustrate some of the key issues relating to the optimal invoicing strategy, Bacchetta and van Wincoop (2002) start with a traditional partial equilibrium approach where the profit functions for the exporter invoicing in the importer's currency, I, and in the exporter's currency, E, are respectively:

$$\Pi^I = Sp^I D(p^I) - C(D(p^I)), \tag{11.11}$$

$$\Pi^E = p^E D(p^E/S) - C(D(p^E/S)), \tag{11.12}$$

where p is the price faced by the importer and is equal to p^I when the importer's currency is used as the invoice medium and p^E when the exporter's currency is used. If the exporter's currency is used for invoicing there is only uncertainty about demand and therefore costs, while if the importer's currency is used there will be uncertainty about the price denominated in the exporter's currency, p^I, but not demand. In this kind of model firms have to compare the expected utility of profits under the two price-setting options, $EU(\Pi^E) - EU(\Pi^I)$. A standard finding in this literature, which Bacchetta and van Wincoop confirm, is that the exporter's (importer's) currency is preferred when Π^E is globally convex (concave) with respect to S because profits are larger (smaller).

Exchange rate variability will clearly affect the variance and expectation of profits but since the first-order derivative of profits with respect to the exchange rate is identical under the two invoicing strategies, the first-order effect on the variance will be the same and so risk aversion does not matter. The effects on expected profits are, of course, different under the two pricing strategies. Pricing in the importer's currency, the profit function is linear in the exchange rate and expected profits are not affected. There are two effects on expected profits when the firm prices in exporter's currency. First, when the elasticity of demand is greater than unity the cost function is convex and a rise in demand will raise costs more than a decline in demand lowers costs and so expected profits will be lower and there will be an incentive to price in the importer's currency. However, to set against this the expected level of demand will also rise, since demand is a convex function of the exchange rate and is proportional to S^μ, where μ is the elasticity of demand; this will raise expected profits when pricing in the exporter's currency. The first effect dominates when $(\eta - 1)\mu > 1$, where η defines the convexity of the cost function.

Bacchetta and van Wincoop extend this base-line model to the situation where the domestic firm is competing with a number of other firms in the same country and in other countries. In the case where all of the firms are in the same country they consider a particular industry where N exporting firms from the home country sell in the market of the foreign country, which is assumed to have N^* exporting firms and the market share of the exporting country is defined as: $n = N/(N + N^*)$. Assuming CES preferences with elasticity $\mu > 1$ among the different products then the demand for firm j is:

$$D(p, P^*) = \frac{1}{N + N^*} \left(\frac{p_j}{P^*}\right)^{-\mu} d^*, \qquad (11.13)$$

where p_j is the price set by the firm measured in the importer's currency and d^* is the level of foreign spending on goods in the industry (equal to the nominal level of spending divided by the industry price index). If it is assumed that a fraction, f, of home country firms sets a price, p^E, in their own (i.e. exporter's) currency, and a fraction $1 - f$ sets price in the importer's currency, p^I, and foreign firms set a price p^{H*}, it can be shown that the overall price index faced by the consumers is given by:[1]

$$P^* = \left((1 - n)(p^{H*})^{1-\mu} + nf(p^E/S)^{1-\mu} + n(1 - f)(p^I)^{1-\mu}\right)^{1/1-\mu}. \quad (11.14)$$

Bacchetta and van Wincoop consider two types of equilibrium: a Nash equilibrium in which each firm makes an optimal invoicing decision conditional on the invoicing decisions of all other firms and, since there will be multiple Nash equilibria, a coordination equilibrium which is the Parato optimal Nash equilibria for the exporting country's firms. The coordination equilibrium is found by using the properties of the profit functions mentioned earlier under the different Nash conditions to see which yields the highest expected utility. Given the demand function (11.13), and defining $\bar{n} = 0.5 - 0.5/\mu(\eta - 1)$, this leads to the following pricing strategies:

- If $\mu(\eta - 1) < 1$, firms price in the exporter's currency;
- If $\mu(\eta - 1) > 1$ and $n < \bar{n}$ firms price in the importer's currency;
- If $\mu(\eta - 1) > 1$ and $n > \bar{n}$ there are three Nash Equilibria: all price in the exporter's currency; all price in the importer's currency; a fraction prices in the exporter's currency, while the rest price in the importer's currency.

In the final case if firms coordinate they will prefer to all price in the exporter's currency if either $\bar{n}$ or their rate of risk aversion are large enough. The three pricing strategies make clear that the market share of the exporting country is crucial in determining the pricing decision – if the market share is small below the cut-off, $\bar{n}$, then the results are unchanged compared to the single exporting firm considered in the partial equilibrium model: if demand is sufficiently price elastic firms price in the importer's currency. More generally, the results show that firms are more likely to price in the exporter's currency if their country's market share is large.

Bacchetta and van Wincoop then go on to consider invoicing practice in the context of a general equilibrium set-up which is in the spirit of the NOEM. The key difference in moving from the partial to general equilibrium setting is that the exchange rate is no longer exogenous. Their variant of the NOEM model is one in which there are two tradable sectors and a non-tradable sector and the only source of uncertainty comes from money supply shocks. They show that the invoicing results are crucially dependent on the assumption regarding wage flexibility. With wages preset Bacchetta and van Wincoop show that the pricing strategies for firms are very similar to those outlined earlier in the case of the partial equilibrium set-up:[2] market share is still the critical factor in determining the invoicing currency.

In a related paper, Devereux *et al.* (2001) use the basic NOEM model of the previous chapter to develop a model of endogenous exchange rate pass-through, where both pass-through and the exchange rate are simultaneously determined and interact with one another. The main distinguishing features of Devereux *et al.* over Bacchetta and van Wincoop is that they focus on exchange rate pass-through and exchange rate volatility and the implications for exchange rate volatility of differences in monetary policies across countries. In the model of Devereux *et al.*, pass-through is endogenous because firms choose the currency in which they set their export prices and, assuming exchange rate volatility increases as the degree of pass-through falls, they demonstrate that there is a unique equilibrium rate of pass-through. Importantly, they show that exchange rate volatility may be substantially affected by the presence of endogenous pass-through. The key results of Devereux *et al.* show that pass-through is related to the relative stability of monetary policy: countries which have relatively low monetary growth have relatively low rates of exchange rate pass-through, while countries with relatively high volatility of money growth have relatively high pass-through rates.

11.4 Stochastic versions of the new open economy macroeconomic model: exchange rate volatility issues revisited

Obstfeld and Rogoff (2000c) use a stochastic version of NOEM model to generate a variant of the forward-looking monetary model considered in Chapter 4. The basic difference here is that the introduction of uncertainty means that the forward-looking reduced form features a risk premium term. Risk, however, has a more pervasive effect in this model, affecting the price-setting behaviour of individual producers and on expected output and international trade flows.

In a stochastic context Obstfeld and Rogoff demonstrate that the solution for the expected value of the log of (world) consumption is:

$$
Ec = \frac{1}{1+\rho} \left\{ \log\left(\frac{\theta-1}{\theta}\right) - E\log\kappa - \frac{1}{2}\sigma_\kappa^2 - 2n(1-n)\sigma_s^2 - \left[2 - \frac{1}{2}(1-\rho)^2\right] \right.
$$
$$
\left. \times \sigma_c^2 - 2n(1-n)(\sigma_{ks} - \sigma_{k*s}) - 2\left[n\sigma_{kc} + (1-n)\sigma_{k*c}\right] \right\},
$$

$$(11.15)$$

where of terms not familiar from the previous chapter, the σ_i^2 terms represent the variance of consumption, c, productivity, k, and the exchange rate, s, respectively, and the σ_{ij} terms represent the corresponding covariance terms. Needless to say, the distinguishing factor between this expression and its certainty equivalent expression is that none of these uncertainty terms appear in the certainty equivalent version. Assuming all shocks are log-normally distributed allows Obstfeld and Rogoff to log-linearise the first-order conditions for consumption and money and using the first-order conditions for money they are able to derive an equation for the exchange rate of the following form:

$$
s_t = \frac{\bar{i}\varepsilon}{1+\bar{i}\varepsilon} \sum_{s=t}^{\infty} \left(\frac{1}{1+\bar{i}\varepsilon}\right)^{s-t} E_t\left[m_s - m_s^* + \frac{v_s - v_s^*}{\bar{i}\varepsilon}\right], \tag{11.16}
$$

where the risk premium, $v_t - v_t^*$, is given by:

$$
v_t - v_t^* = \frac{1}{2}\left(\sigma_{p^*,t}^2 - \sigma_{p,t}^2\right) + \rho(\sigma_{cp^*,t} - \sigma_{cp,t}), \tag{11.17}
$$

and where the subscript p denotes the log of the price level and the overbar above the interest rate term reflects a non-stochastic steady-state value (which arises because the non-linearity of the money equilibrium condition makes it necessary to approximate it in the neighbourhood of a non-stochastic steady state), and ε is the consumption elasticity of the demand for money. The term involving $[v_s - v_s^*]_{s=t}^{\infty}$ is referred to as the 'level' risk premium, and is not exactly equal to the standard forward market risk premium because of the existence of $1/\bar{i}\varepsilon$. There are two key insights here. First, the risk premium can affect the level of the exchange rate, and not just the predictable excess return, which has been studied extensively in the literature (and is considered in some detail in Chapter 15). This is important because it means that higher moments of economic variables can affect the volatility of the exchange rate and not just the first moments – if the forward risk premium is quite volatile, this could have important implications for exchange rate volatility. Second, the effect of the risk premium on the exchange rate may potentially be very large because of the scaling factor $1/\bar{i}\varepsilon$. A rise in the covariance of c and p would lead to a fall in v which, in turn, would produce a fall in the interest rate and from (11.16) an exchange rate appreciation. Obstfeld and Rogoff view this as capturing the idea of a portfolio shift toward the home currency or, equivalently, of a 'safe haven' effect on the home currency.

Obstfeld and Rogoff proceed to solve for the risk premium on the basis that the only source of uncertainty arises from home money supply uncertainty and the home money supply is assumed to follow a random walk process:

$$m_t = m_{t-1} + \mu_t,$$

where $\mu_t \sim \mathcal{N}(0, \sigma_\mu^2)$ for every date t. With this assumption, the risk premium term becomes:

$$v_t - v_t^* = -\sigma_\mu^2 \left[\frac{1-2n}{2} + \frac{n(1+\bar{i}\varepsilon)}{1+\bar{i}} \right]. \tag{11.18}$$

Taken in conjunction with equation (11.16) we see that a rise in the level of home monetary variability leads to both a fall in the level exchange risk premium and the forward exchange rate risk premium. However, for plausible values of $\bar{i}$ and ε the former effect is likely to be much larger than the latter thereby imparting an exchange rate appreciation and considerable exchange rate volatility. Notice that the link here between the risk premium and monetary variability contrasts with the common casual presumption that financial markets attach a positive risk premium to the currency of a country with high monetary volatility. The effect is different in this model because in the sticky price variant, positive monetary shocks lead to increases in global consumption, which means that domestic money can be a hedge, in real terms, against shocks to consumption. Furthermore, higher monetary variability raises the expectation of the future real value of money (other things equal) which is the convexity term (this effect also works in a flexible price model).

Duarte (2003) uses a variant of the two-country NOEM model in which asset markets are incomplete and prices are set one period in advance in the buyer's currency (i.e. local currency pricing) to address the intra-regime volatility issue, introduced in the introduction, that the conditional variance of the real exchange rate changes sharply across exchange rate regimes. In the model, the home agent holds home currency and trades a riskless bond, B, which pays one unit of home currency with certainty one period after issuance, with the foreign agent (i.e. there is a single bond and so asset markets are incomplete). The agent's maximisation problem is summarised as:

$$\max_{c_t,l_t,B_{t+1},M_t} E_0 \left[\sum_{t=0}^{\infty} \beta^t u \left(c_t, 1 - l_t, \frac{M_t}{P_t} \right) \right], \tag{11.19}$$

where the nature of this function should be clear from our previous discussions. This function is maximised subject to a standard budget constraint:

$$P_t c_t + M_t + Q_t F_{t+1} \leq P_t w_t l_t + M_{t-1} + F_t + \Pi_t + T_t, \tag{11.20}$$

$$B_{t+1} \geq -a_t, \tag{11.21}$$

where of terms not previously defined, Q_t denotes the time t-price of one discount bond, Π_t represents firms profits. T_t is money transfers from the government, $P_t w_t l_t$ represents nominal labour earnings and equation (11.21) puts an upper bound, a_t, on the number of one-period bonds that an agent can issue. The first-order condition from this maximisation process for the price of the home bond is

$$Q_t \geq \beta \frac{P_t}{u_{c,t}} E_t \left[\frac{u_{c,t+1}}{P_{t+1}} \right], \tag{11.22}$$

and for the foreign consumers maximisation problem (the bond is denominated in domestic currency):

$$Q_t \geq \beta \frac{s_t P_t^*}{u_{c,t}^*} E_t \left[\frac{u_{c,t+1}^*}{s_{t+1} P_{t+1}^*} \right], \tag{11.23}$$

where $u_{c,t}$ represents the marginal utility function of home consumption in period t and other terms have the same interpretation as before. At any point in time the price of the bonds will be uniquely determined by the unconstrained agent's first-order condition and on combining equations (11.22) and (11.23) an equation for the nominal exchange rate can be obtained as:

$$s_t = \frac{P_t}{u_{c,t}} \frac{u_{c,t}^*}{P_t^*} \frac{E_t[u_{c,t+1}/P_{t+1}]}{E_t[u_{c,t+1}^*/s_{t+1} P_{t+1}^*]}. \tag{11.24}$$

Note the contrast between this equation and that derived from a model where asset markets are complete, such as the Lucas' model considered in Chapter 4. In particular, unlike the standard general equilibrium model considered in that chapter, the nominal exchange rate is an explicit function of expectations of future variables. This follows on from the assumption of incomplete asset (bond) markets and product market segmentation.[3] It then follows that changes in expectations about future variables can translate into changes in the exchange rate without directly affecting other macroeconomic variables, thereby offering an explanation for the excess volatility result. This result would not occur, of course, in a model with complete risk-sharing. It would equally not occur in a model in which goods markets are integrated (either in terms of no product market segmentation, or with product market segmentation where prices are preset in the seller's, rather than the buyer's currency).

Duarte studies the properties of this model in the context of a simulation exercise in which the utility function is fully specified, along with technology and monetary shocks. This exercise clearly generates a sharp increase in the volatility of the real exchange rate following a switch from fixed to flexible rates, with no similar change in the volatilities of output, consumption or trade flows. Therefore the model is able to explain Figures 1.6 and 1.7 introduced in Chapter 1. The intuition for this result is quite simple: because prices are set one period ahead in the buyer's currency, allocation decisions are disconnected, at the time of impact, from unexpected changes in the nominal exchange rate and so the volatilities of output, consumption and trade flows are unaffected.

Duarte and Stockman (2005) exploit the same two-country model used in Duarte (2003) and by writing the equivalent expression to (11.24) for the forward exchange rate, f, are able to rewrite (11.24) as

$$s_t = \frac{Q_t}{Q_t^*}(rp_t + E_t[s_{t+1}]), \tag{11.25}$$

where rp_t is the risk premium defined in the conventional way as $f_t - E(s_{t+1})$. This equation is a first-order stochastic difference equation for the exchange rate and, in words, shows that the expected growth of the exchange rate depends on the household's perception of the relative risk of holding the two nominal assets, rp_t, normalised by the level of the exchange rate. The risk premium is given by:

$$rp_t = \frac{\text{cov}_t(s_{t+1}, u_{c,t+1})}{E_t[u_{c,t+1}]}, \tag{11.26}$$

where $u_{c,t+1}$ denotes the marginal utility of the home household in period $t + 1$. Equation (11.26) shows that the risk premium arises from the covariance between the nominal exchange rate and the marginal utility of consumption. When the next period's covariance between s and $u_{c,t+1}$ is high, the foreign bond tends to pay a high (low) real return when the marginal utility of consumption is also high (low). The foreign bond is therefore more risky to the home agent the lower is $\text{cov}(s_{t+1}, u_{c,t+1})$.

The key prediction of the model is that new information which results in agents revising their perceptions of the risk premium can produce exchange rate volatility without there being any changes in the current macroeconomic variables. Exogenous shocks to money growth and productivity growth, with time-varying second moments, cause endogenous changes in the risk premium. Such shocks result from regime shifts which affect the covariances of shocks, and these generate 'rational speculation' in the sense of altering equilibrium risk premia. The model of Duarte and Stockman generates a strong correlation between changes in exchange rates and changes in risk premia. However, it turns out that the magnitude of the risk premium is too small to match the data and, as a result, the exchange rate changes they produce are also too small. Duarte and Stockman suggest that further modifications to the model, such as modelling the equity-premium and the introduction of irrational speculation, may help to generate sufficient exchange rate variability.

Monacelli (2004) takes a stochastic small open economy version of the NOEM model, in which there is an explicit role for capital accumulation (where capital is assumed to be a function of Tobin's q) and pricing to market, in order to examine the issue of intra-regime volatility. The main novelty of this work is to introduce into this class of model an open economy variant of a Taylor style interest rate monetary rule which allows an analysis of the short-run dynamic effects of a change in the nominal exchange rate regime. Specifically, the equation for the target for the nominal interest rate is:

$$(1 + \bar{i}_t) = \left(\frac{P_{H,t}}{P_{H,t-1}} \right)^{\omega_\pi} Y_t^{\omega_y} S_t^{\omega_s / (1 - \omega_s)}. \tag{11.27}$$

From this expression the monetary authority reacts to the contemporaneous level of the nominal exchange rate (a forward-looking jump variable) and to contemporaneous inflation and output. The use of this rule allows Monacelli to consider fixed and floating exchange rate regimes in the context of the NOEM. If $\omega_s = 0$ this implies a flexible rate regime whereas if $\omega_s \in [0, 1]$ this allows for a range of managed to fixed exchange rates. It is then assumed that the monetary authority smooth interest rates using the following rule:

$$(1 + i_t) = (1 + \bar{i}_t)^{1 - \chi} (1 + i_{t-1})^\chi, \tag{11.28}$$

and by taking a log-linear approximation of these two equations it is possible to obtain:

$$i_t = \bar{\omega}_\pi \pi_{H,t} + \bar{\omega}_y y_t + \bar{\omega}_s s_t + \chi i_{t-1}, \tag{11.29}$$

where $\bar{\omega}_\pi \equiv (1 - \chi)\omega_\pi$, $\bar{\omega}_y = (1 - \chi)\omega_y$, $\bar{\omega}_s = (1 - \chi)(\omega_s / 1 - \omega_s)$, $i_t \approx \log(1 + i_t / 1 + i)$.

The model is then calibrated and solved numerically for the instances of complete and incomplete pass-through. In the complete pass-through case, Monacelli (2004) shows that in moving from fixed to flexible exchange rates there is a proportional rise in the volatility of the nominal exchange rate which is coupled with a rise in the real exchange rate which roughly mimics what we observe in the data. He shows that the interest rate smoothing objective is crucial in generating this result. Furthermore, the close correlation between real and nominal exchange rates in a flexible rate regime is mimicked in this model and these results are robust with respect to the sources of the underlying shocks. However, this version of the model produces a correlation between nominal depreciation and inflation which is too high relative to the actual correlation in the data. Nonetheless, it is demonstrated that this correlation can be made consistent with the data when there is incomplete pass-through of exchange rate changes.

A further attempt to explain the excess volatility of exchange rates using a variant of the NOEM is made by Devereux and Engel (2001). They attempt to shed light on a conjecture of Krugman (1989) that exchange rate volatility is so great because fluctuations in the exchange rate matter so little for the economy. They use a variant of the NOEM in which there is a combination of local currency pricing, heterogeneity in international price setting and in the distribution of goods (e.g. some firms market their products directly in the foreign market and charge a foreign price while some exporters use foreign distributors, charging a price set in the exporter's currency) and, crucially, the existence of noise traders who impart expectational biases into international financial markets. They derive an expression for the unanticipated change in the exchange rate of the following form:

$$\hat{s}_t = \frac{(1 + \sigma/r)(\hat{m}_t - \hat{m}_t^*) + (\sigma/r)v_t}{[\sigma/r + \rho(\theta - (1 - \theta^*))]}, \tag{11.30}$$

where θ is the fraction of home firms that sell directly to households in the foreign country at a foreign price (with $1-\theta$ selling their product to home-based distributors at a home price), θ^* is the fraction of foreign firms that sell directly to households in the home country at a home currency price (with $1 - \theta^*$ selling their product to home-based distributors at a foreign currency price), v is the biasedness in foreign exchange dealers' prediction of the exchange rate due to the existence of noise traders, ρ is the elasticity of inter-temporal substitution, σ is a function of the elasticity of inter-temporal substitution, the intra-temporal elasticity of substitution and a leisure–work parameter. How volatile the exchange rate is with respect to the fundamentals can be gauged by calculating the conditional variance of the exchange rate:

$$\text{Var}_{t-1}(\hat{s}_t) = \frac{(1 + \sigma/r)\text{Var}_{t-1}(\hat{m}_t - \hat{m}_t^*)}{\Phi^2\left[1 - [\lambda\sigma/(r\Phi)]^2\right]}, \quad \Phi = \left[\sigma/r + \rho(\theta - (1 - \theta^*))\right], \tag{11.31}$$

where, of terms not previously defined, $\lambda > 0$ and $\text{Var}_{t-1}(v_t) = \lambda\text{Var}_{t-1}(s_t)$; that is, the volatility of the bias in noise traders' expectations is determined by exchange rate volatility. Given this expression, (11.31) says that the conditional volatility in the exchange rate depends only on fundamentals which in this case are the volatility in relative money supply terms. Given (11.31) it turns out that as $\theta + \theta^* \to 1$ and with $\lambda = 1$, the conditional volatility of the exchange rate rises without bound. This is because in this model the combination of local currency pricing, along with asymmetric distribution of goods and noise trading implies a degree of exchange rate volatility which is far in excess of the underlying shocks.

The basic intuition for this result is that the presence of local currency pricing and domestic distributors tends to remove both the substitution and wealth effects of exchange rate movements at any point in time. In the absence of noise traders an unanticipated shock to the exchange rate will drive a wedge between the real interest rate in the home and foreign country and this in turn will limit the degree of exchange rate movement so that the current account adjusts to maintain expected future levels of consumption. However, with noise traders, of the type assumed in this model, the response of the exchange rate is no longer governed by the inter-temporal current account parameters.

11.5   Empirical evidence on the NOEM

As we have seen, there are voluminous empirical literatures testing PPP and variants of the monetary approach to the exchange rate. Perhaps because of the complexity of the model, there is less in the way of empirical tests of the NOEM. Lane (2001) argues that the VAR-based models, discussed in Chapter 8, can be used to gain insight into the validity of the NOEM class of model. In particular, the VAR models of Clarida and Gali (1994), Eichenbaum and Evans (1995) and MacDonald and Swagel (2000) show that monetary shocks have an effect on the real and nominal exchange rates which is consistent with the predictions of sticky-price models such as the NOEM. Betts and Devereux (1997) add the trade balance to the Eichenbaum and Evans VAR specification (which included US output, the US CPI, US money, a US-based interest differential and the real exchange rate) discussed in Chapter 8 and using calibration methods show that a version of the model in which features PTM matches well the conditional moments in the data while the PPP-based redux model does not do well in this regard. Other VAR-based estimates focus on the relationship between monetary shocks and the current account, which, as we have seen, is a central component of the NOEM (see, for example, Lane (1998) and Lee and Chinn (1998)), and this evidence seems to support the prediction of the NOEM that positive nominal shocks lead to an improvement in the current account.

Another strand in the NOEM empirical literature involves comparing the unconditional moments generated by the model with the unconditional moments of the data. Here the focus is on determining what proportion of aggregate fluctuations can be explained by monetary shocks (see, for example, Chari *et al.* 1998 and Kollmann 1998) and it turns out that monetary shocks only account for a small proportion of aggregate economic fluctuations over a given time interval. However, as Lane (2001) notes, this finding is not inconsistent with the existence of nominal rigidities or an important role for monetary policy in responding to other disturbances; the calibration method therefore is not sufficient to produce an overall assessment of the NOEM model.

A number of researchers have documented evidence that there is a significant link between net foreign assets and the real exchange rates of OECD countries (see Obstfeld and Rogoff 1995, 1996; Gagnon 1996; MacDonald and Ricci 2001). Lane (2001) argues that these findings provide indirect support for the notion that even temporary disturbances can have persistent effects, because current account imbalances alter net foreign assets and, as we have seen at various points in the book, this can generate permanent, or long-lasting, real effects.

Ghironi *et al.* (2003) test a two-country variant of the NOEM model in which cross-country differences in net foreign asset and consumption dynamics are driven by differences in discount factors and steady-state levels of productivity. Their simulation results show that even small and empirically plausible differences in discount factors can impart considerable heterogeneity into net foreign asset positions, and system dynamics, following productivity shocks. In the empirical implementation of their model, Ghironi *et al.* focus on the G3 – Germany, Japan and the US – against the aggregate of the G7 (excluding the home country). A VAR-based approach is used, for a sample period spanning 1977, quarter 1 to 1997, quarter 4, and the key variables included are labour productivity, per capita consumption and net foreign assets. Standard identification methods are used to identify country-specific and global productivity shocks. Ghironi *et al.*'s empirical results show that the dynamic responses of net foreign assets and consumption vary considerably across the G3 and they also argue that the empirical response of the US data are consistent with those of the less patient more productive economy.

Perhaps the most direct test of the NOEM class of models has been provided by Bergin (2004) who estimates, using maximum likelihood methods, a two-country version of the NOEM. The two 'countries' are the US against an aggregate of the rest of the G7 and the variables entering the model are the exchange rate, the current account, output growth, inflation and interest rate deviations; data are quarterly over the period 1973:1 to 2000:4. Bergin demonstrates that the one-step-ahead in-sample predictions for the exchange rate and the current account are able to beat a random walk, although they are not able to beat the predictions from a standard VAR model. The estimated parameter estimates from the model help to shed some light on some of the issues that have arisen in the NOEM class of models. For example, Bergin finds that a very high degree of local currency pricing (see Section 11.2) is needed to explain the actual exchange rate movements in the data set. Bergin also demonstrates that the elasticity of substitution between home and foreign goods is close to unity, which is the value often assumed in theoretical work. Bergin also shows that deviations from UIP are very closely correlated with shocks to marginal utility rather than to monetary shocks, which is at odds with the basic story in many variants of the NOEM.

12 The economics of fixed exchange rates, part 1

Target zone models

So far in this book we have considered the determination of exchange rates when the exchange rate is freely floating. We now turn to the determination of exchange rates when exchange rates are fixed. It may seem odd to consider the determination of a price which is fixed, however, as Svensson and others have argued there is really no such thing as a truly fixed exchange rate (monetary unions aside). If we take the Classical Gold Standard period, in which participating currencies were fixed to each other because they first of all fixed their currency in terms of gold, there was nonetheless some exchange rate flexibility because of the costs of shipping gold between countries and certain opportunity costs (such as the funds tied in shipping gold). These costs set-up bands above and below the central parity which are referred to as a target zone. Admittedly, such bands were very narrow, but nonetheless some have argued (see, for example, Svensson 1994 and Bordo and MacDonald 2005) that they conferred on the government of the day some autonomy in the operation of its monetary policy (we consider this point in more detail later). The existence of target zones in other fixed rate regimes is perhaps clearer since such regimes have explicit bands above and below the central parity (in the Bretton Woods regime currencies were allowed to float by plus or minus 1% relative to the central rate, while in the ERM of the EMS the bands ranged from plus or minus 2.5% to plus or minus 15%). How then are exchange rates determined within such bands?

As Krugman (1991) notes, a naive interpretation of how exchange rates likely behave within a band would be to say that they behave like flexible rates until they hit the edge of the band, whereupon the regime switches to a fixed exchange rate. However, such an interpretation is not correct since the existence of the bands constrains the future behaviour of the exchange rate and if agents are forward-looking this should affect the behaviour of the exchange rate within the band. Expectations formation is therefore a crucial aspect of the determination of target zone exchange rates.

In this chapter we consider the target zone literature. We start in the next section with what is usually referred to as the base-line model, based on the simple flex-price monetary approach equation first introduced in Chapter 4. We then go on to develop the model using a sticky-price variant in Section 12.3. The empirical evidence is considered in Section 12.4.

12.1   The base-line target zone model

Consider a small open economy in which both UIP and PPP are assumed to hold continuously and the exchange rate at any point in time is given by:

$$s_t = m_t + v_t + \alpha E[ds/dt], \tag{12.1}$$

or as

$$s = f + \alpha E[ds/dt], \tag{12.1'}$$

where s is the log of the exchange rate, m is the log of the money supply, v is a shift term capturing velocity shocks, f, the composite fundamental term equals $m + v$ and the last term is, as before, is the expected change in the exchange rate. The velocity term is assumed to be the only exogenous source of exchange rate dynamics and it is assumed to follow a continuous time random walk process:

$$dv = \sigma \, dz. \tag{12.2}$$

Using this assumption facilitates a simple analytic solution and highlights exchange rate dynamics due to the existence of the target zone rather than the predictable future changes in v. Monetary policy in the model is assumed to be passive, which means that the money supply is only altered in order to maintain the target zone. More specifically, the monetary authority reduces m (sells foreign exchange) in order to prevent the exchange rate exceeding $\bar{s}$, the upper edge of the band, and increases m (buys foreign exchange) to prevent s from falling below $\underline{s}$, the lower edge of the band. As long as s lies within the band defined by $\bar{s}$ and $\underline{s}$, the money supply will remain unchanged. The model therefore predicts that any foreign exchange intervention will take place at the bands (so-called marginal intervention) and will not be of the traditional intra-marginal variety that central banks normally adopt. The reason that only marginal intervention is required in this model is because it is assumed that the bands are credible. It is usual to centre the target zone around zero, so $\bar{s} = -\underline{s}$.

Figure 12.1 plots the exchange rate against v and the broken lines define the bands $\bar{s}$ and $-\underline{s}$. Consider first the observed exchange rate behaviour if $m = 0$. If the exchange rate is freely floating, then the earlier assumptions imply that the expected change in the exchange rate must be zero (i.e. the money supply is constant and velocity follows a random walk) and exchange rate behaviour would follow a 45° ray given by FF – a positive shock to velocity produces a proportionate depreciation of the exchange rate, as in the flexible price monetary model. In the presence of the exchange rate bands, however, exchange rate behaviour is described by the S-shaped curve. The curvature of this schedule indicates that in the upper half of the figure the relationship between s and v is concave while in the lower half it is convex. Why? Consider a shock to velocity which takes us to a point such as v_1. At this point, the expected change in v is zero but the expected change in the exchange rate is negative since agents expect the currency depreciation to be

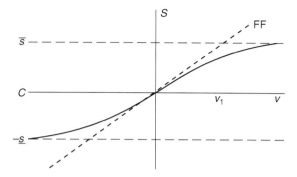

Figure 12.1 The *S* function.

offset in the future. The closer the rate is to the edge of the band the more strongly are such expectations held and therefore the function increases at an increasing rate. A similar argument would apply at the bottom edge of the band and so the relationship between f and s will be bent as it approaches the edge of the band: the S-shaped curve describes the functional relationship between s and f, rather than the 45° ray.

There are two points worth noting from Figure 12.1. First, in the top half of the figure the expected change in the exchange rate is negative, while in the bottom half it is positive. This is possible, despite the fact that m is constant and the expected change in v is zero, because of the curvature of the S function: the concavity of S in the top half allows $E[ds/dt]$ to be negative, and the convexity of S in the bottom half allows $E[ds/dt]$ to be positive. Second, note that the existence of the band has a stabilising effect on the exchange rate since a given shock to velocity has a lesser effect on the exchange rate in the band than in the free float scenario. This is despite the fact that no effort is being made by the monetary authorities to engage in foreign exchange market intervention. This has been referred to by Svensson as the honeymoon effect which follows on from moving from a freely floating system to a target zone arrangement.

12.1.1 A formal analysis of S in the target zone

In this section we consider a more formal analysis of the S curve portrayed in Figure 12.1 (the discussion here follows Krugman 1991). The objective is to determine a relationship for s:

$$s = g(m, v, \bar{s}, \underline{s}), \tag{12.3}$$

which is consistent with (12.1) and the assumed monetary behaviour. Assuming m is constant and s lies in the band then, and as we have seen, the only source of expected changes in s comes from the random movement of v. By the rules of stochastic calculus (and in particular on using Ito's lema) we have:

$$E[ds]/dt = \left(\frac{\sigma^2}{2}\right) g_{vv}(m, v, \bar{s}, \underline{s}),$$
(12.4)

where g_{vv} denotes the second derivative of the function with respect to v. On substituting (12.4) into (12.1) we can obtain:

$$g(m, v, \bar{s}, \underline{s}) = m + v + \left(\frac{\alpha\sigma^2}{2}\right) g_{vv}(m, v, \bar{s}, \underline{s}),$$
(12.5)

and this second order differential equation has a general solution of the form:

$$g(m, v, \bar{s}, \underline{s}) = m + v + Ae^{\rho v} + Be^{-\rho v},$$
(12.6)

where the roots, ρ, are given by:

$$\rho = \left(\frac{2}{\alpha\sigma^2}\right)^{1/2},$$
(12.7)

and A and B are constants to be determined. The problem can be simplified by appealing to symmetry. If $m = 0$ then if the relationship is symmetrical we would expect the relationship to go through the middle of Figure 12.1, where we should have $v = 0$ and $s = 0$. This, of course, can only be true if $B = -A$ and so:

$$g(m, v, \bar{s}, \underline{s}) = m + v + A[e^{\rho v} - e^{-\rho v}].$$
(12.8)

In order to get the S-shaped function of Figure 12.1, A clearly has to be negative (i.e. this will yield a value of s that falls increasingly below $m + v$ for positive v, and increasingly above for negative v). More specifically, the problem of defining A for any given value of m must be one in which the curve defined by (12.8) is tangent to, or smooth pastes, the edges of the band. Krugman shows that for schedules which cross the edge of the band equilibria on the schedule are not consistent, whereas they are consistent on the S-shaped curve. To determine the value of A that makes the curve in (12.8) tangent to the top and bottom of the band, we let $\bar{v}$ be the value of v at which s reaches the top of the band, which gives:

$$\bar{s} = \bar{v} + A[e^{\rho\bar{v}} - e^{\rho\bar{v}}],$$
(12.9)

and

$$A = \frac{-1}{\rho[e^{\rho\bar{v}} + e^{\rho\bar{v}}]},$$
(12.10)

which is clearly negative. The smooth pasting condition of the S curve is in fact well known from the option pricing literature and in the analysis of irreversible investment (see, for example, Dumas 1988). The analogy with option pricing may be illustrated in the following way. Consider a (continuous time) present value formulation of expression (12.1) (see our discussion of such present value formulations of the monetary model in Chapter 4):

$$s_t = \left(\frac{1}{\alpha}\right) \int_t^\infty (m + v)e^{-(1/\alpha)(t-\tau)} d\tau, \tag{12.11}$$

where as in equation (4.6) the current spot rate may be viewed as the present discount value of future realisations of $m + v$, where α is the discounting factor. By differentiating (12.11) with respect to t yields the equation (12.1).

If the price of an asset is given by (12.11), where m is held constant at, say, m_0 then the value of this asset would be:

$$\tilde{s}_t = \left(\frac{1}{\alpha}\right) \int_t^\infty (m_0 + v)e^{-(1/\alpha)(t-\tau)} d\tau, \tag{12.12}$$

and the actual exchange rate, s, may be regarded as a compound asset, that is, the sum of the imaginary asset, whose price is determined by (12.12), and the right to sell the asset at a price $\underline{s}$, plus the obligation to sell at the price $\bar{s}$ on demand. The derivation of the S curve then becomes the combined price of the two options: the requirement to sell on demand becomes more important the higher $\bar{s}$ is, so the price of the compound asset falls below $\bar{s}$ at high v. Conversely, the right to sell the asset at $\underline{s}$ supports the value of the asset at low v.

So far the assumption about the behaviour of the money supply in defence of the target zone has not been made explicit. This behaviour can be illustrated in the following way. Suppose that initially the market is at point 1 on Figure 12.2. There is then a series of positive shocks to velocity which moves the system to a point such as 2. However, at this point any further increases in v would have to be offset by reductions in m so that the exchange rate stays constant as the market

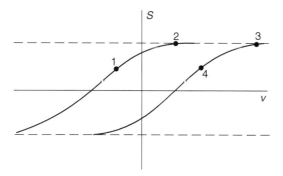

Figure 12.2 Monetary policy and a family of S curves.

moves from 2 to, say, point 3. However, at 3 if there is then a succession of negative shocks, the authorities will not react and the market will therefore move back down a new S curve to a point such as 4. So a new S curve will arise each time the band is reached. An expression for this family of S curves may be derived by assuming that A is determined so that the curve is tangent for some particular m. The whole family of schedules may be defined by:

$$g(m, v, \bar{s}, \underline{s}) = m + v + A[e^{\rho(m+v)} - e^{\rho(m+v)}], \tag{12.13}$$

with the same A. Whenever shocks to v push (12.13) to the edge of the band, m is reduced in order to keep $m + v$ constant and s at the edge of the band. It follows from this that the whole family of S curves can be drawn as a single curve in f/s space, as in Figure 12.3, where the edges of the band now represent a reflecting barrier: if s goes to the edge of the band m adjusts to keep f from going any further.

12.1.2   The sticky-price variant of the target zone model

The base-line target zone model is, as we have seen, based on the flex-price monetary model. Are the predictions of the base-line model modified in the presence of sticky prices? To address this issue, Miller and Weller (1991) take a stochastic variant of the Dornbusch model and we consider their model here. The particular stochastic version of the Dornbusch model is:

$$m - p = \beta_0 y - \beta_1 i, \tag{12.14}$$

$$y = \gamma_1 (s_t - p_t) - \gamma_2 i_t, \tag{12.15}$$

$$dp = \phi(y - \bar{y})dt + \sigma \, dz, \tag{12.16}$$

$$E(ds) = (i^* - i)dt. \tag{12.17}$$

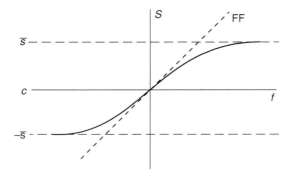

Figure 12.3 The S schedule in S–f space.

Expression (12.14) is the money market condition familiar from previous chapters. The goods market condition is also familiar from Chapter 5, being a simplified version of expression (5.3). Equation (12.16) is a stochastic Phillips curve, or inflation, equation (i.e. a stochastic version of equation 5.13), where dz is a scalar Brownian motion with unit variance, so the term $\sigma\,dz$ is white noise. This expression indicates that inflation is driven by deviations of output from its equilibrium level and by the white noise disturbances. Finally, equation (12.17) is a continuous time version of UIP, where s is defined here as the foreign currency price of a unit of home currency.

As in the sticky-price model considered in Chapter 5, the stochastic version of the model can be expressed as two simultaneous (stochastic) differential equations for the change in the price and exchange rate:

$$
\begin{bmatrix} dp \\ E(ds) \end{bmatrix} = \frac{1}{\Delta} \begin{bmatrix} -\phi(\gamma_2 + \beta_1\gamma_1) & -\phi\beta_1\gamma_1 \\ \beta_0\gamma_1 - 1 & \beta_0\gamma_1 \end{bmatrix} \begin{bmatrix} pdt \\ sdt \end{bmatrix}
$$
$$
+ \frac{1}{\Delta} \begin{bmatrix} \phi\gamma_2 & \phi\beta_1 & 0 \\ 1 & -\beta_0\gamma_1 & \Delta \end{bmatrix} \begin{bmatrix} mdt \\ p^*dt \\ i^*dt \end{bmatrix} + \begin{bmatrix} \sigma\,dz \\ 0 \end{bmatrix}, \tag{12.18}
$$

where $\Delta = \beta_0\gamma_2 + \beta_1$. Again as in the case of the simple sticky-price model considered in Chapter 5 the expression (12.18) can alternatively be written in terms of deviations from equilibrium:

$$
\begin{bmatrix} d\hat{p} \\ d\hat{s} \end{bmatrix} = A \begin{bmatrix} \hat{p}dt \\ \hat{s}dt \end{bmatrix} + \begin{bmatrix} \sigma\,dz \\ 0 \end{bmatrix}, \tag{12.18$'$}
$$

where an over hat denotes a deviation from equilibrium, $z - \bar{z}$, an overbar denotes an equilibrium value and A is the matrix of coefficients on the right-hand-side endogenous variables in (12.18). The existence of a stable saddle path requires that root of A be negative. When $\sigma^2 > 0$ there are a number of functional relationships between s and p which satisfy equation (12.18). In order to obtain a solution Miller and Weller (1991) assume a solution of the form:

$$
s = f(p). \tag{12.19}
$$

By Ito's lemma it follows that:

$$
d\hat{s} = f'(p)d\hat{t} + \frac{\sigma^2}{2} f''(p)dt. \tag{12.20}
$$

By taking expectations of both sides of (12.20) and substituting from (12.18$'$) we obtain the following desired result:

$$
[A_2 - f'(p)A_1] \begin{bmatrix} p \\ f(p) \end{bmatrix} = \frac{\sigma^2}{2} f''(p), \tag{12.21}
$$

where A_1 and A_2 are the respective rows of A. By imposing the boundary condition $f(0) = 0$, solutions which satisfy the symmetry property $f(s) = -f(-s)$ may be obtained. These solutions are the relevant ones for problems with boundary conditions around equilibrium. Figure 12.4 indicates how these boundary conditions tie down a particular solution and the possible trajectories between p and s. The linear relationships SOS' and UOU' describe the stable and unstable saddle paths, respectively, of the deterministic system and are also the solutions to the stochastic system when suitable boundary conditions are imposed. There are also an infinity of other non-linear solutions whose qualitative features are illustrated by the curved lines in Figure 12.4. Beetsma and van der Ploeg (1994) have extended the stochastic sticky-price target zone model of Miller and Weller to include both wage and price stickiness, imperfect substitutability of home and foreign goods and they allow for both marginal and intra-marginal interventions (see our discussions later).

(a) The 'smooth-pasting' condition

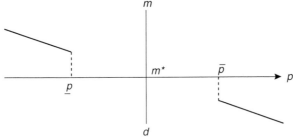

(b) The required monetary regime

Figure 12.4 Smooth pasting in the sticky-price monetary model.

Source: Miller and Weller (1991).

12.1.3   *Empirical evidence on the target zone model*

Generally speaking, empirical tests of the target zone model attempt to assess the validity of the model assumptions and predictions. In this section we first of all present an overview of the extant empirical evidence on the model assumptions before moving on to look at the predictions.

12.1.3.1   *Model assumptions*

The key assumption of the target zone model is, of course, the credibility of the bands. Svensson's (1992a) so-called simplest test of credibility simply involves using the forward exchange rate at different maturities as a measure of expected future exchange rates. These are then simply plotted against the exchange rate bands and, on the basis of the maintained assumption of UIP, if they lie outside the bands this suggests a lack of credibility. Both Svensson (1992a) and Flood, Rose and Mathieson (1991) [hereafter referred to as FRM] show for the ERM experience that forward rate observations lie outside the bands for prolonged periods (the exception being the Dutch guilder).

A related, but more sophisticated, test of credibility involves constructing the so-called drift adjusted measure of credibility. This may be explained in the following way. Consider again the decomposition of the actual exchange rate into two components:

$$s_t \equiv c_t + x_t, \tag{12.22}$$

where c_t denotes the central parity rate and x_t is exchange rate's deviation from central parity. From (12.22) the continuous time expected currency depreciation in a 'fixed rate' regime may be defined as:

$$E_t[ds_t]/dt = E_t[dc_t]/dt + E_t[dx_t]/dt, \tag{12.23}$$

or in discrete time as:

$$E_t \Delta s_{t+k} = E_t \Delta c_{t+k} + E_t \Delta x_{t+k}.$$

Since the empirical literature is based on discrete changes, we work with these in the following. If the central rate is credible, the term Δc_{t+k}^e should be zero and there should be a one-to-one mapping between changes in s and x. Let x_t^l and x_t^u denote the lower and upper limits of an exchange rate's deviation from the central band, then the maximum possible changes within band are given by the following weak inequality:

$$(x_t^l - x_t) \leq E_t \Delta x_t \leq (x_t^u - x_t). \tag{12.24}$$

Since UIP is assumed to hold continuously, a suitable interest differential, $i - i^*$, may be chosen to define $E_t \Delta s_t$. The, so-called, 100% confidence interval for the expected devaluation/realignment may be defined as:

$$(i_t - i_t^*) - (x_t^u - x_t) \le E_t \Delta c_t \le (i_t - i_t^*) - (x_t^l - x_t). \tag{12.25}$$

Note that this is simply a different way of formulating Svensson's simplest test. An alternative and more precise measures of the expected rate of realignment can be obtained using the drift adjustment method, as originally formulated by Bertola and Svensson (1991). In particular, they propose using a simple linear regression equation of the form:

$$x_{t+k} - x_t = \alpha_0 + \alpha_1 x_t + \beta z_t' + v_t, \tag{12.26}$$

where z_t' represents a vector of variables deemed useful for explaining the expected change in the exchange rate within the band. It turns out that in all of the studies which use (12.26) (see Caramazza 1993; Svensson 1993; Rose and Svensson 1994; Hallwood *et al.* 2000) the key significant determinant is x_t; that is, the single determinant of the expected change in band is the current deviation of the exchange rate from the centre. In other words the drift adjustment method adjusts the interest differential by the drift of the exchange rate within the band. The projected values from this regression are adjusted by the equation standard error to produce 95% bounds as:

$$(i_t - i_t^*) - (x_t^{+5} - x_t) \le E_t \Delta c_t \le (i_t - i_t^*) - (x_t^{-5} - x_t). \tag{12.27}$$

When both sides of this inequality are above or below zero this indicates a statistically significant violation of credibility.

Svensson (1993) and Rose and Svensson (1994) present 95% confidence intervals for the ERM target zone experience and some representative examples are reported in Figure 12.5. This shows clear evidence of violations of credibility, although there are also a few periods/currencies when credibility is not violated (most notably, the Dutch guilder towards the end of the ERM experience). As Giovannini (1993) demonstrates, the picture for Bretton Woods is better, although there are still some significant violations of credibility (see Figure 12.6). For the Classical and inter-war gold standards – see Figures 12.7 and 12.8 – there is much less evidence of a lack of credibility as noted by Hallwood *et al.* (1996) and Giovannini (1993), although it is worth noting the apparent lack of credibility for the USD in the period 1879–96. One interesting question concerns what this lack of credibility actually represents. It could, of course, simply indicate a non-credible system, or it could, given the interest differential is being used to back out these estimates, reflect a peso effect or a risk premium. A peso effect (see Chapter 15 for a further discussion) refers to the situation where agents expect an event to occur within the sample period the researcher is examining, but the change does not actually take place (it may take place outside sample). This leads to a biased expectations series. In a perfectly credible target zone regime, as Svensson points out, the interest differential is likely to reflect purely expectational factors and the risk premium

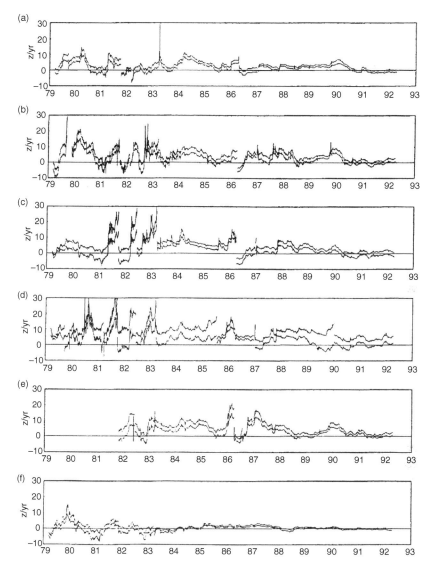

Figure 12.5 Expected rate of devaluation (95% conf.i.): 3 months – (a) BF/DM, (b) DK/DM, (c) FF/DM, (d) IL/DM, (e) IP/DM and (f) NG/DM.

Source: Rose and Svensson (1994).

is likely to be zero. However, in situations of less-than-perfect credibility the risk premium may well be non-zero.

The other key assumption of the model is that intervention should only occur at the bands. Dominguez and Kenen (1991), for example, examine the

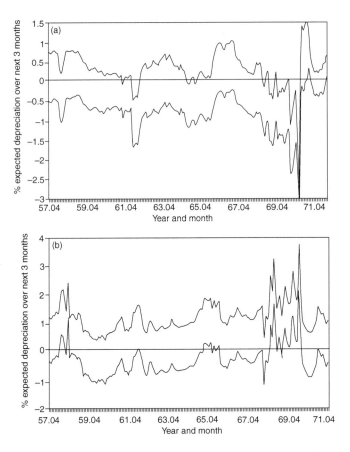

Figure 12.6 Ninety-five confidence intervals for expected depreciation in Bretton Woods:
(a) of deutsche mark (b) of sterling.

Source: Giovannini (1993).

intervention policies of European central banks for the ERM period and find that practically all of the intervention occurs within the band; that is, the intervention is intra-marginal. These findings are reinforced by Giavazzi and Giovannini (1989) and Lindberg and Soderlind (1991).

In sum, then, the model assumptions are not well supported on data for the ERM period, the episode for which the target zone model was originally formulated. However, there is more support for the model especially when other fixed rate regimes are considered, such as the two gold standard episodes.

12.1.4   *Target zone model predictions*

A key prediction of the model is that x_t and $E_t \Delta s_{t+k}$ should be negatively related; that is, if x_t is above the central parity this will generate an expectation of an

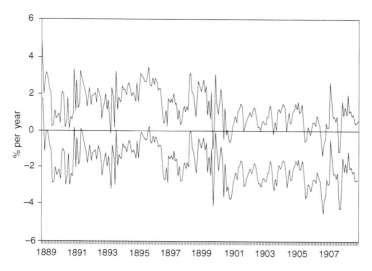

Figure 12.7 Expected realignment rate, 95% CI, franc-sterling, Classical Gold Standard.
Source: Hallwood *et al.* (1996).

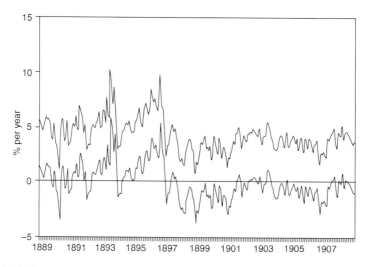

Figure 12.8 Expected realignment rate, 95% CI, dollar-sterling, Classical Gold Standard
Source: Hallwood *et al.* (1996).

exchange rate movement in the opposite direction. Flood *et al.* (1991) present
a range of scatterplots for the ERM experience and show no evidence of a negative relationship. Indeed, correlations between the exchange rate within the
band and the interest differential ($= E_t \Delta s_{t+k}$) are often positive. Giovannini
(1993) confirms this for the Bretton Woods regime, although both Bordo and

MacDonald (2005) and Hallwood *et al.* (1996) report negative relationships for key currencies participating in the Classical Gold Standard regime.

A related prediction to that of negative correlation is the idea that the exchange rate should be mean-reverting within the band – for example, a current depreciation should be offset by an exchange rate movement in the opposite direction. Svensson (1992b) argues that 'mean reversion is an important general property of target zone exchange rates that is independent of the validity of the specific Krugman model.' Perhaps not surprisingly it turns out that there is close correspondence between mean reversion tests and the credibility tests discussed earlier.

Anthony and MacDonald (1998, 1999) propose using univariate tests of mean reversion for both the narrow and wide band ERM experiences. Recognising the well known low power of the Dickey–Fuller class of statistic, they supplement such tests with variance ratio test statistics which are known to be more powerful in a univariate setting. The basic finding in this paper is that the variance ratio statistics show clear evidence of mean reversion for currencies known to be credible, in particular the Dutch guilder and the Danish krone. Furthermore, it turns out that there is as much evidence of mean reversion in the wide band system as in the narrow band system. Hallwood *et al.* (1996) use both variance ratio and Dickey–Fuller type tests for both the Classical and inter-war Gold Standards and report strong evidence of mean reversion with both types of test for both gold standard regimes. For the Classical period the US/UK and FR/UK show very fast and significant mean reversion – for example, within 4 months half of a deviation is extinguished. For the inter-war period they again get clear evidence of mean reversion, although this is not as clear-cut (as fast or as significant) as in the Classical period.

A key feature of the basic target zone model is that there should be a non-linear – S-shaped – function between the exchange rate and the composite fundamental. For the ERM period FRM find little evidence of non-linearities between exchange rates and fundamentals, and, indeed, there is some evidence to suggest that countries which appeared to be more committed to the ERM actually exhibited fewer manifestations of non-linearities. In sum, the *s*/*f* relationship appears to be approximately linear over the entire sample. For the Bretton Woods period Giovannini finds that most of the data, apart from the yen–dollar rate, is consistent with a linear relationship. For the gold standard period (Bordo and MacDonald 2005) there is clear evidence of a non-linear relationship but it is not S-shaped (although this could be due to the existence of gold points).

More formal tests of non-linearity by FRM, using parametric methods, shows clear evidence of statistically significant non-linear relationship, of target zone type effect, for most countries and for most ERM regimes. However, this result also equally holds in the floating rate period, and FRM argue that the non-linearity they capture could be picking up some form of generic misspecification, not specific to target zone. Meese and Rose (1991) use non-parametric methods to test for non-linearities in fixed rate regimes and find little evidence that non-linear models fit the data better than linear models in fixed rate regimes.

The target zone model predicts that the *distribution* of the exchange rate within the band should be U-shaped; that is, the exchange rate should spend most of the time near the edges of band. This follows on from the shape of the functional form and the smooth pasting result. These features imply that the exchange rate is insensitive to fundamentals at the edges of the band. Therefore the exchange rate moves slowly and where it moves slowly it will appear often. In contrast the fundamental moves with constant speed between its bounds and it therefore has a uniform distribution. But in actuality, for the ERM period, exchange rate distributions are hump-shaped (see, for example, FRM and Bertola and Caballero 1992), with most of the mass in the interior of the band and very little at the edges of the bands. Sutherland (1994) notes that in the sticky-price target zone model the distribution function for the exchange rate within the band is ambiguous. This is because in this variant of the model the marginal intervention rule of the central bank has, as in the base-line model, the implication that the distribution of the exchange rate should be U-shaped, while the stickiness of prices implies a hump-shaped distribution. If the latter effect dominates then the distribution will turn out to be hump-shaped. The observed hump-shaped distributions would therefore seem to be supportive of the sticky-price target zone model.

Finally, there is the issue of the interest differential and its position in the band. Credible target zone models imply that the interest differential should be a non-linear deterministic declining function, when graphed against the exchange rate. However, FRM find no clear-cut pattern and in contrast find much evidence of randomness. Since the sticky-price variant does not predict a deterministic relationship between the position of the exchange rate within the band and the interest differential, it would seem to fare better by this metric.

12.1.5   Direct tests of the model

The earlier tests may be regarded as indirect tests of the target zone model. A number of researchers have attempted to test the model directly. For example, Smith and Spencer (1991) use the method of simulated moments (MSM) to test the target zone model using daily data for the DM–lira, over the period 14 January 1987–20 September 1989. The rationale for using simulated method of moments, rather than a generalised method of moments (GMM) estimator, is that in the context of the basic target zone model analytical expressions for the relevant moments may not be known. For example, if the theoretical probability density function of the spot rate was known, standard method of moments could be used to choose the model parameters which minimise the discrepancy between the moments of that density and those of the empirical density. However, in the case of the target zone model the researcher is unlikely to know the theoretical probability density function of the spot rate and so it has to be simulated. A further advantage of the simulation approach is that the unobservability of the fundamental term rules out direct estimation of a non-linear regression model linking the fundamentals to the exchange rate. However, a disadvantage of the simulation approach is that it is less efficient than comparable GMM estimators. In implementing the MSM for the DM–lira, Smith and Spencer find evidence against the target zone model in the sense that the simulated moments did not match the observed moments (in particular, the model predicted greater skewness and kurtosis in exchange rate levels and significantly less kurtosis). Other applications of the MSM estimator to target zone exchange rates are Koedijk *et al.* (1992), who find evidence against the target zone model for a number of currencies, and Lindberg and Soderlind (1991) who find evidence in favour of the model.

12.2   Extensions of the base-line target zone model

As we have seen, the base-line model does not fare very well for the ERM target zone experience. It is perhaps not surprising therefore that a number of modifications have been proposed to the basic Krugman model in order to make it better suited to explaining exchange rate behaviour during this period.

12.2.1   Credibility issues

Perhaps the most obvious extension is that which addresses the evident lack of credibility of the ERM target zone experience. Bertola and Svensson (1993) propose the following modification to allow for a lack of credibility. First, the central parity, *c*, is assumed to jump at the time of the realignment and stays constant between realignments and, second, investors are assumed to be uncertain about the timing and size of realignments. Consider (12.23) again:

$$E_t[ds_t]/dt = E_t[dc_t]/dt + E_t[dx_t]/dt, \tag{12.28}$$

where $E[dc]/dt$ is now a product of two factors: the probability of realignment and the expected size of realignment. If it is assumed that the rate of realignment is exogenous and does not depend directly on the exchange rate, then on subtracting c_t from both sides of (12.1) and on using (12.28) we have:

$$x_t = h_t + \alpha \frac{E_t dx_t}{dt}, \tag{12.29}$$

where

$$h_t \equiv f_t - c_t + \alpha \frac{E_t dc_t}{dt}. \tag{12.30}$$

The first upshot of this modified version of the model is that any relationship between the interest differential and the exchange rate within the band is possible depending on how the expected rate of realignment fluctuates over time and how it is correlated with the exchange rate. Second, new linear exchange rate function is now defined for *x*, *h* and the expected rate of realignment in the band instead of *s*, *f* and the expected total change in the exchange rate, as in the original model. These two relationships are formally the same and if it is further assumed that $E_t dc_t/dt$ follows a Brownian motion process the new exchange rate function will be of exactly same form as in the basic Krugman model, that is, an S-shape. Indeed, the scatterplots reported by FRM show that the relationship between h and x conforms much more closely to the basic target zone shape since the slope is less that unity although it is not S-shaped.

12.2.2 Incorporating intra-marginal interventions

As we have seen, the empirical evidence shows that central banks intervene well within the band; that is, intra-marginal intervention dominates marginal intervention. In the context of less than full credibility, Froot and Obstfeld (1991) and Delgado and Dumas (1993) propose, in addition to marginal intervention, capturing this fact by modelling the expected rate of change of the composite fundamental towards central parity as proportional to its distance from central parity:

$$\frac{E_t dh_t}{dt} = -\gamma h_t, \tag{12.31}$$

where γ is rate of mean reversion. The effect of this modification is illustrated in Figure 12.9. The FF schedule has the same interpretation as before for a free float regime with no intervention. In the case of a traditional managed float where there are no bands and interventions are mean-reverting towards a central parity, the MM schedule would capture the relationship between the fundamental and the exchange rate, where the equation for the MM line is:

$$x_t = \frac{h_t}{1 + \alpha\gamma}. \tag{12.32}$$

The MM schedule clearly indicates that there is a honeymoon effect in the managed-float regime even when there is no exchange rate band: when the exchange rate moves above the central rate the mean-reverting intervention implies the currency is expected to appreciate, which reduces the exchange rate. With

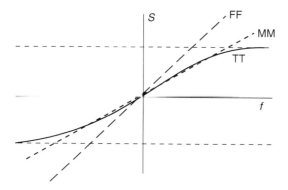

Figure 12.9 Intra-marginal interventions.

explicit bands, along with marginal intervention to defend the bands, the schedule becomes TT which is close to MM but has a slight S-shape and smooth pasting at the edge of the bands. The TT schedule exhibits a slight honeymoon effect but this is clearly much smaller than the honeymoon effect for MM relative to FF. Why? When the exchange rate is above the central parity mean-reverting intervention implies that the currency is expected to appreciate, which attenuates the exchange rate movement. This effect is reinforced by the expected future marginal interventions to prevent the exchange rate moving outside the band. The latter is, of course, the effect in the basic target zone model but it is much less powerful here because the probability of reaching the bands is much smaller.

Lindberg and Soderlind (1991) show that with mean-reverting interventions the unconditional distribution of *h* is truncated normal – that is, hump-shaped – which is, as we have seen, consistent with the empirical evidence. Furthermore, as Svensson (1993) notes, with strong mean-reverting intra-marginal intervention the exchange rate function is close to the linear MM schedule. Using a structural target zone model Lindberg and Soderlind (1991) show that the overall fit of the target zone model with mean-reverting interventions is much better than the basic target zone model.

As Svensson (1993) notes, the earlier modification of the basic target zone model renders the original emphasis on aspects such as smooth pasting, non-linearities and marginal intervention as misplaced. The earlier modelling framework suggests that target zones are much closer in spirit to managed floats with intra-marginal mean-reverting interventions and marginal interventions only occuring on the rare occasions that the exchange rate hits the edge of the band. The upshot of this then is that a target zone should not be seen as a commitment to marginal interventions, but rather as a way of limiting exchange rate volatility with intra-marginal interventions.

12.2.3   *Credibility revisited, 1: modelling credibility violations*

Hallwood, MacDonald and Marsh (2000) [hereafter referred to as HMM] attempt to explain the apparent lack of credibility of the US dollar in the period 1879–96 (Figure 12.8). They present a modelling framework which seeks to disentangle the effect of economic fundamentals, expectational failures, time-varying risk premia and political factors. In an earlier contribution to this issue, Friedman and Schwartz (1963) argued that political factors rather than economic factors explain this.

The model used by HMM splits the interest differential into four components:

$$i_t - i_t^* = [\rho_t^k E_t[\Delta s_{t+k}|\text{deval}] + (1 - \rho_t^k)E_t[\Delta s_{t+k}|\text{nodeval}] + RP_t]. \quad (12.33)$$

The first term on the right hand side of expression (12.33) is the probability of a devaluation, and is assumed to be a function of several economic and political fundamentals:

$$\rho_t^k = f(\text{economic} + \text{political fundamentals}). \tag{12.34}$$

The economic fundamentals are defined as the relative excess growth in the money supply, the Standard and Poor's stock market index, and gold and silver holdings. In particular, a dummy is included if the Sherman Silver purchase act is on the US statutes (1890/7–1893/10) and a zero otherwise. The second dummy takes on a value of one if the bimetallism debate is still active in the US, defined as the period from the start of the period until the defeat in 1896 of William Bryan, the democratic pro-silver presidential candidate.

The second component on the right hand side of (12.33) is the expected rate of change of the exchange rate, conditional on their being no devaluation, and is equivalent to the expected change in the deviation from the centre of the band. The drift adjustment method of Svensson is then used to measure this in the following way:

$$E_t[\Delta s_{t+k}|\text{nodeval}] = E_t[\Delta x_{t+k}|\text{nodeval}] = \beta_1 x_t. \tag{12.35}$$

The third component is the expected rate change of the exchange rate conditional on a devaluation taking place. Since no actual devaluation took place during their sample period, HMM assume that this term is simply equal to a constant:

$$E_t[\Delta s_{t+k}|\text{deval}] = \beta_2. \tag{12.36}$$

Finally, a GARCH (1,1)-in-mean model is used to capture the risk premium. The empirical results from estimating this model are reported in Table 12.1 from HMM. Summarising their results HMM find that the Peso effect – defined as $\rho_t^k E_t[\Delta s_{t+k}|\text{deval}]$ – explains the majority of the interest differential, particularly for the early part of the sample. The key determinants of ρ_t^k are political factors rather than the economic ones – agents predicted a regime change, in particular, monetisation of silver alongside gold. The risk premium turns out to be positive and statistically significant, but relatively small for the period (on average 0.25%). The decomposition of the risk premium into the different components is presented in Figure 12.10 and it is clear that the peso effect explains nearly all of the lack of credibility of the USD for the early part of the sample (see Figure 12.8).

12.2.4 *Credibility revisited, 2: monetary independence in target zones*

Consider the UIP condition under rigidly fixed exchange rates (i.e. a fixed exchange rate with no bands):

$$i_t = i_t^*, \tag{12.37}$$

Table 12.1 FIML estimation results 1890/02–1908/12[a]

Variable	Coefficient	Std error	T-statistic
1. Mean reversion, β_1	−0.260	0.122	−2.132
Size of devaluation			
2. Devaluation size, β_2	0.581	0.020	29.741
Probability of devaluation, γ			
3. Constant	−4.380	0.439	−9.972
4. Money	1.609	1.600	0.969
5. Income	0.060	0.459	0.131
6. Real exchange rate	3.356	0.529	6.345
7. Cotton exports	−0.038	0.024	−1.586
8. S and P index	−1.557	0.341	−4.571
9. Gold reserves	0.009	0.057	0.166
10. Sherman dummy	0.163	0.039	4.234
11. Silver debate dummy	0.686	0.147	4.652
12. Trend	0.004	0.001	4.389
Risk premium			
13. Variance in mean, δ	1.218	0.312	3.907
14. Variance constant, v_1	0.048	0.016	2.915
15. ARCH, v_2	1.196	0.507	2.362
16. Asymmetric ARCH, v_3	−0.907	0.406	−2.232
17. GARCH, v_4	0.331	0.151	2.188

Notes
a The general form of the model is

$$i_t - i_t^* = [(\text{prob. of deval.})(\text{size of deval.}) + (1 - \text{prob. of deval.})(\text{mean reversion})$$
$$+ \text{risk premium}]/k,$$

mean reversion $= \beta_1 x_t$,
size of deval. $= \beta_2$,
prob of deval. $= \Phi(\gamma z_t)$,
risk premium $= \delta h_t$,
$h_t = v_1 + v_2 \varepsilon_{t-1}^2 + v_3 (\varepsilon_{t-1}^2 | \varepsilon_{t-1} < 0) + v_4 h_{t-1}.$

Source: Hallwood, MacDonald and Marsh (2000).

since there are no bands the expected change in the exchange rate is zero and of course there can be no monetary independence. At the other extreme with freely floating exchange rates there may be some, quite considerable, monetary independence to the extent that a non-zero expected change in the exchange rate, $E_t \Delta s_{t+k}$, term enters the UIP condition:

$$i_t = i_t^* + E_t \Delta s_{t+k}. \tag{12.38}$$

The recognition that all historical fixed exchange rate regimes (with the exception of currency board – not regime) have had exchange rate bands means that in principal

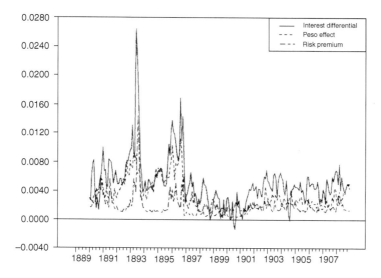

Figure 12.10 Components of the interest differential.
Source: Hallwood, MacDonald and Marsh (2000).

they allow some monetary independence. For example, even if the central rate is credible, $(\Delta E_t c_{t+k} = 0)$ i can rise above or below i^* to the extent that $E_t \Delta x_{t+k}$ is non-zero. For example, if the domestic money supply increases i can fall relative to the foreign rate because of the expectation of an appreciation relative to c; that is, $E_t \Delta x_{t+k} < 0$.

As Svensson (1994), however, stresses there are important limitations to such independence in a target zone. First, the independence can only be temporary since the exchange rate will eventually revert back to the central parity. To put this point differently, the central bank cannot affect the average domestic interest rate over a long period, since on average $E\Delta x$ will be zero in the long term. The upshot of this is that any monetary independence should largely be confined to short maturity interest rates – the yields on long-term interest rates should be little changed. Second, if the assumption that $E_t \Delta c_{t+k}$ is zero is violated this will reduce the degree of monetary independence. In the limit, if $E_t \Delta c_{t+k}$ were to move in an equal and opposite fashion to $E_t \Delta x_{t+k}$ there would be no monetary independence.

Bordo and MacDonald (2005) propose a method for testing how much independence is actually conferred by exchange rate bands in a *credible* target zone. In particular, they focus on arbitrage conditions as given by UIP and the term structure of interest rates. Using cointegration methods they test if the UIP condition holds in the long-run and whether the gap between short and long interest rates is stationary. If these two relationships can be established they then go on to examine the dynamic inter-relationships between short-term interest rates across countries (their system 1), the dynamic inter-relationships between short-term interest rates across countries and the yield gap in the home country (system 2) and how a vector of fundamental variables impact on the interest rate dynamics (system 3). System 1 is designed to gauge how much short-run monetary independence exists with exchange rate bands, system 2 to determine if long rates are affected at all by monetary impulses in an exchange band system, while system 3 is designed to determine to what use monetary independence is used.

As we noted earlier, one key empirical finding to emerge from the target zone literature is the credibility of the gold standard system. Bordo and MacDonald therefore apply their methods to three Classical Gold Standard exchange rates, namely, sterling–franc, sterling–mark and franc–mark, January 1880–December 1913. We focus on their system 2 results here. These results are based on the following vector:

$$x_t = [i_t^s, i_t^{*s}, i_t^l]', \tag{12.39}$$

where i^s denotes the home short rate, i^{*s} is the foreign short rate and i^l is the home long rate. If UIP and the expectations view of the term structure are valid this vector should potentially produce two cointegrating relationships: one a stationary relationship between the home and foreign short rate and, second, a stationary relationship between the home short and long interest rates. In the presence of such cointegration, the so-called Granger Representation Theorem implies that there must exist a vector error correction mechanism (VECM) of the following general form:

$$\Delta i_t^s = -\varphi(i_{t-1}^s - i_{t-1}^{s,*}) - \delta(i_{t-1}^l - i_{t-1}^s) + \sum_{i=1}^{p} \kappa_i \Delta i_{t-i}^s$$

$$+ \sum_{i=1}^{p} p_i \Delta i_{t-i}^{s,*} + \sum_{i=1}^{p} \mu_i \Delta i_{t-i}^{l,*}. \tag{12.40}$$

If the predictions of Svensson about the behaviour of credible bands are correct then we would expect the following in such VECM relationships. First, adjustment back to equilibrium should be rapid, since the Svensson model only allows monetary policy to deviate transitorily from foreign monetary policy; that is, φ should be large in absolute terms. Second, there should be some significant dynamic effects showing interaction between interest rates and, third, the yield gap should open up after a change in i^s, but it is not expected that i^l will adjust much, if at all, to a change in i^s.

For each of the three currencies Bordo and MacDonald (2005) find evidence of two significant cointegrating vectors and the interpretation that these form a UIP and yield gap relationship could not be rejected for any combination. To illustrate the dynamic interactions we focus on the impulse response functions, generated from VECMs, reported in Figure 12.11. Taking the UK–French rates as an example then the figure clearly demonstrates that in the short-run there is not a one-to-one lock between UK and French short interest rates: the 1% increase in

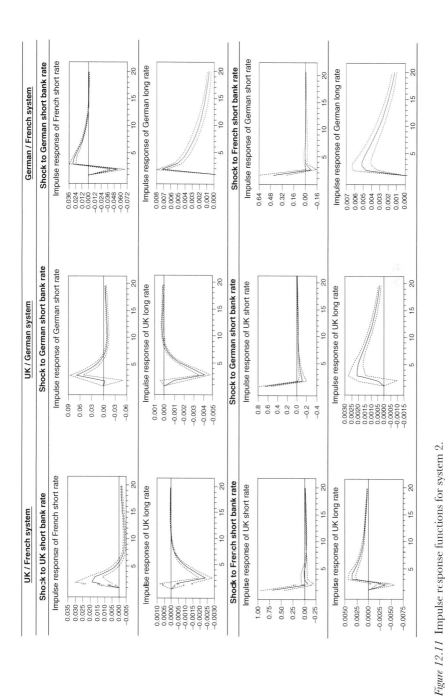

Figure 12.11 Impulse response functions for system 2.

Source: Bordo and MacDonald (2005).

the UK short rate only leads to an approximate 0.1% increase in the French rate and equilibrium is restored after 2 years. UK long rate rises as well, but by a very small amount; again the dynamics die out very rapidly. Interest rates therefore seem to behave in the way predicted by the Svensson model – domestic short-term interest rates can deviate from foreign rates and the yield gap opens up as short rates change. However, such changes are purely transitory, with the average over the three systems being 1 year. The system 3 results of Bordo and MacDonald (2005) indicate that this potential monetary independence could have been used for objectives such as interest rate smoothing.

Bordo and MacDonald (2005) estimate systems 1–3 for the inter-war gold regime standard, a regime which is also known to be credible, and report a similar set of results to that for the Classical Gold Standard. Edison and MacDonald (2003) estimate system 1 for the ERM experience. They show that countries which had a credible commitment to the ERM (at certain times) – Belgium, Denmark, Netherlands – produced adjustment speeds (i.e. the extent of monetary policy freedom) which were similar to the Classical Gold Standard.

The conclusion to arise from the work of Bordo and MacDonald is that for a modern day international monetary system to function effectively, credibility ultimately needs to anchor both short-term interest rate policy and the term structure of interest rates and therefore the question that arises is: is gold, or some other commodity, necessary to provide the credibility anchor, or are there other *mechanisms, institutions and regulations* that can replace gold?

13 The economics of fixed exchange rates, part 2

Speculative attack models and contagion

In this chapter we overview the speculative attack and currency crises literatures. The speculative attack models were originally developed to provide an understanding of currency crisis in Latin America and, in particular, the failure of stabilisation plans in the 1970s and 1980s. The so-called first generation models of Krugman (1979) and Flood and Garber (1984) had at their core the relationship between a fixed exchange rate and inconsistent economic fundamentals, namely, monetary and fiscal policy. In particular, this class of model was designed to show how a combination of fixed exchange rates and excessive money supply growth prior to an attack could push an economy into crises, with the private sector trying to profit from unravelling what they see as inconsistent policies. An alternative perspective on this class of models is to say they demonstrate that currency crises associated with the stabilisation policies pursued in Latin America in the 1970s and 1980s were not a sign of market malfunction, but rather they are the consequence of an inappropriate fiscal–monetary mix pursued by these countries (Jeanne 2000a). A classic application of the first generation model has been to the devaluation of the Mexican peso in 1976 and 1981 (see Blanco and Garber 1986).

However, first generation models are not regarded as particularly well-suited to explaining the behaviour of the Mexican peso in the 1990s and the ERM crisis in 1992–3. In the latter, countries such as France and the UK had pursued a sound monetary–fiscal mix but were nevertheless spectacularly ejected from the ERM arrangement. How may such crises be explained? The so-called second generation models of Obstfeld (1994) and Flood and Marion (1997b, 2000) were designed to tackle these kind of crises.[1] They have two features which distinguish them from first generation models: first, they have a much richer specification of what is a fundamental and this can, in the limit, involve any variable which influences the policy-maker's decision to defend a peg or not. This can include 'hard' fundamentals, such as unemployment, and 'soft' fundamentals, such as the beliefs of foreign exchange market participants (Jeanne 2000). The latter kind of fundamental leads into the second contribution of these models, namely, that they provide a new theory of self-fulfilling speculation and multiple equilibria. The latter feature of these models is designed to show how a speculative attack may apparently be unrelated to fundamentals.

The Latin American and Asian crises of 1995 and 1997 do not seem well explained by the second generation models. For one thing, if the second generation models are correct the abandonment of a fixed peg should allow a country more expansionary macroeconomic policies. However, in the aftermath of the Latin American and Asian crises countries faced severe recessions. Two strands have developed in the speculative attack literature to explain these kind of crises: one is based on a moral hazard argument and the other is based on bank runs producing a currency crisis. These two contributions have been grouped under the label third generation models.

The outline of the remainder of this chapter is as follows. In the next section we discuss the variants of the speculative attack model, ranging from the first generation model to the escape clause model and the third generation model. In Section 13.2 the empirical evidence on the theoretical models is overviewed and this incorporates a review of the recent literature on contagion.

13.1   The theory of a speculative attack

13.1.1   First generation models

The standard first generation model is based on a small open economy with perfect capital mobility and a fixed exchange rate (see Krugman 1979 and Flood and Garber 1984).[2] As in other small open economy models considered elsewhere in this book this implies that the country takes foreign interest rates and prices as parametrically given. It is important to note that in this class of model the monetary policy instrument is domestic credit, rather than the interest rate or the total quantity of money. Additionally, this choice of monetary variable means that monetary and fiscal policy may be interrelated, to the extent that domestic credit evolves in response to fiscal deficits. The money market equilibrium condition is given by a simplified form of the log-linear money demand function first introduced in Chapter 4:

$$m - p = -\alpha(i), \quad \alpha > 0, \tag{13.1}$$

where symbols have the same interpretation as before and the domestic money supply can be decomposed into two central bank assets: d, domestic credit and r, international reserves:

$$m = d + r. \tag{13.2}$$

PPP is assumed to hold continuously:

$$p = p^* + s. \tag{13.3}$$

The assumption of perfect capital mobility is described here by the UIP condition, in which the expected change in the exchange rate has been replaced by the actual change, under the assumption of perfect foresight:

$$i = i^* + \dot{s}. \tag{13.4}$$

As is standard in this kind of monetary model (see the FLMA discussed in Chapter 4), if the exchange rate is flexible it moves to equilibrate the money market. If, however, the exchange rate is fixed at, say, $\bar{s}$ then from (13.3) the domestic price moves one-to-one with the foreign price, the domestic interest rate is locked against the foreign rate and so reserves move to balance the money market. Consider the case where s is fixed at $\bar{s}$ and suppose the home government engages in deficit finance, which requires domestic credit to grow at a constant rate, μ. By substituting (13.2), (13.3) and (13.4) into (13.1) and noting, by assumption, that $i = i^*$ and $\dot{s} = 0$ we obtain:

$$r + d - p^* - \bar{s} = -\alpha \left(i^* \right), \tag{13.5}$$

where d grows at a rate equal to μ, and since it is assumed that the monetary authorities do not attempt to sterilise the consequences of their domestic credit expansion (we consider this assumption again later), r falls at the same rate; that is, $r = -\mu.$ [3] Clearly, the home country will eventually exhaust its foreign exchange reserves and the fixed exchange rate will have to be abandoned. One of the key issues in first generation models is determining when this actually occurs. To answer this question we introduce the concept of a shadow exchange rate, $\hat{s}$, which is the (floating) rate that would prevail if speculators purchased the remaining reserves committed to the peg and the government permanently refrained from foreign exchange intervention. The rate $\hat{s}$ is therefore that rate which balances the money market following an attack in which foreign exchange reserves are exhausted.

From (13.5) it is clear that the exchange rate which solves the post-attack money market has to be consistent with:

$$d - \hat{s} = -\alpha \left(\dot{s} \right), \tag{13.6}$$

where, for simplicity, we have assumed that $i^* = p^* = 0$. Equation (13.6) may be used to obtain a solution for the exchange rate as:

$$\hat{s} = \alpha\mu + d, \tag{13.7}$$

where $\dot{s} = \mu$. A schedule representing (13.7) is plotted in Figure 13.1. Consider two scenarios, depending on whether d is greater or less than d^A. If d is less than d^A, say, and if speculators attack at such a level then post the attack the currency will appreciate and speculators will suffer a capital loss on the reserves they get from the government. In this scenario, therefore, there will be no speculative attack. If, on the other hand, d is greater than d^A and the shadow exchange rate is greater than the fixed rate $-\hat{s} > \bar{s}$ – there is a potential capital gain to speculators for every unit of reserves they purchase from the government. Essentially, speculators will compete for these expected profits and this has the effect of bringing the exchange

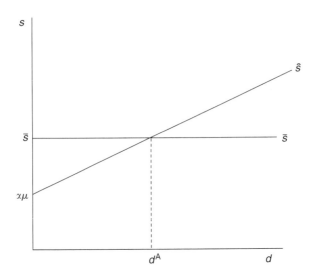

Figure 13.1 First generation speculative attack model.

rate change/crisis forward in time. The implication therefore is that the fixed exchange rate will have to be abandoned *before* the central bank runs out of reserves. Note that in this example the behaviour of private sector individuals is completely rational since each individual agent is better off in participating in the attack to take advantage of the more advantageous (pre-devaluation) exchange rate. From a game-theoretic perspective, attacking the currency is a dominant strategy and one which leads to the speculative attack as the only robust equilibrium (Jeanne 2000a).[4] What then will the timing of the attack be?

Assume that the size of the attack is $-\Delta r$ then from (13.7) we see that the exchange rate begins rising at a rate μ after the attack. The important implication of this is that, given UIP, the domestic interest rate will jump up by μ to reflect the prospective currency depreciation. This, in turn, means that two things adjust in the money market at the time of the attack: high powered money drops by the size of the attack and the demand for domestic currency drops because the domestic interest rate increases to reflect the prospective currency depreciation. Money market equilibrium as given by (13.1) requires that at the instant of the attack the drop in money supply must match the drop in money demand and so:

$$\Delta r = -\alpha\mu. \tag{13.8}$$

If we assume domestic credit is determined by the following process:

$$d_t = d_0 + \mu t, \tag{13.9}$$

and, by implication, reserves follow the same process:

$$r_t = r_0 + \mu t, \tag{13.10}$$

where d_0 and r_0 denote, respectively, the initial stock of domestic credit and reserves and t is a deterministic time trend. At the time of the attack, T, reserves fall to zero and the money market equilibrium at T requires the drop in money supply to match the drop in money demand. So the condition for the timing of the attack becomes:

$$-\Delta r = r_0 - \alpha T = \alpha \mu, \tag{13.11}$$

and by rearranging terms we can solve for the attack time as:

$$T = \frac{r_0 - \alpha \mu}{\mu}. \tag{13.12}$$

Equation 13.12 demonstrates that the timing of the attack is determined by the initial stock of reserves and the rate of credit expansion: the higher the initial stock of reserves, or the lower the rate of credit expansion, the longer it takes before the fixed rate regime collapses. The dynamics of the crisis are illustrated in Figure 13.2, using a diagram from Obstfeld (1994). $T^\wedge$ is the point at which reserves are zero and the point at which the attack would occur, absent expectations. However, with forward-looking expectations the attack time is, as we have seen, brought forward to T^*.

13.1.2 *Modifications to first generation models*

In the crisis of the 1990s the money supply implications of reserve losses were often sterilised and so the condition $\Delta r = -\mu$ did not necessarily hold. However, as Flood and Marion (1997a) point out, as long as this sterilisation is understood by the market no fixed exchange rate regime will be sustainable. To see this note that if the money supply is held constant (i.e., the central bank successfully sterilises all of the reserve loss) we may think of the money market equilibrium condition as:

$$\bar{m} - p^* - \bar{s} = -\alpha(i^*). \tag{13.13}$$

Just after the attack the money market equilibrium condition will be given by:

$$m - p^* - \hat{s} = -\alpha(i^* + \mu). \tag{13.14}$$

On subtracting (13.14) from (13.13) we get:

$$\hat{s} - \bar{s} = \alpha \mu > 0, \tag{13.15}$$

which demonstrates that $\hat{s} > \bar{s}$ no matter how high $\bar{s}$ is set or how great the quantity of reserves are. So this means that no fixed exchange rate regime can

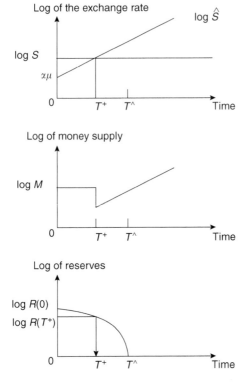

Figure 13.2 The dynamics of the crisis.

Source: Obstfeld (1994).

survive if the sterilisation plans are understood by the market. Despite this, however, we still observe countries fixing their exchange rates and engaging in prolonged periods of sterilisation. How can this be rationalised in the context of the earlier model? Flood *et al.* (1996) argue that to understand this phenomenon the bond market has to be explicitly modelled, along the lines of the portfolio-balance approach discussed in Chapter 7. Essentially, this means replacing the UIP condition (13.4) with:

$$i = i^* + \dot{s} + \lambda, \tag{13.4'}$$

where λ is a risk premium. Now there is an extra jump variable – the risk premium – that can move to clear the market. Flood *et al.* (1996) demonstrate that the risk premium jumps at the time of the crisis to keep the demand for money equal to the constant supply of money.

A number of papers relax the assumption of perfect foresight used in the earlier variant of the first generation model by assuming the domestic credit expansion is stochastic (see, *inter alia*, Flood and Garber 1984; Obstfeld 1986; Dornbusch 1987). This means that the date of the attack becomes uncertain and in the run-up to the attack the domestic interest rate will exhibit a peso effect (see Chapter 15).

In sum, first generation models emphasise the link between fundamentals and a currency crises in a linear framework. Although they have been regarded as well-suited to explaining certain Latin American crises in the 1970s and 1980s they are not deemed to be very useful in understanding currency crises in the 1990s. For example, at the time of the breakup of the ERM in 1992–3 and the Asian meltdown of 1997–8 countries seemed to have sufficient international reserves and sound monetary–fiscal mixes. As we noted in the introduction, the value added of second generation models is that they can explain speculative attacks against a currency even when the underlying fundamentals of that currency appear healthy. In particular, these models make agents' expectations endogenous and introduce important non-linearities.

13.1.3   The base-line second generation model

The paper that started the second generation literature is that of Obstfeld (1986) and his modification to the basic model involves assuming that the second-period monetary policy depends on the government's decision on whether or not to devalue in the first period. This therefore introduces a policy non-linearity into the model and can be illustrated in the following way.

If there is no attack on the currency, domestic credit grows at a rate μ_0 and has a shadow exchange rate associated with it of $\hat{s}_{\mu_0}$. Alternatively, if there is an attack and the currency is devalued domestic credit grows at a rate μ_1, where $\mu_1 > \mu_0$, and the corresponding shadow exchange rate is $\hat{s}_{\mu_1}$. Obstfeld argues that the higher monetary growth in the post-attack scenario could arise if the government is cut-off from borrowing overseas after the attack and has to engage in extra monetisation of its debt. The two scenarios are illustrated in Figure 13.3, where for illustrative purposes we assume $\mu_0 = 0$ so that the fixed rate would survive indefinately for some given d.

Suppose d is to the left of d^B. If there is no attack then the shadow rate will be on the $\hat{s}_{\mu_0}$ schedule while if there is an attack the shadow rate jumps to the $\hat{s}_{\mu_1}$ line which is still below the fixed exchange rate and therefore implies a capital loss for speculators. Therefore in this scenario there will be no incentive to attack and the fixed rate is compatible with domestic credit and survives indefinitely. Suppose now that domestic credit is at a level d^B. With $\mu = \mu_0$ we now have an intersection at C. If speculators attack the rate jumps from C to B and the attack will be successful. However, notice that there is no profit for speculators since there is no immediate capital gain from any reserves purchased from the central bank. So in equilibrium the system could equally be at B or C since there is no incentive to move to point B.

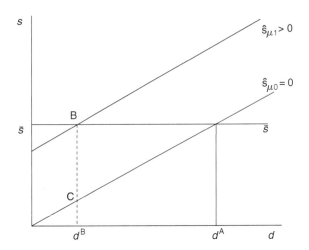

Figure 13.3 Second generation speculative attack model.

If domestic credit is in the range d^A to d^B and speculators were subsumed into a representative agent then an attack would be successful in this range since the economy would move to the new shadow line, there would be a run on the currency and the currency would depreciate. Here the authorities validate the attack ex post by engaging in the higher monetary creation, and this gives an outcome which is observationally equivalent to the kind of attack considered in the first generation model. Here though the crucial difference is that the outcome is being driven by the exogenous 'sunspot' expectations of the representative speculator.

In reality, however, speculators are a group who often have heterogenous beliefs and the coordination of their expectations on the sunpsot variable may not be straightforward. For example, if speculators are individually small and uncoordinated then they will have little market power to individually change the rate and multiple equilibria may still arise. For example, a speculator who believes the currency is overvalued will not attack the currency unless he believes there is a chance the rest of the market has the same expectation and will actually follow suit. In this case the economy could stay indefinitely on the lower shadow line. Alternatively, if all speculators believe the currency should be attacked the attack will, as in the case of the representative agent outcome, force the currency to devalue. In a heterogenous market one way this could occur is if there is one large player – for example, a Soros type figure – who leads the market to its new equilibrium (the coordination issue is discussed later).

Jeanne (2000a) provides a nice critique of the first and second generation speculative attack models. In particular, what is to stop the central bank engaging in unsterilised changes in domestic credit to keep the interest rate at a level which offsets the devaluation expectations and sustains reserves above the minimum level?

The speculative attack models therefore dodge the issue of why monetary authorities who have the power in the run-up to an attack, or at the time of an attack, to raise interest rate do not always do so. By failing to answer this question Jeanne (2000a) argues that the speculative attack model misses an important link in the logic of currency crises. Of course, raising interest rates in this way is costly and it is a comparison of the costs and benefits of raising interest rates which will influence the policy-maker in deciding to maintain a fixed peg. However, in order to address this kind of issue in the context of a speculative attack model, the policy-maker's objective function has to be explicitly modelled (i.e. the policy-maker's actions have to be endogenised). The so-called escape clause model of Obstfeld (1994) attempts to do this.

13.1.4   The escape clause variant of the second generation model

In this section we consider a variant of the escape clause model due to Jeanne (2000a). Such models have also been included in under the rubric of second generation models, although it is important to recognise that the escape clause approach is broader than the second generation model considered in the previous section since it incorporates a wider range of fundamentals and also it addresses the relationship between fundamentals and multiple equilibria. The label 'escape clause' refers to the fact that in this class of model the authorities may escape from the fixed peg if it is placing too high a cost on an important variable in the authorities' objective function, say, the level of unemployment. We now consider this variant of the second generation model, due to Jeanne (2000a), in a little more detail. As in our previous discussion, the essence of this model can be captured by thinking in terms of two periods – prior- and post-attack devaluation. Here the government decides whether to devalue or not depending on the level of unemployment. The latter is determined by a standard expectations-augmented Phillips curve:

$$U_2 = \rho U_1 - \alpha(\pi - \pi^e), \tag{13.16}$$

where U_1 and U_2 are deviations of unemployment from the natural level in periods 1 and 2, respectively, and π is inflation. The decision to devalue in period 2 is obtained by minimising the loss function:

$$L = (U_2)^2 + \delta C, \tag{13.17}$$

where δ is a zero/one dummy variable indicating the policy maker's decision ($=1$ if devaluation, 0 if not) and C is the cost of abandoning the fixed exchange rate. The latter is seen to be a function of, *inter alia*, the effects of increased exchange rate volatility on trade and investment, and the potential loss of anti-inflationary credibility by abandoning the peg and potential retaliatory 'beggar-thy-neighbour' policies. Using (13.16) in (13.17) we see that if there is no expectation of a devaluation by the private sector ($\pi^e = 0$) the government's loss function is $L^D = (\rho U_1 - \alpha d)^2 + C$ if it devalues, and $L^F = (\rho U_1)^2$ if it does not, where d represents the amount of devaluation and since PPP is assumed to hold continuously the domestic rate of inflation equals d if the government devalues and zero if not. Under these circumstances not devaluing will be optimal if:

$$\frac{C}{\alpha d} - 2\rho U_1 > -\alpha d. \tag{13.18}$$

Alternatively, if the private sector expects devaluation, implying $\pi^e = d$, the cost of defending the peg would be $L^F = (\rho U_1 + \alpha d)^2$, while the cost of devaluing would be $L^D = (\rho U_1)^2 + C$. Devaluing will in this case be the optimal strategy if:

$$\frac{C}{\alpha d} - 2\rho U_1 < \alpha d. \tag{13.19}$$

If we define a composite fundamental as:

$$\Phi = \frac{C}{\alpha d} - 2\rho U_1, \tag{13.20}$$

then there are three possible outcomes: $\Phi > \alpha d$ which is a unique equilibrium in which the currency is not devalued; $\Phi < -\alpha d$ which is also a unique equilibrium in which the currency is devalued in the second period; and, third, if $-\alpha d < \Phi < \alpha d$ there are two equilibria – one in which the policy-maker devalues and the other in which he does not. Two important implications follow from this model. When the rate of unemployment U_1 increases, the fixed exchange rate system may switch from a stable to unstable state in which a currency crisis may occur or may even become the sole equilibrium. The intuition for this is that because the loss function is convex in the unemployment rate the government is more inclined to devalue the higher the level of unemployment. So fundamentals can trigger or cause a currency crisis much as in the original first generation model (although the fundamentals here are broader than in that model). But the second implication of the model is that devaluation expectations are not always uniquely determined by fundamentals. In particular, in zone three, where equilibrium is not unique, a devaluation is possible but not certain. The intuition for this multiple equilibrium is that devaluation expectations raise the level of wages and increase the level of unemployment that the government has to accept to maintain the fixed peg which, in turn, increases the possibility of them devaluing. Here, therefore, the devaluation is not triggered by fundamentals per se but rather by the shift in devaluation expectations. As in the second generation models, considered in the previous section, the latter are seen as a reflection of so-called animal spirits, which are usually modelled as a sunspot variable coordinating market participants on high or low devaluation expectations.

Jeanne (2000a) has demonstrated that the results from the earlier model are robust to a number of specification changes, such as a wider specification of the fundamentals set, relaxing the perfect foresight assumption (see, for example, Obstfeld 1994, 1997) and endogenising the opting out cost (de Kock and Grilli 1993 and Bensaid and Jeanne 2000) and the magnitude of the devaluation (see Obstfeld 1994).

Krugman (1996) has criticised the escape clause model for requiring implausible assumptions about the monetary policy channel in order to produce multiple equilibria. He demonstrates that since devaluation expectations have a cost – by raising the ex ante real interest rate – multiple equilibria will not arise as long as the fundamentals deteriorate deterministically over time. The idea being that with deterministic fundamentals the crises can be uniquely determined by backward deduction. However, Jeanne and Masson (2000) show that although for a broad class of models, including that of Krugman (1996), the existence of deterministic or stochastic non-stationarity of the fundamentals does indeed rule out multiple equilibria, an arbitrarily large number can arise if a condition on the fundamentals is satisfied. However, this still begs the question: in such multiple equilibrium models how does the sunspot variable coordinate the activity of speculators? As we have mentioned earlier, this role may fall to the public pronouncements of a Soros type figure which have been known to move markets. The problem with this interpretation, however, is that these kind of people do not always move the market and so how are speculators coordinated in other instances? In the context of an escape clause model, Morris and Shin (1998) have demonstrated how abandoning the hypothesis of common knowledge in favour of a small amount of noise on signals about fundamentals results in the bad equilibrium becoming unique. This kind of argument therefore shifts the weight to the importance of credibility for the survival of the exchange rate, and policy instruments aimed at restoring transparency and common knowledge about fundamentals.

13.1.5   Third generation speculative attack models

Although the label 'third generation' is not universally accepted, there is no doubt that the second generation models were unable to fully explain the Latin American and Asian crises of 1995 and 1997 and so an alternative explanation seems to be required. In particular, if the second generation model is correct devaluing or floating a currency should enable a government to follow more expansionary policies. However, in the aftermath of both the East Asian and Latin America crises countries faced severe recession. Third generation models, therefore, focus on what appear to be the key determinants of these crises, namely, issues relating to financial intermediaries and liquidity effects.

For example, Radelet and Sachs (1998) argue crises in emerging markets are essentially bank runs that work their way through the foreign exchange market. Chang and Velasco (1998a,b) propose this view, suggesting self-fulfilling collapses due to a literal bank run (an alternative route would be through a balance-sheet-driven financial contraction). Another strand in the third generation literature builds on an idea by McKinnon and Pill (1996), who focussed on the role of implicit loan guarantees in generating excessively risky investment. In the context of the currency crises literature, a form of moral hazard arises when the unregulated, or loosely regulated, financial intermediaries of a country have some form of government guarantee (either explicit or implicit). In this kind of scenario the financial intermediaries are able to borrow at low (government backed/linked) interest rates and lend at relatively high rates in risky investment projects. By inflating the price of these risky assets the intermediaries inflate the asset side of their balance sheets which provokes further lending: a classic bubble process arises and when it eventually bursts produces capital flight and sparks a currency crises (see, for example, Corsetti *et al.* 1998 and Edison *et al.* 1998).

Krugman's (1999) variant of the third generation model focuses on a balance sheet approach. In particular, he considers highly leveraged firms holding a large proportion of foreign currency-denominated-debt. If there is then an exogenous capital outflow which results in a currency depreciation which if it is large enough can eliminate the net worth of firms. In imperfect capital markets firms with poor balance sheets cannot invest and so real investment collapses, thereby validating the capital flight. Krugman illustrates this view using a simple variant of the Mundell–Fleming model. The aggregate demand, money market and UIP conditions are given here, respectively, as expressions (13.21) to (13.23) and should be self-explanatory given our discussions in previous chapters.

$$y = D(y, i) + NX(sP^*/P, y), \tag{13.21}$$

$$M/P = L(y, i), \tag{13.22}$$

$$i = i^*. \tag{13.23}$$

The graphical solution to this simple model is given in Figure 13.4, where GG shows how output is determined given the exchange rate and money market equilibrium is represented by the schedule AA. The GG schedule is upward sloping because an exchange rate depreciation increases net exports which, in turn, increases output. The AA schedule indicates all points at which (13.23) satisfied,

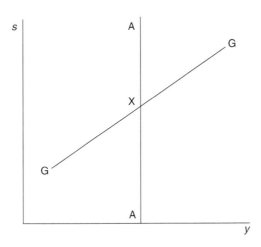

Figure 13.4 Base line MF model.

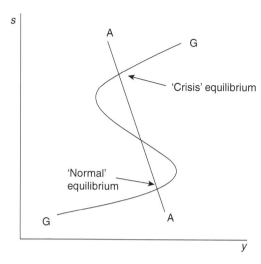

Figure 13.5 Third generation speculative attack model.

given the money market equilibrium condition (13.22). The equilibrium at X is the standard kind of equilibrium when firms are not balance sheet constrained. In the presence of balance sheet constraints expression (13.21) is modified to

$$y = D(y, i, sP^*/P) + NX(sP^*/P, y). \tag{13.24}$$

The real exchange rate now enters the demand function directly to capture the idea that exchange rate changes by influencing the balance sheet, and hence the investment decisions, of firms with a large component of foreign currency-denominated-debt. This kind of demand schedule could produce the GG curve of Figure 13.5. The idea here being that at favourable exchange rates GG has a normal slope (no balance sheet constraints) and at very unfavourable exchange rates (i.e. above) firms with foreign debt are unable to invest at all so there is no influence of balance sheet effects and again the GG schedule has a normal slope. But in the intermediate range balance sheet effects are large enough to outweigh the direct, traditional, net export effects so the exchange rate depreciation is highly contractionary. If, additionally, the central bank has a 'fear of floating', that is, it leans against the wind, then the money market equilibrium condition has to be modified to:

$$M(s)/P = L(y, i), \tag{13.25}$$

where M is assumed to be decreasing in s. This kind of money market relationship gives the backward bending AA curve in Figure 13.5 and raises the possibility of multiple stable equilibria: one with a normal exchange rate and one with a hyper-depreciated rate and bankrupt corporate sector. Since monetary policy becomes more contractionary in the latter case this also produces a fall in output.

Krugman also considers the policy implications of this kind of fourth generation model. In contrast to the conventional wisdom, fiscal expansion rather than fiscal contraction is needed to counteract the kind of capital flight underpinning this kind of model; that is, the GG schedule has to be pushed far enough to the right to produce a stable equilibrium. The important issue here, though, is whether in practice countries will be able to undertake the necessary expansion. Financial support from the IMF, to enable the country to intervene in the foreign exchange market, is ruled out as an option because it amounts to sterilised intervention, which is known to have little more than a transitory impact on exchange rates. The correct monetary reaction involves an initial sharp monetary contraction which in terms of Figure 13.5 pushes AA far enough to avoid the crises equilibrium. Once investors are convinced that the exchange rate is not going to depreciate massively, monetary policy can then be relaxed. Of course the cost of this policy measure is to produce an initial output contraction. Krugman concludes that the best way of ruling out the bad equilibrium is by *force majuere* using capital controls as a temporary measure during the crisis.

13.1.6   *Fourth generation models*

So-called fourth generation models were christened by Krugman (2001) and essentially extend the balance sheet view outlined earlier to incorporate the effect of a range of asset prices, in addition to the exchange rate, on balance sheets. Krugman focuses on a closed economy to make the point that the focus is on domestic asset markets rather than the foreign exchange market. Investment is assumed to be a function of Tobin's q; that is, the ratio of the replacement cost of capital to the equity valuation of capital. Investment through a standard multiplier effect impinges on output (the model is a stripped down model to make the point that balance sheet effects from other sectors of the economy can be as important as the exchange rate effect):

$$y = y(\rho), \tag{13.26}$$

where ρ denotes Tobin's q (we have not used q in the functional forms here to avoid further confusion with the real exchange rate). For simplicity it is assumed that ρ is increasing in output which determines profits, and decreasing in the interest rate:

$$\rho = \rho(\overset{+}{y}, \overset{-}{i}). \tag{13.27}$$

In place of a money demand function Krugman uses a monetary reaction function of the form:

$$i = i(\overset{+}{y}), \tag{13.28}$$

where the central bank raises interest rates if y is high and reduces them if output is low. The goods market equilibrium is given by (13.26) and Krugman assumes that the impact of ρ on y is non-linear: below some level reducing ρ has little effect, simply because gross investment is near zero and cannot go any lower, while above some level raising ρ also has little effect because capacity constraints put a cap on further expansion. This gives a goods market schedule similar to that in the base-line discussion and is given as GG in Figure 13.6. Asset market equilibrium is given by (13.27) – the private sector response – and (13.28) the monetary reaction function. If the monetary authority is sufficiently responsive to changes in output the AA schedule is downward sloping, as in Figure 13.6. If, in contrast, the monetary authority is not sufficiently responsive the AA schedule will be upward sloping, as in Figure 13.7, and we again have multiple equilibria.

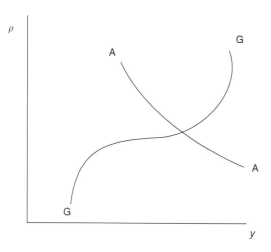

Figure 13.6 Fourth generation speculative attack model (sufficiently responsive monetary authority).

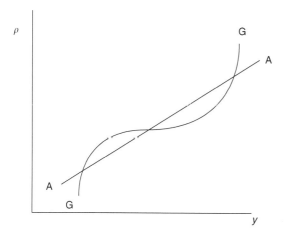

Figure 13.7 Fourth generation speculative attack model (insufficiently responsive monetary authority).

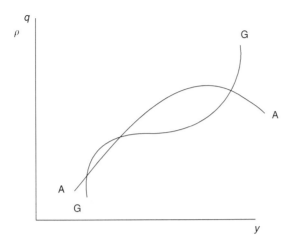

Figure 13.8 Fourth generation speculative attack model (no monetary action case).

In this case some financial crises push the economy to the bad equilibrium and monetary policy is not responsive enough to prevent it from doing so. In the worst case scenario it may be impossible for the authorities to react if the interest rate is, say, already at zero as was the case in Japan. The picture here would look like Figure 13.8. Again, as in the simple balance sheet model considered earlier, a sufficiently large fiscal expansion could rule out the bad equilibrium and put the economy back into a favourable equilibrium.

13.2   Empirical evidence

13.2.1   Estimates of first generation models

Blanco and Graber (1986) use a structural representation of the Krugman (1979) model to explain recurrent episodes of devaluation of the Mexican peso over the period 1973–82. In particular, they derive a formula for the expected change in the exchange rate that includes the objective probability of a devaluation, conditional on the policy adopted by the central bank. They show that when this conditional expectation is above the fixed rate devaluation occurs. The model is a discrete time version of the model outlined in Section 13.1 and has the following structure. The money market equilibrium condition is a more general variant of (13.1):

$$m_t - p_t = \beta + \Omega y_t - \alpha(i_t) + w_t, \tag{13.29}$$

where of terms not previously defined w is a stochastic disturbance to money demand. PPP does not hold exactly in this model and therefore in place of (13.3) we have:

$$p_t = p_t^* + s_t + q_t, \tag{13.30}$$

where, as before, q is the log of the real exchange rate. In the absence of perfect foresight, the discrete time version of UIP is:

$$i_t = i_t^* + E_t(s_{t+1} - s_t). \tag{13.31}$$

Movements in the variables in (13.29) to (13.31) and domestic credit expansion determine the evolution of foreign exchange reserves and the central bank stops defending the fixed exchange rate, $\bar{s}$, when reserves reach a critical level, $\bar{R}$ (measured in foreign currency units). As before, $\hat{s}$ is the shadow exchange rate which becomes visible to the researcher at the time of the attack and, therefore, may also be thought of as the post-devaluation exchange rate. Analogous to the derivation of (13.5), the flexible exchange rate in this model may be obtained by substituting (13.30) and (13.31) into (13.29) to get:

$$\tilde{h}_t = -\alpha E_t \tilde{s}_t + (1 + \alpha)\tilde{s}_t, \tag{13.32}$$

where $\tilde{h}_t \equiv \log[D_t + \bar{R}\exp(\tilde{s})] - \beta - \Omega y_t + \alpha i_t^* - p_t^* - u_t - w_t$. Since $\tilde{h}_t$ is unobservable to the researcher, Blanco and Garber assume $\tilde{h}_t = h_t$, the initial value of $\tilde{h}_t$ that would prevail at time t if the floating rate began at time t. The variable h_t is assumed to follow a first-order autoregressive process as:

$$h_t = \theta_1 + \theta_2 h_{t-1} + v_t, \tag{13.33}$$

where v_t is a white noise process with a normal density function $g(v)$, with zero mean and standard deviation σ. The flexible exchange rate solution may be found by solving the difference equations in (13.32) and (13.33) to obtain:

$$\tilde{s}_t = \mu\alpha\theta_1 + \mu h_t, \tag{13.34}$$

where $\mu = 1/[(1 + \alpha) - \alpha\theta_2]$.[5] Rather than use an optimising rule for the determination of the new exchange rate, Blanco and Garber assume it is given by a simple linear function:

$$\hat{s}_t = \tilde{s}_t + \delta v_t, \tag{13.35}$$

where δ is a non-negative parameter. This rule states that after an attack the central bank will select a new rule equal to the minimum viable rate plus a non-negative amount which depends on the magnitude of the disturbance that forced the collapse. Since when $\hat{s}$ is greater than $\bar{s}$ is equivalent to a devaluation at time t we may use (13.34) and (13.35) to define the probability of devaluation at time $t + 1$, based on information at time t as:

$$pr(\mu\alpha\theta_1 + \mu h_{t+1} + \delta v_{t+1} > \bar{s}), \tag{13.36}$$

where $\bar{s}$ is the time t value of the fixed rate. The devaluation probability may alternatively be expressed as:

$$1 - F(k_t) \equiv pr(v_{t+1} > k_t), \tag{13.37}$$

where $k_t \equiv [1/(\mu + \delta)][\bar{s} - \mu\alpha\theta_1 + \theta_2 h_t]$, and $F(k_t)$ is the cumulative distribution function associated with $g(v)$. Using this probability, the expected future exchange rate may be expressed as the weighted average of the current fixed rate and the rate expected conditional on devaluation, both weighted by the respective probabilities of occurrence:

$$Es_{t+1} = F(k_t)\bar{s} + [1 - F(k_t)]E(\bar{s}_{t+1}|v_{t+1} > k_t). \tag{13.38}$$

Using (13.35) the conditional expectation can be expressed as:

$$E(\hat{s}_{t+1}|v_{t+1} > k_t) = \mu\theta_1(1 + \alpha) + \mu\theta_2 h_t + (\mu + \delta)E(v_{t+1}|v_{t+1} > k_t).^6 \tag{13.39}$$

Since $g(v)$ is assumed to be a normal density function, the unconditional forecast of the exchange rate for period $t + 1$ is:

$$Es_{t+1} = F(k_t)\bar{s} + [1 - F(k_t)][\mu\theta_1(1 + \alpha) + \mu\theta_2 h_t]$$
$$+ \frac{\sigma(\mu + \delta)\exp[-0.5(k_t/\sigma)^2]}{\sqrt{2\pi}}. \tag{13.40}$$

On the basis of (13.37), (13.39) and (13.40) Blanco and Garber draw the following predictions: $[1-F(k_t)]$ is expected to peak immediately before a devaluation; $E_t s_{t+1}$ should be closely correlated with the appropriate forward exchange rate; the conditional forecast should approximate the exchange rate set when a devaluation occurs. The forward rate for the peso is assumed to be generated by the following expression:

$$f_t = Es_{t+1} + \varepsilon_t, \tag{13.41}$$

where ε_t is a zero mean disturbance, orthogonal to the variables in the expression for Es_{t+1}.

Blanco and Garber propose estimating the model in the following way. First, the money market relationship is estimated, along with (13.33), and the estimated parameters are plugged into (13.40) along with starting values for $\bar{R}$ and δ. The values of $\bar{R}$ and δ are then re-estimated by minimising the sum of squared residuals from (13.40) and this process is repeated until the values of $\bar{R}$ and δ converged. Using this methodology, Blanco and Garber confirm that whenever $\hat{s}$ is greater than the fixed rate a devaluation occurs – in the periods 1976:Q3 and 1982:Q2.

The estimated one step ahead probabilities increase quite sharply before each of these devaluations, and decline sharply thereafter. Ninety-five per cent confidence intervals are also constructed for the conditional expected exchange rates (forecasts) and these show that for the 1976:Q3 devaluation the conditional expected exchange rate falls within the confidence interval, but the 1981 devaluation does not.

Cumby and Wijnbergen (1989) use a similar analysis and monthly data to analyse the Argentine crawling peg, 1979–80. Consistent with the basic model, they find that a sharp increase in growth of domestic credit is the main factor triggering an attack on the currency.

13.2.2 *Empirical evidence on self-fulfilling crises and escape clause models*

A number of papers have used Markov–Switching-regime models in an attempt to capture regime changes which are unrelated to fundamentals. For example, Jeanne and Masson (2000) have proposed interpreting the regime shifts identified by such models as jumps between multiple equilibria because the Markov–Switching-regime model can be interpreted as a linear reduced form of a structural escape clause model with sunspots. In particular, Jeanne and Masson (2000) estimate a two-state Markov–Switching model for the French franc–German mark exchange rate over the period 1979–86. They follow the second generation/escape clause literature and include a broader range of fundamentals than in the first generation models. In particular, the probability of devaluation was specified as:

$$\pi_t = \gamma_{s_t} + \beta_u u_t + \beta_b \text{tbal}_t + \beta_r \text{rer}_t + v_t, \tag{13.42}$$

where u represents the unemployment rate, tbal is the trade balance as a ratio of GDP, rer is percentage deviation of the real effective exchange rate from its 1990 level and the dependent variable is the 1 month interest differential between euro-franc and euro-DM instruments, after correction for the expected movement towards the centre of the band using the risk-adjusted method of Svensson (1993) (see Chapter 12). The error term is assumed to be normally distributed with variance σ_v^2. The constant term depends on two potential states (i.e. $s_t = 1$ or 2) and is the term which captures the potential multiple equilibria in this class of model. Assuming this term is constant, estimates of the purely fundamental-based model are recovered using OLS. Jeanne and Masson find that the coefficient estimates recovered are often wrongly signed and the fitted value from this expression does not do a good job of tracking the actual probability of devaluation, particularly in periods associated with speculation. However, when the two-state model is estimated, the fit of the model improves dramatically, all of the coefficients are correctly signed and the actual and fitted probabilities track each other closely, particularly around the periods of speculative pressure. Jeanne and Masson infer from this that the Markov–Switching model provides a better fit for the probability of devaluation than the purely fundamentals-based model because it is capturing sunspot activity.

Jeanne (1997) estimates a variant of (13.42) using maximum likelihood methods for the French franc ERM crises, using monthly data from 1991 to 1993. He finds that the jumps in expectations that occurred in September 1992, the first quarter of 1993 and July 1993 are not well explained by the fundamentals alone but are well explained when a regime switch is allowed for. This is interpreted as *prima facie* evidence that the crises are better interpreted as self-fulfilling. Martinez-Peria (1997) has applied the Markov–Switching methodology, with some success, to a broader range of EMS currencies. Cerra and Saxena (2000) has applied it to the 1997 crises of the Indian rupiah.

However, there have been a number of criticisms levelled against the kind of empirical evidence presented in this section. First, favourable results, such as those generated by Jeanne and Masson from a Markov–Switching model, could simply reflect some form of omitted variable bias. For example, the reduced form of Jeanne and Masson does not contain a variable which first generation models indicate as important, namely, foreign exchange reserves. Second, the reduced-form nature of the model makes it possible to interpret the results in a different way, perhaps due to rational learning. For example, Krugman considers an economy with a steadily rising unemployment rate in which market participants believe the government will devalue when the unemployment rate reaches between 12% and 14%. This means that devaluation expectations will jump up when unemployment reaches 12% and fall back when it exceeds 14%. Such behaviour would be observationally equivalent to a self-fulfilling jump in expectations, but it is simply a reflection of rational learning process. Alternatively, such results could reflect informational asymmetries. For example, in the model of Caplin and Leahy (1994), much as in the market microstructural models of Chapter 14, agents receive private information and do not immediately reveal this to the rest of the market because they have to pay a fixed cost to reallocate their portfolios. When some threshold is reached investors withdraw from a market en mass and the information gets aggregated, thereby precipitating the crash. The informational cascade models of Banerjee (1992); Bikhchandani *et al.* (1992) and Chari and Kehoe (2003) also rely on the dispersal of private information amongst investors. In these models investors receive information sequentially and each investor observes the prior decisions of the last investor in the chain. In these models if the signals are noisy it may be optimal for the investor to ignore her private information and simply imitate the decision made by previous investors. Such repeated imitation could lead to an outcome very similar to that uncovered by the Markov–Switching models. The main problem with models which rely on private information is that most information of relevance to foreign exchange markets is public and of that which is not – such as the order flow – will be disseminated pretty rapidly if it is of sufficient import to result in the collapse of a currency. As we have noted earlier, speculative attack models have also been criticised from a theoretical perspective.

13.2.3   Speculative index approaches

Most other empirical studies of speculative attack models focus on speculative indices. For example, Eichengreen, Rose and Wyplosz (1995) [hereafter ERW] use a panel of 22 OECD countries to analyse the ERM crises. They develop a speculative pressure index along the lines of Girton and Roper's measure of external pressure. In particular, they construct a series emp which is the weighted average of exchange rate and interest rate changes, and the (negative) of reserve changes. If the index reaches two standard deviations above the mean a speculative attack is identified. This variable is regressed on a set of macro-fundamentals. They find that for non-ERM countries there is a significant difference for the relationship between emp and fundamentals for non-ERM countries when they compare tranquil and crises periods but no significant difference for non-ERM countries. They interpret this as suggesting that ERM crises are driven by self-fulfilling events.

Flood and Marion (1997b) criticise the index used by ERW. In particular, they argue that picking out extreme values in terms of the two standard error bounds will miss out any *anticipation* of the crisis which is reflected in the indicators prior to the crises. This simply means that the share of the predictable crisis in the sample may be reduced. Second, if the subsequent post-crisis devaluation is viewed as credible there may be little change in interest rate and reserves at the time of the crisis, or they may revert back to pre-crisis levels quickly so the indicator in averaging across these terms misses the crisis.

For example, Frankel and Rose (1996) use an annual data set, covering the period 1971–92, for 105 developing countries and apply an event-study and probit-regression methods to a set of 16 macro indicators. In sum, they find that crises tend to occur when output growth is low, growth of domestic credit is high, the level of foreign interest rates is high and a low ratio of FDI debt is associated with a high likelihood of a crash. Klein and Marion (1994) use a panel data set for 80 devaluations in South America over the period 1957–91. They find that the monthly probability of abandoning a peg increases with real overvaluation and a declining level of foreign assets – other factors that are important are: the degree of openness, political factors and the amount of time the currency was pegged.

Variants of the speculative index approach have been used by others. For example, Kaminsky and Reinhart (1996) use a variant to develop an 'early warning system' of crises. In particular, a balance of payments crisis is identified when a weighted average[7] of the monthly percentage depreciation in the exchange rate and decline in reserves exceeds its mean by more than three standard deviations. A more qualitative approach is used to define a banking crisis. Such a crisis arises either when bank runs lead to the closure, merging or takeover by the public sector of one or more financial institutions. Alternatively, in the case of no runs the crisis occurs with the closure, merging, takeover or large-scale government assistance of an important financial institution that marks the start of a string of similar outcomes for other financial institutions. Kaminsky and Reinhart (1996) focus on 20 countries in Asia, Europe, Latin America and the Middle East, over the period 1970 to mid-1995. They find that in the 1970s there are a total of 25 balance of payments crises but only 3 banking crises. In contrast, in the 1980s and 1990s the number of banking crises quadruples while the number of balance of payments crises hardly changes.

Using a probit model in which a binary measure (i.e. a 0/1 measure, where the 1 denotes a crisis and is determined by the exchange market pressure variable) of balance of payments crisis is regressed onto their index of banking crisis they find that a banking crisis in a country is a significant determinant of a balance of payments crisis (the converse is not true). Kaminsky and Reinhart (1996) then go on to analyse the evolution of nine macroeconomic variables, 18 months before and after the crises, relative to their behaviour in tranquil times. In sum, they find that balance of payments crises are preceded by recesssions, or below 'normal' economic growth. Monetary policy, reacting perhaps to the recessionary forces, is more expansionary about 6 months before the crises. Finally, the unbacked liabilities of the financial system climb steeply just before the crises.

Kaminsky *et al.* (1997) use 15 monthly indicators to provide an alternative measure of early warning. In particular, when an indicator exceeds a certain threshold value this is interpreted as a warning signal that a currency crisis may take place within the following 24 months. The effectiveness of different indicators is determined on the basis of the following matrix:

Signal performance matrix

	Crisis (within 24 months)	Non-crisis (within 24 months)
Signal A	B
No Signal C	D

Source: Kaminsky *et al.* (1997).

where A is number of months in which an indicator issued a good signal, B is the number of months in which an indicator issued a bad signal or simply 'noise', C is the number of months in which an indicator failed to issue (which would have been a good signal) and D is the number of months in which indicator did not issue a signal (a bad signal). In this context, a perfect indicator would have been one for which A and D > 0, B and C = 0. That is, it would issue a signal in every month that is to be followed by a crisis (A > 0 and C = 0) and it would not issue a signal in every month that is not followed by a crisis (B = 0 and D > 0). The optimal threshold for each indicator is then the value which minimises the so-called noise to signal ratio: [B/B + D] / [A/A + C] which is the ratio between the false signal as a proportion of the number of months in which false signals could have been issued, and good signals as a proportion of all possible good signals that could have been issued. *Ceteris paribus*, the lower is this ratio the better is the indicator. In particular, a signalling device which issues signals randomly would have a ratio equal to one and therefore Kaminsky *et al.* (1997) exclude indicators with a ratio of one and above.

It turns out that the variables that have the best track record as indicators are exports, deviations of the real exchange rate from trend, the ratio of broad money to gross international reserves, output and equity prices (these are all defined as the percentage change in the level of the variable with respect to its level a year before). Variables which produce poor noise to signal ratios and are therefore not used as early warning indicators are the real interest differential, bank deposits, imports and the ratio of lending interest rates to deposit interest rates. It is further demonstrated that of the chosen indicators on average send the first signal between a year and one year and a half before the crises erupt. They therefore conclude that 'the signals approach can be useful as the basis for an early warning system of currency crises'.

Frankel and Rose (1998) refer to a currency crisis as a currency crash and define this as a nominal depreciation of the currency of at least 25% that is also at least a 10% increase in the rate of depreciation. The latter modification is designed to ensure that not all of the often year-by-year devaluations generated by high inflation countries are counted as crises. The explanatory variables of a crisis are: *foreign* variables, interest rates and output; *domestic macroeconomic* indicators, such as output, monetary and fiscal shocks; *external* variables such as exchange rate misalignment, the current account and the level of indebtedness; and the *composition* of debt. The data set consists of annual data over the period 1972–92 for 105 countries. Their definition of a crash yielded 117 different crashes and have a 'slight tendency' to be clustered in the early-to-mid 1980s. Their analysis of this data set consists of two parts, an ocular, 'event-study', analysis and a formal analysis based on a probit model. In terms of the latter, they find statistically significant explanatory power for crises from all of the explanatory variables, apart from the debt variables, using contemporaneous values of the variables. However, when the variables are entered with a single lag they are all, including the debt variables, statistically significant, thereby suggesting that the crises were predictable 1 year ahead. Frankel and Rose demonstrate that their results are robust to a number of sensitivity tests.

Kamin *et al.* (2001) push the EWI further by trying to unravel the relative contribution of domestic and external factors in explaining currency crises. Their approach involves, first, identifying the years in which devaluation crises occur for 26 emerging market countries. As in Kaminsky and Reinhart, this is calculated from an exchange market pressure variable – a weighted average of the US dollar bilateral exchange rate and the change in international reserves – and declines in this index in excess of 1.75 standard deviations in any month indicates a crisis occurred in that year. Probit models are then applied to a pooled annual data set for the crises countries over the period 1981–99 to estimate the probability of a crisis as a function of key macroeconomic variables. The variables capturing domestic variables in these models are: GDP growth, fiscal deficits, bank loans, M2/reserves and external debt. The chosen external variables are: real exchange rates, export growth, foreign direct investment, current accounts, terms of trade, US real short-term interest rates and industrial country growth. The key finding of this paper is that the external factors make a relatively small contribution to the probability of crises relative to the internal factors. However, the external factors make a relatively greater contribution during years in which an actual crisis occurs and probably pushed countries which had poor internal factors into a crisis. They regard these results as favouring a regime of flexible exchange rates for these countries, since such flexibility should help to cushion the impacts of external shocks when they occur (although they recognise that a one size fits all exchange rate policy is not entirely desirable for emerging market countries).

13.2.4   *Contagion*

The East Asian Crises have introduced the term contagion into the lexicon of International Finance. Unfortunately, there is no generally accepted definition of this phenomenon. In general terms the concept is trying to get at the way a crisis in one country gets contemporaneously propagated to nearby countries (i.e. the Asian crises which are generally regarded as starting in Thailand and then rapidly spread to neighbouring countries) and even distant economies (i.e. the Russian crises in 1998 is widely believed to have effected other emerging markets, in South America). The key issue in the contagion literature is to understand if these common attacks are triggered by macroeconomic imbalances (Corsetti *et al.* (1998)) or are unrelated to fundamentals and reflect fad-like, or non-fundamental, behaviour or were both effects present? Alternatively, does contagion simply mean country interdependencies?

One channel which could explain the phenomenon of contagion is trade links. If country a and b have close trading links then a shock to a that forces it to devalue may make it more likely for b also to devalue in order to maintain competitiveness. However, it seems unlikely that trade links by themselves are large enough to be the primary channel of contagion. An alternative explanation for spillovers may lie on the capital account: a liquidity crisis in one market may force third country investors to liquidate positions in other emerging markets.[8] An alternative explanation is that such crises may be due to a common cause such as policies taken in industrial countries which have a common effect on emerging markets. Drazen (1999) has emphasised 'informational spillovers' as being a key source of contagion. For example, the extent to which countries share similar bank regulatory systems, or perhaps other more intangible/unobservable factors, may lead investors to revise their view of a particular country when there is, say, a bank failure or a change in a neighbouring country with a similar banking structure. Such fundamentals are often difficult to measure and come under the category of 'soft' fundamentals. A related informational point is the 'wake up' call of Goldstein (1998). Here the fundamentals were actually bad but investors did not realise this until one country's crises made this evident (the poor state of the banking sector is a case in point). It is possible to imagine these kind of factors explaining the spread of the Asian crises from Thailand to neighbouring countries such as Indonesia, Malaysia and the Phillipines, since these countries shared some common 'weak' fundamentals problems. However, using these channels, it is harder to figure out why it spread to countries such as Hong Kong and Singapore which both had strong fundamentals.

To explain contagion to such countries researchers have resorted to the multiple equilibrium or sunspot theme discussed earlier. The idea being that the sunspot variables that trigger crises are correlated across countries crises will erupt simultaneously across countries regardless of fundamentals (as long as they lie in the zone of multiplicity). Masson (1998), indeed, has argued that this last channel is the only form of contagion and labels interdependencies associated with changes in fundamentals in developed countries as 'monsoonal' effects, while interdependencies among the developed countries themselves are referred to as spillover effects.

In order to separate the monsoonal and spillover effects from the pure contagion effects, Masson (1998) extends the escape clause model of Jeanne (1997) to incorporate interactions between a developed economy and an emerging market economy. The model illustrates three channels which can propagate a crisis: monsoonal effects, represented by a change in the US interest rate or the dollar–yen exchange rate; spillover effects coming from the initial level of the exchange rate of the emerging market; and the potential for contagion coming from the expectation of devaluation in the emerging market country. Using data for 13 emerging markets for the period 1994–96, Masson demonstrates that for most of the countries there is a range of values for the composite fundamental term, Φ, in which multiple equilibria can occur. Of course, this result is only suggestive of his definition of contagion, it cannot be definitive. Much as in the work of Kaminsky *et al.* (1997), discussed earlier, Masson argues that a more refined version of the model (incorporating a broader range of fundamentals) may be used as an early warning indicator of countries that might be vulnerable to multiple equilibria.

A number of researchers have used correlations of movements in financial prices, or returns, to develop measures of contagion (see, *inter alia*, King and Wadwani 1995 and Corsetti *et al.* 1998).[9] The idea being that over a period when investors behave in a herd-like manner across a range of economies, equities, exchange rates and interest rates will react similarly across the group regardless of fundamentals. While such an approach appears intuitive, and is straightforward to implement, it is open to a number of concerns. First, it appears to provide a contemporaneous measure of contagion, whereas ideally one would prefer a measure which helped predict it. Second, a rise in correlations could reflect either herd behaviour or a change in fundamentals affecting a wide swathe of emerging markets. For example, if the crisis in Thailand provided information to investors about potential problems across a wide range of other emerging markets, the higher correlations would not necessarily reflect herd behaviour, in the sense of indiscriminate withdrawal of funds. Recognition of this point has led some to include 'fundamental' contagion (based on links such as trade) into the definition. Such a differentiation, however, can cause confusion as it blurs the focus on the central issue, namely, the importance of herd-like behaviour of investors as opposed to rational responses to changes in fundamentals. Third, on a technical level, larger movements in a series may also tend to create higher correlations, so that such a test may simply be identifying periods of turmoil (see Corsetti *et al.* 1998). Fourth, these correlations have tended to increase over time, suggesting that they may simply be reflecting increasing globalisation in the underlying markets.

As an alternative to using the correlations of returns to measure contagion, Bayoumi *et al.* (2003) propose using the gravity model to capture contagion effects. In particular, they use correlations of equity markets across countries and condition these on distance – the key variable in gravity models – and other gravity approach terms plus macroeconomic fundamentals. Contagion is defined as purely herd-like behaviour (i.e. unconnected with fundamentals) and an increase in contagion is captured by a fall in the absolute value of the coefficient on distance. The data consists of a panel of 16 countries for the period 1991 through to 2001 (data frequency, monthly). Bayoumi *et al.* show that this method is extremely good at identifying periods of 'positive contagion', that is, when capital flowed into emerging countries in a herd-like manner with little or no differentiation based on fundamentals. They also demonstrate that in the run-up to a typical crisis, positive contagion peaks before the crisis actually occurs, and then there is a period during which investors become more sensitive to differences in fundamentals across countries, followed by a renewed period of contagion after the crisis. This basic kind of pattern was demonstrated to hold in the run-up to the Tequila crisis, the Asian crisis and in early 2001 as the Argentinian crisis started to form.

14 The market microstructure approach to the foreign exchange market

Up to this point the focus has been on the macroeconomics of exchange rate behaviour and we have argued, either directly or indirectly, that this focus is a valuable one. However, there are still important issues to address with respect to understanding the daily volume of foreign exchange traded globally and how the price of foreign exchange is actually set in the foreign exchange market. For example, we noted in Chapter 1 that on a day-to-day basis the current BIS estimate of the volume of gross trading in foreign exchange markets on a global basis is approximately \$1.2 trillion,[1] 86% of which occurs between market makers alone. Since the total annual world trade flow is around \$4 trillion it is clearly difficult to explain the massive foreign exchange trade in terms of standard macroeconomic fundamentals and therefore a number of researchers (see, for example, Frankel and Rose 1995a; Flood and Rose 1999; Lyons 2001) have proposed using a microeconomic-based modelling approach, namely, a market microstructure approach. This micro-based approach focuses on an array of institutional aspects of the foreign exchange market, such as price formation, the matching of buyers and sellers (i.e. market makers and brokers) and optimal dealer pricing policies.

As we shall see later, one of the key explanations offered by the microstructural approach for the huge daily volume in foreign exchange trade is the so-called 'hot potato' effect. The idea is that if an initial trade between a customer and a bank produces an unwanted position for the dealer, she will try to offload this to another dealer and this process will continue until an equilibrium, where the initial foreign exchange position is willingly held, is reached. This may be seen as a form of risk management. The interpretation of high volume has important policy implications. For example, if, as many conjecture, high volume is a reflection of speculation some form of tax, such as the Tobin tax of throwing 'sand in the wheels' of international finance, may be the appropriate remedy. But if the volume reflects risk management the tax would impede this and would therefore be undesirable.

Garman (1976) introduced the term market microstructure to define 'moment-to-moment trading activities in asset markets'. O'Hara (1995) gives a more general finance-based definition: 'Market microstructure is the study of the process and outcomes of exchanging assets under explicit trading rules. While much of Economics abstracts from the mechanics of trading, the microstructure literature analyses how specific *trading mechanisms* affect the price formation process.' As we shall see in this chapter, such trading mechanisms may range from the role of a broker as an intermediary in the transaction process to the existence of (or lack of) a centralised trading location. In essence, market microstructure research exploits the structure provided by the existing trading patterns in a particular market and attempts to show how this affects price formation, returns and hence the (informational) efficiency of the market. In the microstructural literature, the focus on price formation is very different to the standard approach taken in the economics literature, where most of the discussion centres on market-clearing or equilibrium prices. In the context of the macroeconomics literature considered in this book this is perhaps at its clearest in the use of the rational expectations assumption, where behaviour out of equilibrium is not considered.

Lyons (2001) fleshes out the general definition of market microstructure, given by O'Hara, and provides a definition which is much more specific to the foreign exchange market. He argues that what distinguishes the micro-approach from the asset market approach, considered extensively in the earlier chapters of this book, is that it relaxes three key assumptions of the asset approach. First, microstructural models recognise that some information relevant to exchange rates is not publicly available. For example, foreign exchange dealers regularly have access to information on trades – the concept of order flow – which gives them inside information on how a currency might move in the future. A good example of this is central bank intervention which gives a trader, or traders, an indication of how the central bank perceives currency developments. Also traders engaged in exporting and importing take positions with foreign exchange dealers and thereby impart information on the evolution of the trade balance that is not available to the general public. This, of course, contrasts with the asset market model where all information is supposed to be publicly available. It is, however, consistent with Fama's definition of strong-form efficiency (see Chapter 15), which encompasses both public and private information. Second, market microstructural models recognise that agents may differ in ways that can affect prices – that is, heterogeneity of expectations is significant. One important way they differ is with respect to expectations formation. In nearly all macro-based models considered in this book, it is assumed that expectations are *homogeneous* and this is usually expressed using the conditional expectations operator, $E(./I_t)$. The essence of micro-based work is that the huge volumes of foreign exchange traded can only be explained by the existence of *heterogeneous* agents. In particular, why would agents trade with each other if they all held the same expectations? The kind of heterogeneity referred to in the microstructure literature may arise from a number of sources, such as differences in information, beliefs, preferences and wealth. Third, and as we noted in the previous paragraph, market microstructure models emphasise that trading mechanisms differ in ways that can affect prices. In sum, Lyons argues that the 'hallmarks' of any market microstructure model are order flow and the bid–ask spread, which is the measure of price.

In this chapter we consider the various aspects of the microstructure literature as it relates to the foreign exchange market, in the following ways. First, we examine to what extent expectations are indeed heterogeneous. To this end we focus on a literature which uses disaggregate exchange rate survey data to gauge the extent of heterogeneity in the foreign exchange market. We then go on to look at some of the characteristics of the foreign exchange market and its key players – that is, we examine the trading mechanisms of the foreign exchange market. Finally, we examine some of the theoretical work on market microstructure.

14.1 Do foreign exchange market participants have heterogeneous expectations? Some answers from the survey data literature

As we have noted, central to the MMH is the existence of heterogeneity amongst foreign exchange market participants. If there is no heterogeneity, then the market microstructural story does not get started. The existence of heterogeneous expectations in the context of the foreign exchange market has been tested extensively using a number of different disaggregate survey data bases. The testing methods tend to follow two basic approaches. The first set of tests involves examining the exchange rate expectations of agents, in terms of their unbiasedness, orthogonality and evolution of expectations. Such tests may be regarded as indirect in the sense that they are not specifically designed to capture heterogeneity. The second set of tests, which we refer to as 'direct' tests, is based on variants of a test due to Ito (1990). Survey data bases have also been used to calculate measures of dispersion which are then related to key microsturcture variables such as volume, volatility and the bid–ask spread.

14.1.1 Indirect tests of heterogeneity

Unbiasedness tests are based on the following kind of equation or some variant of this which adequately addresses stationarity issues (see Chapter 15 for further details):

$$s_{t+k} = \alpha + \beta s^e_{t+k} + \varepsilon_{t+k}, \tag{14.1}$$

where the null hypothesis of unbiasedness is $\alpha = 0$ and $\beta = 1$ and the error term is random. To test unbiasedness, Ito (1990) uses a survey data base, collected by the Japanese Centre for International Finance, which consists of the individual responses (44 in total) of a number of financial and non-financial institutions on their expectations of the yen–dollar exchange rate, 1, 3 and 6 months ahead for the sample May 1985–June 1987. He groups the survey responses into six industrial classifications: banking, security companies, trading companies, companies in the export industries, insurance companies and companies in the import industries. He finds that unbiasedness is rejected for trading companies and insurance companies at the 1-month horizon, for securities and import companies at the 3-month horizon and for all groups, except banks and import industries, at the 6-month horizon. In sum Ito's, unbiasedness tests reveal some evidence of heterogenity in the sense that the rejection of unbiasedness is not universal across company groups and forecast horizons.

MacDonald (1992) uses a disaggregate survey data base supplied by Consensus Forecasts of London, to test the unbiasedness of individual forecasters (sample period October 1989–March 1991). This survey data base is particularly valuable since it contains disaggregate survey responses for three key currencies (dollar–sterling, dollar–mark and dollar–yen) conducted simultaneously in seven financial centres. Although these results tend to confirm unbiasedness tests using aggregate data (which give a strong rejection of unbiasedness – see Chapter 15), in the sense that the vast majority of forecasters do not have unbiased forecasts, there is a significant minority that do produce unbiased forecasts. An interesting aspect of this study is that German forecasters have almost a 100% record in producing unbiased forecasts of the German mark, but produce as biased forecasts as other country forecasters for the non mark currencies. MacDonald and Marsh (1996a), Chionis and MacDonald (2002) have updated the Consensus unbiasedness results (period October 1989–March 1995) and essentially confirm the findings of MacDonald.

Survey-based error orthogonality tests are based on the following equation:

$$s^e_{t+k} - s_{t+k} = \alpha + \beta I_t + \varepsilon_{t+k}, \tag{14.2}$$

where I_t is a publicly available information set and the null hypothesis is $\alpha = 0$ and $\beta = 0$ (for further issue relating to this kind of equation see Chapter 15). Ito (1990) conducts his error orthogonality tests using the forward premium, past forecast errors and the past exchange rate change as informational variables. At the individual level Ito finds that about three-quarters of the individuals in his survey fail the orthogonality test. MacDonald (1992) finds that the forecasters who produce biased forecasts also failed the error orthogonality test (14.2) when the information set consisted of the fourth lagged survey forecast error (the fourth lag was used to avoid potential misalignments which may have produced spurious correlations). MacDonald and Marsh (1996a) and Chionis and MacDonald (2002) have extended and updated the Consensus results of MacDonald using the forward premium as the informational variable; again the null hypothesis of orthogonality was rejected in the vast majority of cases.

14.1.2   *Expectational mechanisms*

The following expression combines three expectational mechanisms, namely, bandwagon, adaptive and regressive (see Chapter 15 for a discussion):

$$\Delta s^e_{t+1} = \omega + \gamma (s_t - s_{t-1}) + \tau (s^e_t - s_t) + \nu (\bar{s}_t - s_t). \tag{14.3}$$

In the context of this equation the null hypothesis of static expectations may be tested as $\gamma = \nu = \tau = 0$. In MacDonald (1992), a comprehensive examination of the expectations formation mechanisms of all of the respondents to the Consensus survey is undertaken. In estimating (14.3) MacDonald found that the null hypothesis of static expectations could not be rejected in the vast majority of cases; however, a significant minority of forecasters displayed evidence of bandwagon effects.

Benassy *et al.* (2003) use the Consensus survey data base, of 3- and 12-month expectations, to examine the adaptive, extrapolative, regressive and mixed expectations models for a panel of 40 foreign exchange dealers. Both fixed-effects and random-effects panel estimators are used to estimate these models. Clear evidence of heterogeneity amongst forecasters is reported, although the vast majority of forecasters have stabilising expectations at both forecast horizons.

14.1.3   *Direct tests of heterogeneity*

The earlier indirect tests of heterogeneity of expectations do seem to indicate evidence of heterogeneity in the sense that not all agents display the same patterns with respect to error orthogonality and unbiasedness – some provide a rejection of the null, some do not. In this sub-section we consider a set of tests which provide a more direct insight into the issue of heterogeneity. In particular, we consider the Ito (1990) test which facilitates testing both individual and idiosyncratic effects.

According to the Ito test, individual-specific effects emanate from a constant bias amongst foreign exchange participants, rather than from the use of different modelling techniques. For example, suppose individual j forms a forecast at time t and this consists of two parts: X_t, based on publicly available information, I_t, and an individual effect, g_j. For a given forecast horizon, the expected exchange rate for the individual will be the sum of these two parts plus an individual random disturbances term u_{jt}:

$$s_{j,t}^e = X_t + g_j + u_{j,t}. \tag{14.4}$$

The average forecast at time t is then:

$$s_{A,t}^e = X_t + g_A + u_{A,t}. \tag{14.5}$$

Using a normalisation such that g_A equals zero and subtracting (14.5) from (14.4) we get:

$$s_{j,t}^e - s_{A,t}^e = g_j + [u_{j,t} - u_{A,t}]. \tag{14.6}$$

An attractive feature of expression (14.6) is that it is unnecessary for the econometrician to know the exact structure of X_t to be able to recover the individual effect. The latter may be obtained from this equation by regressing the difference between an individual and average forecast onto a constant term: a non-zero value of g_j indicates that an individual's forecasts are biased compared to those of the average forecaster. The importance of a so-called 'idiosyncratic effect' may be gauged by incorporating a piece of the common information set – say past exchange rate changes or the forward premium, – into equation (14.6), that is:

$$s^e_{j,t} = X'_t + g'_j + \beta_j \Delta s_{t-1} + u_{j,t}, \tag{14.7}$$

where X'_t is the common forecast based on I less the lagged exchange rate change and g'_j is the new individual bias. Specifying the equivalent equation for the average forecast and subtracting as earlier implies that:

$$s^e_{jt} - s^e_{At} = g'_j + [\beta_j - \beta_A]\Delta s_{t-1} + [u_{jt} - u_{At}]. \tag{14.8}$$

Individual biases exist if in an estimated version of (14.8) $g'_j \neq 0$, while idiosyncratic effects exist if $\beta_j - \beta_A \neq 0$.

In implementing (14.8), Ito (1990) uses the data set described in Section 14.1.1 and finds that there are important differences between the different industrial classifications. In particular, he finds that around half of the forecasters have significant individual effects. This breaks down in the following way. First, exporters and trading companies are significantly heterogeneous for each of the three horizons and this is revealed solely in terms of individual biases (idiosynchratic effects are not significant). Constant biases are also shown to be important for importers at the 1-month horizon and banks at the 6-month horizon. Ito also reported 'group effects' which relate to the fact that forecasters in the export sector are biased towards yen depreciation (relative to others) and importers are biased towards a yen appreciation (relative to others), and this is described as 'wishful expectations'.

Due to the international nature of their database, MacDonald and Marsh (1996b) are able to push the Ito tests a little further. In particular, the Consensus data set allows calculations of the earlier effects with respect to both the overall average and also to the relevant country average. This, in turn, allows an examination, amongst other aspects, of whether individuals are more inclined towards, say, a dollar appreciation than the overall average or their fellow countrymen. The distinction may be important if the information set is not common to all forecasters, due to time zone or language-induced informational differences: averaging within a country is less likely to result in problems arising from such informational asymmetries. MacDonald and Marsh find very strong evidence of heterogeneity for both the 3- and 12-month horizons. Using the country average or the 'world' average does not change this result, and MacDonald and Marsh infer from this that the informational asymmetries between nations are small and insignificant. In contrast to Ito, MacDonald and Marsh also find evidence of idiosynchratic effects using both the forward premium and the exchange rate change.

Having established that forecasters are heterogeneous, MacDonald and Marsh then go on to test whether such differences of opinion translate into different forecast performances using a version of Prentice's reduced rank statistic. Overall they find that differential forecast performance is indicated for all three currencies at both forecast horizons, but is strongest for the 12-month forecasts and especially for the Japanese yen. However, although there are differences in forecasting performance MacDonald and Marsh demonstrate that very few forecasters out-perform a random walk at short horizons, although a substantial number do over longer horizons.

14.2 Institutional description of the market and market classification[2]

In this section we consider some of the institutional aspects of the foreign exchange market, which have a direct bearing on the market microstructure literature. As we have seen, the institutional structure of a market is crucial for proponents of the market microstructural view, since institutional differences can affect the efficiency of pricing and allocation.

As we saw in Chapter 1, the foreign exchange market differs from some other financial markets in having a role for three types of trade: interbank trade, which accounts for the majority of foreign exchange trade; trade conducted through brokers, which represents the second largest proportion of trade; trade undertaken by private customers (e.g. corporate trade), which represents the smallest amount of trade in the foreign exchange market. The latter group have to make their transactions through banks, since their credit-worthiness cannot be detected by brokers.

Cheung and Chinn (1999) use data from a survey of US-based foreign exchange traders to gain further insight into the operation of the foreign exchange market. In particular, their survey 'attempts to ascertain directly how market participants behave, document their experiences, and solicit their views on the workings of the foreign exchange market'. The survey was conducted between October 1996 and November 1997 and out of a total of 1796 market participants mailed, 142 completed questionnaires were returned to the authors. Some interesting results stem from this survey. First, their survey reveals that in 1992 transactions were apportioned equally between interbank and traditional broker trades but by 1996–7 interbank transactions had fallen to about one-third of the total and traditional brokers lost considerable ground to electronic brokers, such that the latter represented 46% of total trade and the former only 17%. Cheung and Chinn also show that traders have a range of what they regard as conventional spreads – five basis points for the Swiss franc and UK pound against the US dollar and three basis points for the German mark and Japanese yen against the US dollar. In practice Cheung and Chinn find that only a small proportion of bid–ask spreads deviate from the convention (we return later to this point)[3]

As Lyons (2001) notes, the foreign exchange market is distinct from other asset markets in a number of ways. For example, in the foreign exchange market there is no physical location where dealers meet with customers. Furthermore, the transparency of trade is quite different to other asset markets such as equity or bond markets. In these national markets, trades usually have to be disclosed by law within minutes of trade taking place, whereas in the foreign exchange market there is no requirement for such disclosure. If order flow is not generally observed then this means the trading process in the foreign exchange market will be less informative than in other markets.

The agents within banks who conduct trade are referred to as market makers, so-called because they make a market in one or more currencies by providing bid and ask spreads for the currencies. The market makers can trade for their own account (i.e. go long or short in a currency) or on behalf of a client, a term which encompasses an array of players from central banks, to financial firms and traders involved in international trade. A foreign exchange broker on the other hand does not trade on her own behalf but keeps a book of market makers limit orders (orders to buy/sell a specified quantity of foreign exchange at a specified price) from which she, in turn, will quote the best bid/ask rates to market makers. The latter are referred to as the brokers' 'inside spread'. The broker earns a profit by charging a fee for their service of bringing buyers and sellers together. Recently, various automated brokerage systems have become popular and one of these is considered in more detail in Section 14.4.2. In sum, then, the foreign exchange market may be thought of as a multiple dealer market.

As Flood (1991) notes, the interbank market may be described as a decentralised, continuous, open bid, double auction market, while the brokered market is a quasi-centralised, continuous, limit book, single auction market. These terms have the following meaning. In the microstructural literature the degree of centralisation of a market is important because it can have an effect on market efficiency. In centralised markets agents trade on the basis of publicly quoted prices and all traders have access to the same trading opportunities. In contrast, a decentralised market is one in which price quotes and transactions are conducted in private amongst agents. It is usually argued that there are efficiency gains from having centralised prices. This follows if it is assumed that trips are costly. With a centralised market N traders would require N trips compared to a decentralised market where the N agents have to negotiate bilaterally leading to a total of $N(N-1)/2$ trips. The decentralised nature of the foreign exchange market would therefore seem to imply an efficiency loss. However, there are other potential efficiency gains from having such a market structure.

The foreign exchange market is referred to as a continuous market in the sense that trade occurs at its own pace, with transactions being processed as they arrive. In contrast, the kind of market featured in most microeconomic models is a call market in which the Walrasian auctioneer calls out a series of prices and receives buy/sell orders at each price. Transactions are then concluded at a price where the quantities supplied and demanded are equal. The distinction between these two kinds of markets is referred to as the degree of *temporal consolidation*. In call markets trading occurs at pre-appointed times (the calls) with arriving orders retained until the next call. In continuous markets trading occurs at its own pace.

Theoretical work (see, for example, Hahn 1984 and Negishi 1962) indicates how the degree of temporal consolidation can affect the performance of a market. For example, with continuous trading, transactions conducted at the start of the trading day can cause shifts in supply and demand which ultimately affect the prices of later transactions. So it is possible for continuous trading to alter allocations, the process of price discovery and the ultimate equilibrium price relative to the Walrasian 'call' equilibrium. To set against this, however, the periodic batching of orders that occur in a call market can also have a deleterious effect on investors, since the difference in time between the placement and settlement of orders can impose real costs on investors. Therefore in such a market agents may be prepared to pay a *liquidity premium* to trade immediately. Also the lack of continuity between calls means that the flow of information is not continuous and this may introduce uncertainty into the period between calls. Lyons (2001) argues that the extent to which trades are actually 'out of equilibrium' or not depends on the amount of information available to the dealer. For example, if the dealer is not initially sure what the buyer–seller imbalance is, then rational trade can occur in the transition to the new equilibrium (i.e. the dealer is unable to trade using all of the information available to the Walrasian auctioneer).

In sum, a trade-off exists between the allocational efficiency of a Walrasian call system and the informational efficiency of a continuous market. As Flood (1991) notes, it is unclear if the microstructure of the foreign exchange market represents a globally optimal balance of these advantages.

As noted earlier, the interbank market is referred to as an open bid market, while the brokered part of the market is a limit book market. The terms open bid and limit book refer to ways in which price is communicated. The extreme form of open bid is the open outcry system of futures exchanges where buy/sell offers are communicated to all agents in the market. The interbank market approximates this since any agent can contact any bank at any time to obtain a price quote. Of course, the bilateral nature of the negotiations means that not all market participants can be simultaneously informed of the current quotes of a market maker. This, of course, can introduce the possibility of genuine arbitrage possibilities if, say, two market makers can be found whose bid–ask spread does not overlap.

The limit order books[4] of brokers may also impart another layer of inefficiency into the foreign exchange market since only the 'best' bid–ask spreads of brokers are revealed to market makers. Knowledge of the concealed limit order would be of potential value to market makers since an unbalanced book would suggest a future price move in one direction or other. The potential search process of an agent searching for the best quote in the foreign exchange market means the agent is prepared to pay a premium to avoid constant access to a counterparty. The existence of this premium, however, suggests that the foreign exchange market does not provide as an efficient means of communicating prices as a fully centralised market.

The classifications single and double auction refer to the nature of the quoted prices. In a single auction market prices are specified either to buy or sell, whereas in a double auction market participants provide both bid and ask prices. In the foreign exchange market the market makers provide the double auction prices while the broker tries to aggregate single auction quotes into inside spreads. As Flood (1991) notes, this issue is related to the degree of centralisation in a market. Since market makers are absent in a single auction market this, combined with transaction costs, produces a tendency towards centralisation of price information, thereby facilitating the search for a counterparty. Decentralisation, on the other hand, leads to a tendency towards double auction prices, which again facilitates the search for a counterparty.

14.3   Exchange rate volatility and volume: a first pass at market microstructure predictions

A central feature of the microstructural literature as it applies to stock markets is the relationship between the volatility of price (a measure of risk) and the volume of trade, a measure of market turnover. It is a stylised fact that in stock markets this relationship is positive, and, as we shall see later, this kind of relationship also appears to hold in foreign exchange markets. Clark (1973) proposed the mixture of distribution hypothesis (MDH) to explain the positive association between price volatility and volume in terms of a common directing factor. In particular, in Clark's model the daily price change is the sum of a random number of within-day price changes. Given this, the variance of the daily price change is a random variable with a mean proportional to the mean number of daily transactions. By arguing that trading volume is related positively to the number of within-day transactions, Clark obtains a positive relationship between trading volume and the variability of the price change.

Tauchen and Pitts (1983) tie the volume–volatility relationship down in the context of a model where the relationship can take on two forms. First, with an increase in the number of traders, market prices, which can be thought of as an average of traders' reservation prices, become less volatile because averaging involves more observations. Second, a positive relationship can occur for a fixed number of traders if higher trading volume reveals higher disagreement among traders, which is associated with higher price variability. This link is seen to be stronger when new information flows to the market at a higher rate. The Tauchen and Pitts model can be formalised in the following way.

The number of traders, N, is assumed to be non-random and fixed for each day. The number of daily equilibria, I, is also random because the number of new pieces of information arriving to the market each day varies significantly. Summing the within-day price changes and trading volumes gives the daily values:

$$\Delta S = \sum_{i=1}^{I} \Delta S_i, \quad \Delta S_i \sim N(0, \sigma_1^2), \tag{14.9}$$

$$V = \sum_{i=1}^{I} V_i, \quad V_i \sim N(\mu_2, \sigma_2^2), \tag{14.10}$$

where both the daily market price change, ΔS, and volume, V, are mixtures of independent normals, with the same mixing variable, I. Conditional on I, the daily price change and volume are:

$$\Delta S_i \sim \mathcal{N}(0, \sigma_1^2 I), \tag{14.11}$$

$$V_i \sim \mathcal{N}(\mu_2 I, \sigma_2^2 I), \tag{14.12}$$

and it follows that an alternative way of writing this bivariate normal mixture model is:

$$\Delta S = \sigma_1 \sqrt{I} \mathcal{Z}_1, \tag{14.13}$$

$$V = \mu_2 I + \sigma_2 \sqrt{I} \mathcal{Z}_2, \tag{14.14}$$

where $\mathcal{Z}_1$ and $\mathcal{Z}_2$ are independent $\mathcal{N}(0,1)$ variables and $\mathcal{Z}_1$, $\mathcal{Z}_2$ and I are mutually independent variables. Given these expressions for the price change and volume the source of the positive relationship between volume and volatility can be seen immediately by taking the covariance of volume and the price change:

$$\begin{aligned} \mathrm{Cov}(\Delta S^2, V) &= E[\Delta S^2 V] - E[\Delta S^2] \, E[V] \\ &= \sigma_1^2 \mu_2 E[I^2] - \sigma_1^2 \mu_2 (E[I])^2 \\ &= \sigma_1^2 \mu_2 \mathrm{Var}[I] > 0, \end{aligned} \tag{14.15}$$

which will hold empirically as long as the number of traders is fixed. As Tauchen and Pitt note, this relationship makes clear that the positive volume–volatility relationship arises because both ΔS^2 and V are positively related to the mixing variable I. If the mixing variable has no variation – $\mathrm{Var}[I] = 0$ – then, of course, the positive volume–volatility relationship would vanish.

In the Tauchen and Pitt model, the variance term σ_1^2 is assumed to depend both on the variance of a 'common' noise component, σ_ϕ^2, agreed upon by all traders, and on the variance of 'disagreement' component, σ_φ^2, scaled by the number of active traders:

$$\sigma_1^2 \equiv \mathrm{Var}[\Delta S_t] = \sigma_\phi^2 + \frac{\sigma_\varphi^2}{N}. \tag{14.16}$$

It then follows that volatility increases with the rate of information flow, I, increases with the common noise, increases with the trader disagreement and decreases with the number of active traders. The volume parameters, in turn, can be written approximately as:

$$\mu_2 = \sigma_\varphi N, \tag{14.17}$$

and

$$\sigma_2^2 = \sigma_\varphi^2 N. \tag{14.18}$$

It therefore follows that turnover increases with the rate of information flow I, with trader disagreement ψ, and with the number of active traders N. As Jorion (1996) notes, although appealing the model has the limitation that the mixing variable is unobservable and that the unknown parameters, σ_ϕ^2, σ_φ^2 and $\mathcal{N}$, likely change over time. In their empirical application of the model to US treasury bill futures, Tauchen and Pitts assumed a lognormal distribution for I and a logistic model for the number of traders and find that the model matches the general trends in the data.

Jorion (1996) tests the mixture of distributions hypothesis of Tauchen and Pitts using deutsche mark currency futures quotes for the period January 1985–February 1992. In particular, he estimates the following regression equation:

$$R_{t+1}^2 = a + b_1\sigma_t^{2,\,\text{ISD}} + b_2 h_{t+1} + b_3 E_t(v) + c[v_{t+1} - E_t(v)] + \varepsilon_{t+1}, \quad (14.19)$$

where R_{t+1}^2 is the variance over the next day of the futures rate, $\sigma^{2,\,\text{ISD}}$ is forecast variance from an option implied standard deviations (ISD) (extracted using Black's (1976) option pricing model), h is a GARCH(1,1) measure of the forecast variance, v is log volume and expected volume is generated using an ARMA time series model. The option data are taken from the Chicago Mercantile Exchange's closing quotes for deutsche mark (DM) currency options and the volume of trading is taken as the total volume of daily trades in DM contracts.

Using equation (14.19) Jorion demonstrates two main results. First, by sequentially regressing the squared return against the two measures of volatility, he shows that they are both positive and statistically significant. However, when both are entered together in the regression only the coefficient on the ISD measure is significantly positive (indeed this is shown to produce an almost unbiased forecast of the next day's variance). Second, he shows that the both expected and unexpected volume are positively related to the volatility measure but that only the unexpected measure is statistically significant, a finding which is consistent with the Tauchen and Pitts model.

14.3.1   *Volatility and volume and survey-based measures of heterogeneity*

The effects of trader heterogeneity, or disagreement, on volume and volatility, as predicted in the Tauchen and Pitts model, have been explored in a number of the papers, discussed in Section 14.1, which use survey data to measure heterogeneity. For example, Frankel and Froot (1990b) measure heterogeneity as the percentage standard deviation of forecasts across respondents in an MMS weekly survey of expectations of the British pound, German mark, Japanese yen and Swiss franc for the period October 1984–February 1988. Trading volume is measured by the weekly number of nearest-term future contracts traded on the IMM of the Chicago Mercantile Exchange and volatility is measured by the squared percentage change each 15 minutes in the futures price, averaged over the week. Using these data

Granger causality tests of the following form are run:

$$\sigma_t = \sum_{i=1}^{p} \alpha_i \sigma_{t-i} + \sum_{i=1}^{p} \beta_i \, \text{svol}_{t-i} + \sum_{i=1}^{p} \varphi_i \, \text{volu}_{t-i} + \varepsilon_t,$$

$$\text{svol}_t = \sum_{i=1}^{p} \alpha_i \sigma_{t-i} + \sum_{i=1}^{p} \beta_i \, \text{svol}_{t-i} + \sum_{i=1}^{p} \varphi_i \, \text{volu}_{t-i} + \varepsilon_t, \qquad (14.20)$$

$$\text{volu}_t = \sum_{i=1}^{p} \alpha_i \sigma_{t-i} + \sum_{i=1}^{p} \beta_i \, \text{svol}_{t-i} + \sum_{i=1}^{p} \varphi_i \, \text{volu}_{t-i} + \varepsilon_t,$$

where σ denotes the standard deviation of exchange rate predictions, svol is their measure of exchange rate volatility, and volu is futures trading volume. Frankel and Froot show that the measure of dispersion Granger causes both volume and volatility in 3 out of the 4 currencies. They also report a high contemporaneous correlation between volume and volatility. Frankel and Froot also demonstrate that the patterns of causality are complex in the sense that volatility also Granger causes dispersion. The finding that dispersion of expectations Granger causes both volume and volatility would seem to provide support for the noise trader paradigm and also for the models of Epps and Epps (1976) and Copeland (1976); also some evidence of bidirectional causality between the heterogeneity of expectations and turnover is reported in MacDonald and Marsh (1996b).

MacDonald and Marsh (1996b) estimate the following reduced form (which they derive from a mean-variance model of trading volume due to Grossman 1976 and Varian 1989):

$$T_t = a + b\sigma(s_{it}^e) + c\sigma(s_t) + dT_{t-1} + \text{seasonals}, \qquad (14.21)$$

where T is turnover, calculated as the daily average dollar value of trade in the relevant IMM futures pit on the Chicago Mercantile Exchange, $\sigma(s_{it}^e)$ is a survey-based measure of expectations (based on the Consensus data set noted earlier) and $\sigma(s_t)$ is the current exchange rate change. This equation is estimated over the period 1989–92 (monthly data frequency) for the USD bilaterals of the German mark, pound sterling and Japanese yen. MacDonald and Marsh find that for both the yen and mark the dispersion of expectations is positive and significant at the 5% level and the standard deviation of the actual exchange rate change also proves to be significant for these currencies. These effects are less clear-cut for the pound sterling, a result which MacDonald and Marsh ascribe to the distortions caused by the pound's entry to and exit from the ERM.

Using Consensus survey data as their measure of dispersion, Chionis and MacDonald (1997) use Granger causality testing methods to examine the interrelationships between volume, volatility and dispersion (for the bilateral US dollar rates of the BP, DM and JY spot rates) as in (14.20). They report 'strong evidence of heterogeneity causing both volume and volatility'. Chionis and MacDonald push their tests further and, in particular, use GARCH modelling to estimate the conditional volatility of the three currencies and they then consider the informational content of the estimated conditional volatility. For example, in the context of the stock market literature, Lamoureux and Lastrapes (1990) have suggested that conditional volatility acts as a good proxy for trading volume. Chionis and MacDonald test this hypothesis for currencies by introducing volume into their estimated GARCH equations. They find that the original GARCH estimates are little changed by the inclusion of volume, thereby casting doubt on the validity of the Lamoureux and Lastrapes (1990) hypothesis for the foreign exchange market.

14.3.2   ARCH- and GARCH-based estimates of conditional volatility and market microstructure

In Chapter 1 we noted that volatility, and particularly the clustering of high frequency exchange rate movements, seems to be adequately captured by ARCH and GARCH models. Such modelling methods have also been used for the specific purpose of gaining extra insight into the validity of the market microstructure hypothesis. We now consider some of these ARCH and GARCH tests of volatility.

Goodhart and Guigale (1993) (Wasserfallen and Zimmerman 1985 conduct a similar study) exploit an hourly exchange rate data base (US dollar bilaterals of pound, DM, yen and Swiss franc) for the period 2 January 1986–July 1986 (a total of 3409 observations), supplied by Money Market Services International. Using ARCH and GARCH methods they demonstrate that exchange rates seem to overshoot, in an exaggerated way, in response to new information and they take this as evidence against the efficient markets hypothesis. They also report that daily peaks in volatility occur at the start of each trading day and a special peak occurs at the overlap of the opening of the New York market and the closing of the European market, which they take to be evidence in favour of the so-called news hypothesis (see Chapter 15). However, they also find that exchange rate volatility is smaller during intervals when trading is smaller, such as weekends and during lunch breaks, and is abnormally large during the first hour of Monday trading for each currency in its domestic market (this holds even when markets are open in other time zones). This suggests that either residents have a comparative advantage at processing news of their own currencies or perhaps trading itself generates volatility. Neither of these interpretations is consistent with the conventional definition of market efficiency, although from our discussions earlier it should be clear that they are consistent with the market microstructure view of informational asymmetries.

A number of researchers have sought to determine if the volatility clustering in foreign exchange markets, discussed in Chapter 1, has as its source clustering in information flows. For example, Engle *et al.* (1990) examine four separate foreign exchange market locations: Europe, New York, Pacific and Tokyo. Under the assumption that information arrivals in each of the markets are uncorrelated with arrivals in other markets, a test of increased volatility spilling over from one market to another is regarded as *prima facie* evidence that information processing is the source of the volatility clustering. Such volatility spillovers are referred to by Engle *et al.* as 'meteor showers'. Using intra-daily data on the yen–dollar exchange rate they show that each market's volatility is indeed significantly affected by changes in the volatility in the other markets (with the exception of the Tokyo market) and this is taken as supportive of their information processing hypothesis. Baillie and Bollerslev (1991) confirm the meteor shower hypothesis using hourly data on four US dollar bilaterals. However, they also find some evidence for the importance of market-specific volatility, and the volatility during the day is shown to exhibit a distinct and very similar pattern across currencies: increases in volatility occur around the opening of the London, New York and Tokyo markets.

14.4   Market microstructure and two key variables: the bid–ask spread and order flow

In contrast to the macro-based approach to exchange rate modelling considered at some length in this book, Lyons (2001) argues central to the micro-based approach are two key variables (what he refers to as the hallmarks of the micro-based approach), namely, the bid–ask spread and order flow. In this section we consider each of these key microstructural variables in some detail.

14.4.1   The bid–ask spread – some theoretical considerations

The bid–ask spread, as we have seen, can be thought of as an important measure of transaction costs and is also an important reflection of trading mechanisms. As Lyons (2001) notes, although there are other important indicators of the trading environment data on spreads are readily available, often on a high frequency basis, for most financial markets, including the foreign exchange market. As Flood (1991) notes, the existence of a bid and ask price for a currency (indeed for any financial asset) seems a violation of the efficient markets hypothesis (EMH) since it implies the existence of two prices on the same commodity. There are, however, a number of ways of reconciling these two prices with the EMH. First, there is the dealer services argument, originally formalised by Demsetz (1968). In this, agents are prepared to pay a dealer compensation for the costs of acting as a specialist – the jobbers turn – so that they may obtain what Demsetz referred to as *predictable immediacy*. This concept is linked to that of liquidity. For example, in a busy market a continuous stream of buyers and sellers would generate predictable immediacy as a by-product of their trading and such liquidity would be a public good. Since the foreign exchange market has no apparent barriers to entry or exit, and can support a large number of market makers, its liquidity will be close to a public good and the bid–ask spread will simply cover the cost of processing orders and not monopoly rents for predictable immediacy.

A second explanation for the bid–ask spread was originally proposed by Bagehot (1971) and relates to adverse selection. In this set-up, as before, traders are prepared to pay a *liquidity premium* for the service of predictable immediacy. However, in this model traders have inside, or asymmetric, information about, say, a potential arbitrage opportunity, and can engage in favourable speculation against the market maker. The adverse selection arises because in a market with competing market makers, the one who interacts with the trader with inside information is the loser. In a decentralised market with no consensus on price, setting a single price is a dangerous strategy for a trader because he is vulnerable to the inside arbitrage opportunity. By setting a bid–ask spread the market maker allows a tolerance for error and it is easier to get spreads to overlap (which would represent a consensus) than to get a scalar price to overlap. The spread therefore gives the market maker some degree of protection from adverse selection arbitrage. Bagehot (1971) argued that the losses incurred by the market maker from the better-informed traders must be compensated by the less well-informed traders, and this idea has been formalised in the asymmetric information models of, for example, Admati and Pfleider (1988) and Subrahmanyam (1991) and we consider these models and their predictions here.

In the model of Admati and Pfleider (1988), there are three types of agents: informed traders, who only trade on terms advantageous to them; discretionary liquidity traders who must trade over the trading day, but have some discretion at what point in the day to trade; non-discretionary liquidity traders who must trade at a given time during the day, irrespective of cost. In high volume periods both informed and discretionary traders are attracted to trade. The informed are attracted because they are better able to disguise their activity due to the behaviour of the uninformed traders. The discretionary liquidity traders are also attracted at this point because the increased activity amongst the informed traders implies increased competition amongst them and the cost of trading is lowered for the uninformed. Using this model they are able to explain some of the stylised facts of the NYSE stock market: the high volume exhibited at the open and close of trade is explained by the earlier kind of equilibrium mechanism while the concurrent high variance at open and close follows on from the increased activity of the informed traders who exploit previously private information.

Subrahmanyam (1991) builds on the model of Admati and Pfleider (1988) to show that their key result, that increased activity by the informed trader lowers the costs to the uninformed who pay the price of the informed, depends on the assumption that the informed traders are risk neutral. If, in contrast, the informed traders are risk averse then Subrahmanyam shows that increased activity by them actually leads to an *increase* in the trading costs of liquidity traders.

A further way in which this has been modelled is in terms of inventory considerations. For example, in the so-called random walk inventory model (starting with Barnea and Logue 1975) the market maker has a desired inventory level (equal to zero) and a constant spread is shifted up and down on a price scale to ensure that the expected change in inventory is always zero; hence the level of inventory follows a random walk. However, this has the unpleasant consequence that the market maker inevitably becomes bankrupt. This follows because market makers face finite capitalisation levels which, in turn, force upper and lower bounds on the level of allowable inventories. When inventory follows a random walk it will reach the upper or lower bounds in a finite number of trades, with a probability of one (see Ross 1983). Dynamic optimisation models (see, for example, Amihud and Mendelson 1980 and Ho and Stoll 1981) resolve this problem. In such models the market maker faces a stochastic order flow and will optimise his bid–ask spread over time by shifting both the bid and ask downward (upward) and increase the width of the spread when a positive (negative) inventory has accumulated.

For example, in the price-inventory model of Amihud and Mendelson (1980) a market maker is faced with buy and sell order flows and these flows are assumed to arrive as independent Poisson processes. The buy and sell arrival rates, defined as d and x, respectively, are assumed to be a function of the bid, B, and ask, A, prices quoted by the broker:

$$d = D(A) \quad \text{and} \quad x = X(B). \tag{14.22}$$

The inventory level is denoted by k:

$$k \in \{-\Sigma, \ldots, \Lambda\},$$

where Σ and Λ denote the largest allowable short and long positions, respectively, and d_k an x_k denote the order arrival rates when prices are set as functions of the inventory level:

$$d_k = D(A(k)) \quad \text{and} \quad x_k = X(B(k)). \tag{14.23}$$

The expected time at position k is given by the Poisson process known as $1/(d_k + x_k)$. Given this, the probability that the next order will be a buy (sell) order is $d_k/(d_k + x_k)$ $(x_k/(d_k + x_k))$. Hence the expected cash flow per unit of time at position k is given by:

$$Q(k) = \left[\frac{d_k}{d_k + x_k} \cdot A(k) - \frac{x_k}{d_k + x_k} \cdot B(k) \right] \cdot (d_k + x_k)$$
$$= d_k \cdot A(k) - x_k \cdot A(k). \tag{14.24}$$

The objective of the market maker is to maximise the expected profit per unit of time, as given by:

$$\pi = \sum_{k=-\Sigma}^{\Lambda} \Phi_k Q(k),$$

where Φ is the probability of being at inventory level k. The solution to the optimising problem gives values for $A(k)$ and $B(k)$. The market maker controls inventory by adjusting prices up (down) to make an investor sale (purchase) more likely when the inventory level is low (high). As the inventory nears its bounds the spread must widen to avoid the issue of inventory following a random walk.

The earlier discussion deals with market maker spreads – the determination of brokers spreads are usually analysed separately. As we have seen, a brokered spread is the combination of the best bid and best ask price received by the broker as separate limit orders. Cohen *et al.* (1979) model limit orders as if they are generated by 'yawl' distributions, named after their resemblance to a sailing boat. Such distributions are argued to satisfy heuristics for the incentives of investors placing limit orders (see also Cohen *et al.* 1981). However, such models have been developed for the stock market, where brokerage is seen as a service providing predictable immediacy. As we noted earlier, in our discussion of market makers, this is not such an issue in the foreign exchange market since there are a large number of market makers capable of providing this immediacy. Instead, as Flood (1991) notes, one key advantage of a bank trading through a broker is that the name of the bank remains anonymous until a deal is agreed and at that stage only the counterparty knows the identity of the bank. Such anonymity is valuable because in revealing a buy–sell position a market maker is potentially at a disadvantage compared to the situation where he does not need to reveal his position.[5] Additionally, anonymity can be advantageous to market makers who would not normally contact each other directly. However, a theoretical model of anonymity has still to be developed and therefore the determination of the broker bid–ask spreads in the foreign exchange market is less well understood than that of market maker spreads.

14.4.2   *Empirical evidence on the bid–ask spread*

As we have seen, an implication of the inventory-carrying cost models is that the costs in such models arise as a result of market makers having open positions in currencies and they can be related to price risk, interest rate costs and trading activity. In terms of price risk, the idea is that as exchange rate volatility increases, risk-averse traders will increase the bid–ask spread in order to offset the increased risk of losses. There is a lot of evidence in support of this positive relationship between the spread and volatility. For example, Fieleke (1975), Overturf (1982) and Glassman (1987) all show that spreads increase with recent volatility. Using GARCH-based methods to model exchange rate uncertainty, Glassman (1987), Boothe (1988) and Bollerslev and Melvin (1994) and Bessembinder (1994) show that spreads are positively correlated with GARCH-expected volatility. In the study of Jorion (1996), discussed in Section 14.3, the implied volatility from option prices is shown to be positively related to the spread and, indeed, it is shown to be a superior measure of volatility compared to the GARCH models used in other studies. Using a term structure effect as a proxy for the cost of capital from investing in short-term investments, Bessembinder (1994) shows that this has little effect on the spread.

A number of studies have also shown that trading activity is an important determinant of the spread. For example, Glassman (1997) and Bessembinder (1994) and Jorion (1996) show that at time when markets are known to be less volatile– at weekends and holidays – spreads tend to increase. Trading activity can also be captured by volume and Cornell (1978) has argued that volume should be negatively related to the spread because of economies of scale leading to more efficient processing of trades and greater competition amongst market makers. Jorion (1996), in turn, argues that this implies that expected volume should also be negatively related to the spread, a relationship which is formally captured in the model of Easley and O'Hara (1992). Furthermore, unexpected trading volume, since it reflects contemporaneous volatility through the mixture of distribution hypothesis, should be positively related to bid–ask spreads. In the context of the study discussed in Section 14.3, Jorion (1996) confirms the negative relationship between volatility and expected volume and he interprets these results as a confirmation that bid–ask spreads reflect primarily inventory carrying costs that depend primarily on price uncertainty and trading activity.

Hseih and Kleidon (1996) empirically examine the predictions from the standard informational asymmetry models of Admati and Pfleiderer (1988) and Subrahmanyam (1991), discussed earlier. In particular, Hseih and Kleidon (1996) use the data of Bollerslev and Domowitz (1993) (these data are Rueters indicative bid–ask quotes for the period 9 April–30 June 1989), in two markets, London and New York. They show that the volume and volatility in these markets follows the same U-shaped pattern as in the NYSE: volume and volatility is much greater at the open and close of business. However, they also show that the bid–ask spread actually goes up at the open and close of markets and this is at odds with the key prediction of the Admati and Pfleiderer (1988) model. Subrahmanyam argues that this kind of result is consistent with his extension of the model to risk-averse traders: the increased trading by informed traders results in lower market liquidity and higher costs. However, Hseih and Kleidon (1996) argue that the asymmetric information models of Admati and Pfleiderer (1988) and Subrahmanyam (APS) are not consistent with foreign exchange data on spreads and volatility for two reasons. First, Subrahmanyam's extension of the Admati and Pfleiderer model is at the cost of loosing the main prediction of their model, namely, the concentrated trading equilibrium to account for simultaneous high volume and high volatility. Second, another interesting feature of the empirical evidence presented by Hseih and Kleidon (1996) is that they find that at the time of the close of the London market, when volume and volatility is high, there is no corresponding high volume and volatility pattern in New York and this contradicts the kind of assymetric information model of APS where knowledge of the economic structure is common even in the presence of idiosynchratic information.

Hseih and Kleidon (1996) propose two alternative explanations for the kind of results that they report. First, they propose using a broader class of information models and, in particular, those models which relax the assumption that traders have perfect knowledge about the preferences and beliefs of other traders in the market. What they have in mind is that with differential information sets at the start of a day's trade, market participants need to get a 'feel' for the market at that time. The most important elements of this feel are participants in the market at that point in time and their trading behaviour immediately prior to the trading period. Hsieh and Kleidon (1996) go on to argue that 'traders report that, until they have got a feel for the market they are uncertain of their view and hence, for example, of whether they will be going long or short one or another currency in their early trading during the day. This translates into initial high spreads, with rapidly changing quotes as traders develop their view for the current trading period.' This kind of behaviour would explain the combination of high volatility–volume at the start of the day's trade. To explain the same phenomenon at close of trade, they appeal to inventory-based models.

It is well known that many market makers cannot hold a net open position overnight. Therefore traders who have to close out a position at the end of the day will, as close of trade approaches, have increasingly inelastic demand to trade (assuming, of course, that they have accumulated foreign exchange during the day) and are more likely to accept a relatively poor price to accomplish trade. The effects of inventory on prices are now well known (see Garman 1976 and Ho and Stoll 1983 for stock markets and Lyons 1995 for the foreign exchange market): high quote volatility and spreads at close of trade are linked to the activity of traders who are attempting to close out their positions.

The bid–ask data used in academic research often involves using so-called indicative quotes rather than actual price at which trade takes place. Does the use of the former as a proxy for the latter matter? Goodhart *et al.* (1996) address this issue by analysing a day (16 June 1993) in the life of the Reuters 2000–2 automated electronic trading system. This dealing system allows a bank dealer to enter, buy and or sell prices directly into the system thereby avoiding the need for a human, voice-based, broker (and it is therefore seen as more cost effective). The D2000–2 records the *touch*, which is the highest bid and lowest ask. This differs importantly from indicative foreign exchange pages which show the latest update of the bid and ask entered by a single identified bank. The system also shows the quantity that the bank was willing to deal in, which is shown in integers of $1 million. The limit orders are also stored in these systems, but are not revealed. A member of the trading system (i.e. another bank) can hit either the bid or ask via his own computer terminal. The trading system then checks if the deal is prudential to both parties and if it is the deal goes ahead, with the transaction price being posted on the screen. Associated with the price is the change in the quantity of the bid (ask) and also in the price offered if the size of the deal exhausts the quantity offered at the previous price.

A continuous record of all transactions was available to Goodhart *et al.* for the USD/JPY, DM/JPY, USD/CHF, DEM/CHF, USD/DEM, DEM/FRF. In particular, a record of actual, trades, prices at which they took place and volumes. They find that the time series properties of the quote series follow a negative MA1 process, transaction prices appear to follow a random walk, and that the sequence of trades at the bid and ask is non-normally distributed (in particular, it has a fat-tailed distribution). They also find that there is a strong two-way relationship between the frequency of quote revisions and the frequency of transactions within a period. They attribute the underlying cause of this relationship to the arrival of new information. They also demonstrate that when a deal exhausts the quantity on offer this then affects volatility, spreads and quote revision. Perhaps the most interesting aspect of this study is the comparison between the properties of the actual transactions prices culled from the 2000–2 with the indicative bid–ask quotes contained on the Reuters FXFX page. They find that the levels of the two prices (i.e. average of bid–ask) have very similar properties but that the behaviour of the touch from the 2000–2 is very different from the bid–ask spread derived from the FXFX, and so using the latter would give a very poor indication of how market spreads evolve over time.

In their study, referred to earlier, Cheung and Chinn (1999) show that traders have a range of what they regard as conventional bid–ask spreads – five basis points for the Swiss franc and UK pound against the US dollar and three basis points for the German mark and Japanese yen against the US dollar and in practice they find that only a small proportion of bid–ask spreads deviate from the convention. They note that the most popular reason for adopting the conventional spread is to 'maintain an equitable and reciprocal trading relationship', since offering quotes with a conventional spread is one of the key ways a trader can establish his reputation. Of those dealers who do deviate from the convention the majority offer narrower spreads and this is because some professional dealers like to demonstrate to customers they are able to bear greater risk by offering a tighter price. The most cited reason for deviating from the conventional spread and increasing the spread is a 'thin and hectic market' which is seen as reflecting increased volatility and uncertainty. For example, 43% of the responses claimed 'increased market volatility', before/after a major news release and 'unexpected change in market activity' as the main driving forces of uncertainty. This kind of result seems to match the results of Jorion (1996) that there is a correlation between volatility and bid–ask spreads. Trading profits turn out to play only a minor role in setting spreads and this is because dealers make most of their money on rate changes rather than from the spread itself.

Cheung and Chinn (1999) also find that the DM/USD and Yen/USD markets are fairly competitive in terms of the make up of the players. However, the smaller dollar–pound and Swiss franc markets are much more dominated by the larger banks. The large players are perceived by the survey respondents to have a better customer and market network which give them better information on order flow and the activity of other trading banks. This would seem to reinforce Lyons' (1997) view that order flow can be used to explain trading volume.

14.4.3   Order flow – how does it affect price?

Perhaps the key variable in the microstructural approach is order flow, which is the conduit through which the actions and interactions of individuals is revealed. It is Lyons' second hallmark of the microstructural approach. Order flow is transaction volume that is signed. That is, if an agent approaches a bank dealer and buys (sells) 1000 euros, the transaction volume is 1000 and the order flow +1000 (−1000). Summing the order flow over time indicates if there has been net selling (negative sum) or net buying (positive sum) over a period. In terms of a broker order, flow has a slightly different interpretation since they, as we have seen, have a limit order book containing limit orders. The latter are the passive side of any transaction (as in the last example where the quoting dealer is on the passive side of the transaction). Orders to a broker which require immediate action – market orders – generate the signed order flow described earlier.

In the foreign exchange market order flow is important since it conveys information to market makers (and researchers) about views of agents involved in buying and selling foreign exchange. In other words, agents' views of economic fundamentals and non-fundamentals, be they noise or technical analysis, are transmitted through order flow. If this view is correct it has the radical implication that even if one is interested in the determination of exchange rates in terms of macroeconomic fundamentals, it is simpler to focus directly on order flow rather than the large range of macroeconomic fundamentals discussed elsewhere in the book.

A figure from Lyons (2001) illustrates the importance of order flow. Figure 14.1 shows that information processing has two stages. First, non-dealers, such as hedge funds, interpret fundamentals and this shows up in order flow. In a second stage non-dealers' interpretation of order flow determines the price. Since not all information is private in foreign exchange markets, foreign exchange dealers can, of course, learn about influences on price from publicly available information. However, even if all information is publicly available, order flow can be important in conveying information if different dealers *interpret* information differently (what Lyons refers to as the mapping between the information set and prices may not be publicly known). But as we have said, not all information in foreign exchange markets is publicly available. Private information can also be transmitted through order flow when a central bank places an order with a dealer for foreign exchange. Exporters and importers can also signal through order flow information about how the current account is likely to evolve, information which would not otherwise be privy to dealers.

In one of the first foreign exchange microstructural models, Lyons (1991) models customer order flow as the source of information asymmetry amongst dealers. The main result in this paper is to show that the greater the market power and risk-aversion of dealers, the less revealing are prices. Lyons (1995) derives an estimatable reduced-form equation from an extension of a model by Madhavan and Smidt (1991) which is designed to capture the way that order flow affects price in microstructure theory through the inventory-control and asymmetric-information channels (as discussed in the previous section). Lyons (1995) uses data from

Figure 14.1 The two stages of information processing.

Source: Lyons (2001).

The Rueters D2000–1 trading system for 5 trading days of the week 3–7 August 1992, from the start of trading at 8.30 am to 1.30 pm Eastern Standard Time. The data set has three components: the first includes the time-stamped quotes, prices and quantities for all the direct inter-dealer transactions of a single DM/USD dealer; the second is the same dealer's position cards which include all indirect (i.e. brokered) transactions; the final component includes the time-stamped prices and quantities for transactions involving a leading broker operating in the same market as the dealer (but not the same individual as the dealer). The estimated reduced-form equation is:

$$\Delta P_{it} = \beta_0 + \beta_1 Q_{it} + \beta_2 I_{it} + \beta_3 I_{it-1} + \beta_4 D_{it} + \beta_5 D_{it-1} + \beta_6 B_t + \beta_1 v_{it-1} + v_{it},$$

(14.25)

where ΔP_{it} is the change in the incoming transaction price of the DM/USD over the period $t-1$ to t, Q_{it} is the incoming order (flow) transacted at dealer i's quoted prices which is positive for purchase and negative for sales; I is dealer i's inventory at the end of period t. D is an indicator variable with value 1, if the incoming order is a purchase, and -1 if a sale; B is the net quantity of third party brokered trading over the previous two minutes which is positive for buyer-initiated trades and negative for seller-initiated trades. The estimated version of (14.25) is:

$$\Delta P_{it} = -1.30 + 1.44\ Q_{it} - 0.98\ I_{it} + 0.79\ I_{it-1}$$
$$\underset{(0.96)}{} \quad \underset{(3.10)}{} \quad \underset{(3.59)}{} \quad \underset{(3.00)}{}$$
$$+ 10.15\ D_{it} - 8.93\ D_{it-1} + 0.69\ B_t - 0.09\ v_{it-1} + v_{it} \quad R^2 = 0.23,$$
$$\underset{(4.73)}{} \quad \underset{(6.12)}{} \quad \underset{(2.21)}{} \quad \underset{(2.55)}{}$$

(14.26)

where t-ratios are in brackets. The coefficients on the information variables – Q and B – and the coefficients on the inventory variables – I_t and I_{t-1} – are correctly signed and statistically significant. For example, the size of β_1 implies that the dealer widens his spread by about 2.8 (1.4 doubled) pips per $10 million (the increment traded) to protect against adverse selection. The inventory-control coefficient, β_3, indicates that the dealer changes his DM/USD rate by about 0.8 pips for every $10 million of net open position. The coefficients on the indicator variables, D_t and D_{t-1}, which measure the effective spread for Q_{it} when it is close to zero, are very significant and correctly signed. The stong inventory control effect on price that Lyons reports contrasts with prior work on the NYSE and futures markets. Lyons speculates that the information captured by the information channel may be information about aggregate inventories (as opposed to the idiosynchratic inventories under the inventory channel).

In a follow-up paper, Lyons (1996) uses the same model structure and data set as in Lyons (1995) in an attempt to discriminate between two views of trading intensity: the event uncertainty view and the so-called 'hot potato' view. The former view indicates that trades are more informative when trading intensity is high, while the latter predicts that trades are more informative when trading intensity is low. The work of Easley and O'Hara (1992) gives a justification for the former prediction. In their model when new information is received by a trader there is some probability, ρ, that an informed trader has received 'good news' and a probability $(1 - \rho)$ of no new information. Easley and O'Hara show that if there is no trade at time t a rational dealer raises the probability that he attaches to the no-information event and lowers the probability of news having occurred. Conversely, if there is a large volume of trade at time t the dealer will raise the probability of news having occurred. The 'hot potato' prediction is based on the informational asymmetry view of Amanti and Pfleiderer (1988), discussed earlier. Recall that in this model discretionary liquidity traders try to minimise their losses to informed traders by clustering together in their trading. Owing to this clustering, trades occurring when intensity is high tend to be less informative.

These predictions are tested using equation (14.25) where the focus is on the information on order flow given by β_1. In particular, Lyons (1996) tests whether the coefficient β_1 is sensitive to inter-transaction time and, if so, in which direction. The event uncertainty view predicts a higher value of β_1 when inter-transaction times are short, while the hot potato (liquidity) hypothesis predicts a lower value of β_1 when inter-transaction times are short. In practice this is achieved by introducing a dummy variable into equation (14.25):

$$\Delta P_{it} = \beta_0 + \beta_1 s_t Q_{it} + \beta_1' l_t Q_{it} + \beta_2 I_{it} + \beta_3 I_{it-1} + \beta_4 D_{it}$$
$$+ \beta_5 D_{it-1} + \beta_6 B_t + \beta_1 v_{it-1} + v_{it}, \tag{14.27}$$

where, of variables not defined previously, s_t equals 1 if inter-transaction time is short and is 0 otherwise. The dummy l_t is 0 if inter-transaction time is short, and is 1 otherwise. Lyons' estimates of (14.27) show strong support for the hot potato hypothesis in the sense that the β_1 coefficient, which measures the information effect of incoming trades with short inter-transaction times, is insignificant, while β_1', which measures the information effect of incoming trades with short inter-transaction times, is significant. Lyons' pushes his test further by exploring another implication of the hot potato hypothesis, namely, that clustered trading is more likely to be of the hot potato variety if trades follow in the same direction. The s dummy in (14.27) now equals 1 if inter-transaction time is both short and the previous incoming trade has the same direction. An o dummy is introduced which takes a value of 1 if inter-transaction time is both short and the previous incoming trade has the opposite direction. Lyons finds that the β_1 coefficient times s is insignificant whilst the β_1 coefficient times o is significant, evidence which he interprets as favourable to the hot potato hypothesis. Lyons also finds evidence that trades which occur when quote intensity is high are significantly more informative than trades occurring when quoting intensity is low and he interprets this as evidence that the hot potato and event uncertainty views of order flow are complementary: both effects are operative in the market but the hot potato effect simply dominates when trading is most intense.

As in the work of Lyons (1996), Yao (1998) analyses D2000–1 data for a single New York dealer for the period 1 November–8 December, 1995 (25 days of trade). In addition to the advantage of the longer time period compared to Lyons, Yao's dealer also has a substantial volume of trade with non-dealer customers (25% relative to 1% in the case of the Lyons data set) making his mix of trade more representative of the market average.

Evans (1997) also uses Reuters D 2000–1 data, sourced from a customised feed at the Bank of England, on interbank trading for the period 1 May–31 August, 1996. In particular, he has access to time-stamped tick-by-tick data on all transactions for nine USD bilateral currencies (the price, a bought-and-sold indicator and cumulative trading volume). This data has the advantage over that of Lyons and Yao since it contains 24 hour transaction data on the whole of the interbank market, rather than one dealer, and makes it possible to analyse order flow's role in price determination for the overall market. As Lyons (2001) notes, the fact that this data set spans such a long time span, and for so many currencies, is important since it allows analysing exchange rate determination from more of an asset price perspective than is possible with the other data sets and, second, it permits analysis of intra-day patterns with more precision than prior studies (noted earlier) which used indicative quotes. However, to set against these advantages, the data set only consists of transaction prices, rather than the spread, and also does not include the inventory position of dealers. Although the data is date-stamped to the second decimal place, it is not necessarily continuous and for this reason Evans analyses the data on a 5 minute by 5 minute basis. He shows that there is pronounced heterogeneity across the markets in the sense that, in terms of transactions, the DM is a much more active market than either the guilder or krona.

The nature of the data allows Evans to construct measures of market-wide demand for currencies of the form:

$$D_t = \frac{(\text{Number of dollar purchases}) - (\text{Number of dollar sales})}{\text{Number of dollar purchases} + \text{sales}}, \qquad (14.28)$$

and he finds that there is a strong statistically positive correlation between this excess demand measure and the change in the exchange rate. Evans argues that the source of this correlation can be traced to an informational asymmetry between traders during bilateral conversations. In particular, the nature of the foreign exchange market – decentralised trading, lack of transparency and heterogenous information – means that there is a tendency of under-adjustment of quotes with respect to excess demand and the lack of transparency stops traders from observing the extent to which the arrival of private information is correlated across the market. This, in turn, creates the informational asymmetry referred to earlier.

Using a VAR analysis, Evans also examines the interactions between the transaction prices, quantities and quotes. This analysis suggests that the posting of quotes is a distinct activity rather than an adjunct of trading, although the data also indicate that quote and trading activity are not made independently from each other. Furthermore, changes in trading activity within the interbank market significantly affect quotes, while innovations in quote activity affect transactions. These complex interactions are not consistent with any extant microstructure model.

Evans and Lyons (2002) re-examine the portfolio-balance approach to the exchange rate, discussed in Chapter 7, in a market microstructure setting. They set-up what they call a micro-portfolio-balance model which is designed to show how the dealing process reveals information contained in order flow. The model has N foreign exchange dealers and a continuum of non-dealer customers, assumed to be the public. Within each day, there are assumed to be three rounds of trading: the first round where dealers trade with the public; the second round where dealers trade among themselves to spread risk; and round three in which dealers trade for a second time with the public to share risk more widely. After T trading days the payoff to holding foreign exchange on day $T + 1$ is V, which is composed of a series of realised payoff increments, R:

$$V = \sum_{t=1}^{T+1} R_t, \tag{14.29}$$

where R_t are assumed normal $(0, \sigma_R^2)$ and iid and are publicly observable at the start of the trading day. In this model these increments are interpreted as the flow of macroeconomic information. Once the dealers observe R_t they then give quotes for their public customers. For dealer i the quote in round one of day t is S_{it}. In equilibrium Evans and Lyons show that all dealers choose to quote the same price, namely, S_t^1. On the basis of this, each dealer receives a customer order realisation C_{it}^1, where $C_{it}^1 < 0$ denotes a customer sale, and these realisations are assumed to be normally distributed. A key feature of the C_{it}^1 realisations is that they are not publicly observable and are uncorrelated with the stream of payoff increments, R_t. This means that order flow only contains discount rate information and not information on payoffs. Since their model rules out inventory effects at the daily frequency, the discount rate information is necessarily about portfolio-balance effects.

In round two each dealer simultaneously and independently quotes a two-way price for other dealers and these quotes are available to all dealers in the market. As in the round one set-up, it is assumed that all dealers set the same price, S_t^2. Each dealer then simultaneously and independently trades on other dealer quotes and at the end of round two all dealers observe the net inter-dealer order flow on that day:

$$X_t = \sum_{i=1}^{N} T_{it}, \tag{14.30}$$

where T_{it} denotes the (net) inter-dealer trade initiated by dealer i in round two of day t. The order flow information is important in the model because it conveys the size and sign of the public order flow in the first round. At the start of round three, dealers simultaneously and independently quote a scaler two-way price, S_t^3, and these quotes are observable and available to the public. It is assumed by Evans and Lyons that dealers set prices in such a way that the public willingly absorbs all dealer imbalances so that each dealer ends the day with no net positions. In contrast to round one, the public dealing in round two is non-stochastic. In order to be able to set prices in round three, dealers therefore need to know the total position that the public needs to absorb (which they learn from X_t) and the risk-bearing capacity of the public.

On the basis of this set-up, Evans and Lyons demonstrate that the price at the end of day t is given by:

$$S_t = \sum_{\tau=1}^{t} R_\tau + \lambda \sum_{\tau=1}^{t} X_\tau, \tag{14.31}$$

and therefore the change in price from end of day $t - 1$ to end of day t can be written as:

$$\Delta S_t = R_t + \lambda X_t, \tag{14.32}$$

where λ is a positive constant which depends on the aggregate risk-bearing capacity of the public and λX_t is the portfolio-balance effect. The version of equation (14.32) that Evans and Lyons estimate is:

$$\Delta s_t = \beta_1 \Delta(i_t - i_t^*) + \beta_2 X_t + \kappa_t, \tag{14.33}$$

where $R_t = \Delta(i_t - i_t^*)$ and X_t is order flow and other variables have their usual interpretation. This equation is estimated using the daily data set from Evans (1997) (discussed earlier) for the DM–USD and yen–USD exchange rates. Evans and Lyons find that the coefficient on order flow is correctly signed and statistically significant in both exchange rate equations and that the equations have high explanatory power in terms of the coefficients of variation (0.64 and 0.45, respectively, for the DM and yen). They find that the majority of this explanatory power comes from order flow rather than the change in the interest differential (indeed the interest differential is insignificant in the DM equation). But does this result not simply imply that demand is driving price? Lyons suggests not and emphasises that standard macroeconomic models effectively say that order flow is not needed to move price. The fact that order flow explains such a large proportion of price underscores the inadequacy of the public information framework.

Evans and Lyons (2001) consider a variant of the model presented earlier to disentangle the information about two portfolio-balance effects – temporary and persistent portfolio-balance effects – on the exchange rate. In contrast to equation (14.33), their model involves regressing exchange rate changes onto the lagged price change (instead of the change in the interest differential) and order flow. These variables are taken from the Reuters D 2000–1 system and are for the DM/USD for the 4-month period starting in 31 August, 1996. They interpret the coefficient on the order flow term as the temporary portfolio-balance channel, while the coefficient on the lagged price change captures the persistent portfolio-balance channel. Evans and Lyons show that both effects are significant, although the latter accounts for the majority of order flow's impact effect, and this is seen as resurrecting the portfolio-balance approach. They also show that trades have the most price impact when the flow of macroeconomic news is strong. This is also shown to apply to intervention trades as well, as long as they are sterilised, secret and provide no policy signal.

In an attempt to understand if it is information flows – and particularly the split between private and public information – that drive order flow, Evans and Lyons (2003) analyse the effect of macroeconomic news on order flow (which is distinct from the question of whether volume is determined by news). The effect of news on exchange rates is considered in Chapter 15. The Evans and Lyons paper differs from that body of work by considering a broader set of macro-news and by using an approach based on state-dependent heteroscedasticty, rather than an event-study approach. This approach follows Rigobon and Saack (2003) and involves using generalised method of moments (GMM) to identify the relative importance of the direct and indirect effects from news by allowing the variances of shocks to order flow and price to depend separately on the rate of news. The basic hypothesis in the paper is that news affects exchange rates through order flow because market participants draw different inferences (i.e. are heterogeneous) from common macro-data. Both daily and intra-daily data on the exchange rate change and order flow are drawn from the Reuters D2000–1 dealing system for the DM–USD over the period 1 May–31 August 1996. As we have seen, this data is time-stamped tick-by-tick data and involves a full 24-hour trading day. The data on news is extracted from the Reuter's Money Market Headline News screen.

The model of Evans and Lyons (2003) allows for three sources of exchange rate variation. The first is the standard effect of public news, as captured by the models in Chapters 4 and 5, in which news impacts onto price immediately and directly, with no role for order flow. The second source is the indirect effect of news operating on the price via order flow, while the third source of exchange rate variation is due to order flow unrelated to news arrival. Evans and Lyons find that while all three sources of price variation are statistically significant but that two-thirds of the price effect from macro-news comes via order flow while the remaining third comes from the standard direct effect. They also report evidence which is indicative of uni-directional causality between news and exchange rates.

Cao *et al.* (2003) set about answering the following question: in a market, such as the foreign exchange market, with symmetric information about fundamentals, can information-based trade still arise? In particular, in such a market does inventory information impact on price? Their answer to this question is a resounding 'yes'. Their analysis clarifies that price effects arising from non-fundamentals trades are of three types: a transitory, idiosyncratic, effect which is the so-called inventory effect from microstructure theory; a transitory effect common to all market makers; and a permanent effect which is common to all traders. Using the intra-daily data from the Reuters D2000–1 dealing system for the DM–USD they show that inventory information has both transitory and permanent price effects. In particular, a $1 billion positive shock to inter-dealer order flow permanently increases the DM–USD by 0.25 to 0.45 of a pfenning. These permanent effects are also shown to contribute significantly to the variance of permanent price changes, which range from 15% to 30%. Cao *et al.* also show that the transitory effects from inventory information account for between 43% and 89% of the price change at horizons from 30 minutes to 2 hours.

Killeen *et al.* (2000) use a variant of the Evans and Lyons (2002) model to show that exchange rate volatility is high when exchange rates are flexible due to the information content of order flow. In particular, with floating exchange rates, the elasticity of public demand is low, due to the higher volatility and risk aversion that higher volatility entails. This allows the portfolio-balance effect of Evans and Lyons to come into play and allows order flow to provide information about these effects. With a perfectly credible fixed exchange rate the elasticity of public demand becomes infinite and the portfolio effect disappears.

The Killeen, Lyons and Moore (KLM) hypothesis is tested using daily cumulative net order flow data from the Electronic Broking System (EBS), for the German mark–French franc market for the year of 1998. In the weekend of May 2/3 of that year the 11 countries who eventually participated in EMU were made known and the date the internal conversion rates for the euro was also announced. KLM interpret the period post-May 2/3 as one in which EMU was perfectly credible and show that the time series properties of the relationship are very different pre- and post-May 2/3. In particular, the exchange rate seems to become disconnected from order flow post-May 2/3 (in the period up to May 1998 there is a strong positive correlation between cumulative net order flow and the exchange rate). This disconnect is confirmed by formal time series analysis (stationarity and cointegration-based tests). For example, KLM demonstrate that in the first 4 months of 1998, the exchange rate, order flow and the interest differential are non-stationary, but in the post-May period the exchange rate is stationary (the other variables continue to be non-stationary).

14.5 Combining macro-fundamentals with market microstructure

In an interesting and important paper Bacchetta and Wincoop (2003) build on the idea from the market microstructure literature that the heterogeneity of investors may be important for an understanding of exchange rate dynamics over and above that contained in macro-fundamentals. In particular, they introduce two types of investor heterogeneity, that have been associated with order flow, into a standard variant of the monetary model considered in Chapter 4. The first type is the heterogeneous information of market participants about future macro-fundamentals – a dispersion effect – and the second is heterogeneity due to non-fundamentals. The latter includes noise traders and rational traders who trade for non-speculative reasons such as liquidity trades, or trades associated with differential access to private investment opportunities. Models which incorporate both of these heterogeneity effects are referred to as 'noisy rational expectations models' (see the overview in Brunnermeier 2001). As Townsend (1983) notes such models are difficult to solve because of the problem of 'infinite regress' – 'asset prices depend on higher order expectations of fundamentals: expectations of other investors' expectations, expectations of expectations of other investors' expectations, and so on. The dimension of these higher order expectations increases with the horizon, leading to infinite regress for an infinite horizon model' (Bacchetta and Wincop 2003).

In the context of a two-country monetary model of the type considered in Chapter 4, Bacchetta and Wincoop (2003) introduce a continuum of investors on the interval [0,1], each having different expectations and use a risk-adjusted variant of the UIP condition to derive an expression for the equilibrium exchange rate as:

$$s_t = \frac{1}{1+\alpha} \sum_{k=0}^{\infty} \left(\frac{\alpha}{1+\alpha}\right)^k \overline{E}_t^k \left(f_{t+k} - \alpha \gamma \sigma_{t+k}^2 b_{t+k}\right), \tag{14.34}$$

where the fundamental, f_t, equals $(m_t - m_t^*)$, b is the stock of foreign bonds, σ_t^2 is the variance of the nominal exchange rate, γ is a parameter from the demand function for bonds and α is the interest semi-elasticity of the demand for money (the term $\gamma \sigma_{t+k}^2 b_{t+k}$ may be thought of as a risk premium). $\overline{E}_t$ is the average rational expectation across all investors, $\overline{E}_t^0(x_t) = x_t, \overline{E}_t^1(x_{t+1}) = \overline{E}_t(x_{t+1})$ and higher order expectations are defined in the following way:

$$\overline{E}_t^k(x_{t+k}) = \overline{E}_t \overline{E}_{t+1} \ldots \overline{E}_{t+k-1}(x_{t+k}). \tag{14.35}$$

In the present value version of the monetary model considered in Chapter 4 the current (period t) exchange rate is the present discounted value of the current fundamental and the expectation of the fundamental in all future periods. In the current variant of this formula the current exchange rate depends upon the current fundamental, the average expectation of the fundamental at $t + 1$, the average expectation of the fundamental at $t + 2$ and so on. A basic feature of this kind of heterogeneous model is that the expectations of other investors' expectations matter and the law of iterated expectations does not hold, that is, $\overline{E}_t \overline{E}_{t+1}(s_{t+2}) \neq \overline{E}_t(s_{t+2})$. In dynamic systems this leads to the infinite regress problem of Townsend (1983) – in the limit as the discounting horizon goes to infinity the dimensionality of the expectation term also goes to infinity.

Using the base-line expression, and some assumptions about the time series properties of the information structure, Bacchetta and Wincoop then go on to show how information heterogeneity produces both a magnification effect on the exchange rate and endogenous persistence of the impact of non-fundamentals trade on the exchange rate. The model can only be solved analytically when $T = 1$. In order to solve the model when $T > 1$ numerical simulation methods have to be used. Using a benchmark calibration and assuming that both fundamentals and non-fundamentals follow an autoregressive process, they demonstrate that there is a substantial magnification effect as a result of information dispersion and a substantial part of this seems to be attributable to the role of higher order expectations due to the infinite regress. They also show that the heterogeneity introduces exchange rate persistence compared to a model in which there is homogeneous expectations. In particular, the half-life of the impact of the non-fundamental shock is three periods in their modelling exercise.

Bacchetta and Wincoop also explain a number of other stylised facts using their simulated results. For example, they show that there is a very weak link in the short-to medium-run between the macro-fundamentals and the exchange rate change, but that in the longer-run the relationship is much tighter. This is explained in two ways. First, in the short-run the relative contribution of non-fundamental shocks is large but small in the long-run. The exchange rate is also affected through future fundamentals that are not yet available and this effect is also more prominent in the short-run. As we noted in Chapter 6, one key feature of present value models is that the exchange rate or spread should be an optimal predictor of future fundamentals. In practice, though, as we saw in Chapter 6 exchange rates are only weak predictors of future fundamentals and this is consistent with the model of Bacchetta and Wincoop because most of the short-run volatility of exchange rates is associated with non-fundamentals shocks which are not useful for explaining future fundamentals. Bacchetta and Wincoop also use their model to demonstrate how information dispersion contributes to explaining the apparent excessive volatility of exchange rates with respect to fundamentals.

Evans and Lyons (2004) present a very interesting hybrid model which combines key elements of the general equilibrium class of models considered earlier in the book and the microstructural approach considered in this chapter. The general equilibrium component of the model has a number of novel features such as the incompleteness of financial markets (as in the Duarte and Stockman 2001 paper considered in Chapter 11) and the incorporation of social learning. The model is able to explain many of the key exchange rate puzzles considered through-out the book, such as the excess volatility puzzle and the disconnection between macro-fundamentals and exchange rates.

15 Spot and forward exchange rates and the forward premium puzzle

In this chapter we consider the literature on the efficiency of the forward foreign exchange market. Although the literature relating to this concept is voluminous, in essence it focuses on a very simple relationship between spot and forward exchange rates. More specifically, central to this literature is the concept that the forward exchange rate is the market's consensus of the expected exchange rate and is an unbiased forecast of the future spot exchange rate. The next section of this chapter considers the basic spot forward relationship and we note that the empirical evidence indicates that the forward rate is in fact a biased predictor of the future spot rate. In Section 15.2 we outline the so-called Fama decomposition, which seeks to explain the biasedness result in terms of time-varying risk premia, and we also consider issues of irrational expectations and small sample biases in the context of this decomposition. In Section 15.3 we return to the general equilibrium model of Chapter 4 and the portfolio-balance model of Chapter 7 in order to examine the role of time-varying risk premia as the key explanation for biasedness. In Section 15.4 expectational reasons for the failure of the biasedness result are discussed in greater detail. Issues relating to the empirical implementation of the hypothesis are considered in Section 15.5 and in Section 15.6 we consider the usefulness of survey data in explaining the forward premium puzzle.

15.1 Unbiasedness of the forward exchange rate: the joint hypothesis of market efficiency

The forward exchange rate may be decomposed into an expected exchange rate component, s^e_{t+k}, and a term, ω, which is usually referred to in this literature as a risk premium (i.e. in a world of risk-averse agents the investor has to pay a premium in buying forward exchange in period t relative to its expected spot price in period $t + k$) but may, more generally, be thought of as a 'wedge':

$$f_t = s^e_{t+k} + \omega_t. \tag{15.1}$$

In the standard *joint* hypothesis of market efficiency it is usual to assume that agents are risk neutral and therefore:

$$f_t = s^e_{t+k}. \tag{15.1'}$$

If, additionally, agents are assumed to form their expectations rationally, so that $E_t s_{t+k} = s^e_{t+k}$ and $s_{t+k} = E_t s_{t+k} + u_{t+k}$, where u_{t+k} is a purely random term, then under this joint hypothesis:

$$s_{t+k} = f_t + u_{t+k}, \tag{15.2}$$

and the forward rate is an optimal predictor of the future spot rate. In principle, this relationship may be tested by running the following regression:

$$s_{t+k} = \alpha + \beta f_t + v_{t+k}, \tag{15.3}$$

where unbiasedness implies $\alpha = 0/\beta = 1$ and with non-overlapping data $E_t(v_{t+k}) = 0$. With overlapping data, that is, where the maturity of the forward contract is greater than the observational frequency, the error term would be expected to be serially correlated and have a moving average structure of order $k - 1$. It is important to note that such autocorrelation is not inconsistent with efficiency, and is usually accounted for in empirical studies using a generalised method of moments estimator. Since s and f are likely to be non-stationary (this issue is discussed later) a popular alternative to (15.3) involves subtracting the log exchange rate from both sides of the expression to obtain:

$$s_{t+k} - s_t = \alpha_0 + \alpha_1 (f_t - s_t) + v_{t+k},$$

which, for a one-period maturity, can be written as:

$$\Delta s_{t+1} = \alpha_0 + \alpha_1 (f_t - s_t) + \omega_{t+1}. \tag{15.4}$$

Expression (15.4) states that the forward premium should be an unbiased predictor of the exchange rate change if $\alpha_0 = 0/\alpha_1 = 1$. As we shall see later, there is, in fact, a controversy regarding the stationarity of the forward premium term. For the time being we assume this term is stationary and if the estimate of α_1 is assumed to be consistent we can write the probability limit of the estimate of α_1 as:

$$p \lim(\hat{\alpha}_1) = \alpha_1 = \frac{\text{Cov}(f_t - s_t, \Delta s_{t+1})}{\text{Var}(f_t - s_t)}.$$

Since it is assumed that agents are rational, and therefore $\Delta s_{t+1} = E_t \Delta s_{t+1} + u_{t+1}$, and since u_{t+1} is uncorrelated with period-t information we may alternatively rewrite the covariance term as:

$$\text{Cov}(f_t - s_t, \Delta s_{t+1}) = \text{Cov}(f_t - s_t, E_t \Delta s_{t+1}).$$

There are a very large number of estimates of α_1 for different currencies and time periods (see, *inter alia*, MacDonald and Taylor 1989) and these studies produce a preponderance of estimates of α_1 which are closer to -1 than $+1$. For example, Froot and Thaler (1990) demonstrate that averaging α_1 over 75 published produces a value of -0.88. We present an example of an estimated version of expression (15.4) here, from Fama (1984), for the Swiss franc–US dollar:

$$\Delta s_{t+k} = \underset{(0.42)}{0.81} - \underset{(0.50)}{1.15}(f_t - s_t) + u_t. \tag{15.5}$$

How may this stylised result be explained? There are essentially two potential explanations: it is either caused by some form of expectational failure, which can range from simple irrationality through to a 'peso' effect, or learning, or simply a time-varying risk premium. These alternative explanations may be illustrated using the so-called Fama (1984) decomposition, but before considering this we outline some other ways of testing the informational efficiency of the forward exchange rate.

Forward market efficiency has also been tested using the rational forecast error (alternatively labelled in the literature, later, as the excess return premium or the rational risk premium $- s_{t+1} - f_t$). By regressing this error onto lagged information we may obtain alternative, and potentially stronger, tests of efficiency. A so-called weak-form test of efficiency[1] would simply involve regressing the current forecast error onto past forecast errors:

$$s_{t+1} - f_t = \delta_0 + \sum_{i=0}^{p} \lambda_i(s_{t-i} - f_{t-i-1}) + \omega_t, \tag{15.6}$$

where the null hypothesis would be $\delta_0 = 0$ and $\sum_{i=0}^{p} \lambda_i = 0$. A stronger test would involve running the following regression:

$$s_{t+1} - f_t = \delta_0 + \sum_{i=1}^{p} \lambda_i X_{t-i} + \omega_t, \tag{15.7}$$

where X is an $n \times 1$ vector containing any publicly available information, such as money supplies, forecast errors from other foreign exchange markets, and so on. The joint null hypothesis in this case would be $\delta_0 = 0$ and $\sum_{i=1}^{p} \lambda_i = 0$ and this would be interpreted as a semi-strong-form test of efficiency. Using the terminology of Fama (1970) a strong-form test of efficiency would involve including non-publicly available, or inside, information in the information set, X_t (the issue of inside information is not addressed further in this chapter but is considered in Chapter 14).

15.2   Decomposing the forward premium puzzle: the Fama decomposition

In an important and influential paper, Fama (1984) demonstrated that the empirical finding of forward rate biasedness may be attributable either to the existence of a time-varying risk premium, or to some form of expectational failure – be it learning, peso effects or 'irrationality'. To see this, consider Fama's 'complementary regression' to (15.4), namely:

$$f_t - s_{t+k} = \alpha_2 + \alpha_3(f_t - s_t) + v_{t+k}, \tag{15.8}$$

where the left-hand-side term represents the so-called rational expectations risk premium – $\lambda_t = f_t - s_{t+k}$ – (i.e. the risk premium defined when agents form their expectations rationally), $p\lim(\hat{\alpha}_1) = 1 - \alpha_3$ and the p lims of α_1 and α_3 can be written as (given rational expectations and the definition of the risk premium):

$$\alpha_1 = \frac{\text{var}(E_t s_{t+k} - s_t) + \text{cov}(\lambda_t, E_t s_{t+k} - s_t)}{\text{var}(\lambda_t) + \text{var}(E_t s_{t+k} - s_t) + 2\text{cov}(\lambda_t, E_t s_{t+k} - s_t)}, \tag{15.9}$$

$$\alpha_3 = \frac{\text{var}(\lambda_t) + \text{cov}(\lambda_t, E_t s_{t+k} - s_t)}{\text{var}(\lambda_t) + \text{var}(E_t s_{t+k} - s_t) + 2\text{cov}(\lambda_t, E_t s_{t+k} - s_t)}, \tag{15.10}$$

where the denominator in these expressions is simply an expansion of $\text{Var}(f_t - s_t)$. In the extreme case where λ_t and $E_t s_{t+k} - s_t$ are uncorrelated, α_3 would capture the component of the variance of the forward premium due to the variance of the risk premium and α_1 would capture the variance of forward premium due to the expected change in the exchange rate. The formula for α_3 suggests that low estimated values of α_1 can be explained, with rational expectations, if $\text{var}(\lambda_t)$ is large ($\alpha_1 = 1 - \alpha_3$). However, more realistically, allowing for a non-zero correlation between λ_t and $E_t s_{t+k} - s_t$ how may a negative value of α_1 be explained? Since the denominator in (15.9) and (15.10) must be non-negative (i.e. they are expansions of a variance term) and the variance term in the numerator is positive, it must follow that $\text{Cov}(\lambda_t, E_t s_{t+k})$ is negative and greater than $\text{var}(E_t s_{t+k} - s_t)$ in absolute value. Given α_3, this, in turn, implies:

$$\text{var}(\lambda_t) > \text{var}(E_t s_{t+k} - s_t).$$

Indeed a finding that $\alpha_1 < 0.5$ will ensure this result, as can be demonstrated. The variance of the risk premium can be written as:

$$\text{Var}(\lambda_t) = \text{Var}(F_t \wedge s_{t+1}) + \text{Var}(f_t - s_t) - 2\text{Cov}(f_t - s_t, E_t \Delta s_{t+1}).$$

By substituting this expression, and then the formula for α_1 into the left hand side of the earlier inequality, we can obtain:

$$\frac{\text{Cov}(f_t - s_t, E_t \Delta s_{t+1})}{\text{Var}(f_t - s_t)} = \alpha_1 < 1/2, \tag{15.11}$$

which becomes the relevant hypothesis to test.

15.2.1   *Small sample bias*

The earlier discussion assumes a consistent estimate of α_1 and that there is direct link between α_1 and α_3. In small samples, however, it may be that a finite sample bias exists which drives a wedge between these terms. For example, in finite samples we have:

$$\hat{\alpha}_1 = \frac{\mathrm{Cov}(\widehat{f_t - s_t}, \Delta s_{t+k})}{\mathrm{Var}(\widehat{f_t - s_t})},$$

where $\hat{}$ again denotes an estimate and we now have:

$$\hat{\alpha}_1 = 1 - \hat{\alpha}_3 - \hat{\alpha}_{ss},$$

where:

$$\hat{\alpha}_{ss} = \frac{\mathrm{Cov}(f_t - s_t, \widehat{E_t s_{t+k}} - s_{t+k})}{\mathrm{Var}(\widehat{f_t - s_t})},$$

which may be thought of as a small sample expectational failure (in large samples plim $\alpha_{ss} = 0$). The α_{ss} term can arise for two reasons related to differences in agents' information sets, relative to that of the econometrician, namely, learning and 'peso' effects. With learning there is a change in the stochastic process governing s_t which agents only learn about gradually and in this case the econometrician, who analyses the data ex post, has more information than agents. This effect generates a positive correlation between $E\Delta s$ and $f - s$ and this implies a positive value of α_{ss}, which goes to zero in large samples.

In the peso interpretation, agents have more information than the econometrician – agents form expectations using the correct distribution of the exchange rate, but ex post the sample does not contain all of the events that agents think will occur with the correct frequency of occurrence. The best known example of this is where agents expect a large depreciation of s, so $E_t s_{t+k} - s_t$ is high and correspondingly $f_t - s_t$, is high, but the expected change does not occur in sample and so α_{ss} is positive. A classic example of this is the behaviour of the Mexican peso in the early 1970s in which a persistently high home relative interest rate differential (which with covered interest parity is equivalent to the forward premium) was combined with a fixed exchange rate and an expected devaluation which did not actually occur until the late 1970s. So an econometrician testing (15.4), using data up to before the devaluation, would have found the forward premium to be biased because of a positive α_{ss} term.

15.2.2   *Irrational expectations*

Both of the earlier effects should, of course, disappear in large samples. However, this need not follow if what is driving the result are irrational expectations. In this case the market's subjective probability distribution of s is not the same as the true distribution because $E_t^m \neq E_t$ where E_t^m is the market expectation and so

$$\lambda_t^{ir} = f_t - E_t^m(s_{t+1}),$$

where λ_t^{ir} denotes the 'irrational' risk premium and $\hat{\alpha}_1 = 1 - \hat{\alpha}_3 - \hat{\alpha}_{ss} - \hat{\alpha}_{ir}$, where

$$\hat{\alpha}_3 = \frac{\mathrm{Cov}(\widehat{E_t^m s_{t+1} - s_{t+1}}) + \mathrm{Var}(\widehat{\lambda_t^{ir}})}{\mathrm{Var}(\widehat{f_t - s_t})},$$

$$\hat{\alpha}^{ss} = \frac{\mathrm{Cov}(f_t - s_t, \widehat{E_t s_{t+1} - E_t s_{t+1}})}{\mathrm{Var}(\widehat{f_t - s_t})},$$

and

$$\hat{\alpha}_{ir} = \frac{\mathrm{Cov}(f_t - s_t, \widehat{E_t^m s_{t+1} - E_t s_{t+1}})}{\mathrm{Var}(\widehat{f_t - s_t})}.$$

The latter will be positive if $f - s$ is correlated with the expected error. When the consensus estimate of the future exchange rate is above what is rational and this results in a higher forward premium this will produce a positive α_{ir}. So positive values of $\hat{\alpha}_3$, $\hat{\alpha}_{ss}$ and $\hat{\alpha}_{ir}$ can all contribute to a finding that $\hat{\alpha}_1$ is less than unity. We have a more formal discussion of expectational issues in the following section.

15.3 The forward premium puzzle, the risk premium and the Lucas general equilibrium model

In this section we focus on explanations for the biasedness result which exploit the existence of a risk premium and, in particular, emphasise risk premium approaches based on the general equilibrium model of Lucas and also the portfolio-balance model.

15.3.1 The Lucas model and the general equilibrium approach to the risk premium

Consider again a variant of the first-order condition from the Lucas model derived in Chapter 5:

$$\frac{S_t P_t^*}{P_t} = \frac{u_{c_t}^*}{u_{c_t}}, \tag{15.12}$$

where terms have the same interpretation as before. If we now assume an arbitrary asset i which has a home currency price V_t^i and a payoff in period $t+1$ of $V_{t+1}^i + D_{t+1}^i$, where D has the interpretation of either a coupon payment or dividend. The foregone marginal utility from investing in this asset is $V_t^i u_{c_t}/P_t$ and the expected marginal utility of the payoff is $E_t[\beta u_{c_t}(V_{t+1}^i + D_{t+1}^i)/P_{t+1}]$. Equating the marginal benefit to the marginal cost produces an expression that must be satisfied by all equilibrium returns defined in terms of the home currency:

$$E_t(Q_{t+1}R_{t+1}^j) = 1 \quad \forall_j, \tag{15.13}$$

where $R_{t+1}^i \equiv (V_{t+1}^i + D_{t+1}^i)/V_t^i$ and $Q \equiv [\beta u_{c_{t+1}} P_t/u_{c_t}P_{t+1}]$ is the so-called pricing kernel. This expression may be related to the forward rate in the following way. If R_{t+1}^f is the nominal interest rate on a risk free discount bond paying one unit of home money, M, in period $t+1$ ($= (1 + i)$) (a certain payoff) and so the price of such an asset is simply:

$$1/R_{t+1}^f = E_t(Q_{t+1}), \tag{15.14}$$

or

$$1 = E_t(Q_{t+1}R_{t+1}^f),$$

equally we can think of this condition holding for an interest differential:

$$1/R_{t+1}^f - 1/R_{t+1}^c = E_t(Q_{t+1}), \tag{15.15}$$

or

$$0 = E_t(Q_{t+1}(R_{t+1}^f - R_{t+1}^c)).$$

For the equivalent foreign position we have:

$$1/R_{t+1}^{f*} = E_t\{\beta u_{c_{t+1}}^* P_t^*/u_{c_t}^* P_{t+1}^*\} \equiv E_t(Q_{t+1}^*),$$

or

$$1/R_{t+1}^{f*} = E_t(Q_{t+1}^*). \tag{15.16}$$

By exploiting the familiar covered interest parity (CIP) condition – $(1 + i_t) = (1 + i_t^*)(F_t/S_t)$ – (15.14) and (15.16) may be rewritten as:

$$F_t = S_t R_{t+1}^f/R_{t+1}^{f*} = S_t E_t(Q_{t+1}^*)/E_t(Q_{t+1}). \tag{15.17}$$

As Lewis (1995) notes, this relationship between the spot and forward exchange rate is quite general and to solve for the forward rate using the specific form of the Lucas model requires substituting (15.12) or the monetary extension of (15.12), derived in Chapter 4, which we use here:

$$F_t = S_t R_{t+1}^f/R_{t+1}^{f*} = \left[\frac{u_{c_t}^*}{u_{c_t}}\frac{M_t}{M_t^*}\frac{y_t^*}{y_t}\right] E_t(Q_{t+1}^*)/E_t(Q_{t+1}). \tag{15.18}$$

The earlier relationships can be used to re-express the Fama result that the variance of the risk premium is greater than the variance of the expected change in the exchange rate – $\text{var}(\lambda_t)$ is $> \text{var}(E_t s_{t+k} - s_t)$ as:

$$\text{Var}\{E_t(Q^*_{t+1}/Q_{t+1}) - [E_t(Q^*_{t+1})/E_t(Q_{t+1})]\} > \text{Var}\{E_t(Q^*_{t+1}/Q_{t+1})\}. \tag{15.19}$$

In words, expression (15.19) indicates that the risk premium is the difference between the ratio of expected marginal rates of substitution in consumption and the expectation of this ratio and the variance of this difference exceeds the variance of the expected ratio of marginal rates of substitution.

From (15.15), and by exploiting the CIP condition, a further implication of (15.15) is

$$E_t\left(Q_t\frac{S_{t+1} - F_t}{S_t}\right) = 0, \tag{15.20}$$

which may be rewritten to give an alternative interpretation of the forward premium as:

$$E_t\left(\frac{S_{t+1} - F_t}{S_t}\right) = \text{Cov}\left(Q_t; \frac{S_{t+1} - F_t}{S_t}\middle| I_t\right)[-E_t(Q_t)]^{-1}, \tag{15.21}$$

or

$$\frac{F_t}{S_t} = E_t\left(\frac{S_{t+1}}{S_t}\right) - \text{Cov}\left(Q_t; \frac{S_{t+1} - F_t}{S_t}\middle| I_t\right)[-E_t(Q_t)]^{-1},$$

where the risk premium is the second term on the right hand side and this clearly implies that the forward rate need not be an unbiased predictor of the future spot rate. Note that in this model this biasedness result can occur even with risk-neutral agents, a situation characterised by the linearity of the utility function underlying (15.21).

15.3.2 Testing the general equilibrium risk premium model

A number of researchers have empirically implemented the general equilibrium approach to modelling the risk premium and we consider the various tests in this subsection.

15.3.2.1 Direct (error orthogonality) tests

Mark (1985) considers a variant of equation (15.15), in which the return is defined as the forward forecast error:[2]

$$E_t\left(Q_t\frac{S_{t+1} - F_t}{S_t}\right) = 0. \tag{15.22}$$

In order to estimate (15.22) the utility function has to be explicitly parameterised and Mark uses a constant relative risk aversion (CRRA) utility function of the form:

$$U(C_t) = \delta C_t^{1-\gamma}/(1 - \gamma), \quad \gamma < 1, \tag{15.23}$$

where γ is the coefficient of relative risk aversion. If the ratio of consumption in t to consumption in $t + 1$ is c_{t+1} then from (15.23) the ratio of marginal utilities of consumption is simply c_{t+1}^{γ}. Mark uses a generalised method of moments (GMM) estimator to estimate γ from a set of orthogonality conditions for the USD bilateral exchange rate of the CD, DM, NG, ST over the period March 1973–July 1983. Six different instrument sets are used to estimate the orthogonality conditions, and overall the overidentifying restrictions are rejected. Furthermore, in all cases the estimate of γ tends to be quite large – in the region of 12 to 50 – which is much greater than the ball park figure for risk aversion which is usually taken to be around two, although the reported standard errors on γ are also large, implying that the hypothesis that it is zero cannot be rejected.

Hodrick (1989) presents an updated and extended version of Mark's study to cover seven exchange rates over the period 1973, quarter 3 to 1987, quarter 4. Two numeraire currencies are used, namely, the US dollar and UK pound. When the dollar is used, Hodrick reports an estimated value of γ which is, as in Mark (1985), very large and implausible, although the overidentifying restrictions are not rejected. Interestingly, with the pound as numeraire γ is estimated as 2.15 and the overidentifying restrictions are not rejected.

Modjtahedi (1991) follows the approach of Mark (1985) using a variety of different forward rate maturities and also obtains implausible estimates of γ and finds the overidentifying restrictions are rejected. Kaminsky and Peruga (1988) also confirm Mark's finding using a multivariate orthogonality test. Backus et al. (1993) exploit a utility function which is non-separable to revisit the test of Mark (1985), but they also find the estimated value of γ is too large and the overidentifying restrictions are again rejected.

In sum, then, the 'direct tests', based on an explicit parameterisation of utility, of the general equilibrium model are not very supportive of the risk premium interpretation, both because the estimated values of the risk aversion parameter are implausibly large and, in general, the overidentifying restrictions are rejected.

15.3.2.2   Latent variable tests

So-called latent variable tests of the general equilibrium risk premium rely on a reformulation of expression (15.14) as:

$$E_t(R_{t+1}^j) = \frac{1}{E_t(Q_{t+1})} - \frac{\text{Cov}_t(Q_{t+1}, R_{t+1}^j)}{E_t(Q_{t+1})}.$$

If R_{t+1}^0 is the return on an asset that has a zero conditional covariance with Q_{t+1}, then

$$E_t(R_{t+1}^0) = \frac{1}{E_t(Q_{t+1})},$$

and

$$E_t(R_{t+1}^j - R_{t+1}^0) = \frac{-\text{Cov}_t(Q_{t+1}, R_{t+1}^j)}{E_t(Q_{t+1})}. \tag{15.24}$$

If it is assumed that agents can trade an asset whose return is the minimum second moment return (see Hodrick 1987) – $R_{t+1}^m = Q_{t+1}/E_t(Q_{t+1})^2$ – then Hansen and Richard (1984) demonstrate that any return, R_{t+k}^b, on the mean-variance frontier can be written as a weighted average of R_{t+1}^m and R_{t+1}^0:

$$R_{t+1}^b = \sigma_t R_{t+1}^m + (1 - \sigma_t) R_{t+1}^0. \tag{15.25}$$

With these relations it is possible to rewrite equation (15.14) in CAPM form as:

$$E_t(R_{t+1}^j - R_{t+1}^0) = \beta_t^j (R_{t+1}^b - R_{t+1}^0), \tag{15.26}$$

where

$$\beta_t^j = \frac{\text{Cov}_t(R_{t+1}^b, R_{t+1}^j)}{\text{Var}_t(R_{t+1}^b)}.$$

An alternative way of demonstrating this result (see Lewis 1995) is as follows. Since relationship (15.14) holds for any asset with return j, it must also hold for the risk free rate and we can write (15.15) as:

$$E_t\{Q_{t+1}(R_{t+1}^j - R_{t+1}^f)\} = E_t\{Q_{t+1}ex_{t+1}^j\} = 0, \tag{15.27}$$

where $ex_{t+1}^j \equiv R_{t+1}^j - R_{t+1}^f$ and R_{t+1}^f is the risk free rate. Using the definition of covariances and (15.14), equation (15.27) can be rewritten as:

$$E_t(ex_{t+1}^j) = -\text{Cov}_t(R_{t+1}^j, Q_{t+1})R_{t+1}^f. \tag{15.28}$$

and since this holds for any asset, such as the benchmark return:

$$E_t(ex_{t+1}^b) = -\text{Cov}_t(R_{t+1}^b, Q_{t+1})R_{t+1}^f. \tag{15.29}$$

And by substituting out for the risk free rate we get a similar expression to (15.26), namely:

$$E_t(ex_{t+1}^j) = [\text{Cov}_t(R_{t+1}^j, Q_{t+1})/\text{Cov}_t(R_{t+1}^b, Q_{t+1})]E_t(ex_{t+1}^b), \tag{15.30}$$

where R^b is the benchmark return and R is the risk free rate.

Hansen and Hodrick (1983) test (15.26) by assuming that the conditional covariances between returns and the marginal rate of substitution move in proportion across assets over time. With this assumption the ratios of covariances in (15.24) or β in (15.26) are constant. Their approach may be viewed as a latent variable approach because R^b is unobservable and it implies a set of overidentifying restrictions. With β assumed constant, and forward forecast errors used as instruments, Hansen and Hodrick find that the overidentifying restrictions are not rejected. However, in an alternative set of tests Hodrick and Srivastava (1984) find that the overidentifying restrictions are rejected when $f - s$, the forward premium, is used as an instrument. There are a large number of other tests of the latent variable model and these produce mixed results (see also Hodrick and Srivastava 1986; Campbell and Clarida 1987; Giovannini and Jorion 1987). However, even tests which do not reject the overidentifying restrictions are unable to provide a measure of how much of the forward premium puzzle is explained by the risk premium term. Cumby (1990) and Lewis (1991) argue that one reason for the rejections of the model could be due to the auxiliary assumption that covariances move in proportion to each other. They note that this condition only seems to hold at longer horizons and when long horizon returns are used there is less evidence of rejection; however, this failure to reject at long horizons could simply reflect the low power of the test.

15.3.2.3   Hansen–Jaganathan bounds

The Hansen–Jaganathan approach uses combinations of excess returns to provide a lower bound on the volatility of the inter-temporal marginal rate of substitution in consumption – the Q_t term. This lower bound is seen as a useful empirical tool for comparing excess returns – here the excess return from taking a forward position – with the implications of a particular model, in this case the general equilibrium model of Lucas. The derivation of these bounds may be illustrated in the following way (see, for example, Lewis 1995). Consider again (15.27):

$$E_t\{Q_{t+1}ex_{t+1}\} = 0,$$

where the j superscript has been dropped.

If it is assumed that Q_t can be written in terms of a simple linear projection as:

$$Q_{t+1} = \delta_0 + \delta'ex_{t+1} + e_{t+1}, \tag{15.31}$$

where e is the error term. Using the standard OLS formulae the parameter vector can be written as:

$$\delta = \sum^{-1}[E(Q_{t+1}ex_{t+1}) - E(Q_{t+1})E(ex_{t+1})], \tag{15.32}$$

which given (15.27) implies

$$= -\sum^{-1}E(Q_{t+1})E(ex_{t+1}),$$

where $\sum$ is the variance, or variance covariance matrix (if ex is a vector) of ex.

By substituting (15.32) into (15.31) and noting that the variance of e_t must be positive we obtain a variance inequality of the following form:

$$\sigma^2(Q_{t+1}) > [E(Q_{t+1})]^2 E(ex_{t+1})' \sum^{-1} E(ex_{t+1}), \tag{15.33}$$

or

$$\sigma(Q_{t+1})/E(Q_{t+1}) > [E(ex_{t+1})' \sum^{-1} E(ex_{t+1})]^{1/2}, \tag{15.33'}$$

which is the Hansen–Jaganathan bounds. Bekaert and Hodrick (1992) estimate Hansen–Jaganathan bounds as in (15.33') using a variety of different measures of equity and foreign exchange returns in the US, UK, Japan and Germany and find that the bounds are in the range of 0.6–0.7. However, as Lewis (1995) notes for these bounds to be consistent with the Lucas (1982) model a risk aversion parameter in excess of 140 would be required, which is far too large.

15.3.2.4   *ARCH/GARCH tests*

Domowitz and Hakkio (1985) propose using an ARCH framework to estimate the representative agent model. Specifically, by imposing some structure on the Lucas model, they propose the following modelling framework. Equation (15.4) is rewritten as:

$$s_{t+1} - s_t = \lambda_t + \beta(f_t - s_t) + \varepsilon_{t+1}, \tag{15.34}$$

and the risk premium is assumed to be a function of the conditional variance of the forecast error:

$$\lambda_t = \beta_0 + \theta h_{t+1}, \tag{15.35}$$

where

$$\varepsilon_{t+1}|I_t \sim \mathcal{N}(0, h_{t+1}^2),$$

and

$$h_{t+1}^2 = \alpha_0^2 + \sum_{j=1}^{n} \alpha_j^2 \varepsilon_{t+1-j}^2.$$

Domowitz and Hakkio estimate this relationship for five currencies for the recent float and find strong evidence of ARCH effects (i.e. significant non-zero α_j coefficients), but the null hypothesis of no risk premium ($\beta_0 = \theta = 0$) cannot be rejected for any of the currencies studied. Kaminsky and Peruga (1988) argue that this may be due to the failure of Domowitz and Hakkio to capture the contemporaneous correlations across exchange markets. To account for such correlation Kaminsky and Peruga estimate a multivariate ARCH representation to estimate the risk premium and they find they can strongly reject their null of no risk premium. In sum, representative agent models of the risk premium, with rational expectations, do not appear to shed much light on whether it is a risk premium which explains the forward premium puzzle.

15.3.3   *Portfolio-balance approach to measuring risk*

The essence of the portfolio-balance model, discussed in Chapter 7, may be summarised as:

$$B_t S_t F_t^{-1} = \gamma (i_t - i_t^* - \Delta s_{t+k}^e), \tag{15.36}$$

which states that relative home to foreign bond supplies are determined by the excess return, which on the basis of covered interest parity, may be thought of as a risk premium. By assuming that agents are rational, an inversion of (15.36) produces:

$$i_t - i_t^* - \Delta s_{t+k} = \gamma^{-1} (B_t S_t F_t)^{-1} + \upsilon_{t+k}, \tag{15.37}$$

which may be rewritten as:

$$i_t - i_t^* - \Delta s_{t+k} = \beta_0 + \beta_1 (B_t S_t F_t)^{-1} + u_{t+k}, \tag{15.38}$$

which predicts that the risk premium, or excess return, is driven by the relative supplies of bonds. A number of researchers have exploited a different, although related, portfolio literature to that used to derive the portfolio-balance model in Chapter 7 in order to place restrictions on the parameters in (15.38). This related literature seeks to explain the composition of investors' portfolios and involves considering an investor who maximises a function of their mean and variance over the coming period (the earliest variants of this approach are Stultz 1981 and Adler and Dumas 1983). Here we consider a version of the two-country model as set out in Engel (1994) in which agents can invest in two assets: home and foreign country bonds. More specifically, individuals in the home country at time t are assumed to maximise a function of the mean and variance of their portfolio:

$$E_t(W_{t+1}) - \frac{\phi}{2W_t} \mathrm{Var}_t(W_{t+1}), \tag{15.39}$$

where ϕ is related to the coefficient of relative risk aversion and in this set-up investors like to have a higher return but dislike variance. If ω represents the fraction of wealth invested in the foreign country bonds, then:

$$E_t(W_{t+1}) = W_t[(1 + i_t)(1 - \omega_t) + (1 + i_t^*)\omega_t E_t(S_{t+1}/S_t)], \tag{15.40}$$

and

$$\mathrm{Var}_t(W_{t+1}) = W_t^2(1 + i_t^*)^2 \omega_t^2 \mathrm{Var}_t(S_{t+1}/S_t),$$

where it is assumed that the only form of uncertainty comes from the value of the exchange rate in the next period. The first-order condition for this model can be written as:

$$(1 + i_t^*)E_t(S_{t+1}/S_t) - (1 + i_t) = \phi\omega_t(1 + i_t^*)^2\text{Var}_t(S_{t+1}/S_t). \qquad (15.41)$$

Asssuming that $\ln(s_{t+1}) \equiv s_{t+1}$ is conditionally normally distributed, expression (15.41) can be written as:

$$E_t(s_{t+1}) - s_t + i_t^* - i_t + 0.5 \cdot \text{Var}_t(s_{t+1}) = \phi\omega_t\text{Var}_t(s_{t+1}). \qquad (15.42)$$

An analogous expression to (15.42) can be derived for investors in the foreign country who maximise a function of the mean and variance of wealth in foreign terms:

$$-E_t(s_{t+1}) + s_t - i_t^* + i_t + 0.5 \cdot \text{Var}_t(s_{t+1}) = \phi(1 - \omega_t^*)\text{Var}_t(s_{t+1}), \qquad (15.43)$$

where ω_t^* represents the fraction of wealth that foreigners invest in their own bonds. If μ is the share of total wealth held by domestic residents, then by multiplying equation (15.42) by ω_t and equation (15.43) by ω_t^* and adding the resulting expressions together, the following expression may be obtained:

$$E_t(s_{t+1}) - s_t + i_t^* - i_t = [-0.5 + (1-\phi)(1-\mu_t) + \phi(\mu_t\omega_t + (1-\mu_t)\omega_t^*)]$$
$$\times \text{Var}_t(s_{t+1}), \qquad (15.44)$$

where the term $\mu_t\omega_t + (1 - \mu_t)\omega_t^*$ is the value of foreign bonds held in the world as a fraction of world wealth which we define as $\bar{\omega}_t$ and so (15.44) may be written more compactly as:

$$E_t(s_{t+1}) - s_t + i_t^* - i_t = \text{Var}_t(s_{t+1})[(1-\phi)(1-\mu_t) - 0.5] + \phi\text{Var}_t(s_{t+1})\bar{\omega}_t, \qquad (15.45)$$

where the home–foreign bond differential is related to the share of foreign bonds in world wealth, to the share of wealth held by domestic residents and to the variance of the exchange rate. As Engel (1996) points out equation (15.45) can be thought of as a restricted version of equation (15.38). This can be seen more clearly by rewriting (15.38) using the terminology underlying (15.45):

$$E_t(s_{t+1}) - s_t + i_t^* - i_t = \alpha_t + \delta_t(1 - \mu_t) + \gamma_t\bar{\omega}_t. \qquad (15.46)$$

In the standard portfolio-balance model considered in Chapter 7 and represented by (15.36) and (15.46) the time-varying parameters α_t, δ_t and γ_t are not restricted. The key distinguishing feature of the mean-variance version of the portfolio-balance model is that these terms are restricted and in the following way:

$$\alpha_t = -0.5 \cdot \text{Var}_t(s_{t+1}),$$
$$\delta_t = (1 - \phi) \cdot \text{Var}_t(s_{t+1}),$$

and

$$\gamma_t = \phi \text{Var}_t(s_{t+1}).$$

The majority of the papers in the mean-variance portfolio-balance approach involve estimating variants of equation (15.45) and testing the restrictions that (15.46) imposes on (15.45). It is worth noting that one of the big empirical advantages of this approach is that it only requires information on the value of total bonds held in the world denominated in each country, and the share of wealth in each country, rather than the value of bonds denominated in each country and held in each country (the latter data are much less readily available than the former).

Frankel (1982a,b, 1983), Lewis (1988) and Rogoff (1984) present estimates of variants of (15.38) (i.e the standard unconstrained portfolio-balance equation) for a variety of currencies and time periods and essentially find no evidence of a statistically significant link between excess returns and bond holdings.

Engel and Rodriguez (1989) estimate a version of (15.45) for the demand for government bonds for six countries. Since they assume all investors evaluate returns in the same terms, the equation they estimate is equivalent to (15.42) and the variance is modelled using an ARCH model and also models which relate the variance to economic data. The estimates of ϕ turn out to be either insignificantly different from zero or negative and therefore do not offer support to the mean-variance approach. Giovannini and Jorion also offer GARCH-based estimates of (15.42) which are also unsupportive of the mean-variance approach since the estimates of the coefficient of risk aversion are insignificant. Other unsupportive estimates of this approach have been produced by Lyons (1988), Thomas and Wickens (1993), Engel and Rodriguez (1993) and Tesar and Werner (1994).

By incorporating a home country bias effect, as in equation (15.45), and using a GARCH process to model volatility, Engel (1994) produces a reasonably plausible estimate of the coefficient of risk aversion which is marginally significant; however, the risk premiums implied by estimates of equation (15.45) 'are more than an order of magnitude greater than those from the estimated CAPM' (Engel 1996). Black and Salemi (1988) do not assume the first-order maximisation condition from the consumers' maximisation problem holds exactly and add an error term to (15.45) and this produces a statistically significant value of ϕ of 4.08, but they do not provide estimates of the size of the implied risk premiums and how they relate to estimates derived from equation (15.45). Lewis, however, reports estimates of a version of the model which is subject to an error term, but in contrast to Black and Salemi she finds no evidence in support of the model.

The empirical evidence which exploits a risk premium to explain the forward premium puzzle is evidently not clear-cut with respect to the significance of a risk premium in explaining the forward premium puzzle. Indeed the preponderance of estimates reported in this section does not support the risk premium interpretation. Can the puzzle therefore be explained by some form of expectational failure? We now consider the evidence on such an interpretation.

15.4   Expectational explanations for the forward premium puzzle: learning, peso effects and irrationality

In this section we return to the question of whether expectational failures explain the forward premium puzzle and, in particular, consider three aspects of expectational failure, namely: learning, peso effects and irrationality.[3]

15.4.1   Rational learning

With rational learning, agents are fully rational but they take time to understand a once-and-for-all shift in the underlying distribution of the economy – due, say, to a change in the monetary regime which produces an exchange rate appreciation – and this can explain the forward rate biasedness result. This may be demonstrated more formally in the following way. Define the term $E_t(s_{t+1}/O)$ as the expected future exchange rate conditional on the old regime, and $E_t(s_{t+1}/N)$ as the expected future exchange rate conditional on the new regime and assume that $E_t(s_{t+1}/O) > E_t(s_{t+1}/N)$. In this case the expected future exchange rate at time t will be a probability weighted average of the two expected values:

$$E_t s_{t+1} = (1 - \phi_t)E_t(s_{t+1}/N) + \phi_t E_t(s_{t+1}/O), \tag{15.47}$$

where ϕ_t is the markets' assessed probability at time t that monetary policy is based on the old regime. The evolution of ϕ_t is assumed to be based on a rational learning process – as new information on the regime becomes available (i.e. as the currency appreciates after the regime change) ϕ_t decreases over time and the plim of ϕ_t goes to zero as the time dimension goes to ∞. During the learning period this will generate persistent forecast errors, which can be demonstrated by subtracting (15.47) from the realised exchange rate to obtain:

$$s_{t+1}^N - E_t s_{t+1} = \eta_{t+1} = s_{t+1}^N - E_t(s_{t+1}/N) - \phi_t[E_t(s_{t+1}/N) - \phi_t E_t(s_{t+1}/O)], \tag{15.48}$$

and

$$\eta_{t+1} = \eta_{t+1}^N - \phi_t \kappa_{t+1},$$

where s_{t+1}^N indicates a realisation of the exchange rate from process N, $\eta_{t+1}^N \equiv [s_{t+1}^N - E_t(s_{t+1}/N)]$ and $\kappa = [E_t(\Delta s_{t+1}/O) - E_t(\Delta s_{t+1}/N)]$,[4] which is the difference between the expected future exchange rate changes, conditional on each regime. Although the mean of the first term will be zero, the mean of the second term will not be in a finite sample so η_t is negative as long as $\phi_t > 0$. In this situation even if the 'true' risk premium were zero, the rational expectations risk premium, λ, need not be zero because of the existence of forecast errors, and we can rewrite the formula for α_3:

$$\alpha_3 = \frac{\text{var}(\eta_{t+1}) + \text{cov}(\eta_t, E_t s_{t+k} - s_t)}{\text{Var}(f_t - s_t)}.$$

From this expression, the covariance term has to be negative to explain the forward premium puzzle which it will be with learning if the probability weighted average of the exchange rate in the old regime exceeds its counterpart in the new regime:

$$\text{Cov}(\eta_{t+1}, E_t \Delta s_{t+1}) = \phi_t[(1 - \phi_t)\text{Var}(E_t \Delta s_{t+1}^N) - \phi_t \text{Var}(E_t \Delta s_{t+1}^O)].$$
(15.49)

Of course, this covariance term goes to zero over time if agents are truly rational. However, if agents are in fact irrational this term need not go to zero, even in the limit. Lewis (1989) has argued that learning can explain about 50% of the behaviour of excess returns.[5]

15.4.2 Peso effects

As we have seen, a peso effect refers to anticipated future regime changes, rather than learning about a past regime change, and this can be more precisely defined in the following way, using the expected exchange rate:

$$E_t s_{t+1} = (1 - \psi_t)E_t(s_{t+1}/C) + \psi_t E_t(s_{t+1}/A),$$
(15.50)

where ψ_t represents the probability that the regime will shift from the current regime (C) to an alternative regime (A) that may be realised in the future. As long as the regime does not materialise the exchange rate will be generated by the current regime and the forecast error will be:

$$s_{t+1}^C - E_t s_{t+1} = \eta_{t+1} = (s_{t+1}^c - E_t(s_{t+1}/C)) + \psi_t[E_t(s_{t+1}/C) - E_t(s_{t+1}/A)]$$
$$\times \eta_{t+1} = \eta_{t+1}^C - \psi_t \kappa_{t+1},$$
(15.51)

where now η_{t+1}^C is the forecast error conditional upon C and $\kappa_{t+1} = [E_t(s_{t+1}/C) - E_t(s_{t+1}/A)]$. In a similar vein to our derivation for learning, this forecast error could also provide another explanation for the biasedness result. Indeed, using a calibrated model, Evans and Lewis (1995) show how peso effects can generate the typical kind of numbers reported in the literature for α_1.

15.5   Empirical issues

In this section we briefly survey a number of empirical papers which provide an alternative explanations for the forward premium puzzle.

15.5.1   Liquidity effects

Many, if not all, of the empirical studies referred to earlier relate to developed countries which have relatively low inflation environments compared to developing countries which, in general, may be thought of as high inflation environments. The significance of this is that in low inflation environments interest rates are more likely to reflect liquidity effects, while in high inflation countries interest rates will reflect Fisher, or expected inflation, effects: regressing the change in the exchange rate on the interest differential/forward premium is likely to produce a negative association for developed countries (the forward premium puzzle), but the correctly signed relationship for the developed country. Bansal and Dahlquist (2000) explore this idea by analysing a panel of 28 countries, consisting of both developed and developing countries (January 1976–May 1998). They consider a state-dependent regression of the following form:

$$\Delta s_{it+1} = \alpha_{i0} + \alpha_{il}^+ (f_{it} - s_{it})^+ + \alpha_{il}^- (f_{it} - s_{it})^- + \varepsilon_{it+1}, \tag{15.52}$$

where:

$$(f_{it} - s_{it})^+ = (f_{it} - s_{it}) \text{ if } (f_{it} - s_{it}) > 0 \text{ or } 0 \text{ if } (f_{it} - s_{it}) \leqslant 0,$$
$$(f_{it} - s_{it})^- = (f_{it} - s_{it}) \text{ if } (f_{it} - s_{it}) \leqslant 0 \text{ or } 0 \text{ if } (f_{it} - s_{it}) > 0,$$

and the exchange rate is the dollar–foreign currency rate so $f - s$ will be positive when the US interest rate is above the foreign rate and negative when the foreign rate is above the US rate. Bansal and Dahlquist (2000) find, first, that although the forward rate is a biased predictor when all countries are pooled the evidence of a forward premium puzzle $- \alpha_1 < 0.5 -$ only exists for high income economies (in particular, G7 countries); for emerging markets and developing countries they cannot reject the hypothesis that $\alpha_1 = 0.5$. Their second finding is that when the interest differential is negative (foreign rate greater than US and so a negative state exists) the estimated value of α_1 is insignificantly different from unity across all country groups in the state and the forward premium puzzle arises. Third, for high income countries coefficients are significantly different between the $-$ and $+$ states and therefore this is indicative of non-linearity; for emerging markets they cannot reject the hypothesis that these coefficients are the same.

15.5.2   *Weak exogeneity*

Although, as we have seen, the most popular way of testing forward rate unbiasedness involves using expression (15.4), repeated here:

$$\Delta s_{t+1} = \alpha_0 + \alpha_1(f_t - s_t) + \omega_{t+1}, \tag{15.4}$$

there is a debate about the stationarity of the forward premium term, $f_t - s_t$. (see Baillie and Bollerslev 1994; Crowder 1994; and MacDonald and Marsh 1999 and the references in Chapter 8 to the UIP/PPP hypothesis) and this has led researchers to start with the levels equation (15.3), repeated here:

$$s_{t+k} = \beta_0 + \beta_1 f_t + v_{t+k}. \tag{15.3}$$

Since s and f are non-stationary variables a number of researchers have suggested testing equation (15.3) using cointegration methods (see Hakkio and Rush 1989 and Liu and Maddala 1992) and these studies find that the null of no cointegration is rejected for a number of currencies and, furthermore, the studies find that the two series are cointegrated with a cointegrating vector 1, −1.

However, in the presence of cointegration, MacDonald and Moore (2000) raise the question of whether in fact the benchmark equation such as (15.4) is an appropriate framework for testing the unbiasedness of the forward exchange rate. For example, if f and s are cointegrated and, therefore $f - s$ is stationary, then a VECM representation of the following form must exist:

$$\Delta s_t = \alpha_s(s_{t-1} - \beta_1 f_{t-1} - \beta_0) + \sum_{i=1}^{k-1} b_{si}\Delta s_{t-i} + \sum_{i=1}^{k-1} c_{si}\Delta s_{t-i} + \varepsilon_{st}, \tag{15.53}$$

$$\Delta f_t = \alpha_f(s_{t-1} - \beta_1 f_{t-1} - \beta_0) + \sum_{i=1}^{k-1} b_{fi}\Delta s_{t-i} + \sum_{i=1}^{k-1} c_{fi}\Delta f_{t-i} + \varepsilon_{ft}.$$

Johansen (1995) has demonstrated that it is invalid to estimate dynamic equations of (15.53) separately unless there is evidence of weak exogeneity. So what does this imply for the estimation of the standard equation? For (15.4) to be a valid representation, α_f in this system would have to be zero, thus ensuring that a single equation estimator is valid. In order to see the restrictiveness of (15.4), consider equation (15.54):

$$\Delta s_t = b_o \Delta f_t + \alpha_s(s_{t-1} - \beta_1 f_{t-1} - \beta_0) + \sum_{i=1}^{k-1} b_i \Delta s_{t-1} + \sum_{i=1}^{k-1} c_i \Delta f_{t-i} + \varepsilon_t,$$

$$\tag{15.54}$$

and let $\begin{bmatrix} \sigma_{ss} & \sigma_{sf} \\ \sigma_{fs} & \sigma_{ff} \end{bmatrix}$ be the var–covar of $(\varepsilon_{st}\varepsilon_{ft})$. It follows then that the parameters in (15.4) are related to (15.3) as follows:

$$b_0 = \sigma_{sf}\sigma_{ff}^{-1}, \; b_i = b_{si} - \sigma_{sf}\sigma_{ff}^{-1}bf_i, \; c_i = c_{si} - \sigma_{sf}\sigma_{ff}^{-1}cf_i,$$

and the noise term $\varepsilon_t = \varepsilon_{st} - \sigma_{sf}\sigma_{ff}^{-1}\varepsilon_{ft}$. That equation (15.4) is a special case of (15.53) can be seen by rearranging (15.53) as:

$$\Delta s_t = -\alpha_s \beta_0 - \alpha_s(s_{t-1} - f_{t-1}) + b_0\Delta f_1 + \alpha_s(1 - \beta_1)f_{t-1}$$

$$+ \sum_{i=1}^{k-1} b_i \Delta s_{t-i} + \sum_{i=1}^{k-1} c_i \Delta f_{t-1} + \varepsilon_t, \tag{15.55}$$

which will degenerate to (15.1) when $b_0 = 0$, $\beta_1 = 1$, $b_i = 0$, $c_i = 0$, $i = 1, \ldots, (k-1)$. $b_0 = 0$ means that the contemporaneous cross-equation covariance in the VAR of the spot and forward rate, σ_{sf}, in the vector autoregression of the spot and forward rate must be zero. And the lag length in the VAR, given $b_i = 0$, $c_i = 0$, must be unity. So for equation (15.1) to be valid the following conditions must hold:

1   The spot and forward rate must be cointegrated.
2   The slope of the cointegrating vector must be unity.
3   The forward rate must be weakly exogenous – the derivative market must drive the underlying market.
4   The cross-equation residual covariance in the VECM must be zero.
5   The lag length of the VECM must be exactly 1.

MacDonald and Moore consider to what extent these conditions are met for 10 currencies against the USD and DM, for the period 1978–1994. In the vast majority of cases it turns out that it is in fact the spot rate change that is weakly exogenous and *not* the forward rate and so the forward rate puzzle may simply be a function of the chosen regression equation rather than saying anything else.

The MacDonald and Moore finding is consistent with McCallum's (1994) interpretation of the forward premium puzzle. McCallum argues that if central banks target the interest rate according to the function:

$$i_t - i_t^* = \lambda(s_t - s_{t-1}) + \sigma(i_{t-1} - i_{t-1}^*) + \xi_t, \tag{15.56}$$

and if the risk premium follows a first-order autoregressive process, with coefficient ρ, the coefficient in the basic forward premium representation will be equal to $(\rho - \sigma)^{-1}\lambda$, and if ρ is small relative to σ this would give a negative coefficient in the standard forward premium unbiasedness equation.

Abadir and Talmain (2005) demonstrate that the forward premium puzzle may be explained because of a failure of researchers to model the non-linear long memory properties of the series used to test the unbiasedness of the forward premium.

They propose transforming the basic equation using the autocorrelation function and generalised least squares. They demonstrate that as a result of this transformation the coefficient is insignificantly different from unity. However, they also demonstrate that the error term in the estimated version of (15.4) is strongly serially correlated (they do not use overlapping contracts) which represents a violation of the basic efficiency hypothesis.

15.6   The advantages of survey data in unravelling forward rate bias

As we have seen, a key problem with standard tests of forward rate unbiasedness is that they are tests of a joint hypothesis that agents are risk neutral and form their expectations rationally. The existence of survey data bases offers an independent measure of exchange rate expectations and, in principle, a way round the joint hypothesis problem and it has now been widely used to unravel the separate constituents of the joint hypothesis and also to test other hypothesis about the behaviour of exchange rates and expectations formation.

With access to an independent source of expectations, the rational expectations assumption can be replaced with:

$$\Delta s_{t+k} = \Delta s_{t+k}^e + \varepsilon_{t+k}, \tag{15.57}$$

where Δs_{t+k}^e is now the (subjective) market expectation. Frankel and Froot (1987, 1989) were the first to take the mean or median value from a survey data base as their measure of Δs_{t+k}^e. The existence of an independent measure of expectations should allow a different separation of the risk and expectational parameters/coefficients to that discussed in Section 15.2. For example, as we have seen the p lim of α_1 is:

$$\alpha_1 = \frac{\text{Cov}(fp_t, \Delta s_{t+k})}{\text{Var}(fp_t)}.$$

And on using expression (15.57) in this formulae we can obtain:

$$\alpha_1 = \frac{\text{Cov}(s_{t+k}^e - s_t, fp_t) + \text{Cov}(\varepsilon_{t+k}, fp_t)}{\text{Var}(fp_t)} \tag{15.58}$$

where the terms in the numerator indicate the two potential reasons why α_1 may differ from unity. Using the definition of the risk premium given in Section 15.1 we have:

$$\alpha_1 = 1 - \alpha_\omega - \alpha_e,$$

where:

$$\alpha_\omega = \frac{\text{Var}(\omega_t) + \text{Cov}(\omega_t, s^e_{t+k} - s_t)}{\text{Var}(fp_t)},$$

$$\alpha_e = \frac{\text{Cov}(\varepsilon_{t+k}, s^e_{t+k} - s_t) + \text{Cov}(\varepsilon_{t+k}, fp_t)}{\text{Var}(fp_t)}.$$

The existence of independent survey data means that the expectations terms can, in principle, be recovered from the data. We say in principle because, of course, survey expectations may not equal the 'true' expectation for a number of reasons such as the imperfect synchronisation of survey responses, the use of a consensus response such as the mean or median, which is extracted from only a fraction of market participants. However, as long as the survey expectation and the true expectation are only separated by a random measurement error, regression-based estimates which utilise the survey expectations to extract α_ω and α_e will have valid properties. On this basis the α_e term may be recovered from the following regression:

$$s^e_{t+k} - s_{t+k} = \alpha_0 + \alpha_e(f_t - s_t) + \omega_{t+1}, \tag{15.59}$$

and α_ω may be recovered as $1 - \alpha_\kappa$, from:

$$s^e_{t+k} - s_t = \alpha_0 + \alpha_\kappa(f_t - s_t) + \omega_{t+1}. \tag{15.60}$$

The α_κ term in (15.60) would be expected to be greater than 1 to explain the forward premium puzzle.

A variety of researchers (see, *inter alia*, Dominguez 1986; Frankel and Froot 1989; MacDonald and Torrance 1990; Chinn and Frankel 1994) have estimated equation (15.59) using a variety of different data sets (e.g. Money Market Services, the *Economist* and *The Currency* digest) for a number of US dollar bilateral currencies and for different forecast horizons (such as, 1, 3, 6 and 12 month). These results clearly indicate that the estimate of α_e is strongly significant suggesting that it is one of the expectational stories which explain the rejection of the null. One exception to these set of results is the paper by Cavaglia *et al.* (1993a). They use survey data for six DM bilateral rates and show that the estimates of α_e are only significant in one case. Their results, generated for a period coinciding with the ERM period, perhaps demonstrate that the relative fixity of DM bilaterals during the sample period increased the predictability of spot rates and thereby the efficiency of these markets.

A variety of researchers have estimated equation (15.60) (see, *inter alia*, MacDonald and Torrance 1988, 1990; Frankel and Froot 1989; Cavaglia *et al.* 1993a; Chinn and Frankel 1994) and the significance of the results seems to hinge crucially on whether the survey data was source in the US or UK. For example, Frankel and Froot (1989, 1990b) use Money Market Services data sourced in the US and find α_κ to be insignificantly different from zero although the estimate of α_0 is significant, suggesting a constant risk premium. Evidence derived by MacDonald and Torrance (1988a, 1990) using Money Market Services (UK) indicates that both α_K and α_0 are significant, thereby offering support for the existence of time-varying risk premia.

This latter finding seems at odds with the evidence reported in Section 15.3 but does seem to be a function of the use of survey data to measure the risk premium since Dominguez and Frankel (1993), Giorgianni (1996) and MacDonald (2000d) show that measures of the risk premium defined using survey data are related to the conditional variances of certain fundamentals such as money supplies and inflation Cavaglia *et al.* (1993b) model the risk premium using time series models in the ARMA class and report evidence that the AR(1) model appears best for almost all currency horizons.

Much as in the studies reported in previous sections, which use the forward rate to test unbiasedness and error orthogonality conditions, survey data has been subject to similar scrutiny. Unbiasedness tests are based on the following kind of equation, or a variant in first differences:

$$s_{t+k} = \alpha + \beta_u s^e_{t+k} + \varepsilon_{t+k}, \tag{15.61}$$

where the null hypothesis of unbiasedness is $\alpha = 0$ and $\beta_u = 1$ and the error term is random. Unbiasedness tests have been implemented by Dominguez (1986), Frankel and Froot (1987), MacDonald and Torrance (1988a), MacDonald (1988), MacDonald and Marsh (1996a), Cavaglia *et al.* (1993a), Chinn and Frankel (1994), and Kim (1997). All of these papers, with the exception of Cavaglia *et al.*, concentrate exclusively on US dollar bilaterals and consider more than one forecast horizon and all report a very clear rejection of unbiasedness in the sense that the β_u term is statistically less than unity.

Survey-based error orthogonality tests have also been conducted and these are based on the following equation:

$$s^e_{t+k} - s_{t+k} = \alpha + \beta I_t + \varepsilon_{t+k}, \tag{15.62}$$

where I_t is a publicly available information set and the null hypothesis is $\alpha = 0$ and $\beta = 0$. When the forward premium is the only variable in the information set such tests are equivalent to testing (15.59) and, as we have seen, such tests produce a rejection of the error orthogonality condition. When only the lagged error term is included in the information set, Dominguez (1986) and MacDonald (1990) and MacDonald and Torrance (1988b) find few rejections of the orthogonality property for short horizons (i.e. 1 to 2 weeks). However, at horizons of 1 month and longer there is more evidence of rejection of weak-form orthogonality (see MacDonald and Torrance 1988b; MacDonald 1990, 1992; Gan and Wong 1993; Benassy and Raymond 1994; Sobiechowski 1996; Lim and McKenzie 1998). In sum, the results from the unbiasedness and error orthogonality tests are again strongly suggestive that it is some form of expectational failure that is behind the forward rate biasedness result.

The above survey-based studies exploit aggregate survey data basis. A number of related studies have exploited disaggregate survey data. Since the disaggregate literature has a direct bearing on the market microstructure literature we have considered this work in Chapter 14.

15.6.1   Testing expectations formation

Survey data has also been used to test if expectations are stabilising or not (along the lines suggested in Milton Friedman's classic case for flexible exchange rates, discussed earlier).[6] In other words, does an exchange rate depreciation today induce the expectation of a future appreciation (which would be stabilising) or an appreciation in the same direction (which would be destabilising)? Clearly, to the extent the forward rate is a pure reflection of expectations it could be used for this purpose, but as we have seen it will be a contaminated measure in this regard if risk is important. Three types of expectations processes are common in the literature: extrapolative, adaptive and regressive.

So-called extrapolative expectations arise when agents extrapolate a current change of the exchange rate into a future change in the same direction and can be captured by the following mechanism:

$$\Delta s^e_{t+k} = \varphi(s_t - s_{t+1}), \quad \varphi > 0. \tag{15.63}$$

With regressive expectations a current exchange rate depreciation/appreciation is expected to be reversed in the future and may be captured by:

$$\Delta s^e_{t+k} = \phi(\bar{s}_t - s_t), \quad 0 < \phi < 1. \tag{15.64}$$

With adaptive expectations agents adapt their expectations to the current forecast error as in:

$$\Delta s^e_{t+k} = \lambda(s^e_t - s_t), \quad 0 < \lambda < 1. \tag{15.65}$$

These kind of relationships have been tested by, *inter alia,* Frankel and Froot (1987), MacDonald and Torrance (1988a), Cavaglia *et al.* (1993a), Prat and Uctum (1994a). The upshot from these tests is that, in general, at horizons longer than 3 months–6 and 12 months – expectations are found to be stabilising (i.e. some form of regressive or extrapolative expectations dominate extrapolative expectations but at shorter horizons), but at shorter horizons – 1 week, 2 weeks, 1 month and 3 months   there is clear evidence of destabilising expectations. One explanation for the difference between the long and the short end of the market is that the individuals providing these kinds of forecasts base their short-term forecasts on chartism and extrapolative methods. Results from a mixed model in which elements of regressive, adaptive and extrapolative expectations are combined essentially confirm this finding (see Benassy-Quere *et al.* 2003).

The consistency of expectations is another way in which the survey-generated measures of expectations have been assessed. In essence, consistency means that the subjective expectation of the exchange rate formed at $t + i$ for period $t + k$ ($k > 1$) is the same as that produced for a one-period ahead forecast formed at period t but iterated forward to $t + i$. Froot and Ito (1989), using a survey data base generated by the *Economist* and Cavalgia *et al.* (1993a) and Verschoor and Wolff (2001, 2002) using survey data generated by BIC reject consistency for a number of currencies across a variety of forecast horizons.

15.7   News in the foreign exchange market

We close this chapter by considering a number of studies which try to assess the impact of new information or 'news' in the foreign exchange market. This seems an appropriate juncture at which to consider this literature since such studies use the forward exchange rate as a measure of the expected exchange rate and also survey expectations have also been used to generate the news. The essential idea underlying such tests is that if the foreign exchange market is efficient all current information should be discounted into the current price and what moves the price period by period is the arrival of new information, such as new information on the money supply or prices. Tests which use the forward exchange rate to test the impact of news generally use a variant of:

$$s_{t+1} - f_t = \kappa_0 + \kappa_1 (z_{t+1} - z_{t+1}^e) + u_t, \tag{15.66}$$

where the term in square brackets is the news and κ_1 is expected to be significantly positive or negative depending on the particular news variable. Frenkel (1981) was the first to test a version of (15.66) and he generated interest rate news by subtracting an actual interest rate differential using the fitted value of an autoregression of an interest differential. He finds a significantly positive association for interest rate news, a finding he attributes to news about inflation.

Edwards (1982, 1983) implements a version of (15.66) for the flexible price monetary model, and news is generated using time series methods for relative money, relative income and relative interest rates and reports statistically significant, and, in general, correctly signed news terms. MacDonald (1983a,b) also estimates a news version of the monetary model and although he finds many contemporaneous news terms to be significant, many are wrongly signed. Furthermore, he finds that lagged news is also a significant determinant of the current forecast error and this is attributed to some form of expectational failure. Hartley (1983) argues that equation (15.66) should be estimated jointly with the equation used to derive the news since this will generate more efficient estimates. However, his results turn out to be disappointing, with none of the estimate news coefficients being statistically significant. Bomhoff and Korteweg (1983) generates a successful news variant of the monetary model, using a multi-state kalman filter to generate news, and Branson (1983) also provides empirical support for a news-based version of the portfolio-balance model (using a VAR-based approach to generate estimates of the expected values).

In contrast to the earlier studies, which use time series methods to generate the news, Dornbusch (1980) uses survey data from an OECD data base to generate news about current accounts and interest rates. The news terms appear statistically significant and correctly signed. A number of other studies have followed Dornbusch's lead and used survey data to generate news measures of fundamentals; however, the literature is somewhat separate to the earlier in the sense that the dependent variable is the change in the exchange rate at the time the relevant news occurs. Specifically:

$$s_t^a - \hat{s}_t = a_0 + a_1(z_t^a - \hat{z}_t^e) + w_t, \tag{15.67}$$

where s_t^a denotes the exchange rate at the time of the news announcement, $\hat{s}_t$ is the spot rate immediately after the announcement, $\hat{z}_t^e$ denotes the expected fundamental recorded just before the announcement and z_t^a is the announcement of the fundamental. Starting with Cornell (1983) and Engel and Frankel (1984) a number of researchers have implemented (15.67) using announcements of monetary growth by central banks (such tests were developed at the time when central banks were involved in monetary targeting). The idea underpinning such tests is simple: if a central bank overshoots its monetary target what do agents infer from this? Will they tighten monetary policy in the future to get their monetary growth back in line or will they fail to control the money supply in the future. If the former view prevails agents will expect a rise in the nominal interest rate which with sticky produces should produce an exchange rate appreciation – this is the so-called policy anticipation effect of Urich and Wachtel (1981) – and the coefficient on the news term in (15.67) should be negative. Evidence using US (see, for example, Cornell 1983 and Engel and Frankel 1984) and UK (see, for example, MacDonald and Torrance 1988, 1989 and Goodhart 1988) survey data strongly supports the policy anticipation effect. More recent work on news in the foreign exchange market takes a market microstructure perspective and this is considered in Chapter 14.

Notes

1 Introduction: some basic concepts and stylised facts and the case for (and against) floating exchange rates

1 The weights used in our examples of the construction of a NEER and REER are arithmetic. In practice, however, geometric weights are often preferred because a geometric average treats increases and decreases in exchange rates symmetrically and is not affected by the choice of base year.

2 For a more complete analysis of the MABP and, in particular, the assumptions underlying the approach see Hallwood and MacDonald (2000).

3 A lucid account of this view is given in Johnson (1977). For some empirical estimates see Genberg (1978).

4 Also notice from equation (1.3) that even if $\Delta D = 0$ the money supply may still be changing if reserves are changing due, perhaps, to excessive domestic credit expansions in other countries. By having a freely floating exchange rate the home country would effectively insulate itself from such foreign monetary impulses.

5 In the Classical Gold standard period participating countries defined their currencies in terms of one ounce of gold which, in turn, meant the bilateral exchange rate of the two countries was fixed. However, the costs (both direct and indirect) of shipping gold between countries defined the gold points, which were effectively the upper and lower limits within which the exchange rate could move without generating arbitrage. In other words, the gold points defined a kind of neutral band within which it was not profitable to ship gold between countries.

6 The classic discussion of equilibria is to be found in Marshall (1923) in the context of his treatment of reciprocal demand or offer curves.

7 More precisely, the Marshall-Lerner condition is predicated on the following assumptions: there is assumed to be only one export and one import good; the elasticity of supply of exports and imports are infinite; trade is initially balanced; the home country is at full employment. For some empirical evidence supportive of the J-curve effect see Artus and Young (1979). For further information on the Marshall-Lerner condition see Hallwood and MacDonald (2000).

8 One problem, however, with the Tsiang analysis lies in its compartmentalization of the different activities of traders. In the real world the hypothetical agents we deal with in the next section are liable to indulge in all three roles simultaneously. For present purposes it will prove useful to trade-off this added realism for greater simplicity and clarity.

9 Operating in the spot market a speculator requires access to the funds for speculation more or less immediately. Operating in the forward market, however, he only requires to fulfil any margin requirements imposed by his broker (which may, for example, be 10% of his total transaction). The opportunity cost therefore of operating in the forward market is much less than the cost of spot market operations.

10 Thus on this definition a test of whether CIP holds or not would be a test of perfect capital mobility.

11 Skewness relates to the third moment of the distribution.

12 In order to check that the significant ARCH/GARCH effects are not a reflection of mispecified models for the conditional mean, Diebold and Nason (1990) and Meese and Rose (1991) use non-linear methods to show that the model-based exchange rate forecasts cannot outperform a martingale.

13 Hausman *et al.* (2004) demonstrate that the real exchange rates of developing countries are approximately three times more volatile than the real exchange rate of industrial countries and that the difference in volatility across developing and developed countries cannot be explained by the larger shocks (both real and nominal) facing developing countries nor in their susceptibility to currency crises.

14 In the post-1997 period the IMF has significantly revised and upgraded its official approach to classifying exchange rate arrangements.

15 As Reinhart and Rogoff (2002) have argued, and as we shall see in Chapter 7, there are a number of different measures of dollarisation.

16 This section draws on Hallwood and MacDonald (2000).

17 Bilateral trade intensity can be measured as either total bilateral trade divided by the sum of total world trade of the bilateral partners, or divided by the sum of the partners GDPs (Frankel and Rose 1998).

18 Business cycle correlation can be measured as the correlation between country pairs of residuals from various detrending methods – as in Frankel and Rose (1998). An alternative method of measuring the degree of macroeconomic correlation between pairs of countries is that of Blanchard and Quah (1989). In a vector autoregression of real GDP and inflation rates they use identifying restrictions in a way such that temporary and permanent shocks can be identified and the correlation between countries calculated. Bayoumi and Eichengreen (1992) were among the first to apply this methodology to judge whether sets of countries were suitable for monetary union.

19 But not the capital account as financial integration may work in the opposite direction (see below).

20 Using instrumental variables, where the instruments for trade intensity are chosen from the gravity trade model (distance between countries, and dummies for adjacency and common language) they find in an illustrative regression that an increase in trade intensity by one standard deviation from the mean of the data increases the bilateral correlation of business cycles from about 0.22 to 0.35.

21 Relatedly, Kalemli-Ozcan *et al.* (2001) find empirical support for the hypothesis that national and regional specialisation increases as, respectively, international and inter-regional capital market integration increases.

22 Hughes-Hallett and Piscitelli (2002) derive sets of conditions where *joining* a currency union positively affects business cycle correlation between the members. In the context of the UK, the significant theoretical result is that following the creation of a monetary union, correlation will increase when the home economy (say, Scotland) is small in relation to the other members (in the rest of the UK) and is not subjected to large cyclical disturbances.

2 Purchasing power parity and the PPP puzzle

1 This chapter, and the next, draw on MacDonald (1995a).

2 The relatively slow mean reversion of the real exchange rate may be explicable in the context of a real model where real shocks are predominant. However, real shocks are not well suited to explaining the volatility of the real exchange rate (see Chapter 8).

3 Such costs are usually defined broadly to include both direct transportation costs and indirect costs such as opportunity cost.

4 Although the split between traded and non-traded goods is often portrayed as dichotomous, the dividing line is often fuzzy and depends on transactions costs. So a good that was in the past non-traded may become traded due to some innovation in transaction costs. For this reason, in their open economy macroeconomic models, Obstfeld and Rogoff (1995) prefer using a continuum of goods whose degree of tradability depends on transaction costs.

5 It is important to note that β, and therefore $\bar{q}$, will not equal zero if price indices are used instead of price levels.

6 MacDonald (1985) also presents regression-based evidence favourable to the PPP hypothesis for the 1920s experience with floating exchange rates.

7 They distinguish between these terms by the inclusion or exclusion of product/country fixed effects in their panel tests: relative LOOP includes fixed effects while the tests of absolute PPP excludes these terms and therefore tests if prices differences are converging towards zero in the long-run.

8 See Jorion and Sweeney (1996) and Papell (1997) for a further discussion.

9 The relationship between the level of economic development and the half-life has been explored by Cheung and Lai (2000b) Using World Bank (per capita income) classifications of low-, medium- and high-income countries and data from the current floating period Cheung and Lai show that the median half life for high income (largely European countries) is 3.3 years, but for low income countries it is 1.4 years (this result is confirmed by Cashin and McDermott 2003). They then attempt to explain persistence for different country groupings in terms of the usual suspects: inflation, productivity, openness and government spending. Cheung and Lai find that countries with higher inflation (low income for the sample) have higher mean reversion speeds and that productivity differences do not seem to explain differing mean reversion speeds (although they use per capita GDP as their measure of productivity). Relatedly, Hausman *et al.* (2004) report that industrialized economies have, on average, a lower standard deviation of the innovations to the real exchange and that this cannot be attributed to the magnitude of shocks facing developing countries.

3 The economics of the PPP puzzle

1 Our derivation of the Balassa-Samuelson model is based on Asea and Cordon (1994) which in turn, is based on Balassa (1964).

2 Hsieh (1982) defines productivity in the traded sector as the ratio of the index of manufacturing to employed man-hours in manufacturing, Marston uses labour productivity while DeGregorio and Wolf (1994) employ the OECD sectoral data base to build measures of total factor productivity in the traded and non-traded sectors.

3 In an empirical study, Bergin *et al.* (2004) demonstrate that the Balassa-Samuelson effect only exists when data for the last 50 years is used; using data further back than 50 years the effect disappears.

4 Firms are assumed to be engaged in Bertrand competition with other firms and so treat q_t as exogenous.

5 Choudhri *et al.* (2005) consider the performance of a range of New Open Economy Macroeconomic models (NOEM)considered in Chapters 9 and 10, in explaining the degree of pass-through in a wide variety of prices. Using a VAR-based approach they show that the best fitting model incorporates a number of different strands in the NOEM literature, such as sticky prices, sticky wages, distribution costs and a combination of local and producer currency pricing.

6 In reality, the distribution sector delivers both intermediate inputs to the firms that use them in the final stage of production and final goods to consumers. For the sake of simplicity, we assume that intermediate inputs are used only in the tradable sector and

that distribution of final goods is necessary only in the tradable sector; relaxation of these assumptions would deliver qualitatively identical results. This choice of assumptions is also in line with the fact that most non-tradable activities (utilities, social services) have a vertically integrated distribution sector.

7 The model is similar to that of Devereux (1999).

8 The net effect of the distribution sector would be positive if $\phi < (1 - \gamma)\alpha/((1 - \alpha)\gamma)$. Note that if $\phi = 0$ and $\gamma = 1$, the distribution sector would disappear from the model and we would obtain the usual Balassa-Samuelson framework, where the exponent of the relative productivity of both tradables and non-tradables is α and $-\alpha$. In our model, the relative productivity of the tradable sector presents two differences with respect to a basic Balassa-Samuelson model: on the one hand, it has a smaller effect, as its impact on wages is less than proportional; on the other hand it has an additional positive effect, as its impact on wages also raises the consumption price of tradables via the employment cost of the distribution sector. Note also that the sum of all the exponents in the RER expression is zero. Allowing for intermediate inputs in the non-tradable sector would lower the exponents (and hence the impact) of the productivities in both tradable and non-tradable sectors.

9 The MacDonald and Ricci model does not feature policy or preference shocks, which can have an independent effect on the relative price of traded to non-traded goods in the short-run.

10 The effect of home bias on the relative price of tradables has been highlighted by Backus *et al.* (1992). The symmetric effect of productivity and mark-up (i.e. product market competition) has been discussed by Obstfeld and Rogoff (2000b).

11 See Bergin *et al.* (2004) for an alternative model.

12 See Ricci (1999) for an economic geography model investigating the relation between agglomeration effects and comparative advantage (based on different productivities across countries and sectors).

13 We introduced the notation of the nominal exchange rate for convenience in order to facilitate comparison with the macroeconomic literature on the real exchange rate. In this model, however, the nominal exchange rate is a redundant variable and can be set to one so that each variety has the same price in both locations.

14 Note that in our framework the expenditure bias is assumed via the choice of δ. However, it may also be derived endogenously via the introduction of the trade costs, as in many economic geography models.

15 The parameter θ_{sk} is directly related to the elasticity of substitution of demand for the respective variety (which equals $1/(1 - \theta_{sk})$) and inversely related to the equilibrium economies of scale (as proxied by the ratio of average cost, equal to the optimal price, and marginal cost) in the respective sector.

16 Using an empirically based real exchange rate, such as a geometric average of the prices of tradables and non-tradables (with weights given by the relative expenditures on the two components), would yield a simpler expression, and similar conclusions to those in Section 2.6 would be obtained.

17 The competitiveness measure in the non-tradable is found to be collinear with the one in tradables, and its effect dominated by the first one. Hence, specific implications for such measure cannot be derived.

4 The flexible price monetary approach to the exchange rate

1 By Walras's law, if the two money markets are in equilibrium so too must the 'composite' bond market.

2 In particular, U is assumed to be bounded, continuously differentiable, increasing in both arguments and strictly concave.

3 The fact that the utility function and the discount factor are common across countries means that differences across countries can only result, if at all, from differences in endowments.

4 This can be derived most easily by substituting c_{yt} into (4.1) to get and differentiating the resulting expression with respect to c_y. Similar Euler equations can be derived for the purchases of home and of foreign equities by differentiating the resulting expression with respect to ω_y and ω_y^*.

5 The sticky-price monetary model

1 The fiscal policy induced shift in the IS curve with flexible exchange rates is conducted purely for pedagogic reasons, since with perfect capital mobility the domestic interest rate is continually tied to the foreign rate and thus the IS curve cannot shift.

2 See Cushman and Zha (1997) for an empirical implementation of the Mundell–Fleming model using a structural VAR approach.

3 This is essentially the 'Dutch disease' issue addresses by Forsyth and Kay (1980).

4 Thus

$$\left.\frac{\delta q}{\delta 1}\right|_{i=0} = \frac{-\beta_0}{\alpha_2 \beta_1}.$$

5 For instance,

$$\left.\frac{\delta q}{\delta 1}\right|_{\dot{q}=0} = \frac{1}{\beta_1 (\alpha_1 - \pi \alpha_2)}.$$

6 As Buiter and Miller (1981), demonstrate, a unique stable saddle path requires the existence of one stable and one unstable root. A necessary and sufficient condition for this to hold is that the determinant of the A matrix in (5.39) be negative. A sufficient condition for this is that π should be sufficiently small, which is what we have assumed.

7 Of course, our representation here is rather crude since in the UK, for example, the Medium Term Financial Strategy was defined in terms of monetary contraction in the current and also future periods. For a full discussion of the implications this has for this model, particularly when a government's credibility is questioned, see Buiter and Miller (1981a).

8 One rather unappealing feature of this story is that it assumes that the rate of money growth continually equals the expected inflation rate. Few 'moderate monetarists' (such as Milton Friedman and David Laidler) would deny that there is a lag between the adjustment of price expectations and a monetary slowdown. In the context of this model a failure of μ to continually equal $\dot{m}$ would exacerbate the recession. A recent statement of Laidler's position on the adjustment of expectations to monetary growth is given in Laidler (1985).

6 The monetary approach to the exchange rate: an empirical perspective

1 Driskell does not use an instrumental variable estimator to account for potential simultaneity between s and m' on the grounds that the Swiss franc's float was relatively clean for this period (due to currency substitution the Swiss authorities adopted a managed float in the period after 1977 – see Vaubel 1980).

2 The monetary model has also been estimated in a structural context by Kearney and MacDonald (1987, 1988).

3 These results are from MacDonald and Taylor (1993).
4 Relative prices appear here since this approach allows for deviations from PPP.
5 Note that this relationship has the constraint that money enters in real terms imposed, a constraint which is not rejected for this data set.
6 Notice that in these sub systems the Fisher conditions are not 'pure' Fisher conditions in the sense that the coefficient on the interest rate term is not minus unity. However, in the gross, or overall, system these coefficients can be restricted to minus one.
7 The dynamic one-step-ahead out-of-sample forecasts for each of the equations in the La Cour and MacDonald system performed impressively since only 5 (out of 168) of the forecasted values lie outside the 95% confidence intervals (none lay outside the bands in the exchange rate equation) and the directional ability of the forecasts also proved to be extremely good. The formal one-step-ahead restrictions test for the restricted VECM model (which takes account of the variance of the estimated parameters and their correlation) had a p-value of approximately 0.5.
8 Alternatively, we could work with a vector error correction model consisting of the vector $[\Delta x_t, \Delta s_t, \zeta_t]'$, but information contained in this vector is preserved in a bivariate VAR of $[\Delta x_t, \zeta_t]'$ or $[\Delta s_t, \zeta_t]'$.
9 Flood and Rose (1999) conduct a similar exercise using the change in the exchange rate and the composite monetary variable as the key variables.

7 Currency substitution models and the portfolio balance approach to the exchange rate

1 Girton and Roper (1981), were the first to introduce the term currency substitution.
2 Such currencies are assumed to be non-interest-bearing.
3 In practice agents will hold a portfolio of money and non-money assets. We shall leave inclusion of the latter in a theory of exchange rate determination until Chapter 8.
4 For example, Laney *et al.* (1984), argue that in 1981 US foreign currency holdings amounted to US$3 billion, whereas total narrowly defined money amounted to over US$400 billion. For a further discussion of the empirical evidence on CS see Chapter 9.
5 McKinnon (1982, p. 327).
6 Underlying the assumption that $\dot{m}^e$ is equal to $\dot{s}^e$ is a further assumption that expected income growth is equal to zero. This type of assumption has been termed monetary super-neutrality by Artis and Currie (1981).
7 Equation (7.14) is a condition for asset market equilibrium because via the wealth identity, (7.12), only one of equations (7.13) and (7.13') can be independent.
8 Kouri (1976), considers other shocks, such as a tax-financed increase in government expenditure and the dynamics of adjustment from short-run equilibrium to the steady state under expectational schemes.
9 A once-and-for-all increase in the price level, unaccompanied by a monetary expansion, results in a proportionate increase in the exchange rate and price level.
10 The empirical relevance of the CS concept will be discussed in Section 7.5.
11 Strictly speaking the asset demand equations (7.38) to (7.40), should be real demands and equation (7.37) should be real wealth, but the assumed homogeneity of asset demands to wealth ensures that the price deflator drops out.
12 For simplicity we assume that the government taxes all domestic residents' interest earnings on domestic bonds.
13 Notice that this definition of the price level differs from that used in the MF model since the exchange rate enters directly. This assumption has important implications for the results in this chapter.
14 Examples of portfolio balance models in which expectations are assumed rational are Dornbusch and Fischer (1980); Branson (1983) and Branson and Buiter (1983).

15 This result is familiar in closed economy models where the existence of an outside asset, which is regarded as wealth by the private sector, will result in non-homogeneity between money and prices n the long run.
16 We noted in Chapter 6 that researchers who have correctly identified the dynamic processes in the simple monetary model have been successful in beating a random walk in an out-of-sample forecasting context.

8 Real exchange rate determination: theory and evidence

1 Additionally, the β term contains income, or expenditure, elasticities. It is relatively straightforward to unravel β in terms of the underlying income, or expenditure, and price elasticities. This is not done here because it would not affect our analysis in any significant way; see Mussa (1984) for a further discussion.
2 Note that (8.10) is perfectly consistent with the condition of risk-adjusted uncovered interest rate parity given in (8.5). Thus it is straightforward to rewrite (8.5) in real terms, as we discuss later, where we have a relationship between the expected change in the real exchange rate, real interest rates and a risk premium. The risk premium in (8.5) exists because foreign assets are imperfect subsititutes for domestic (non-money) assets. This is captured in (8.10) by the term $\mu(\hat{A} - A)$.
3 More specifically: $\eta = (1/2) \cdot \{r^* + (\beta/\alpha) + [r^* + (\beta/\alpha)^2 + 4 \cdot (\mu\beta/\alpha)]^{-1/2}\} > (r^* + (\beta/\alpha))$.
4 Coughlin and Koedjik (1990) find some evidence for cointegration for one of the currencies in their data set, namley the German mark–US dollar.
5 Throop (1994), using an error correction relationship for the real exchange rate/real interest rate relationship reports some evidence for cointegration on the basis of the estimated t-ratio on the error correction term; however, this is not significant on the basis of a small sample correction.
6 Our discussion here is based on Stockman (1995).
7 As in Rogers (1999) and Weber (1998), MacDonald (1999b) advocates a wider range of shocks (both demand and supply shocks) and also a completely different way of estimating the effects of the shocks. In particular, MacDonald points out that in systems which are relatively rich in terms of the numbers of shocks the cointegratedness of the system must be recognised. The existence of significant cointegrating vectors is then used to impose a set of long-run restrictions. The impulse response functions and variance decompositions are then calculated using the generalised impulse response approach of Pesaran. This approach appears to give a more balanced approach.

9 Equilibrium exchange rates: measurement and misalignment

1 The balance of payments is given by the sum of the current, ca, and capital accounts, cap, which with flexible exchange rates must sum to zero. The current balance may be written as: $ca_t = \alpha_1 (s_t - p_t + p_t^*) + \alpha_2 y_t - \alpha_3 y_t^* + i_t' nfa_t$, where the first three terms reflect the influence of the real exchange rate and home and foreign income on net exports and the last term is net interest payments on net foreign assets. The capital account is assumed to be a function of net interest yields adjusted for the expected change in the exchange rate – $cap_t = \mu(i_t - i_t^* - E_t\Delta s_{t+k})$. Using these expressions for the current and capital accounts and solving for the real exchange rate we obtain expression (9.1).

10 The new open economy macroeconomics and exchange rate behaviour

1 If, for example, $\theta < 1$ then as Helpman and Krugman (1985) note marginal revenue would be negative, which is inconsistent with the assumption of monopolistic consumption.

2 Here the j superscript does not appear because we have imposed symmetry on the identical agents within each country.

3 Where $1 + i_t = (P_{t+1})/(P_t)(1 + r_{t+1})$.

4 Note also that equilibrium is characterised by a situation in which the following transversality condition holds:

$$\lim_{T \to \infty} R_{t,t+T} \left(B_{t+T+1} + \frac{M_{t+T}}{P_{t+T}} \right) = 0.$$

5 That is, from (10.11) we have $1 = \beta(1+r)$ and therefore there is no consumption tilting in steady state.

6 S', the steady-state change in the exchange rate, appears here as the representation of the expected exchange rate change in period $t + 1$, given the assumption that the model gets back to steady state in one period.

7 This equation is derived by using equations (10.31), (10.39), (10.35) and (10.36) with home and foreign government spending subtracted and using (10.49).

8 Hau (2000) introduces non-traded goods into the two-country redux model, considered in the last section. He demonstrates that this introduction increases the size of the initial exchange rate movement in response to a monetary shock (because non-traded prices are tied down by the sticky nominal wage assumption, a larger exchange rate movement is required to get a given change in the aggregate price level).

9 Therefore, we do not need to consider the production of the traded good.

11 The new open economy macroeconomic model: pricing to market and exchange rate volatility redux

1 This follows from substituting the assumed pricing patterns into the following industry price index for the foreign country:

$$P^* = \left(\sum_{i=1}^{N+N^*} \frac{1}{N + N^*} \, p_i^{1-\mu} \right)^{1/(1-\mu)}.$$

2 The key difference is that the term $\mu(\eta - 1)$ is replaced with $(\mu - 1)(\eta - 1)$, because the exchange rate is no longer exogenous and so the demand risk associated with invoicing in the exporter's currency has been reduced.

3 For example, in a model with a complete set of state-contingent nominal assets, complete risk-sharing across markets implies that $s_t = (P_t/u_{c,t})(u_{c,t}^*/P_t)$.

13 The economics of fixed exchange rates, part 2: speculative attack models and contagion

1 We follow this terminology here, although see Jeanne (2000) for a critique and an alternative taxonomy.

2 For a variant of the first generation model with currency substitution, see Sawada and Yotopoulos (2000).

3 As Jeanne (2000) notes, this assumption can be justified by the fact that reserve flows move very suddenly at the time of an attack and this does not leave the authorities much time to intervene.

4 Obstfeld (1994) provides a rigorous game-theoretic analysis of a speculative attack using a model with two large speculators.

5 This follows from assuming that $\alpha\theta_2/(1 + \alpha) < 1$ and ruling out speculative bubbles.

6 Where

$$E(v_{t+1}|v_{t+1} > k_t) = \int_{k_t}^{\infty} \frac{vg(v)}{1 - F(k_t)} dv.$$

7 The weights ensure that the two components of the index have equal weights.
8 Pavlova and Rigobon (2003) devlop a two-country two-good model in which the real exchange rate, stock and bond prices ate jointly determined. The model predicts that stock market prices are correlated internationally even though their dividend processes are independent, providing a theoretical argument in favour of financial contagion.
9 This paragraph draws on Bayoumi *et al.* (2003).

14 The market microstructure approach to the foreign exchange market

1 As we stressed in Chapter 1 this figure comprises the total of spot, forward, swaps, futures and options; the figure of spot transactions is about one-half the total.
2 This section draws on Flood (1991).
3 A companion paper by Cheung *et al.* (2000) uses UK-based survey questionire data.
4 An example of a limit order is: 'buy 1000 euros when the euro dollar rate reaches 1.2'. Such orders are collected in a book and then the best buy price becomes the bid and best sell price the ask.
5 See Kubaraych (1983) and Burnam (1991).

15 Spot and forward exchange rates and the forward premium puzzle

1 The definitions weak- and semi-strong form efficiency are from Fama (1970); see Fama (1990) for an alternative definition of informational efficiency.
2 Equation (15.22) can be derived by taking the difference uncovered and covered investments in the risk free asset and by dividing by the foreign nominal return and the discount factor.
3 This section draws on the discussion in Lewis (1995).
4 The expression may be written in terms of changes since the period t exchange rate is in the current information set.
5 Gourinchas and Tornell (2004) show that the forward premium puzzle arises from a systematic distortion in investors beliefs about the interest rate process; this distortion can also explain the delayed overshooting puzzle introduced in Chapter 8.
6 Surveys of this literature are provided by Tagaki (1991) and MacDonald (2000b).

References

Abadir, K.M. and G. Talmain (2005), 'Autocorrelations of Series and of their Transforms', *Journal of Econometrics*, 124, 227–52.

Abuaf, N. and P. Jorion (1990), 'Purchasing Power Parity in the Long Run', *Journal of Finance*, 45, 157–74.

Adler, M. and B. Dumas (1983), 'International Portfolio Choice and Corporate Finance: A Synthesis', *Journal of Finance*, 48, 1887–908.

Adler, M. and B. Lehmann (1983), 'Deviations from Purchasing Power Parity in the Long Run', *Journal of Finance*, 38 (December), 1471–87.

Admati, A. and P. Pfleiderer (1988), 'A Theory of Intraday Trading Patterns: Volume and Price Variability', *Review of Financial Studies*, 1, 3–40.

Agenoir, P.-R., R. Flood and N. Marion (1992), 'A Survey of Speculative Attack Models', IMF Staff Papers.

Ahking, F.W. (1990), 'Further Results on Long-run Purchasing Power Parity in the 1920s', *European Economic Review*, 34, 913–19.

Alberola, E., S.G. Cervero, J. Lopez, J. Humberto and A. Ubide (1999), 'Global Equilibrium Exchange Rates – Euro, Dollar, "Ins," "Outs," and Other Major Currencies in a Panel Cointegration Framework', IMF Working Papers 99/175, International Monetary Fund.

Aliber, R.Z. (1973), 'The Interest Parity Theory: A Reinterpretation', *Journal of Political Economy*, 81, 1451–9.

Allen, P.R. and P.B. Kenen (1980), *Asset Markets, Exchange Rates, and Economic Integration: A Synthesis* (Cambridge: Cambridge University Press).

Allen, P.R. and J.L. Stein (1995), *Fundamental Determinants of Exchange Rates* (Oxford: Oxford University Press).

Amihud, Y. and H. Mendelson (1980), 'Dealership Markets: Market-making with Inventory', *Journal of Financial Economics*, 8, 31–53.

Anthony, M. and R. MacDonald (1998), 'On the Mean-Reverting Properties of Target Zone Exchange Rates: Some Evidence from the ERM', *European Economic Review*, 42, 1493–523.

Anthony, M. and R. MacDonald (1999), 'The Width of the Band and Exchange Rate Mean Reversion: Some Further ERM-Based Results', *Journal of International Money and Finance*, 18, 411–28.

Argy, V. and P. De Grauwe (eds) (1990), *Choosing an Exchange-Rate Regime: The Challenge for Smaller Industrial Countries* (Washington: Institute of International Economics).

Arnold, I., C. de Vries and R. MacDonald (2005), 'Fundamental Volatility is Regime Specific', mimeo, University of Glasgow.

Artis, M. and M. Lewis (1981), *Monetary Control in the United Kingdom* (Oxford: Philip Allan).

Artis, M.J. and D.A. Currie (1981), 'Monetary, Targets and the Exchange Rate: A Case for Conditional Targets', in W.A. Eltis and P.J.N. Sinclair (eds), *The Money Supply and the Exchange Rate* (Oxford: Oxford University Press).

Artis, M.J. and M. Ehrmann (2000), 'The Exchange Rate: A Shock Absorber or Source of Shocks? A Study of Four Open Economies', CEPR Discussion Paper No. 2550.

Artus, J.R. and J.H. Young (1979), 'Fixed and Flexible Exchange Rates: A Renewal of the Debate', *IMF Staff Papers*, 26, 654–98.

Asea, P.K. and W.M. Cordon (1994), 'The Balassa–Samuelson Model: An Overview', *Review of International Economics*, 2, 191–200.

Bacchetta, P. and E. van Wincoop (2001), 'Trade Flows, Prices and the Exchange Rate Regime', in *Revisiting the Case for Flexible Exchange Rates*, Bank of Canada conference, 213–31.

Bacchetta, P. and E. van Wincoop (2002), 'A Theory of the Currency Denomination of International Trade', NBER Working Paper No. 9039.

Bacchetta, P. and E. van Wincoop (2003), 'Can Information Heterogeneity Explain the Exchange Rate Determination Puzzle?', NBER Working Paper No. 9498, National Bureau of Economic Research, Inc.

Bacchetta, P. and E. van Wincoop (2004), 'A Scapegoat Model of Exchange Rate Fluctuations', NBER Working Paper No. 10245.

Backus, D. (1984), 'Empirical Models of the Exchange Rate: Separating the Wheat from the Chaff', *Canadian Journal of Economics*, 17, 824–46.

Backus, D., P.J. Kehoe and F.E. Kydland (1992), 'Dynamics of the Trade Balance and the Terms of Trade: The S-curve', NBER Working Paper No. 4242.

Backus, D., A. Gregory and C. Telmer (1993), 'Accounting for Forward Rates in Markets for Foreign Currency', *Journal of Finance*, 48, 1887–908.

Bagehot, W. (1971), 'The Only Game in Town', *Financial Analysts Journal*, 27 (March/April), 12–17.

Baillie, R.T. and T. Bollerslev (1989), 'The Message in Daily Exchange Rates: A Conditional Variance Tale', *Journal of Business and Economic Statistics*, 7, 297–305.

Baillie, R.T. and T. Bollerslev (1991), 'Intra-day and Inter-market Volatility in Foreign Exchange Rates', *Review of Economic Studies*, 58(3), 565–85.

Baillie, R.T. and T. Bollerslev (1994), 'Cointegation, Fractional Cointegration and Exchange Rate Dynamics', *The Journal of Finance*, 49, 737–45.

Baillie, R.T. and D.D. Selover (1987), 'Cointegration and Models of Exchange Rate Determination', *International Journal of Forecasting*, 3(1), 43–51.

Balassa, B. (1964), 'The Purchasing Power Parity Doctrine: A Reappraisal', *Journal of Political Economy*, 72, 584–96.

Banerjee, A.V. (1992), 'A Simple Model of Herd Behaviour', *The Quarterly Journal of Economics*, 107(3), 798–817.

Banerjee, A., J. Dolado, J. Galbraith and D. Hendry (1986), 'Exploring Equilibrium Relationships in Econometrics Through Static Models: Some Monte Carlo Evidence', *Oxford Bulletin of Economics and Statistics*, 48 (August 1986), 253–77.

Banerjee, A., J. Dolado, J. Galbraith and D. Hendry (1993), *Co-Integration, Error Correction, and the Econometric Analysis of Non-Stationary Data* (Oxford: Oxford University Press).

Bank for International Settlements (2001), Triennial Survey, Basle: BIS.

Bansal, R. and M. Dahlquist (2000), 'The Forward Premium Puzzle: Different Tales from Developed and Emerging Markets', *Journal of Monetary Economics*, 51, 115–44.

Barnea, A. and D.E Logue (1975), 'The Effect of Risk on the Market-maker's Spread', *Financial Analysts Journal*, 31 (November/December), 45–9.

Barr, D. (1984), 'Exchange Rate Dynamics: An Empirical Analysis', LSE Discussion Paper No. 200.

Barrell, R. and S. Wren-Lewis (1989), 'Fundamental Equilibrium Exchange Rates for the G7', CEPR Discussion Paper No. 323.

Barrell, R., P. Soteri, P. Westaway and S. Wren-Lewis (1991), 'Evaluating the UK's Choice of Entry Rate into the ERM', *Manchester School of Economics and Social Studies*, Supplement, 1–22.

Barrios, S., M. Brulhart, R.J.R Elliott and M. Sensier (2001), 'A Tale of Two Cylces: Cofluctuations Between UK Regions and the Euro Zone', Corresponding author Marius.Brulhart@hec.unil.ch

Baxter, M. (1994), 'Real Exchange Rates and Real Interest Rate Differentials: Have we Missed the Business Cycle Relationship?', *Journal of Monetary Economics*, 33, 5–37.

Baxter, M. and A. Stockman (1989), 'Business Cycles and the Exchange-rate System', *Journal of Monetary Economics*, 23, 377–400.

Bayoumi, T. and B. Eichengreen (1992), 'Shocking Aspects of European Monetary Integration', CEPR Working Paper, 643.

Bayoumi, T. and R. MacDonald (1998), 'Deviations of Exchange Rates from Purchasing Power Parity: A Story Featuring Two Monetary Unions', IMF Working Paper No. 98/69 (Washington: International Monetary Fund, March 1998), IMF Staff Papers, 1999.

Bayoumi, T., P. Clark, S. Symansky and M. Taylor (1994), 'The Robustness of Equilibrium Exchange Rate Calculations to Alternative Assumptions and Methodologies', in J. Williamson (ed.), *Estimating Equilibrium Exchange Rates*, Washington: Institute of International Economics.

Bayoumi, T., G. Fazio, M. Kumar and R. MacDonald (2003), 'Fatal Attraction: Measuring Contagion in Good times and Bad', IMF working Paper No. 03/80.

Bec, F., M. Ben-Salem and R. MacDonald (2006), 'Real Exchange Rates and Real Interest Rates: A Nonlinear Perspective', *Rescherches Economiques de Louvain*, 72, 177–94.

Beetsma, R.M. and F. van der Ploeg (1994), ' Intramarginal Interventions, Bands and the Pattern of EMS Exchange Rate Distributions', *International Economic Review*, 17, 339–53.

Bekaert, G. and R.J. Hodrick (1992), 'Characterising Predictable Components in Excess Returns on Equity and Foreign Exchange Markets', *Journal of Finance*, 47, 467–510.

Benassy, A. and H. Raymond (1994), 'The Heterogeneity of Exchange Rate Expectations According to Survey Data', Thema Working Paper 9418.

Benassy-Quere, A., S. Larribeau and R. MacDonald (2003), 'Models of Exchange Rate Expectations: How Much Heterogeneity?', *Journal of International Financial Markets, Institutions and Money*, 13, 113–36.

Benigno, G. and C. Theonissen (2003), 'Equilibrium Exchange Rates and Supply-side Performance', *The Economic Journal*, 113, C103–C124.

Bensaid, B. and O. Jeanne (2000), 'Self Fulfilling Currency, Crises and Central Bank Independence', *Scandinavian Journal of Economics*, 102(4), 605–20.

Bergin, P. (2000), 'One Money One Price? Pricing to Market in a Monetary Union' (available from www.econ.ucdavis.edu/faculty/bergin/research/index.html).

Bergin, P.R. (2004), 'How Well can the New Open Economy Macroeconomics Explain the Current Account?' NBER Working Paper No. 10356.

Bergin, P.R. and R.C. Feenstra (2000), 'Pricing-to-Market, Staggered Contracts, and Real Exchange Rate Persistence' (available from www.econ.ucdavis.edu/faculty/bergin/research/index.html).

Bergin, P., R. Glick and A.M. Taylor (2004), 'Productivity, Tradability and the Long-run Price Puzzle', NBER Working Paper No. 10569.

Bergstrand, J.H. (1991), 'Structural Determinants of Real Exchange Rates and National Price Levels: Some Empirical Evidence', *American Economic Review* (March), 325–34.

Bertola, G. and R.J. Cabellero (1992), 'Target Zones and Realignments', *American Economic Review*, 82, 520–36.

Bertola, G. and L.E.O. Svensson (1993), 'Stochastic Devaluation Risk and the Empirical Fit of Target-Zone Models', *Review of Economic Studies*, 60(3), 689–712.

Bessembinder, H. (1994), 'Bid–Ask Spreads in the Interbank Foreign Exchange Markets', *Journal of Financial Economics*, 35, 317–48.

Betts, C. and M. Devereux (1996), 'The Exchange Rate in a Model of Pricing to Market', *European Economic Review*, 40, 1007–21.

Betts, C. and M. Devereux (2000), 'Exchange Rate Dynamics in a Model of Pricing to Market', *Journal of International Economics*, 50, 215–44.

Beveridge, S. and C.R. Nelson (1981), 'A New Approach to the Decomposition of Economic Time Series into Permanent and Transitory Components, with Particular Attention to the Measurement of Business Cycles', *Journal of Monetary Economics*, 7, 151–74.

Bikhchandani, S., D. Hirshleifer and I. Welch (1992), 'A Theory of Fads, Fashion, Custom, and Cultural Change as Informational Cascades', *Journal of Political Economy*, 100, 992–1026.

Bilson, J.F.O. (1978a), 'Rational Expectations and the Exchange Rate', in Jacob A. Frenkel and Harry G. Johnson (eds), *The Economics of Exchange Rates: Selected Studies* (Reading, MA: Addison-Wesley), 75–96.

Bilson, J.F.O. (1978b), 'The Monetary Approach to the Exchange Rate – Some Empirical Evidence', *IMF Staff Papers*, 25, 201–23.

Black and Salemi (1988), 'FIML Estimation of the Dollar Deutschemark Risk Premium in a Portfolio Balance Model', *Journal of International Money and Finance*, 25, 250–70.

Blanchard, O. (1981), 'Output, the Stock Market and Interest Rates', *American Economic Review*, 71, 132–43.

Blanchard, O. (1984), 'Current and Anticipated Deficits, Interest Rates and Economic Activity', *European Economic Review*, 25, 7–27.

Blanchard, O. and R. Dornbusch (1984), 'US Deficits, the Dollar and Europe', *Banca Nationale Del Lavoro*, 25, 89–113.

Blanchard, O. and D. Quah (1989), 'The Dynamic Effects of Aggregate Demand and Supply Disturbances', *American Economic Review*, 79, 655–73.

Blanco, H. and P. Garber (1986), 'Recurrent Devaluation and Speculative Attacks on the Mexican Peso', *Journal of Political Economy*, 94, 148–66.

Blough, S.R. (1992), 'The Relationship Between Power and Level for Generic Unit Root Tests in Finite Samples', *Journal of Applied Econometrics*, 7, 295–308.

Blundell-Wignall, A. and F. Browne (1991), 'Increasing Financial Market Integration: Real Exchange Rates and Macroeconomic Adjustment', OECD Working Paper No. 65.

Bollerslev, T. (1986), 'Generalised Autoregressive Conditional Heteroskedasticity', *Journal of Econometrics*, 31, 307–27.

Bollerslev, T. and I. Domowitz (1993), 'Trading Patterns and Prices in the Interbank Foreign Exchange Market', *Journal of Finance*, 48(5), 511–21.

Bollerslev, T. and M. Melvin (1994), 'Bid–Ask Spreads and Volatility in the Foreign Exchange Market: An Empirical Analysis', *Journal of International Economics*, 36(3–4), 355–72.

Bollerslev, T., R.Y. Chou and K.F. Kroner (1992), 'ARCH Modeling in Finance: A Review of the Theory and Empirical Evidence', *Journal of Econometrics*, 52, 5–59.

Bomhoff, E.S. and P. Korteweg (1983), 'Exchange Rate Variability and Monetary Policy under Rational Expectations', *Journal of Monetary Economics*, 11, 169–206.

Boothe, P. (1988), 'Exchange Rate Risk and the Bid–Ask Spread: A Seven Country Comparison', *Economic Inquiry*, 26(3), 485–92.

Boothe, P. and D. Glassman (1987), 'The Statistical Distribution of Exchange Rates: Empirical Evidence and Economic Implications', *Journal of International Economics*, 22, 297–319.

Bordo, M.D. and R. MacDonald (2003), 'The Inter-War Gold Exchange Standard: Credibility and Monetary Independence', *Journal of International Money and Finance*, 22, 1–32.

Bordo, M.D. and R. MacDonald (2005), 'Violations of the "Rules of the Game" and the Credibility of the Classical Gold Standard, 1880–1914', NBER Working Paper No. 6115, and *Journal of Monetary Economics*, 52, 307–27.

Branson, W.H. (1969), 'The Minimum Covered Interest Differential Needed for International Arbitrage Activity', *Journal of Political Economy*, 77, 1028–35.

Branson, W.H. (1977), 'Asset Markets and Relative Prices in Exchange Rate Determination', *Sozialwissenschaftliche Annalen*, Band 1.

Branson, W.H. (1983), 'Macroeconomic Determinants of Real Exchange Risk', in R.J. Herring (ed.), *Managing Foreign Exchange Risk* (Cambridge: Cambridge University Press), 33–74.

Branson, W.H. and W. Buiter (1983), 'Monetary and Fiscal Policy with Flexible Exchange Rates', in J.S. Bhandari and B.H. Putnam (eds), *Economic Interdependence and Flexible Exchange Rates* (Cambridge: MIT press), 251–85.

Branson, W.H., H. Haltunen and P. Masson (1977), 'Exchange Rates in the Short Run', *European Economic Review*, 10, 395–402.

Breuer, J.B. (1994), 'An Assessment of the Evidence on Purchasing Power Parity', in John Williamson (ed.), *Estimating Equilibrium Exchange Rates* (Washington, DC: Institute for International Economics), 245–77.

Brigden, A., B. Martin and C. Salmon (1997), 'Decomposing Exchange Rate Movements According to the Uncovered Interest Parity Condition', *Bank of England Quarterly Bulletin*, November, 377–89.

Buiter, W.H. (2000), 'Optimal Currency Areas: Why Does the Exchange Rate Regime Matter', *Scottish Journal of Political Economy*, 47, 213–50.

Buiter, W.H. and M.H. Miller (1981a), 'Monetary Policy and International Competitiveness: The Problem of Adjustment', *Oxford Economic Papers*, 33, 143–75.

Buiter, W.H. and M.H. Miller (1981b), 'Real Exchange Rate Overshooting and the Output Cost of Bringing Down Inflation', Discussion Paper No. 204, Department of Economics, University of Warwick.

Buiter, W.H. and D.D. Purvis (1983), 'Oil Disinflation and Export Competitiveness: A Model of the "Dutch Disease"', in J. Bandari and B.H. Putnam (eds), *Economic Interdependence and Flexible Exchange Rates* (Cambridge, MA: MIT Press).

Burnam, J.B. (1991), 'Current Structure and Recent Developments in Foreign Exchange Markets', in S.J. Khoury (ed.), *Recent Developments in International Banking and Finance Vol. IV*, (Amsterdam: Elsevier), 123–53.

Burstein, A.T., J.C. Neves and S. Rebelo (2000), 'Distribution Costs and Real Exchange Rate Dynamics During Exchange-rate-based-stabilizations', mimeo, Northwestern University.

Caballero, R. and A. Krishnamurthy (2000), 'Dollarization of Liabilities: Underinsurance and Domestic Financial Underdevelopment', NBER Working Paper No. 7792.

Calvo, G. and C. Reinhart (2002), 'Fear of Floating', *The Quarterly Journal of Economics*, 117(2), 379–408.

Calvo, G.A. and C.A. Rodriguez (1977), 'A Model of Exchange Rate Determination under Currency Substitution and Rational Expectations', *Journal of Political Economy*, 85, 3, 261–78.

Calvo, G. and C. Vegh (1992), 'Currency Substitution in Developing Countries – An Introduction', IMF Working Paper No. 92/40.

Campa, J.M. and L.S. Goldberg (2002), 'Exchange Rate Pass Through into Import Prices: A Macro or Micro Phenomenon', NBER Working Paper No. 8943.

Campbell, J.Y. and R.H. Clarida (1987a), 'The Dollar and Real Interest Rates', *Carnegie-Rochester Conference Series on Public Policy*, 27 (Autumn), 103–40.

Campbell, J.Y. and R.H. Clarida (1987b), 'The Term Structure of Euromarket Interest Rates: An Empirical Investigation', *Journal of Monetary Economics*, 19, 25–44.

Campbell, J.Y. and P. Perron (1991), 'Pitfalls and Opportunities: What Macroeconomists Should Know About Unit Roots', in Olivier Jean Blanchard and Stanley Fisher (eds), *NBER Economics Annual 1991* (Cambridge: MIT Press).

Campbell, J.Y. and R.J. Shiller (1987), 'Cointegration and Tests of Present Value Models', *Journal of Political Economy*, 95, 1062–88.

Canzoneri, M.B. and B. Diba (1993), 'Currency Substitution and Exchange Rate Volatility', *Journal of International Economics*, 35, 351–65.

Canzoneri, M.B., R.E. Cumby and B. Diba (1996), 'Relative Labour Productivity and the Real Exchange Rate in the Long Run: Evidence for a Panel of OECD Countries', *Journal of International Economics*, 47, 245–66.

Cao, H.H., R.K. Lyons and M.D.D. Evans (2003), 'Inventory Information', NBER Working Paper No. 9893, National Bureau of Economic Research, Inc.

Caplin, A. and J. Leahy (1994), 'Business as Usual, Market Crashes, and Wisdom After the Fact', *American Economic Review*, 84, 548–65.

Caramazza, F. (1993), 'French–German Interest Rate Differentials and Time-varying Realignment Risk', *IMF Staff Papers*, 40(3) (September), 567–83.

Cashin, P. and J.M.C. Dermott (2003), 'An Unbiased Appraisal of Purchasing Power Parity', *IMF Staff Papers*, 50(3), 1–25.

Cassel, G. (1928), *Foreign Investments*, Lectures of the Harris Foundation, University of Chicago Press.

Cavaglia, S., W.F.C. Verschoor and C.C.P. Wolff (1993a), 'Further Evidence on Exchange Rate Expectations', *Journal of International Money and Finance*, 27, 78–98.

Cavaglia, S., W.F.C. Verschoor and C.C.P. Wolff (1993b), 'On the Biasedness of Forward Foreign Exchange Rates: Irrationality or Risk Premia?', *Journal of Business*, 67, 321–43.

Cerra, V. and S.C. Saxena (2000), 'Contagion, Monsoons, and Domestic Turmoil in Indonesia: A Case Study in the Asian Currency Crisis', IMF Working Paper No. 60.

Chadha, B. and E. Prasad (1997), 'Real Exchange Rate Fluctuations and the Business Cycle', *International Monetary Fund, Staff Papers*, 44(3), 328–55.

Chang, R. and A. Velasco (1998a), 'The Asian Liquidity Crisis', NBER Working Paper No. 6606

Chang, R. and A. Velasco (1998b) 'Financial Crises in Emerging Markets: A Canonical Model', NBER Working Paper No. 6606.

Chan-Lau, J.A., D. Mathieson and J.Y. Yao (2002), 'Extreme Contagion in Equity Markets', IMF Working Paper No. 98.

Chari, V.V. and P.J. Kehoe (2003), 'Financial Crises as Herds: Overturning the Critiques', NBER Working Paper No. 9658, National Bureau of Economic Research, Inc.

Chari, V.V., P.J. Kehoe and E. McGrattan (1998), 'Sticky Price Models of the Business Cycle: Can the Contract Multiplier Solve the Persistence Problem', NBER, 5809.

Cheung, Y.-W. and M.D. Chinn (1999), 'Macroeconomic Implications of the Beliefs and Behavior of Foreign Exchange Traders', NBER Working Paper No. 7417.

Cheung, Y.-W. and K.S. Lai (1993), 'Long-run Purchasing Power Parity During the Recent Float', *Journal of International Economics*, 34 (February), 181–92.

Cheung, Y.-W. and K.S. Lai (2000a), 'On the Purchasing Power Parity Puzzle', *Journal of International Economics*, 52, 321–30.

Cheung, Y.-W. and K.S. Lai (2000b), 'On Cross-country Differences in the Persistence of Real Exchange Rates', *Journal of International Economics*, 50, 375–97.

Cheung, Y.-W., M. Chinn and E. Fujii (1999), 'Market Structure and the Persistence of Sectoral Real Exchange Rates', mimeo, University of California at Santa Cruz.

Cheung, Y.-W., M. Chinn and I.W. Marsh (2000), 'How do UK-Based Foreign Exchange Dealers Think their Market Operates?' NBER Working Paper 7524.

Cheung, Y.-W., M. Chinn and A.G. Pascual (2005), 'Empirical Exchange Rate Models of the Nineties: Are any Fit to Survive?' *Journal of International Money and Finance*, 24(7), 1150–75.

Chinn, M. (1997), 'Sectoral Productivity, Government Spending and Real Exchange Rates: Empirical Evidence for OECD Countries', chapter 7, in R. MacDonald and J. Stein (eds), *Equilibrium Exchange Rates* (Amsterdam: Kluwer Press).

Chinn, M. (1998), 'Long Run Determinants of East Asian Real Exchange Rates', Federal Reserve Bank of St. Francisco, April.

Chinn, M. and J. Frankel (1994), 'Patterns in Exchange Rate Forecasts for Twenty-five Currencies', *Journal of Money Credit and Banking*, 26, 760–67.

Chinn, M. and L. Johnston (1999), 'Real Exchange Rate Level, Productivity and Demand Shocks: Evidence from a Panel of 14 Countries', NBER Discussion Paper No. 5709.

Chinn, M. and R. Meese (1995), 'Banking on Currency Forecasts: How Predictable is the Change in Money?', *Journal of International Economics*, 38, 161–78.

Chinn, M. and G. Meredith (2004), 'Monetary Policy and Long Horizon Uncovered Interest Parity', *IMF Staff Papers*, 51(3), 404–30.

Chionis, D. and R. MacDonald (1997), 'Some Tests of Market Microstructure Hypotheses in the Foreign Exchange Market', *Journal of Multinational Financial Management*, 7, 203–29.

Chionis, D. and R. MacDonald (2002), 'Aggregate and Disaggregate Measures of the Foreign Exchange Risk Premium', *International Review of Economics and Finance*, 11, 57–84.

Chortareas, G.E. and R.L. Driver (2001), 'PPP and the Real Exchange Rate–Real Interest Rate Differential Puzzle Revisited: Evidence from Non-stationary Panel Data', Bank of England Working Papers 138.

Choudhri, E.U., H. Faruqee and D.S. Hakura (2005), 'Explaining the Exchange Rate Pass-through in Different Prices', *Journal of International Economics*, 65, 349–74.

Choudhri, T., R. McNown and M. Wallace (1991), 'Purchasing Power Parity and the Canadian Float in the 1950s', *Review of Economics and Statistics*, 73 (August), 558–63.

Christiano, L.J. and M. Eichenbaum (1992), 'Liquidity Effects and the Monetary Transmission Mechanism', *American Economic Review*, American Economic Association, 82(2), 346–53.

Chrystal, A. and R. MacDonald (1996), 'Exchange Rates, Financial Innovation and Divisia Money: The Sterling/Dollar Rate 1972–1990', *Journal of International Money and Finance*, 14, 493–513.

Clarida, R. and J. Gali (1994), 'Sources of Real Exchange Rate Fluctuations: How Important are Nominal Shocks?', *Carnegie-Rochester Series on Public Policy*, 41, 1–56.

Clark, P.B. and R. MacDonald (1998), 'Exchange Rates and Economic Fundamentals: A Methodological Comparison of BEERs and FEERs', IMF Working Paper No. 98/67 (Washington: International Monetary Fund, March).

Clark, P.B. and R. MacDonald (2000), 'Filtering the BEER: A Permanent and Transitory Decomposition', IMF Working Paper No. 00/144 (Washington: International Monetary Fund) and *Global Finance Journal*, 215, 29–56.

Clark, P.K. (1973), 'A Subordinate Stochastic Process Model with Finite Variance for Speculative Prices', *Econometrica*, 41, 135–55.

Clark, T.E. and E. van Wincoop (2001), 'Borders and Business Cycles', *Journal of International Economics*, 55, 59–85.

Clostermann, J. and W. Friedmann (1998), 'What Drives the Real Effective D-Mark Exchange Rate?', *Konjunkturpolitik, Applied Economics Quarterly*, 44, 207–30.

Clostermann, J. and B. Schnatz (2000), 'The Determinants of the Euro–Dollar Exchange Rate – Synthetic Fundamentals and a Non-existing Currency', Deutsche Bundesbank Working Paper No. 02/00.

Cochrane, J.H. (1988), 'How Big is the Random Walk in GNP?', *Journal of Political Economy*, 96 (October), 893–920.

Cochrane, J.H. (1990), 'Univariate vs. Multivariate Forecasts of GNP Growth and Stock Returns', NBER Working Paper No. 3427.

Cochrane, J.H. (1991), 'A Critique of the Application of Unit Root Tests', *Journal of Economic Dynamics and Control*, 15, 275–84.

Cohen, D. and C. Wyplosz (1989), 'The European Monetary Union: An Agnostic Evaluation', CEPR Discussion Paper No. 306.

Cohen, K.J., S.F. Maier, R.A. Schwartz and D.K. Whitcomb (1979), 'Market Makers and the Market Spread: A Review of the Recent Evidence', *The Journal of Financial and Quantitative Analysis*, 14, 813–35.

Cohen, K.J., S.F. Maier, R.A. Schwarz and D.K. Whitcomb (1981), 'Transaction Costs, Order Placement Strategy, and Existence of the Bid–Ask Spread', with, *The Journal of Political Economy*, April 1981, 287–305. Reprinted in Hans Stoll (ed.) *Microstructure: The Organization of Trading and Short Term Price Behavior* (London: Edward Elgar), 76–94.

Copeland, T.E. (1976), 'A Model of Asset Trading under the Assumption of Sequential Information Arrival', *Journal of Finance*, 31, 1149–68.

Cornell, B. (1978), 'Determinants of the Bid–Ask Spread on Forward Foreign Exchange Contracts under Floating Exchange Rates', *Journal of International Business Studies*, 9 (Fall), 33–41.

Cornell, B. (1983), 'Money Supply Announcements and Interest Rates: Another View', *Journal of Business*, 56, 109–13.

Corsetti, G. and P. Pesenti (2001), 'Welfare and Macroeconomic Interdependence', *Quarterly Journal of Economics*, 116, 421–45.

Corsetti, G.M., P. Pesenti and N. Roubini (1998), 'What Caused the Asian Currency and Financial Crisis?', Temi di Discussione – Banca d'Italia No. 343.

Cosandier, P.A. and B.R. Laing (1981), 'Interest Rate Parity Tests: Switzerland and Some Major Western Countries', *Journal of Banking and Finance*, 5, 187–200.

Coughlin, C.C. and K. Koedijk (1990), 'What do we Know about the Long-run Real Exchange Rate?', *St. Louis Federal Reserve Bank Review*, 72 (January/February), 36–48.

Crowder, W.J. (1994), 'Foreign Exchange Market Efficiency and Common Stochastic Trends', *Journal of International Money and Finance*, 13, 551–64.

Crucini, M., C. Telmer and M. Zachariadis (1998), 'What can we Learn from Deviations from the Laws of One Price?', mimeo, Carnegie Mellon.

Cuddington, J.T. (1982), 'Currency Substitution: A Critical Survey from a Portfolio Balance Perspective', IIES No. 241.

Cuddington, J.T. (1983), 'Currency Substitution, Capital Mobility and Money Demand', *Journal of International Money and Finance*, 2, 111–33.

Cuddington, J.T. and S.K. Otoo (1990), 'Choice of Exchange Rate Regime: A Multinomial Logit Model', Georgetown University Working Paper No. 90-18.

Cumby, R.E. (1990), 'Consumption Risk and International Equity Returns: Some Empirical Evidence', *Journal of International Money and Finance*, 9, 181–92.

Cumby, R.E. (1996), 'Forecasting Exchange Rates and Relative Prices with the Hamburger Standard', NBER No. 5675.

Cumby, R.E. and J. Huizinga (1990), 'The Predictability of Real Exchange Rate Changes in the Short Run and in the Long Run', NBER Working Paper No. 3468.

Cumby, R.E. and M. Obstfeld (1981), 'Exchange Rate Expectations and Nominal Interest Rates: A Test of the Fisher Hypothesis', *Journal of Finance*, 36, 697–703.

Cumby, R.E. and M. Obstfeld (1984), 'International Interest-rate Linkages under Flexible Exchange Rates: A Review of Recent Evidence', in J.F.O. Bilson and R.C. Marston (eds), *Exchange Rate Theory and Practice* (Chicago, IL: Chicago University Press).

Cumby, R.E. and S. van Wijnbergen (1989), 'Financial Policy and Speculative Runs with a Crawling Peg', *Journal of International Economics*, 17, 111–27.

Cushman, D.O. (2006), 'A Portfolio Balance Approach to the Canadian–US Exchange Rate', mimeo, Westminster College.

Cushman, D.O. and T. Zha (1997), 'Identifying Monetary Policy in a Small Open Economy under Flexible Exchange Rates', *Journal of Monetary Economics*, 39(3), 433–48.

Cushman, D.O., S. Lee and T. Thorgeirsson (1997), 'Maximum Likelihood Estimation of Cointegration in Exchange Rate Models for 7 Inflationary OECD Countries', *Journal of International Money and Finance*, 15, 337–68.

Darby, M.R. (1980), 'Does Purchasing Power Parity Work?', NBER Working Paper No. 607 (Cambridge, MA: National Bureau of Economic Research, December 1980).

Davidson, J. (1985), 'Econometric Modelling of the Sterling Effective Exchange Rate', *Review of Economic Studies*, 211, 231–40.

Davutyan, N. and J. Pippenger (1985), 'Purchasing Power Parity did not Collapse During the 1970s', *American Economic Review*, 75, 1151–8.

De Grauwe and W. Vanhaverbeke (1993), 'Is Europe an Optimum Currency Area?: Evidence from Regional Data', in P. Masson and M. Taylor (eds), *Policy Issues in the Operation of Currency Areas* (Cambridge: Cambridge University Press).

DeGregorio, J. and H. Wolf (1994), 'Terms of Trade, Productivity and the Real Exchange Rate', NBER Working Paper No. 4807.

DeGregorio, J., A. Giovannini and H. Wolf (1994), 'International Evidence on Tradables and Nontradables Inflation', *European Economic Review*, 44, 1225–44.

de Kock and Vittorio Grilli (1993), 'Fiscal Policies and the Choice and Exchange Rate Regime', *Economic Journal*, 103: 347–58.

Delgado, F.A. (1991), 'Hysteresis, Menu Costs and Pricing with Random Exchange Rates', *Journal of Monetary Economics*, 28, 461–89.

Delgado, F.A. and B. Dumas (1993), 'Monetary Contracting and the Design of Sustainable Exchange Rate Zones', *Journal of International Economics*, 34 , 201–24.

De Long, J. Bradford, A. Shleifer, L.H. Summers and R.J. Waldmann (1990), 'Noise Trader Risk in Financial Markets', *Journal of Political Economy*, 98, 703–38.

Demsetz, H. (1968), 'The Cost of Transacting', *Quarterly Journal of Economics*, 82, 33–53.

Detken, C., A. Dieppe, J. Henry, F. Smets and C. Marin (2000), 'Determinants of the Effective Real Exchange Rate of the Synthetic Euro: Alternative Methodological Approaches', *Australian Economic Papers*, 41(4), 404–36.

Devereux, M.B. (1999), 'Review of International Economics. Real Exchange Rate Trends and Growth: A Model of East Asia', UBC Departmental Archives 99–05, UBC Department of Economics.

Devereux, M.B. and C. Engel (1998), 'Fixed Versus Floating Exchange Rates: How Price Setting Affects the Optimal Choice of Exchange-rate Regime', NBER Working Paper No. 6867.

Devereux, M.B. and C. Engel (2001), 'Endogenous Currency Price Setting in a Dynamic Open Economy Model', mimeo, University Wisconsin-Madison.

Devereux, M.B., C. Engel and P.E. Storgaard (2001), 'Endogeneous Exchange Rate Pass-through When Nominal Prices Are Set in Advance', *Journal of International Economics*, 63, 263–91.

Dickey, D.A. and W. Fuller (1979), 'Distribution of the Estimators for Autoregressive Time Series with a Unit Root', *Journal of the American Statistical Association*, 74 (June), 427–31.

Diebold, F.X. (1988), *Empirical Modeling of Exchange Rate Dynamics* (New York: Springer Verlag).

Diebold, F.X. and J.M. Nason (1990), 'Nonparametric Exchange Rate Prediction', *Journal of International Economics*, 28, 315–32.

Diebold, F.X. and M. Nerlove (1989), 'The Dynamics of Exchange Rate Volatility: A Multivariate Latent Factor ARCH Model', *Journal of Applied Econometrics*, 4, 1–21.

Diebold, F.X., S. Husted and M. Rush (1991), 'Real Exchange Rates under the Gold Standard', *Journal of Political Economy*, 99 (December), 1252–71.

Dixit, A.K. (1989), 'Hysteresis, Import Penetration, and Exchange Rate Pass Through', *Quarterly Journal of Economics*, 104, 205–28.

Dixit, A.K. and J. Stiglitz (1977), 'Monopolistic Competition and Optimal Product Diversity', *American Economic Review*, 67, 367–89.

Dominguez, K.M. (1986), 'Are Foreign Exchange Forecasts Rational? New Evidence from Survey Data', *Economics Letters*, 21, 277–82.

Dominguez, K.M. and J.A. Frankel (1993), 'Does Foreign-exchange Intervention Matter? The Portfolio Effect', *American Economic Review*, 83, 1356–69.

Dominguez, K.M. and P. Kenen (1991), 'On the Need to Allow for the Possibility that Governments do not Mean What they say – Interpreting the Target Zone Model in the Light of EMS Experience', NBER Paper No. 3670.

Domowitz, I. and C. Hakkio (1985), 'Conditional Variance and the Risk Premium in the Foreign Exchange Market', *Journal of International Economics*, 19, 47–66.

Dooley, M. and P. Isard (1982), 'A Portfolio-Balance Rational-Expectations Model of the Dollar–Mark Exchange Rate', *Journal of International Economics*, 12, 257–76.

Doornik, J. and H. Hansen (1994), 'A Practical Test of Multivariate Normality', unpublished paper (Oxford: Nuffield College).

Dornbusch, R. (1976), 'Expectations and Exchange Rate Dynamics', *Journal of Political Economy*, 84, 1161–76.

Dornbusch, R. (1979), 'Monetary Policy under Exchange Rate Flexibility', in *Managed Exchange Rate Flexibility: The Recent Experience*, Federal Reserve Bank of Boston, 90–122.

Dornbusch, R. (1980), 'Exchange Rate Economics: Where do we Stand?', *Brookings Papers on Economic Activity*, 1, 143–94.

Dornbusch, R. (1982), 'Flexible Exchange Rates and Interdependence', *IMF Staff Papers*, 30, 3–30.

Dornbusch, R. (1987), 'Exchange Rates and Prices', *American Economic Review*, 77, 93–106.

Dornbusch, R. (2001), 'Fewer Monies, Better Monies', NBER Working Paper No. 8324.

Dornbusch, R. and S. Fischer (1980), 'Exchange Rates and the Current Account', *American Economic Review*, 70, 960–71.

Dornbusch, R. and P. Krugman (1978), 'Flexible Exchange Rates in the Short Run', *Brookings Papers on Economic Activity*, 3, 357–84.

Drazen, A. (1999), 'Political Contagion in Currency Crises', NBER Working Paper No. 7211, National Bureau of Economic Research.

Driskell, R.A. (1981), 'Exchange Rate Dynamics: An Empirical Investigation', *Journal of Political Economy*, 89(2), 357–71.

Driskell, R.A. and S.M. Sheffrin (1981), 'On the Mark: Comment', *American Economic Review*, 71, 1068.

Driver, R. (2000), 'Evaluating Alternative Exchange Rate Regimes', mimeo, Bank of England.

Driver, R. and S. Wren-Lewis (1998), 'Real Exchange Rates for the Year 2000' (mimeo, Washington, DC: Institute for International Economics).

Driver, R. and S. Wren-Lewis (1999), 'FEERs: A Sensitivity Analysis', in R. MacDonald and J. Stein (eds), *Equilibrium Exchange Rates* (Boston, MA: Kluwer).

Duarte, M. (2003), 'Why Don't Macroeconomic Quantities Respond to Exchange Rate Variability?', *Journal of Monetary Economics*, 50, 889–913.

Duarte, M. and A.C. Stockman (2005), 'Rational Speculation and Exchange Rates', *Journal of Monetary Economics*, 52, 3–29.

Dumas, B. (1988), 'Pricing Physical Assets Internationally', NBER Working Paper No. 2569.

Dumas, B. (1992), 'Dynamic Equilibrium and the Real Exchange Rate in a Spatially Separated World', *Review of Financial Studies*, 5, 153–80.

Easley, D. and M. O'Hara (1992), 'Time and the Process of Security Price Adjustment', *Journal of Finance*, American Finance Association, 19, 64–90.

Eastwood, R.K. and A.J. Venables (1982), 'The Macroeconomic Implications of a Resource Discovery in an Open Economy', *The Economic Journal*, 92, 285–99.

Edison, H.J. (1985), 'Purchasing Power Parity: A Quantitative Reassessment of the 1920s Experience', *Journal of International Money and Finance*, 4 (September), 361–72.

Edison, H.J. (1987), 'Purchasing Power Parity in the Long Run: A Test of the Dollar/Pound Exchange Rate (1890–1978)', *Journal of Money, Credit and Banking*, 19 (August), 376–87.

Edison, H.J. and B. Diane Pauls (1993), 'A Re-assessment of the Relationship between Real Exchange Rates and Real Interest Rates: 1974–90', *Journal of Monetary Economics*, 31 (April), 165–87.

Edison, H.J. and R. MacDonald (2003), 'Credibility and Interest Rate Discretion in the ERM', *Open Economies Review*, 14, 351–68.

Edison, H.J. and W.R. Melick (1995), 'Alternative Approaches to Real Exchange Rates and Real Interest Rates: Three Up and Three Down', Board of Governors of the Federal Reserve System, International Finance Papers No. 518.

Edison, H.J., P. Luangaram and M. Miller (1998), 'Asset Bubbles, Domino Effects and "Lifeboats": Elements of the East Asian Crisis', CEPR Discussion Paper No. 1866.

Edwards, S. (1982), 'Exchange Rates, Market Efficiency and New Information', *Economics Letters*, 9, 377–82.

Edwards, S. (1983), 'Exchange Rates and "News": A Multi-currency Approach', *Journal of International Money and Finance*, 3, 211–24.

Edwards, S. (1989), *Real Exchange Rates, Devaluation, and Adjustment* (Cambridge, MA: MIT Press).

Edwards, S. and I. Magendzo (2003), 'A Currency of One's Own? An Empirical Investigation on Dollarization and Independent Currency Unions', NBER Working Paper No. 9514.

Edwards, S. and E. Yeyati (2003), 'Flexible Exchange Rates as Shock Absorbers', NBER Working Paper No. 9867.

Egert, B., L. Halpern and R. MacDonald (2005), 'Equilibrium Exchange Rates in Transition Economies: Taking Stock of the Issues', CEPR Working Paper No. 4809. *Journal of Economic Surveys*, 20, 257–324.

Eichenbaum, M. and C.L. Evans (1995), 'Some Empirical Evidence on the Effects of Shocks to Monetary Policy on Exchange Rates', *Quarterly Journal of Economics*, 101, 975–1009.

Eichengreen, B., A. Rose and C. Wyplosz (1995), 'Exchange Market Mayhem: The Antecedants and Aftermath of Speculative Attacks', *Economic Policy*, 21, 249–312.

Elbadawi, I. (1994), 'Estimating Long-Run Equilibrium Real Exchange Rates', in J. Williamson (ed.), *Fundamental Equilibrium Exchange Rates* (Washington, DC: International Economics Institute).

El-Gamal, M.A. and D. Ryu (2006), 'Short Memory and the PPP Hypothesis', *Journal of Economic Dynamics and Control*, 30, 361–91.

Enders, W. (1988), 'ARIMA and Cointegration Tests of PPP under Fixed and Flexible Exchange Rate Regimes', *Review of Economics and Statistics* (August 1988), 504–08.

Engel, C. (1993), 'Real Exchange Rates and Relative Prices: An Empirical Investigation', *Journal of Monetary Economics*, 32, 35–50.

Engel, C. (1994), 'Tests of CAPM on an International Portfolio of Bonds and Stocks', in J. Frankel (ed.), *The Internationalisation of Equity Markets* (Chicago, IL: University of Chicago Press).

Engel, C. (1996a), 'Long-run PPP may not Hold after all', *National Bureau of Economics*, Working Paper No. 5646.

Engel, C. (1996b), 'The Forward Discount Anomaly and the Risk Premium: A Survey of Recent Evidence', *Journal of Empirical Finance*, 3, 123–92.

Engel, C. (1999), 'Accounting for US Real Exchange Rate Changes', *Journal of Political Economy*, 107, 507–38.

Engel, C. (2000a), 'Long-run PPP may not Hold after all', *Journal of International Economics*, 57, 243–73.

Engel, C. (2000b), 'Local Currency Pricing and the Choice of Exchange Rate Regime', *European Economic Review*, 44, 1449–72.

Engel, C. and J. Frankel (1984), 'Why Interest Rates React to Money Supply Announcements: An Explanation from the Foreign Exchange Market', *Journal of Money Credit and Banking*, 17, 321–7.

Engel, C. and A.P. Rodriguez (1989), 'Tests of International CAPM with Time Varying Covariances', *Journal of Applied Econometrics*, 4, 119–38.

Engel, C. and A.P. Rodriguez (1993), 'Tests of Mean Variance Efficiency of International Equity Markets', *Oxford Economic Papers*, 45, 403–21.

Engel, C. and J.H. Rogers (1996), 'How Wide is the Border?', *American Economic Review*, 86, 1112–25.

Engel, C. and K.D. West (2004), 'Accounting for Exchange Rate Variability in Present Value Models when the Discount Factor is Nearer One', NBER Working Paper No. 10267.

Engel, C., M.K. Hendrickson and J.H. Rogers (1997), 'Intranational, Intracontinental, and Intraplanetary PPP', *Journal of the Japanese and International Economies*, 11, 480–501.

Engle, R.F. (1982), 'Autoregressive Conditional Heteroscedasticity with Estimates of the Variance of UK Inflation', *Econometrica*, 50, 987–1008.

Engle, R.F. and C.W.J. Granger (1987), 'Co-integration and Error Correction: Representation, Estimation, and Testing', *Econometrica*, 55(March), 251–76.

Engle, R.F., T. Ito and W.-L. Lin (1990), ' Meteor Showers or Heat Waves? Heteroskedastic Intra-daily Volatility in the Foreign Exchange Market', *Econometrica*, Econometric Society, 58(3), 525–42.

Epps, T.W. and M.L. Epps (1976), 'The Stochastic Dependence of Security Price Changes and Transaction Volume: Implications for the Mixture-of-Distributions Hypothesis', *Econometrica*, 44, 305–21.

Ethier, W. (1973), 'International Trade and the Forward Exchange Market', *American Economic Review*, 63, 494–503.

Evans, G. (1989), 'A Measure of the U.S. Output Gap', *Economics Letters*, 29, 285–89.

Evans, G. and K. Lewis (1995), 'Do Long-term Swings in the Dollar Affect Estimates of the Risk Premium?', *Review of Financial Studies*, 8, 122–31.

Evans, M.D.D. and R.K. Lyons (2001), 'Portfolio Balance, Price Impact, and Secret Intervention', NBER Working Paper No. 8356, National Bureau of Economic Research, Inc.

Evans, M.D.D. and R.K. Lyons (2002), 'Order Flow and Exchange Rate Dynamics', *Journal of Political Economy*, 110, 170–80.

Evans, M.D.D. and R.K. Lyons (2003), 'How is Macro News Transmitted to Exchange Rates?', NBER Working Paper No. 9433, National Bureau of Economic Research, Inc.

Evans, M.D.D. and R.K. Lyons (2004), 'A New Micro Model of Exchange Rate Dynamics', NBER Working Paper No. 10379, National Bureau of Economic Research, Inc.

Fama, E.F. (1970), 'Efficient Capital Markets: A Review of Theory and Empirical Work', *Journal of Finance*, 25, 383–417.

Fama, E.F. (1984), 'Forward and Spot Exchange Rates', *Journal of Monetary Economics*, 14, 319–28.

Fama, E.F. (1990), 'Stock Returns, Expected Returns, and Real Activity', *Journal of Finance*, 45(4), 1089–108.

Fama, E.F. and K.R. French (1988), 'Permanent and Temporary Components of Stock Prices', *Journal of Political Economy*, 96 (April), 246–73.

Faruqee, H. (1995), 'Long-run Determinants of the Real Exchange Rate: A Stock-flow Perspective', *Staff Papers, International Monetary Fund*, 42 (March), 80–107.

Faruqee, H., P. Isard and P.R. Masson (1999), 'A Macroeconomic Balance Framework for Estimating Equilibrium Exchange Rates', in R. MacDonald and J. Stein (eds), *Equilibrium Exchange Rates*, chapter 4 (Boston, MA: Kluwer).

Feenstra, R.C. and J.D. Kendall (1997), 'Pass-through of Exchange Rates and Purchasing Power Parity', *Journal of International Economics*, 43, 237–61.

Feige, E.L. (2003), 'The Dynamics of Currency Substitution, Asset Substitution and de facto Dollarization and Euroization in Transition Countries', *Comparative Economic Studies*, 45, 358–83.

Feige, E.L. and J. Dean (2002), 'Dollarization and Euroization in Transition Countries: Currency Substitution, Asset Substitution, Network Externalities and Irreversibility', mimeo, University of Wisconsin-Madison.

Fieleke, N.S. (1975), 'Exchange-rate Flexibility and the Efficiency of the Foreign-exchange Markets', *Journal of Financial and Quantitative Analysis*, 10(3) (September), 409–28.

Fischer, A.M. (1989), 'Unit Roots and Survey Data', *Oxford Bulletin of Economics and Statistics*, 51, 451–63.

Fischer, S. (2001), 'Distinguished Lecture on Economics in Government-exchange Rate Regimes: Is the Bipolar View Correct?', *The Journal of Economic Perspectives*, 15, 3–24.

Fisher, E.O'N. and J.Y. Park (1991), 'Testing Purchasing Power Parity under the Null Hypothesis of Co-integration', *Economic Journal*, 101 (November), 1476–84.

Fleming, J.M. (1962), 'Domestic Financial Policies under Fixed and Floating Exchange Rates', *IMF Staff Papers*, 369–79.

Flood, M. (1991), 'Microstructure Theory and the Foreign Exchange Market', *Federal Reserve Bank of St Louis Quarterly Review*, November/December, 52–70.

Flood, R.P. (1981), 'Explanations of Exchange Rate Volatility and Other Empirical Regularities in Some Popular Models of the Foreign Exchange Market', *Carnegie-Rochester Series on Public Policy*, 15, 219–50.

Flood, R.P. and P. Garber (1984), 'Collapsing Exchange Rate Regimes: Some Linear Examples', *Journal of International Economics*, 17, 1–14.

Flood, R.P. and N. Marion (1997a), 'Perspectives on the Recent Currency Crisis Literature', IMF Research Department Seminar.

Flood, R.P. and N. Marion (1997b), 'Policy Implications of Second Generation Crisis Models', *IMF Staff Papers*, 44(3), 333–90.

Flood, R.P. and N. Marion (2000), 'Self-fulfilling Risk Predictions: An Application to Speculative Attacks', *Journal of International Economics* , 50, 245–68, 263.

Flood, R.P. and A.K. Rose (1995), 'Fixing Exchange Rates: A Virtual Quest for Fundamentals', *Journal of Monetary Economics*, 36, 3–37.

Flood, R.P. and A.K. Rose (1999), 'Understanding Exchange Rate Volatility without the Contrivance of Macroeconomics', *Economic Journal*, 109, F660–F672.

Flood, R.P., A.K. Rose and D. Mathieson (1991), 'An Empirical Exploration of Exchange Rate Target Zones', *Carnegie-Rochester Series on Public Policy*, 35 (Amsterdam: North Holland).

Flood, R.P., P. Garber and C. Kramer (1996), 'Collapsing Exchange Rate Regimes: Another Linear Example', *Journal of International Economics*, 41, 223–34.

Forni, M. and L. Reichlin (2001), 'Federal Policies and Local Economies: Europe and the US', *European Economic Review*, 45, 109–34.

Forsyth, P.J. and J.A. Kay (1980), 'The Economic Implications of North Sea Oil Reserves', *Fiscal Studies*, 1, 1–28.

Frankel, J.A. (1979), 'On the Mark: A Theory of Floating Exchange Rates Based on Real Interest Differentials', *American Economic Review*, 69, 610–22.

Frankel, J.A. (1982a), 'A Test of Perfect Substitutability in the Forward Exchange Market', *Southern Economic Journal*, 46, 1083–101.

Frankel, J.A. (1982b), 'In Search of Exchange Risk Premium: A Six Currency Test Assuming Mean-variance Optimization', *Journal of International Money and Finance*, 1, 255–74.

Frankel, J.A. (1982c), 'The Mystery of the Multiplying Marks: A Modification of the Monetary Model', *Review of Economics and Statistics*, 87, 216–30.

Frankel, J.A. (1983), 'Monetary and Portfolio-balance Models of Exchange Rate Determination', in J.S. Bhandari, B.H. Putnam and J.H. Levin (eds), *Economic Interdependence and Flexible Exchange Rates* (Cambridge, MA: MIT Press).

Frankel, J.A. (1984), 'Tests of Monetary and Portfolio Balance Models of Exchange Rate Determination', in J.F.O. Bilson and R.C. Marston (eds), *Exchange Rate Theory and Practice* (Chicago: Chicago University Press), 239–59.

Frankel, J.A. (2003), 'Experience of and Lessons from Exchange Rate Regime in Emerging Economies', NBER Working Paper No. 10032, National Bureau of Economic Research, Inc.

Frankel, J.A. and K.A. Froot (1987), 'Using Survey Data to Test Standard Propositions Regarding Exchange Rate Expectations', *American Economic Review*, 77 (March 1987), 133–53.

Frankel, J.A. and K.A. Froot (1989), 'Interpreting Tests of Forward Discount Bias Using Survey Data on Exchange Rate Expectations', *Quarterly Journal of Economics*, 104 (February), 139–61.

Frankel, J.A. and K.A. Froot (1990a), 'Chartists, Fundamentalists, and the Demand for Dollars', in A.S. Courakis and M.P. Taylor (eds), *Private Behavior and Government Policy in Interdependent Economies* (Oxford: Clarendon Press).

Frankel, J.A. and K.A. Froot (1990b), 'Exchange Rate Forecasting Techniques, Survey Data, and Implications for the Foreign Exchange Market', NBER Working Paper No. 3470.

Frankel, J.A. and R. Meese (1987), 'Are Exchange Rates Excessively Variable?', in S. Fischer (ed.), *NBER Macroeconomics Annual* (Cambridge: MIT Press), 117–53.

Frankel, J.A. and D. Romer (1999), 'Does Trade Cause Growth?', *American Economic Review*, 89, 379–99.

Frankel, J.A. and A. Rose (1995a), 'A Survey of Empirical Research on Nominal Exchange Rates', in S. Grossman and K. Rogoff (eds), *The Handbook of International Economics*, 3 (Amsterdam: North Holland).

Frankel, J.A. and A. Rose (1995b), 'A Panel Project on Purchasing Power Parity: Mean Reversion within and between Countries', NBER Working Paper No. 5006, February 1995 (Cambridge, MA: National Bureau of Economic Research).

Frankel, J.A. and A.K. Rose (1996), 'Currency Crashes in Emerging Markets: Empirical Indicators', CEPR Discussion Paper No. 1349, C.E.P.R. Discussion Papers.

Frankel, J.A. and A.K. Rose (1998), 'The Endogeneity of the Optimum Currency Area', *The Economic Journal*, 108(July), 1009–25.

Fratianni, M. and L.M. Wakeman (1982), 'The Law of One Price in the Eurocurrency Market', *Journal of International Money and Finance*, 1, 307–23.

Frenkel, J.A. (1976), 'A Monetary Approach to the Exchange Rate: Doctrinal Aspects and Empirical Evidence', *Scandinavian Journal of Economics*, 200–24.

Frenkel, J. (1980), 'Exchange Rates, Price, and Money: Lessons from the 1920s', *American Economic Review, Papers and Proceedings*, 70 (May 1980), 235–42.

Frenkel, J. (1981), 'Flexible Exchange Rates, Prices and the Role of "News": Lessons from the 1970s', *Journal of Political Economy*, 89 (August 1981), 665–705.

Frenkel, J.A. and H.G. Johnson (1976), *The Monetary Approach to the Balance of Payments* (London: Allen and Unwin).

Frenkel, J.A. and R.M. Levich (1975), 'Covered Interest Arbitrage: Unexploited Profits?', *Journal of Political Economy*, 83, 325–38.

Frenkel, J.A. and R.M. Levich (1977), 'Transaction Costs and Interest Arbitrage: Tranquil Versus Turbulent Periods', *Journal of Political Economy*, 85, 1209–24.

Frenkel, J.A. and M.L. Mussa (1980), 'The Efficiency of Foreign Exchange Markets and Measures of Turbulence', *American Economic Review*, 70, 374–81.

Frenkel, J. and M.L. Mussa (1986), 'Exchange Rates and the Balance of Payments', in R. Jones and P. Kenen (eds), *Handbook of International Economics*, 2 (Amsterdam: North Holland).

Frenkel, J. and M.L. Mussa (1988), 'Asset Markets, Exchange Rates, and the Balance of Payments', chapter 14, in E. Grossman and K. Rogoff (eds), *Handbook of International Economics*, 3 (Amsterdam: North Holland).

Frenkel, J.A. and L. Rodriguez (1982), 'Exchange Rate Dynamics and the Overshooting of Hypothesis', *IMF Staff Papers*, 1–30.

Frieden, J.P.G. and E. Stein (2001), 'Politics and Exchange Rates: A Cross Country Approach to Latin America', Research Network Working Paper, R-421 (Washington, DC: Inter-American Development Bank).

Friedman, M. (1953), 'The Case for Flexible Exchange Rates', in M. Friedman (ed), *Essays in Positive Economics* (Chicago, IL: Chicago University Press).

Friedman, M. (1990), 'Bimetallism Revisited', *Journal of Economic Perspectives* 4(4) (Fall), 85–104.

Friedman, M. and A.J. Schwartz (1963), *A Monetary History of the United States, 1867–1960* (Chicago, IL: Chicago University Press).

Friedmann, W. and J. Clostermann (1997), 'Determinants of the Real D–Mark Exchange Rate', mimeo, Deutsche Baundesbank.

Frommel, M., R. MacDonald and L. Menkhoff (2005), 'Do Fundamentals Matter for the D–Mark/Euro–Dollar? A Regime Switching Approach', *Global Finance Journal*, 15, 321–35.

Froot, K.A. and T. Ito (1989), 'On the Consistency of Short-run and Long-run Exchange Rate Expectations', *Journal of International Money and Finance*, 8, 487–510.

Froot, K.A. and M. Obstfeld (1991), 'Exchange-rate Dynamics under Stochastic Regime Shifts: A Unified Approach', *Journal of International Economics*, 31(3–4), 203–29.

Froot, K.A. and K. Rogoff (1985), 'Perspectives on PPP and Long-run Real Exchange Rates', in R.W. Jones and P.B. Kenen (eds), *Handbook of International Economics*, 3 (Amsterdam: North Holland), 679–747.

Froot, K. and R. Thaler (1990), 'Anomolies: Foreign Exchange', *Journal of Economic Perspectives*', 4, 179–92.

Froot, K., M. Kim and K. Rogoff (1995), 'The Law of One Price over 700 Years', NBER Working Paper No. 5132.

Fuller, W.A. (1976), *Introduction to Statistical Time Series* (New York: Wiley).

Gagnon, J. (1996), 'Net Foreign Assets and Equilibrium Exchange Rates: Panel Evidence', International Finance Discussion Paper No. 574.

Galati, G. (2001), 'Why Has Global FX Turnover Declined? Explaining the 2001 Triennial Survey', *Bank for International Settlements Quarterly Review 0112*, 1–25.

Gan, W.B. and K.S. Wong (1993), 'Exchange Rate Expectations and Risk Premium in the Singapore/US Dollar Exchange Rate: Evidence from Survey Data', *Applied Financial Economics*, 3(4), 365–73.

Garman, M.B. (1976), 'A General Theory of Asset Valuation under Diffusion State Processes', Research Program in Finance Working Paper No. 50, University of California at Berkeley.

Genberg, H. (1978), 'Purchasing Power Parity under Fixed and Flexible Exchange Rates', 8, 247–76.

Ghironi, F., T.B. Iscan and A. Rebucci (2003), 'Productivity Shocks and Consumption Smoothing in The International Economy', Boston College Working Paper No. 565.

Ghosh, A. (1991), 'Accounting for Real Exchange Rate Movements in the Short-run and in the Long-run', mimeo, Princeton University.

Ghosh, A. and H. Wolf (1994), 'Pricing in International Markets: Lessons from the Economist', NBER Working Paper No. 4806.

Ghosh, A. and H. Wolf (2001), 'Imperfect Exchange Rate Pass-through: Strategic Pricing and Menu Costs', CESifo Working Paper No. 436.

Ghosh, A.R., A.-M. Gulde and H.C. Wolf (1997), 'Does the Nominal Exchange Rate Regime Matter?', NBER Working Paper No. 5874.

Ghosh, A.R., A.-M. Gulde and H.C. Wolf (2003), *Exchange Rate Regimes: Choices and Consequences* (Cambridge, MA: MIT Press).

Giavazzi, F. and A. Giovannini (1989), *Limiting Exchange Rate Flexibility: The European Monetary System* (Cambridge, MA: MIT Press).

Giorgianni, L. (1996), 'On Expectations and Risk Premia in Foreign Exchange Markets: Evidence From Survey Data', PhD dissertation, University of Pennsylvania.

Giovannini, A. (1988), 'Exchange Rates and Traded Goods Prices', *Journal of International Economics*, 24, 45–68.

Giovannini, A. (1993), 'Bretton Woods and Its Precursors: Rules Versus Discretion in the History of International Monetary Regimes', in M.D. Bordo and B. Eichengreen (eds), *A Retrospective on the Bretton Woods System* (Chicago, IL: University of Chicago Press).

Giovannini, A. and P. Jorion (1987), 'Interest Rates and Risk Premia in the Stock and Foreign Exchange Markets', *Journal of International Money and Finance*, 6, 234–46.

Girton, L. and A. Roper (1977), 'A Monetary Model of Exchange Market Pressure Applied to the Postwar Canadian Experience', *The American Economic Review*, 67, 537–48.

Glassman, D. (1987), 'Exchange Rate Risk and Transactions Costs: Evidence from Bid–Ask Spreads', *Journal of International Money and Finance*, 6, 479–90.

Glen, J.D. (1992), 'Real Exchange Rates in the Short, Medium and Long Run', *Journal of International Economics*, 33 (August), 147–66.

Godfrey, L.G. (1988), *Misspecification Tests in Econometrics* (Cambridge: Cambridge University Press).

Goldberg, L.S. and C. Tille (2005), 'Vehicle Currency Use in International Trade', NBER Working Paper No. 11127.

Goldberg, P.K. and M.M. Knetter (1997), 'Goods Prices and Exchange Rates: What Have We Learned?', *Journal of Economic Literature*, 35, 1243–72.

Goldstein, M. (1998), *The Asian Financial Crisis: Causes, Cures, and Systemic Implications*, Institute for International Economics, Washington DC.

Goldstein, M. and M. Khan (1985a), 'Income and Price Effects in Foreign Trade', chapter 20, in R. Jones and P.B. Kenen (eds), *Handbook in International Economics*, 2 (Amsterdam: Elsevier), 1041–5.

Goldstein, M. and M.S. Khan (1985b), 'Income and Price Effects in Foreign Trade', chapter 20, in Ronald W. Jones and Peter B. Kenen (eds), *Handbook of International Economics*, 2 (Amsterdam: Elsevier), 1041–105.

Goodhart, C. (1988), 'The Foreign Exchange Market: A Random Walk with a Dragging Anchor', *Economica*, 55(220) (November), 437–60.

Goodhart, C. and M. Guigale (1993), 'From Hour to Hour in the Foreign Exchange Market', in C.A.E. Goodhart and R. Payne (eds), *Empirical Studies with High-frequency Data* (London: Palgrave Macmillan).

Goodhart, C. and R. Payne (1996), 'Microstructural Dynamics in an Electronic Foreign Exchange Broking System', *Journal of International Money and Finance* (December), 15, 829–52.

Goodhart, C., T. Ito and R. Payne (1996), 'One Day in June 1993: A Study of the Workings of the Reuters' 2000–2 Electronic Foreign Exchange Trading System', in J. Frankel, G. Galli and A. Giovannini (eds), *The Microstructure of Foreign Exchange Markets* (Chicago, IL: University of Chicago Press).

Gourinchas, P.-O. and A. Tornell (2004), 'Exchange Rate Puzzles and Distorted Beliefs', *Journal of International Economics*, 64, 303–33.

Granger, C.W. and J. Gonzalo (1995), 'Estimation of Common Long-memory Components in Cointegrated Systems', *Journal of Business Economics and Statistics*, 13, 27–35.

Granger, C.W. and T. Terasvirta (1993), *Modelling Non-linear Economic Relationships* (Oxford: Oxford University Press).

Gray, M.R. and S.Turnovsky (1979), 'The Stability of Exchange Rate Dynamics under Perfect Myopic Foresight', *International Economic Review*, 20, 643–60.

Grilli, V. and G. Kaminsky (1991), 'Nominal Exchange Rate Regimes and the Real Exchange Rate: Evidence from the United States and Great Britain, 1885–1986', *Journal of Monetary Economics*, 27 (April 1991), 191–212.

Grilli, V. and N. Roubini (1992), 'Liquidity and Exchange Rates', *Journal of International Economics*, 32, 339–52.

Grilli, V. and N. Roubini (1996), 'Liquidity Models in Open Economies: Theory and Empirical Evidence', *European Economic Review*, 21, 847–59.

Groen, J.J.J. (2000), 'The Monetary Exchange Rate Model as a Long-run Phenomenon', *Journal of International Economics*, 52(2), 299–319.

Groen, J.J.J. (2002), 'Cointegration and the Monetary Exchange Rate Model Revisited', *Oxford Bulletin of Economics and Statistics*, 64(4), 361–80.

Guidotti, P.E. and C.A. Rodriguez (1992), 'Dollarization in Latin America: Gresham's Law in Reverse?', *International Monetary Fund Staff Papers*, 39, 518–44.

Guillermo, C. and C.M. Reinhart (2002), 'Fear of Floating', *The Quarterly Journal of Economics*, 117(2), 379–408.

Hacche, G. and J. Townend (1981), 'Exchange Rates and Monetary Policy: Modelling Sterling's Effective Exchange Rate', in W. Eltis and A. Sinclair (ed.), *The Money Supply and the Exchange Rates* (Oxford: Oxford University Press).

Haggan, V. and T. Ozaki (1981), 'Modelling Nonlinear Random Vibrations Using and Amplitude-dependent Autoregressive Time Series Model', *Biometrika*, 68, 189–96.

Hahn, F.H. (1984), *Equilibrium and Macroeconomics* (Oxford: Blackwell).

Hakkio, C. (1986), 'A Reexamination of Purchasing Power Parity', *Journal of International Economics*, 17, 265–77.

Hakkio, C.S. and M. Rush (1989), 'Market Efficiency and Cointegration: An Application to the Sterling and Deutschemark Exchange Rates', *Journal of International Money and Finance*, 8, 75–88.

Hallwood, C.P. and R. MacDonald (2000), *International Money and Finance* (Oxford: Blackwell, 3rd edition).

Hallwood, P., R. MacDonald and I.W. Marsh (1996), 'Credibility and Fundamentals: Were the Classical and Inter-war Gold Standards Well-behaved Target Zones?', in T. Bayoumi, B. Eichengreen and M. Taylor (eds), *Modern Perspectives on the Gold Standard* (Cambridge: Cambridge University Press).

Hallwood, P., R. MacDonald and I.W. Marsh (2000), 'Realignment Expectations and the US Dollar, 1890–1897: Was there a "Peso Problem"', *Journal of Monetary Economics*, 46, 605–20.

Halpern, L. and C. Wyplosz (1997), 'Equilibrium Exchange Rates in Transition Economies', *International Monetary Fund Staff Papers*, 44, 430–61.

Halpern, L. and C. Wyplosz (2001), 'Realignment Expectations and Real Exchange Rates in the 2000s; The Balassa–Samuelson Connection', mimeo, University of Geneva.

Hansen, B. (1990), 'A Powerful Simple Test for Cointegration Using Cochrane–Orcutt', mimeo, University of Rochester.

Hansen, B.E. (1992), 'Tests for Parameter Instability in Regression with I(1) Processes', *Journal of Business and Economic Statistics*, 10 (July 1992), 321–35.

Hansen, L.P. (1982), 'Large Sample Properties of Generalized Method of Moments Estimators', *Econometrica*, 50, 1029–54.

Hansen, L.P. and R. Hodrick (1983), 'Risk Averse Speculation in the Forward Exchange Market: An Econometric Analysis of Linear Models', in J.A Frenkel (ed.), *Exchange Rates and International Macroeconomics* (Chicago, IL: Chicago University Press).

Hansen, L.P. and S. Richard (1984), 'A General Approach for Deducting Testable Restrictions Implied by Asset Pricing Models', mimeo, University of Chicago.

Hansen, L.P. and K. Singleton (1982), 'Generalized Instrumental Variables Estimation of Nonlinear Rational Expectations Models', *Econometrica*, 50, 1269–86.

Hartley, P.R. (1983), 'Rational Expectations and the Foreign Exchange Market', in J.A. Frenkel (ed.), *Exchange Rates and International Macroeconomics* (Chicago, IL: Chicago University Press).

Haskel, J. and H. Wolf (2001), 'The Law of One Price – A Case Study', *Scandinavian Journal of Economics*, 103, 545–58.

Hau, H. (2000), 'Exchange Rate Determination: The Role of Factor Price Rigidity and Nontradables', *Journal of International Economics*, 50(2), 421–47.

Hausman, R., U. Panizza and R. Rigobon (2004), 'The Long-run Volatility Puzzle of the Real Exchange Rate', NBER Working Paper No. 10751.

Haynes, S.E. and J.A. Stone (1981), 'On the Mark: Comment', *American Economic Review*, 71, 1060–7.

Heckscher, E.F. (1916), 'Vaxelkursens Grundval vid Pappersmyntfot', *Ekonomisk Tidskrift*, 18, 309–12.

Heller, R. (1978), 'Determinants of Exchange Rate Practices', *Journal of Money Credit and Banking*, 10, 308–21.

Helpman, E. and P. Krugman (1985), *Market Structure and Foreign Trade* (Boston: MIT Press).

Hendry, D.F and G. Mizon (1993), 'Evaluating Dynamic Econometric Models by Encompassing the VAR', in P.C.B. Phillips (ed.), *Models, Methods and Applications of Econometrics* (Oxford: Blackwell), 272–300.

Hinkle, L.E. and P.J. Montiel (eds) (1999), *Exchange Rate Misalignment: Concepts and Measurement for Developing Countries* (Washington DC: World Bank).

Ho, T. and H. Stoll (1983), 'The Dynamics of Dealer Markets under Competition', *Journal of Finance*, 38, 1053–74.

Hodrick, R.J. (1978), 'An Empirical Analysis of the Monetary Approach to the Determination of the Exchange Rate', in J.A. Frenkel and H.G. Johnson (eds), *The Economics of Exchange Rates* (Reading, MA: Addison-Wesley), 97–116.

Hodrick, R.J. (1987), *The Empirical Evidence on the Efficiency of Forward and Futures Markets* (London: Harwood).

Hodrick, R.J. (1989), 'Risk, Uncertainty and Exchange Rates', NBER Working Paper No. 2429, National Bureau of Economic Research, Inc.

Hodrick, R. and S. Srivastava (1984), 'An Investigation of Risk and Return in Forward Foreign Exchange', *Journal of International Money and Finance*, 3, 1–29.

Hodrick, R. and S. Srivastava (1986), 'The Covariation of Risk Premiums and Expected Future Spot Rates', *Journal of International Money and Finance*, 5, S5–S22.

Hoffman, M. and R. MacDonald (2000), 'Real Exchange Rate Decompositions', mimeo, University of Glasgow.

Hoffman, M. and R. MacDonald (2005), 'A Re-examination of the Link between Real Exchange Rates and Real Interest Rate Differentials', mimeo, University of Glasgow.

Hoffman, D.L and D.E. Schlagenhauf (1983), 'Rational Expectations and Monetary Models of Exchange Rate Determination: An Empirical Examination', *Journal of Monetary Economics*, 11, 247–60.

Hooper, P. and J. Morton (1982), 'Fluctuations in the Dollar: A Model of Nominal and Real Exchange Rate Determination', *Journal of International Money and Finance*, 1 (April 1982), 39–56.

Hsieh, D. (1982), 'The Determination of the Real Exchange Rate: The Productivity Approach', *Journal of International Economics*, 12, 355–62.

Hsieh, D. (1988), 'The Statistical Properties of Daily Foreign Exchange Rates: 1974–1983', *Journal of International Economics*, 24, 129–45.

Hsieh, D. (1989), 'Modeling Heteroskedasticity in Daily Foreign Exchange Rates', *Journal of Business and Economic Statistics*, 7, 307–17.

Hsieh, D. and A. Kleidon (1996), 'Bid–Ask Spreads in Foreign Exchange Markets: Implications for Models of Asymmetric Information', in J. Frankel, G. Galli and A. Giovannini (eds), *The Microstructure of Foreign Exchange Markets* (Cambridge: National Bureau of Economic Research), 41–65.

Huang, R.D. (1981), 'The Monetary Approach to the Exchange Rate in an Efficient Foreign Exchange Market: Tests Based on Volatility', *Journal of Finance*, 36, 31–41.

Hughes-Hallett, A. and L. Piscitelli (2002), 'Does Trade Integration Cause Convergence?', *Economics Letters*, 75, 165–70.

Huizinga, J. (1987), 'An Empirical Investigation of the Long-run Behaviour of Real Exchange Rates', in *Carnegie-Rochester Conference Series on Public Policy*, 27, 149–214.

Husted, S. and R. MacDonald (1998), 'Monetary-based Models of the Exchange Rate: A Panel Perspective', *Journal of International Financial Markets, Institutions and Money*, 8, 1–19.

Husted, S. and R. MacDonald (1999), 'The Monetary Model Redux', mimeo, University of Strathclyde.

Im, K.S., H. Pesaran and Y. Shin (1995), 'Dynamic Linear Models for Heterogeneous Panels', Cambridge Working Paper in Economics, 9503.

Imbs, J.H.M., M. Ravn and H. Rey (2002), 'PPP Strikes Back: Aggregation and the Real Exchange Rate', NBER Working Paper No. 9372.

Isard, P. (1977), 'How Far can we Push the "Law of One Price"?' *American Economic Review*, 67 (December 1977), 942–8.

Isard, P. (1978), 'Exchange Rate Determination: A Survey of Popular Views and Recent Models', *Princeton Studies in International Finance*, No. 42 (Princeton, NJ: Princeton University Department of Economics, International Finance Section).

Isard, P. and H. Faruqee (eds) (1998), 'Exchange Rate Assessment: Extensions of the Macroeconomic Balance Approach', IMF Occasional Paper No. 167.

Ito, T. (1990), 'Foreign Exchange Rate Expectations: Micro Survey Data', *American Economic Review*, 80 (June 1990), 434–39.

Ito, T., P. Isard and S. Symansky (1997), 'Economic Growth and Real Exchange Rate: An Overview of the Balassa–Samuelson Hypothesis in Asia', in T. Ito and A.O. Krueger (eds), *Changes in Exchange Rates in Rapidly Developing Countries* (Chicago, IL: Chicago University Press), 109–28.

Jeanne, O. (1997), 'Are Currency Crises Self-fulfilling?: A Test', *Journal of International Economics*, 43, 263–86.

Jeanne, O. (1999), 'Currency Crises: A Perspective on Recent Theoretical Developments', CEPR Discussion Paper Series No. 2170.

Jeanne, O. (2000a), 'Currency Crises: A Perspective on Recent Theoretical Developments', Special Papers in International Finance No. 20, Princeton University.

Jeanne, O. (2000b), 'The IMF: An International Lender of Last Resort?', *IMF Research Bulletin*, 40, 20–31.

Jeanne, O. and P. Masson (2000), 'Currency Crises, Sunspots and Markov–Switching Regimes', *Journal of International Economics*, 50, 327–50.

Johansen, S. (1988), 'Statistical Analysis of Cointegrating Vectors', *Journal of Economic Dynamics and Control*, 12, 231–54.

Johansen, S. (1995), *Likelihood-based Inference in Cointegrated Vector Autoregressive Models* (Oxford: Oxford University Press).

Johansen, S. and K. Juselius (1990), 'Testing Structural Hypothesis in a Multivariate Cointegration Analysis of the PPP and the UIP for the UK', *Journal of Econometrics*, 53, 211–44.

Johansen, S. and K. Juselius (1992), 'Maximum Likelihood Estimation and Inference on Cointegration – with Applications to the Demand for Money', *Oxford Bulletin of Economics and Statistics*, 52, 169–210.

Johansen, S. and K. Juselius (1994), 'Identification of the Long-run and the Short-run Structure. An Application to the ISLM Model', *Journal of Econometrics*, 63, 7–36.

Johnson (1977), 'The Monetary Approach to the Balance of Payments: A Non Technical Guide', *Journal of International Economics*, 7, 251–68.

Jorion, P. (1996), 'Risk and Volume in the Foreign Exchange Market', in Frankel, Galli and Giovannini (eds), *The Microstructure of the Foreign Exchange Market* (Chicago, IL: University of Chicago Press).

Jorion, P. and R. Sweeney (1996), 'Mean Reversion in Real Exchange Rates: Evidence and Implications for Forecasting', *Journal of International Economics*, 40, 112–30.

Juselius, K. (1995), 'Do Purchasing Power Parity and Uncovered Interest Rate Hold in the Long Run, *Journal of Econometrics*, 69, 211–40.

Juselius, K. and R. MacDonald (2004), 'The International Parities between Japan and the USA', *Japan and the World Economy*, 16, 17–34.

Juselius, K. and R. MacDonald (2007), 'International Parity Relationships and a Non-stationary Real Exchange Rate. Germany Versus the US in the Post Bretton Woods Period', forthcoming in V. Morales (ed.), *Recent Issues in International Macroeconomics* (New York: Nova Publications).

Kalemli-Ozcan, S., B.E. Sorenson and O. Yosha (2001), 'Economic Integration, Industrial Specialization and the Asymmetry of Macroeconomic Fluctuations', *Journal of International Economics*, 55, 107–37.

Kamin, S., J. Schindler and S. Samuel (2001), 'The Contribution of Domestic and External Factors to Emerging Market Devaluation Crises: An Early Warning Systems Approach', International Finance Discussion Paper, Board of Governors of the Federal Reserve System.

Kaminsky, G. and R. Peruga (1988), 'Risk Premium and the Foreign Exchange Market', mimeo, San Diego: University of California.

Kaminsky, G. and R. Peruga (1990), 'Can a Time-varying Risk Premium Explain Excess Returns in the Forward Market for Foreign Exchange?', *Journal of International Economics*, 28(1/2) (February 1990), 47–70.

Kaminsky, G.L. and C.M. Reinhart (1996), 'The Twin Crises: The Causes of Banking and Balance-of-payments Problems', International Finance Discussion Paper No. 544, Board of Governors of the Federal Reserve System.

Kaminsky, G., S. Lizondo and C.M. Reinhart (1997), 'Leading Indicators of Currency Crisis', IMF Working Paper No. WP/97/79.

Kawai, M. and H. Ohara (1998), 'Nonstationarity of Real Exchange Rates in the G7 Countries: Are They Cointegrated with Real Variables?', *Journal of Japanese and International Economies*, 11, 523–47.

Kearney, C. and R. MacDonald (1987), 'Intervention and Sterilisation under Floating Exchange Rates: The UK 1973–1983', *European Economic Review*, 30, 345–64.

Kearney, C.P. and R. MacDonald (1988), 'Asset Markets, the Current Account and Exchange Rate Determination: An Empirical Analysis of the Sterling/Dollar Exchange Rate, 1973–1983', *Australian Economic Papers* (December), 213–32.

Kearney, C. and R. MacDonald (1990), 'Rational Expectations, Bubbles and Monetary Models of the Exchange Rate: The Australian/US dollar Rate during the Recent Float', *Australian Economic Papers*, 44, 1–20.

Kenen, P. (1963), 'The Theory of Optimum Currency Areas: An Eclectic View', in R. Mundell and A. Swoboda (eds), *Monetary Problems in the International Economy* (Chicago, IL: Chicago University Press).

Killeen, W.P., R.K. Lyons and M.J. Moore (2001), 'Fixed Versus Flexible: Lessons from EMS Order Flow', NBER Working Paper No. 8491.

Kim, S. and N. Roubini (2000), 'Exchange Rate Anomolies in the Industrial Countries: A Solution with a Structural VAR Approach', *Journal of Monetary Economics*, 46, 561–86.

Kim, Y. (1990), 'Purchasing Power Parity in the Long-run: A Cointegration Approach', *Journal of Money, Credit and Banking*, 22 (November 1990), 491–503.

King, M. and S. Wadwani (1995), 'Transmission of Volatility between Stock Markets', *The Review of Financial Studies*, 3, 5–33.

Klein, M.W. and N.P. Marion (1994), 'Explaining the Duration of Exchange-rate Pegs', NBER Working Paper No. 4651.

Knetter, M. (1989), 'Price Discrimination by US and German Exporters', *American Economic Review*, 79, 198–209.

Knetter, M. (1993), 'International Comparisons of Pricing-to-Market Behaviour', *American Economic Review*, 83, 473–86.

Koedijk, K.G., M.M.A. Scahfgans and C.G. de Vries (1990), 'The Tail Index of Exchange Rate Returns', *Journal of International Economics*, 29, 93–108.

Koedijk, K.G., P.A. Stork and C.G. de Vries, (1992), 'An EMS Target Zone Model in Discrete Time', *Journal of Applied Econometrics*, 13(1), 31–48.

Kollmann, R. (1998), 'US Trade Balance Dynamics: The Role of Fiscal Policy and Productivity Shocks and of Financial Linkages', *Journal of International Money and Finance*, 17, 637–69.

Kouretas, G. (1997), 'Identifying Linear Restrictions on the Monetary Exchange Rate Model and the Uncovered Interest Parity: Cointegration for the Canadian Dollar', *Canadian Journal of Economics*, 30, 875–90.

Kouri, R. (1976), 'The Exchange Rate and the Balance of Payments in the Shortrun and in the Long Run: A Monetary Approach', *Scandinavian Journal of Economics*, 78 (2), 280–304.

Kravis, I. and R. Lipsey (1978), 'National Price Levels and the Prices of Tradeables and Non-tradeables', *American Economic Review (papers and proceedings)*, 78, 474–8.

Kravis, I. and R. Lipsey (1983), *Toward an Explanation of National Price Levels*, Princeton Studies in International Finance No. 52.

Kremers, J. and T.D. Lane (1991), 'Economic and Monetary Aggregation and the Demand for Money in the EMS', *International Monetary Fund Staff Papers*, 37, 777–805.

Krugman, P.R. (1978), 'Purchasing Power Parity and Exchange Rates: Another Look at the Evidence', *Journal of International Economics*, 8, 397–407.

Krugman, P.R. (1979), 'A Model of Balance of Payments Crisis', *Journal of Money Credit and Banking*, 11, 311–25.

Krugman, P. (1980), 'Vehicle Currencies and the Structure of International Exchange', *Journal of Money, Credit and Banking*, 12, 513–26.

Krugman, P.R. (1987), 'Pricing to Market when the Exchange Rate Changes', in S.W. Arndt and J.D. Richardson (eds), *Real-financial Linkages among Open Economics* (Cambridge, MA: MIT Press), 49–70.

Krugman, P. (1989), *Exchange Rate Instability* (Cambridge, MA: MIT Press).

Krugman, P. (1990), *Rethinking International Trade* (Cambridge, MA: MIT Press).

Krugman, P. (1991), 'Target Zones and Exchange Rate Dynamics', *Quarterly Journal of Economics*, 56, 669–82.

Krugman, P. (1993), 'Lessons of Massachusetts for EMU', in F. Giavazzi and F. Torres (eds), *The Transition to Economic and Monetary Union in Europe* (New York: Cambridge University Press), 241–61.

Krugman, P. (1996), 'Are Currency Crises Self-fulfilling?', *NBER Macroeconomics Annual*, 5, 20–41.

Krugman, P. (1999), 'Balance Sheets, the Transfer Problem, and Financial Crises', in P. Isard, A. Razin and A. Rose (eds), *International Finance and Financial Crises, Essays in Honor of Robert P. Flood* (Amsterdam: Kluwer).

Krugman, P. (2001), 'Crises: The Next Generation', Unpublished Manuscript.

Kubaraych, R.M. (1983), *Foreign Exchange Markets in the United States*, Federal Reserve Bank of New York.

Kugler, P. and C. Lenz (1990), 'Chaos, ARCH and the Foreign Exchange Market: Empirical Results from Weekly Data', mimeo, Volkswirtschaftliches Institut, Zurich.

Kugler, P. and C. Lenz (1993), 'Multivariate Cointegration Analysis and the Long-run Validity of PPP', *Review of Economics and Statistics*, 75, 180–4.

La Cour, L. and R. MacDonald (2000), 'Modelling the ECU against the US Dollar: A Structural Monetary Interpretation', *Journal of Business Economics and Statistics* (September), 18, 56–70.

Laidler, D. (1985), 'Monetary Policy in Britain – Successes and Shortcomings', *Oxford Review of Economic Policy*, 1, 44–57.

Lamoureux, C.G. and W.D. Lastrapes (1990), 'Persistence in Variance, Structural Change and the GARCH Model', *Journal Business and Economic Statistics*, 8, 225–34.

Lane, P.R. (1998), 'What Determines the Nominal Exchange Rate? Some Cross Sectional Evidence', *Canadian Journal of Economics*, 118–38.

Lane, P.R. (2001), 'The New Open Economy Macroeconomics: A Survey', *Journal of International Economics*, 54 (2), 235–66.

Laney, L.O., C.D. Radcliffe and T.D. Willett (1984), 'Currency Substitution: Comment', *Southern Economic Journal*, 50, 1196–200.

Lastrapes, W.D. (1989), 'Weekly Exchange Rate Volatility and US Monetary Policy Regimes: An Application of the ARCH Model', *Journal of Money Credit and Banking*, 21, 66–77.

Lastrapes, W.D. (1992), 'Sources of Fluctuations in Real and Nominal Exchange Rates', *Review of Economics and Statistics*, 74, 530–9.

Layard, R., W. Buiter, C. Huhne, W. Hutton, P. Kenen and A. Turner (2000), 'The Case for the Euro', Britain in Europe Campaign, London.

Lee, J. and M.D. Chinn (1998), 'The Current Account and the Real Exchange Rate: A Structural var Analysis', NBER Working Paper No. 6495.

Levin, A. and C.-F. Lin (1992, 1994), 'Unit Root Tests in Panel Data: Asymptotic and Finite Sample Properties' (Unpublished; Washington: Federal Reserve Board of Governors).

Levy-Yeyati, E. and F. Sturzeneger (2002), 'Classifying Exchange Rate Regimes: Deeds vs Words', mimeo, IMF.

Lewis, K. (1988), 'Testing the Portfolio Balance Model: A Multilateral Approach', *Journal of International Economics*, 24, 109–27.

Lewis, K. (1989), 'Can Learning Affect Exchange Rate Behaviour: The Case of the Dollar in the Early 1990s?', *Journal of Monetary Economics*, 23, 79–100.

Lewis, K. (1991), 'The Behaviour of Eurocurrency Returns Across Different Holding Periods and Monetary Regimes', *Journal of Finance*, 45, 1211–36.

Lewis, K. (1995), 'Puzzles in International Financial Markets', in E. Grossman and K. Rogoff (eds), *The Handbook of International Economics*, 3, North-Holland.

Lim, G.C. and C.R. McKenzie (1998), 'Testing the Rationality of Expectations in the Australian Foreign Exchange Market Using Survey Data with Missing Observations', *Applied Financial Economics*, 8(2), 181–90.

Lindberg, H. and P. Soderlind (1991), 'Testing the Basic Target Zone Model on Swedish Data', Institute of International Economics Paper 448.

Linder, S.B. (1961), *An Essay on Trade and Transformation* (New York: Wiley).

Liu, P.C. and G.S. Maddala (1992), 'Rationality of Survey Data and Tests for Market Efficiency in the Foreign Exchange Markets', *Journal of International Money and Finance*, 11, 366–81.

Lo, A.W. and A.C. MacKinley (1988), 'Stock Market Prices do not Follow Random Walks: Evidence From a Simple Specification Test', *Review of Financial Studies*, 1 (Spring 1988), 41–66.

Loopesko, B.E. (1984), 'Relationships among Exchange Rates, Intervention, and Interest Rates: An Empirical Investigation', *Journal of International Money and Finance*, 3, 257–78.

Lothian, J. (1997), 'Multi-country Evidence on the Behaviour of Purchasing Power Parity under the Current Float', *Journal of International Money and Finance*, 21, 37–51.

Lothian, J. and M. Taylor (1995), 'Real Exchange Rate Behaviour: The Recent Float from the Behaviour of the Past Two Centuries', *Journal of Political Economy*, 102, 130–43.

Lothian, J. and L. Wu (2003), 'Uncovered Interest Rate Parity over the Past Two Centuries', mimeo, Fordham University.

Lucas, R.E. (1982), 'Interest Rates and Currency Prices in a Two-Country World', *Journal of Monetary Economics*, 10, 335–60.

Lutkepohl, H. (1993), *Introduction to Multiple Time Series Analysis* (Berlin: Springer-Verlag).

Lyons, R.K. (1988), 'Tests of the Foreign Exchange Risk Premium Using the Expected Second Moments Implied by Option Pricing', *Journal of International Money and Finance*, 7, 91–108.

Lyons, R.K. (1991), 'Private Beliefs and Informational Externalities in the Foreign Exchange Market', Papers 91–17 (Columbia, SC: Graduate School of Business).

Lyons, R.K. (1993), 'Tests of Microstructural Hypothesis in the Foreign Exchange Market', NBER Working Paper No. 4471.

Lyons, R.K. (1995), 'Tests of Microstructural Hypotheses in the Foreign Exchange Market', *Journal of Financial Economics*, Elsevier, 39(2–3), 321–51.

Lyons, R.K. (1996), 'Optimal Transparency in a Dealer Market with an Application to Foreign Exchange', *Journal of Financial Intermediation*, Elsevier, 5(3), 225–54.

Lyons, R.K. (1997), 'A Simultaneous Trade Model of the Foreign Exchange Hot Potato', *Journal of International Economics*, Elsevier, 42(3–4), 275–98.

Lyons, R.K. (2001), *The Microstructure Approach to Exchange Rates* (Cambridge, MA: MIT Press).

McCallum, B. (1994), 'A Reconsideration of the Uncovered Interest Parity Relationship', *Journal of Monetary Economics*, 33, 105–32.

McCurdy, T. and I. Morgan (1987), 'Tests of the Martingale Hypothesis for Foreign Currency Futures with Time-varying Volatility, *International Journal of Forecasting*, 3, 131–48.

McCurdy, T. and I. Morgan (1988), 'Testing the Martingale Hypothesis in Deutsche Mark Futures with Models Specifying the Form of Heteroskedasticity', *Journal of Applied Econometrics*, 3, 187–202.

MacDonald, R. (1983a), 'Some Tests of Rational Expectations Hypothesis in the Foreign Exchange Market', *Scottish Journal of Political Economy*, 30, 235–50.

MacDonald, R. (1983b), 'Tests of Efficiency and the Impact of News in Three Foreign Exchange Markets', *Bulletin of Economic Research*, 35(2), 123–44.

MacDonald, R. (1985), 'The Norman Conquest of $4.86 and the Asset Approach to the Exchange Rate', *Journal of International Money and Finance*, 4, 373–87.

MacDonald, R. (1988a), *Floating Exchange Rates: Theories and Evidence* (London: Unwin-Hyman).

MacDonald, R. (1988b), 'Purchasing Power Parity: Some Long Run Evidence from the Recent Float', *The Economist*, 136, 239–52.

MacDonald, R. (1990a), 'Exchange Rate Economics', in G. Bird (ed.), *The International Financial Regime* (London: Academic Press).

MacDonald, R. (1990b), 'Are Foreign Exchange Market Forecasters Rational?: Some Survey-based Tests', *The Manchester School of Economic and Social Studies*, 58, 229–41.

MacDonald, R. (1992), 'Exchange Rate Survey Data: A Disaggregated G-7 Perspective', *Manchester School of Economic and Social Studies*, 60 (June), 47–62.

MacDonald, R. (1993), 'Long-run Purchasing Power Parity: Is it for Real?', *Review of Economics and Statistics*, 75 (November), 690–5.

MacDonald, R. (1995a), 'Long-run Exchange Rate Modeling: A Survey of the Recent Evidence', *Staff Papers, International Monetary Fund*, 42(3), 437–89.

MacDonald, R. (1995b), 'Random Walks, Real Exchange Rates and Panel Unit Root Tests', *Economics Letters*, 50, 7–11.

MacDonald, R. (1997), 'What Determines Real Exchange Rates?: The Long and The Short of It', *International Financial Markets, Institutions and Money*, 8, 117–53.

MacDonald, R. (1998), 'Expectations Formation and Risk in Three Financial Markets', in G. Prat and F. Gaurdes (eds), *The Usefulness of Survey Data in Measuring Expectations* (London: Elgar).

MacDonald, R. (1999a), 'Exchange Rates: Do Fundamentals Matter?', *Economic Journal*, 109, F673–F691.

MacDonald, R. (1999b), 'Asset Market and Balance of Payments Characteristics: An Eclectic Exchange Rate Model for the Dollar, Mark, and Yen', *Open Economies Review*, 10(1), 5–30.

MacDonald, R. (2000a), 'Concepts to Calculate Equilibrium Exchange Rates: An Overview', Discussion Paper No. 3/00 Deutsche Bundesbank.

MacDonald, R. (2000b), 'On Risk and Rationality in Three Financial Markets: Surveying What the Surveys Say', *Journal of Economic Surveys*, 14, 69–100.

MacDonald, R. (2000c), 'Is the Foreign Exchange Market Risky? Some New Survey-based Results', *Journal of Multinational Financial Management*, 3, 1–14.

MacDonald, R. (2000d), 'Is the Foreign Exchange Market Risky?: Some New Survey-based Evidence', *Journal of International Financial Management*, 7, 203–24.

MacDonald, R. (2001), 'The Role of the Exchange Rate in Economic Growth: A Euro Area Perspective', in J. Smets and M. Dombrecht (eds), *How to Promote Economic Growth in the Euro Area* (London: Edward Elgar).

MacDonald, R. (2002), 'Modelling the Long-run Real Effective Exchange Rate of the New Zealand Dollar', *Australian Economic Papers*, 41(4), 519–37.

MacDonald, R. and P. Macmillan (1994), 'On the Expectations View of the Term Structure, Term Premia and Survey-based Expectations', *The Economic Journal*, 104, 1070–86.

MacDonald, R. and I.W. Marsh (1993), 'The Efficiency of Spot and Futures Stock Indices: A Survey Based Perspective', *The Review of Futures Markets*, 12(2), 431–54.

MacDonald, R. and I.W. Marsh (1994a), 'On Long- and Short-run Purchasing Power Parity', in J. Kaehler and P. Kugler (eds), *Econometric Analysis of Financial Markets* (Heidelberg, Germany: Physica-Verlag), 23–46.

MacDonald, R. and I.W. Marsh (1994b), 'Combining Exchange Rate forecasts: What is the Optimal Consensus Measure?', *Journal of Forecasting*, 13 (May), 313–32.

MacDonald, R. and I.W. Marsh (1996a), 'Heterogeneite Des revisionnistes: Une Exploration Des Anticipations Sur Le March Des Changes', *Economie et Prevision*, 125, 109–16.

MacDonald, R. and I.W. Marsh (1996b), 'Foreign Exchange Market Forecasters are Heterogeneous: Confirmation and Consequences', *Journal of International Money and Finance* (September), 15, 665–85.

MacDonald, R. and I.W. Marsh (1997), 'On Casselian PPP, Cointegration and Exchange Rate Forecasting', *Review of Economics and Statistics* (November), 70, 655–64.

MacDonald, R. and I.W. Marsh (1999), *Exchange Rate Modelling* (Boston, MA: Kluwer).

MacDonald, R. and I.W. Marsh (2004), 'A Tripolar Forecasting Model of Bilateral Exchange Rates', *Journal of International Money and Finance*, 23, 99–111.

MacDonald, R. and M. Moore (1996), 'Long-run Purchasing Power Parity and Structural Change', *Economie Appliquee*, XLIX, 11–48.

MacDonald, R. and M. Moore (2000), 'The Spot-forward Relationship Revisited: An ERM Perspective', *Journal of International Financial Markets, Institutions and Money*, 11, 29–52.

MacDonald, R. and J. Nagayasu (1999), 'The Long-run Relationship between Real Exchange Rates and Real Interest Differentials: A Panel Study', IMF Staff Papers.

MacDonald, R. and L. Ricci (2001), 'PPP and the Balassa–Samuelson Effect: The Role of the Distribution Sector', IMF Working Paper No. 01/38.

MacDonald, R. and L. Ricci (2003), 'Purchasing Power Parity and New Trade Theory', IMF Working Paper No. 02/32.

MacDonald, R. and L. Ricci (2004), 'Estimation of the Equilibrium Real Exchange Rate for South Africa', IMF Working Paper No. WP/03/44 and *South African Journal of Economics*, 72(2), 282–304.

MacDonald, R. and P. Swagel (2000), 'Business Cycle Influences on Exchange Rates: Survey and Evidence', World Economic Outlook, Supporting Studies, 129–59.

MacDonald, R. and M.P. Taylor (1989), 'The Term Structure of Forward Foreign Exchange Rate Premiums', *The Manchester School of Economic and Social Studies*, 58, 54–65.

MacDonald, R. and M.P. Taylor (1991), 'The Monetary Model of the Exchange Rate: Long-run Relationships and Coefficient Restrictions', *Economics Letters*, 37, 179–85.

MacDonald, R. and M.P. Taylor (1992), 'Exchange Rate Economics: A Survey', *IMF Staff Papers*, 1–57.

MacDonald, R. and M.P. Taylor (1993), 'The Monetary Approach to the Exchange Rate: Rational Expectations, Long-run Equilibrium and Forecasting', *IMF Staff Papers*, 40, 89–107.

MacDonald, R. and M.P. Taylor (1994), 'The Monetary Model of the Exchange Rate: Long-run Relationships, Short-run Dynamics and How to Beat a Random Walk', *Journal of International Money and Finance*, 13, 276–90.

MacDonald, R. and T.S. Torrance (1987a), 'Monetary Policy and the Real Interest Rate: Some UK Evidence', *The Scottish Journal of Political Economy*, 35, 361–71.

MacDonald, R. and T.S. Torrance (1987b), 'Sterling M3 Surprises and Asset Prices', *Economica*, 54, 505–15.

MacDonald, R. and T.S. Torrance (1988a), 'On Risk, Rationality and Excessive Speculation in the Deutschemark–US Dollar Exchange Market: Some Evidence Using Survey Data', *Oxford Bulletin of Economics and Statistics*, 50(2), 1–17.

MacDonald, R. and T.S. Torrance (1988b), 'Covered Interest Parity and UK Monetary "News" ', *Economics Letters*, 26, 53–6.

MacDonald, R. and T.S. Torrance (1988c), 'Exchange Rates and the "News": Some Evidence Using UK Survey Data', *The Manchester School*, 56(1), 69–76.

MacDonald, R. and T.S. Torrance (1989), 'Some Survey Based Tests of Uncovered Interest Parity', in R. MacDonald and M.P. Taylor (eds), *Exchange Rates and Open Economy Macroeconomics* (Oxford: Blackwell).

MacDonald, R. and T.S. Torrance (1990), 'Expectations Formation and Risk in Four Foreign Exchange Markets', *Oxford Economic Papers*, 42, 544–61.

MacDonald, R. and C. Wojcik (2004), 'Catching Up: The Role of Demand, Supply and Regulated Price Effects on the Real Exchange Rates of Four Accession Countries', *The Economics of Transition*, 12(1), 153–79.

MacDonald, R. and R.Young (1986), 'Decision Rules, Expectations and Efficiency in Two Foreign Exchange Markets', *De Economist*, 134, 42–60.

Machlup, F. (1972), 'The Case for Floating Exchange Rates', in G.N. Halm (ed.), *Approaches to Greater Flexibility of Exchange Rates* (Princeton, NJ: Princeton University Press).

McKinnon, R.I. (1963), 'Optimum Currency Areas', *American Economic Review*, 53, 717–25.

McKinnon, R. (1979), *Money in International Exchange: The Convertible Currency System* (Oxford: Oxford University Press).

McKinnon, R. (1982), 'Currency Substitution and Instability with World Dollar Standard', *American Economic Review*, 72, 320–33.

McKinnon, R. (1988), 'Monetary and Exchange Rate Policies for International Financial Stability: A Proposal', *Journal of Economic Perspectives*, 2, 83–103.

McKinnon, R.I. and H. Pill (1996), 'Credible Liberalizations and International Capital Flows: The Overborrowing Syndrome', in T. Ito and A.O. Krueger (eds), *Financial Deregulation and Integration in East Asia* (Chicago, IL: Chicago University Press).

McKinnon, R.I. and H. Pill (1999), 'Exchange-rate Regimes for Emerging Markets: Moral Hazard and International Overborrowing', *Oxford Review of Economic Policy*, 15(3), 19–37.

Madhavan, A. and S. Smidt (1991), 'A Bayesian Model of Intraday Specialist Pricing', *Journal of Financial Economics*, 30, 99–134.

Makrydakis, S., P. de Lima, J. Claessens and M. Kramer (2000), 'The Real Effective Exchange Rate of the Euro and Economic Fundamentals: A BEER Perspective', mimeo, ECB.grang.

Mann, C.L. (1986), 'Prices, Profit Margins and Exchange Rates', *Federal Reserve Bulletin* (June), 366–79.

Mark, N.C. (1990), 'Real and Nominal Exchange Rates in the Long-run: An Empirical Investigation', *Journal of International Economics*, 28, 115–36.

Mark, N.C. (1995), 'Exchange Rates and Fundamentals: Evidence on Long-horizon Predictability', *American Economic Review*, 85, 201–18.

Mark, N.C. (1997), 'Fundamentals of the Real Dollar–Pound Rate 1871–1994', in R. MacDonald and J. Stein (eds), chapter 8, *Equilibirum Exchange Rates* (Amsterdam: Kluwer Press).

Mark, N.C. (2001), *International Macroeconomics and Finance* (Oxford: Blackwell).

Mark, N.C. and D. Sul (2001), 'Nominal Exchange Rates and Monetary Fundamentals: Evidence from a Small Post-Bretton Woods Panel', *Journal of International Economics*, 53(1), 29–52.

Mark, N.M. (1985), 'On Time-varying Risk Premia in the Foreign Exchange Market: An Econometric Analysis', *Journal of Monetary Economics*, 16, 3–58.

Marshall, A. (1923), *Money Credit and Commerce* (London: MacMillan).

Marston, R.C. (1976), 'Interest Arbitrage in the Eurocurrency Markets', *European Economic Review*, 7, 1–13.

Marston, R. (1990a), 'Systematic Movements in Real Exchange Rates in the G-5: Evidence on the Integration of Internal and External Markets', *Journal of Banking and Finance*, 14, 1023–44.

Marston, R. (1990b), 'Pricing to Market in Japanese Manufacturing', *Journal of International Economics*, 29, 217–36.

Martinez Peria, M. (1997), 'Understanding Devaluations in Latin America: A "Bad Fundamentals" Approach', CIDER Working Paper C97086.

Masson, P. (1998), 'Contagion: Monsoonal Effects, Spillovers, and Jumps between Multiple Equilibria', in P.R. Agenor, M. Miller, D.Vines and A.Weber (eds), *The Asian Financial Crisis: Causes, Contagion, and Consequences* (Cambridge, UK: Cambridge University Press).

Masson, P.R. and M.P. Taylor (eds) (1993), *Policy Issues in the Operation of Currency Areas* (Cambridge: Cambridge University Press).

Masson, P.R., J. Kremers and J. Horne (1994), 'Net Foreign Assets and International Adjustment: The United States, Japan and Germany', *Journal of International Money and Finance*, 13(1), 27–40.

Meese, R. (1986), 'Testing for Bubbles in Exchange Markets: A Case of Sparkling Rates', *Journal of Political Economy*, 94, 345–73.

Meese, R. and K. Rogoff (1983), 'Empirical Exchange Rate Models of the Seventies: Do they Fit out of Sample?', *Journal of International Economics*, 14, 3–24.

Meese, R. and K. Rogoff (1984), 'The Out-of-Sample Failure of Empirical Exchange Rate Models: Sampling Error or Misspecification?', in J.A. Frenkel (ed.), *Exchange Rates and International Macroeconomics* (Chicago: Chicago University Press), 67–109.

Meese, R. and K. Rogoff (1988), 'Was it Real? The Exchange Rate-Interest Differential Relation Over the Modern Floating-rate Period', *Journal of Finance*, 43, 933–48.

Meese, R. and A. Rose (1990), 'Non-linear, Nonparameter Nonessential Exchange Rate Estimations', *American Economic Review*, 80, 192–6.

Meese, R. and A. Rose (1991), 'An Empirical Assessment of Nonlinearities in Models of Exchange Rate Determination', *Review of Economic Studies*, 58, 603–19.

Melvin, M. (1985), 'Choice of an Exchange Rate Regime System and Macroeconomic Stability', *Journal of Money Credit and Banking*, 17, 467–78.

Michael, P., A.R. Nobay and D.A. Peel (1997), 'Transaction Costs and Nonlinear Adjustment in Real Exchange Rates: An Empirical Investigation', *Journal of Political Economy*, 105, 4.

Micossi, S. and G.M. Milesi-Ferretti (1994), 'Real Exchange Rates and the Prices of Nontradable Goods', IMF Working Paper No. 94/19.

Milhoj, A. (1987), 'A Conditional Variance Model for Daily Observations of an Exchange Rate', *Journal of Business and Economics Statistics*, 5, 99–103.

Miller, M. and P. Weller (1991), 'Exchange Rate Bands with Price Inertia', *Economic Journal* (November), 101, 127–41.

Minford, P. (1977), 'North Sea Oil and the British Economy', *The Banker*, 12, 23–7.

Modjtahedi, B. (1991), 'Multiple Maturities and Time-varying Risk Premia in Forward Exchange Markets: An Econometric Analysis', *Journal of International Economics*, 30, 69–86.

Monacelli, T. (2004), 'Into the Mussa Puzzle: Monetary Policy Regimes and the Real Exchange Rate in a Small Open Economy', *Journal of International Economics*, 62, 191–217.

Montiel, P. (1999), 'Exchange Rate Policy and Macroeconomic Management in ASEAN Countries', in L.E. Hinkle and P. Montiel (eds), *Exchange Rate Misalignment* (New York: Oxford University Press).

Moore, M.J. (1993), 'System of Bilateral Real Exchange Rates', *Applied Economics*, 25 (September), 1161–6.

Morris, S. and Hyun Song Shin (1998), 'Unique Equilibrium in a Model of Self-fulfilling Currency Attack', *American Economic Review*, 88(3), 587–97.

Mundell, R.A. (1961), 'A Theory of Optimum Currency Areas', *American Economic Review*, 51, 657–65.

Mundell, R.A. (1962), 'The Appropriate Use of Monetary and Fiscal Policy for Internal and External Balance', *IMF Staff Papers*, 9, 70–9.

Mundell, R.A. (1963), 'Capital Mobility and Stabilization Policy under Fixed and Flexible Exchange Rates', *Canadian Journal of Economics and Political Science*, 29, 475–85.

Mundell, R.A. (1968), *International Economics* (New York: Macmillan).

Mussa, M. (1979), 'Empirical Regularities in the Behaviour of Exchange Rates and Theories of the Foreign Exchange Market', in *Carnegie-Rochester Conference Series on Public Policy*, 11, 9–57.

Mussa, M. (1982), 'A Model of Exchange Rate Dynamics', *Journal of Political Economy*, 90, 74–104.

Mussa, M. (1984), 'The Theory of Exchange Rate Determination', in J.F.O. Bilson and R.C. Marston (eds), *Exchange Rate Theory and Practice*, NBER Conference Report (Chicago, IL: Chicago University Press).

Mussa, M. (1986), 'Nominal Exchange Rate Regimes and the Behaviour of Real Exchange Rates: Evidence and Implications', *Carnegie-Rochester Conference Series on Public Policy*, 26, 1–50.

Negishi, T. (1962), 'The Stability of a Competitve Economy', *Econometrica*, 31, 635–69.

Obstfeld, M. (1984), 'Balance-of-payments Crises and Devaluation', *Journal of Money Credit and Banking*, 16(2), 208–17.

Obstfeld, M. (1985), 'Floating Exchange Rates: Experiences and Prospects', *Brookings Papers on Economic Activity*, 2, 369–450.

Obstfeld, M. (1986), 'Rational and Self-fulfilling Balance-of-payment Crises', *American Economic Review*, 76(1), 72–81.

Obstfeld, M. (1987), 'Peso Effects and Speculative Bubbles and Tests of Market Efficiency', NBER Working Paper No. 2203.

Obstfeld, M. (1989), 'Competitiveness, Realignment, and Speculation: The Role of Financial Markets', in F. Giavazzi and A. Giovannini (eds), *Managing Exchange Rate Flexibility: The European Monetary System* (Cambridge: MIT Press).

Obstfeld, M. (1994), 'The Logic of Currency Crises', NBER Working Paper Series No. 4640.

Obstfeld, M. (1996), 'Models of Currency Crises with Self-fulfilling Features', *European Economic Review*, 40(3–5), 1037–47.

Obstfeld, M. (1997), 'Destabilizing Effects of Exchange Rate Escape Clause', *Journal of International Economics*, 43(1–2), 61–77.

Obstfeld, M. (1998), 'The Global Capital Market: Benefactor of Menace?', *Journal of Economic Perspectives*, 12, 9–30.

Obstfeld, M. and K. Rogoff (1995), 'Exchange Rate Dynamics Redux', *Journal of Political Economy*, 103, 624–60.

Obstfeld, M. and K. Rogoff (1996), *Foundations of International Macroeconomics* (Cambridge, MA: MIT Press).

Obstfeld, M. and K. Rogoff (2000a), 'The Six Major Puzzles in International Macroeconomics: Is there a Common Cause', NBER Working Paper No. 7777.

Obstfeld, M. and K. Rogoff (2000b), 'New Directions for Stochastic Open Economy Models', *Journal of International Economics*, 50, 117–53.

Obstfeld, M. and K. Rogoff (2000c), 'Risk and Exchange Rates', NBER Working Paper No. 6694.

Obstfeld, M. and K. Rogoff (2001a), 'Risk and Exchange Rates', NBER Working Paper 6694.

Obstfeld, M. and K. Rogoff (2001b), 'Perspectives on OECD Economic Integration: Implications for US Current Account Adjustment', in *Global Economic Integration: Opportunities and Challenges* (Kansas City, MO: FRB), 169–208.

Obstfeld, M. and A. Stockman (1985), 'Exchange Rate Dynamics', in R. Jones and P. Kenen (eds), *Handbook of International Economics*, 2 (Amsterdam: North Holland).

Obstfeld, M. and A.M. Taylor (1997), 'Nonlinear Aspects of Goods-market Arbitrage and Adjustment: Hecksher's Commodity Points Revisited', *Journal of Japanese and International Economies*, 11, 441–79.

O'Connell, P. (1998a), 'Market Frictions and Relative Traded Goods Prices', *Journal of International Money and Finance*, 17, 71–95.

O'Connell, P. (1998b), 'The Overvaluation of Purchasing Power Parity', *Journal of International Economics*, 44, 1–19.

O'Connell, P. and S.-J. Wei (1997), 'The Bigger they are the Harder they Fall: How Price Differences across US Cities Are Arbitraged', NBER Working Paper 6089.

Officer, L.H. (1976), 'The Purchasing Power Parity Theory of Exchange Rates: A Review Article', Staff Papers, International Monetary Fund, 23, 1–60.

Oh, K.-Y. (1996), 'Purchasing Power Parity and Unit Root Test Using Panel Data', *Journal of International Money and Finance*, 15, 405–18.

O'Hara, M. (1995), *Market Microstructure Theory* (Cambridge: Blackwell).

Oomes, N.K. (2001), 'Essays on Network Externalities and Aggregate Persistence', PhD Dissertation, University of Wisconsin.

Ostry, J.D. and C.M. Reinhart (1991), 'Private Saving and Terms of Trade Shocks: Evidence from Developing Countries', IMF Working Papers 91/100, International Monetary Fund.

Overturf, S.F. (1982), 'Risk, Transactions Charges, and the Market for Foreign Exchange Services', *Economic Inquiry*, 20(2), 291–302.

Papell, D.H. (1997), 'Searching for Stationarity: Purchasing Power Parity Under the Current Float', *Journal of International Economics*, 41, 313–32.

Papell, D.H. and H. Theodoris (1997), 'The Choice of Numeraire Currency in Panel Tests of Purchasing Power Parity', mimeo, University of Houston.

Patel, J. (1990), 'Purchasing Power Parity as a Long-run Relation', *Journal of Applied Econometrics*, 5 (October–December), 367–79.

Pavlova, A. and R. Rigobon (2003), 'Asset Prices and Exchange Rates', NBER Working Paper No. 9834.

Pedroni, P. (1997), 'Panel Cointegration: Asymptotic and Finite Sample Properties of Pooled Time Series Tests with an Application to the PPP Hypothesis', mimeo, Indiana University.

Pedroni, P. (2001), 'PPP in Cointegrated Panels', *Review of Economics and Statistics*, 4, 727–31.

Perron, P. and T.J. Vogeslang (1992), 'Nonstationarity and Level Shifts with and Application to Purchasing Power Parity', *Journal of Business and Economic Statistics*, 10 (July), 301–20.

Pesaran, H. (1989), 'Consistency of Short-term and Long-term Expectations', *Journal of International Money and Finance*, 8, 511–20.

Phillips, P.C.B. and B.E. Hansen (1990), 'Statistical Inference in Instrumental Variables Regression with I(1) Processes', *Review of Economic Studies*, 57, 99–125.

Prat, G. (1994), 'La Formation des Anticiaptions Boursieres', *Economie et Prevision*, 112, 101–25.

Prat, G. and R. Uctum (1996), 'FF/$ Exchange Rate Expectations Formation: Analysis of the Hypothesis of Changes in Processes over Time', in proceedings of the Third International Conference, Forecasting Financial Markets: New Advances for Exchange Rates, Interest Rates and Asset Management, London, 27–29 March.

Prat, G. and R. Uctum (1997), 'La Formation des Anticipations de Change', mimeo, University of Paris.

Putnam, B.H. and J.R. Woodbury (1980), 'Exchange Rate Stability and Monetary Policy', *Review of Business and Economic Research*, 15, 1–10.

Quah, D. (1994), 'Exploiting Cross-section Variation for Unit Root Inference in Dynamic Data', *Economics Letter*, 44(1), 9–19.

Radelet, S. and J. Sachs (1998), 'The Onset of the Asian Crisis', NBER Working Paper Series No. 6680.

Razin, A. and Y. Rubinstein (2005), 'Exchange Rate and Capital Market Regimes: Resolution to Confounding Effects on Macroeconomic Performance', mimeo, Cornell University.

Reinhart, C.M. and K.S. Rogoff (2002), 'The Modern History of Exchange Rate Arrangements: A Reinterpretation', NBER Working Paper No. 8963.

Reinhart, C.M., K.S. Rogoff and M.A. Savastano (2003), 'Addicted to Dollars', NBER Working Paper No. 10015.

Rey, H. (2001), 'International Trade and Currency Exchange', *Review of Economic Studies*, 68(2), April 2001, 443–64.

Ricci, L. (1999), 'Economic Geography and Comparative Advantage: Agglomeration Versus Specialization', *European Economic Review*, 43, 357–77.

Rigobon, R. and B. Sack (2002), 'The Impact of Monetary Policy on Asset Prices', Finance and Economics Discussion Series 2002–4, Board of Governors of the Federal Reserve System (US).

Rogers, J.H. (1999), 'Monetary Shocks and Real Exchange Rates', *Journal of International Economics*, 49(2), 269–88.

Rogers, J.H. and M. Jenkins (1995), 'Haircuts or Hysteresis? Sources of Movements in Real Exchange Rates', *Journal of International Economics*, 38, 339–60.

Rogoff, K. (1984), 'On the Effects of Sterilised Intervention: An Analysis of Weekly Data', *Journal of Monetary Economics*, 14, 123–50.

Rogoff, K. (1992), 'Traded Goods, Consumption Smoothing and the Random Walk Behaviour of the Real Exchange Rate', NBER Working Paper No. 4119.

Rogoff, K. (1996), 'The Purchasing Power Parity Puzzle', *Journal of Economic Literature*, XXXIV, 647–68.

Rogoff, K. (1999), 'Monetary Models of Dollar/Yen/Euro Nominal Exchange Rate: Dead or Undead', *Economic Journal*, 109, F655–9.

Rogoff, K.S., A.M. Husain, A. Mody, R. Brooks and N. Oomes (2004), 'Evolution and Performance of Exchange Rate Regimes', IMF, Occasional Paper No. 229.

Roll, R. (1979), 'Violations of Purchasing Power Parity and their Implications for Efficient International Commodity Markets', in M. Sarnat and G.P. Szegö (eds), *International Finance and Trade*, 1 (Cambridge, MA: Ballinger), 133–76.

Rose, A. (2000), 'One Money, One Market: The Effect of Common Currencies on Trade?', *Economic Policy*, 30, 1–50.

Rose, A.K. and Engel (2000), 'Currency Unions and International Integration', NBER Working Paper No. 7872.

Rose, A.K. and L.E.O. Svensson (1994), 'European Exchange Rate Credibility Before the Fall', *European Economic Review*, 38(6), 1185–1216.

Ross, S. (1983), *Introduction to Stochastic Dynamics* (New York: Academic Press).

Salvatore, D., J. Dean and T. Willett (eds) (2003), *The Dollarization Debate* (New York: Oxford University Press).

Samuelson, P. (1964), 'Theoretical Problems on Trade Problems', *Review of Economics and Statistics*, 46, 145–54.

Sarantis, N. (1994), 'The Monetary Exchange Rate Model in the Long-run: An Empirical Investigation', *Weltwirtschaftlishes Archiv*, 698–711.

Sawada, Y. and P.A. Yotopoulos (2000), 'Currency Substitution, Speculation and Financial Crises: Theory and Empirical Analysis', mimeo, Central Bank of Greece.

Schinasi, G. and P. Swamy (1987), 'The Out-of-sample Forecasting Performance of Exchange Rate Models when Coefficients are Allowed to Vary', International Finance Discussion Papers, 301, Board of Governors of the Federal Reserve System.

Sercu, P.U. and V. Hulle (1995), 'The Exchange Rate in the Presence of Transaction Costs: Implications for Tests of Purchasing Power Parity', *Journal of Finance*, 50, 1309–19.

Sheffrin, S. and T. Russel (1984), 'Sterling and Oil Discoveries: The Mysteries of Nonappreciation', *Journal of International Money and Finance*, 3, 311–26.

Shiller, R.J. (1980), 'Do Stock Prices Move too much to be Justified by Subsequent Changes in Fundamentals?', *American Economic Review*, 71, 421–36.

Smith, G.W. and M.G. Spencer (1991), 'Estimation and Testing in Models of Exchange-rate Target Zones and Process Switching', in P. Krugman and M. Miller (eds), *Exchange Rate Targets and Currency Bands* (Cambridge: Cambridge University Press), 211–39.

Smith, P. and M. Wickens (1990), 'Assessing Monetary Shocks and Exchange Rate Variability with a Stylised Econometric Model of the UK', in A.S. Courakis and M.P. Taylor (eds), *Private Behaviour and Government Policy in Interdependent Economies* (Oxford: Oxford University Press).

Sobiechowski, D. (1996), 'Rational Expectations in the Foreign Exchange Market: Some Survey Evidence', *Applied Economics*, 28, 1601–11.

Sohmen, E. (1961), *Flexible Exchange Rates* (Chicago, IL: University of Chicago Press).

Sohmen, E. (1967), 'Fiscal and Monetary Policies under Alternative Exchange Rate Systems', *Quarterly Journal of Economics*, 81, 515–23.

Spinelli, F. (1983), 'Currency substitution, flexible exchange rates and the case for international monetary cooperation, International Monetary Fund, *Staff Papers*, 30, 4, 755–83.

Stein, J. (1994), 'The Natural Real Exchange Rate of the United States Dollar and Determinants of Capital Flows', in J. Williamson (ed.), *Equilibrium Exchange Rates* (Washington, DC: Institute of International Economics).

Stein, J. (1999), 'The Evolution of the Real Value of the US Dollar Relative to the G7 Currencies', in R. MacDonald and J. Stein (eds), chapter 3, *Equilibirum Exchange Rates* (Amsterdam: Kluwer Press).

Stein, J. and P.R. Allen (1995), *Fundamental Determinants of Exchange Rates* (Oxford: Oxford University Press).

Stein, J. and K. Sauernheimer (1997), 'The Real Exchange Rate of Germany', in J. Stein (ed.), *Globalisation of Markets* (Bonn: Physica-Varlag).

Stock, J.H. (1987), 'Asymptotic Properties of Least Squares Estimators of Cointegrating Vectors', *Econometrica*, 55 (September), 1035–56.

Stock, J.H. and M.W. Watson (1988), 'Testing For Common Trends', *Journal of the American Statistical Association*, 83 (December), 1097–107.

Stockman, A. (1980), 'A Theory of Exchange Rate Determination', *Journal of Political Economy*, 88, 673–98.

Stockman, A. (1987), 'The Equilibrium Approach to Exchange Rates', Federal Reserve Bank of Richmond *Economic Review*, 7, 12–30.

Stockman, A. (1988), 'Real Exchange Rate Variability under Pegged and Floating Nominal Exchange Rate Systems: An Equilibrium Theory', *Carnegie-Rochester Conference Series on Public Policy*, 29, 259–94.

Stockman, A. (1995), 'Sources of Real Exchange-rate Fluctuations: A Comment', *Carnegie-Rochester Conference Series on Public Policy*, 41, 57–65.

Strauss, J. (1995), 'Real Exchange Rates, PPP and the Relative Price of Nontraded Goods', *Southern Economic Journal*, 61, 991–1005.

Strauss, J. (1996), 'The Cointegrating Relationship Between Productivity, Real Exchange Rates and Purchasing Power Parity', *Journal of Macroeconomics*, 18, 299–313.

Stultz, R. (1981), 'A Model of International Asset Pricing', *Journal of Financial Economics*, 9, 383–406.

Subrahmanyam, A. (1991), 'A Theory of Trading in Stock Index Futures', *Review of Financial Studies*, 4, 17–52.

Subrahmanyam, A. (1994), 'Circuit Breakers and Market Volatility: A Theoretical Perspective', *Journal of Finance*, 49, 237–54.

Sutherland, A. (1994), 'Target Zone Models with Price Inertia: Solutions and Testable Implications', *Economic Journal*, Royal Economic Society, 104(422), 96–112.

Svensson, L.E.O. (1992a), 'The Foreign Exchange Risk Premium in a Target Zone with Devaluation Risk', *Journal of International Economics*, 33(1–2), 21–40.

Svensson, L.E.O. (1992b), 'An Interpretation of Recent Research on Exchange Rate Target Zones', *Journal of Economic Perspectives*, 6, 119–44.

Svensson, L.E.O. (1993), 'Assessing Target Zone Credibility : Mean Reversion and Devaluation Expectations in the ERM, 1979–1992', *European Economic Review*, 37(4), 763–93.

Svensson, L. (1994), 'Why Exchange Rate Bands?: Monetary Independence in Spite of Fixed Exchange Rates', *Journal of Monetary Economics*, Elsevier, 33(1), 157–99.

Svensson, L.E. and S. van Wijnbergen (1989), 'Excess Capacity, Monopolistic Competition and International Transmission of Monetary Disturbances', *Economic Journal*, 99, 785–805.

Swoboda, A. (1968), 'The Euro–Dollar Market: An Interpretation', *Essays in International Finance*, 64, International Finance Section (Princeton, NJ: Princeton University).

Swoboda, A. (1969a), 'Problems of the International Monetary System', in R. Mundell and A. Swoboda (eds), *Monetary Problems of the International Economy* (Chicago, IL: Chicago University Press).

Swoboda, A. (1969b), 'Vehicle Currencies and the Foreign Exchange Market: The Case of the Dollar', in R.Z. Aliber (ed.), *The International Market for Foreign Exchange* (New York: Praeger).

Tagaki, S. (1991), 'Exchange Rate Expectations: A Survey of Survey Studies', *International Monetary Fund Staff Papers*, 38, 156–83.

Tauchen, G.E. and M. Pitts (1983), 'The Price Variability–Volume Relationship on Speculative Markets', *Econometrica*, 51, 485–505.

Taylor, M.P. (1989), 'Covered Interest Arbitrage and Market Turbulence', *Economic Journal*, 99, 376–91.

Taylor, M.P. and M. Iannazzotto (2001), 'On the Mean-reverting Properties of Target Zone Exchange Rates: A Cautionary Note', *Economics Letters*, 71, 117–29.

Taylor, M.P. and McMahon (1988), 'Long-run Purchasing Power Parity in the 1920s', *European Economic Review*, 32, 179–97.

Taylor, M.P. and L. Sarno (1998), 'Real Exchange Rates under the Recent Float: Unequivocal Evidence of Mean Reversion', *Economics Letters*, 60, 131–7.

Taylor, M.P., D. Peel and L. Sarno (2001), 'Nonlinear Mean-reversion in Real Exchange Rates: Toward a Solution to the Purchasing Power Parity Puzzle', *International Economic Review*, 42, 1015–42.

Tesar, L. and I. Werner (1994), 'International Equity Transactions and US Portfolio Choice', in J. A. Frankel (ed.), *The Internationalization of Equity Markets* (Chicago, IL: Chicago University Press).

Thomas, S.H. and M.R. Wickens (1993), 'An International CAPM for Bonds and Equities', *Journal of International Money and Finance*, 12, 390–412.

Throop, A. (1994), 'A Generalised Incovered Interest Rate Parity Model of Real Exchange Rates', Federal Reserve Bank of San Francisco, mimeo.

Tille, C. (2001), 'The Role of Consumption Substitutability in the International Transmission of Monetary Shocks', *Journal of International Economics*, 53, 421–44.

Tsay, R.S. (1989), 'Testing and Modeling Threshold Autoregressive Processes', *Journal of the American Statistical Association*, 84, 231–40.

Tsiang, S.C. (1959), 'The Theory of Foreign Exchange and Effects of Government Intervention on the Forward Exchange Market', *IMF Staff Papers*, VII, 75–106.

Urich, T.J. and P. Wachtel (1981), 'Market Response to Weekly Money Supply Announcements in the 1970s', *Journal of Finance*, 36, 1063–72.

Vaubel, R. (1980), 'International Shifts in the Demand for Money, their Effects on Exchange Rates and Price Levels and their Implications for the Preannouncements of Monetary Expansion', *Weltwirtschaftliches Archiv*, 116, 1–44.

Verschoor, W.F.C. and C.C.P. Wolff (2001), 'Scandinavian Forward Discount Bias Risk Premia, *Economics Letters*, 73, 65–72.

Verschoor, W.F.C. and C.C.P. Wolff (2002), 'Scandinavian Exchange Rate Expectations', *Applied Economics Letters*, 9, 111–16.

de Vries, C.G. (1994), 'Stylized Facts of Nominal Exchange Rate Returns', in F. Van der Ploeg (ed.), *The Handbook of International Macroeconomics* (Oxford: Blackwell).

Wadhwani, S. (1984), 'Are Exchange Rates Excessively Volatile?', Centre for Labour Economics, Discussion Paper No. 198, London School of Economics.

Wadhwani, S. (1999), 'Currency Puzzles', mimeo, Bank of England.

Wallace, M.S. (1979), 'The Monetary Approach to Flexible Exchange Rates in the Short-run: An Empirical Test', *Review of Business and Economic Research*, 5, 98–102.

Wasserfallen, W. and H. Zimmerman (1985), 'The Behaviour of Intra Daily Foreign Exchange Rates', *Journal of Banking and Finance*, 9, 55–72.

Weber, A. (1998), 'Sources of Purchasing Power Disparities between the G3 Economies', *Journal of Japanese and International Economies*, 11, 548–83.

Wei, S.-J. and D. Parsley (1995), 'Purchasing Power Disparity during the Recent Floating Rate Period: Exchange Rate Volatility, Trade Barriers and Other Culprits', NBER Working Paper No. 5032, *Quarterly Journal of Economics*, 14, 1211–36.

Westerfield, J.M. (1977), 'An Examination of Foreign Exchange Risk under Fixed and Floating Rate Regimes', *Journal of International Economics*, 7, 181–200.

Whitt, J.A. (1992), 'The Long-run Behaviour of the Real Exchange Rate: A Reconsideration', *Journal of Money, Credit and Banking*, 24 (February), 72–82.

Williamson, J. (1983a), *Estimating Equilibrium Exchange Rates* (Washington, DC: Institute for International Economics).

Williamson, J. (1983b), *The Exchange Rate System* (Washington, DC: Institute for International Economics).

Williamson, J. (1988), 'Managing the Monetary System', in P.B. Kenen (ed.), *Managing the World Economy: Fifty Years After Bretton Woods* (Washington, DC: Institute for International Economics).

Wilson, C.A. (1979), 'Anticipated Shocks and Exchange Rate Dynamics', *Journal of Political Economy*, 87(3), 639–47.

Wolff, C. (1987), 'Time-varying Parameters and the Out-of Sample Forecasting Performance of Structural Exchange Rate Models', *Journal of Business and Economics Statistics*, 5, 87–97.

Woo, W.T. (1985), 'The Monetary Approach to Exchange Rate Determination under Rational Expectations: The Dollar–Deutschemark Rate', *Journal of International Economics*, 18, 1–16.

Wren-Lewis, S. (1992), 'On the Analytical Foundations of the Fundamental Equilibrium Exchange Rate', in Colin P. Hargreaves (ed.), *Macroeconomic Modelling of the Long Run* (London: Edward Elgar).

Wren-Lewis, S. (1998), 'How Robust Are FEERs?', in R. MacDonald and J. Stein (eds), chapter 5, *Equilibirum Exchange Rates* (Amsterdam: Kluwer Press).

Wu, Y. (1996), 'Are Real Exchange Rates Nonstationary? Evidence from a Panel Data Set', *Journal of Money Credit and Banking*, 28, 54–63.

Yao, J. (1998), 'Market Making in the Interbank Foreign Exchange Market', New York University, Salomon Center Working Paper No. S-98-3.

Index